DATE DUE

DE 16			

DEMCO 38-296

ENCYCLOPEDIA OF ADOLESCENCE

edited by

RICHARD M. LERNER
ANNE C. PETERSEN
JEANNE BROOKS-GUNN

Volume II
M – INDEX

GARLAND PUBLISHING, INC.
NEW YORK & LONDON
1991

Library of Congress Cataloging-in-Publication Data

Encyclopedia of adolescence / edited by Richard M. Lerner, Anne C. Petersen,
   Jeanne Brooks-Gunn.
        p. cm. — (Garland references library of the social sciences; vol. 495)
      Includes index.
      ISBN 0-8240-4378-2
      1. Adolescence—Encyclopedias. I. Lerner, Richard M. II. Petersen, Anne C.
   III. Brooks-Gunn, Jeanne. IV. Series: Garland reference library of the
   social sciences; vol. 495.
      HQ796.E58   1991
      305.23'5—dc20   90-14033
                                                                          CIP

Design by Alison Lew

Printed on acid-free, 250-year-life paper

Manufactured in the United States of America

ENCYCLOPEDIA OF ADOLESCENCE

Volume II

Maternal Employment Influences on Adolescent Development

Jacqueline V. Lerner
The Pennsylvania State University

Laura E. Hess
Max Planck Institute for Human Development and Education

The influence that the mother's absence from the home has on her child's development has received much attention by researchers (Hoffman, 1979). Investigators of the effects of maternal employment on infants and young children have been primarily concerned with the quality of the alternative care situation and the quality of the mother-child relationship. That is, many researchers believe that it is not maternal employment per se that may affect child development. Rather, what is believed to be at issue is how a mother's employment affects her relationship with her child and how that relationship, in turn, influences the child's development (Lerner & Galambos, 1986). In addition, the type and quality of alternative care that is needed when a mother is employed is also thought to affect the child's development.

The concern with how maternal employment influences the child shifts focus during adolescence. No longer is the central issue one of the quality of alternative care or infant-mother attachment. School-aged children spend a smaller proportion of their time with their mother, the father becomes more involved in their lives, and other groups—such as peers, teachers, and other adults—become socializers of the child. Thus, the influence of a mother's employment on her adolescent's development is modified by a host of variables from one family to the next, among them the quality of the husband-wife and parent-child relationships, the nature and number of sibling relationships, and the support available to both parents and children from the extended family and the community.

Still another important factor is the effect of timing of employment on adolescent development. Adolescence may appear to the mother as the optimal time to begin working outside the home because her child is becoming more self-sufficient and is placing significantly fewer demands on her. However, although the adolescent may be striving to prove independence and autonomy, he or she is adjusting to a number of complex changes, and his or her mother's entrance into the labor force may pose an added threat to his or her security. Conversely, a young adolescent whose mother has been employed throughout his or her childhood may welcome the freedom, independence, and added responsibilities brought on by the mother's absence.

Another important distinction is the difference between full-time and part-time employment effects. Clearly the demands and responsibilities (household chores, care of younger siblings, etc.) placed on an adolescent whose mother is gone forty hours a week differ from those placed on the son or daughter of a mother who is gone only five or ten hours a week. This distinction has been largely ignored in maternal employment research. Although considering these factors may provide useful information about how mother-adolescent relationships may differ from family to family and across different employment situations, it ignores the processes by which mothers influence adolescent development.

To illustrate, despite many inconsistent findings, many scholars agree that maternal employment status may not be the most salient influence on the child's development. Rather, research has pointed to a mother's satisfaction with her role, and not whether she is employed, as exerting the strongest influence on the developing child (Lerner & Galambos, 1986). Such findings underscore the use of a focus on processes linking maternal employment to adolescent development.

The work of Lerner and Galambos (1985) and the results of the Lerner and Lerner Pennsylvania Early Adolescent Transitions Study (PEATS) provide support for a model of such processes. This model proposes that the process by which role satisfaction influences child development is through the quality of the mother-child relationship. In other words, mothers who are more satisfied with their roles (regardless of whether they are working) are

more likely to interact positively with their children, leading to a higher quality mother-child relationship and more positive child outcomes. Thus, a mother's staying home or going to work outside the home will not ensure high-quality mother-adolescent interactions, but satisfaction with the roles of mother, employee, and wife (among others) is likely to influence positively the quality of the mother-adolescent relationship. In turn, a strong, supportive mother-adolescent relationship is likely to relate positively to the early adolescent's development of a strong sense of self or identity across a number of roles in a variety of contexts: as a child in a family, as a friend in a peer group, and as a student in a school.

Research Findings

Research that has looked at the relationship between maternal employment and adolescent development can be divided into three major areas: the relationship between maternal employment and delinquency, the relationship between maternal employment and the adolescent's intellectual and academic performance, and the relationship between maternal employment and adolescent personal and social adjustment.

MATERNAL EMPLOYMENT AND DELINQUENCY ▪ A predominant issue in the maternal employment research of the 1950s and 1960s was delinquency, and this issue is still of concern. Is the lack of supervision created by the mother's employment associated with higher rates of delinquency in the children of these employed mothers? The answer to this question is not clear. It appears that mother's employment itself does not seem to be related to delinquency, but the pattern of her employment and the adequacy of supervision do seem to be related. Gleuck and Gleuck (1957) found no relationship in a lower-class sample between son's delinquency and maternal employment. Higher rates of delinquency were associated with inadequate supervision and employed mothers; however, the sons of occasionally employed mothers were more likely not to be delinquent. In contrast, McCord, McCord, and Thurber (1963) found no difference in the adequacy of supervision in employed- and nonemployed-mother families. Also, Nye (1958) found that both very high and very low amounts of supervision were moderately related to delinquency.

Some sex differences have been found in regard to the influence of inadequate supervision on children. Woods (1972), in a study of lower-class fifth-grade children, found that inadequate supervision had no adverse effect on boys, but unsupervised girls showed lower school adjustment on tests of social relations and cognitive abilities. Complicating this issue further, maternal employment, adequacy of supervision, and delinquency do not seem to be systematically related across all socioeconomic classes. Nye (1963) found that delinquency was related to maternal employment in a middle-class sample, but no such relationship was found in a lower-class sample. This study did not assess supervision, however.

In the Gleuck and Gleuck (1957) study, the mother's pattern of employment was also found to influence her child's delinquent behavior. Gleuck and Gleuck found no tendency for sons of regularly employed mothers to be delinquent; however, the sons of occasionally employed mothers were more likely to be delinquent. Even more important, perhaps, is the fact that these occasionally employed mothers were characterized as divorced or having

poor marriages or having husbands with poor work habits and emotional disturbances. Therefore delinquency in this group would seem to be related more to family instability or the father's inadequacies.

In a recent study of midwestern fifth, sixth, eighth, and ninth graders, Steinberg (1986) examined variations in after-school experiences and their relationship to negative peer influence. These after-school arrangements included at home with parent; at home in self-care; adult supervised at friend's, neighbor's, or relative's home; adult supervised at school; unsupervised at home or at a friend's home; or "hanging out." Steinberg found that children who reported home after school without a parent present were not significantly different from children who were supervised by their parents at home after school; however, children who were unsupervised at a friend's house or who described themselves as hanging out were more likely to engage in antisocial activities than the at-home groups. In addition, self-care children whose parents knew where they were and self-care youngsters who were raised authoritatively (characterized by high parental responsiveness and high demandingness) were less susceptible to negative influences than their peers. Some sex differences also emerged in Steinberg's study. For example, he found that girls who were on their own after school were more susceptible to peer pressure and more likely to engage in antisocial activity than were their adult-supervised peers.

In sum, the relationship between maternal employment and delinquency may be reduced to the relationship between adequacy of supervision and delinquency. Although some data point to the notion that lower-class working mothers provide less adequate supervision and that this is linked to delinquency, the data are not solid, and no evidence exists stating that the children of working mothers are more likely to be delinquent. What is needed is more in-depth research on the adequacy of supervision and child development and how this adequacy of supervision may be related to maternal employment status.

MATERNAL EMPLOYMENT AND THE ADOLESCENT'S INTELLECTUAL AND ACADEMIC PERFORMANCE ■

One characteristic of the child that has been most often examined in relation to maternal employment is academic achievement and intelligence. The premise that employed mothers do not have sufficient time to supervise their child's homework and academic pursuits has served to initiate such research.

Several studies using lower-class, black, or single-parent families demonstrated a relationship between maternal employment and intelligence in early adolescent children. For example, Woods (1972), in her study of fifth graders, found that full-time employed mothers had children with higher IQ scores on the California Test of Mental Maturity. Conversely, Hutner (1972) found no significant differences in children's IQ scores based on whether their mothers worked. She did find, however, that there was a direct, positive, and significant relationship between the educational attainment of the mother and the child's IQ, scholastic aptitude, and academic achievement. In this study, the mother's educational attainment was directly related to both parents' and teachers' expectations and aspirations for the child's attainment. Here, it was educational level of the mother and expectations for the child that related to the child's academic outcomes, and not maternal employment status. Hence, we may venture to say that the highly educated mother who is employed and holds high expectations for her child's

achievement probably compensates for her time away from the child and ensures that he or she is properly supervised and guided in the academic arena. Hutner's (1972) results clearly support the notion that maternal employment itself is unlikely to have a consistent, direct effect on early adolescent functioning.

Other studies provide inconsistent results—that is, relations that seem dependent on the age and sex of the child, the socioeconomic status of the family, the prestige of the mother's job, and the mother's role satisfaction. Jones, Lundsteen, and Michael (1967) matched children on social class, sex, age, and IQ and then compared the reading skills of children whose mothers were either full-time housewives or employed in professional jobs. They found that the children of the employed women were more proficient in reading. These parents spend more time in reading activity with the children and had more plans for the children's education. There were also more books in the home, and the mothers were better educated. Another study (Frankel, 1964) also found a difference between employed and professionally employed mothers of intellectually gifted adolescent boys. Frankel matched low and high achievers on IQ and found that low achievers were more likely to have employed mothers, but high achievers were more likely to have professional mothers. For high-school–aged children, most studies find no differences in school achievement based on whether the mother is employed (Keidel, 1970; Nelson, 1969).

Lerner, Hess, and Tubman (1986) examined the influences of timing of employment and part-time or full-time employment on the school grades of a sample of lower-middle-class sixth graders. Mothers were asked to report if they were employed part time or full time or not employed at each of four stages in their child's life: infancy, preschool years, grade school years (up to 5th grade), and currently. A few significant relationships with the child's academic and psychosocial functioning emerged. First, full-time employment during the child's infancy was associated with lower grade point averages in first grade. There was no difference in the first-grade grade point average of the children whose mothers either worked part time or were not employed. In addition, full-time maternal employment while the child was in sixth grade was associated with lowered grade point averages in the children. Again, there was no distinction between the children of the nonemployed or employed part-time mothers. Although these grade point average differences were significant, they were not substantial, ranging from two-tenths to six-tenths of a point.

Although these findings show a direct influence of work status on the child's academic performance, they should be interpreted with caution. First, there was no long-term influence of maternal employment on the child's academic performance. That is, working full time in infancy was related to performance only in first grade and not to performance later. It could be that the children who showed a decrement in grade point average in first grade were also having difficulty adjusting to school, although data does not exist to clarify this. For the sixth graders, it may be that the mothers of the group who showed a lower grade point average had just begun to work, although only 14% of the mothers showed this employment pattern. Most mothers (63.5%) stayed employed once they started working. Only 4.6% of the mothers of this sample showed an alternating pattern of going from employed to nonemployed and back to employed status or vice versa during the child's life.

The Lerner et al. (1986) study also found that satisfaction of the mother was more powerfully related to the child's academic performance than was maternal employment status. When maternal role difficulty and role satisfaction were related to child outcomes, they were more powerful predictors than work status alone. For example, the mother's report of being satisfied with child care arrangements and the division of labor for household chores was most related to the child having a higher grade point average. In turn, mothers who reported being dissatisfied had children with lower grade point averages. Hoffman (1979) also found that maternal satisfaction exerted a stronger influence on children's school achievement. She found that the elementary school children of employed mothers scored lower on teacher-rated performance than children of nonemployed mothers. It should be noted that in this study, the children of satisfied employed mothers had lower IQs than a matched nonemployed sample, but there were no IQ differences between the children of dissatisfied nonemployed or employed mothers.

Thus, research evidence suggests that maternal employment itself is unlikely to have a consistent, direct effect on early adolescent intellectual and academic performance. Rather, other variables in the child's context, such as social class, mother's and father's education, mother's role satisfaction, mother's job characteristics, and the child's motivations and abilities, to name a few, interact with maternal employment and mediate its influence on the child.

MATERNAL EMPLOYMENT AND ADOLESCENT PERSONAL AND SOCIAL ADJUSTMENT ■ The research findings are relatively clear regarding maternal employment influences on adolescent psychosocial functioning: employed mothers of adolescents are happier, more satisfied, and more likely to encourage independence in their children than are

nonemployed mothers (Hoffman, 1979). This may also be true of mothers who are not employed but have interests and activities outside the home, but these mothers and their children have not been systematically studied, so conclusions are harder to draw for this group. Studies of mothers who work outside the home during the child's adolescence have found daughters to be more outgoing, independent, and motivated and to appear better adjusted on social and personality measures. Adolescent sons also show better social and personality adjustment, have better family relations, and show better interpersonal relations at school. And both sons and daughters are less likely to show sex-role stereotypes than do children from families in which the mother is not employed (Hoffman, 1979).

The context of maternal employment fits well with the needs of the early adolescent. Particularly true for daughters, children are exposed to the new adult roles they will occupy. It is very likely that daughters will be employed while they are mothers and equally likely that sons will be married to a female who will be employed most of her adult life. Therefore, the presence of an employed mother affects the daughter by directly modeling her adult role, and it affects the son by the changes in the father's role that accompany maternal employment. Adolescent children are also given more household responsibilities when their mothers are employed, and this has been found to contribute to their positive self-esteem (Smokler, 1975).

Lerner et al. (1986) investigated the influences of maternal work status, role difficulty, and satisfaction on early adolescents' perceived competence in several areas and found several interesting relationships. First, when mothers reported that they were experiencing little role difficulty and high role satisfaction, their children reported themselves as being more athletically competent. This finding was stronger for males than females. Similarly, when mothers were satisfied with the division of labor in the house with respect to child care, the adolescent reported a higher level of perceived scholastic competence than did the adolescents of mothers who were not satisfied. In addition, the mother's satisfaction with the division of labor for household chores was positively related to the child's conduct as rated by his or her teacher, indicating that higher satisfaction was linked with more positive conduct. Along the same lines, a high level of maternal satisfaction with child care was related to high teacher-rated scholastic competence for the child.

In turn, these findings point to the importance of going beyond work status in evaluating the child's development. The mother's emotional state, satisfaction, and role difficulty contribute in important ways to the child's functioning whether or not the mother is employed.

Conclusions

Research to date has stressed to those concerned with the influences of maternal employment on early adolescent development that there is rarely a direct link between work status and the child's development. Rather, other characteristics in the family context or the child's own characteristics typically have more of an influence on the child's development than the mother's employment status. For example, the type and quality of supervision the child receives after school, the quality of the parent-child relationship, and the mother's role satisfaction are all more powerful predictors of the child's development than is maternal employment status. We recognize, however, that maternal employment can affect the mother's satisfaction and role difficulty in many ways. So, too, can nonemployment, as in the case of the mother who prefers to be employed but is not.

In sum, recent studies have demonstrated the need for concerned researchers and practitioners to go beyond work status and to examine the processes by which work status influences child development. Of course, the child's functioning can be influenced by many other factors in the context or in the individual child. Maternal employment is only one aspect of the child's world that has been shown to exert an influence on the child's development. One needs to examine other influences as well as those related to the mother's employment situation to understand fully how maternal employment influences adolescent development.

References

Frankel, E. (1964). Characteristics of working and non-working mothers among intellectually gifted high and low achievers. *Personnel and Guidance Journal, 42*, 776–780.

Gleuck, S., & Gleuck, E. (1957). Working mothers and delinquency. *Mental Hygiene, 41*, 327–352.

Hoffman, L. W. (1979). Maternal employment: 1979. *American Psychologist, 34*, 859–865.

Hutner, F. C. (1972). Mother's education and working: Effect on the school child. *Journal of Psychology, 82*, 27–37.

Jones, J. B., Lundsteen, S. W., & Michael, W. B. (1967). The relationship of the professional employment status of mothers to reading achievement of sixth-grade children. *California Journal of Educational Research, 43*, 102–108.

Keidel, K. C. (1970). Maternal employment and ninth grade achievement in Bismarck, North Dakota. *Family Coordinator, 19*, 95–97.

Lerner, J. V., & Galambos, N. L. (1985). Maternal role satisfaction, mother-child inter-action, and child temperament. *Developmental Psychology, 21*, 1157–1164.

Lerner, J. V., & Galambos, N. L. (1986). Child development and family change: The influences of maternal employment on infants and toddlers. In L. P. Lipsitt & C. Rovee-Collier (Eds.), *Advances in infancy research* (Vol. 4, pp. 39–86). Hillsdale, NJ: Lawrence Erlbaum Associates.

Lerner, J. V., Hess, L. E., & Tubman, J. (1986, March). *Maternal employment, maternal role satisfaction, and early adolescent outcomes*. Paper presented at the First Meeting of the Society for Research on Adolescence, Madison, Wisconsin, March 21–23.

McCord, J., McCord, W., & Thurber, E. (1963). Effects of maternal employment on lower-class boys. *Journal of Abnormal and Social Psychology, 67*, 177–182.

Nelson, D. D. (1969). A study of school achievement among adolescent children with working and non-working mothers. *Journal of Educational Research, 62*, 456–457.

Nye, F. I. (1958). *Family relationships and delinquent behavior*. New York: Wiley.

Smokler, C. S. (1975). *Self-esteem in pre-adolescent and adolescent females*. Unpublished doctoral dissertation, University of Michigan, Ann Arbor.

Steinberg, L. (1986). Latch-key children and susceptibility to peer pressure: An ecological analysis. *Developmental Psychology, 22*, 433–439.

Woods, M. B. (1972). The unsupervised child of the working mother. *Developmental Psychology, 6*, 14–25.

See Also

Employment; Parenthood and Marriage in Adolescence: Associations with Educational and Occupational Attainment; Unemployment; Vocational Development and Choice in Adolescence; Vocational Training.

Maturational Timing Variations in Adolescent Girls, Antecedents of

Jeanne Brooks-Gunn
Educational Testing Service

The transition to adolescence is that period of life when a child is transformed physically into an adult and is expected to exhibit at least some behaviors indicative of this new status. What strikes any observer is the large variability in the onset and timing of puberty. In this entry, the antecedents of maturational variability are explored, using girls' menarcheal age as the focus. This focus is necessary because virtually all of the research on antecedents of maturational timing use menarche as the marker. The same is not true for work on the consequences of maturational variation, as markers such as the growth spurt and the onset and timing of secondary sexual characteristics are used to document variation.

Genetic and Environmental Influences on Maturational Timing

Clearly, both genetic and environmental factors play a role in the timing of maturation. Menarcheal age of mothers and daughters is related, with correlations typically ranging from .30 to .45 (Brooks-Gunn & Warren, 1988; Zacharias & Wurtman, 1969).

Nutrition, leanness, and exercise/activity are believed to be the most relevant environmental factors (Brooks-Gunn & Reiter, 1990). The secular trend in menarcheal age, which has been documented for Western cultures (Eveleth & Tanner, 1976), is typically used as evidence for the role of nutrition and corresponding weight (in fact, for Western countries, the secular trend seems to have flattened in the past 20 years). Menarcheal age is higher in times of famine and in poorer segments of societies, particularly those in which nutrition is not adequate for maturational-linked weight gains (Eveleth & Tanner, 1976). However, limits seem to be inherent in the delay of menarche associated with weight (and presumably nutrition). For example, as Garn (1980) has demonstrated, even girls who weigh less than 47 kilograms do begin to menstruate in the adolescent years, with all of them reaching menarche by age 18 or 19.

In some instances, physical conditions influence maturational timing variation. Hypothyroidism, blindness, and retardation advance menarche, and thyrotoxicosis and muscular development retard it (see Brooks-Gunn, 1988, p. 106, and Warren, 1983, for reviews). Some of these effects may be mediated by exercise or activity patterns and weight. For example, blind and retarded children may exhibit lower activity levels and/or may weigh more than nonhandicapped children, which in turn could influence maturational timing. Hypothyroidism, which involves the metabolic process, may result in heavier children, with weight acting as the mediator of maturational timing. Such hypotheses have not been directly tested, however.

Number of children in the family and high altitude also are predictors of menarcheal age (Frisch & Revelle, 1973; Malina, 1988). The reasons for these differences are not fully understood.

Prediction of Delayed Menarche: The Case of Athletes

Another approach to the study of tempo variation antecedents focuses on groups who are likely to have delayed menarche, such as elite athletes or young adolescents with anorexia nervosa. In both instances menarcheal ages are later than population norms would predict. Delayed menarche is a common characteristic of many groups of female athletes, especially those who compete nationally. Delays of one or two years are reported for gymnasts, figure skaters, dancers, and runners (Frisch et al., 1981; Malina, 1983; Warren, Brooks-Gunn, Hamilton, Hamilton, & Warren, 1986). Delays are less likely to be seen in athletes such as swimmers (Brooks-Gunn, Burrow, & Warren, 1988). The mean ages of menarche do vary across studies, with these differences being attributed, in part, to the type of sport, the competitiveness of the individual athlete, and the process of selection for particular sports. Little is known about the characteristics of sports that may result in a greater incidence of menarcheal delays (Malina, 1983).

Both genetic and environmental factors probably account for menarcheal delays seen in athletes. The stringent selection process for elite athletes may make it more likely that late maturing girls will become athletes. The physical characteristics associated with delayed menarche—relatively narrow hips, long legs, and lower weight for height (McNeill & Livson, 1963; Tanner, 1962)—may render an individual girl more suited for most competitive athletics. Selection for certain physical characteristics, if it occurs (and most coaches say it does), is probably for leanness and a linear body build, not delayed menarche per se (Hamilton, Brooks-Gunn, Warren, & Hamilton, 1988). Early maturing girls may be at a special disadvantage in many sports (Malina, 1975), although few studies have directly examined this premise (Brooks-Gunn, Attie, Burrow, Rosso, & Warren, 1989).

As found in samples of athletes, environmental factors possibly associated with delayed menarche include weight and body mass, intensity and duration of exercise, and restricted food intake (Brooks-Gunn, Warren, & Hamilton, 1987; Houston, 1980; Malina, 1983). However, it is difficult to assess the relative effects of such factors because they are often interrelated, because large variation in these factors is found in samples of athletes, and because not all studies of athletes report associations between these factors and delayed menarche (Frisch et al., 1981; Malina, 1983). In a classic longitudinal study where weight and exercise were carefully monitored over several years, adolescent dancers were most likely to begin menstruating when they were not dancing (most often because of injuries), even when no corresponding increase in weight occurred during these periods of inactivity (Warren, 1980). This study demonstrates the importance of exercise, independent of weight, in menarcheal timing. Another example is that initiating training prior to menarche may be associated with later menarche than initiating training after menarche, at least in some groups of athletes (Frisch et al., 1981).

Comparing the characteristics of adolescents in different athletic groups helps explain variations in menarcheal age across different sports. At least two dimensions of sports endeavor are likely to be associated with menarcheal age. One is the body size and shape preferred by a particular athletic endeavor, and the other is the energy expended in training for a sport. Although sports are similar in that high standards of technical proficiency are demanded of all first-class athletes, they differ in terms of requirements for body shape and size.

Low weight is required of gymnasts, figure skaters, and dancers, all of whom are likely to have delayed maturation. In contrast, low weight is not demanded of swimmers, volleyball players, and some other athletes. Requirements for thinness sometimes go beyond what is necessary for the performance of a certain athletic endeavor, becoming an aesthetic preference. The most obvious example is the ballet dancer who, unless she is very thin, will not be accepted into a national company regardless of talent. While body size is to a large part genetically determined (Stunkard et al., 1986), it is also influenced by environmental factors (Garn & Clark, 1976). Diet, exercise, or a combination of the two affect body size (Stern & Lowney, 1986).

Another dimension that is important is amount of energy expended. While most elite athletes train four or more hours a day, sports differ on caloric expenditure, making it more likely that athletes engaged in activities requiring high caloric expenditure will find it easier to maintain a low weight than those in sports using less energy, assuming similar duration of training and levels of cardiovascular fitness.

In order to examine the effects of energy expended and weight demands on menarcheal delays, one study compared adolescents engaging in three sports: dance (low energy expended and low weight demands), figure skating (high energy expended and low weight demands), and swimming (high energy expended and no weight demands). Menarcheal delays were more common in the two groups that had low weight requirements than the one that did not. At the same time, the dancers were more likely to diet than the figure skaters, perhaps because in the absence of high energy expenditure, limiting food consumption was necessary to maintain low weights (Brooks-Gunn, Burrow, & Warren, 1988).

Although dieting behavior seems to be associated with delayed menarche and secondary amenorrhea (Brooks-Gunn, Warren, & Hamilton, 1987), little is known about actual nutritional intake and menarcheal delays. In a study of adult elite dancers, high eating problem scores were associated with low levels of protein and fat intake (Hamilton, Brooks-Gunn, & Warren, 1986). In another study, prepubertally trained college athletes consumed fewer calories, specifically less fat and protein, than did postpubertally trained athletes (Frisch et al., 1981).

Conclusion

In brief, antecedents of tempo variations include genetic and environmental components. What is of interest here is the fact that a girl's behavior might alter the genetic timetable for tempo. This may be best illustrated by the athlete who has chosen a sport for which very low weights are required, for which training begins at an early age, or for which large amounts of energy are expended.

References

Brooks-Gunn, J. (1988). Antecedents and consequences of variations in girls' maturational timing. In E. R. McAnarney & M. Levine (Eds.), *Early adolescent transitions* (pp. 101–121). New York: Heath.

Brooks-Gunn, J., Attie, I., Burrow, C., Rosso, J. T., & Warren, M. P. (1989). The impact of puberty on body and eating concerns in different athletic and nonathletic contexts. *Journal of Early Adolescence, 9*(3), 269–290.

Brooks-Gunn, J., Burrow, C., & Warren, M. P. (1988). Attitudes toward eating and body weight in different groups of female adolescent athletes. *International Journal of Eating Disorders, 7,* 749–758.

Brooks-Gunn, J., & Reiter, E. O. (1990). The role of pubertal processes in the early adolescent transition. In S. Feldman & G. Elliott (Eds.), *At the threshold: The developing adolescent.* (pp. 16–53). Cambridge: Harvard University Press.

Brooks-Gunn, J., & Warren, M. P. (1988). Mother-daughter differences in menarcheal age in adolescent dancers and nondancers. *Annals of Human Biology, 15*(1), 35–43.

Brooks-Gunn, J., Warren, M. P., & Hamilton, L. H. (1987). The relationship of eating disorders to amenorrhea in ballet dancers. *Medicine and Science in Sports and Exercise, 19*(1), 41–44.

Eveleth, P. B., & Tanner, J. M. (1976). *Worldwide variation in human growth.* London: Cambridge University Press.

Frisch, R. E., Gotz-Welbergen, A. V., McArthur, J. W., Albright, T., Witschi, J., Bullen, B., Birnholz, J., Reed, R. B., & Hermann, H. (1981). Delayed menarche and amenorrhea of college athletes in relation to age of onset of training. *Journal of the American Medical Association, 246,* 1559–1590.

Frisch, R. E., & Revelle, R. (1973). Components of weight at menarche and the limitation of the adolescent growth spurt in girls: Estimated total water, lean body weight, and fat. *Human Biology, 45,* 469–483.

Garn, S. M. (1980). Continuities and change in maturational timing. In O. Brim & J. Kagan (Eds.), *Constancy and change in human development* (pp. 113–162). Cambridge: Harvard University Press.

Garn, S. M., & Clark, D. C. (1976). Trends in fatness and the origins of obesity. *Pediatrics, 57,* 443–456.

Hamilton, L. H., Brooks-Gunn, J., & Warren, M. P. (1986). Nutritional intake of female dancers: A reflection of eating problems. *International Journal of Eating Disorders, 5,* 925–934.

Hamilton, L. H., Brooks-Gunn, J., Warren, M. P., & Hamilton, W. G. (1988). The role of selectivity in the pathogenesis of eating disorders. *Medicine and Science in Sports and Exercise, 20*(6), 560–565.

Houston, M. E. (1980). Diet, training, and sleep: A survey study of elite Canadian swimmers. *Canadian Journal of Applied Sport Science, 5,* 161–163.

Malina, R. M. (1975). Anthropometric correlates of strength and motor performance. *Exercise and Sport Sciences Review, 3,* 249–274.

Malina, R. M. (1983). Menarche in athletes: A synthesis and hypothesis. *Annals of Human Biology, 10,* 1–24.

Malina, R. M. (1988). The adolescent growth spurt and sexual maturation. In M. Shangold & G. Mirkin (Eds.), *Women and Exercise: Physiology and sports medicine* (pp. 120–128). Philadelphia: F. A. Davis.

McNeill, D., & Livson, N. (1963). Maturation rate and body build in women. *Child Development, 34*, 25–32.

Stern, J. S., & Lowney, P. (1986). Obesity: The role of physical activity. In K. D. Brownell & J. P. Foreyt (Eds.), *Handbook of eating disorders: Physiology, psychology, and treatment of obesity, anorexia, and bulimia* (pp. 145–158). New York: Basic Books.

Stunkard, A. J., Sorensen, T. I. A., Hanis, C., Teasdale, T. W., Chakraborty, R., Schull, W. J., & Schulsinger, F. (1986). An adoption study of obesity. *New England Journal of Medicine, 314*, 193–198.

Tanner, J. M. (1962). *Growth at adolescence: With a general consideration of the effects of hereditary and environmental factors upon growth and maturation from birth to maturity* (2nd ed.). Oxford: Blackwell Scientific Publications.

Warren, M. P. (1980). The effects of exercise on pubertal progression and reproductive function in girls. *Journal of Clinical Endocrinology and Metabolism, 51*, 1150–1157.

Warren, M. P. (1983). Physical and biological aspects of puberty. In J. Brooks-Gunn & A. C. Petersen (Eds.), *Girls at puberty: Biological and psychosocial perspectives* (pp. 3–28). New York: Plenum Press.

Warren, M. P., Brooks-Gunn, J., Hamilton, L. H., Hamilton, W. G., & Warren, L. F. (1986). Scoliosis and fractures in young ballet dancers: Relationship to delayed menarcheal age and secondary amenorrhea. *New England Journal of Medicine, 314*, 1348–1353.

Zacharias, L., & Wurtman, R. J. (1969). Age at menarche: Genetic and environmental influences. *New England Journal of Medicine, 280*, 868–875.

See Also

Cognitive Abilities and Physical Maturation; Growth Spurt, Adolescent; Maturational Timing Variations in Adolescent Girls, Consequences of; Menarche and Body Image; Menarche, Secular Trend in Age of; Menstrual Cycle; Physical Status and Timing in Early Adolescence, Measurement of; Pubertal Development, Assessment of; Puberty, Body Fat and; Puberty Education; Puberty, Endocrine Changes at; Puberty, Hypothalamic-Pituitary Changes of; Puberty, Precocious, Treatment of; Puberty, Sport and; Spatial Ability and Maturation in Adolescence; Spermarche.

Portions of this article first appeared in Brooks-Gunn, J. (1988), Antecedents and consequences of variations in girls' maturational timing, in M. D. Levine & E. R. McAnarney (Eds.), Early Adolescent Transitions (pp. 102–121), Lexington, MA: D. C. Heath; and in Brooks-Gunn, J. (1988), "Antecedents and consequences of variations in girls' maturational timing," Journal of Adolescent Health Care, 9 (5), 365–373.

Maturational Timing Variations in Adolescent Girls, Consequences of

Jeanne Brooks-Gunn

Educational Testing Service

Until recently, not much was known about the consequences of girls being early or late maturers, in part due to the disparities in measuring tempo and findings of earlier studies (Faust, 1986; Peskin, 1967). It has been hypothesized that being on time is more advantageous than being off time, and that early maturing girls are at more of a disadvantage than late maturers because the former are more deviant compared to their male and female classmates. Most current research suggests that most timing effects have to do with being early, not late (Brooks-Gunn, Petersen, & Eichorn, 1985). Maturation-timing influences can be seen in girls' physical development, preparation for and feelings about menarche, body image and self-image, deviant behavior, and relationships with parents and peers, as discussed in this entry.

Early maturers weigh more and are slightly shorter than late maturers when pubertal growth is complete. These differences remain throughout life (Garn, 1980). Early maturers may not be as prepared for pubertal change as are late maturers. Approximately 10–15% of white adolescent girls report not being prepared for menarche (i.e., not given information and not having parents discuss it (Ruble & Brooks-Gunn, 1982)). The early maturer may not receive as much factual information as the late maturer because health education classes typically occur at the end of fifth grade or in the sixth grade, after the early maturer has already had menarche. In addition, mothers, who are a girl's most likely primary source of information about puberty and menarche, may be less likely to discuss changes with their early maturing daughters (Brooks-Gunn & Ruble, 1982). Early maturers are less likely to report that their fathers know their menarche and are less likely to directly tell their fathers about it (Brooks-Gunn, 1987). Because girls in part seem to choose close girlfriends on the basis of physical status (Brooks-Gunn, Samelson, Warren, & Fox, 1986), early maturing girls may have a smaller network of intimate friends. All of these potential influences may affect the early maturing girls' attitudes about menstruation, which continue to be more negative, and their menstrual symptoms, which are more severe than one-time or late maturing girls, even in later adolescence (Brooks-Gunn & Ruble, 1982).

Early maturing girls seem to have a poorer body image than on-time or late maturing girls, at least when global measures of body image and weight-related measures are used (Tobin-Richards, Boxer, & Petersen, 1983). This is true of girls in elementary school, junior high school, and senior high school (Blyth, Simmons, & Zakin, 1985; Duncan, Ritter, Dornbusch, Gross, & Carlsmith, 1985). In addition, higher eating-problem scores are found among early maturing girls compared to on-time and late maturing girls, and this lasts throughout the adolescent years (Brooks-Gunn & Warren, 1985). In part, such differences are due to the following: Body build appears to be related to peer evaluations and prestige; being thin is a desirable condition for almost all adolescent girls; and dieting is a common response to the current cultural demands for thinness (Attie & Brooks-Gunn, 1987, 1989; Brooks-Gunn, Attie, Burrow, Rosso & Warren, 1989). Early maturing girls, by virtue of being somewhat heavier, do not conform to the cultural values that promote thinness. Thus, it is not surprising that they may have a less positive body image than do late maturing girls (Attie & Brooks-Gunn, 1989).

Maturation status by itself, however, does not seem to affect overall self-esteem. Instead, self-esteem appears to be affected simultaneously by the occurrence of physical and social changes (Simmons & Blyth, 1987).

Early maturers may engage in "adult behaviors" (such as smoking, drinking, and intercourse) at a younger age than later maturing girls, as reported in the large prospective Swedish study of Magnusson and colleagues (Magnusson, Stattin, & Allen, 1985). This may be due, in part, to the fact that early maturers tend to associate with older peers. Perhaps by virtue of their physical appearance, some early maturers seek out (or are sought out by) older peers, who are more likely to engage in such behaviors. Long-term consequences of engaging in such behaviors at young ages is currently being studied by Magnusson et al. (1985).

Early maturers seem to be somewhat more advanced with respect to dating than are on-time or late maturers, at least in middle school (Magnusson et al., 1985; Simmons, Blyth, & McKinney, 1983). However, pubertal status does not seem to be associated with dating behavior, suggesting that maturation vis-a-vis one's peers plays a larger role than the actual maturation status (Gargiulo, Attie, Brooks-Gunn, & Warren, 1987).

Currently, several investigators are pursuing the issue of family adaptation to early adolescence as a function of pubertal status (Brooks-Gunn & Zahaykevich, 1989; Paikoff, Brooks-Gunn & Warren, in press). Observation of family interactions and self-report measures have been collected on seventh-grade girls and their parents, and divided into four groups: menarche more than 12 months ago; menarche 6–11 months ago; menarche within the last 6 months; and premenarcheal (Hill, 1988; Hill, Holmbeck, Marlow, Green, & Lynch, 1985). Results suggest that "perturbations," to borrow a term used by Hill, occur immediately following menarche. Girls who have just begun to menstruate are perceived as less accepting and the family as more controlling when compared with the premenarcheal and more postmenarcheal girls. Of particular interest are the results of those girls who reached menarche over a year earlier. They resemble the immediate postmenarche group in terms of reporting strain in parent-child relations. The authors hypothesize that these findings may be due to the early maturation status of the girls in the group reaching menarche a year ago (i.e., menarche in the sixth grade or earlier).

Early maturers may exhibit more psychopathology than on-time or late maturers, as found in two studies (Brooks-Gunn & Warren, 1985; Petersen & Crockett, 1985). They may also exhibit less impulse control and poorer emotional tone (i.e., more depressive affect). In a study that used hormone status to define early and late maturation, earlier maturing girls, as defined by follicle-stimulating hormone levels, had higher psychopathology and depressive affect scores than on-time or late-maturing girls. However, no associations were found between emotional function and other hormones (Susman et al., 1985). In another study measuring hormones, the most rapid rises in estradiol hormone was associated with relatively high levels of depressive affect, irrespective of maturational timing (Brooks-Gunn & Warren, 1989; Warren & Brooks-Gunn, 1989). These effects persist one year later (Paikoff, Brooks-Gunn & Warren, in press). Thus, psychopathology and poor emotional tone (which may be indicative of a mild depressive affect) may be associated with early maturation in young adolescent girls. Additionally, early maturing girls who experience negative family and school events are more likely to exhibit depressive affect than later maturing girls who experience negative events (Brooks-Gunn, Warren, & Rosso, in press). In yet another study, late maturation was a "protective" factor against depressive affect (Baydar, Brooks-Gunn, & Warren, in press).

Although early maturation may be a risk factor, several caveats are in order. First, the effects appear to be small. Second, our understanding of maturation timing effects is greatly enhanced by the notion of on-time and off-time events. Neugarten (1979), in particular, discussed how the life cycle is perceived in terms of a set of norms about what events should occur and when. Critical to this notion is the individual's perception of timeliness, as well as actual timing. That is, an event may be perceived to be on-time or off-time depending on a variety of factors, such as one's reference group, the cohort in which one finds oneself, the importance to the individual of being in the "correct" phase, and an individual's perception of the on-time range (Lerner, 1985; Tobin-Richards, Boxer, & Petersen, 1983). Third, an early maturer may be at most risk when the requirements of a particular social context and a girl's physical and behavioral characteristics are mismatched. On-time dancers are a case in point. With regard to the general peer group, they are on-time and should not exhibit any particular problems; however, they do not have the characteristics deemed ideal by the dance world. That they do look quite different physically from late maturers is probably a consequence of having higher weights and less control over eating than the profession demands (Brooks-Gunn et al., 1989; Brooks-Gunn & Warren, 1985).

Only certain behaviors seem to be affected by timing of maturation. Cultural standards seem to play a role. Of all of the psychological factors studied, body image is most affected by early maturation. Clearly, the demand for thinness, to the point of desiring to be below one's supposed ideal weight for height, contributes to the potential difficulties an early maturing girl may face (Attie, Brooks-Gunn, & Petersen, in press). Since the entire repertoire of adolescent behaviors have not been examined vis-a-vis the timing of maturation, other behaviors may also be influenced.

References

Attie, I., & Brooks-Gunn, J. (1987). Weight concerns as chronic stressors in women. In R. C. Barnett, L. Biener, & G. K. Baruch (Eds.), *Gender and stress* (pp. 218–254). New York: Free Press.

Attie, I., & Brooks-Gunn, J. (1989). The development of eating problems in adolescent girls: A longitudinal study. *Developmental Psychology, 25,* 70–79.

Attie, I., Brooks-Gunn, J., & Petersen, A. C. (1990). The emergence of eating problems: A developmental perspective. In M. Lewis & S. Miller (Eds.), *Handbook of developmental psychopathology* (pp. 409–420). New York: Plenum Press.

Baydar, N., Brooks-Gunn, J., & Warren, M. P. (in press). Determinants of depressive symptoms in adolescent girls: A four-year longitudinal study. *Developmental Psychology.*

Blyth, D. A., Simmons, R. G., & Zakin, D. F. (1985). Satisfaction with body image for early adolescent females: The impact of pubertal timing within different school environments. *Journal of Youth and Adolescence, 14,* 207–225.

Brooks-Gunn, J. (1987). Pubertal processes and girls' psychological adaptation. In R. M. Lerner & T. T Foch (Eds.), *Biological-psychosocial interactions in early adolescence: A life-span perspective* (pp. 123–153). Hillsdale, NJ: Lawrence Erlbaum Associates.

Brooks-Gunn, J., Attie, I., Burrow, C., Rosso, J. T., & Warren, M. P. (1989). The impact of puberty on body and eating concerns in different athletic and nonathletic contexts. *Journal of Early Adolescence, 9*(3), 269–290.

Brooks-Gunn, J., Petersen, A. C., & Eichorn, D. (1985). Special Issue: Time of maturation and psychosocial functioning in adolescence. *Journal of Youth and Adolescence, 14,* (3/4).

Brooks-Gunn, J., & Ruble, D. N. (1982). The development of menstrual-related beliefs and behaviors during early adolescence. *Child Development, 53,* 1567–1577.

Brooks-Gunn, J., Samelson, M., Warren, M. P., & Fox, R. (1986). Physical similarity of and disclosure of menarcheal status to friends: Effects of age and pubertal status. *Journal of Early Adolescence, 6,* 3–14.

Brooks-Gunn, J., & Warren, M. P. (1985). Effects of delayed menarche in different contexts: Dance and nondance students. *Journal of Youth and Adolescence, 14,* 285–300.

Brooks-Gunn, J., & Warren, M. P. (1989). Biological contributions to affective expression in young adolescent girls. *Child Development, 60,* 372–385.

Brooks-Gunn, J., Warren, M. P., & Rosso, J. T. (in press). The impact of pubertal and social events upon girls' problem behavior. *Journal of Youth and Adolescence.*

Brooks-Gunn, J., & Zahaykevich, M. (1989). Parent-child relationships in early adolescence: A developmental perspective. In K. Kreppner & R. M. Lerner (Eds.), *Family systems and life-span development* (pp. 223–246). Hillsdale, NJ: Lawrence Erlbaum Associates.

Duncan, P. D., Ritter, P. L., Dornbusch, S. M., Gross, R. T., & Carlsmith, J. M. (1985). The effects of pubertal timing on body image, school behavior, and deviance. *Journal of Youth and Adolescence, 14,* 227–235.

Faust, M. S. (1960). Developmental maturity as a determinant in prestige of adolescent girls. *Child Development, 31,* 173–186.

Gargiulo, J., Attie, I., Brooks-Gunn, J., & Warren, M. P. (1987). Dating in middle school girls: Effects of social context, maturation, and grade. *Developmental Psychology, 23,* 730–737.

Garn, S. M. (1980). Continuities and change in maturational timing. In O. Brim & J. Kagan (Eds.), *Constancy and change in human development* (pp. 113–162). Cambridge: Harvard University Press.

Hill, J. P. (1988). Adapting to menarche: Familial control and conflict. In M. Gunnar (Ed.), *Development during the transition to adolescence* (Vol. 21, pp. 43–77). Hillsdale, NJ: Lawrence Erlbaum Associates.

Hill, J. P., Holmbeck, G. N., Marlow, L., Green, L., & Lynch, M. E. (1985). Menarcheal status and parent-child relations in families of seventh-grade girls. *Journal of Youth and Adolescence, 14*, 301–316.

Lerner, R. M. (1985). Adolescent maturational changes and psychosocial development: A dynamic interactional perspective. *Journal of Youth and Adolescence, 14*, 355–372.

Magnusson, D., Stattin, H., & Allen, V. L. (1985). Biological maturation and social development: A longitudinal study of some adjustment processes from mid-adolescence to adulthood. *Journal of Youth and Adolescence, 14*, 267–283.

Neugarten, B. L. (1979). Time, age, and life cycle. *American Journal of Psychiatry, 136*, 887–894.

Paikoff, R. L., Brooks-Gunn, J., & Warren, M. P. (in press). Effects of girls' hormonal status on effective expression over the course of one year. *Journal of Youth and Adolescence*.

Peskin, H. (1967). Pubertal onset and ego functioning. *Journal of Abnormal Psychology, 72*, 1–15.

Petersen, A. C., & Crockett, L. (1985). Pubertal timing and grade effects on adjustment. *Journal of Youth and Adolescence, 14*, 191–206.

Ruble, D. N., & Brooks-Gunn, J. (1982). The experience of menarche. *Child Development, 53*, 1557–1566.

Simmons, R. G., & Blyth, D. A. (1987). *Moving into adolescence: The impact of pubertal change and school context.* New York: Aldine DeGruyter.

Simmons, R. G., Blyth, D. A., & McKinney, K. L. (1983). The social and psychological effects of puberty on white females. In J. Brooks-Gunn & A. C. Petersen (Eds.), *Girls at puberty: Biological and psychosocial perspectives* (pp. 229–272). New York: Plenum Press.

Susman, E. J., Nottelmann, E. D., Inoff-Germain, G. E., Dorn, L. D., Cutler, G. B., Jr., Loriaux, D. L., & Chrousos, G. P. (1985). The relation of relative hormonal levels and physical development and social-emotional behavior in young adolescents. *Journal of Youth and Adolescence, 14*, 245–264.

Tobin-Richards, M. H., Boxer, A. M., & Petersen, A. C. (1983). The psychological significance of pubertal change: Sex differences in perceptions of self during early adolescence. In J. Brooks-Gunn & A. C. Petersen (Eds.), *Girls at puberty: Biological and psychosocial perspectives* (pp. 127–154). New York: Plenum Press.

Warren, M. P., & Brooks-Gunn, J. (1989). Mood and behavior at adolescence: Evidence for hormonal factors. *Journal of Clinical Endocrinology and Metabolism, 69*(1), 77–83.

See Also

Cognitive Abilities and Physical Maturation; Growth Spurt, Adolescent; Maturational Timing, Antecedents of in Girls; Menarche and Body Image; Menarche, Secular Trend in Age of; Menstrual Cycle; Physical Status and Timing in Early Adolescence, Measurement of; Pubertal Development, Assessment of; Puberty, Body Fat and; Puberty Education; Puberty, Endocrine Changes at; Puberty, Hypothalamic-Pituitary Changes of; Puberty, Precocious, Treatment of; Puberty, Sport and; Spatial Ability and Maturation in Adolescence; Spermarche.

Portions of this article appeared in Brooks-Gunn, J. (1988). Antecedents and consequences of variations in girls' maturational timing. Journal of Adolescent Health Care, 9, 365–373. In addition, an expanded version was published as: Antecedents and consequences of variations in girls' maturational timing. (1988). In M. Levine & E. R. McAnarney (Eds.), Early adolescent transitions (pp. 101–121). Lexington, MA: D.C. Heath Publications.

Measuring Physical Status and Timing in Early Adolescence

Jeanne Brooks-Gunn
Educational Testing Service

Michelle P. Warren
St. Luke's-Roosevelt Hospital Center

In order to understand the effects of puberty, it is necessary to examine some of the physical parameters related to maturation. This entry reviews anthropomorphic measures and secondary sexual characteristics associated with puberty in terms of their usefulness for psychological research and measurement.

Anthropomorphic Measures

BONE AGE ∎ Skeletal maturation is typically measured by an X-ray of the bones, usually the wrist and hand, less commonly the knee and long bones. Based on epiphyseal fusion of different bone centers and osseous maturation, bone status has been extensively studied (Styne & Grumbach, 1978). Radiographs are made of the hand and wrist and compared to norms published in the Greulich and Pyle (1959) atlas or the more recent norms of

Tanner and colleagues (Tanner, Whitehouse, Marshall, Healy, & Goldstein, 1975). Reproductions enable the skeletal age of the child to be identified and compared to his or her chronological age. Height predictions can also be made with this data by using tables from a variety of sources (Acheson, Fowler, Fry, et al., 1963; Bayley & Pinneau, 1952; Roche, 1974; Roche, Davila, & Eyman, 1971; Roche, French, & Davila, 1971; Tanner et al., 1975).

Bone age has been used as a status and timing measure. The early growth studies all used bone X-rays for timing classifications (Jones & Bayley, 1950; Jones & Mussen, 1958; Peskin, 1973). However, it is not as salient to the adolescent as other changes, since skeletal growth changes are not directly observed.

HEIGHT ∎ The most common anthropomorphic measure is standing height. Other measures for which extensive data have been collected include foot, leg, hand, and trunk length (Tanner & Whitehouse, 1976). Typically, changes in height over age are assessed using curve-fitting techniques (Bock, Wainer, Petersen, Thissen, Murray, & Roche, 1973; Thissen, Bock, Wainer, & Roche, 1976). In addition, maximum velocity and age at the peak of the growth spurt are examined (Faust, 1977; Malina, 1978). The interest in velocity changes necessitates charting a child's height from middle childhood onwards— for girls, from age 8 or 9, and for boys, from age 9 or 10.

Measurement of height is straightforward. In order to minimize measurement errors, it is advisable to take two or three readings using a T-square and a tape measure, and then compute an average. Percentiles are available for age, gender, and pubertal status (Hamill, Drizd, Johnson, Reed, & Roche, 1976; Hamill, Johnston, & Lemeshow, 1973; National Center for Health Statistics, 1976; Tanner & Whitehouse, 1976). Self-report data are fairly accurate (correlations with actual height are in the 90s), even for young adolescents (Brooks-Gunn, Warren, Gargiulo, & Rosso, 1987). Peak height velocity is moderately related to other pubertal indices. Peak height velocity may be used to classify subjects as early, on-time, and late maturers (Faust, 1977).

WEIGHT ■ Weight, like height, increases through pubertal growth, with a weight spurt around the time of peak height velocity (Malina, 1978; Parizkova, 1976; Tanner & Whitehouse, 1976) often occurring after the growth spurt. However, much less is known about the weight spurt, and peak velocities typically are not charted (for an exception, see Tanner & Whitehouse, 1976). Thus, weight is represented as an absolute, as a ratio related to height,

or as a percentile. Percentile ratings take into account age and height, since weight increases with both during childhood and adolescence. Few norms are available by sexual maturation stages, even though weight varies as a function of secondary sexual status, even when age is controlled. Absolute weight or ideal weight using percentiles are used in most studies.

Measuring weight is relatively straightforward. Error of measurement is approximately ±2% with portable balance scales and ±4% with bathroom scales. If a bathroom scale is used, it should be calibrated after every two or three weighings. Individual variabilities also may result from observer error in reading the scale. Self-reports are surprisingly accurate, at least within five pounds (Brooks-Gunn et al., 1987). Almost all discrepancies for girls are in the direction of under-reporting, which is not surprising given the cultural ideal of thinness.

BODY FAT AND MUSCLE ■

Rapid weight gain is associated with an accumulation of body fat in girls and with increased muscle mass in boys (Tanner, 1968, 1974). The increases occur throughout sexual maturation, with the most rapid rise in body fat typically occurring in Tanner Stages 4 and 5 and in muscle circumference in Tanner Stages 3 and 4 (Gross, 1984). Gains in muscle circumference are seen closely following peak height velocity (Malina, 1978; Tanner, 1968). In addition, maximal strength of muscle occurs about one year after peak height velocity in boys (Stolz & Stolz, 1951), with more variability seen for girls (Faust, 1977).

Body fat may be measured by examining skinfold thickness or by hydrostatic weighing. Measurement of skinfolds are made on one side of the body at four sites:

biceps, triceps, iliac crest, and the subscapula area. The sum of these four skinfolds can be read off a table adjusted for sex and age (Durnin & Wormersley, 1974; Merrow, 1967; Wilmore & Behnke, 1970; Young, Sipin, & Rose, 1968). Measurements are taken at each site three times and the average computed. Sometimes only the upper arm skinfold is measured (Merrow, 1967). Norms are available for children (Seltzer, Goldman, & Mayer, 1965; Tanner & Whitehouse, 1975) and for adolescents over 16 (Durnin & Wormersley, 1974; Merrow, 1967; Wilmore & Behnke, 1970; Young et al., 1968). The two criteria used for defining fatness and thinness are: (1) skinfold thickness exceeding one standard deviation from the mean for their age and gender group (Seltzer et al., 1965) and (2) 10% of all children of each sex who have the thickest and thinnest skinfolds, using a minimum skinfold thickness of obesity and a maximum for thinness (Stunkard, d'Aquili, Fox, & Filion, 1972). Although skinfold thickness measurement is non-invasive, it takes extensive training and is only moderately reliable. Three measurements per site are taken because of the unreliability.

Secondary Sexual Characteristics

The progression of secondary sexual characteristics has been carefully documented by Tanner (1962, 1968, 1978) and colleagues. For girls, changes in breast and body hair development, and for boys, changes in body hair, changes in facial hair, voice lowering, penis development, and testicular volume, have been examined. Data are most complete for pubic hair development in both sexes, breast development in girls, and penile development and testicular volume in boys.

SEXUAL MATURATION STAGES ■

Following Reynold and Wines (1948, 1951), Tanner devised a system for rating the amount of growth in breasts and pubic hair for girls and in the penis and pubic hair for boys. This system superimposes stages upon a continuous process, as Tanner has noted. Such a system allows for classification of an individual's amount of growth as well as for comparison across cohorts and with other pubertal processes. Thus, the "Tanner stages," as they are often termed, do not represent qualitative changes, but a characterization of quantitative change. Schematic drawings and written explanations of the five stages of development have been developed; Stage 1 is prepubertal and Stage 5 postpubertal for each sex.

Typically, the adolescent's development is rated by a pediatrician or nurse-practitioner during a physical examination. Often, each breast is rated separately and the average score computed, given that development across breasts is sometimes asynchronous. With training, inter-observer reliability is adequate. The rating of breast development has been criticized for not discriminating among areolar contours, papillary elevation, and breast fat. Breast fat is problematic in that large variations exist for females in Stage 5. However, as a general measure, the breast ratings do discriminate among pre-pubertal, pubertal, and post-pubertal girls.

Other measurement techniques have been developed, given the reluctance of some adolescents to have a physical examination, feelings of parents, and school concerns (Brooks-Gunn, in press). To overcome these difficulties, several investigators have developed alternative techniques for Tanner staging. In one, nude photographs of the child are taken (front and profile positions). Sexual maturation ratings made from photographs are fairly reliable, although some difficulties arise when using black and white rather than color pictures (Petersen, 1976). Photographs may be as objectionable to school personnel, parents, and adolescents as are physical examination (and perhaps even more so). Another approach is to ask adolescents or parents to rate current physical development using photographs or schematic drawings of the five sexual maturation stages. These attempts have been successful in medical and school settings and correlate well with nurse-practitioner ratings (Brooks-Gunn, Warren, Rosso, & Gargiulo, 1987; Duke, Litt, & Gross, 1980; Morris & Udry, 1980). Mothers' ratings using schematic drawings are also quite accurate for daughters (Brooks-Gunn et al., 1987).

The Tanner stages may be profitably used in psychological studies of pubertal status or timing. In some, the two Tanner measures are averaged (Duncan, Ritter, Dornbusch, Gross, & Carlsmith, 1985); in others, they are analyzed separately (Brooks-Gunn & Warren, 1988). We suggest that analyses be conducted separately if investigators have any interest in possible hormonal influences (pubic hair growth being more androgen dependent and breast growth being more estrogen dependent) or in socially-mediated effects (breast but not pubic hair growth being directly observable by others).

Tanner ratings also have been used to classify on-time and off-time maturers. Using the National Health Survey data, the Tanner cut-offs for defining early, on-time, and late maturers by gender and age have been calculated (Gross, 1984); 20% of the sample was classified as early, 60% as on time, and 20% as late (Attie & Brooks-Gunn, 1989; Gargiulo et al., 1987).

MENARCHE ▪ Menarche, or the onset of menstruation, occurs relatively late in

the maturational sequence, typically after the peak growth spurt, between Tanner Stages 4 and 5, and in the middle of the fatweight spurt (Marshall & Tanner, 1969). The events that initiate normal puberty development and culminate in menarche and normal cyclicity in girls are not well understood. Research suggests that the events are probably initiated in the central nervous system (CNS) which releases the toxic inhibitory control of gonadotropin luteinizing and follicle stimulating hormone secretions from the pituitary.

Self-reports of menarche are quite accurate, across all birth cohorts and ages (Garn, 1980). However, around the time of menarche, a few girls may misreport menarche. In one study of 50 girls called every 10–12 weeks to see if they had begun to menstruate, two said they had begun, but in a subsequent interview stated that they had not (Brooks-Gunn & Ruble, 1982). In another study of 87 junior high school students, 89% of the mothers and daughters agreed as to the girls' menarcheal status. Six girls denied menarche had occurred when it had (according to mother), and three did not know or declined to say, while their mothers said it had not occurred (Petersen, 1983).

The psychological significance of menarche has been extensively studied (Brooks-Gunn, 1984; Brooks-Gunn & Reiter, 1990). In addition, more timing studies have used menarche than all other maturation events combined (Brooks-Gunn, Petersen, & Eichorn, 1985; Greif & Ulman, 1982). However, almost all studies use different criteria to define groups (Brooks-Gunn, 1989; Brooks-Gunn & Warren, 1985).

Thus, menarche is a useful measure, as it is easily collected, raises few concerns with parents, school administrators, or girls themselves, and is reliably ascertained via self-report. However, as it occurs relatively late in the pubertal process, it is not adequate for the classification of status or timing in girls under age 12 or under seventh grade.

PUBERTAL CLASSIFICATIONS ■
Instead of measuring changes specific to breast, body hair, menarche, and penile development, Petersen, Crockett, Richards, and Boxer (1988) have developed an interview to assess six aspects of sexual maturation in girls and boys. For boys, the six are height growth, foot growth, skin changes, voice changes, facial hair, and body hair. For girls, the six are height growth, foot growth, skin changes, body hair, breast development, and menarche. Young adolescents are asked if they have begun to develop in each area using a four-point scale (from "1" = "no, not at all," to "4" = "yes, a lot"), with the exception of menarche (coded dichotomously with "1" = premenarcheal and "4" = postmenarcheal). Based on the scale scores, subjects are classified as prepubertal, early pubertal, midpubertal, or post-pubertal (Petersen, 1983). Boys are considered prepubertal if they reported no development on voice, pubic hair, and facial hair, early pubertal if they reported initial development on one or two of the three events (or advanced development on one but no development on the other two), and mid-pubertal if some development had begun on all three (or advanced development on one or two and no development on the others). Girls are classified as prepubertal if they have not begun to develop breasts or pubic hair and are premenarcheal, early pubertal if they are premenarcheal but have begun breast *or* pubic hair development; midpubertal if they are premenarcheal but have developed some breasts *and* pubic hair. Alpha coefficients for the scales are high (Petersen et al., 1988). These scales are not synonomous with Tanner ratings (Brooks-Gunn et al., 1987).

Conclusions
First, any one measure will not accurately represent an individual's current status. No particular measure will necessarily characterize pubertal status better than another. Indeed, the choice of a particular measure depends on the purpose of the study, the feasibility of obtaining accurate measures, and the importance of distinguishing between biological processes and the social significance of the event. Second, classification systems are superimposed on continuous events. Third, some measures are highly related to one another, while others are not. Weight and body fat are not good proxies for maturational status generally, while peak height velocity is. Fourth, inter-rater reliability is an issue for many measures, even those that seem relatively straightforward. In summary, the choice of a physical parameter and measurement technique is contingent upon the purpose of the study, the density of measurement points, the concerns of the school and community, staff availability, and collaborative arrangements with pediatricians (Brooks-Gunn, in press; Brooks-Gunn & Reiter, 1990). If a developmental perspective is taken, then repeated physical measurements are necessary. In some cases (e.g., secondary sexual characteristics), prospective data must be collected.

References
Acheson, R. M., Fowler, G., & Fry, E. I., et al. (1963). Studies in the reliability of assessing skeletal maturity from X-rays. *Human Biology, 35,* 317–349.

Attie, I., & Brooks-Gunn, J. (1989). The development of eating problems in adolescent girls: A longitudinal study. *Developmental Psychology, 25*(1), 70–79

Bayley, N., & Pinneau, S. R. (1952). Tables for predicting adult height from skeletal age:

Revised for use with the Greulich-Pyle hand standards. *Journal of Pediatrics, 40,* 423–441.

Bock, R. D., Wainer, H., Petersen, A. C., Thissen, D., Murray, J., & Roche, A. F. (1973). A parameterization for individual human growth curves. *Human Biology, 45,* 63–80.

Brooks-Gunn, J. (1984). The psychological significance of different pubertal events to young girls. *Journal of Early Adolescence, 4,* 315–327.

Brooks-Gunn, J. (1988). Antecedents and consequences of variations in girls' maturational timing. *Journal of Adolescent Health Care, 9*(5), 365–373.

Brooks-Gunn, J. (in press). Barriers and impediments to conducting research with young adolescents. *Journal of Youth and Adolesence.*

Brooks-Gunn, J., Petersen, A. C., & Eichorn, D. (Eds.). (1985). Time of maturation and psychosocial functioning in adolescence. *Journal of Youth and Adolescence, 14* (Volumes 3 and 4).

Brooks-Gunn, J., & Reiter, E. O. (1990). The role of pubertal processes in the early adolescent transition. In S. Feldman & G. Elliott (Eds.), *At the threshold: The developing adolescent* (pp. 16–53). Cambridge: Harvard University Press.

Brooks-Gunn, J., & Ruble, D. N. (1982). The development of menstrual-related beliefs and behaviors during early adolescence. *Child Development, 53,* 1567–1577.

Brooks-Gunn, J., & Warren, M. P. (1985). Measuring physical status and timing in early adolescence: A developmental perspective. (Special issue on pubertal timing.) *Journal of Youth and Adolescence, 14*(3), 163–189.

Brooks-Gunn, J., & Warren, M. P. (1988). The psychological significance of secondary sexual characteristics in 9- to 11-year-old girls. *Child Development, 59,* 161–169.

Brooks-Gunn, J., Warren, M. P., Rosso, J., & Gargiulo, J. (1987). Validity of self-report measures of girls' pubertal status. *Child Development, 58,* 829–841.

Duke, P. M., Litt, I. F., & Gross, R. T. (1980). Adolescents' self-assessment of sexual maturation. *Pediatrics, 66,* 918–920.

Duncan, P. D., Ritter, P. L., Dornbusch, S. M., Gross, R. T., & Carlsmith, J. M. (1985). The effects of pubertal timing on body image, school behavior, and deviance. (Special issue on pubertal timing.) *Journal of Youth and Adolescence, 14*(3), 227–235.

Durnin, J. V. G. A., & Wormersley, J. (1974). Body fat assessed from total body density and its estimation from skinfold thickness: Measurement on 481 men and women aged 16 to 72 years. *British Journal of Nutrition, 72,* 77–97.

Faust, M. S. (1977). Somatic development of adolescent girls. *Monographs of the Society for Research in Child Development, 42* (Serial No. 169).

Gargiulo, J., Attie, I., Brooks-Gunn, J., & Warren, M. P. (1987). Dating in middle school girls: Effects of social context, maturation, and grade. *Developmental Psychology, 23*(5), 730–737.

Garn, S. M. (1980). Continuities and change in maturational timing. In O. Brim & J. Kagan (Eds.), *Constancy and change in human development* (pp. 113–162). Cambridge: Harvard University Press.

Greif, E. B., & Ulman, K. J. (1982). The psychological impact of menarche on early adolescent females: A review of the literature. *Child Development, 53,* 1413–1430.

Greulich, W. W., & Pyle, S. I. (1959). *Radiographic atlas of skeletal development of the hand and wrist* (2nd ed.). Stanford: Stanford University Press.

Gross, R. T. (1984). Patterns of maturation: Their effects on behavior and development. In M. D. Levine & P. Satz (Eds.), *Middle childhood: Development and dysfunction* (pp. 47–62). Baltimore: University Park Press.

Hamill, P. V. V., Drizd, T. A., Johnson, L. L.,

Reed, R. A., & Roche, A. F. (1976). NCHS growth charts. *Monthly Vital Statistics Reports, 25*(1).

Hamill, P. V. V., Johnston, F. E., & Lemeshow, S. (1973). *Bodyweight, stature, and sitting height: White and Negro youths 12–17 years* (U.S. DHEW Publication No. (HR#) 74-1608, Series 11, No. 126). Washington, DC: U.S. Government Printing Office.

Jones, M. C., & Bayley, N. (1950). Physical maturing among boys as related to behavior. *Journal of Educational Psychology, 41*, 129–148.

Jones, M. C., & Mussen, P. H. (1958). Self-conceptions, motivations, and interpersonal attitudes of early and late-maturing girls. *Child Development, 19*, 491–501.

Malina, R. M. (1978). Adolescent growth and maturation: Selected aspects of current research. *Yearbook of Physical Anthropology* (Vol. 21, pp. 63–94).

Marshall, W. A., & Tanner, J. M. (1969). Variations in the pattern of pubertal changes in girls. *Archives of Disease in Childhood, 44*, 291–303.

Merrow, S. B. (1967). Triceps skin-fold thickness of Vermont adolescents. *American Journal of Clinical Nutrition, 20*, 978.

Morris, N. M., & Udry, J. R. (1980). Validation of a self-administered instrument to assess stage of adolescent development. *Journal of Youth and Adolescence, 9*, 271–280.

Parizkova, J. (1976). Growth and growth velocity of lean body mass and fat in adolescent boys. *Pediatrics Research, 10*, 647–650.

Peskin, H. (1973). Influence of the developmental schedule of puberty on learning and ego functioning. *Journal of Youth and Adolescence, 2*, 273–290.

Petersen, A. C. (1976). Physical androgyny and cognitive functioning in adolescence. *Developmental Psychology, 12*, 524–533.

Petersen, A. C. (1983). Menarche: Meaning of measures and measuring meaning. In S. Golub (Ed.), *Menarche* (pp. 63–76). Lexington, MA: Lexington Books/D. C. Heath.

Petersen, A. C., Crockett, L., Richards, M., & Boxer, A. (1988). A self-report measure of pubertal status: Reliability, validity, and initial norms. *Journal of Youth and Adolescence, 17*, 117–133.

Reynolds, E. L., & Wines, J. V. (1948). Individual differences in physical changes associated with adolescence in girls. *American Journal of Disease in Childhood, 75*, 329–350.

Reynolds, E. L., & Wines, J. V. (1951). Physical changes associated with adolescence in boys. *American Journal of Disease in Childhood, 82*, 529–547.

Roche, A. F. (1974). Differential timing of maximum length increments among bones within individuals. *Human Biology, 46*, 145–157.

Roche, A. F., French, N. Y., & Davila, D. H. (1971). Areolar size during pubescence. *Human Biology, 43*, 210–223.

Roche, A. F., Davila, D. H., & Eyman, S. L. (1971). A comparison between Greulich-Pyle and Tanner-Whitehouse assessments of skeletal maturity. *Radiology, 98*, 273–280.

Seltzer, C. C., Goldman, R. F., & Mayer, J. (1965). The triceps skinfold as a predictive measure of body density and body fat in obese adolescent girls. *Pediatrics, 136*, 212–218.

Stolz, H. R., & Stolz, L. M. (1951). *Somatic development of adolescent boys.* New York: Macmillan.

Stunkard, A. J., d'Aquili, E., Fox, S., & Filion, R. D. L. (1972). Influence of social class on obesity and thinness in children. *Journal of the American Medical Association, 221*, 579–584.

Styne, D. M., Grumbach, M. M. (1978). Puberty in the male and female: Its physiology and disorders. In S. S. C. Yen & R. B. Jaffe (Eds.), *Reproductive endocrinology, physiology, pathophysiology, and clinical management* (pp. 189–240). Philadelphia: B. Saunders.

Tanner, J. M. (1962). *Growth at adolescence.* Springfield, IL: Thomas.

Tanner, J. M. (1968). Growth of bone, muscle, and fat during childhood and adolescence. In G. A. Lodge & G. E. Lamming (Eds.), *Growth and development of mammals* (pp. 3–18). New York: Plenum Press.

Tanner, J. M. (1974). Sequence and tempo in the somatic changes in puberty. In M. M. Grumbach, G. D. Grave, & F. E. Mayer (Eds.), *Control of the onset of puberty* (pp. 448–470). New York: Wiley.

Tanner, J. M. (1978). Physiological control of puberty. *Medical Clinics of North America,* 62, 351–366.

Tanner, J. M., & Whitehouse, R. H. (1976). Clinical longitudinal standards for height, weight, height velocity, weight velocity and the stages of puberty. *Archives of Disease in Childhood,* 51, 170–179.

Tanner, J. M., Whitehouse, R. H., Marshall, W. A., Healy, M. J. R., & Goldstein, H. (1975). *Assessment of skeletal maturity and prediction of adult height.* (TW2 Method) London: Academic Press.

Thissen, D., Boch, R. D., Wainer, H., & Roche, A. F. (1976). Individual growth in stature. A comparison of four growth studies in the U. S. A. *Annals of Human Biology,* 3, 529–542.

Wilmore, J. H., & Behnke, A. R. (1970). An anthropometric estimation of body density and lean body weight in young women. *American Journal of Clinical Nutrition,* 23, 267.

Young, C. M., Sipin, S. S., & Rose, D. A. (1968). Density and skinfold measurements: Body composition of preadolescent and adolescent girls. *Journal of the American Dietetic Association,* 53, 25.

See Also

Cognitive Abilities and Physical Maturation; Growth Spurt, Adolescent; Maturational Timing, Antecedents of in Girls; Maturational Timing Variations in Adolescent Girls, Consequences of; Menarche and Body Image; Menarche, Secular Trend in Age of; Menstrual Cycle; Pubertal Development, Assessment of; Puberty, Body Fat and; Puberty Education; Puberty, Endocrine Changes at; Puberty, Hypothalamic-Pituitary Changes of; Puberty, Precocious, Treatment of; Puberty, Sport and; Spatial Ability and Maturation in Adolescence; Spermarche.

Portions of this article appeared as Brooks-Gunn, J., & Warren, M. P. (1985), Measuring physical status and timing in early adolescence: A developmental perspective. Journal of Youth and Adolescence, 14(3), 163–189.

Memory

Joseph M. Fitzgerald
Wayne State University

The study of memory development in adolescence has been a curiously neglected topic. Although memory factors clearly play a role in such adolescent behaviors as academic performance, formal reasoning, and identity formation, neither researchers nor theorists have devoted much attention to specifying that role. The available research can be divided into three areas: normative changes in the basic capacity of memory, the development of memory strategies and strategy usage in academic performance, and developmental changes in the nature of memories about one's own experiences (autobiographical memory).

Two standard instruments are available for assessing basic memory capacity in adolescence, the Wechsler Memory Scale—Revised (WMS–R) (Russell, 1975) and the Digit Span subtest of the Wechsler Intelligence Scale for Children—Revised (WISC–R) (Wechsler, 1986). The norms for both of these instruments indicate that the average level of performance increases by approximately 10% from early to late adolescence. Norms for the WMS–R developed by Curry, Logue, and Butler (1986) suggest that males recall more items than females, but these sex differences are not reflected in performance on the Digit Span test of the WISC–R.

Perhaps the most interesting aspect of the WISC–R norms is the increasing variability in performance during adolescence. Although the average level of performance does increase steadily, it is apparent that some individuals are experiencing dramatic improvement, while others are falling further behind the group average. This is illustrated by comparing the norms at ages 6, 10, and 16. In Figure 1, we present the average Digit Span Score for five levels of performance for each age group. These levels range from the very low (−2 Standard Deviations) to average (0) to very high (+2 Standard Deviations). From age 6 to age 16 the range of performance has increased from 10 points to 17, and those individuals at the top end of the distribution recall 67% more information than the average individual. The reasons for such differential improvement have not been isolated but they may be related to the increased use of memory strategies by some individuals and the failure to effectively use such strategies by others.

Some aspects of memory performance can clearly be altered through the use of such mnemonic devices as rehearsal, imagery, and organizational strategies such as clustering together related words. Research on memory development (Kail & Hagen, 1977) has centered on the increased

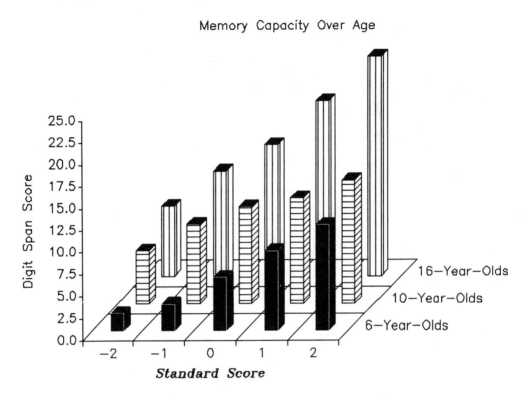

FIGURE 1 Average Digit Span for five levels of performance for each age group.

usage of such strategies with increasing age and the development of an awareness of the impact of using such strategies on performance. This later ability has been termed metamemory.

Unfortunately for students of adolescent development, many memory studies compare the performance of 5-year-olds, 8-year-olds, and college students. This type of design has generally shown that the youngest children did not spontaneously use memory strategies and could not use them effectively after short periods of training. School-age children could use them, albeit with a great deal of inconsistency, after training. College students are more consistent in employing memory strategies, although it is clear that many college students do not have a high awareness of the impact of such strategies and remain inconsistent in their usage. The image of

memory development in adolescence remains very obscure. Clearly, many adolescents develop useful memory skills that allow them to perform well, but beyond that generalization little is known.

The relationship between memory performance, age, and academic achievement is one important topic for future research on adolescent development. College students who have a clear awareness of the effectiveness of memory strategies and actually use such strategies perform better in the college classroom (Leal, 1987). This suggests that many adolescents might benefit from training in memory strategies. Such training, particularly long-term training, would increase the probability of academic success and might indirectly influence the probability of dropping out of school and perceptions of self-competence. It is clear that simply exposing children and adolescents to a memory strategy will not necessarily improve their performance. In fact, using a new, unfamiliar strategy may require so much effort that performance will not improve at all or actually be hampered (Bjorklund & Harnishfegger, 1987).

A third set of memory studies in adolescence addresses autobiographical memory. These studies have been concerned with both the temporal distribution and the content of autobiographical memories. In one type of study, adolescents are presented with a stimulus and asked to recall an autobiographical memory that they associate with that stimulus (e.g., think of the first memory that comes to mind in association with the word *river*). On this task, individuals of all ages show a very strong recency bias (i.e., most memories are from the past month). This bias is even more evident in adolescence than other ages (Fitzgerald & Lawrence, 1984). The primary frame of reference for most adolescents appears to be the past thirty days.

The recency effect is also reflected in survey research. When adolescents are asked to report life-events, many more are reported from the recent past than from the more remote (greater than 6 months) past (Monck & Dobbs, 1985). Given the potential for considerable variation in adolescent experience, the heightened bias of adolescents toward recency may contribute to temporal instability of the self-concept. For example, an adolescent who generally sees himself as *socially competent* may alter his/her self-perception on the basis of recent failures to find a date or to get along with a teacher.

Autobiographical memories have also been studied in the context of studies of the relationship between the content of early childhood memories and personality variables. This relationship has been a focal point in Adlerian research (e.g., Clay, 1982). In such studies, the content of the earliest recollection is rated on a number of characteristics (e.g., does the memory report contain themes of trust), which are then correlated with the results of a personality test or some other psychosocial variable. It is not clear, however, that using earliest recollections is any more useful in assessment than using memories of more recent vintage.

A more general approach to the analysis of memories in assessment is provided by McAdams (1987). He has developed coding schemes for intimacy and achievement motivation and has applied this scheme to a variety of memory types, including extremely positive (peak) and extremely negative (nadir) experiences. He finds that relative to scores based on the coding of peak experiences, scores based on earliest recollections are actually less predictive of other measures of intimacy and achievement motivation.

In summary, knowledge of adolescent memory development remains very limited. Although it is clear that various aspects of memory performance change during adolescence, neither the mechanisms nor the impact of those changes have been sufficiently studied to allow for an incorporation of an image of memory development into more comprehensive theories of adolescent development.

References

Bjorklund, D. F., & Harnishfegger, K. K. (1987). Developmental differences in the mental effort requirements for the use of an organizational strategy in free recall. *Journal of Experimental Child Psychology, 44*, 109–125.

Clay, W. (1982). The relationship between early recollections and behavior patterns. *Individual Psychology, 38*, 223–237.

Curry, J. F., Logue, P. E., & Butler, B. (1986). Child and adolescent norms for Russell's

Revision of the Wechsler Memory Scale. *Journal of Clinical Child Psychology, 15*, 214–220.

Fitzgerald, J. M., & Lawrence, R. (1984). Autobiographical memory across the life-span. *Journal of Gerontology, 39*, 692–698.

Kail, R. V., & Hagen, J. W. (Eds.). (1977). *Perspectives on the development of memory and cognition.* Hillsdale, NJ: Lawrence Erlbaum Associates.

Leal, L. (1987). Investigation of the relation between metamemory and university students' examination performance. *Journal of Educational Psychology, 79*, 35–40.

McAdams, D. (1987). *Power, intimacy, and the life story.* New York: Guilford.

Monck, E., & Dobbs, R. (1985). Measuring life-events in an adolescent population: Methodological issues and related findings. *Psychological Medicine, 15*, 841–850.

Russell, E. W. (1975). A multiple scoring method for assessment of complex memory functions. *Journal of Consulting and Clinical Psychology, 43*, 800–809.

Wechsler, D. (1986). *Manual for The Wechsler Intelligence Scale for Children.* New York: Psychological Corporation.

See Also

Cognition, Adolescent; Cognition and Health; Cognitive Abilities and Physical Maturation; Cognitive and Psychosocial Gender Differences, Trends in; Cognitive Development; Egocentrism Theory and the "New Look" at the Imaginary Audience and Personal Fable in Adolescence; Formal Operational Thinking and Identity Resolution; Illness, Adolescents' Conceptualization of; Inhelder, Barbel; Introspectiveness, Adolescent; Piaget, Jean; Relativistic Thinking in Adolescence; Reasoning, Higher-Order, in Adolescence; Reasoning in the Adolescent; Scientific Reasoning, Adolescent; Social Intelligence in Adolescence; Spatial Ability and Maturation in Adolescence.

Menarche And Body Image

Elissa Koff
Jill Rierdan
Wellesley College

Menarche, or the first menstruation, experienced by the average American girl at 12.8 years of age (with the normal range between 10 and 16 years), occurs relatively late in the course of pubertal development. It succeeds, sometimes by several years, a number of other significant prepubertal and pubertal changes, including rapid gains in fat, height, and body width, alterations in body proportions, the development of breasts, and the growth of pubic hair (Faust, 1977; Tanner, 1978; Warren, 1983). While the feminizing changes of puberty thus begin long before menarche, and continue for some time thereafter, it is the onset of menstruation that is experienced by most girls as the landmark event of puberty. This is not surprising, as it is unique in the context of pubertal change: menarche usually occurs suddenly and without premonition, and virtually alone among the physical changes of puberty it involves a tangible and rather spectacular product whose first appearance can be dated quite precisely. Menarche is thus the most sharply defined and dramatic physical change of puberty and is universally perceived as a harbinger of reproductive maturity and fertility.

Menarche also is viewed as having profound psychological consequences. A number of influential clinical (mainly psychoanalytic) writers (e.g., Deutsch, 1944; Kestenberg, 1967; Ritvo, 1977), have commented on the significance of menarche for personality development; this view is perhaps best articulated by Kestenberg (1967), who conceives of menarche as a normative developmental crisis. Drawing primarily from clinical case materials, Kestenberg describes the premenarcheal state most broadly as one of confusion and disequilibrium. In contrast, the postmenarcheal state is seen as one in which girls are increasingly able to organize their body sensations, feelings, and thoughts, and to express themselves with greater clarity. For Kestenberg, menarche is the necessary organizer which serves to crystallize and define girls' biological and psychological experience. Premenarcheal confusion about body image and sexual identification gives way to postmenarcheal acceptance of womanhood, with a corresponding reorganization of body image and clarification of the sexual role.

Interviews with pre- and postmenarcheal adolescents (Whisnant & Zegans, 1975) corroborate these clinical impressions. Postmenarcheal girls identified several notable personal changes following the advent of menstruation. They reported experiencing themselves as more womanly, as accepting their bodies as feminine, and as beginning to reflect upon their future reproductive roles. Girls stated that menarche provided "proof" that they really were women, a sentiment echoed in a clinical vignette reported by Hart and Sarnoff (1971).

As has been noted, menarche is but one of a series of momentous changes that co-occur throughout puberty. It is unique in that it is a discontinuous event embedded in a series of more gradual changes; it also is the event most closely identified with adult reproductive potential. Some researchers interested in the psychological concomitants of adolescent girls' development have focused on puberty in general, assessing pubertal development by reference to girls' standing along a number of physical dimensions, one of which is menarcheal status. Others of these researchers, particularly those influenced by the clinical-developmental literature, have concentrated more narrowly on the psychological significance of menarche. Each approach has advantages and limitations. The more broadly based examination of puberty better encompasses the multidimensional, asynchronous, and complex nature of the pubertal experience, and yields a more comprehensive picture of adolescent psychological development (e.g., Brooks-Gunn, 1987; Petersen, 1987; Simmons & Blyth, 1987). It does not, however, allow the degree of specificity that the use of a single discrete marker of puberty affords, nor does it permit assessment of hypotheses

about the particular and unique impact of menarche among a variety of maturational changes. This latter approach is exemplified in this review. The studies reported below all view menarche as the watershed pubertal event, and assess its significance in relation to one particular psychological domain, body image.

Body image generally relates to how individuals view and assign meaning to their own bodies (Fisher, 1986). Implicit in this definition is the assumption that the organization of body experience is multi-dimensional and that body image will vary across time and situations and with body maturation and change. There is evidence that body image changes in relation to changes in pubertal status (e.g., Crockett & Petersen, 1987; Dreyer, Hulac, & Rigler, 1971); the studies below consider whether changes in body image are associated specifically with changes in menarcheal status.

In exploring this issue, a number of techniques have been employed to assess body image, including recognition of one's own body, self-reports of personal responses to the body (e.g., satisfaction, perceived attractiveness), interviews, and projective measures. One of the most frequently used procedures is the human figure drawing task. Two important assumptions underlie the use of this projective technique: one is that the human figure drawing is a valid (albeit indirect) index of body image, and the other is that body growth and configurational changes are reflected in human figure drawings (Fisher, 1986; Swensen, 1968). One way to assess developmental changes in body image is to measure the sexual differentiation (Haworth & Normington, 1961) of male and female drawings produced by subjects differing along such dimensions as age, sex, physical and/or cognitive maturity.

Employing such a procedure, Koff, Rierdan, and Silverstone (1978) examined drawings of pre- and postmenarcheal girls of the same age at two points in time, six months apart, an approach that allowed the comparison of drawings produced by the same girl before and after the onset of menstruation. Postmenarcheal girls' drawings were more sexually differentiated than those of premenarcheal girls, and a greater percentage of the postmenarcheal girls drew their own sex first, interpreted to mean greater self-identification as female. The most notable changes were observed in the drawings of girls whose menarcheal status changed during the course of the study. There was a significant increase in the sexual differentiation of their drawings at the second testing; in contrast to their earlier, more childlike productions, the newly postmenarcheal girls drew more womanly figures with breasts and curves (examples of these drawings can be seen in Koff, 1983), suggesting that menarche functions to precipitate a change in body image toward greater sexual maturity over and above that associated with other more gradual pubertal changes.

In a second study, Rierdan and Koff (1980) observed that there seemed to be several phases in girls' responses to menarche. There was a trend for girls within six months of menarche to exhibit heightened awareness of sexual differentiation and greater clarity of sexual identification in comparison to girls who were postmenarcheal for more than six months. It was suggested that awareness of sexual differentiation and female identity peaks immediately after menarche and diminishes thereafter as the girl integrates a sense of herself as sexually mature into a broader psychosocial identity.

To further elucidate girls' beliefs about changes that would be associated with menarche, Koff, Rierdan, and Jacobson (1981) used another projective technique, the sentence completion task, and asked pre- and postmenarcheal girls to complete a series of sentence stems in response to the cue "Ann just got her period for the first time." Two sentence stems were of particular relevance to the issues of reorganization of body image and sexual identification, "When Ann looked at herself in the mirror that night . . ." and "Ann regarded her body as. . . ." The sentiments expressed by the girls in this study were consonant with the data from the human figure drawing studies and with the interview data reported by Whisnant and Zegans (1975), and suggested that girls expect immediate bodily changes attendant upon the first period. The majority of girls agreed that Ann "had changed; thought she looked older; saw herself in a different way" upon looking in the mirror that night. They also agreed that Ann's body was "more mature; a woman's body; grown up; different; older."

Using a quite different method, Collins and Propert (1983) examined the role of menarche in girls' recognition of photographs of their bodies. Adolescent girls, like young adults, were best at recognizing frontal views of their bodies. Premenarcheal girls were the least accurate, menarcheal girls (onset of menstruation within a year of the study) were somewhat more accurate, and postmenarcheal girls (more than one year postmenarche) were indistinguishable from older subjects. Unfortunately, subjects' ages varied widely, so that menarcheal status was confounded with age. A replication of this study with a design similar to that used by Koff, Rierdan, and Silverstone (1978) would permit a clearer test of the reorganization hypothesis.

Yet another approach to body image involves evaluation of the subjective experiences of the body through such measures as Body Cathexis (Secord & Jourard, 1953), an index of how satisfied one is with various body characteristics. This measure, like several of the others reported above, reveals an effect of menarche on body image generally, and on satisfaction with aspects of the body associated with sexual maturation (e.g., breasts, weight, waist, and hips) more specifically. Koff, Rierdan, and Stubbs (1986) measured body satisfaction in pre- and postmenarcheal girls, and found postmenarcheal girls to be less satisfied with their bodies overall than premenarcheal girls. Different patterns of relationship between menarcheal status and body image emerged when particular body characteristics were considered. In keeping with the overall finding, postmenarcheal girls were significantly less satisfied with their weight, waist, and hips than premenarcheal girls, but, in contrast to the overall finding, they were significantly more satisfied with their breasts. Results also differed as a function of the timing of girls' menarche. For example, younger postmenarcheal girls (early maturers) were markedly less satisfied with their weight than older postmenarcheal girls.

This last result indicates the importance of timing of menarche (or puberty) for certain dimensions of psychological functioning. Whether a girl is early, on-time, or late with respect to her peers' development has been shown to have significant consequences for her body image. For example, Blyth, Simmons, and Zakin (1985) found early maturing girls to be considerably less satisfied than late maturers with their weight, and Tobin-Richards, Boxer, and Petersen (1983) found that girls who perceived themselves to be early maturers (regardless of their actual status) were less positive about their bodies. The work of Simmons and Blyth (e.g., Simmons & Blyth, 1987) also has demonstrated that the particular context (e.g., school setting) in which pubertal change occurs significantly affects girls' experi-ences of and responses to the bodily changes of puberty.

In general, the pattern of results concerning the impact of menarche on body image supports clinical speculation that menarche has an organizing effect upon body experience and sexual identity. There may be a particularly heightened articulation of body image immediately after menarche, which decreases as girls become less preoccupied with their bodies; concomitantly, increasing familiarity with the pubescent body over time, together with increasing cognitive maturity, seems to lead toward more accurate body perception as girls enter late adolescence and adulthood. Positive developments in accuracy and organization of body image are not generally paralleled by increasingly positive evaluations of the body. In this way, menarche may be said to have both a disruptive and an integrative impact on body image. Findings of Blyth et al. (1986), Koff et al. (1986), and Tobin-Richards et al. (1983) suggest that these generalizations may need to be tempered as research continues to explicate the importance of personal variables (e.g., timing of menarche, girls' attractiveness), behavioral variables (e.g., dating patterns), and situational variables (e.g., type of school system) as mediators or moderators of the impact of menarche on body image.

References

Blyth, D. A., Simmons, R. G., & Zakin, D. F. (1985). Satisfaction with body image for early adolescent females: The impact of pubertal timing within different school environments. *Journal of Youth and Adolescence, 14,* 207–225.

Brooks-Gunn, J. (1987). Pubertal processes and girls' psychological adaptation. In R. M. Lerner & T. T. Foch (Eds.), *Biological-psychosocial interactions in early adolescence* (pp. 123–153). Hillsdale, NJ: Lawrence Erlbaum Associates.

Collins, J., & Propert, D. (1983). A developmental study of body recognition in adolescent girls. *Adolescence, 18*, 767–774.

Crockett, L. J., & Petersen, A. C. (1987). Pubertal status and psychosocial development: Findings from the Early Adolescence Study. In R. M. Lerner & T. T. Foch (Eds.), *Biological-psychosocial interactions in early adolescence* (pp. 173–188). Hillsdale, NJ: Lawrence Erlbaum Associates.

Deutsch, H. (1944). *The psychology of women* (Vol. 1). New York: Grune & Stratton.

Dreyer, A. S., Hulac, V., & Rigler, D. (1971). Differential adjustment to pubescence and cognitive style patterns. *Developmental Psychology, 4*, 456–462.

Faust, M. S. (1977). Somatic development of adolescent girls. *Monographs of the Society for Research in Child Development, 42* (Serial No. 169).

Fisher, S. (1986). *Development and structure of the body image* (Vol. 1). Hillsdale, NJ: Lawrence Erlbaum Associates.

Hart, M., & Sarnoff, C. A. (1971). The impact of menarche: A study of two stages of organization. *Journal of the American Academy of Child Psychiatry, 10*, 257–271.

Haworth, M. R., & Normington, C. J. (1961). A sexual differentiation scale for the D-A-P Test. *Journal of Projective Techniques, 25*, 441–450.

Kestenberg, J. S. (1967). Phases of adolescence, parts 1 and 2. *Journal of the American Academy of Child Psychiatry, 6*, 426–463, 577–611.

Koff, E. (1983). Through the looking glass of menarche: What the adolescent girl sees. In S. Golub (Ed.), *Menarche: The transition from girl to woman* (pp. 77–86). Lexington, MA: Lexington Books.

Koff, E., Rierdan, J., & Jacobson, S. (1981). The personal and interpersonal significance of menarche. *Journal of the American Academy of Child Psychiatry, 20*, 148–158.

Koff, E., Rierdan, J., & Silverstone, E. (1978). Changes in representation of body image as a function of menarcheal status. *Developmental Psychology, 14*, 635–642.

Koff, E., Rierdan, J., & Stubbs, M. (1986, March). Menarche, body satisfaction, and self-concept. Poster presented at meeting of the Society for Research on Adolescence, Madison, WI.

Petersen, A. C. (1987). The nature of biological-psychosocial interactions: The sample case of early adolescence. In R. M. Lerner & T. T. Foch (Eds.), *Biological-psychosocial interactions in early adolescence* (pp. 35–61). Hillsdale, NJ: Lawrence Erlbaum Associates.

Rierdan, J., & Koff, E. (1980). Psychological impact of menarche: Integrative versus disruptive change. *Journal of Youth and Adolescence, 9*, 49–57.

Ritvo, S. (1977). Adolescent to woman. In H. P. Blum (Ed.), *Female psychology: Contemporary psychoanalytic views*. New York: International Universities Press.

Secord, P. F., & Jourard, S. M. (1953). The appraisal of body cathexis: Body-cathexis and the self. *Journal of Consulting Psychology, 17*, 343–347.

Simmons, R. G., & Blyth, D. A. (1987). *Moving into adolescence*. Hawthorne, NY: Aldine de Gruyter.

Swensen, C. H. (1968). Empirical evaluations of human figure drawings: 1957–1966. *Psychological Bulletin, 70*, 20–44.

Tanner, J. M. (1978). *Fetus into man: Physical growth from conception to maturity*. Cambridge, MA: Harvard University Press.

Tobin-Richards, M. H., Boxer, A. M., & Petersen, A. C. (1983). The psychological significance of pubertal change: Sex differences in perceptions of self during early adolescence. In J. Brooks-Gunn & A. C. Petersen (Eds.), *Girls at puberty: Biological and psychosocial perspectives* (pp. 127–154). New York: Plenum Press.

Warren, M. P. (1983). Physical and biological

aspects of puberty. In J. Brooks-Gunn & A. C. Petersen (Eds.), *Girls at puberty: Biological and psychosocial perspectives* (pp. 3–28). New York: Plenum Press.

Whisnant, L., & Zegans, L. (1975). A study of attitudes toward menarche in white middle-class American adolescent girls. *American Journal of Psychiatry, 132,* 809–814.

See Also

Cognitive Abilities and Physical Maturation; Growth Spurt, Adolescent; Maturational Timing, Antecedents of in Girls; Maturational Timing Variations in Adolescent Girls, Consequences of; Menarche, Secular Trend in Age of; Menstrual Cycle; Physical Status and Timing in Early Adolescence, Measurement of; Pubertal Development, Assessment of; Puberty, Body Fat and; Puberty Education; Puberty, Endocrine, Changes at; Puberty, Hypothalamic-Pituitary Changes of; Puberty, Precocious, Treatment of; Puberty, Sport and; Spatial Ability and Maturation in Adolescence; Spermarche.

Menarche, Secular Trend in Age of

James M. Tanner
University of London

During at least the last 150 years the average age of menarche, the first menstrual period, has decreased in the populations of the industrialized or "developed" countries. Modern data on menarche is collected by what is called the "status quo" method. An accurate sampling is made of all girls aged 9 to 16 in a given city, country, or geographical area and each individual is simply asked her date of birth and whether she has yet experienced a menstrual period (usually defined as bleeding for at least three days). The percentage of girls responding in the affirmative for successive six-month age periods is plotted, and yields a sigmoid curve. The age at which 50% of the girls were postmenarcheal is then estimated, using the statistical technique of probits. (Longitudinal studies giving exact date of menarche have shown that the distribution of age at menarche, at least under good environmental conditions, is Gaussian.) This method is so easy to apply that we now have an enormous list of ages of menarche, including practically all populations in the world (Eveleth & Tanner, 1990). The method yields a standard error of the mean and a test also for homogeneity of the populations examined.

But the status quo method has only been in use since the middle 1950s. Before then most studies relied on questioning adult women—often those admitted to hospital for childbirth—as to their recollection of their age when menstruation occurred for the first time. Some studies are available on the accuracy of this recollection. In a Swedish longitudinal study, 339 girls whose dates were accurately known were questioned some four years after the event. Despite the fact that these girls had participated in a prolonged study that paid particular attention to all aspects of development, the correlation between recollected and true age was only 0.81; less than two-thirds recalled the date to within three months of the true one. In a similar study, at the Harvard University School of Public Health, a correlation of 0.78 was found between the true date and the date recollected 19 years later. Thus recollected ages have to be dealt with cautiously.

Using historical data may also produce sampling problems. Young women attending a certain hospital in the 1870s, for example, may be exclusively from the lower class (since most middle-class women in Europe had their labors at home at that time), while all social classes might be represented in the same hospital during the 1920s.

In spite of these cautions, the data gives rather clear-cut results. Table 1, taken from my *A History of the Study of Human Growth*, lists most of the data available for Europe in the 19th century. Working women had a later menarche than middle-class women, by something approaching two years. The figures for Danish women have recently been carefully reassessed by Helm and Helm (*Annals of Human Biology*, 1987, p. 371). In 1840–50 the average age of menarche for working women was as high as 17.2 years. From 1860 on there was a fairly rapid reduction, amounting to about 0.3 years per decade, so that by 1920 age 15.0 was the average figure. By 1950 the value had fallen to about 13.5. Thereafter the change slowed down; the figure for 1983 was 13.0. Figure 1 summarizes some of the main data.

More detail is available for the city of Oslo, Norway. This data shows that the trend has not always been as linear as it appears in Figure 1. Brudevoll (1973), randomly selected the records of 50 women for each year from the archives of the Oslo City Maternity Hospital and plotted the average recollected age of menarche of these patients year by year. Figure 2 shows the data, with a 21-point moving average line put in. There was a sharp drop between girls born about 1860 and those born about 1880, followed by a period of little change. Then a second sharp drop occurred between those born in 1900 and those born in 1940. There has been little change in the last 30 years.

Brudevoll reports the data in terms of date of birth, and this may well paint a truer historical picture than reporting in terms of date of menarche. The secular trend to earliness is a response to amelioration of the conditions of life, particularly increase of food and decrease of infection. Age at menarche, the end-point of the growth process, is influenced by all the conditions in the preceding years of fetal life and childhood. There is some evidence, however, that it is especially the conditions of the early years, around birth to two, which play the major role (as they do in the secular increase in body size also).

North American data is more limited. About 1890 patients in a Boston and a St. Louis practitioners' dispensary had a recollected age of 14.2 years (see Tanner, 1981); college women had a mean of 13.5 years. Wyshak (1983) studied a large number of mostly middle-class Americans all over the U.S.A. in the course of an epidemiological survey and found a secular trend of 3.2 months per decade between women born around 1920 and those born around 1940. The value for those born in 1940 and later was 12.5, but no further decline has occurred—12.5 is still the expected value for middle-class white Americans.

The greatest of all secular trends in menarche occurred in Japan. From 1900 to 1935 the trend was slight, and from 1935 to 1950 the trend actually reversed, with age at menarche increasing. Then, in improving postwar conditions, there was a decline of some 11 months per decade until 1975, when the trend leveled out to practically zero. The secular change in age at peak height velocity was similar (Marshall & Tanner, 1986).

In a population growing up under optimal circumstances from the points of view of nutrition, infection, exercise, and psychological well-being, age at menarche is a genetically determined characteristic (being simply an element of the more general characteristic called growth tempo). In some developed countries something like these conditions have obtained for several decades, and it seems that menarche has

TABLE 1
AVERAGE AGES OF MENARCHE IN UNITED KINGDOM, SCANDINAVIA, GERMANY, AND RUSSIA IN THE NINETEENTH CENTURY

	YEAR OF MENARCHE (APPROX.)	MEAN AGE AT MENARCHE	PLACE	AUTHOR
Working women				
UK	1815	15.2	Manchester	Roberton (1830)
	1835	15.6	Manchester	Whitehead (1847)
	1830	15.1	London	Guy (1845)
	1830	14.9	London mostly	Murphy (1844–45)
	1855	15.0	London	Rigden (1869)
	1910	15.0	Edinburgh	Kennedy (1933)
Scandinavia,	1785	16.6	Göttingen	Osiander (1795)
Germany, and Russia	1835	16.4	Copenhagen	Ravn (1850)
	1850	16.8	Copenhagen	Hannover (1869)
	1850	16.4	Berlin	Krieger (1869)
	1850	16.8	Munich	Hecker (1864)
	1865	16.6	Bavaria	Schlichting (1880)
	1870	15.6	Oslo	Brudevoll et al. (1979)
	1875	15.7	Russia	Grüsdeff (1894)
	1875	16.5	Helsinki	Malmio (1919)
	1890	15.7	Stockholm	Essen-Möller; in Lenner (1944)
	1895	16.2	Berlin	Schaeffer (1908)
	1900	16.2	Schleswig	Heyn (1920)
	1900	16.0	Helsinki	Malmio (1919)
	1900	14.6	Oslo	Brudevoll et al. (1979)
Middle class				
UK	1835	14.3	Manchester	Whitehead (1847)
	1890	14.4	London	Giles (1901a)
Scandinavia, Germany, and Russia	1820	15.0	Norway	Brundtland and Walløe (1976)
	1835	14.4	Copenhagen	Ravn (1850)
	1875	14.4	Russia	Grüsdeff (1894)
	1895	14.4	Berlin	Schaeffer (1908)

Note: The average date of year of menarche has been calculated from the probable mean age of the women studied: it has an error of up to five years.

reached or very nearly reached its lower threshold; the secular trend has stopped. (There are differences between populations in the value of this threshold: it is about 13.0 for North-West European popula-tions, for example, but nearer 12.3 for Mediterranean European populations). Similarly, in socially advanced countries, such as Norway and Sweden, there are no differences in age at menarche between

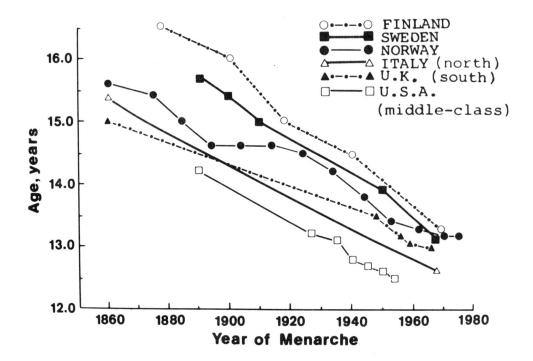

FIGURE 1 Secular changes in age at menarche, 1860–1980 (from Marshall and Tanner, 1986).

children growing up in manual workers' families and those in nonmanual workers' households. But in most other countries, lower-class age of menarche lags behind middle- and upper-class age of menarche.

In the developing countries the trend in age at menarche, which may be zero, is a good guide to whether conditions of life are being ameliorated. Thus economic historians have been interested to interpret data such as those shown in Figure 2, in terms of the history of industrialization. Statistics on age at menarche are one of the most easily obtained indicators of economic well-being.

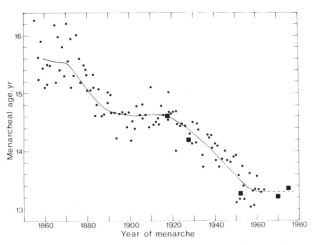

FIGURE 2 Mean menarcheal age for working-class women (up to 1945; thereafter middle-class also) in Oslo from 1860 to 1975. Recollection data; each point represents the average of about 50 maternity clinic patients. The squares represent status-quo probit-fitted data on Oslo schoolgirls. The curve is a 21-term moving average until 1960. Redrawn from Brudevoll, Liestol, and Walloe (1979).

References

Brudevoll. (1973). *Annals of Human Biology.*

Eveleth, P. B., & Tanner, J. M. (1990). *Worldwide variation in human growth.* (2d Ed.) Cambridge: Cambridge University Press.

Marshall, W. A. & Tanner, J. M. (1986). Puberty. In F. Falkner & J. M. Tanner (Eds.), *Human Growth* (2nd ed., Vol. 2, pp. 171–209). New York: Plenum Press.

Tanner, J. M. (1981). *A history of the study of human growth.* Cambridge: Cambridge University Press.

Wyshak. (1983). *Annals of Human Biology.*

See Also

Menstrual Cycle

Kathryn E. Hood
The Pennsylvania State University

Menstruation is the external sign of internal events that produce periodic ovulation in females. It occurs during the reproductive cycle only in human and nonhuman primates. Hormonal changes produced by the ovulatory cycle influence courtship, mating, and implantation of the fertilized ovum or ova in the lining of the uterus, which then may be followed by pregnancy, parturition, lactation, and intensive caregiving to offspring. The ovulatory, or menstrual cycle, organizes the sequential events necessary for ovulation to occur, and prepares the reproductive system for possible pregnancy.

The timing of the internal events that induce and support ovulation involve several organs of the reproductive system. The two ovaries containing the ova are each 2 to 4 cm long, suspended in the abdomen. The pituitary gland, located just under the brain, receives 90% of its blood supply from a special system of vessels connecting it to areas of the brain in the hypothalamus, areas involved in regulating the menstrual cycle. Cells in each of these areas produce and release into the blood hormones that influence the function of other areas. Figure 1 represents a typical pattern of changes in hormones during a 28-day menstrual cycle.

The follicular phase of the cycle begins with the maturation of several ova, induced by FSH (follicle stimulating hormone) from the anterior pituitary gland. The ovarian cells surrounding each maturing ovum grow to produce a sphere or follicle that secretes estrogens. After 5 to 7 days of maturation, the largest follicles are fluid-filled sacs which move to the surface of the ovary. Of these maturing ova, only one or two are released in each ovulatory cycle in humans. As the "dominant" follicle ripens, it synthesizes and secretes into the bloodstream very high levels of estrogens, which are carried to the hypothalamus and pituitary. After several days of exposure to rising levels of estrogens from the developing follicle, the pituitary and hypothalamus are sensitized, and, when estrogen reaches peak levels, a dramatic response is triggered. The hypothalamus releases GnRH (gonadotropin-releasing hormone) into the portal vessel system to the anterior pituitary. Within minutes, GnRH causes a surge of LH (luteinizing hormone, a gonadotropin) to be released from the pituitary and carried in the bloodstream to the ovary. In response to LH, the follicle opens to release the ovum into the abdominal cavity, and ciliated cells in the oviduct, or Fallopian tube, create currents sufficient to draw the ovum into the opening leading to the uterus or womb. The cells of the ovarian follicle are transformed, or "luteinized," to begin

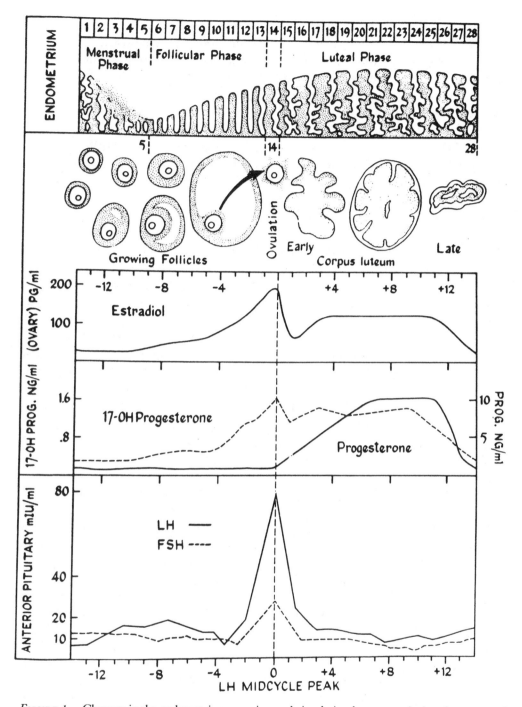

FIGURE 1   Changes in the endometrium, ovaries, and circulating hormones during the menstrual cycle. (Reproduced from Turner & Bagnara (1976) courtesy of W. B. Saunders Co.)

secreting progesterone instead of estrogen. This transformation of the follicle into the "corpus luteum" marks the beginning of the luteal phase of the menstrual period. Under the influence of circulating progesterone from the corpus luteum, the endometrial lining of the uterus is enriched and enlarged. This bed of nutrients will support implantation into the uterine wall, if the ovum is fertilized.

The fertilized ovum, egg plus sperm, acts to create a favorable environment for its own development. HCG (human chorionic gonadotropin), a hormone secreted by the fertilized ovum, sustains the activity of the corpus luteum for 6 to 8 weeks until the developing placenta begins to produce progesterone. When an ovum receives an x chromosome from a sperm, the cells that will become that female's ova begin to differentiate at fetal age 14 days, and migrate to the site of the future ovary at fetal age 30 to 40 days. Fetal ova all go into meiotic division and are arrested in prophase; meiosis I is not completed until many years later, shortly before each ovum is ovulated. Meiosis II is initiated only at fertilization.

If the ovum is not fertilized, the corpus luteum grows for about 9 days and then regresses. When the diminishing corpus luteum ceases secretion of progesterone, the succulent endometrial lining separates from the uterine wall and flows out of the body through the vagina, the long tubular muscle leading from the uterus. This flow, menstruation, may last from 3 to 8 days in humans. A small amount of blood and uterine tissue (about 3 ml daily) is lost, and the uterine lining is renewed. The pituitary gland begins to produce FSH, and a new set of follicles begins to mature to initiate the next ovulatory cycle.

The timing of these sequential events is regulated by chemical messengers, such as the hormones LH and progesterone, with receptor cells for each hormone in the target tissues. Follicular growth results initially from the tonic release of FSH, and the secretion of estrogens from the developing follicle increases the number of estrogen receptors in the follicle and in target tissues in the hypothalamus and pituitary. This process "up-regulates" the system, rendering tissues more sensitive to estrogen effects. Similarly, FSH up-regulates FSH and estrogen receptors in the follicle. LH increases the number of LH receptors in the follicle, and limits the FSH-estrogen cycle by decreasing or "down-regulating" the number of estrogen receptors. In addition, progesterone counterbalances the effects of estrogens, down-regulating the sensitivity of the system by decreasing the number of both estrogen and progesterone receptors. In this way the ovarian follicle controls the timing of the cycle. Hormone effects on target tissues depend on the timing of antecedent events. For example, the effects of progesterone in the hypothalamus and the uterus depend on prior estrogen priming. Further discussion of these dynamics are found in Campbell and Turek, 1981; Cutler and Garcia, 1980; Feder, 1981a, 1981b; and Mahesh, 1985; also see Southam and Gonzaga, 1965.

Several key questions of ovarian regulation remain. How is the one dominant follicle "selected"? Because of its large size and increased blood flow and exposure to FSH? How is the development of other follicles inhibited? How is the follicle induced to release the ovum? The timing of the appearance and disappearance of the corpus luteum is the most reliable feature of the cycle. What controls the regression of the corpus luteum? Answers will come from the continuous discovery of new bioactive substances and new feedback loops by modern research techniques in hormone radioimmunoassay and systematic animal research. For example, prostaglandins may play important intermediary roles in the events of the cycle. Prostaglandin-inhibiting drugs, such as ibuprofen, are useful for alleviating menstrual cramps.

The current understanding of the female reproductive cycle is of very recent origin. A historian of science notes that "until the 1930's, standard medical advice books recommended that to *avoid* conception women should have intercourse during the middle of their menstrual cycles—i.e., during days twelve through sixteen, now known as the period of *maximum* fertility. Until the 1930s, even the outlines of our modern understanding of the hormonal control of ovulation was unknown" (Laqueur, 1987, p. 3). Previously, menstruation had been wrongly equated with animal estrus or "heat," which in dogs is accompanied by vaginal bleeding. The primate menstrual cycle is distinguished from the estrus cycle of other animals by the elaborate preparation of the uterine lining for implantation, and the periodic loss and renewal of the lining.

External factors such as social contacts, stress, and diet also control the menstrual cycle. Day length and season regulate the ovulatory cycle in conjunction with circadian pacemakers in animals. Whether humans show seasonal reproduction is debatable. Evidence for a lunar effect on human cycles was reported by Cutler (1980). In human and nonhuman animals, extreme conditions such as starvation (anorexia), obesity, or psychological stress may temporarily alter or abolish the ovulatory cycle. Social factors may influence the ovulatory cycle. Close association with males (Cutler, Preti, Kreiger, Huggins, Garcia, & Lawley, 1986) or with females (McClintock, 1971, 1981; Preti, Cutler, Garcia, Huggins, & Lawley, 1986) may alter the timing of the cycle, and developmentally may advance or delay the onset of ovulatory cycles.

Whether the ovulatory cycle changes social behavior is a focus of current controversy. In nonhuman animals the time of ovulation is obvious because of external changes (such as vaginal swelling in some primate species) or because of visible courtship and mating behaviors. Humans are thought to be unique because ovulation is "silent," or nonobvious, and because sexual behavior is not restricted to the period of ovulation (but see Adams, Gold, and Burt, 1978, and the discussion in Daly and Wilson, 1983). The popular stereotype of "PMS" (premenstrual syndrome) is undergoing refinement by new scientific inquiry. Recent rigorous studies of menstrual-behavioral relationships do not find behavioral or mood swings in women that overshadow social and cultural influences. Premenarcheal adolescents' expectations about menstrual cycle discomfort tend to be worse than their actual experiences after menarche (Ruble & Brooks-Gunn, 1987; also see Golub, 1983). Women usually do not find menstruation to be debilitating (Brooks-Gunn & Ruble, 1986; Golub & Harrington, 1981).

References

Adams, D. B., Gold, A. R., & Burt, A. D. (1978). Rise in female-initiated sexual activity at ovulation and its suppression by oral contraceptives. *New England Journal of Medicine, 299*, 1145–1150.

Brooks-Gunn, J., & Ruble, D. N. (1986). Men's and women's attitudes and beliefs about the menstrual cycle. *Sex Roles, 14,* 287–299.

Campbell, C. S., & Turek, F. W. (1981). Cyclic function of the mammalian ovary. In J. A. Schoff (Ed.), *Handbook of behavioral neurobiology: Biological rhythms*, (Vol. 4), (pp. 523–546). New York: Plenum.

Cutler, W. B. (1980). Lunar and menstrual phase locking. *American Journal of Obstetrics and Gynecology, 137*, 834–839.

Cutler, W. B., & Garcia, C. R. (1980). The psychoneuroendocrinology of the ovulatory cycle of women: A review. *Psychoneuroendocrinology, 5*, 89–111.

Cutler, W. B., Preti, G., Kreiger, A., Huggins, G. R., Garcia, C. R., & Lawley, H. J. (1986). Human axillary secretions influence women's menstrual cycles: The role of donor extract from men. *Hormones and Behavior, 20*, 463–473.

Daly, M., & Wilson, M. (1983). *Sex, evolution, and behavior* (2nd ed.), pp. 318–321. Boston: Willard Grant.

Feder, H. H. (1981a). Experimental analysis of hormone actions on the hypothalamus, anterior pituitary, and ovary. In N. T. Adler (Ed.), *Neuroendocrinology of reproduction: Physiology and behavior* (pp. 243–278). New York: Plenum.

Feder, H. H. (1981b). Estrous cyclicity in mammals. In N. T. Adler (Ed.), *Neuroendocrinology of reproduction: Physiology and behavior* (pp. 279–349). New York: Plenum.

Golub, S. (1983). *Lifting the curse of menstruation: A feminist appraisal of the influence of menstruation on women's lives.* New York: Haworth.

Golub, S., & Harrington, D. M. (1981). Premenstrual and menstrual mood changes in adolescent women. *Journal of Personality and Social Psychology, 41*, 961–965.

Laqueur, T. (1987). Orgasm, generation, and the politics of reproductive biology. In C. Gallagher & T. Laqueur (Eds.), *The making of the modern body: Sexuality and society in the nineteenth century* (pp. 1–41). Berkeley and Los Angeles: University of California Press.

Mahesh, V. B. (1985). The dynamic interactions between steroids and gonadotropins in the mammalian ovulatory cycle. *Neuroscience and Biobehavioral Reviews, 9*, 245–260.

McClintock, M. K. (1971). Menstrual synchrony and suppression. *Nature* (London), *229*, 244–245.

McClintock, M. K. (1981). Social control of the ovarian cycle and the function of estrous synchrony. *American Zoologist, 21*, 243–256.

Preti, G., Cutler, W. B., Garcia, C. R., Huggins, C. R., & Lawley, H. J. (1986). Human axillary secretions influence women's menstrual cycles: The role of donor extract of females. *Hormones and Behavior, 20*, 474–482.

Ruble, D. N., & Brooks-Gunn, J. (1987). Perceptions of menstrual and premenstrual symptoms: Self-definitional processes at menarche. In B. E. Ginsburg & B. F. Carter (Eds.), *Premenstrual syndrome: Ethical and legal implications in a biomedical perspective* (pp. 237–251). New York: Plenum.

Southam, A. L., & Gonzaga, F. P. (1965). Systemic changes during the menstrual cycle. *American Journal of Obstetrics and Gynecology, 91*, 142–165.

Turner, C. D., & Bagnara, J. T. (1976). *General endocrinology* (6th ed.). Philadelphia: W. B. Saunders.

See Also

Cognitive Abilities and Physical Maturation; Growth Spurt, Adolescent; Maturational Timing, Antecedents of in Girls; Maturational Timing Variations in Adolescent Girls, Consequences of; Menarche and Body Image; Menarche, Secular Trend in Age of; Physical Status and Timing in Early Adolescence, Measurement of; Premenstrual Syndrome (PMS); Pubertal Development, Assessment of; Puberty, Body Fat and; Puberty Education; Puberty, Endocrine Changes at; Puberty, Hypothalamic-Pituitary Changes of; Puberty, Precocious, Treatment of; Puberty, Sport and; Spatial Ability and Maturation in Adolescence; Spermarche.

Minority and Female Participation in Math and Science, Increase in: The Importance of the Middle School Years

Beatriz Chu Clewell

Educational Testing Service

That minorities (blacks and Hispanics) and females are underrepresented in the math- and science-related professions in the United States is well documented (Malcom, Aldrich, Hall, Boulware, & Stern, 1984; National Science Board, 1985; National Science Foundation, 1988; Pearson, 1987). What is not as well known, however, are the causes for underrepresentation. And even less is known regarding effective strategies to solve this problem. This entry will focus on factors affecting the underrepresentation of blacks, Hispanics, and females in math and science up through the high school years, with special emphasis on middle school, and suggest intervention strategies to address the problem.

The Math/Science Career Pipeline

Berryman (1983), in charting the math/science career pathway, identified the major points along the educational and career pipeline where students are most in danger of being lost. In order to participate in math or science careers students have to develop an interest in math or science, acquire the necessary skills to do well in math and science courses, enroll in a sufficient number of these courses in high school, and persist in a math and science major through college. Her analyses indicate that before the ninth grade, membership in the scientific talent pool may be defined more by quantitative interests than by skills. By the 12th grade, however, membership is defined both by interest and by significantly higher math achievements. This distinction continues through graduate school. According to Berryman, the talent pool seems to reach its maximum size before high school, although migration into the pool continues to occur during grades 9 through 12. After high school, however, she states that "migration is almost entirely out of, not into, the pool" (1983, p. 7).

The implications of this research for intervention strategies suggest that, in order to increase the talent pool of minorities and females, intervention prior to the ninth grade is important; and that this intervention should focus on fostering interest in math and science. At this time students should also be encouraged and prepared to enroll in an academic track and to take advanced math and science courses once they get to high school. After the ninth grade, however, the development of quantitative skills assumes greater importance.

Intervention by the middle school level is crucial to the issue of enlarging the scientific talent pool. Development of effective intervention strategies depends on a thorough knowledge of the target populations at this stage of life, including their attitudes toward math and science, their achievement levels in these subjects, and the characteristics that distinguish this age group—the preadolescents—from other students.

Barriers to Participation

Several factors contribute to low minority and female participation in science and engineering careers. These factors can be grouped as follows: (1) negative attitudes regarding math and science and/or lack of information regarding careers in these and related fields; (2) low levels of achievement in math and science courses; and (3) lack of participation in advanced math and science courses at the high school level (Clewell, 1987). Not only are minorities and females affected differentially by these factors, but these factors come into play at different points along the pipeline for each of the two groups.

ATTITUDES ■ Research has established that negative attitudes toward math and science, as well as lack of information regarding careers in these fields, represent barriers to participation by both minorities and females in math and science (Armstrong, 1980; Boswell, 1985; Brush, 1979; Eccles et al., 1985; Fennema & Sherman, 1977a, 1977b; Johnson, 1981; Miller & Remick, 1978; Schreiber, 1984; Thomas, 1986). Although research has suggested a relationship between positive attitudes toward mathematics and better performance on math tests (Armstrong, 1980; Boswell & Katz, 1980; Creswell, 1980; Fennema, 1976; Tsai & Walberg, 1983), researchers have expressed doubt concerning whether positive attitudes determine performance or vice versa (Bernreuter, 1980; Berryman, 1983; Lockheed, Thorpe, Brooks-Gunn, Casserly, & McAloon, 1985).

For girls at the middle school level, the evidence seems to favor attitudes influencing achievement (Berryman, 1983; Boswell, 1985; Sherman, 1980). Most researchers agree that girls' interest in science or math as a career, as well as their positive attitude toward these subjects, suffer a decline as they reach middle school (Hill & Lynch, 1983; Schreiber, 1984), coinciding with a decline in achievement scores. Reasons for this decline in interest include an image of science as a male domain (or as an inappropriate activity for females) (Armstrong, 1980; Bossert, 1981; Fox, 1976; MacCorquodale, 1984; Schreiber, 1984); the perception that these subjects are not "useful" for the future (Armstrong, 1980; Boswell & Katz, 1980; Fennema & Sherman, 1978); negative messages from important others in girls' lives—peers, teachers, and parents (Casserly, 1975; Fennema, 1976; Fox, 1976; Lee, 1984); sex-role socialization (Schreiber, 1984); and lack of science experiences (Kahle & Lakes, 1983).

For blacks, the picture is different. Although black students display positive attitudes toward science (Jacobowitz, 1983; James & Smith, 1985; Kahle, 1982), these attitudes seem to be unrelated to achievement, exposure to math/science experiences, or perceptions of the usefulness of science or science careers (Jacobowitz, 1983; Johnson, 1981; Kahle, 1982). Like girls, blacks express positive attitudes toward science in the early grades, but these positive attitudes decline as they grow older (Fleming & Malone, 1982; James & Smith, 1985).

For minority students, attitudes also differ according to sex. Rakow (1985) found that black and Hispanic students had positive attitudes toward science and that for nine-year-olds sex, not ethnicity, appeared to be a better predictor of science attitudes. For all three groups of nine-year-olds—white, blacks, and Hispanics—the males had more positive attitudes than the females. Hispanic females had the least positive attitudes of any group.

ACHIEVEMENT/ PERFORMANCE ■

Data from tests administered in mathematics and science show that white males consistently outperform both girls and minorities. Although girls obtain approximately the same math achievement scores in elementary school as do males (Maccoby & Jacklin, 1974), by high school males surpass them on such scores. This tendency increases with age (Mullis, 1975). According to data from the National Assessment of Educational Progress (NAEP) for 1973, 1978, and 1986, male and female math scores differed very little at ages 9 and 13, but males had higher scores at age 17 (Dossey, Mullis, Lindquist, & Chambers, 1988; Levine & Ornstein, 1983). A study of sex-related achievement differences in precollege science found that although on the surface differences between the sexes seem small, at the higher cognitive levels the differences favoring senior high males are quite large (Kahl, Malone, & Fleming, 1982). The study concluded that women are at a disadvantage with respect to being on track for postsecondary programs and ultimately careers in science. Reporting on the results of the 1986 National Assessment in Science, NAEP revealed that the science performance gap between males and females persists and that no progress had been made in closing this gap (Mullis & Jenkins, 1988).

Attitudinal factors have been mentioned as some of the reasons for girls' lower achievement levels. Sherman (1980) concluded that sex-role factors influencing attitudes were most important in creating sex-related differences in math performance. Other research has suggested that differences in extracurricular experiences in math and science and course-taking may be responsible for the lower female achievement (Fennema & Sherman, 1977a, 1977b; Fox, 1976). Other reasons given are that girls lag behind boys in the development of cognitive skills necessary to perform well in math and science; that girls develop logical thinking abilities later than boys (Graybill, 1975) and that they lag behind boys in reaching understanding of concepts of volume and density (Howe & Shayer, 1981); and that they may perform differently from boys on measures of spatial ability, field dependence/independence, or Piagetian formal reasoning (Armstrong, 1980; Fennema & Sherman, 1978; Linn & Pulos, 1983; Sherman, 1980; Treagust, 1980). External learning factors such as classroom environment and classroom interaction have also been cited as factors influencing sex differences in achievement (Lockheed & Hall, 1976; Morse, 1982; Webb, 1984). The consensus, however, is that there is no single explanation to account for all the observed differences (Linn & Pulos, 1983).

Recent research has shown that Asian and white students outperform black and Hispanic students in mathematics and has noted that this pattern is found as early as the third grade (Gross, 1988). Evidence from this study suggests that once a student falls below the standard level of performance for a grade, it is unlikely that he or she will ever catch up. This is particularly true for black and Hispanic students (Gross, 1989). Data gathered from the NAEP assessments of mathematics and science for 1976–77 and 1977–78, respectively, show that the percentage of black students able to respond successfully to all the science and math exercises ranges from 11 to 17 percentage points below the national mean percentage (Holmes, 1982). A more recent national assessment conducted by the Minnesota Science Assessment and Research Project (MSARP) in 1981–82 revealed that even at age nine white students scored 12% higher than black and Hispanic students (Rakow & Walker, 1985). Encouraging, however, is the fact that this assessment also found that black 9- and 13-year-olds improved in science achievement and that the black-white performance gap narrowed somewhat (National Assessment of Educational Progress, 1984). This trend continued in the 1986 assessment, which reported improvement in science achievement for blacks and Hispanics at all three age levels (Mullis & Jenkins, 1988).

There has been less research on reasons for differential minority performance on tests of math and science than there has been on sex differences in performance. Learner characteristics such as cognitive style and locus of control as factors influencing minority achievement have been the subject of some research. A number of studies have found significantly greater field independence among Anglo-American children compared to Mexican-American children (Buriel, 1975; Kagan & Zahn, 1975; Kagan, Zahn, & Gealy, 1977; Ramirez & Price-Williams, 1974; Sanders, Scholz, & Kagan, 1976). Minority group members have also been cited as tending to have an external locus of control, whereas Anglo-Americans tend to have an internal locus of control (Alexander, 1977; Brown, Rosen, Hill, & Olivas, 1980; Coleman et al., 1966; Joe, 1971; Lefcourt, 1966). These ethnic-related differences in learner characteristics have implications for minority achievement in math and science. Both field independence and internal locus of control have been positively related to achievement in math and science (Kagan & Zahn, 1975; Rowe, 1973; Witkin, Moore, Goodenough, & Cox, 1977).

Culture and language affect achievement of minority students in science and math. Llabre and Cuevas (1983) found that students should be tested in the language of instruction. Brown, Fournier, and Mayer (1977), in looking at differential performance levels of Mexican-Americans and Anglos in science, concluded that culture and language seem to be useful indicators of differences in cognitive development. They suggested that the time required to develop facility in a new language and new cultural environment may cause a lag in the development of logical thinking. Several studies have investigated the effect of English language proficiency and bilingualism on Hispanic students' achievement in mathematics, with mixed results, reporting both negative and beneficial effects of bilingualism on achievement in mathematics (Myers & Milne, 1988). There is some evidence that level of English proficiency rather than bilingualism is the determining factor in mathematics achievement (MacCorquodale, 1988; Nielsen & Fernandez, 1982; So & Chan, 1982). One problem in determining the effect of language on achievement is the confusion of language with other processes that affect learning, such as characteristics of a culture, socio-economic status, and classroom interaction (MacCorquodale, 1988). Group membership should not be confused with linguistic characteristics (DeAvila, 1988). An excellent discussion of the linguistic and cultural influences on the learning of mathematics is contained in a volume edited by Cocking and Mestre (1988).

There are also a number of factors that affect achievement in science and math for all middle school students. Objectives for middle school science should recognize the physical and intellectual development of students. For example, the typical middle school class is likely to contain a few students who are concrete operational and a few who are formal operational, with the majority being in some transitional phase between the two stages (Juraschek, 1983).

Research on adolescents and on effective middle schools has identified physical, social, emotional, and cognitive needs of young adolescents (Hill, 1980; Lipstiz, 1977). These are the needs that an educational program for this age group should take into account if it wishes to be effective: diversity; self-exploration and self-definition; meaningful participation in school and community; social interaction with peers and adults; physical activity; a sense of competence and achievement; and structure and clear limits (Dorman, 1981).

PARTICIPATION IN ADVANCED MATH AND SCIENCE

COURSES ■ Precollegiate preparation is an important factor influencing female and minority participation in mathematics- and science-related careers. Researchers report that black and Hispanic students are less likely than white students to enroll in an academic track in high school (National Science Foundation,

1988; Oakes, 1985; Orum, 1986). This virtually disqualifies them from continuing along the pipeline that leads to higher education. Even when minority (with the exception of Asian) students do enroll in an academic track, they, as do white females, tend to take fewer advanced level mathematics and science courses that would prepare them to major in science and math in college (Davis, 1989; National Science Foundation, 1988).

Intervention Strategies: Implications from Research

Research on factors that affect minority and female access to math and science careers can inform the development of effective intervention strategies and approaches. In the following section, implications for intervention are organized according to the barriers they address.

ATTITUDES ■ The work of Berryman (1983) and others suggest that by middle school girls' negative attitudes toward math and science begin to affect their performance in these subjects. Cultivation of interest and positive attitudes, then, should be the primary focus of intervention efforts for girls at the middle school level. These efforts should counteract girls' perceptions of science and math as a male domain, affirming the appropriateness of these careers for women. The use of role models, materials portraying women as scientists, and information on careers in math and science are effective strategies. Intervention approaches should also focus on providing social support and acceptance for the doing of math and science by girls on the part of their peers, teachers, and parents. Finally, middle school girls should be provided with access to out-of-school science experiences such as field trips, visits to science museums, science clubs, and other such activities.

Studies by several researchers (Berryman, 1983; Jacobowitz, 1983; James & Smith, 1985; Kahle, 1982) have found that the black students' attitudes toward math and science seem unrelated to achievement or perceptions of the usefulness of careers in these fields. Also, research has found that the positive attitudes of black students toward science in the early grades suffer a decline by the time they reach middle school (Fleming & Malone, 1982; James & Smith, 1985). Less is known regarding attitudes of Hispanic students. Although MacCorquodale (1984) reports that the self-image of Mexican-Americans is likely to discourage their interest in participating in science, 9-year-old Hispanics had positive attitudes toward science. Research on minority attitudes suggests somewhat different strategies for intervention. Activities to improve math and science skills are an important component of intervention to sustain minority interest in these subjects. For black students, intervention on attitudes should begin before the seventh grade. For black and Hispanic students, intervention efforts should include role models and career information as well as exposure to more science experiences, activities, and hobbies both in and out of school. Attention should be paid to sex differences. Parents, teachers, and counselors should be made aware of the importance of their role in encouraging minority students to participate in math and science.

ACHIEVEMENT/ PERFORMANCE ■ Although girls' performance does not decline until junior high or after, minority student achievement in math and science is lower than that of whites by the age of 9. Implications from the research on both female and minority performance suggest similar interventions, although focus on the improvement of minority performance should begin much earlier. Also important to the development of effective strategies is an awareness of the middle school learner's physical and intellectual development. Instructors should adapt their teaching methods and courses to accommodate varying stages of cognitive development as well as different cognitive styles and locus of control orientations. Learning activities combining the inquiry/discovery method, direct use of materials (manipulatives), as well as progression from the concrete to the abstract, facilitate learning for this age group (Georgia State Department of Education, 1982; Juraschek, 1983; Padilla, 1983). Teachers should be aware of how their expectations, attitudes, behavior, and interactions with students affect achievement. Girls should be exposed to male-oriented science activities, both in and out of school. Math and science instruction for students with limited English proficiency should take into account the role of language in learning. The use of cooperative goal structures with a high level of peer interaction and small-group activities are also effective strategies (Johnson & Johnson, 1974).

PARTICIPATION IN ADVANCED MATH AND SCIENCE COURSES ■ Although this is not an intervention that can be directly applied before the high school years, research indicates that minorities' and females' failure to enroll in advanced courses is an important reason for their underrepresentation in math and science majors in college. Intervention during middle school should focus on preparing and encouraging these students to enroll in an academic track and, while there, to take advanced level science and mathematics.

Realization that the roots of exclusion from math- and science-related careers begins before the high school years for minority and female students has resulted in a growing focus on intervention in middle school (Clewell, Thorpe & Anderson, 1987; Lockheed et al., 1985). Effective intervention, however, must be grounded in a thorough knowledge of the target population.

References

Alexander, S. (1977). Locus of control and sex role expectations in black and white, female and male children. *Dissertation Abstracts International, 38*(2), 957–B.

Armstrong, J. M. (1980). *Achievement and participation in mathematics: An overview. Report of a two-year study* (Grant No. NIE–G–77–0061). Washington, DC: National Institute of Education.

Bernreuter, J. D., III. (1980). *A study of self-concept and achievement of inner city black seventh grade students as influenced by values clarification lessons in science.* Unpublished doctoral dissertation, University of Northern Colorado.

Berryman, S. F. (1983). *Who will do science? Trends and their causes in minority and female representation among holders of advanced degrees in science and mathematics.* New York: Rockefeller Foundation.

Bossert, S. T. (1981). Understanding sex differences in children's classroom experiences. *Elementary School Journal, 81,* 254–266.

Boswell, S. L. (1985). The influence of sex-role stereotyping on women's attitudes and achievement in mathematics. In S. F. Chipman, L. R. Brush, & D. M. Wilson (Eds.), *Women and mathematics: Balancing the equation* (pp. 175–197). Hillsdale, NJ: Lawrence Erlbaum Associates.

Boswell, S. L., & Katz, P. A. (1980). *Nice girls don't study mathematics* (Grant No. NIE–G–79–0023). Washington, DC: National Institute of Education. (ERIC Document Reproduction Service No. ED 188 888)

Brown, G. H., Rosen, N. L., Hill, S. T., & Olivas, M. A. (1980). *The condition of education for Hispanic-Americans.* Washington, DC: National Center for Educational Statistics. (ERIC Document Reproduction Service No. ED 188 853)

Brown, R. L., Fournier, J. F., & Mayer, R. H. (1977). A cross-cultural study of Piagetian concrete reasoning and science concepts among rural fifth-grade Mexican- and Anglo-American students. *Journal of Research in Science Teaching, 14,* 329–334.

Brush, L. R. (1979). Avoidance of science and stereotypes of scientists. *Journal of Research in Science Teaching, 16*(3), 237–241.

Buriel, R. (1975). Cognitive styles among three generations of Mexican-American children. *Journal of Cross-Cultural Psychology, 6,* 417–429.

Casserly, P. L. (1975). *An assessment of factors affecting female participation in advanced placement programs in mathematics, chemistry, and physics.* Unpublished manuscript. Princeton, NJ: Educational Testing Service.

Clewell, B. C. (1987). What works and why: Research and theoretical bases of intervention programs in math and science for minority and female middle school students. In A. B. Champagne & L. E. Hornig (Eds.), *Students and science learning* (pp. 95–135). Washington, DC: American Association for the Advancement of Science.

Clewell, B. C., Thorpe, M. E., & Anderson, B. T. (1987). *Intervention programs in math, science, and computer science for minority and female students in grades four through eight.* Princeton, NJ: Educational Testing Service.

Cocking, R. R., & Mestre, J. P. (Eds.). (1988). *Linguistic and cultural influences on learning mathematics.* Hillsdale, NJ: Lawrence Erlbaum Associates.

Coleman, J. S., Campbell, E. Q., Hobson, C.,

Partland, J., Mood, A. M., Weinfeld, F. P., & York, R. L. (1966). *Equality of educational opportunity*. Washington, DC: U.S. Department of Health, Education, and Welfare.

Creswell, J. L. (1980). *A study of sex-related differences in mathematics: Achievement of black, Chicano, and Anglo adolescents*. Houston, TX: University of Houston. (ERIC Document Reproduction Service No. ED 189 029)

Davis, J. D. (1986). *The effect of mathematics course enrollment on racial/ethnic differences in secondary school mathematics achievement* (NAEP Report 86–EMC). Princeton, NJ: Educational Testing Service.

Davis, J. D. (1989). The mathematics education of black high school students. In W. Pearson, Jr. & H. K. Bechtel (Eds.), *Blacks, science, and American education*. New Brunswick, NJ: Rutgers University Press.

DeAvila, E. A. (1988). Bilingualism, cognitive functioning, and language minority group membership. In R. R. Cocking & J. P. Mestre (Eds.), *Linguistic and cultural influences on learning mathematics* (pp. 101–121). Hillsdale, NJ: Lawrence Erlbaum Associates.

Dorman, G. (1981). *Middle grades assessment program*. Chapel Hill, NC: Center for Early Adolescence, University of North Carolina.

Dossey, J. A., Mullis, I. V. S., Lindquist, M. M., & Chambers, D. L. (1988). *The mathematics report card: Are we measuring up? Trends and achievement based on the 1986 national assessment*. Princeton, NJ: Educational Testing Service.

Eccles (Parsons), J., Adler, T. F., Futterman, R., Goff, S. B., Kaczala, C. M., Meece, J. L., & Midgley, C. (1985). Self-perceptions, task perceptions, socializing influences, and the decision to enroll in mathematics. In S. F. Chipman, L. R. Brush, & D. M. Wilson (Eds.), *Women and mathematics: Balancing the equation* (pp. 95–121). Hillsdale, NJ: Lawrence Erlbaum Associates.

Gross, S. (1988). *Participation and performance of women and minorities in mathematics: Findings by gender and racial/ethnic group (Vol. 1)* (Grant No. MDR-8470384). Rockville, MD: Montgomery County Public Schools.

Gross, S. (1989, March). *Early mathematics performance and achievement: The beginning of a downward spiral for blacks and Hispanics*. Paper presented at the annual meeting of the American Educational Research Association, San Francisco, CA.

Fennema, E. (1976). *Influences of selected cognitive, affective, and educational variables on sex-related differences in mathematics learning and studying* (Grant No. P-76-0274). Washington, DC: National Institute of Education.

Fennema, E., & Sherman, J. (1977a). Sex-related differences in mathematics achievement, spatial visualization, and affective factors. *American Educational Research Journal, 14*, 51–71.

Fennema, E., & Sherman, J. (1977b). Sexual stereotyping and mathematics learning. *Arithmetic Teacher, 24*, 369–372.

Fennema, E., & Sherman, J. (1978). Sex-related differences in mathematics achievement and related factors: A further study. *Journal for Research in Mathematics Education, 9*(3), 189–203.

Fleming, M. L., & Malone, M. R. (1982). A meta-analysis of the relationships between student characteristics and student outcomes in science. In R. D. Anderson, S. R. Kahl, G. V. Glass, M. L. Smith, M. L. Fleming, & M. R. Malone (Eds.), *Science meta-analyses project: Vol. 2. Final report* (pp. 211–288). Boulder, CO: University of Colorado, Laboratory for Research in Science and Mathematics Education. (ERIC Document Reproduction Service No. ED 223 476)

Fox, L. H. (1976). *The effects of sex role socialization on mathematics participation and achievement* (Contract NO. FN17-400-76-0114). Washington, DC: National Institute of Education.

Georgia State Department of Education. (1982). *Teaching middle school science.* Atlanta: Office of Instructional Services. (ERIC Document Reproduction Service No. ED 220 281)

Graybill, L. (1975). Sex differences in problem-solving ability. *Journal of Research in Science Teaching, 12,* 341–346.

Hill, J. P. (1980). *Understanding early adolescence: A framework.* Carrboro, NC: Center for Early Adolescence, Department of Maternal and Child Health, School of Public Health.

Hill, J. P., & Lynch, M. E. (1983). The intensification of gender-related role expectations during early adolescence. In J. Brooks-Gunn & P. L. Peterson (Eds.), *Girls at puberty* (pp. 201–228). New York: Plenum Press.

Holmes, B. J. (1982). Black students' performance in the national assessments of science and mathematics. *Journal of Negro Education, 51,* 392–405.

Howe, A. C., & Shayer, M. (1981). Sex-related differences on a task of volume and density. *Journal of Research in Science Teaching, 18*(2), 169–175.

Jacobowitz, T. J. (1983). Relationship of sex, achievement, and science self-concept to the science career preferences of black students. *Journal of Research in Science Teaching, 20,* 621–628.

James, R. K., & Smith, S. (1985). Alienation of students from science in grades 4–12. *Science Education, 60*(1), 39–45.

Joe, V. C. (1971). Review of the internal-external control construct as a personality variable. *Psychological Reports, 28,* 619–640.

Johnson, D. W., & Johnson, R. T. (1974). Instructional goal structure: Cooperative, competitive, or individualistic. *Review of Educational Research, 44*(2), 213–240.

Johnson, R. C. (1981). *Psychosocial influences on the math attitudes and interests of black junior high school students.* Unpublished manuscript.

Juraschek, W. (1983). Piaget and middle school mathematics. *School Science and Mathematics, 83*(1), 4–13.

Kagan, S., & Zahn, G. L. (1975). Field dependence and the school achievement gap between Anglo-American and Mexican-American children. *Journal of Educational Psychology, 67,* 643–650.

Kagan, S., Zahn, G. L., & Gealy, J. (1977). Competition and school achievement among Anglo-American and Mexican-American children. *Journal of Educational Psychology, 69,* 432–441.

Kahl, S. R., Malone, M. R., & Fleming, M. L. (1982, March). *Sex-related differences in pre-college science: Findings of the science meta-analysis project.* Paper presented at the annual meeting of the American Educational Research Association, New York. (ERIC Document Reproduction Service No. ED 216 909)

Kahle, J. B. (1982). Can positive minority attitudes lead to achievement gains in science? Analyses of the 1977 National Assessment of Educational Progress, Attitudes toward Science. *Science Education, 66,* 539–546.

Kahle, J. B., & Lakes, M. K. (1983). The myth of equality in science classrooms. *Journal of Research in Science Teaching, 29*(2), 131–140.

Lee, M. K. (1984). Debunking the Cinderella myth. *Educational Forum, 48,* 334.

Lefcourt, H. M. (1966). Internal versus external control of reinforcement: A review. *Psychological Bulletin, 65,* 206–220.

Levine, D. U., & Ornstein, A. C. (1983). Sex differences in ability and achievement. *Journal of Research and Development in Education, 16*(2), 66–72.

Linn, M. C., & Pulos, S. (1983). Male-female differences in predicting displaced volume: Strategy usage, aptitude relationships, and experience influences. *Journal of Educational Psychology, 75*(1), 86–96.

Lipsitz, J. (1977). *Growing up forgotten: A review of research and programs concerning early adolescence.* Lexington, MA: D. C. Heath.

Llabre, M. M., & Cuevas, G. (1983). The effects of test language and mathematical skills assessed on the scores of bilingual Hispanic students. *Journal of Research in Mathematics Education, 14*, 318–324.

Lockheed, M. E., & Hall, K. P. (1976). Conceptualizing sex as a status characteristic: Applications to leadership training strategies. *Journal of Social Issues, 32*(3), 111–124.

Lockheed, M. E., Thorpe, M., Brooks-Gunn, J., Casserly, P., & McAloon, A. (1985). *Sex and ethnic differences in middle school mathematics, science, and computer science: What do we know?* Princeton, NJ: Educational Testing Service.

Maccoby, E., & Jacklin, C. (1974). *The psychology of sex differences.* Palo Alto, CA: Stanford University Press.

MacCorquodale, P. (1984, August). *Self-image, science, and math: Does the image of the "scientist" keep girls and minorities from pursuing science and math?* Paper presented at the 79th Annual Meeting of the American Sociological Association, San Antonio, Texas.

MacCorquodale, P. (1988). Mexican-American women and mathematics: Participation, aspirations, and achievement. In R. R. Cocking & J. P. Mestre (Eds.), *Linguistic and cultural influences on learning mathematics* (pp. 137–160). Hillsdale, NJ: Lawrence Erlbaum Associates.

Malcom, S. M., Aldrich, M., Hall, P. Q., Boulware, P., & Stern, V. (1984). *Equity and excellence: Compatible goals* (AAAS Publication No. 84-14). Washington, DC: American Association for the Advancement of Science, Office of Opportunities in Science.

Miller, K., & Remick, H. (1978). Participation rates in high school mathematics and science courses. *Physics Teacher, 16*, 280–282.

Morse, L. W. (1982, March). *Classroom interaction as related to junior high school students' achievement in science.* Paper presented at the annual meeting of the American Educational Research Association, New York.

Mullis, I. V. S. (1975). *Educational achievement and sex discrimination.* Denver, CO: National Assessment of Educational Progress.

Mullis, I. V. S., & Jenkins, L. B. (1988). *The science report card: Elements of risk and recovery. Trends and achievement based on the 1986 national assessment.* Princeton, NJ: Educational Testing Service.

Myers, D. E., & Milne, A. M. (1988). Effects of home language and primary language on mathematics achievement: A model and results for secondary analysis. In R. R. Cocking & J. P. Mestre (Eds.), *Linguistic and cultural influences on learning mathematics* (pp. 259–293). Hillsdale, NJ: Lawrence Erlbaum Associates.

National Science Board. (1985). *Science indicators.* Washington, DC: U.S. Government Printing Office.

National Science Foundation. (1988). *Women and minorities in science and engineering* (NSF 88-301). Washington, DC: Author.

Nielsen, F., & Fernandez, R. M. (1982). *Achievement of Hispanic students in American high schools: Background characteristics and achievement.* Washington, DC: U.S. Government Printing Office.

Oakes, J. (1985). *Keeping track: How schools structure inequality.* New Haven, CT: Yale University Press.

Orum, L. S. (1986). *The education of Hispanics: Status and implications.* Washington, DC: National Council of La Raza.

Padilla, M. J. (1983). Formal operations and middle/junior high school science education. In M. J. Padilla (Ed.), *Science and the early adolescent* (pp. 13–16). Washington, DC: National Teachers Association.

Pearson, W., Jr. (1987). The graduate education and careers of underrepresented minorities in science and engineering. In L. S. Dix (Ed.), *Minorities: Their underrepresentation and career differentials in science and engineering* (pp. 133–149). Washington, DC: National Academy Press.

Rakow, S. J. (1985). Minority students in science. *Urban Education, 20*(1), 103–113.

Rakow, S. J., & Walker, C. L. (1985). The status of Hispanic-American students in science: Achievement and exposure. *Science Education, 69*, 557–565.

Ramirez, M., & Price-Williams, D. R. (1974). Cognitive styles of children of three ethnic groups in the United States. *Journal of Cross-Cultural Psychology, 5*, 212–219.

Rowe, M. B. (1973). *Teaching science as continuous inquiry.* New York: McGraw-Hill.

Sanders, M. L., Scholz, J. P., & Kagan, S. (1976). Three social motives and field-independence-dependence in Anglo-American and Mexican-American children. *Journal of Cross-Cultural Psychology, 7*, 451–462.

Schreiber, D. A. (1984). *Factors affecting female attitude formation toward science: Specific reference to 12–14 year old female adolescents and their affective orientation toward middle school science.* Unpublished master's thesis, University of Cincinnati, Cincinnati, Ohio.

Sherman, J. (1980). *Women and mathematics: Summary of research from 1977–1979* (Final Report, Contract No. G–77–0063). Washington, DC: National Institute of Education. (ERIC Document Reproduction Service No. ED 145 312.)

So, A. Y., & Chan, K. S. (1982). *What matters? A study of the relative impact of language background and socioeconomic status on reading and achievement.* Los Alamitos, CA: National Center for Bilingual Research.

Thomas, G. E. (1986). Cultivating the interest of women and minorities in high school mathematics and science. *Science Education, 70*, 31–43.

Treagust, D. F. (1980). Gender-related differences in spatial representational thought. *Journal of Research in Science Teaching, 17*(2), 91–97.

Tsai, S., & Walberg, H. J. (1983). Mathematics achievement and attitude productivity in junior high school. *Journal of Educational Research, 76*(5), 267–272.

Webb, N. M. (1984). Sex differences in interaction and achievement in cooperative small groups. *Journal of Educational Psychology, 76*(1), 33–44.

Witkin, H., Moore, C., Goodenough, D., & Cox, P. (1977). Field-dependent and field-independent cognitive styles and their educational implications. *Review of Educational Research, 47*, 1–64.

See Also

Black Adolescents At-Risk: Approaches to Prevention; Black Adolescents, the Impact of Federal Income Assistance Policies on; Black Female Adolescents, Socialization of; Drug Use, Minority Youth and; Health and Substance Abuse in Adolescence: Ethnic and Gender Perspectives; Hispanic Adolescents: Identity, Minority Development of; Sexual Behavior in Black Adolescents, Initiation of; Socialization of African-American Adolescents.

Moodiness, Adolescent

Reed Larson

University of Illinois at Urbana/Champaign

It is commonly believed that adolescents experience greater emotional fluctuations in their daily lives than other age groups. This conception of teenagers as emotionally variable or "moody" is expressed by psychoanalysts, social psychologists, educators, and novelists, as well as by laypersons and teenagers themselves. Research addressing this belief indicates that teenagers do experience wider and more frequent daily emotional fluctuations than adults, but that their emotional variability is no greater than that of children.

In lay terminology, the word "moody" is sometimes used to denote that adolescents are more despondent, withdrawn, or negative, and indeed evidence suggests that they experience more frequent dysphoric states than do children. It is important to recognize, however, that the emotional swings of adolescents are not just comprised of gloomy negative states, but also include surgent positive states of excitement, joy, and love. Adolescents experience both more negative and more extreme positive states than do adults.

Cultural and Historical Variations

The conception of young people as "passionate" and emotionally changeable is not confined to our historical era, nor to Western society. Aristotle wrote that the young "are heated by Nature as drunken men by wine" (Fox, 1977). In the philosophy of Confucius, which played a major role through much of Chinese history, youth is a period when one's "blood and vital humors" are not yet settled (Wei-Ming, 1976). The Gusii of Kenya, typical of many tribal societies, group male youth and young adults into an age category, *omomura*—once the warrior class—who are considered to be high-spirited, aggressive, and potential troublemakers (Levine, 1980). At the core of this prevalent conception of youth is a belief that young people lack perspective on events, respond to them emotionally, and have less control of their passions. In contrast, age and experience allow adults to respond to daily events with greater equanimity and self-control.

This conception or stereotype of adolescents as emotional has also been documented in the contemporary United States. In two studies in which Americans were asked to describe the "typical teenager," youth were described as impulsive, unstable, and wild (Hess & Goldblatt, 1957; Musgrove, 1963). What is striking is that adolescents also held this stereotype of themselves.

The occurrence of these cultural beliefs or stereotypes, of course, is not conclusive evidence that young people in these various societies actually are more emotional. But the presence of such beliefs undoubtedly provides license for youth to be so; in other words, such beliefs are likely to be self-fulfilling. It has been suggested that the typification of the young as emotional serves an age-graded social organization in which youth are denied major responsibility because of their changeability (whether real or projected), and older adults are seen as the ones capable of making rational decisions (Lewin, 1938). This interpretation suggests the hypothesis that in a society where youth are expected to fill adult roles and carry important responsibilities they will be less moody, and indeed Margaret Mead's (1928) portrayal of Samoan adolescence appears to support this prediction, though her evidence has been subject to question (Freeman, 1983).

Moodiness in Modern Conceptions of Adolescence

The belief that adolescence is a time of emotionality was introduced into modern academic discourse by G. Stanley Hall (1904), who portrayed youth as oscillating between extremes of egotism and self-doubt, selfishness and altruism, wisdom and folly, among other bi-polarities. Psychoanalytic thinkers, who had discovered extreme emotionality in their adolescent patients, contributed two explanations for this variability. First, puberty was hypothesized to bring a dramatic increase in primary drive that destabilizes the control over impulses achieved by the preadolescent ego (Freud, 1962). Second, the adolescent's developmental task of establishing autonomy from his or her parents requires a violent thrusting away from dependency upon them, inevitably accompanied by cycles of regression when this dependency is temporarily revived (Blos, 1961). Hence,

in the psychoanalytic view, emotionality, particularly emotionality of a turbulent nature, is an indication that development is proceeding according to plan, while an absence of emotionality is a sign that development is arrested (Jacobson, 1961).

For Hall and the psychoanalytic theorists, adolescent emotionality was part of a normative condition of personality disequilibrium, commonly identified as "storm and stress." Researchers have discredited the thesis that storm and stress is normative and developmentally beneficial, showing that the typical teenager does not experience extreme conflict with his or her parents (Hill & Holmbeck, 1986; Montemayor, 1986), that the great majority of teenagers report feeling happy with their lives (Offer, Ostrov, & Howard, 1981), and that an untroubled adolescence is associated with better, not worse, adjustment in subsequent years (Ducek & Flaherty, 1981; Offer & Offer, 1975).

Nonetheless, until recently the narrower hypothesis—that adolescents are more emotionally variable—has not been tested, and the prediction that such emotionality might be associated with puberty, deindividuation from the family, or other changes and life stresses associated with this age period has remained open to study.

Empirical Data on Adolescent's Daily Moods

The most direct information on adolescents' emotionality comes from research in which respondents reported on their affective experience at random times during the day in response to random signals received via a pager. Larson, Csikszentmihalyi and Graef (1980) used data obtained by this means to compare 75 high-school-aged adolescents with 107 adults. They found that adolescents reported wider daily mood variability, including both higher highs and lower lows. They also found that adolescents' strongest emotional states did not last very long, typically dissipating within half an hour, while adults' strong states often lasted an hour, two hours, or more. In other words, while adolescents experienced more extreme states, these states were more transient.

Corroboration of these differences between adolescents and adults is provided by several studies employing one-time questionnaire measures, in which adolescents and young adults reported more extreme emotional states in their recent experience than did older adults (Bradburn, 1969; Campbell, 1981; Diener, Sandvik & Larsen, 1985). Taken as a whole, these results suggest that the emotionality of adolescents represents one end of a trend toward diminished emotional variability across the adult life span, though not all researchers agree with this conclusion (Malatesta, 1981).

Comparison between adolescents and children is provided by a second study employing the pager time-sampling method. Larson and Lampman-Petraitis (1989) compared the daily moods reported by a sample of 473 5th to 9th graders (ages 9–15) and found no difference in emotional variability across this age period for boys and only a small, marginally significant increase in variability for girls. They did find, however, that both older girls and boys reported fewer extreme positive and more moderately negative states than their younger counterparts. By having participants rate the emotions they perceived in pictures of faces, they were also able to demonstrate that these age differences could not be attributed to age differences in response sets. These findings indicate a downward shift in average daily mood state with entry into adolescence, but suggest that the emotional variability of adoles-

cence is largely a continuation of a childhood condition, not a new state of affairs associated with this age period.

These findings from self-report studies need to be complemented by research employing behavioral and physiological measures of emotional arousal.

Relation of Adolescents' Moods to other Variables

Research has begun to evaluate hypotheses about the causes and correlates of adolescents' mood patterns. Contrary to prior theory, this work has found little or no relationship between moods and pubertal change. Analyzing data from the above-mentioned study of 5th-9th graders, Richards and Larson (submitted) found that pubertal maturation related to more frequent feelings of being "in love," but not to more generalized mood states. Likewise, several studies found no relationship between pubertal status and one-time measures of moods (Buchanan & Eccles, submitted), although two of these studies did find small associations between hormonal levels and moods (Brooks-Gunn & Warren, 1989; Inoff-Germain, Arnold, Nottelmann, Susman, Cutler & Chrousos, 1988).

There is support for the hypothesis that adolescent emotionality is related to the increased change and life stress associated with this stage of life. The time sampling study of 5th-9th graders shows modest associations between occurrence of negative events in an adolescent's life and dysphoric and variable moods (Larson & Ham, 1989), a relationship also evident in the study of high-school-aged teens (Larson, Csikszentmihalyi, & Graef, 1980; see also Brooks-Gunn & Warren, 1989). In addition, Csikszentmihalyi and Larson (1984) show that the emotional changeability of adolescents, as compared to adults, is partly related to the greater pace of their daily lives—to the fact that they switch between activities and contexts more rapidly than do adults.

The final question is whether the more variable and dysphoric moods of adolescents are related to personality disequilibrium and maladjustment, as theorists have suggested. A set of mixed and modest correlations suggest that while these mood patterns are normative in adolescence, extreme variability and dysphoria are related to signs of maladjustment. Among high school students, Larson, Csikszentmihalyi and Graef (1980) found no correlation of mood variability with average mood and control, but did find small correlations with poorer school performance and lower general motivation. In the study of young adolescents, Richards, Casper and Larson (1990) found an association of lower and more variable moods with disturbed eating attitudes among girls, a finding that may anticipate a strong pattern of moodiness found among adult bulimic women (Johnson & Larson, 1983). These researchers also found an association of lower and more variable moods with depression in young adolescents (Larson, Raffaelli, Richards, Ham & Jewell, 1990). These relationships, however, are not strong enough to suggest that variability in a specific adolescent, particularly variability that includes both positive and negative swings, is related to personality disequilibrium.

For many teenagers wide and rapid fluctuations between positive and negative moods appear to be a natural and healthy part of their lives. Mood variability is related to features of a peer-oriented life-style: to spending more time with friends, thinking about heterosexual relationships more often, and spending more time outside the home (Larson et al., 1980). Because many things in their daily life are new to them (the first kiss, the first time out with the car on one's

own), it is not surprising that they react more intensely. Because they have not yet established a firm sense of self, they do not have a core sense of internal continuity that prevents them from oscillating quickly from a positive state to a negative one and back again. In most cases, then, the emotionality that typifies adolescence is not storm and stress, but more likely reflects the change, uncertainty, and excitement associated with this time of life.

References

Blos, P. (1961). *On adolescence.* New York: Free Press.

Bradburn, N. (1969). *The structure of psychological well-being.* Chicago: Aldine.

Brooks-Gunn, J., & Warren, M. P. (1989). Biological and social contributions to negative affect in young adolescent girls. *Child Development, 60,* 40-55.

Buchanan, C. M., & Eccles, J. S. (submitted). Evidence for activational effects of hormones on moods and behavior at adolescence.

Campbell, A. (1981). *The sense of well-being in America: Recent patterns and trends.* New York: McGraw-Hill.

Csikszentmihalyi, M., & Larson, R. (1984). *Being adolescent.* New York: Basic Books.

Diener, E., Sandvik, E., & Larsen, R. J. (1985). Age and sex effects for emotional intensity. *Developmental Psychology, 21,* 542-546.

Ducek, J., & Flaherty, J. (1981). The development of the self-concept during the adolescent years. *Monographs of the Society for Research in Child Development, 46* (serial no. 191).

Fox, V. (1977). Is adolescence a phenomenon of modern times? *Journal of Psychohistory, 1,* 271-290.

Freeman, D. (1983). *Margaret Mead and Samoa: The making and unmaking of an anthropological myth.* Cambridge: Harvard University Press.

Freud, S. (1962). *Three essays on the theory of*

sexuality (translated by J. Strachey). New York: Basic Books (originally published 1905).

Hall, G. S. (1904). *Adolescence*. New York: Appleton.

Hess, R., & Goldblatt, I. (1957). The status of adolescence in American society: A problem in social identity. *Child Development, 28*, 459–468.

Hill, J. P., & Holmbeck, G. N. (1986). Attachment and autonomy during adolescence. In G. J. Whitehurst, (Ed.), *Annals of child development* (Vol. 3, pp. 145–189). Greenwich, CT: JAI Press.

Inoff-Germain, G., Arnold, G. S., Nottelmann, E. D., Susman, E. J., Cutler, G. B., & Chrousos, G. P. (1988). Relations between hormone levels and observational measures of aggressive behavior of young adolescents in family interactions. *Developmental Psychology, 24*, 129–139.

Jacobson, E. (1961). Adolescent moods and the remodeling of psychic structures in adolescence. *Psychoanalytic Study of the Child, 16*, 164–183.

Johnson, C., & Larson, R. (1983). Bulimia: An analysis of moods and behavior. *Psychosomatic Medicine, 44*, 341–347.

Larson, R., Csikszentmihalyi, M., & Graef, R. (1980). Mood variability and the psychosocial adjustment of adolescents. *Journal of Youth and Adolescence, 9*, 469–490.

Larson, R., & Ham, M. (1989, April). Stressful events and adolescents' mood states. Paper presented at the Biennial Meetings of the Society for Research on Child Development, Kansas City.

Larson, R., & Lampman-Petraitis, C. (1989). Daily emotional states as reported by children and adolescents. *Child Development, 60*, 1250–1260.

Larson, R., Raffaelli, M., Richards, M., Ham, M., & Jewell, L. (1990). The ecology of depression in early adolescence: A profile of daily psychological states and activities. *Journal of Abnormal Psychology, 99*, 92–102.

Levine, R. A. (1980). Adulthood among the Gusii of Kenya. In N. Smelser & E. Erikson (Eds.), *Themes of work and love in adulthood* (pp. 77–104). Cambridge: Harvard University Press.

Lewin, K. (1938). Field theory and experiment in social psychology: Concepts and methods. *American Journal of Sociology, 44*, 868–896.

Malatesta, C. Z. (1981). Affective development over the lifespan: Involution or growth? *Merrill-Palmer Quarterly, 27*(2), 145–173.

Mead, M. (1928). *Coming of age in Samoa*. New York: Morrow.

Montemayor, R. (1986). Family variation in parent-adolescent storm and stress. *Journal of Adolescent Research, 1*, 15–31.

Musgrove, F. (1963). Intergenerational attitudes. *British Journal of Sociology and Clinical Psychology, 2*, 209–223.

Offer, D., & Offer, J. (1975). *From teenage to manhood*. New York: Basic Books.

Offer, D., Ostrov, E., & Howard, K. I. (1981). *The adolescent*. New York: Basic Books.

Richards, M., & Larson, R. (submitted). Pubertal development and daily emotional well-being in young adolescents.

Richards, M., Larson, R., & Casper, R. (1990). Weight and eating concerns among young adolescent boys and girls. *Journal of Adolescent Health Care, 11*, 203–209.

Wei-ming, T. (1976). The Confucian perception of adulthood. *Daedalus: Journal of the American Academy of Arts and Sciences, 105*, 109–123.

See Also

Affective Disorders; Depression in Adolescence, Gender Differences in; Developmental Psychopathology and the Adolescent; Fears and Phobias in Adolescence; Psychophysiological/Psychosomatic Problems; Schizophrenia in Adolescence and Young Adulthood, Antecedents/Predictors of; Turmoil, Adolescent.

Moral Development in Adolescence

Shawn L. Ward

Le Moyne College

The study of moral development is one of the oldest topics of interest to those curious about human nature. Moral development concerns rules and conventions centered around what people should do in their interactions with other people. In examining these rules and conventions, four domains will be considered. First, how do adolescents reason about these rules. The theories of Piaget and Kohlberg will be presented as leading explanations of the reasoning powers used to justify moral decisions. The next consideration will be the issue of how people actually behave in moral situations. The discussion will then move to how adolescents feel about their thoughts and actions and how these feelings affect moral development. Finally, the nature of moral education will be addressed.

Moral Reasoning: The Cognitive-Developmental Perspective

The cognitive-developmental model is oriented toward the intellectual structures that an individual uses in determining moral behavior. This model is a maturational model: just as adolescents' intellectual structures change from preoperational to concrete operational to formal operational structures, the quality of moral structures changes as the individual matures. Theorists from this perspective hold that moral judgments precede moral behaviors, but do not always lead to such behaviors. In other words, an individual may analyze a situation and make a moral judgment, but then behave in a way that is not in accord with that judgment.

Piaget (1965) described moral development as moving from other-oriented (heteronomous) to self-oriented (autonomous) moral judgments. Early in cognitive development moral judgments are based on an understanding of what parents or those in authority see as moral. The moral structures are not based on any inherent understanding of morality but on a set of external demands to conform to what is right and acceptable. Moral structures in this early stage of moral development are oriented toward obedience to authority and are seen as rigid and unalterable. As children mature (approximately at age 10), Piaget argued, their moral structures become more flexible and internally defined. Right and wrong are now defined in light of a more general moral sense. This second level of moral reasoning is a natural outgrowth of intellectual maturation; in an environment that permits social growth, the child will normally make the transition to this level of moral thinking.

Kohlberg's (1981) description of moral development overlaps Piaget's theory and extends it into adolescence and adulthood. He proposes a universal, invariant sequence, a six-stage model wherein each stage reflects a more advanced social perspective and logical structure. The first two stages form the preconventional level. Adolescents at this level conceive of rules and social expectations as being external to the self. In stage 1—punishment-obedience orientation—right is defined by literal obedience to authority and the avoidance of punishment and physical damage. In stage 2—instrumental-relativist orientation—right is defined as serving one's own interests and desires and letting others do likewise.

The conventional level includes stages 3 and 4. Adolescents at this level identify with or have internalized the conventions and social expectations of others, including authorities. These authorities may be traditional authority institutions or alternate figures that offer other sets of values. In stage 3—mutual interpersonal orientation—right is defined as concern for shared feelings, expectations, and agreements that take primacy over individual interests. In stage 4—law and order orientation—focus is on the maintenance of the social order and the welfare of society or the group by obeying the law and doing one's duty.

The remaining two stages form the postconventional or principled level. At this level adolescents differentiate themselves from the rules and expectations of others and think in terms of self-chosen principles. Stage 5—prior rights and social contract orientation—has utilitarian overtones in that right is defined by mutual standards that have been agreed upon by the whole society and by basic rights and values. In stage 6—universal ethical principle orientation—right is defined as accordance with self-chosen, logically consistent principles that are abstract and ethical and that all humanity should follow. It should be noted that stage 6 had been dropped from the theory except as a theoretical construct because of its absence in Kohlberg's longitudinal data (Colby, Kohlberg, Gibbs, & Lieberman, 1983).

Kohlberg's justice-oriented theory of moral development has not gone without strong criticism. The question of gender differences in moral reasoning has attracted much debate (Brabeck, 1983; Rest, 1979; Walker, 1984). Gilligan (1982) has challenged Kohlberg's strong emphasis on justice and fairness as the basis for moral reasoning. In Gilligan's view, women are more likely than men to base their moral judgments on the consequences for the individuals involved and on obligations to care for and avoid hurting others. Gilligan argues that these qualities of care and responsibility are inadequately assessed by the scoring system used to measure an individual's status in Kohlberg's stages of moral development. Gilligan also disagrees with the use of abstract hypothetical dilemmas. She prefers researchers to study moral decisions that are a result of the subject's real-life dilemmas.

The empirical support for Gilligan's claims has been mixed. Brabeck (1983), after surveying the literature on moral reasoning, empathy, and altruism, concluded that sex differences in morality are at best minimal and are not consistently found. From the results of a meta-analysis, Walker (1984) reported that the overall pattern of sex difference in moral reasoning is nonsignificant. However, this finding is the result of collapsing across all age groups, when in fact the only age groups that fit this issue are the adolescent and adult populations. Baumrind (1986) warned that general searches for sex differences across stages may lead to the conclusion of no sex differences or only minimal sex differences, when in fact the possibility remains that a significant sex difference does exist at a particular stage or level but not across all stages or levels. For example, several studies (Bussey & Maughan, 1982; Kuhn, Langer, Kohlberg, & Haan, 1977) have suggested that Stage 3 is the modal stage for women, and Stage 4 is the modal stage for men.

The majority of the research reviewed has employed the traditional Kohlbergian tasks and interview style. More recent empirical work has directly compared the justice orientation with the care and responsibility orientation. Friedman, Robinson, and Friedman (1987) used traditional moral dilemmas and 12 considerations for how the protagonist should respond. Six of the statements were derived from Kohlberg's postconventional level and the remaining statements corresponded to Gilligan's description of moral reasoning. No sex differences were found on either type of moral reasoning. However, other studies have reported differences when moral judgment tasks other than Kohlberg's were used (Lonky, Roodin, & Rybash, 1988), or when self-report dilemmas were rated and resolved (Ford & Lowery, 1986).

Another area of increased interest is the relationship between moral judgment and social conventional reasoning (Damon, 1983; Turiel, 1974). While moral judgments are based on cognitive disequilibrium, social conventional reasoning deals with discrepancies between behaviors and social norms. Researchers have found that

young children are cognizant of social conventions and are capable of discriminating between social conventions (for example, sex roles, dress codes) and moral transgressions (for example, stealing, cheating) earlier than Kohlberg had predicted. The inclusion of social conventional reasoning broadens the scope of adolescent reasoning beyond issues of justice and allows for the consideration of such diverse social issues as sexuality and intimacy.

Moral Behavior: Social Learning Perspective

Hartshorne and May (1928-30) observed moral responses of thousands of children who were given the opportunity to lie, cheat, and steal, in a variety of settings—at home, in school, at social events, and during athletics. One finding reported was that children behave in situations that call for moral judgment by reacting in specific rather than consistent ways. In a review of the research since this discovery, Lickona (1976) reported a replication of the general finding but added that there are some children that exhibit integration or consistency in behavior across moral situations.

Social learning theorists (Bandura & Walters, 1963) see moral behaviors as the result of learning. The moral values adolescents display result from expectations of what will lead to reinforcement. In this case, reinforcement typically takes the form of social approval. Those people with whom adolescents wish to associate establish norms of acceptable behavior, which they selectively reinforce. An example of this process may be found in the general influence of the peer group, which is generally assumed to reach a peak in adolescence. It is the peer group that plays an increasing role as a source of values and as a controller and reinforcer of behavior (Damon, 1983).

Moral Affect

The psychoanalytic perspective on moral development basically proposes that an adolescent's moral structures emerge from anxieties over conflicts between an ideal moral code and the adolescent's perceived reality. Hence, moral development is a continuous series of moves to balance the impact of the emerging superego or conscience. Perhaps the most salient conflict during adolescence is between the adolescent's need to establish emotional independence from parents and the desire to retain the secure, dependent relationship of childhood. Moral development during adolescence becomes a progressive struggle to establish new standards or social norms to replace those of the parents.

Erikson (1968) has emphasized the "identity crisis" of adolescence and the subsequent ethical consolidation in adulthood as important phases of moral development. For Erikson, the adolescent's search for an indentity requires a sense of purpose. As the adolescent is confronted with a range of new social concerns, including relational considerations, a sense of moral vulnerability abounds. Research has focused on the essential features of self and identity to clarify our understanding of the crisis (Damon, 1983).

Martin Hoffman (1983) has proposed a view of moral development that attempts to synthesize both cognitive and affective processes and offers an explanation for the motivation of moral behavior. This view stresses the importance of the integration of young adolescents' capacity for empathic arousal, which they have had all along, with their newly emerging cognitive awareness of themselves and others. The perceived contrast between the other's well-being and one's own is seen as producing a potential force toward moral action.

The focus is on the empathic response of the adolescent to another's distress. The effectiveness of empathy and anticipatory guilt as a motivator of prosocial behavior is dependent upon the level of cognitive development. To account for prosocial behavior, Hoffman has focused on the discipline styles of authoritarian, permissive, and authoritative parents. These encounters provide conflicts between moral requirements and moral desires and subsequent negotiations. Hoffman points out that although discipline may be multidimensional, it is the inductive features, found in the authoritative parenting style, that provide the cognitive content of prosocial norms.

Moral Education

Empirically, formal education has been one of the most consistent and powerful correlates of moral development. In the longitudinal study by Colby et al. (1983), years of formal education in adults correlated .53 and .60 with Kohlberg's index of moral judgment. In many individual studies education is consistently a strong correlate of moral judgment (for a review, see Rest, 1979). Rest and Thoma (1985) completed a longitudinal study comparing low-education and high-education groups, as designated by the number of years in college attendance. The high-education group showed increasing gains over several 2-year intervals, while the low-education group showed a leveling off. The question remains, what in fact is present in the college environment to account for this difference? An obvious starting point is the curriculum.

The implementation of moral education curricula has not gone without controversy. In the middle 1970s Kohlberg established the Just Community school. In the Just Community, emphasis was placed on considering realistic issues that arise in school, the nature of moral behavior as well as moral thought, and the active role of teachers as moral advocates. The goal for moral development was geared toward increasing student responsibility to the community, which corresponds to stage 4 in Kohlberg's theory. The results were mixed. Although students participating in this program did advance their moral reasoning, their advancement was not greater than students who simply participated in moral discussion programs.

Amid criticism for the use of abstract hypothetical dilemmas and the perceived societal shift from a concern for others to a greater concern for self, Kohlberg (1981) reconsidered his moral discussion approach. Kohlberg felt the urgency for the creation of a moral atmosphere in schools and so he developed the Moral Atmosphere Interview. This interview presents dilemmas that are intended to reflect the typical concerns of an adolescent.

The current consensus regarding thought, action, and feelings of moral development in adolescence were explored. It is clear that no one single approach explains the complexity of adolescent moral development. Rather, an integrated model is the most effective means to begin understanding moral development.

References

Bandura, A., & Walters, R. H. (1963). *Social learning and personality development*. New York: Holt, Rinehart, & Winston.

Baumrind, D. (1986). Sex differences in moral reasoning: Response to Walker's (1984) conclusion that there are none. *Child Development, 57,* 511–521.

Brabeck, M. (1983). Moral judgment: Theory and research on differences between males and females. *Developmental Review, 3,* 274–291.

Bussey, K., & Maughan, B. (1982). Gender differences in moral reasoning. *Journal of Personality and Social Psychology, 42,* 701–706.

Colby, A., Kohlberg, L., Gibbs, J., & Lieberman, M. (1983). A longitudinal study of moral judgment. *Monographs of the Society for Research in Child Development, 48*(1–2, No. 200).

Damon, W. (1983). *Social and personality development*. New York: Norton.

Erikson, E. (1968). *Identity: Youth and crisis*. New York: Norton.

Ford, M. R., & Lowery, C. R. (1986). Gender differences in moral reasoning: A comparison of the use of justice and care orientations. *Journal of Personality and Social Psychology, 50,* 777–783.

Friedman, W. J., Robinson, A. B., & Friedman, B. L. (1987). Sex differences in moral judgments? A test of Gilligan's theory. *Psychology of Women Quarterly, 11,* 37–46.

Gilligan, C. (1982). *In a different voice*. Cambridge: Harvard University Press.

Hartshorne, H., & May, M. A. (1928–30). *Studies in the nature of character*. New York: Macmillan.

Hoffman, M. L. (1983). Affective and cognitive processes in moral internalization. In E. T. Higgins, D. N. Ruble, & W. W. Hartup (Eds.), *Social cognition and social development: A sociocultural perspective* (pp. 236–274). Cambridge: Cambridge University Press.

Kohlberg, L. (1981). *Essays on moral development: The philosophy of moral development* (Vol. 1). San Francisco: Harper & Row.

Kuhn, D., Langer, J., Kohlberg, L., & Haan, N. (1977). The development of formal operations in logical and moral judgment. *Genetic Psychology Monographs, 95,* 97–188.

Lickona, T. (1976). Research on Piaget's theory of moral development. In T. Lickona

(Ed.), *Moral development: Current theory and research* (pp. 219–240). New York: Holt, Rinehart & Winston.

Lonky, E., Roodin, P. A., & Rybash, J. M. (1988). Moral judgment and sex role orientation as a function of self and other presentation mode. *Journal of Youth and Adolescence, 17,* 189–195.

Piaget, J. (1965). *The moral development of the child.* New York: Free Press (translated by Marjorie Gabain, original work published 1932).

Rest, J. R. (1979). *Development in judging moral issues.* Minneapolis: University of Minnesota Press.

Rest, J. R., & Thoma, S. J. (1985). Relation of moral judgment development to formal education. *Developmental Psychology, 21,* 709–714.

Turiel, E. (1974). Conflict and transition in adolescent moral development. *Child Development, 45,* 14–29.

Walker, L. J. (1984). Sex differences in the development of moral reasoning: A critical review. *Child Development, 55,* 677–691.

See Also

Cults, Adolescence and; Prosocial Development in Adolescence; Religion and Adolescence.

Mothers, Adolescent and Their Young Children

Tiffany Field

University of Miami Medical School

Research suggests that the teenage mother and her offspring are at risk primarily due to social, educational, and economic factors. Given prenatal care similar to that given the adult mother, the neonatal outcome for teenagers' offspring is reportedly similar. It appears that the factors that augur against desirable outcomes for the teenage mother and her offspring are the mother's lesser education, her less viable socioeconomic status, and related undesirable attitudes toward childbearing and childrearing.

Most of the research on the problem of teenage pregnancy is focused on the undesirable socioeconomic outcomes of the mother. Investigations of teenage offspring have typically reported only neonatal outcomes, noted to be similar to the outcomes for neonates of adult women when the teenage mother receives prenatal intervention (McLaughlin, Sandler, Sherrod, & Vietze, 1979; Osofsky & Osofsky, 1970). The longer-term outcomes of teenage offspring are uncertain since in most cases both the intervention and investigative efforts have ceased during the neonatal period.

The literature on teenage mothers fairly consistently shows negative long-term socioeconomic consequences for early childbearing, including lower levels of education and greater dependency on public assistance (see Furstenberg, 1976). Widely cited retrospective studies suggest that, as infants, teenagers' offspring are subjected to less educated parents who have relatively limited knowledge and unrealistic expectations regarding developmental milestones and relatively punitive childrearing attitudes (DeLissovoy, 1973). DeLissovoy describes teenage parents as being "uneducated, intolerant, impatient, insensitive, irritable, and prone to use both verbal and physical punishment." The adolescents in this study showed unrealistic expectations concerning the development of their infants; for example, they expected their infants to sit alone at 6–12 weeks, as compared to the developmental norm of 7 months, and to be toilet-trained by 6 months.

Teenagers' preschool offspring have been described as "unable to complete the preschool inventory because of severe physical and psychological handicaps" (Furstenberg, 1976); later, as school-age children, they are unable to maintain grade-appropriate reading levels (Oppel & Royston, 1971). Oppel and Royston compared the offspring of 86 mothers who gave birth when they were less than age 18 with the offspring of mothers who delivered at age 18 or older. The groups were matched on socioeconomic status, race, parity, and birthweight of the offspring. The children were given IQ tests at age 8. The IQ scores of the two groups differed by a few points, a difference that only approached significance. In other areas, however, their differences were marked. Only 29% of the children of the younger mothers, as opposed to 50% of the children of older mothers, were reading at grade level. In addition, the mothers under age 18 were less likely to rear their children during the first 6-to-8 years. The children showed more behavioral problems and were underweight, shorter, and delayed in reading at grade level.

Data from large-scale studies in New York City (Dryfoos & Belmont, 1978), the National Collaborative Perinatal Project (Broman, 1979), and Great Britain (Record, McKeown, & Edwards, 1969) suggest that holding socioeconomic status constant, maternal youth is a significant contributor to deflated later childhood IQ scores. These authors suggest that the IQ scores of the offspring of the teenage mothers at ages 7–11 are disadvantaged by the socioeconomic status of the mothers, and are at an additional disadvantage due to maternal age. Broman (1979) reported a higher incidence of cerebral palsy and battered child syndrome among the offspring of teenagers. In addition, children of the adolescent mothers were more often living in foster or adoptive homes, and their mothers were less often married, had a relatively low level of education, and were frequently receiving public assistance.

Because these problems combined to place the offspring of teenage mothers at significant risk for later developmental problems, a large number of teenage preg-nancy intervention programs have been mounted and have been the subject of descriptions and evaluations (Furstenberg, 1976; Furstenberg, Brooks-Gunn, & Morgan, 1987; Howard, 1968; Lyons, 1968; McMurray, 1968; Murdock, 1968; Osofsky & Osofsky, 1970). These projects have rarely provided control group data, and the effects they have described are limited to the immediate postpregnancy outcome. Despite their limitations, these prenatal intervention projects have influenced a growing trend to incorporate teenage pregnancy programs into community-supported health and educational services. Most intervention programs relating to teenage pregnancy risk factors have been directed at the prenatal and neonatal course of the mothers and infants. Although the teenage mothers are physiologically immature relative to the adult mother, the prenatal programs designed to prevent obstetrical complications apparently minimize these complications. Prenatal intervention studies (McLaughlin et al., 1979; Osofsky & Osofsky, 1970) report no biological disadvantage to teenage offspring whose mothers have received comprehensive prenatal services. However, they do find that teenage mothers are less verbal in interactions with their infants and suggest that mother-infant interactions may well be an important problem area (Osofsky & Eberhart-Wright, 1988). Despite the uneventful neonatal outcomes following prenatal intervention, the long-term negative outcomes suggest that intervention is ceasing at the point at which the need for intervention appears to be most critical. Thus, while prenatal intervention programs may markedly attenuate perinatal medical risk factors for the teenage mother and her offspring, they do not solve the longer-term social and educational consequences for both mother and offspring.

Programs that have continued intervention for teenagers and their offspring following delivery report a reduction in high school drop-out rates and recidivism (Hardy, King, Shipp, & Welcher, 1981) as well as more optimal developmental outcomes for teenage offspring (Badger, 1981). The postnatal intervention program conducted by Hardy suggests that recidivism was reduced to 11% in the 18 months following delivery, and extremely high high school drop-out rates were reduced by the intervention. Unfortunately, even with intervention, the high school drop-out rates are still high and the reading scores of the mothers significantly depressed.

In a review of this literature Field and her colleagues (Field, Widmayer, Stringer, & Ignatoff, 1980) argued that the interventions apparently were not sufficiently intensive to impact on both the mother and her infant. Thus, they mounted a biweekly home-based parent training program in infant stimulation for teenage mothers and their offspring that involved intensive instruction in child care practices, infant stimulation, and developmental milestones. The mothers were instructed to dedicate 30 minutes per day to engaging in stimulation exercises with their infants. A number of positive effects emerged as follows: (1) at four months the intervention infants showed more optimal growth, developmental test performance, and face-to-face interactions; (2) the mothers rated their infants' temperament more optimally, expressed more realistic developmental milestones and childrearing attitudes, and received higher ratings on face-to-face interactions; and (3) at eight months the intervention group received more optimal Bayley mental, home stimulation, and infant temperament scores. However, a number of problems appeared to persist for the mothers of this home-based intervention program despite the positive effects of the program on early infant development and mother-infant interactions. These problems included: (1) failure of mothers to return to school or seek job training/employment; (2) continuing poor financial status of the teenage mothers; and (3) conflicts in the home between the teenager and her own mother regarding childrearing responsibilities and attitudes.

In an attempt to address these problems a center-based intervention program was organized to provide: (1) nursery care for the infants of teenage mothers, and (2) paid job training for the mothers as teacher aide trainees in the same nursery. The authors hoped that this program would improve the mothers' socioeconomic status by giving them financial support, job training, incentives to return to work or seek postschool employment, a stimulating place to leave their infants while in school or at work, education in childrearing and early stimulation, and additional time and experience with their own and others' infants. This program offered the same parent training in infant stimulation, developmental milestones, and childrearing attitudes as had been offered in the home-based intervention program, but in addition provided daycare, job training, and counseling and thereby was expected to have an effect on the mothers' socioeconomic problems. This center-based intervention group was then compared with the following groups: (1) a biweekly home-based intervention program providing parent training and infant stimulation, and (2) a control group receiving no intervention. The entire intervention program was provided for 80 low-income, black teenage mothers during their infants' first six months. Half of the mothers were visited biweekly in their homes to be instructed in caregiving and in sensory motor/interaction exercises, and half were trained as teachers' aides in a medical school infant nursery that provided care for their infants and infants of medical faculty. The mothers' wages were paid by the Comprehensive Employment Training Act.

Growth and development during the first two years were superior for the infants whose mothers received training, particularly those who received paid parent training as teachers' aides in the infant nursery. For example, at one year, the weight of the infants receiving stimulation in either program as well as the Bayley mental scale scores and the Bayley motor scale scores were superior to those of the infants in the control group. In addition, the return to work/school rate was superior for those home-based intervention mothers and even greater for those who were receiving wages as teachers' aides. In addition, the repeat pregnancy rate was lower for the home-based intervention mothers as compared to the control mothers (9% versus 19%) and still lower for those mothers trained as teachers' aides in the intervention nursery (1%). At two years, the weight continued to be lower for the control group infants, as did the Bayley mental and motor scores; at this time, the return to school rate was 34% for the control group, 53% for the home-based intervention group, and 87% for the nursery teachers' aide group; and the repeat pregnancy rate was 39% for the control group, 27% for the home-based intervention group, and 13% for the nursery teachers' aide group. Interestingly, the infant nursery teenage mothers subsequently pursued medical paraprofessional training such as nurse's aide and medical tech training rather than nursery school teacher training, probably because they had used the medical faculty parents as role models for their own careers.

Despite these positive outcomes for both the teenage mothers' education and socioeconomic status as well as reduced repeat pregnancy, and their offspring's significantly greater growth and development, no long-term affects were noted for this infant intervention at grade-school age (Stone, Bendell, & Field, in press). In this grade-school follow-up study of the infants who had received home-based and infant nursery center-based interventions, those children who had received intervention were not performing any better than their control group peers at grade school age. In addition, the mothers who had received intervention did not sustain their socioeconomic and educational advantage over this long-term period. The authors noted that socioeconomic status appeared to be a more potent variable in the long-term follow-up data than early intervention, and suggested that the intensive early interventions had given these mothers unrealistic expectations as well as less relevant coping skills for the continuing socioeconomic disadvantages they experienced.

In addition to the apparently very strong impact of socioeconomic status, other factors affecting the outcomes of the teenage mothers and their offspring are ethnicity, type of family (nuclear versus extended) and being a primary versus secondary caregiver. In a study investigating these other pertinent factors (Field, Widmayer, Adler, & DeCubas, 1990) the researchers found that being reared by a Cuban mother (as opposed to a black American mother), living in a nuclear family (as opposed to an extended family), and being a secondary caregiver (as opposed to a primary caregiver) appeared to have positive effects when considering mothers' social support systems and childrearing attitudes and mother-infant dyads' play interaction behaviors. However, a downward trend in mothers' stimulation and infants' development and language production scores over the second year of life in the sample at large (Cuban and black American mothers, nuclear and extended families, and primary and secondary caregivers) suggest that teenage parenting may have negative consequences irrespective of context variables like childrearing culture and family constellation over the long term. Nonetheless, the emergence of strong effects of these variables on mothers' attitudes and mother-child play highlights the importance of further investigation of these teenage parenthood context variables.

Thus, the data from the literature and our research combine to suggest that over the short term, at least through the infancy of the teenage offspring, intensive interventions can impact on the infants' development and the mothers' socioeconomic status and education in positive ways. Other factors, such as having the social support of being married and being a secondary caregiver, also appear to have positive short-term effects. However, over the long term, by school age no advantages are noted for teenage mothers and infants who received early intervention. Perhaps the interventions have been too short, perhaps undesirable socioeconomic conditions will always be too overwhelming, and perhaps the teenage mother, who is basically still a child herself, will always be disadvantaging herself and her offspring by becoming a mother prematurely.

References

Badger, E. (1981). Effects of parent education program on teenage mothers and their offspring. In K. G. Scott, T. Field, & E. G. Robertson (Eds.), *Teenage parents and their offspring* (pp. 283–316). New York: Grune & Stratton.

Broman, S. (1979). Seven-year outcome of 4,000 children born to teenagers in the U.S. In K. G. Scott, T. Field, & E. Robertson (Eds.), *Teenage parents and their offspring* (pp. 195–226). New York: Grune & Stratton.

DeLissovoy, V. (1973). Child care by adolescent parents. *Children Today, 2*, 22–25.

Dryfoos, J., & Belmont, L. (1978). Long-term development of children born to New York City teenagers. Unpublished manuscript, Columbia University, New York.

Field, T., Widmayer, S., Adler, S., & DeCubas, M. (in press). Teenage parenting in different cultures, family constellations and caregiving environments. *Infant Mental Health Journal.*

Field, T., Widmayer, S., Stringer, S., & Ignatoff, E. (1980). Teenage, lower-class, black mothers and their preterm infants: An interventions and developmental follow-up. *Child Development, 51*, 426–436.

Furstenberg, F. F. (1976). The social consequences of teenage pregnancy. *Family Perceptives, 8*, 148–164.

Furstenberg, F. F., Jr., Brooks-Gunn, J., & Morgan, S. P. (1987). *Adolescent Mothers in Later Life.* New York: Cambridge University Press.

Hardy, J., King, T. M., Shipp, D. A., & Welcher, D. W. (1981). A comprehensive approach to adolescent pregnancy. In K. G. Scott, T. Field, & E. G. Robertson (Eds.), *Teenage parents and their offspring* (pp. 265–282). New York: Grune & Stratton.

Howard, M. (1968). Multidisciplinary services for school-age pregnant girls. *American Journal of Orthopsychiatry, 15*, 193–197.

Lyons, D. J. (1968). Developing a program for pregnant teenagers through the cooperation of school, health department, and federal agencies. *American Journal of Public Health, 58*, 2225–2230.

McLaughlin, J., Sandler, H. M., Sherrod, K., & Vietze, P. M. (1979). Social-psychological characteristics of adolescent mothers and behavioral characteristics of their first-born infants. Unpublished manuscript, Peabody College, Nashville.

McMurray, G. L. (1968). Project Teen Aid: A community action approach to services for pregnant unmarried teenagers. *American Journal of Public Health, 58*, 1848–1853.

Murdock, C. G. (1968). The unmarried mother and the school system. *American Journal of Public Health, 58*, 2217–2224.

Oppel, W., & Royston, A. B. (1971). Teenage births: Some social, psychological, and physical sequelae. *American Journal of Public Health, 61,* 751–756.

Osofsky, J. D., & Eberhart-Wright, A. (1988). Affective exchanges between high risk mothers and infants. *International Journal of Psychoanalysis, 69,* 221–231.

Osofsky, H., & Osofsky, J. (1970). Adolescents as mothers: Results of a program for low-income pregnant teenagers with some emphasis upon infants' development. *American Journal of Orthopsychiatry, 40,* 825–834.

Record, R. G., McKeown, T., & Edwards, J. G. (1969). The relation of measured intelligence to birth order and maternal age. *Annals of Human Genetics, 33,* 61–69.

Stone, W., Bendell, D., & Field, T. (in press). The effect of socioeconomic status on teenage mothers and children who received early intervention. *Journal of Applied Developmental Psychology.*

See Also

Childbearing, Adolescent: Obstetric and Filial Outcomes; Childbearing, Teenage: Effects on Children; Childbirth and Marriage, Adolescent: Associations with Long-Term Marital Stability; Fathers, Adolescent; Fathers, Teenage; Parental Behavior, Adolescent; Parenthood and Marriage in Adolescence: Associations with Educational and Occupational Attainment; Pregnancy and Childbearing: Effects on Teen Mothers; Pregnancy in Adolescence, Interventions to Prevent.

The author would like to thank the children and mothers who participated in her study. This research was supported by an NIMH Research Scientist Development Award #MH00331.

Motivation and Self-Perceptions, Changes in

Jacquelynne S. Eccles
University of Colorado

There has been growing concern with adolescents at risk. Evidence from a variety of sources suggests that the junior high school years mark the beginning of a downward spiral that leads some adolescents to academic failure and school dropout (see Eccles & Midgley, 1988, for review). Although the effects are not so extreme for most adolescents, there is evidence of a gradual decline in academic motivation over the early adolescent years on a variety of indicators of motivation (see Eccles & Midgley, 1988). These declines are reviewed here and possible reasons for these declines are discussed briefly.

Attitudes toward School

In general, there is a gradual decline in students' attitudes toward school and academic subjects (Eccles & Midgley, 1989; Eccles, Midgley, & Adler, 1984; Epstein & McPartland, 1976). For example, Larson (1982) found a decline in students' satisfaction with their school and teachers across grades six to eight. Similarly, students rated "because I have to" as a more important reason for attending school after they had moved into junior high school than they had rated it a year earlier while they were still in elementary school (Eccles, Reuman, Wigfield, & MacIver, 1987).

These decreases, however, vary in magnitude across various studies depending on the particular subject area being rated (Eccles et al., 1984) and the type of school and/or instructional format (Larson, 1982), suggesting that the age/grade differences in attitudes toward one's school are influenced by the *nature* of the school environment one is in. In particular, when comparisons are made, the declines are more extreme for students moving into traditional junior high schools than for children moving into either a nontraditional junior high school or a middle school, or staying in a K–8 school (Larson, 1982). This pattern is especially true for some of the more subtle indicators of students attitudes toward school, such as their feelings of anonymity (Blyth, Simmons, & Carlton-Ford, 1983), their participation in extracurricular activities (Blyth, Simmons, &

Carlton-Ford, 1983), and truancy (Nielsen & Gerber, 1979).

Self-Perceptions: Self-Esteem and Self-Concept

Findings regarding self-perceptions are both more interesting and less consistent. In their classic study, Simmons, Rosenberg, and Rosenberg (1973) found that early adolescents, compared to children in grades 3–6, exhibited heightened self-consciousness, instability of self-image, lower confidence in their academic ability, slightly lower global self-esteem, and more frequent depressive affect. Furthermore, the 12-year-olds in a seventh grade junior high school evidenced more disturbance in self-image and confidence than the 12-year-olds in a sixth grade elmentary school, suggesting that the age differences are influenced by the educational environments experienced by the early adolescents.

Subsequent studies assessing change in self-perceptions have yielded a mixed pattern of results. For example, Eccles et al. (1984) found a decline in children's confidence in their math abilities across grades 6–12 that was especially marked at the junior high school transition. Similarly, Eccles, Wigfield, Flanagan, Miller, Reuman, and Yee (1989) found a decline in general self-esteem between grades 6 and 7 when the children moved from elementary school to junior high school. In contrast, several investigators have failed to find age-related declines in either children's general self-esteem/confidence or children's confidence in their abilities in specific domains (Connell, 1980; Dusek & Flaherty, 1981; Harter, 1982). The failure to find short-term developmental changes is especially characteristic of general measures of self-concept

and of longitudinal studies that follow children for 2 or 3 years. Consequently, it appears that the grade-related decline found by Eccles et al. (1984) and the school structure-related decline found by Simmons et al. (1973) are not universal. In addition, several investigators have found different patterns of change associated with children's estimates of their competence in various domains. Longitudinal declines, especially in grades 5–8 and especially with transition to junior high school, are most extreme for children's ratings of their social and physical competence and for satisfaction with their body (Eccles & Midgley, 1989; Eccles et al., 1989; Schulenberg, Asp, & Petersen, 1984; Simmons & Blyth, 1987).

Both sex and pubertal status have also emerged as significant influences on the nature of change in early adolescents' self-perceptions, suggesting that some children are more vulnerable to the negative effects of the junior high school environment than others. For example, Simmons and her colleagues, in their longitudinal study of children in grades 6 to 10, reported that girls who move into a junior high school at seventh grade evidence a decline in their self-esteem that is not matched by either girls moving from sixth to seventh grade in a K–8 school or by boys in making either transition (Simmons & Blyth, 1987). Although not consistent across all studies, a similar pattern of sex differences in the response to the junior high school transition has been reported in several studies (e.g., Larson, 1982; Simmons et al., 1973). When reported, these sex differences appear to reflect the greater vulnerability of relatively more mature girls (at this age more mature means showing signs of pubertal development and some interest in dating), particularly on measures assessing physical or social self-concept and/or general self-esteem

(Simmons & Blyth, 1987; Simmons, et al., 1973). It should be noted, however, that several longitudinal studies report neither sex nor pubertal status effects (e.g., Petersen & Crockett, 1985) or report even more complex patterns of interactions involving both sex and academic ability level (Eccles et al., 1987).

Although less common, studies assessing the relationship of self-perception to other variables have yielded a more consistent pattern. For example, even though there were no significant grade-level differences in the level of perceived competence, Harter (1982) found the lowest correlation between school performance and perceived academic competence among seventh graders (most of whom were in their first year of junior high school). Similarly, O'Connor (1978) found the greatest discrepancy between children's real and ideal self-images among sixth graders who had just made the transition to a middle school. These results suggest that children's standards for self-evaluation may be disrupted when they move to a new school environment. Longitudinal studies offer some support for this hypothesis. For example, Harter, Whitesell, and Kowalski (1987) found the strongest negative relationship of anxiety to perceived intellectual competence and to intrinsic motivation among early adolescent children who had just undergone a school transition into either a middle school or a junior high school.

Self-Related Affective Reactions: Anxiety, Worry, and Affective Response to Performance

Several investigators have assessed developmental changes in early adolescents' affective reactions to school. Although there are fewer studies of these changes than of changes in self-perceptions, the findings are rather consistent for general measures. Cross-sectional studies find that early adolescent children report higher levels of test anxiety, more self-consciousness, and more extreme worries about their performance than younger children (e.g., Buhrmester, 1980; Harter et al., 1987; Hill, 1980). The one study focusing directly on school transition effects suggests that transitions rather than grade level changes may be responsible for the increases in worry and anxiety, as well as for a decline in early adolescents' positive response to their academic performance (Harter et al., 1987).

Motivational Orientation

The final set of achievement-related beliefs to be reviewed here are associated with motivational orientation. Three different sets of constructs have been investigated: locus of control/knowledge of control, intrinsic versus extrinsic motivation, and general achievement motivation. The results across all three constructs are fairly consistent and seem to be linked quite directly to the middle school/junior high school transition when they emerge. In general, early adolescents, following a transition into either a middle school or a junior high school, have lower achievement motivation (Prawat, Grissom, & Parish, 1979), appear more extrinsically motivated and less intrinsically motivated (deCharms, 1980; Harter, 1982; Harter et al., 1987), feel less in control of their outcomes (deCharms, 1980), and are more likely to report that they do not understand the causes of their outcomes (Connell, 1980).

Summary and Possible Causes

Although not entirely consistent, the existing developmental evidence suggests that some children become less positive toward school in general, less confident in their own academic abilities, more anxious about performance evaluation, and less intrinsically motivated as they enter the adolescent years. These findings suggest that something unique may be going on during early adolescence and that it may interact with the nature of school transitions in affecting the motivation of early adolescents (see Carnegie Council on Adolescent Development, 1989).

A variety of explanations have been offered to explain these negative changes. Some have suggested that declines such as these result from the intrapsychic upheaval assumed to be associated with early adolescent development (e.g., Blos, 1965). This view assumes that there is something unique about early adolescence that leads to an increase in motivational and behavioral problems and that this something is located within the developing adolescent.

Others have suggested that it is the coincidence of the timing of the junior high school transition with pubertal development that accounts for the decline (e.g., Blyth et al., 1983; Simmons & Blyth, 1987). Drawing upon cumulative stress theory, these theorists suggest that declines in motivation result from the multiple stressors of pubertal development combined with a major school transition. They suggest that pubertal development is itself stressful because it is associated with major biological, morphological, and social changes. Similarly, making a major school transition is stressful because it also involves many changes. Compounding these sources of stress is likely to result in negative motivational outcomes.

Eccles and her colleagues have suggested that the quality of the junior high school environment may account for the declines. Drawing upon Person-Environment Fit theory, they propose that these declines result from the fact that junior high schools are not providing developmentally appropriate educational environments for early adolescents (Eccles et al., 1984; Eccles & Midgley, 1989). More specifically, they suggest that there may be a mismatch between the developing needs of the early adolescent and the opportunities afforded them by the junior high school environment. Imagine two trajectories: one a developmental trajectory of student growth, the other a trajectory of environmental change across the school years. Eccles and Midgley (1989) suggest that there will be positive motivational consequences when these two trajectories are in synchrony with one another. In contrast, negative motivational consequences will result if the two trajectories are out of synchrony. This should be particularly true if the environment is developmentally regressive; that is, if it affords the children fewer opportunities for continued growth than previous environments.

Eccles and Midgley (1988) go on to argue that changes in both the school and the classroom environment could contribute to the declines in adolescents' motivation and achievement-related beliefs that often occur coincidentally with the transition into junior high school. In particular, they argue that many early adolescents experience increases in the following characteristics as they move from elementary school to junior high school: the size of student body, the extent of both departmentalization and ability grouping, the use of competitive motivational strategies, the amount of teacher control and whole class instruction, and the rigor in grading coupled with an increased focus on normative grading standards. Early adolescents also typically experience decreases in the following: the extent to which their teachers both trust the students and have a positive sense of teaching efficacy, the opportunities they have for autonomy and participation in decision making, and the opportunities they have for continuous close, personalized contact with particular teachers and with their own friends. Eccles and Midgley (1989) argue that these changes are *particularly* harmful at early adolescence precisely because they emphasize competition, social comparison, and ability self-assessment at a time of heightened self-focus; they decrease decision making and choice at a time when the desire for control is growing; they emphasize lower level cognitive strategies at a time when the ability to use higher level strategies is increasing; and they disrupt social networks at a time when adolescents are especially concerned with peer relationships and may be in special need of close adult friendships.

References

Blos, P. (1965). The initial stage of male adolescence. *Psychoanalytic Study of the Child, 20*, 145–164.

Blyth, D. A., Simmons, R. G., & Carlton-Ford, S. (1983). The adjustment of early adolescents to school transitions. *Journal of Early Adolescence, 3*, 105–120.

Buhrmester, D. (1980). *Assessing elementary-aged children's anxieties.* Unpublished masters thesis, University of Denver, Denver, CO.

Carnegie Council on Adolescent Development. (1989). *Turning points: Preparing American youth for the 21st century.* New York: Carnegie Corporation.

Connell, J. P. (1980). *A multidimensional measure of children's perceptions of control.* Unpublished manuscript, University of Denver, Denver, CO.

deCharms, R. (1980). The origins of competence and achievement motivation in personal causation. In L. J. Fyans (Ed.), *Achievement motivation: Recent trends in theory and research* (pp. 22–23). New York: Plenum Press.

Dusek, J. B., & Flaherty, J. F. (1981). The development of self-concept during the adolescent years. *Monographs of the Society for Research in Child Development, 46.*

Eccles, J. S., & Midgley, C. (1989). Stage/environment fit: Developmentally appropriate classrooms for early adolescents. In R. E. Ames & C. Ames (Eds.), *Research on motivation in education* (Vol. 3, pp. 139–186). New York: Academic Press.

Eccles, J., Midgley, C., & Adler, T. (1984). Grade-related changes in the school environment: Effects on achievement motivation. In J. G. Nicholls (Ed.), *The development of achievement motivation* (pp. 283–331). Greenwich, CT: JAI Press.

Eccles, J. S., Reuman, D. A., Wigfield, A., & MacIver, D. (1987). *Changes in early adolescents' beliefs and self-perceptions.* Paper presented at the annual meeting of the American Educational Research Association, Washington, DC.

Eccles, J. S., Wigfield, A., Flanagan, C. A., Miller, C., Reuman, D. A., & Yee, D. (1989). Self-concepts, domain values, and self-esteem. Relations and changes at early adolescence. *Journal of Personality, 57*, 283–310.

Epstein, J. L., & McPartland, J. M. (1976). The concept and measurement of the quality of school life. *American Educational Research Journal, 13*, 15–30.

Harter, S. (1982). The Perceived Competence Scale for Children. *Child Development, 53*, 87–97.

Harter, S., Whitesell, N., & Kowalski, P. (1987). *The effects of educational transitions on children's perceptions of competence and motivational orientation.* Unpublished manuscript, University of Denver, Denver, CO.

Hill, K. T. (1980). Motivation, evaluation, and educational test policy. In L. J. Fyans (Ed.), *Achievement motivation: Recent trends in theory and research* (pp. 34–95). New York: Plenum Press.

Larson, J. C. (1982). *Middle schools evaluation.* Rockville, MD: Montgomery County Public Schools.

Nielsen, A., & Gerber, D. (1979). Psychosocial aspects of truancy in early adolescence. *Adolescence, 14*, 313–326.

O'Connor, J. L. (1978). Perceptions of self, ideal self, and teacher feelings in preadolescent children. *Elementary School Guidance and Counseling, 13*, 88–92.

Petersen, A. C., & Crockett, L. (1985). Pubertal timing and grade effects on adjustment. *Journal of Youth and Adolescence, 14*, 191–206.

Prawat, R. S., Grissom, S., & Parish, T. (1979). Affective development in children, grades 3 through 12. *Journal of Genetic Psychology, 135*, 37–49.

Schulenberg, J. E., Asp, C. E., & Petersen, A. C. (1984). School from the young adolescent's perspective: A descriptive report. *Journal of Early Adolescence, 4*, 107–130.

Simmons, R. G., & Blyth, D. A. (1987). *Moving into adolescence: The impact of pubertal change and school context.* Hawthorne, NY: Aldine de Gruyter.

Simmons, R. G., Blyth, D. A., Van Cleave, E. F., & Bush, D. (1979). Entry into early adolescence: The impact of school structure, puberty, and early dating on self-esteem. *American Sociological Review, 44*, 948–967.

Simmons, R. G., Rosenberg, F., & Rosenberg, M. (1973). Disturbance in the self-image at adolescence. *American Sociological Review, 38*, 553–568.

See Also

Emotion, Gender Differences in; Emotional Development.

Multivariate, Replicated, Single-Subject, Repeated Measures Design: Studying Change in the Adolescent

Sherry E. Corneal
John R. Nesselroade
Pennsylvania State University

Adolescence, while not necessarily a period of storm and stress, is generally characterized as a time of rapid intraindividual change. Changes occur along several dimensions and involve particular tasks identified with this period in the life span. The tasks of adolescence include moving toward autonomy, broadening and solidifying identity, deepening relationships, exploring sexuality, and considering vocational choices. The questions asked with regard to adolescence are similar to the questions asked by researchers of all periods of the life span: what are individual trajectories like? how are individuals similar in their developmental trajectories and how do they differ? what are the processes involved in change? We attempt to answer these questions by searching for regularities and patterns in human behavior.

Context plays an important role in development. According to the life-span developmental perspective, development is influenced not only by the context surrounding the individual (both proximal and distal), but also by the quality or type of connections present between contexts (for example, communication between school and family). This perspective acknowledges the influence of the individual in shaping the context and stresses the reciprocal influence between the developing individual and an ever-changing context (Belsky, Lerner, & Spanier, 1984; Bronfenbrenner, 1979). Although development is probabilistic in that trajectories are determined by the interaction of the unique characteristics of both the individual and context, it is not chaotic. Instead, one's developmental trajectory is constrained and facilitated by coherent, internal organizational properties that allow for constancy and variability to exist simultaneously (see Capra, 1977; Ford, 1988; Prigogine & Stengers, 1984). The coexistence of these states results in patterns of variability or order through fluctuations. Development, then, is a complex and dynamic process in which we could expect to find patterns of variables to describe change. To attempt to capture the richness of its expression directs us to use research designs that involve multiple variables, many individuals, and numerous occasions of measurement.

A variety of research methods exist; the method one uses depends upon the theoretical issue of interest. When the issue of interest is development, the method of choice should be one that directly examines change. In addition, a desirable methodology would be one that would enable the researcher to examine behavior in sufficient detail to arrive at a thorough picture of the individual's experience. Thus, the design should include a multivariate assessment of an individual's behavior over an extended period of time and the investigation should be replicated over a number of individuals. The present entry is devoted to the explication of a methodology that includes these requisites and is particularly suited to the detailed study of change. That methodology is identified as the multivariate, replicated, single-subject, repeated measures (MRSRM) design.

Data Collection Strategies

The goal of developmental research is to describe and explain systematic intraindividual change across the life span and to examine interindividual differences and similarities in intraindividual change (Baltes, Reese, & Nesselroade, 1977). We understand behavior to be a complex and dynamic phenomenon. Therefore, it is best understood by using a multivariate approach across a time-ordered observation sequence. Ideally, then, developmental re-

search should involve not only the study of individuals measured on a number of variables to unravel the complexity of behavior, but also repeated observations over an extended period of time in order to capture the dynamic quality of behavior. Just as we carefully consider person sampling requirements and the choice of measures we use to get at particular behaviors, thoughtful consideration should be given to the frequency and rate of our data collection. The validity of generalizations are a direct result of the researcher's choice of data collection strategy.

The strategies available for data collection have been aptly described by Cattell (1966) with his Basic Data Relations Matrix. This matrix or "data box" is a three-dimensional representation of data collection strategies and the six pairwise correlational techniques that are used with them (see Figure 1). Each technique involves computing correlations between entities of one dimension over elements of a second dimension with the third dimension fixed at one level. For example, one computes correlations between variables over people measured at one occasion. The generalizability with respect to the fixed dimension in each technique will be limited. Ideally, developmental research should include a good representation of the time dimension. Since in R- and Q-techniques time is the dimension fixed at one level, these two techniques are limited for developmentalists. P-, O-, S-, and T-techniques, which require multiple times of measurement, are best suited for the study of change.

R-technique is the most commonly used data collection strategy; analyses associated with this technique focus on patterns of covariation among different variables among a group of people measured at one point in time. The fixed dimension, then, is time and if, on the basis of such data, one generalizes to other occasions, the implicit

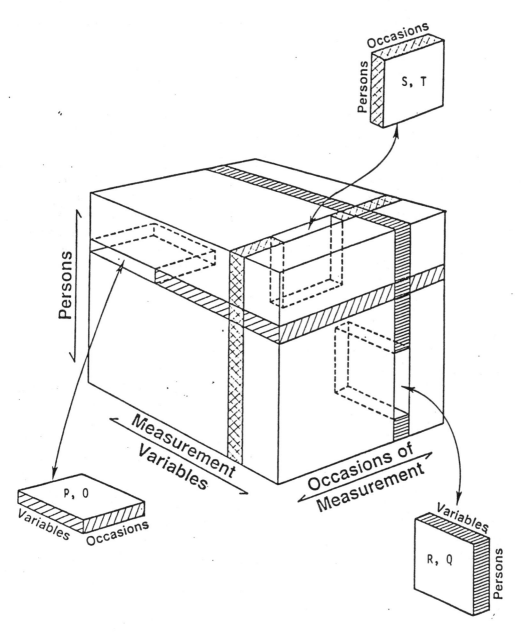

FIGURE 1.   Three-Dimensional Covariation Chart or Data Box

assumption is that the single occasion of measurement is representative of all possible occasions and that variability in responses on other unmeasured occasions is due to error. In contrast, P-technique analyses focus on patterns of covariation among several variables within the individual over many occasions. By using P-technique we are able to examine how the behavior of the individual changes over time. P-technique has been described as the "logical way to study change" (Bereiter, 1963) and is the data collection strategy used in the multivariate, replicated, single-subject, repeated measures design (MRSRM).

The MRSRM Design

The MRSRM is a form of single-subject research design that utilizes multivariate assessment repeated over many occasions of measurement. This design provides information about change within a person by focusing on intraindividual variability manifested over time and situations. Multiple variables are sampled to identify how variables are organized into patterns and multiple occasions are sampled to identify how patterns are organized and change across time. In this design, then, the modes most heavily sampled are occasion and variable. Each of two or more persons studied is a replication. The matter of generalizability across persons is a concern to be addressed at some point in the study of a given behavioral phenomenon but, as has been argued elsewhere, it need not always be the initial concern (Nesselroade & Ford, 1985; Zevon & Tellegen, 1982). The strength of the MRSRM strategy is that it provides the researcher with the data with which to identify fundamental patterns of organization within the individual that can support a more informed search for generalizability across persons. It has been suggested that the number of replications necessary to establish a valid basis for generalizing across people could be considerably smaller than the number needed for group designs if a sound information base is first established (Nesselroade & Ford, 1985).

Providing a sound base for generalizing across persons is part of the MRSRM design. A single-subject design allows the researcher to reap the benefits of the detailed study of an individual (i.e., an idiographic approach) while exploring interindividual differences and similarities (i.e., a nomothetic approach) through replication (Zevon & Tellegen, 1982).

Intraindividual Change

Just as a multivariate assessment of behavior is important to understand fully a particular phenomenon, multiple occasions of measurement are crucial in distinguishing between temporary change, permanent change, and change within boundaries. Generally, developmental research has tried to capture the stability of a given phenomenon over time, but stability has been characterized by change within boundaries or systematic change across time. Seemingly stable attributes, such as locus of control (Roberts & Nesselroade, 1986), work values (Schulenberg, Vondracek, & Nesselroade, in press), and temperament (Hooker, Nesselroade, Nesselroade, & Lerner, 1987), have been found to exhibit coherent, day-to-day variability. Stability, then, is still present but can now be conceptualized as a kind of dynamic stability that constitutes the process of change. From our personal experience we understand that internal and external conditions can affect the degree and quality of our responses from day to day and yet we retain a sense of stability or predictability regarding the boundaries of our responses. Just as a clinician requires multiple sessions to make an accurate evaluation of a client, a researcher should obtain multiple observations to describe behavior accurately.

The idea of variability within boundaries has been termed "steady state hum," a term that reflects the idea that an individual may be characterized by a certain trait (e.g., aggressiveness) but that trait may fluctuate within certain limits (e.g., certain contexts or physiological conditions) or ranges (middle to lower end of a scale). It follows that a one-time assessment might provide a misleading representation of an individual's characteristics or behavior. Intensive short-term tracking of selected variables as they vary together over time can provide a far richer view of the individual's behavior or experience. The MRSRM design enables the researcher to make inferences about the individual's general status on particular variables and how the individual's status appears to change across time and contexts. A comparison of change patterns can then be made across individuals. This approach is illustrated in a recent study that involved change patterns in adolescent subjects.

Corneal and Nesselroade (1988) used an MRSRM design to explore intraindividual variability in emotional response patterns of the stepchild both within and between two households: the mother's and that of the stepfamily. This pilot study involved two replicates. The subjects were two 12-year-old boys. Both children lived with their mothers in a single-parent home and visited on a regular basis in the homes of their remarried fathers. Using a standardized questionnaire, each boy reported his emotional reactions to events that occurred on a day-to-day basis. Each boy's responses were factor analyzed to determine the complexity and nature of response patterns; one factor analysis was done of the responses in the home of the mother; and another was done of the responses in the remarried father's home. The analyses uncovered a different emotional response pattern (i.e., how emotions varied together across time) from one household to the next for each stepchild with a more complex pattern in the stepfamily household. The analyses demonstrated two kinds of intraindividual change as evidenced by (1) a coherent factor pattern for each boy

within each household and (2) different factor patterns for each child in the two households, but also showed consistent interindividual similarities and differences in the numbers of dimensions involved in those changes. Interindividual differences were found in the number of factors required to describe each child's experience in each household (i.e., in mothers' household, 2 for Child A and 3 for Child B; in the stepfamily household, 3 for Child A and 4 for Child B). Interindividual similarity was demonstrated in that, as each boy moved from one family context to the other, an additional factor was required to describe the occasion-to-occasion variability manifested on the same set of measurement variables.

Although the majority of MRSRM studies to date have involved factor analysis as the statistical tool of choice, other analytic techniques, such as multivariate time series analysis, are available to the researcher interested in examining behavior change processes with an MRSRM design. In addition to factor analysis, the Corneal and Nesselroade study used a repeated measures ANOVA to examine mean differences in emotional responses between children, across mothers' and stepfamilies' households, and to examine and compare the change patterns of each child as he moved from one household to the other. A 2 (Child A, Child B) by 2 (mother's household, stepfamily's household) repeated measures ANOVA was performed on each of six emotions to test the effect of child on emotion, household on emotion, and in addition, to test an interaction effect of child and household on emotion. Once again, intraindividual change was examined and interindividual differences and similarities in those intraindividual changes were uncovered. In order to conceptualize how the P-technique data are handled, one should substitute "occasions" for "people" in his or her thinking about covariation patterns. In other words, the concern is how behaviors vary together across time rather than across people.

It has been demonstrated that the MRSRM research design provides information about occasion to occasion changes in variables within the individual and allows for comparisons of those change patterns across individuals. It follows that this design is well-suited for examining important questions involved in the study of adolescent development by providing a detailed picture of the adolescent's experience which can then be compared to the experience of other adolescents. Not only is this method useful to examine and describe short- or long-term change, but when used with stimulus controlled experimental arrangements (Cattell & Scheier, 1961) or causal modeling techniques (Nesselroade & McArdle, 1986) it also enables the researcher to develop explanatory accounts of change.

Although psychologists have advocated the utility of P-technique factor analysis as a method to study change since the 1940s, the method has been used infrequently relative to other methods. We believe the reasons for its underuse are twofold. First, there has been a tendency for those who publish P-technique studies to present their results with a methodological rather than substantive emphasis which, quite simply, appeals to a smaller, less diverse audience of readers. Second, researchers have made generalizing across persons their primary concern and given little attention to the validity of temporal, or contextual, generalization. Both require our attention. With the MRSRM, generalizability across persons is considered along with generalizability across occasions by combining both idiographic and nomothetic approaches. The merging of the two approaches holds great appeal for many students of human development who sense that individuals must be studied in depth to be understood in general.

References

Baltes, P., Reese, H., & Nesselroade, J. (1979). *Life-span developmental psychology: Introduction to research methods.* Monterey, CA: Brooks/Cole.

Belsky, J., Lerner, R. M., & Spanier, G. B. (1984). *The child in the family.* Reading, MA: Addison-Wesley.

Bereiter, C. (1963). Some persisting dilemmas in the measurement of change. In C. W. Harris (Ed.), *Problems in measuring change* (pp. 3–20). Madison, WI: University of Wisconsin Press.

Bronfenbrenner, U. (1979). *The ecology of human development.* Cambridge: Harvard University Press.

Capra, F. (1977). *The tao of physics.* New York: Bantam Books.

Cattell, R. B. (1966). The data box: Its ordering of total resources in terms of possible relational systems. In R. B. Cattell (Ed.), *Handbook of multivariate experimental psychology* (pp. 69–129). Chicago: Rand McNally.

Cattell, R. B., & Scheier, I. H. (1961). *The meaning and measurement of neuroticism and anxiety.* New York: Ronald Press.

Corneal, S., & Nesselroade, J. R. (1988). A stepchild's emotional experience across two households: An investigation of response patterns by P-technique factor analysis. Unpublished manuscript.

Ford, D. (1988). *Humans as self-constructing living systems: A developmental perspective on personality and behavior.* Hillsdale, NJ: Lawrence Erlbaum Associates.

Hooker, K., Nesselroade, D. W., Nesselroade, J. R., & Lerner, R. M. (1987). The structure of intraindividual temperament in the context of mother-child dyads: P-technique factor analyses of short-term change. *Developmental Psychology, 23,* 332–346.

Nesselroade, J. R., & Ford, D. (1985). P-technique comes of age: Multivariate, replicated, single-subject designs for research on older adults. *Research on Aging, 7*, 46–80.

Nesselroade, J. R., & McArdle, J. J. (1986). Multivariate causal modeling in alcohol use research. *Social Biology, 32*, 272–296.

Prigogine, I., & Stengers, I. (1984). *Order out of chaos.* New York: Bantam Books.

Roberts, M. L., & Nesselroade, J. R. (1986). State variability in locus of control measures: P-technique factor analysis of short-term change. *Journal of Research in Personality, 20*, 529–545.

Schulenberg, J. E., Vondracek, F. W., & Nesselroade, J. R. (in press). Patterns of short-term changes in individuals' work values: P-technique factor analyses of intraindividual variability. *Multivariate Behavioral Research.*

Zevon, M. A., & Tellegen, A. (1982). The structure of mood change: An idiographic/nomothetic analysis. *Journal of Personality and Social Psychology, 43*, 111–122.

See Also

Change, Cumulative; Genetic Change.

Neurodevelopmental Variation and Dysfunction in Adolescence

Adrian D. Sandler
Melvin D. Levine
William L. Coleman
University of North Carolina

Growing evidence indicates that many children and adolescents experience stress, underachievement, or failure in school, at home, and in the community because they harbor one or more of the "high prevalence-low severity" developmental dysfunctions of childhood (Levine, 1982). These variations in central nervous system higher cortical function are often subtle and insidious in their manifestations. They commonly impede the acquisition of academic skills and make it difficult for certain students to keep pace with the evolving demands that confront them as they progress through school. Secondary behavioral and affective complications are commonly encountered in adolescence. These high prevalence-low severity developmental dysfunctions are closely related to the concept of learning disability.

Neurodevelopmental Variation and Dysfunction

In the clinical evaluations of adolescents with learning problems, it is helpful to use a paradigm (Table 1) that includes seven basic neurodevelopmental functions that are considered to be essential foundations of learning: selective attention; memory; simultaneous/sequential arrangement; language; higher order cognition; neuromotor function; and social cognition. Each of these functions includes constituent elements of performance, which are compiled from reviews of research articles from the fields of special education, cognitive psychology, developmental psychology, neurology, psycholinguistics, developmental pediatrics, and others. Students differ

TABLE 1
KEY NEURODEVELOPMENTAL FUNCTIONS AND SOME OF THEIR PERFORMANCE ELEMENTS

NEURODEVELOPMENTAL FUNCTIONS

	SELECTIVE ATTENTION	MEMORY	SEQUENTIAL ARRANGEMENT	LANGUAGE	HIGHER ORDER COGNITION	NEUROMOTOR FUNCTIONS	SOCIAL COGNITION
CORE ELEMENTS	Prioritization Arousal control Consistency control Self-monitoring	Registration Active working memory Consolidation Retrieval	Spatial ability Sequential ability	Phonology Semantics Morphology Syntax Pragmatics	Conceptualization Abstraction Inference Rules Creativity	Input Feedback Praxis Engram	Perspective taking Prediction Monitoring Attributions
STRATEGIC ELEMENTS	Reflection Tentativeness Planfulness	Mnemonic strategy application	Previewing Reviewing	Sentence formulation Verbal mediation Narrative skills	Problem-solving Flexibility Deduction	Motor planning	Availability of social strategies
FLUENCY VOLUME CONTROL	Tempo control Task persistence	Automatization Chunk size Synchrony	Processing speed Chunk size Production speed	Processing speed Chunk size Production speed	Reasoning speed Ideational flow	Motor speed Stamina	Speed of response Pacing interactions
META AWARENESS	Insight into patterns of attention control	Understanding one's memory	Recognizing and using preferred arrangements	Understanding different uses of one's language	Ability to think about thinking	Using motor skills flexibly for specific tasks	Knowledge of social skills and perception by others.

markedly from each other with respect to these neurodevelopmental functions and performance elements, and empirical observation reveals wide diversity in their patterns of strengths and weaknesses. Students who exhibit significant weaknesses in certain performance elements may experience considerable stress or failure as a result. At this point, a variation becomes a neurodevelopmental dysfunction.

When dealing with our paradigm of neurodevelopmental dysfunction, some broader implications need to be recognized. First, neurodevelopmental dysfunctions invade multiple domains. For example, memory impairments may affect progress in mathematics, writing, and spelling, and the mastery of certain content areas. Second, neurodevelopmental dysfunctions may not construe learning disabilities. Gross motor delays, for example, may not significantly affect an adolescent's learning or compro-

mise his school work. A student with a language dysfunction may become highly adept and creative with nonverbal reasoning and visual-spatial awareness, and such strengths may actually help to define the student's career pathway. Third, neurodevelopmental dysfunctions occur in multiple different forms and combinations. One research project found that most children doing poorly in school tended to endure clusters of dysfunctions rather than discrete single deficits (Levine, Oberklaid, & Meltzer, 1981). Such diversity is obscured by generic labels, such as "the LD adolescent," which imply a stereotype.

Peers, Family, and Society

The adolescent years represent a critical and often neglected period in the development of school children. Appreciation of the unique developmental shifts of adolescence is essential to the understanding of school failure. Early adolescence is a time of intensified social pressure: peer groups emerge and set the standards for behavior, values, and communication at a time when boys and girls are experimenting with varying degrees of autonomy from their families. Additional stresses, such as family conflicts, divorce and remarriage, drug abuse, and unintended pregnancy may have significant impact on an adolescent's neurodevelopmental dysfunctions and school performance.

Personality, Attributions, and Motivation

An adolescent's beliefs, motivations, and affect clearly influence academic performance. A thorough understanding of learning problems in adolescents must take account of temperament (Carey & Earls, 1988) and "person variables" (Flavell & Wellman, 1977), such as intentions, attri-

butions, and beliefs about one's competence and learning abilities. The relationship between academic self-perceptions and subsequent motivation and performance has been explored in Diener and Dweck's work (1978, 1980) on "learned helplessness." Many studies have shown that learning-disabled students tend to perceive that they have little control over success and failure, and that failure is generally due to lack of ability, while success is due to factors beyond personal control, or "flukes" (Pearl, Bryan & Donohue, 1980). The interplay of neurodevelopmental dysfunctions, behavior, personality factors, and academic performance is illustrated with regard to attention deficits in Figure 1.

Changing Demands and Expectations

Adolescence is a time when accelerated and intensified demands are made upon developing central nervous systems. School is characterized by rapidly growing expectations that impose arduous strains on attention, memory, speed of processing infor-

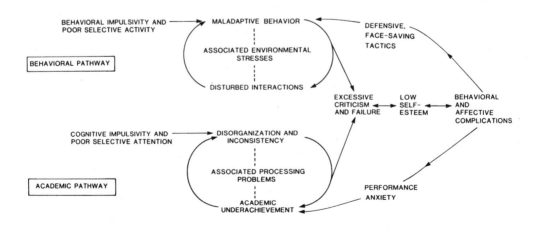

FIGURE 1   Attention Deficits: Cyclic Pathways of Failure and Maladaptation

mation, language facility, and reasoning skill (Levine & Jordan, 1987). Adolescents are confronted with a growing emphasis on written output. They are required to use multistep processes that demand effective sequencing of data or operations. Late elementary and junior high school students encounter a growing demand for rapid retrieval memory (Kail, 1984), often entailing simultaneous demands (e.g., the need for unaided recall of spelling, punctuation, grammar, and capitalization with the flow of words and ideas during writing). They face an increasing need to synthesize material from multiple sources and through multiple processing modalities. Furthermore, students are presented with more complex language and abstract conceptualization (Wiig & Semel, 1975). Methods and metacognitive strategies become increasingly important as aids to assimilation and output, and students are expected to be able to mobilize the skills they mastered earlier in a flexible, efficient, and automatized manner.

Academic performance may decline sharply in adolescence because capacities are exceeded or evolving expectations tap neurodevelopmental functions that were not stressed previously. It is possible, and not uncommon, to uncover insidious "sleeper effects" during early adolescence: preexisting areas of developmental vulnerability may emerge as a direct consequence of the stringency and complexity of demands.

Outcomes—The Toll on Self-Esteem

Compared with normally achieving controls, adolescents with learning disabilities display lower self-esteem, greater anxiety about school, a greater tendency to emotional lability, and an inability to establish satisfactory peer relationships (Koppitz, 1971; McGrath, 1977; Rosenthal, 1973; Silver, 1974). Many students navigate the transitions and demands of adolescence without difficulty. But for some youngsters who harbor neurodevelopmental dysfunctions the passage is turbulent, and a cycle of disillusionment, loss of self-esteem, and antisocial behavior sets in. Although such calamitous outcomes are not a direct consequence of learning problems, they are more likely to occur in the setting of chronic success deprivation and underachievement. The literature concerning the relationships between learning disabilities and juvenile delinquency (Karniski, Levine, Clarke, Palfrey, & Meltzer, 1982), for example, lends support to this argument. The links between teenage functional morbidity and learning deserve further study because of their enormous preventive and therapeutic implications.

Common Adolescent Dysfunctions and Their Effects

Endless patterns of neurodevelopmental dysfunction predispose adolescents to academic failure. Nine commonly encountered phenomena that may occur in varying contexts and combinations are reviewed here.

ATTENTION DEFICITS ■ Attention deficits are the most prevalent developmental dysfunction in adolescence (Weiss & Hechtman, 1986). While overactivity commonly diminishes in adolescence, traits associated with overactivity persist or worsen; these include restlessness, an insatiable appetite for intense experiences, difficulty in delaying gratification, impersistence at tasks, distractibility, inconsistency, problems with planning and organization, and a tendency to tire during sustained cognitive effort (Table 2). An adolescent with attention deficits may have no trouble focusing upon highly motivating pursuits, but when he attempts to focus on details that are less alluring, problems with concentration emerge (Coleman & Levine, 1988).

A cardinal feature of adolescents with attention deficits is their performance inconsistency. At times a student may be highly productive, while at other times she accomplishes nothing. Such inconsistency is perplexing and creates problems for her; the presumption of her parents and teachers

that she can do better further aggravates the situation.

MEMORY IMPAIRMENTS ■

A common source of underachievement in this age group resides in impairments of retrieval (Levine & Zallen, 1984; Sternberg & Wagner, 1982). Many adolescents display prolonged latencies of response time, and their access to stored information is imprecise and labored (Torgesen, 1985). The problem has a powerful impact upon reading, writing, spelling, and mathematics. In some cases a student may have tenuous revisualization skills, such that he is

TABLE 2

ACADEMIC IMPACTS OF ATTENTION DEFICITS IN ADOLESCENCE:
ASSOCIATED PROBLEMS AND SYMPTOMS

CHARACTERISTICS	MANIFESTATIONS
Associated processing problems	May have visual-spatial, temporal-sequential, language, or reasoning problems. Discrete compensatory skills may be evident
Associated memory problems	Divergent memory usually stronger than convergent memory. Difficulty with content-rich subjects, especially those emphasizing cumulative knowledge and skills
Cognitive fatigue	Tendency to tire early in school day, especially with passive listening tasks. Often associated with "sleep arousal imbalance"
Fine motor dysfunction	May result from impulsive and hurried style, poor motor memory, or poor motor planning
Ineffective self-monitoring	Poor execution of quality control over work. "Careless errors" often noted. Ineffective study skills
Excessive motivation dependency	Inordinate motivational intensity required to sustain attention to routine tasks
Disorganization	Affects tasks that require organized, systematic routines (e.g., management of time and materials). Lack of strategies or flexibility may be noted
Performance inconsistency	Day-to-day or even hour-to-hour variation in learning, behavior, and sometimes mood patterns for no apparent reason
Impersistence	Poor on-task performance in both quality and quantity. Difficulty finishing assignments
Poor selective attention	Difficulty in distinguishing the salient detail from irrelevant or trivial. Distractibility is major concern
Abhorrence of or inattention to detail	Tendency to be cursory or superficial. May be good generalizers or conceptual thinkers

able to spell words correctly in isolation, but his brittle visual retrieval breaks down and mis-spellings abound when he is faced with the demands of writing a paragraph.

A key variable is the extent to which youngsters develop effective memory strategies. As students progress through elementary and junior high school, their skills as memory tacticians expand. Some adolescents with memory impairments manifest deficits in their use of subvocalization, clustering, and other memory strategies.

Many adolescents with attention deficits have trouble selectively retaining information and skills. In many instances, they fail to focus intently and their recall is vague, superficial, or inaccurate. They may focus upon incidental stimuli, thereby retaining irrelevant or trivial data.

DELAYED AUTOMATIZATION ■

By early adolescence students are commonly assumed to have rendered automatic many of the skills attained earlier in their education. This allows for greater speed of processing and for the completion of more complex problem solving. There is evidence that the maximum growth in such speed and automaticity occurs between the ages of 8 and 10 years (Kail, 1984). Those students who have delayed acquisition of these skills and capabilities may assume an overly mechanical approach to tasks. Academic production may be slow and laborious, ultimately resulting in a sacrifice of ideation, incentive, and motivation (Sternberg & Wagner, 1982).

GRAPHOMOTOR DYSFLUENCY ■
Some students endure significant problems meeting demands for written output because they harbor one or more fine motor dysfunctions that impede writing (Levine, 1987). The manifestations of such dysfluency include the production of written material with far less sophistication of ideation than that which the student is able to express orally, a tendency toward highly abbreviated writing, and written output that is inordinately slow.

Graphomotor dysfluency most commonly stems from eye-hand coordination problems, fine motor dyspraxia (difficulty with the implementation of motor plans), or finger agnosia (poor proprioceptive and kinesthetic feedback during writing). Students with finger agnosia are unable to track the movements of the pencil effectively unless they engage in close visual monitoring, and they are likely to adopt unusual and maladaptive pencil grasps that cause fatigue ("writer's cramp").

LANGUAGE DISORDERS ■
A broad spectrum of language dysfunctions may be observed in adolescents (Table 3). Receptive language disabilities impair effective interpretation of spoken or written ideas. Such problems may occur as a result of poor auditory attention, hearing deficits, or central auditory processing problems. Other youngsters have trouble appreciating language cues, including grammatical construction, syntax, intonation, and rhythm (Larson & McKinley, 1987). During early adolescence new linguistic subtleties and structures are presented and mastered. The essential difference between the sentences "Ann *knows that* Bill plays the piano" and "Mary *knows whether* John plays basketball" is apparent to most adolescents. Youngsters who arrive at adolescence without having mastered such nuances are likely to be disoriented in the classroom as they strive to follow directions and process information. In some instances they may tune out and become inattentive.

Expressive language difficulties can be equally debilitating. Some students with

TABLE 3
LANGUAGE PROCESSING:
COMMON DEVELOPMENTAL DYSFUNCTIONS

DYSFUNCTION	DESCRIPTION
Weak verbal attention	Poor listening skills; fatigue and distractibility in highly verbal settings
Weak verbal memory	Possible weaknesses of word memory (vocabulary), sentence and passage recall, semantic coding in memory, verbal sequential recall, and memory for language rules
Phonological imperception	Problems with discrimination, phonetics, sound-symbol association (for reading), and foreign languages
Semantic and morphological disorders	Impoverished vocabulary, restrictive word meanings, poor reading comprehension, and trouble with word problems in mathematics
Syntactic weaknesses	Poor sentence comprehension; difficulty interpreting word order and grammar
Problems with pragmatics	Trouble discerning speakers' true meanings or intentions in social contexts; possible social failure; overly literal interpretation
Poor metalinguistic awareness	Varies with age: early trouble with sound segmentation and blending; later difficulties with figurative language, ambiguity, irony, and paradox
Weaknesses of verbal reasoning	Difficulty reasoning with language; deficient verbal problem-solving skills

word-finding and sentence formulation weakness may live in perpetual fear of being called upon in class. The slowness, imprecision, and hesitancy with which they express themselves is a constant source of frustration and embarrassment. Deficits of verbal pragmatics (the use of language for social communication) can have a major impact upon socialization and life adjustment.

TENUOUS CONCEPTUALIZATION ▪ The
Piagetian stage of formal operations entails a growing capacity to appreciate abstract conceptual material. Some students, however, tend to be delayed in arriving at Piagetian stages; they persist in their immature tendencies to view things on a concrete level (Derr, 1985).

A struggling adolescent may exhibit concept formation that is incomplete or tenuous. He might proceed through an algebra course without fully understanding what an equation is. Conscientious students can deploy rote memory and imitation, thereby minimizing conceptualization. Ultimately, however, such an approach can be associated with an inability to transfer learning, to apply what is learned to meet demands for practical or creative applications, and to succeed in more advanced course work.

Tenuous conceptualization may be a pervasive problem for some students. In other cases it may be content- or modality-specific. Some adolescents may be able to conceptualize, but only nonverbally. A student may have a firm grasp on various geometrical interrelationships, for example, but have real problems dealing with verbal concepts such as "taxation without representation." Poor nonverbal conceptualization, on the other hand, is a common source of difficulty in mathematics and certain science courses.

PASSIVE LEARNING ▪ The volume and complexity of academic demands makes the acquisition of efficiency and facilitating strategies exceedingly helpful to the adolescent student. Torgesen (1982) has described certain students as "inactive learners," underachievers who fail to engage in the strategies needed for effective learning. An adolescent with poor memory strategies may have difficulty knowing what she needs to study for an examination, which techniques to utilize for the active learning of new material, and how to test herself.

Highly proficient students not only have facilitative strategies, but also tend to have available to them multiple alternative strategies, so that if one technique fails, other options remain. Many underachieving students have one method available and apply this method rigidly. When this approach fails, they become discouraged, they guess, and they lose interest. Interestingly, it has been found that students who lack multiple alternative strategies in the cognitive domain are prone to similar problems with respect to social performance (Richard & Dodge, 1982). They lack flexibility in their social strategies, which can ultimately result in difficulties with peer and adult interactions.

ORGANIZATIONAL DEFICIENCIES ▪ It is not unusual to hear of an adolescent who has "organizational problems." Although sometimes considered to be trivial annoyances, such difficulties can have a major impact upon academic performance and life adjustment at home and in school. Several forms of organizational disarray are commonly present in this age group (Levine, 1987). First, there are students who exhibit material disorganization. They have problems with the "props" required for school; it is difficult for them to keep track of papers and books, and they tend to forget what they need to bring home to complete assignments. Other students have impairments of temporal-sequential organization. Often they have endured a lifelong history of sequencing deficiencies. It may have been hard for them to deal with time concepts, such as telling time and using temporal prepositions with accuracy. In early adolescence they may have poor narrative skills and difficulty learning events or ideas in their proper sequence. Deadlines may be particularly hard to meet, and class schedules hard to master. Organizational problems may stem from difficulties with selective attention. Impulsivity, inattention to detail, and distractibility engender careless errors, poor planning, and fluctuating forgetfulness.

DISABILITIES OF SOCIALIZATION ▪ A wide range of environmental and cultural factors can influence an adolescent's social relationships, but there is increasing evidence that certain cognitive functions underlie socialization (Bryan & Bryan, 1977). Many adolescents have a tendency to commit social acts impulsively so that they are often unintentionally offensive to peers and adults. Some have trouble foreseeing the social consequences of their actions. They repeatedly say and do things that jeopardize their reputations, or fail to apply accepted rules of interaction. Some may have great difficulty taking other's perspectives. Their extreme egocentricity is offensive, resulting in increasing alienation and isolation. Typically, the lonely youngster has no idea why

he lacks friends. Impaired social feedback may compromise his social standing still further, in that he may commit one faux pas after another without realizing that he is offending his peers.

It should be emphasized that the phenomena cited above are not mutually exclusive. In fact, students with academic underachievement are more likely to exhibit clusters of problems than discrete deficits.

References

Bryan, T. H., & Bryan, J. H. (1977). The social-emotional side of learning disabilities. *Behavior Disorders, 2,* 141–145.

Carey, W. B., & Earls, F. (1988). Temperament in early adolescence: Continuities and transitions. In M. D. Levine & E. R. McAnarney, (Eds.), *Early adolescent transitions,* pp. 23–36. Lexington, MA: D. C. Heath.

Coleman, W. L., & Levine, M. D. (1988). Attention deficits in adolescence: Description, evaluation, and management. *Pediatrics in Review, 9*(9), 287–298.

Denckla, M. G. (1984). Developmental dyspraxia: The clumsy child. In M. D. Levine & P. Satz (Eds.), *Middle childhood: Development and dysfunction,* pp. 245–260. Baltimore: University Park Press.

Derr, A. M. (1985). Conservation and mathematics achievement in the learning disabled child. *Journal of Learning Disabilities, 18,* 333–336.

Diener, C. L., & Dweck, C. S. (1978). An analysis of learned helplessness: Continuous changes in performance, strategy, and achievement cognitions following failure. *Journal of Personality and Social Psychology, 36,* 451–462.

Diener, C. L., & Dweck, C. S. (1980). An analysis of learned helplessness: 2. The processing of success. *Journal of Personality and Social Psychology, 39,* 940–952.

Flavell, J. H., & Wellman, H. M. (1977). Metamemory. In R. V. Kail & J. W. Hagen (Eds.), *Perspectives on the development of memory and cognition.* Hillsdale, NJ: Lawrence Erlbaum Associates.

Kail, R. V. (1984). *The development of memory in children.* San Francisco: Freeman.

Karniski, W. M., Levine, M. D., Clarke, S., Palfrey, J. S., & Meltzer, L. J. (1982). A study of neurodevelopmental findings in adolescent delinquents. *Journal of Adolescent Health Care, 3,* 151–159.

Koppitz, E. M. (1971). *Children with learning disabilities: A five year follow-up study.* New York: Grune and Stratton.

Larson, V. L., & McKinley, N. L. (1987). *Communication assessment and intervention strategies for adolescents.* Eau Claire: Thinking Publications.

Levine, M. D. (1982). The low severity-high prevalence disabilities of childhood. In L. Barness (Ed.), *Advances in pediatrics,* pp. 529–554. Chicago: Yearbook Publishers.

Levine, M. D. (1987). *Developmental variation and learning disorders.* Cambridge, MA: Educators Publishing Service.

Levine, M. D., & Jordan, N. C. (1987). Neurodevelopmental dysfunctions: Their cumulative interactions and effects in middle childhood. In J. J. Gallagher & C. T. Ramey (Eds.), *The malleability of children.* Baltimore: Paul H. Brookes.

Levine, M. D., Oberklaid, F., & Meltzer, L. J. (1981). Developmental output failure: A study of low productivity in school age children. *Pediatrics, 67,* 18–25.

Levine, M. D., & Zallen, B. G. (1984). The learning disorders of adolescents: Organic and non-organic failure to strive. *Pediatric Clinics of North America, 31,* 345–369.

McGrath, M. (1977). *Characteristics of learning-disabled and learning-inhibited adolescents.* Paper presented at the 1977 Annual Meeting of the Society for Adolescent Medicine, Chicago.

Pearl, R., Bryan, T., & Donohue, M. (1980). Learning disabled children's attributions for success and failure. *Learning Disability Quarterly, 3,* 3–9.

Richard, B. A., & Dodge, A. (1982). Social maladjustment and problem solving in school aged children. *Journal of Consulting and Clinical Psychology, 50,* 226–233.

Rosenthal, J. H. (1973). Self-esteem in dyslexic children. *Academic Therapy, 9,* 27–39.

Silver, L. B. (1974). Emotional and social problems of children with developmental disabilities. In R. E. Weber (Ed.), *Handbook on learning disabilities.* Englewood Cliffs, NJ: Prentice/Hall.

Sternberg, R. J., & Wagner, W. J. (1982). Automatization failure in learning disabilities. *Topics in Learning and Learning Disabilities, 2*(2), 1–11.

Torgesen, J. K. (1982). The learning disabled child as an inactive learner. *Topics in Learning and Learning Disabilities, 2*(1), 45–52.

Torgesen, J. K. (1985). Memory processes in reading-disabled children. *Journal of Learning Disabilities, 18,* 350–355.

Weiss, G., & Hechtman, L. (1986). *Hyperactive children grown up.* New York: Guilford Press.

Wiig, E. H., & Semel, E. M. (1975). Productive language abilities in learning disabled adolescents. *Journal of Learning Disabilities, 8,* 578–586.

See Also

AIDS and Adolescents; AIDS and HIV Infection in Adolescents: The Role of Education and Antibody Testing; Asthma in Puberty and Adolescence; Cystic Fibrosis in Puberty and Adolescence; Diabetes; Gynecomastia; Illness, Adolescents' Conceptualization of; Illness, Chronic; Injury during Adolescence, Risk Factors for; Injuries, Unintentional: Gender Differences in Accidents; Premenstrual Syndrome (PMS); Scoliosis; Sexually Transmitted Diseases in Adolescence; Spina Biffida, the Adolescent with.

Nineteenth-Century America, Adolescence In

Susan M. Juster
Maris A. Vinovskis
University of Michigan

Something happened to American youth between 1790 and 1890. That much at least historians of the American family are agreed upon. What exactly this change entailed, and the extent of its reach, remains open to interpretation. Whether adolescence as the term is understood today was a creation of the nineteenth-century social and industrial order (Demos, 1986; Demos & Demos, 1969; Elder, 1980; Graff, 1985; Kett, 1977), or whether that order merely transformed the parameters of an existing category of social identity (Beales, 1975; Hiner, 1975; Thompson, 1984), the period between the Revolutionary War and the hardening of industrial capitalism has come to be seen as the critical era in the history of youth and adolescence.

Disputes over the timing of the emergence of the modern concept of adolescence conceal a broader disagreement over how to define adolescence and its relationship to the institutional structure in which it operates. Historians have been strongly influenced in their study of past life stages by the work of Philippe Aries (1962) and Erik Erikson (1968). The Aries thesis—that childhood as

we know it is the creation of modern middle-class society—has led historians to seek the roots of the contemporary view of adolescence in the social and economic history of the family. But those scholars who follow Erikson's model of psychological development see adolescence as a universal stage in human development that transcends any particular historical juncture. Both approaches have contributed to our understanding of the social and biological parameters of adolescence in historical settings, but it is significant that the term "adolescence" itself was first coined in the early twentieth century, in G. Stanley Hall's pioneering work, *Adolescence: Its Psychology and Its Relations to Anthropology, Sociology, Sex, Crime, Religion, and Education* (1904). Only since the early 1900s has it been possible to attempt a history of "adolescence" per se, and those scholars who posit an essential continuity in the experience of youth (characterized always and everywhere by anxiety, liminality, and rebelliousness) from colonial to modern times must account for the absence of an adequate vocabulary to explain this experience until the end of the nineteenth century.

Colonial Americans certainly had a conceptual vocabulary that distinguished "youth" from adulthood, but this stage of life connoted neither a fixed age span nor a uniform set of experiences. Rather, the term was used loosely to describe persons between the ages of 10 and 25 or even 30 who might occupy a variety of positions in the social and economic life of their communities. Apprentices, schoolboys, farmhands, servants—all were lumped together in the amorphous category of youth regardless of the nature of their activities or the degree to which they remained dependent on parental or other adult authorities. Two leading historians of adolescence in the past have urged a reformulation of the terms that we apply to various life stages in premodern societies; rather than age-specific categories such as "teenager," Joseph Kett (1977) and Michael Katz (1975) have suggested that life stages be distinguished by the degree of dependency or autonomy present in young people's lives. Thus, Kett recommends the term "semidependency" to describe the status of youth in colonial America, while Katz—emphasizing the other side of this ambiguous position—labels this period of life "semiautonomy." Both terms suggest an in-between status that retains characteristics of both the posterior and the anterior stages, rather than a tightly bound category with definite beginning and end points. Few historians would dispute this portrait of colonial youth, though some have taken issue with the implication that transitions to adulthood were less disruptive and conflictual in the past because they were less defined. Evidence of rowdy colonial youth groups and rebellious apprentices has been tendered to counteract the view of premodern adolescence as a relatively tranquil and unproblematic stage of life.

The key features of the nineteenth-century transformation of the experience of adolescence are the emergence of age-graded criterion for demarking youth and youthful behaviors; the gradual institutionalization of both educational and social activities among the young; and a marked tendency to segregate the young in age-bounded environments removed from adult concerns and activities. These developments do not comprehend the entire extent of the transformation, however. For not only was the actual experience of youth substantially different, but the social perception of youth as an ideal was also fundamentally reworked in the postrevolutionary era. The perception of youth as a particularly dangerous and unstable period of life owed as much to anxieties about the precarious status of the revolutionary resolution of authority as to the realities of antebellum adolescent life. The striking parallel between the political struggle of a maturing colony for independence from the "mother" country and the generational struggle of young men against the patriarchal authority of their fathers was not lost on contemporary observers; subsequent historians (Fliegelman, 1982; Yazawa, 1985) have been no less quick to draw attention to this confluence of political and familial metaphors. The relationship of ideas about youth with actual material changes in the condition of the young themselves can best be seen by examining religious, medical, occupational, and educational attitudes toward and experiences of adolescents in the half century between the Revolutionary War and the Civil War.

For G. Stanley Hall and Edwin Starbuck, two of the leading theorists of adolescent psychology in early twentieth-century America, religious conversion constituted a universal adolescent experience, a necessary step in the central process of identity formation. Seventeenth-century Puritan divines would have disagreed fundamentally with this assertion. The Puritan notion that regeneration was a gradual, uneven process begun with the early practice of critical self-examination in childhood and not fully (if ever) resolved until adulthood, had given way under the impact of successive waves of revivalism to the early nineteenth-century view that conversion was a spontaneous, instantaneous experience most suited to Christians of an impressionable age rather than mature saints. The view that religious conversion became a predominantly adolescent rite of passage with the evangelicalization of Protestantism in the eighteenth and nineteenth centuries has not really been challenged by historians. Both statistical and literary evidence seems to substantiate the claims of the evangelical clergy that the First and especially the Second Great Awakenings were characterized by large numbers of youthful converts, marking a departure from earlier patterns of church membership that was as irreversible as it was publicized (Cott, 1975; Greven, 1972; Kett, 1977; Moran, 1972; Walsh, 1971). Yet there is also contradictory evidence that this interpretation has been overdrawn, if not actually misconceived. Using a series of indices to measure trends in ages of conversions, several scholars (Grossbart, 1989; Juster, 1989; Shiels, 1985) have recently argued that the experience of conversion in the revivalist era was too diffused and ill-defined to constitute a meaningful rite of passage. Rather, the persistence of mature conversion even in the face of mass proselytizing among youth stands out as the common feature of the evangelical order even into the nineteenth century. How can these two divergent views be reconciled?

The confusion seems to derive from a disjuncture of perception and fact that marks so much of the contemporary view of adolescence in the antebellum period; while teenage conversions were statistically not dramatically more important in the

nineteenth century than in the eighteenth, there was a new perception of conversion in the evangelical community as a particularly violent and emotional experience that seemed to express the ambivalent position of youth in American society. Revivalists consciously exploited this association of spontaneous conversion with the emotional instability of youth, a strategy which only heightened opponents' fears that the "new measures" of revivalist preachers would aggravate the tendency toward social and sexual dissolution already present in American youth. Both pro- and antirevivalist writers, in other words, articulated a new ideal of youth as emotionally and sexually unstable to their respective religious agendas (Schwartz, 1974). The pervasiveness and intensity of the evangelical preoccupation with youth accounts for the similar bias in historical accounts of the "new" phenomenon of teenage conversion.

This view of adolescence as an unusually turbulent and disjunctive experience, in which expectations and abilities were no longer synchronized but rather operated in a state of constant friction, was encouraged by medical theories that stressed the physiological and psychological imbalances preinscribed in the youthful constitution. Drawing upon a theory of physiological development described by one historian (Barker-Benfield, 1973) as "the spermatic economy," physicians and alienists (the nineteenth-century term for psychiatrists) constructed a model of human growth that stressed the need for conserving vital energies in the period of puberty. The natural inclination toward "dissipation" exhibited especially by pubescent boys, most commonly linked in advice literature with masturbation, came to occupy a prominent place in antebellum anxieties about the dangers of youth. Several scholars (Hare, 1962; Neuman, 1975; Rosenberg, 1973) have argued that the growing preoccupation of medical theorists with "self-abuse" or masturbation in the period 1800–1835 reflects concern over the widening gap between biological maturity and social adulthood; while the age of menarche and puberty steadily dropped in the nineteenth century, the age of marriage for both males and females rose (Vinovskis, 1988). Parents, especially in middle-class families, faced the challenge of controlling the sexual behavior of young people who had reached physical maturity but still could not marry for social and economic reasons.

The alarming gap between the onset of puberty and the safe confinement of sexual desires in the institution of marriage was perceived as but one aspect of a larger social problem of precocity. The Victorian inclination to view the human organism as a "closed energy system in which overstimulation of one faculty drained the others of vitality" prompted fears that precocity was in fact a sign of disease. Critics, spurred to action by the popularity of "infant schools" in the 1820s and 1830s, accused nineteenth-century parents of endangering the physical and mental health of their children by sending them to school at premature ages, exposing them to excessive academic competitions, and forcing them into hasty and ill-conceived career paths before they were ready (Kett, 1978; May & Vinovskis, 1977). The efforts of the evangelical churches to institutionalize youthful piety in Sunday school and college revivals were attacked on similar grounds of inducing precocity; Amariah Brigham claimed in 1835 that revivals actually drove adolescent girls to insanity (Kett, 1978). This sudden interest in the potentially debilitating effects of all forms of youthful precocity was symptomatic of both rising fears of social disintegration engendered by the individualist ethos of Jacksonian society and more tangible signs that opportunities for early (hence unhealthy) advancement were in

fact opening up, especially for middle-class adolescents.

"Spermatic" theories of energy conservation were not ideologically neutral, of course. The medical advice literature of the antebellum period exhibits a definite class content that cannot be ignored in discussions of the history of adolescence. R. R. Neuman (1975, p. 8) argues that middle-class sexual morality drew an economic analogy between the reckless "spending" of sperm in the act of masturbation and moral and physical bankruptcy: "self-control, self-denial, and the postponement of sexual gratification were regarded as the biological and physiological equivalents of economic savings and capital accumulation." In this context, parental worries about the mental and physical effects of "self-abuse" reflected deeper anxieties about the disturbing tendency of middle-class youth to deviate from cultural and class norms of proper behavior. As options multiplied in the expanding commercial economy of the mid-nineteenth century (Demos, 1986; Demos & Demos, 1969), middle-class young men faced new career and personal alternatives that encouraged independence of will. Middle-class parents would have found comfort in the contemporary medical interpretation of the adolescent desire for autonomy—expressed symbolically through the act of masturbation—as a form of "moral insanity" rather than willful disobedience. That middle-class girls were presumed to be unaffected by such willful excesses can be attributed to their relative marginality in the commercial economy; although jobs for single young women proliferated in industry (Dublin, 1979) and teaching (Bernard & Vinovskis, 1977) after 1820, paid employment for most was a transitory experience and largely peripheral to their primary career as wives and mothers (Boylan, 1985).

The study of schooling has proved the most fruitful forum for exploring the impact of class, ethnicity, race, and gender on adolescent experiences in nineteenth-century America. The development of educational institutions designed specifically to cater to youthful needs and abilities was a central feature of the nineteenth-century project to reform society, but—like other reform movements—generated considerable controversy. In the antebellum period schools became the primary if not exclusive site for the education of children, most of whom encountered the common school system at some point in their lives by the time of the Civil War (Kaestle & Vinovskis, 1981; Katznelson & Weir, 1985). School attendance figures for various occupational strata have been offered to chart the influence of class in structuring opportunities for public education. In his now classic study of mid-nineteenth-century Newburyport, Massachusetts, Thernstrom (1964, p. 23) concluded that "[t]he relentless pressure of poverty—stemming from the depressed age level for common labor and from sharp seasonal fluctuations in employment opportunity—forced the children of Newburyport's laborers into the job market at an early age. . . . Opportunities for formal education past the age of ten or eleven, as a result, were effectively nil for working-class children." A reanalysis (Vinovskis, 1985) of that community in 1860, however, reveals that approximately 90% of children aged 11 or 12 from unskilled households attended school, as did a considerable proportion of those aged 13–17 (79.2% of thirteen-year-olds and 12.8% of seventeen-year-olds). There thus appears to be a smaller differential in school attendance among different occupational groups than earlier studies had suggested (Angus & Mirel, 1985).

To raise the issue of the trade-off between wages and education in the decision to send children to school is not to argue for a simple dichotomy that classifies education and work as mutually exclusive categories in the lives of nineteenth-century youth. Indeed, one of the most striking features of the period is the degree to which school and work remained complementary activities for many young people. Seasonal patterns of school attendance that allowed boys to pursue a rudimentary education while fulfilling their work chores persisted into the second half of the century, though the system was gradually undermined by the efforts of educational reformers to impose uniform standards of school attendance. The flexibility and looseness that characterized antebellum education was a major casualty of the pedagogical regime that triumphed by the late nineteenth century, substituting age-segregated groups and standardized curricula for the hodgepodge of ages and abilities that had coexisted in the colonial and antebellum classroom (Kett, 1977; Modell, Furstenberg, & Hershberg, 1976; Vinovskis, 1987a).

Nonetheless, this process was not experienced uniformly by all groups in American society. Perhaps the greatest shortcoming in the secondary literature on nineteenth-century adolescence and education is the almost complete disregard of the black experience in America. Prior to 1860, what little education black slaves received was largely informal and provided by their families and the larger slave community on the plantation (Webber, 1978); white masters provided only enough training to carry out assigned tasks, with perhaps some instruction in the rudiments of literacy, usually in the context of religious instruction (Berrol, 1985). In their teens, slave children were incorporated almost immediately as full-time workers into the plantation economy and assigned tasks deemed appropriate to their gender and physical development (Fogel & Engerman, 1974). Free blacks in antebellum America received more formal education than bondsmen, but they were barred from regular public schools and relegated to segregated institutions (Kaestle, 1983). Although a few blacks were able to attend integrated schools in some northern communities, their education rarely progressed beyond the common school; once out of the classroom, they faced severe racial discrimination in the labor market (Schultz, 1973), and as a result were restricted largely to unskilled occupations (Horton & Horton, 1979).

Following emancipation at the close of the Civil War, educational opportunities for blacks in the South underwent significant expansion, but the quality of that education continued to be markedly inferior to that available to whites as white Southerners regained control of their state and local governments (Link, 1986). Nevertheless, the large national gap in rates of literacy between blacks and whites did narrow after 1860, and a few black youth were even able to attend high schools or colleges. Even well-educated blacks in post–Civil War America, however, could not compete effectively with whites for skilled or white-collar positions because racial discrimination in the labor market persisted (Lane, 1986; Pleck, 1979).

The discouraging story of black education in nineteenth-century America is part of the larger story of the generally feeble state of advanced educational opportunities for most segments of American youth. Since few antebellum communities had public high schools or private academies, most adolescents did not receive any education beyond the common school (Angus, 1981, 1988). Yet in a few sections of the country, most notably New England, high school education was available to a larger proportion of teenagers than previous historians had imagined. Nearly one out of every five youths in Essex County, Massachusetts, in 1860 attended either a public

high school or a private academy, but most stayed for only a short time before dropping out to enter the labor force (Vinovskis, 1987b). By the end of the century, secondary education had expanded throughout the United States, but still only 6.3% of seventeen-year-olds in 1900 graduated from high school (U.S. Bureau of the Census, 1975). While some youths from foreign-born or working-class backgrounds attended nineteenth-century high schools, the primary beneficiaries were children from native and middle-class homes. Middle-class parents responded to the increasing demand for educated white-collar jobs created by the maturing capitalist order by sacrificing the wage-earning potential of their sons to the benefits of an extended education. At the same time, daughters in middle-class households—rendered increasingly superfluous as domestic assets by a declining birth rate and the availability of cheap Irish servants—began to populate the public high schools at a greater rate than ever before.

As this discussion suggests, nineteenth-century boys and girls experienced similar changes in their roles and activities, yet often for very different reasons. Middle-class parents in the end may have consented to prolong the schooling of both their sons and daughters, but in the former's case such consent was encumbered with reciprocal (though often unstated) obligations while in the latter's it was readily and freely offered. The psychic burden imposed on nineteenth-century sons by the recognition that their advanced schooling had been acquired at the expense of their family's often marginal financial status may have accounted for the greater hostility exhibited by adolescent boys toward authority figures both in school and in the workplace. Stories of student disorders at the college level are rampant in the literature on nineteenth-century school life: the entire sophomore class of Harvard was expelled in 1832 for "unlawful combination" (Pease & Pease, 1980); students at Brown University stoned the president's house almost nightly in the 1820s (Demos, 1986); University of Virginia students engaged in at least 9 or 10 collective riots between 1831 and 1850, including the murder of a senior professor (Wagoner, 1986); and at Yale, one tutor died of stab wounds inflicted by students in 1843, and serious town-gown riots flared up in 1841, 1854, and 1858 (Allmendinger, 1973, 1975). This litany of riot and rebellion has been explained by historians as reflective of the growing inadequacy of a disciplinary scheme modeled on parental authority and intended for a relatively small (and elite) segment of the American population. As institutions of higher learning opened their doors in the nineteenth century to poorer students and older ones, conflicts between students and masters over the nature and extent of institutional authority ensued.

That these conflicts were, at bottom, reenactments of domestic struggles within the middle-class family between resentful adolescents and anxious parents seems at least plausible. Family relations between parents and children were not unaffected by the economic and social revolutions that figure so prominently in histories of the period. Nineteenth-century youth, it has been argued, achieved greater autonomy in making the critical decisions of their age: choice of marriage partner, choice of residence, choice of occupation (Henretta, 1973; Smith, 1973). With this freedom came ambivalence, and not a little confusion. To help young people navigate their way through the array of possibilities open to them, institutions of self-improvement began to appear in the Jacksonian era. Libraries, lyceums, literary societies, mechanics' institutes, and didactic publications of all kinds, including sermons, lectures, and religious tracts, proliferated in the 1830s and 1840s (Cohen, 1986; Cremin, 1980; Halttunen, 1982). Though initially established as voluntary associations administered by and for young people themselves, such self-help agencies gradually lost their voluntaristic nature over the course of the century and came increasingly under the sponsorship of adult organizers. Christian youth groups such as the Epworth League, which counted over one million members by 1895, Christian Endeavor, numbering 660,000 members in 1890, and the YMCA—the quintessential youth society—testify to the trend toward institutionalization under adult aegis of all aspects of adolescent life, social as well as educational.

This picture of adolescence as increasingly circumscribed and codified into a uniform set of experiences by 1890 is not a particularly encouraging one. Historians have been generally agreed in their condemnation of the late nineteenth-century resolution of the ambiguous status of youth as rigid, homogenizing, and repressive. The broad latitude of choice that characterized early nineteenth-century youth was replaced by, in Demos's words (1986, p. 105), a "broad-gauge standardization of youthful experience." Yet Demos cautions against a too negative reading of this process. The confinement of adolescents to age-segregated activities removed from adult norms allowed a true youth "subculture" to flourish for the first time. In a manner analogous to the growth of feminist consciousness posited by Nancy Cott (1977) as a consequence of the sealing off of feminine behavior in a "separate sphere" of domesticity, peer-consciousness among young people was the unavoidable result of age-segregation within sites of socialization. That little has been written about the evolution of adolescent consciousness—a sense of belonging to a group of peers with similar needs and aspirations—among young people reflects a bias on the part of historians to focus attention on the agencies of social reform rather than on the targets themselves. John Gillis's (1974, p. 204) comments in a review of several studies of late industrial reformers serve as a fitting conclusion of this survey of adolescence in nineteenth-century America: "Until historians begin to treat youth not only as subject to but participant in its own history, their studies must necessarily remain incomplete and inconclusive."

References

Allmendinger, D. F., Jr. (1973). The dangers of antebellum student life. *Journal of Social History*, 7, 75–85.

Allmendinger, D. F., Jr. (1975). *Paupers and scholars: The transformation of student life in nineteenth-century New England*. New York: St. Martin's Press.

Angus, D. I. (1981). A note on the occupational backgrounds of public high school students prior to 1940. *Journal of Midwest History of Education Society*, 9, 158–183.

Angus, D. I. (1988). Conflict, class, and the nineteenth-century public high school in the cities of the Midwest, 1845–1900. *Curriculum Inquiry*, 18, 7–31.

Angus, D. I., & Mirel, J. (1985). From spellers to spindles: Work-force entry by the children of textile workers, 1888–1890. *Social Science History*, 9, 123–143.

Aries, P. (1962). *Centuries of childhood: A social history of family life*. (Robert Baldick, Trans.). New York: Vintage. (Original work published 1960.)

Barker-Benfield, B. (1973). The spermatic economy: A nineteenth-century view of sexuality. *Feminist Studies*, 1, 45–74.

Beales, R., Jr. (1975). In search of the historical child: Miniature adulthood and youth in colonial New England. *American Quarterly*, 27, 379–398.

Bernard, R. M., & Vinovskis, M. A. (1977). The female school teacher in ante-bellum Massachusetts. *Journal of Social History*, 10, 332–345.

Berrol, S. (1985). Ethnicity and American children. In J. M. Hawes & N. R. Hiner (Eds.), *American childhood: A research guide and historical handbook* (pp. 343–375). Westport, CT: Greenwood Press.

Boylan, A. M. (1985). Growing up female in young America, 1800–1860. In J. M. Hawes & N. R. Hiner (Eds.), *American childhood: A research guide and historical handbook* (pp. 153–184). Westport, CT: Greenwood Press.

Cohen, D. (1986). Arthur Mervyn and his elders. *William and Mary Quarterly* (3rd ser.), 43, 362–380.

Cott, N. F. (1975). Young women in the Second Great Awakening. *American Quarterly*, 3, 15–29.

Cott, N. F. (1977). *The bonds of womanhood: "Woman's sphere" in New England, 1780–1835*. New Haven, CT: Yale University Press.

Cremin, L. (1980). *American education: The national experience, 1763–1876*. New York: Harper and Row.

Demos, J. (1986). *Past, present, and personal: The family and the life course in American history*. New York: Oxford University Press.

Demos, J., & Demos, V. (1969). Adolescence in historical perspective. *Journal of Marriage and the Family*, 31, 632–638.

Dublin, T. (1979). *Women at work: The transformation of work and community in Lowell, Massachusetts, 1826–1860*. New York: Columbia University Press.

Elder, G. H., Jr. (1980). Adolescence in historical perspective. In J. Adelson (Ed.), *The handbook of adolescent psychology* (pp. 3–46). New York: Wiley.

Erikson, E. (1968). *Identity: Youth and crisis*. New York: Norton.

Fliegelman, J. (1982). *Prodigals and pilgrims: The American revolution against patriarchal* authority, 1750–1800. Cambridge: Cambridge University Press.

Fogel, R. W., & Engerman, S. L. (1974). *Time on the cross: The economics of American Negro slavery* (2 vols). Boston: Little Brown.

Gillis, J. R. (1974). Youth in history: Progress and prospects. *Journal of Social History, 7*, 201–207.

Graff, H. J. (1985). Early adolescence in antebellum America: The remaking of growing up. *Journal of Early Adolescence, 5*, 411–427.

Greven, P., Jr. (1972). Youth, maturity, and religious conversion: A note on ages of converts in Andover, Massachusetts, 1711–1749. *Essex Institute Historical Collections, 108*, 119–134.

Grossbart, S. R. (1989). Seeking the divine favor: Conversion and church admission in eastern Connecticut, 1711–1832. *William and Mary Quarterly*, 3d ser., *46*, 696–740.

Hall, G. S. (1904). *Adolescence and psychology and its relations to physiology, anthropology, sociology, sex, crime, religion, and education* (2 vols.). New York: D. Appleton.

Halttunen, K. (1982). *Confidence men and painted women: A study of middle-class culture in America, 1830–1870.* New Haven, CT: Yale University Press.

Hare, E. H. (1962). Masturbatory insanity: The history of an idea. *Journal of Mental Science, 108*, 1–2.

Henretta, J. (1973). *The evolution of American society, 1700–1815.* Lexington, MA: D. C. Heath.

Hiner, N. R. (1975). Adolescence in eighteenth-century America. *History of Childhood Quarterly, 3*, 253–280.

Horton, J. O., & Horton, L. E. (1979). *Black Bostonians: Family life and community struggle in the antebellum North.* New York: Holmes and Meier.

Juster, S. (1989). "In a different voice": Male and female narratives of religious conversion in post-revolutionary America. *American Quarterly, 41*, 34–62.

Kaestle, C. F. (1983). *Pillars of the republic: Common schools and American society, 1780–1860.* New York: Hill and Wang.

Kaestle, C. F., & Vinovskis, M. A. (1981). *Education and social change in nineteenth-century Massachusetts.* Cambridge: Cambridge University Press.

Katz, M. B. (1975). *The people of Hamilton, Canada West.* Cambridge: Harvard University Press.

Katznelson, I., & Weir, M. (1985). *Schooling for all: Class, race, and the decline of the democratic ideal.* New York: Basic Books.

Kett, J. F. (1977). *Rites of passage: Adolescence in America, 1790 to the present.* New York: Basic Books.

Kett, J. F. (1978). Curing the disease of precocity. In J. Demos & S. S. Boocock (Eds.), *Turning points: Historical and sociological essays on the family* (pp. S183–S211). Chicago: University of Chicago Press.

Lane, R. (1986). *Roots of violence in black Philadelphia, 1860–1900.* Cambridge: Harvard University Press.

Link, W. A. (1986). *A hard country and a lonely place: Schooling, society, and reform in rural Virginia, 1870–1920.* Chapel Hill, NC: University of North Carolina Press.

May, D., & Vinovskis, M. A. (1977). "A ray of millenial light": Early education and social reform in the infant school movement in Massachusetts, 1820–1840. In T. K. Hareven (Ed.), *Family and kin in American urban communities, 1800–1940* (pp. 62–99). New York: Watts.

Modell, J., Furstenberg, F. F., Jr., & Hershberg, T. (1976). Social change and transitions to adulthood in historical perspective. *Journal of Family History, 1*, 7–32.

Moran, G. F. (1972). Conditions of religious conversion in the First Society of Norwich, Connecticut, 1718–1744. *Journal of Social History, 5*, 331–343.

Neuman, R. R. (1975). Masturbation, madness, and the modern concepts of childhood and adolescence. *Journal of Social History, 9*, 1–27.

Pease, W. H., & Pease, J. H. (1980). Paternal dilemmas: Education, property, and patrician persistence in Jacksonian Boston. *New England Quarterly, 53*, 146–167.

Pleck, E. H. (1979). *Black migration and poverty: Boston, 1865–1900.* New York: Academic Press.

Rosenberg, C. (1973). Sexuality, class, and role in nineteenth-century America. *American Quarterly, 25*, 151–152.

Schultz, S. K. (1973). *The culture factory: Boston public schools, 1789–1860.* New York: Oxford University Press.

Schwartz, H. (1974). Adolescence and revivals in ante-bellum Boston. *Journal of Religious History, 8*, 144–158.

Shiels, R. (1985). The scope of the Second Great Awakening: Andover, Massachusetts, as a case study. *Journal of the Early Republic, 5*, 223–246.

Smith, D. S. (1973). Parental power and marriage patterns: An analysis of historical trends in Hingham, Massachusetts. *Journal of Marriage and the Family, 35*, 419–428.

Starbuck, E. D. (1899). *The psychology of religion: An empirical study of the growth of religious consciousness.* New York: C. Scribner's Sons.

Thernstrom, S. (1964). *Poverty and progress: Social mobility in a nineteenth-century city.* Cambridge: Harvard University Press.

Thompson, R. (1984). Adolescent culture in Colonial Massachusetts. *Journal of Family History, 9*, 127–144.

U.S. Bureau of the Census. (1975). *Historical statistics of the United States: Colonial times to 1970, bicentennial edition* (2 parts). Washington, DC: U.S. Government Printing Office.

Vinovskis, M. A. (1985). *Patterns of high school attendance in Newburyport, Massachusetts, in 1860.* Paper presented at the American Historical Association Annual Meeting, New York.

Vinovskis, M. A. (1987a). Family and schooling in colonial and nineteenth-century America. *Journal of Family History, 12*, 19–37.

Vinovskis, M. A. (1987b). *Have we underestimated the extent of antebellum high school attendance?* Paper presented at the History of Education Annual Meeting, New York.

Vinovskis, M. A. (1988). *An "epidemic" of adolescent pregnancy? Some historical and policy perspectives.* New York: Oxford University Press.

Wagoner, J. L., Jr. (1986). Honor and dishonor at Mr. Jefferson's university: The antebellum years. *History of Education Quarterly, 26*, 155–179.

Walsh, J. (1971). The Great Awakening in the First Congregational Church of Woodbury, Connecticut. *William and Mary Quarterly*, 3rd Ser., *28*, 543–562.

Webber, T. L. (1978). *Deep like the rivers: Education in the slave quarter community, 1831–1865.* New York: Norton.

Yazawa, M. (1985). *From colonies to commonwealth: Familial ideology and the beginnings of the American republic.* Baltimore: Johns Hopkins University Press.

See Also

Colonial America, Adolescence in; History of Research on Adolescence; Menarche, Secular Trend in Age of; Preindustrial World, Adolescence in; Twentieth-Century America, Adolescence in.

Nutrient Intake
of Female Adolescents

J. Harriett McCoy
Mary Alice Kenney
University of Arkansas-Fayetteville

Nutrient intake is only one of numerous factors that affect humans' health. Moreover, reports of nutrient intake alone do not provide information about the influence of given intakes on present or future health. Growth and development occur more rapidly during adolescence than during any preadult, postnatal phase of the life span except the first year of life. The relation of endocrine secretions to growth and development is well known; endocrine secretions adapt to malnutrition (Brasel, 1980). Therefore, nutrient intakes during adolescence, when the final growth and development of the body occur, have the potential to affect a person's physiologic status throughout life. Females' intakes of nutrients during adolescence have been related to their reproductive success in later life (Manocha, 1972, p. 171) and to their resistance to the effects of aging on the skeleton (Sandler et al., 1985). Therefore, information about female adolescents' nutrient consumption, and about the sources of the nutrients, is needed. The information must be renewed periodically, especially for nutrients that have been related to health problems in later life, because the

social changes that affect teenagers' life styles also impact upon their eating habits.

Recommended Dietary Allowances (RDAs) and "estimated safe and adequate daily intakes" for a number of nutrients needed by female adolescents and other population groups (National Research Council (U. S.) [NRC], 1989) are often used as standards for evaluating nutrient consumption. Intakes near 100% of RDA or within the range of estimated safe and adequate intake for all nutrients listed are desirable. The RDAs "are the levels of intake of essential nutrients that, on the basis of scientific knowledge, are judged by the Food and Nutrition Board to be adequate to meet the known nutrient needs of practically all healthy persons" (NRC, 1989, p. 10). More scientific information exists about humans' quantitative needs for those nutrients that have assigned RDAs than about those for which "safe and adequate" ranges of intakes have been estimated. Except for energy, the quantities represented by the RDAs exceed the basic nutrient requirements of most healthy people, so failure to consume 100% of the RDAs does not necessarily mean that a female adolescent will ever develop a nutrient deficiency. However, habitually consuming either considerably less or more of a nutrient than recommended increases the probability that a girl will develop nutrition-related health problems at some time during her life.

Needs for energy vary greatly among individuals because of differences in physical activity, body size, and other factors that can significantly affect the body's use of energy. The RDAs for energy represent the average energy needs for adolescent girls in the United States who are of median size and may differ considerably from any individual girl's energy need. Consumption of energy from energy-supplying nutrients should equal the amount of energy used by a body of desirable size for the girl's height and skeletal size so that acquisition and/or maintenance of that desirable size is supported. Nutrient consumption is sometimes evaluated as a ratio of the amount of a nutrient consumed to the energy (kilocalories) consumed; the relationship is often described as nutrient density. A high ratio of nutrient to energy (i.e., high nutrient density) suggests desirable eating habits that support the consumption of foods that supply more nutritional value than energy alone.

Osteoporosis is a major threat to the health of aging women. Nutrients that have roles in bone formation and maintenance have been studied as possible etiological influences for osteoporosis. A retrospective study related the life-long calcium intakes of postmenopausal white women to their bone densities at the time of the study (Sandler et al., 1985). Bone densities were greater for those women who had consumed milk with every meal during childhood and adolescence than for those who had not. To increase the likelihood that dietary calcium will be adequate to support the formation of maximum bone density during the years of skeletal formation, the

most recent RDA recommends that females between 11 and 24 years old should consume 1200 milligrams of calcium (NRC, 1989); the previous recommendation was 1200 milligrams through age 18 years only (National Research Council [NRC], 1980). Teenage girls consumed two-thirds or less of the 1980 RDA (NRC, 1980) of 1200 milligrams of calcium (McCoy, Kenney, Kirby, Disney et al., 1984; National Center for Health Statistics [NCHS], 1977). Older teenage girls consumed less calcium than younger teenage girls consumed and their diets were less dense in calcium relative to energy consumed (McCoy, Kenney, Kirby, Disney et al., 1984; NCHS, 1977). Although the diets of black girls often provide less calcium than those of whites (McCoy, Kenney, Kirby, Disney et al., 1984; NCHS, 1977), black women as a group are not as seriously affected by osteoporosis in old age as white women (Garn, 1970), indicating that factors other than diet are also involved. Low calcium intake is associated with low consumption of dairy foods (milk, cream, ice cream, cheese), especially by black, rural, or older teenage girls (Kenney et al., 1986). Cherokee Indian teenage girls had calcium intakes (Story, Tompkins, Bass & Wakefield, 1986) that were similar to those reported for whites (McCoy, Kenney, Kirby, Disney et al., 1984; NCHS, 1977).

Anemia, related to folic acid deficiency, has been identified in significant numbers of pregnant adolescents (Bailey, Mahan & Dimperio, 1980); the RDA for folic acid doubles in pregnancy (NRC, 1980; NRC, 1989). However, in 1980, the RDAs were set at 400 and 800 micrograms, respectively, for non-pregnant and for pregnant adolescents (NRC, 1980). In 1989, the RDAs were reduced to 150 and 180 micrograms, respectively, for girls 11–14 years and for older ones and to 400 micrograms during pregnancy for all ages.

Some studies have shown that defective folate metabolism correlates with a higher incidence of problems in pregnancies (Smithells, Sheppard & Schorah, 1976). Because folic acid has a critical role in the cell division that supports growth, teenage girls' intake of this vitamin is of interest with respect to their own bodies and with respect to the potential carryover, via food habits and physical status, to their fetuses during current or later pregnancies. Teenage girls' intakes of folic acid are frequently low, often less than 50% of the RDA (Clark, Mossholder & Gates, 1987; McCoy, Kenney, Kirby, Disney et al., 1984). Furthermore, low intakes may impair health to some degree since biochemical indicators suggest that significant numbers of girls have less than adequate folic acid status (Clark et al., 1987; McCoy, Dutram & Watkins, 1986) even though they are not necessarily anemic. Income was related to folate status in some (Bailey et al., 1980; Bailey, Wagner, Christakis, & Davis, 1982; McCoy, Kenney, Kirby, Disney et al., 1984) but not in all studies (Clark et al., 1987). One study reported that the folic acid intake of teenage girls increased at a rate of 3.3 mcg/\$1000 increment in per capita family income; this increase is partly attributable to greater use of folate-containing vitamin supplements with greater income (McCoy, Kenney, Kirby, Disney et al., 1984). Research has shown a high incidence of poor folacin status in low-income, pregnant teenagers (Bailey et al., 1980).

Numerous studies have documented the high frequency of diets among teenage girls that provide less than the RDA for iron (Bailey et al., 1982; Greger et al., 1978; Kenney, 1985; Liebman et al., 1983; Looker, Sempos, Johnson & Yetley, 1987; McCoy, Kenney, Kirby, Disney et al., 1984; NCHS, 1977; Viglietti & Skinner, 1987). The incidence of physiological iron

deficiency depends upon what clinical test is used to diagnose it, but studies show that from 1–12% of adolescent females may be physiologically iron deficient (Bailey et al., 1982; Greger et al., 1978; Kenney, 1985; Liebman et al., 1983).

Other nutrients that are likely to be low in teenage girls' diets are iodine (McCoy, Kenney, Kirby, Disney et al., 1984), vitamin D (McCoy, Kenney, Kirby, Disney et al., 1984), vitamin B-6 (Driskell et al., 1985; Kirksey, Keaton, Abernathy & Greger, 1978; McCoy, Kenney, Kirby, Disney et al., 1984), zinc (Greger et al., 1978; Kenney et al., 1984; McCoy, Kenney, Kirby, Disney et al., 1984), magnesium (Greger, Gruner, Ethyre, Abernathy & Sickles, 1979; Huber, Disney & Mason, 1981; McCoy, Kenney, Kirby, Disney et al., 1984), vitamin A (McCoy, Kenney, Kirby, Disney et al., 1984; NCHS, 1977), and pantothenic acid (Eissenstat, Wyse & Hansen, 1986; McCoy, Kenney, Kirby, Disney et al., 1984).

Adolescence may be a critical period in the development of cardiovascular disease, so dietary factors that have been implicated in the risk for development of this disease are important to consider. Comparisons to U.S. Dietary Goals (USDG) showed intakes by southern adolescent girls that exceeded USDG for total, saturated, and monounsaturated fat; refined sugar; and sodium, and intakes that were below the USDG for total and complex carbohydrates and for natural sugars (McCoy, Kenney, Kirby, Chopin et al., 1984). Cholesterol intake was within the USDG range and polyunsaturated fat intake approached the USDG. Other researchers have reported small but significant relationships among intakes of some of these nutrients and plasma lipid levels (Morrison et al., 1980).

Eating habits of adolescent girls that have important effects upon their nutrient intakes include whether or not they eat breakfast (Morgan, Zabik, & Stampley, 1986), their meal and snacking habits (McCoy et al., 1986), whether or not they participate in school lunch programs (Chopin et al., 1985), dieting behavior (Dwyer, Feldman & Mayer, 1976), and consumption of "fast foods" (Shannon & Parks, 1980). The relative impacts of these eating habits on nutrient intake vary to some degree due to racial, ethnic, and geographic factors. However, nutrient intakes of many adolescent females in the United States could be improved considerably simply by increasing their intakes of dark green leafy vegetables (good sources of folic acid, vitamin A value, magnesium, and fiber) and of low-fat dairy products (good sources of calcium and of vitamin D, if fortified). The RDA for iron is high enough at 15 mg (NRC, 1989) that it requires careful planning if a teenage girl is to meet the iron recommendation from food alone without consuming excessive amounts of energy.

Teenagers' eating behavior is affected by biological, psychological, cognitive, social, and developmental changes that are occurring during this stage of the life cycle, yet there have been relatively few large-scale, multidimensional studies of their eating behavior and nutritional health. The need to conduct such studies is apparent, since habits formed during this critical, relatively early phase of the life cycle can potentially affect lifetime health and well-being.

References

Bailey, L. B., Mahan, C. S., & Dimperio, D. (1980). Folacin and iron status in low-income pregnant adolescents and mature women. *American Journal of Clinical Nutrition, 33*, 1997–2001.

Bailey, L. B., Wagner, P. A., Christakis, G. J., &

Davis, C. G. (1982). Folacin and iron status of adolescents from low-income rural households. *Nutrition Research, 2*, 397–407.

Brasel, J. A. (1980). Endocrine adaptation to malnutrition. *Pediatric Research, 14*, 1299–1303.

Chopin, L., Lewis, H., McCoy, H., Kirby, A. L., Kenney, M. A., Adams, O. L., Clark, A. J., Disney, G., Ercanli, F. G., Glover, E., Korslund, M., Liebman, M., Moak, S., Stallings, S., Schilling, P., & Ritchey, S. J. (1985). Contributions of the school lunch and the evening meal to the nutrient intakes of adolescent girls. *School Food Service Research Review, 9*, 20–24.

Clark, A. J., Mossholder, S., & Gates, R. (1987). Folacin status in adolescent females. *American Journal of Clinical Nutrition, 46*, 302–306.

Driskell, J. A., Clark, A. J., Bazzarre, T. L., Chopin, L. F., McCoy, J., Kenney, M. A., & Moak, S. W. (1985). Vitamin B-6 status of southern adolescent girls. *Journal of the American Dietetic Association, 85*, 46–49.

Dwyer, J., Feldman, J. J., & Mayer, J. (1976). Adolescent dieters: who are they? *American Journal of Clinical Nutrition, 20*, 1045–1056.

Eissenstat, B. R., Wyse, B. W., & Hansen, R. G. (1986). Pantothenic acid status of adolescents. *American Journal of Clinical Nutrition, 44*, 931–937.

Garn, S. M. (1970). *The earlier gain and the later loss of cortical bone in nutritional perspective.* Springfield, IL: Charles C. Thomas.

Greger, J. L., Gruner, S. M., Ethyre, G. M., Abernathy, R. P., & Sickles, V. (1979). Dietary intake and nutritional status in regard to magnesium of adolescent females. *Nutrition Reports International, 20*, 235–243.

Greger, J. L., Higgins, M. M., Abernathy, R. P., Kirksey, A., DeCorso, M. B., & Baligar, P. (1978). Nutritional status of adolescent girls in regard to zinc, copper, and iron. *American Journal of Clinical Nutrition, 31*, 269–275.

Huber, H. G., Disney, G. W., & Mason, R. L. (1981). Urinary excretion and dietary intake of magnesium in girls. *Nutrition Reports International, 23*, 127–133.

Kenney, M. A. (1985). Factors related to iron nutrition of adolescent females. *Nutrition Research, 5*, 157–166.

Kenney, M. A., McCoy, J. H., Kirby, A. L., Carter, E., Clark, A. J., Disney, G. W., Floyd, C. D., Glover, E. E., Korslund, M. K., Lewis, H., Liebman, M., Moak, S. W., Ritchey, S. J., & Stallings, S. F. (1986). Nutrients supplied by food groups in diets of teenaged girls. *Journal of the American Dietetic Association, 86*, 1549–1555.

Kenney, M. A., Ritchey, S. J., Culley, P., Sandoval, W., Moak, S., & Schilling, P. (1984). *American Journal of Clinical Nutrition, 39*, 446–451.

Kirksey, A., Keaton, K., Abernathy, R. P., Greger, J. L. Vitamin B-6 nutritional status of a group of female adolescents. (1978). *American Journal of Clinical Nutrition, 31*, 946–954.

Liebman, M., Kenney, M. A., Billon, W., Clark, A. J., Disney, G. W., Ercanli, F. G., Glover, E., Lewis, H., Moak, S. W., McCoy, J. H., Schilling, P., Thye, F., & Wakefield, T. (1983). The iron status of black and white female adolescents from eight Southern states. *American Journal of Clinical Nutrition, 38*, 109–114.

Looker, A. C., Sempos, C. T., Johnson, C. L., & Yetley, E. A. (1987). Comparison of dietary intakes and iron status of vitamin-mineral supplement users and nonusers, aged 1–19 years. *American Journal of Clinical Nutrition, 46*, 665–672.

Manocha, S. L. (1972). *Malnutrition and retarded human development.* Springfield, IL: Charles C. Thomas.

McCoy, J. H., Dutram, K. L., & Watkins, A. L. (1986). Dietary intakes and serum folate concentrations of teenage girls. *Federation Proceedings, 45*, 705.

McCoy, J. H., Kenney, M. A., Kirby, A. L., Chopin, L. F., Clark, A. J., Disney, G. W., Ercanli, F. G., Glover, E. E., Korslund, M. K., Liebman, M., Moak, S. W., Ritchey, S. J., Stallings, S. F., & Wakefield, T. (1984). Southern adolescent girls' consumption of energy, energy-supplying nutrients, cholesterol and sodium. *Nutrition Reports International, 30*, 1343–1353.

McCoy, J. H., Kenney, M. A., Kirby, A., Disney, G., Ercanli, F. G., Glover, E., Korslund, M., Lewis, H., Liebman, M., Livant, E., Moak, S., Stallings, S. F., Wakefield, T., Schilling, P., & Ritchey, S. J. (1984). Nutrient intakes of female adolescents from eight southern states. *Journal of the American Dietetic Association, 84*, 1453–1460.

McCoy, J. H., Moak, S., Kenney, M. A., Kirby, A., Chopin, L., Billon, W., Clark, A., Disney, F. G., Glover, E., Korslund, M., Lewis, H., Ritchey, S. J., Schilling, P., Shoffner, S., & Wakefield, T. (1986). Snacking patterns and nutrient density of snacks consumed by southern girls. *Journal of Nutrition Education, 18*, 61–66.

Morgan, K. J., Zabik, M. E., & Stampley, G. L. (1986). Breakfast consumption patterns of U.S. children and adolescents. *Nutrition Research, 6*, 635–646.

Morrison, J. A., Larsen, R., Glatfelter, L., Boggs, D., Burton, K., Smith, C., Kelly, K., Mellies, M. J., Khoury, P., & Glueck, C. J. (1980). Interrelationships between nutrient intake and plasma lipids and lipoproteins in schoolchildren aged 6 to 19: The Princeton school district study. *Pediatrics, 65*, 727–734.

National Center for Health Statistics. Abraham, S., Carroll, M. D., Dresser, C. M., & Johnson, C. L. (1977). *Dietary Intake Findings, United States, 1971–74.* Series 11-No. 202. (DHEW Publ. No. (HRA) 77-1647). Public Health Service. Washington, DC: U.S. Government Printing Office.

National Research Council. Committee on Dietary Allowances, Food and Nutrition Board. (1980). *Recommended dietary allowances* (9th rev. ed.). Washington, DC: National Academy of Sciences.

National Research Council (U.S.). Subcommittee on the Tenth Edition of the RDAs. (1989). *Recommended dietary allowances* (10th ed.). Washington, DC: National Academy Press.

Sandler, R. B., Slemenda, C. W., La Porte, R. E., Cauley, J. A., Schramm, M. M., Barresi, M. L., & Kriska, A. M. (1985). Postmenopausal bone density and milk consumption in childhood and adolescence. *American Journal of Clinical Nutrition, 42,* 270–274.

Shannon, B. M., & Parks, S. C. (1980). Fast foods: A perspective on their nutritional impact. *Journal of the American Dietetic Association, 76,* 242–247.

Smithells, R. W., Sheppard, S., & Schorah, C. J. (1976). Vitamin deficiencies and neural tube defects. *Archives of Disease in Childhood, 51,* 944–950.

Story, M., Tompkins, R. A., Bass, M. A., & Wakefield, L. M. (1986). Anthropometric measurements and dietary intakes of Cherokee Indian teenagers in North Carolina. *Journal of the American Dietetic Association, 86,* 1555–1560.

Viglietti, G. C., & Skinner, J. D. (1987). Estimation of iron bioavailability in adolescents' meals and snacks. *Journal of the American Dietetic Association, 87,* 903–908.

See Also

Nutrition in Adolescent Girls.

Nutrition in Adolescent Girls

Judith Freedland
Johanna Dwyer
New England Medical Center Hospitals

Nutrition Objectives for Adolescents

Our ultimate health goal for adolescents is to ensure that today's youth experience more favorable health throughout their lives than did their forebears. In the last 25 years American attitudes toward health promotion and disease prevention have undergone radical changes: some of these changes favor better health; others do not.

American adolescents face different forms of malnutrition than did their grandparents. Inadequate diets leading to starvation, undernutrition, or classical vitamin and mineral deficiencies (with the exception of iron-deficiency anemia) are far less common today than they were at the turn of the century. Problems such as food allergies, intolerances, and hypersensitivities, chronic diseases—especially of the gastrointestinal tract—and eating disorders, such as anorexia nervosa and bulimia, do still sometimes give rise to secondary undernutrition, but fortunately these problems are rare. Today, it is problems of affluence that prevail. Inappropriate diets caused by overnutrition, imbal-ances, and toxicities (including alcohol abuse) are common and may be on the upswing in all social classes (Dwyer, 1986).

In 1979, the surgeon general of the United States published a report entitled *Healthy People*. Nutrition was designated as one of the five principle areas in which it was felt improvements would promote better health and prevent disease in the population. Age-specific goals to be achieved by the end of the 1980s were established (Miller & Stephenson, 1987). In 1980 more specific strategies were spelled out in the U.S. Public Health Service's forward plan for 1980–1990, entitled *Promoting Health, Preventing Disease: Objectives for the Nation*. Table 1 summarizes national nutrition-related objectives for adolescents and strategies for reaching them. It also provides a recap of progress to date in meeting these goals, drawing upon the findings of more current studies.

Maintain Desirable Body Weight

Obesity significantly increases health risks, including cardiovascular disease, hypertension, and diabetes, and decreases life expectancy (Burton & Willis, 1985). During childhood and adolescence obesity also has immediate negative social and psychological effects. Since we do not know how to cure obesity, whenever possible our strategy must be to attempt to prevent it.

Adolescent girls often overemphasize decreasing food intakes by the use of very low-calorie weight-reduction diets. Such diets may be nutritionally inadequate and do little to solve the teenager's long-term fatness problem. A better approach is to follow a moderately low-calorie diet (1200 calories or higher), coupled with a more physically active life-style.

To maintain desirable weight levels during adolescence, moderation in food intake and a physically active life-style are necessary. Adolescent girls in particular tend to be sedentary—especially after puberty. Fewer sedentary activities and more energy-expensive activities, such as walking, need to built into daily life. Only about 25% of adolescent girls are involved in competitive sports over the course of a year, compared to 50% of adolescent boys (McKeag, 1986). High school sports programs that concentrate on vigorous aerobic activities, such as cycling, swimming, and tennis, are especially useful in obesity prevention. In addition to increasing energy outputs over the short run, vigorous activities that people can do on their own enhance fitness and recreation over the entire life span (American Dietetic Association, 1987). Active life-styles also contribute positively to good nutritional status. As energy outputs rise, intakes of energy and also protein, vitamins, and minerals usually increase. This makes it easier to assure that needs for protective nutrients are being met. Regular physical activity combined with moderation in energy intake allows one to reach and then maintain normal fatness levels (Dwyer, 1986; Stern & Lowney, 1986).

Positive correlations exist between childhood and adolescent obesity and sedentary activity. Television viewing is one sedentary activity that is especially highly correlated with obesity. Several consequences of television viewing may contribute to obesity: calorie outputs while watching television are only slightly above resting metabolic rates, little time is left over for more vigorous activities, and snacking while television viewing is encouraged by frequent food commercials of high calorie items, so that energy intakes are higher among heavy TV viewers (Dietz & Gortmaker, 1985).

Eating Disorders

Eating disorders, such as anorexia nervosa, bulimia, laxative abuse, and self-induced vomiting, are especially common among today's adolescent girls. The many psychological, nutritional, and behavioral problems associated with these disorders include a disturbed body image and a preoccupation bordering on obsession with low weight and thinness. Extreme weight loss may eventually lead to muscle wasting among anorexics. Electrolyte disturbances, sore throat, and destruction of dental enamel due to the acid vomitus are common among self-induced vomiters. Constipation alternating with diarrhea are problems among laxative abusers (Dwyer, 1985; Kirkley, 1986). Moreover, neither laxative abuse nor self-induced vomiting are effective means for achieving weight control.

Because anorexia and bulimia often become chronic, and denial by the patient and family complicates treatment, early recognition is critical. Once the illness has been identified, the goal is to help the patient regain physical health, reduce symptoms, increase self-esteem, and to begin to reach satisfactory nutritional status. The patient

TABLE 1

NATIONAL GOALS, OBJECTIVES, STRATEGIES, AND
PROGRESS TO DATE FOR IMPROVING ADOLESCENT
NUTRITIONAL HEALTH IN THE 1980s

GOALS	PROGRESS TO DATE:	STRATEGIES
Healthy People: The Surgeon General's Report on Health Promotion and Disease Prevention.		
-Improve health and health habits, and, by 1990, reduce deaths among those aged 15 to 24 by at least 20 percent, to fewer than 92 per 100,000.	Since 1977 the death rate for young adults ages 15 to 24 has continued to decline. In 1984 the death rate was 97 per 100,000 for this population.	-Reduce alcohol and drug misuse. -Reduce teenage pregnancy, sexually transmittable disease, and mental health problems, including suicide and homicide.

OBJECTIVES FOR 1990	PROGRESS TO DATE:	RECOMMENDED STRATEGIES:
In Improved Nutrition: Promoting Health, Prevention Disease, Objectives for the Nation.		
-Mean serum cholesterol level in children aged 1 to 14 should be at or below 150 mg/dl.	Concerted efforts have been made toward the attainment of these goals. Unfortunately, data regarding progress is often unavailable or lacking. Direct measures of the nutrition knowledge of American consumers is not available, however measures of recent trends in food consumption patterns reveal that many of the changes are consistent with current recommendations for improved nutrition. A majority of the efforts made to improve nutrition related information and education involve state and local education agencies, school food service personnel and numerous programs funded by several U.S.D.A. agencies and Department of Education initiatives.	-Improve Nutrition-Related Information and Education. All appropriate sectors—the health system, schools, the media private industry, and government—must help parents and children understand what constitutes a diet that is health promoting to avoid deficiencies, imbalances, excesses of nutrients or energy, and to minimize dietary risk factors for disease.
-75% of the population should be able to identify the principal dietary factors known or strongly suspected to be related to heart disease, high blood pressure, dental caries, and cancer.		
-All states include nutrition education as part of required comprehensive health education in elementary and secondary schools.		Comprehensive school-based health education programs should include a major emphasis on nutrition.
-No public elementary or secondary school and no medical facility offers highly cariogenic foods or snacks in vending machines, in school breakfast or lunch program.		Major manufacturers, distributors, and marketers of food must undertake steps not only to ensure that nutritious foods are widely

TABLE 1 (*continued*)

OBJECTIVES FOR 1990	PROGRESS TO DATE:	RECOMMENDED STRATEGIES:
	Data on the actual number of schools and programs involved are not available.	available, but also to help educate the public about the importance and the components of a nutritious diet. -Integrate nutrition in health care services. Policies of both the public and private health care sectors should ensure that nutrition services become an integral part of health services for mothers and children, directed both at health promotion and disease prevention and at treatment and rehabilitation. Health care providers should give specific consideration to their patients' nutrition-related needs as part of the full range of health services offered and organize their practices so that they are closely linked to nutrition services and professionals in their community to make appropriate referrals to meet their patients' nutritional needs.

can proceed to develop a more realistic body image and work on other skills involving personal and social development. Nutritional therapy restores an appropriate weight and nutritional status, thus restoring physical health and alleviating some of the abnormal psychological symptoms (Dwyer, 1985; Kirkley, 1986).

Energy, Protein, Vitamins, and Minerals

Nutrient recommendations by chronological age provided by the U.S. Recommended Daily Allowances (RDA) provide the best guidelines for appropriate amounts of these nutrients during puberty. Physiologic age correlates better with energy and most nutrient needs than does chronological age during adolescence, but nutrient recommendations based on physiological age are not yet available. Table 2 lists the RDAs for female adolescents (Committee on Dietary Allowances, Food, and Nutrition Board, 1989).

PROTEIN ■ The current RDA is 0.8 gm protein per kilogram of body weight (Committee on Dietary Allowances, Food, and Nutrition Board, 1989). This need is more than met by the typical American

TABLE 2
RECOMMENDED DIETARY ALLOWANCES OF
NUTRIENTS FOR FEMALE ADOLESCENTS

		FEMALES		PREGNANT FEMALES	
		11–14 YR	15–18 YR	11–14 YR	15–18 YR
Weight	(kg)	45	66	46	55
Energy	(Kcal)	2200	2100	2500	2400
Protein	(g)	45	46	76	76
Vitamin A	(ug R.E.)	800	800	1000	1000
Vitamin D	(ug)	5000	5000	5000	5000
Vitamin E	(mg T.E.)	8	8	10	10
Vitamin C	(mg)	50	60	70	80
Folacin	(ug)	400	400	800	800
Niacin	(mg)	15	14	17	16
Riboflavin	(mg)	1.3	1.3	1.6	1.6
Thiamine	(mg)	1.1	1.1	1.5	1.5
Vitamin B	(mg)	1.8	2.0	2.4	2.6
Vitamin B	(ug)	3.0	3.0	4.0	4.0
Calcium	(mg)	1200	1200	1600	1600
Phosphorus	(mg)	1200	1200	1600	1600
Iodine	(ug)	150	150	175	175
Iron	(mg)	18	18	18+	18+
Magnesium	(mg)	300	300	450	450
Zinc	(mg)	15	15	20	20

Adapted from Food and Nutrition Board, National Research Council: Recommended Dietary Allowances, Washington, D.C. National Academy of Sciences, 1985.

adolescent's diet. Eating more protein than needed provides no particular advantage to athletes, or, for that matter, to any adolescent (McArdle, Katch & Katch, 1986).

DIETARY FAT ■ Sedentary life-styles, high blood sugar, high blood pressure, smoking, consumption of diets high in excess calories, saturated fats, and cholesterol—all are preventable factors that increase risk for cardiovascular disease. The advisability of a prudent diet low in cholesterol, total fats, and saturated fats for American adolescents, especially for high-risk adolescents, is now well supported (Dwyer, 1986). The prudent diet recommended by the American Heart Association is one in which average daily con-sumption of cholesterol is no more than 300 mg, with no more than 30–35% of calories derived from fat and less than 10% derived from saturated fat. The P/S of approximately 1.0 and a reduction in salt intake is also called for (Committee on Nutrition of the American Heart Association, 1978). The American Academy of Pediatrics recommendations for childhood and adolescence are more liberal, with 30–40% of calories coming from fat and no specific saturated fat goal (American Academy of Pediatrics, Committee on Nutrition, 1986). Since there is little risk associated with lower dietary fat levels in adolescents, and benefits may be great, the ultimate target for calories from fats should probably be 30% (Dwyer, 1986).

SUGAR AND STARCH ▪ The caries rate is declining, thanks to fluoridation of water supplies, better oral hygiene, and other preventive dental measures. Recommendations by the American Academy of Pediatric Dentistry (AAPD) for the primary prevention of dental caries are fluoridation of the water supply, oral hygiene, including regular toothbrushing with a fluoride-containing dentifrice as well as flossing, and diet management. Diet management includes diet analysis and modification of frequency and type of carbohydrate intake to keep cariogenic exposure to a minimum (American Academy of Pediatric Dentistry, 1987).

Excessive intake of sugar is associated with an increased risk of dental caries, but sugar intake is neither the single nor the most critical factor in causation of dental caries. Caries attack rates are correlated best with frequent consumption of cariogenic carbohydrates between and at meals (Bibby, 1975). Frequent snacking between meals with sugary confections, sugary baked goods, and sugar-sweetened drinks is common among adolescents. Indeed, adolescence is the peak age for consumption of many snack foods. Milk and milk products, most meat and poultry, nuts, eggs, fresh or water-packed fruits, vegetables, and unsweetened fruits—all have low cariogenicity and are good sugar substitutes (Dwyer, 1986).

The American Diabetes Association recommends adolescent diets that keep fat calories to 30% or less, with 50–65% of calories coming from carbohydrate; furthermore, at least half of the carbohydrates should come from foods with a low glycemic index and/or high dietary fiber, such as legumes and most whole-grain cereals (Brink, 1988).

DIETARY FIBER ▪ Dietary fiber helps promote normal laxation. Current recommendations are for 15 grams or more per day. This is best achieved by a diet emphasizing whole-grain cereals, breads, high-fiber vegetables (broccoli, celery, etc.), and fruits whose seeds and skins are consumed (U.S. Department of Health and Human Services, 1986). Natural food sources of fiber rather than fiber supplements are recommended.

SODIUM ▪ The current recommended safe and adequate range for sodium intake is 900 to 2700 mg per day for adolescents (Committee on Dietary Allowances, Food, and Nutrition Board, 1989). The specific role of dietary sodium in the etiology of hypertension is unclear. However, epidemiological and experimental evidence suggest that it is associated with high blood pressure levels. Sodium reduction beginning in childhood or adolescence may help to reduce the risk of high blood pressure in later life in individuals who are sensitive to sodium.

The first step toward lowering sodium intake in the diet of teenagers is to avoid salting food. As much as a third of sodium intake comes from salting food. Fast food and convenience foods are especially high in sodium. Naturally low-sodium foods or specially produced reduced-sodium products, such as low-sodium cheeses, crackers, potato chips, and meat products, can be substituted in the diet (Witschi, Ellison & Doane, et al., 1985). Good, low-sodium snacks include fresh fruits, raw vegetables, yogurt, unsalted nuts, and unsalted popcorn. Commercially prepared foods, such as canned soups, frozen dinners, instant cereals, and fast food items tend to be high in sodium and should be avoided or used in moderation.

Reducing or eliminating sodium while cooking, and substituting herbs and spices for salt to flavor foods, can also help reduce sodium intake. Since few teenagers do much cooking this is a measure that the cook must implement.

IRON ■ Moderate or severe iron deficiency anemia is now rare in the United States except among adolescent girls (Dwyer, 1986). The RDA for iron for adolescent girls is 18 mg/day, assuming 10% absorption. The RDA for adolescent males is 10 mg/day. The sex difference is due to menstrual iron losses (Committee on Dietary Allowances, Food, and Nutrition Board, 1989).

In the National Health and Nutritional Examination Survey II (NHANES II) of 1976–1980 and in the National Food Consumption Survey (NFCS) of 1977, estimates of the iron intake of young women were about 10–11 mg/day, or only about 60% of the RDA (National Center for Health Statistics, 1981; Pao, Mickle & Burk, 1985). To increase iron intake at least one serving of meat, fish, or poultry should be consumed daily. This assures that good amounts of the most readily absorbable form of iron, heme iron, is provided. Including a vitamin C source, such as citrus fruits or juices, with meals can further increase inorganic iron absorption from plant foods (Monsen, Hallberg, Layrisse, et al., 1978). Among the plant sources of iron, fortified breakfast cereals, soybeans, black beans, garbanzo beans, and pinto beans are especially good.

Pregnant adolescent girls have an additional sizable need for iron owing to expansion of blood volume during pregnancy, deposition of fetal iron stores and other tissues, and the need for maternal reserves in the event of extensive blood loss during parturition (Dwyer, 1987).

CALCIUM ■ Needs for calcium, which are accelerated by healthy muscular and skeletal growth during adolescence, are greater during the second decade of life than in either childhood or adulthood. Adolescent girls' calcium intakes tend to be lower than the RDA after 11 or 12 years of age. For example, NHANES II revealed that girls 12–14 years of age consumed an average of about 800mg/day or 66% of the RDA, while girls 15–17 years of age consumed only 700mg/day (National Center for Health Statistics, 1981).

Inadequate calcium intake during adolescence may prevent the attainment of peak bone density in early life, one factor that may predispose the individual to osteoporosis in old age (National Dairy Council, 1984). Some adolescents suffering from long-standing amennhorea due to either anorexia nervosa or the emaciation associated with extreme chronic exercise schedules may also develop decreased bone densities in early adulthood. Lack of exercise may also adversely affect calcium balance.

Milk and other milk products are the best source of calcium, because they provide a high amount of calcium in a highly bioavailable form. Three to four servings a day of low-fat milk products and other calcium-containing foods, such as leafy green vegetables (collard greens, kale, turnip greens, and bokchoy), help meet the elevated needs of adolescents. Calcium-fortified milks, juices, and cereals may also be helpful, although the amount of calcium they provide varies (National Dairy Council, 1984).

Diet for Female Athletes

Energy demands for athletes are based on the individual's resting metabolic rate plus an additional factor for the intensity, duration, frequency, and type of activity involved. A diet of 50–55% calories from carbohydrates, 30% of calories from fat, and 15–20% of calories from protein, with water to quench thirst, provides all the necessary nutrients for optimal athletic performance. Body weight should remain within desirable levels to assure normal endocrine function. Megadoses of vitamins, minerals, or protein supplements do not enhance performance.

The consumption of a high carbohydrate diet (50–55% of calories) two of three days prior to an event is referred to as carbohydrate loading. This builds up glycogen stores and provides a ready source of glucose during exercise of long duration. Carbohydrate loading is only beneficial to athletes participating in endurance or multiple event competitions, such as long distance marathons or triathlons, who must rely on glycogen stores for a long time. Carbohydrate loading should be used very selectively by adolescents (Nutrition and Physical Fitness, 1980).

Only extremely severe forms of iron deficiency anemia (eq 6–8 gm/dl), which are rare in the United States, impair work performance and presumably athletic performance. Other inborn anemias, such as sickle cell anemia, which are not caused by dietary factors, may also influence performance ability (Ederton, Gardner, Ottira, et al., 1979). However, these are also quite rare.

Hydration is essential for efficient energy metabolism. The best fluid for satisfying the fluid needs of the athlete, including losses through sweating, is water. Sufficient water needs to be consumed to maintain precompetition weight. If body weight declines during exercise, more water is needed (Morgan, 1984).

Adolescent Pregnancy

Recommendations for energy intake and weight gain in pregnant adolescents should take into account their prepregnant body weight and physical activity. In general, pregnant teenagers do well with pregnancy weight gains that are a good deal higher than those of older women. This is especially true for very young teenagers. Very lean girls need a higher than average weight gain. Obese girls also need to gain weight during pregnancy (Dwyer, 1987). Energy intakes should be adequate to support an average weight gain of 24–30 pounds plus an increment of 2–3 pounds or more extra for those who are less than 3–5 years postmenarche, and therefore still growing themselves (Jacobson, 1983).

Several key nutrients are often low in pregnant adolescents. These include energy, protein, calcium, iron and vitamin A (Dwyer, 1987). Protein needs increase during pregnancy. The current RDA are 76 grams of protein per day for adolescents under 19, and 74 grams for older girls from the second month until term; the RDAs compare with 46 grams of protein for nonpregnant teens (McArdle, Katch & Katch, 1986). Some experts suggest that even higher protein intakes (by about 10 gm) may be justified (Jacobson, 1983).

Calcium and iron are often low in adolescent girls' diets, even before they become pregnant. Supplements of these minerals are usually prescribed for pregnant teenagers to ensure adequate intake. In addition folic acid supplements are recommended, and, for high-risk adolescents who are likely to have especially poor diets, a multivitamin supplement (Dwyer, 1987).

Conclusion

Adolescence is a time of rapid growth and many social and physical changes. It is marked by an increased need for certain protective nutrients to meet the increased requirements for the pubertal growth spurt and the onset of menarche. Besides basic nutrient concerns, which apply to all female adolescents, additional nutritional challenges may arise due to pregnancy, obesity, eating disorders, and participation in athletics. The recommendations provided in this article are in line with the Recommended Daily Allowances and with the Dietary Guidelines for Americans (U.S. Department of Agriculture and U.S. Department of Health and Human Services, 1985).

References

American Academy of Pediatric Dentistry. (1987). Guidelines for dental health of the adolescent—May, 1986. *Pediatric Dentistry*, 9, 247-251.

American Academy of Pediatrics, Committee on Nutrition. (1986). Prudent life-style of children: Dietary fat and cholesterol. *Pediatrics*, 78, 521-525.

American Dietetic Association (1987). Position paper: Nutrition for physical fitness and athletic performance for adults. *Journal of the American Dietetic Association*, 87, 933-934.

Bibby, B. G. (1975). The cariogenicity of snack foods and confections. *Journal of the American Dental Association*, 90, 121-132.

Brink, S. J. (1988). Pediatric, adolescent, and young adult nutrition issues in IDDM. *Diabetes Care*, 11, 192-200.

Burton, T. B., & Willis, R. F. (1985). Health implications of obesity: An NIH consensus development conference. *Journal of the American Dietetic Association*, 85, 1117-1121.

Committee on Dietary Allowances, Food, and Nutrition Board. (1989). *Recommended dietary allowances*. Washington, DC: National Academy of Sciences.

Committee on Nutrition of the American Heart Association. (1978). Diet and coronary heart disease. *Circulation*, 58, 762A-764A.

Dietz, W. H., & Gortmaker, S. L. (1985). Do we fatten our children at the television set? Obesity and television viewing in children and adolescents. *Pediatrics*, 75, 807-812.

Dwyer, J. T. (1985). Nutritional aspects of anorexia nervosa and bulimia. In S. W. Emmett (Ed.), *Theory and treatment of anorexia nervosa*, (pp. 3-5). New York: Brunner/Mazel.

Dwyer, J. T. (1986). Promoting good nutrition for today and the year 2000. *Pediatric Clinics of North America*, 33, 799-819.

Dwyer, J. T. (1987). Maternal nutrition in pregnancy. In R. Grand & W. B. Diets (Eds.), *Pediatric nutrition* (pp. 205-222). Boston: Butterworth's.

Ederton, V. R., Gardner, G. W., Ottira, J. et al. (1979). Iron-deficiency anemia and its effect on worker productivity and activity patterns. *British Medical Journal*, 2, 1546-1549.

Jacobson, H. N. (1983). Pregnancy in adolescence. *Clinical Nutrition*, 2, 15-19.

Kirkley, B. G. (1986). Bulimia: Clinical characteristics, development, and etiology. *Journal of the American Dietetic Association*, 84, 468-472.

McArdle, W. D., Katch, F. I., & Katch, V. I. (1986). Vitamins, minerals, and water. In *Exercise physiology* (pp. 48-54). Philadelphia: Lea and Febiger.

McKeag, B. B. (1986). Adolescents and exercise. *Journal of Adolescent Health Care*, 7, 121S-129S.

Miller, S. A., & Stephenson, M. G. (1987). The 1990 national nutrition objectives: Lessons for the future: *Journal of the American Dietetic Association*, 87, 1665-1667.

Monsen, E. R., Hallberg, L., Layrisse, M. et al. (1978). Estimation of available dietary iron. *American Journal of Clinical Nutrition*, 31, 131-141.

Morgan, B. L. G. (1984). Nutritional needs of the female adolescent. *Women Health*, 9, 15-28.

National Dairy Council. (1984). Calcium: A

summary of current research for the health professional. Chicago: National Dairy Council.

National Center for Health Statistics. (1981). *Plan and operation of the Second National Health and Nutrition Examination Survey 1976–1980* (Vital and Health Statistics, Series 1, no. 15). Washington, DC: U.S. Government Printing Office.

Office of the Assistant Secretary for Health. (1979). *Healthy People: The Surgeon General's Report on Health Promotion and Disease Prevention* (DHEW Publication No. (PSH) 79–55071). Washington, DC: U.S. Government Printing Office.

Pao, E. M., Mickle, S. J., & Burk, M. C. (1985). One-day and 3-day nutrient intakes by individuals—Nationwide Food Consumption Survey findings, Spring 1977. *Journal of the American Dietetic Association, 85,* 313.

Select Panel for the Promotion of Child Health. (1980). *Better health for our children: A national strategy: Vol. 1. Summary and recommendations: The Report of the Select Panel for the Promotion of Child Health to the United States Congress and the Secretary of Health and Human Services.* Washington, DC: U.S. Department of Health and Human Services Office of the Assistant Secretary for Health and Surgeon General, Publication No. 79–55071.

Stern, J. S., & Lowney, P. (1986). Obesity: The role of physical activity. In K. Brownell & J. Foreyt (Eds.), *Handbook of Eating Disorders.* New York: Basic Books.

U.S. Department of Agriculture and U.S. Department of Health and Human Services. (1985). *Dietary guidelines for Americans.* Washington, DC: U.S. Government Printing Office.

U.S. Department of Health and Human Services. (1980). Promoting health/preventing disease: Objectives for the nation. Washington DC: U.S. Government Printing Office.

U.S. Department of Health and Human Services. (1986a). *Health United States, 1986.* Washington, DC: U.S. Government Printing Office.

U.S. Department of Health and Human Services. (1986b). *Cancer control objectives for the nation 1985–2000* (National Cancer Institute, NCI Monographs No. 2). Washington, DC: U.S. Government Printing Office.

Witschi, J. C., Ellison, R. C., Doane, D. D. et al. (1985). Dietary sodium reduction among students: Feasibility and acceptance. *Journal of the American Dietetic Association, 85,* 816–821.

(1980). Nutrition and physical fitness. *Journal of the American Dietetic Association, 76,* 437.

A Report of the Scientific Community's Views on Progress in Attaining the Public Health Service Objectives for Improved Nutrition in 1990. Bethesda, MD: Life Sciences Research Office Federation of America Societies For Experimental Biology.

See Also

Nutrient Intake of Female Adolescents.

Partial support by a Culpeper Foundation Grant and Grant MCJ 9120 of the U.S. Department of Health and Human Services to Dr. Dwyer for the preparation of this entry is gratefully acknowledged.

Parent-Adolescent Relations

Laurence Steinberg
Temple University

Although the popular stereotype of the adolescent's family as a crucible of intrafamilial tension and hostility persists, this portrait has not been confirmed in most empirical studies of adolescents and their parents (e.g., Kandel & Lesser, 1972; Offer, 1969; Youniss & Smollar, 1985). Nevertheless, recent research on the family at adolescence has shown that the second decade of the child's life—and in particular, the first few years of this decade—is an important time for the realignment and redefinition of family ties (Hill, 1980). Parent-child relationships do not seem to be reconstituted in any dramatic way during the transition from childhood into adolescence, but they nevertheless are transformed in subtle, yet important, respects (Collins, 1988). This entry examines the nature of, and influences on, this set of relational transformations.

It is difficult to consider the empirical literature on parent-child relations in adolescence without acknowledging the profound influence that psychoanalytic models have had in shaping and defining the empirical agenda (Freud, 1958). According to this view, the process of detachment, triggered by the biological changes of puberty, is characterized by intrafamilial storm and stress, and adolescent rebellion is viewed as both inevitable and normative. The development of autonomy during adolescence is conceptualized as autonomy from parents; parent-adolescent conflict is seen as both a normative manifestation of the detachment process and as a necessary stimulus to the process; and parent-adolescent harmony, at least in the extreme, is viewed as developmentally stunting and symptomatic of intrapsychic immaturity.

One particularly important legacy of the psychoanalytic view is the notion that conflict and detachment, rather than harmony and attachment, characterize normal family life during this period of development. As a result, most research has been biased toward the study of the extent to which, the ways in which, and the reasons that adolescents and parents grow apart, to the exclusion of research on the ways in which close family ties are maintained during the second decade (Hill & Holmbeck, 1986). This imbalance is especially ironic in light of research on representative populations of adolescents and parents indicating that harmony is a far more pervasive feature of family life during adolescence than is contentiousness and that the values and attitudes of adults and youth are more alike than different (Conger, 1981).

The weight of the empirical evidence to date indicates that the portrait of family storm and stress painted by most psychoanalytic writers is unduly pessimistic. Only a very small proportion of families—somewhere between 5 and 10%—experience a dramatic deterioration in the quality of the parent-child relationship during adolescence (Rutter, Graham, Chadwick, & Yule, 1976). The view that adolescent detachment and family strain are inherent features of family life during adolescence may accurately describe families of adolescents with problems, but does not appear to apply to the normal population of young people and their parents. There is reason to believe, therefore, that families who experience a marked worsening in the quality of their relationships during adolescence are likely in need of professional attention. It is not known whether estimates of the prevalence of family problems, derived almost exclusively from studies of first-born adolescents from white, middle-class families, can be generalized to other populations, but there is little reason to assume, a priori, that family relations are inherently more strained in nonwhite, non–middle-class households. It does appear, however, that stormy or distant parent-adolescent relationships, while not normative, are more prevalent among single-parent households and stepfamilies (Montemayor, 1986).

In essence, empirical studies argue against the view that familial strain during adolescence is normative. There also is strong evidence in the empirical literature against the view that detachment from family ties during adolescence is desirable. Indeed, adolescents who report feeling relatively closer to their parents score higher than their peers on measures of psychosocial development, including self-reliance and other indicators of responsible inde-

pendence; higher on measures of behavioral competence, including school performance; higher on measures of psychological well-being, including self-esteem; and lower on measures of psychological or social problems, including drug use, depression, and deviant behavior (e.g., Barnes, 1984; Maccoby & Martin, 1983). In contrast, there is no support in studies of nonclinical populations of adolescents and parents that relationships can be so close as to be "enmeshing." In view of the clear and consistent evidence that detachment from family ties during adolescence is neither normative nor desirable, it is important to ask why this notion persists. Part of the problem may inhere in the media's portrayal of adolescents and their parents, which may exaggerate the prevalence and severity of parent-adolescent conflict and downplay the existence of parent-adolescent harmony.

Although the storm and stress view has not been supported in studies of normal populations of young people and their parents, virtually all scholars writing about family relations in adolescence agree that transformations in the parent-child relationship do occur during this period; that families vary in the ways in which their relationships are transformed; and that these variations in relational transformations are likely to be important influences on the young person's mental health and behavior. According to several writers, early adolescence, in particular, is a temporary period of perturbation, adaptation, or realignment in the family system. These periods, which typically occur around the onset of puberty, are characterized by heightened bickering and squabbling and diminished levels of positive interaction (Steinberg, 1988). Research has identified two developments in particular that appear to be related to the genesis of relational perturbations at early adolescence: the physical changes of puberty (e.g., Steinberg, 1987) and the cognitive changes associated with the development of more advanced levels of reasoning (e.g., Smetana, 1988). However, because these perturbations in family relations typically do not threaten the emotional cohesion of the parent-child bond, the fact that families pass through such periods should not be taken as evidence of adolescent detachment. Indeed, numerous writers have asked whether and how periods of realignment—even when accompanied by conflict—may contribute in positive ways to the psychosocial development of the adolescent (Cooper, 1988).

A good deal of research has examined variations in adolescent development as a function of variations in family relations, and the literature is surprisingly consistent in this regard. Generally speaking, adolescents thrive developmentally when their family environment is characterized by warm relationships in which individuals are permitted to express their opinions and assert their individuality and in which parents expect mature behavior and set and enforce reasonable rules and standards (Grotevant & Cooper, 1986; Maccoby & Martin, 1983). This constellation of warmth, democracy, and demandingness has been labeled "authoritative" (Baumrind, 1967). According to several comprehensive reviews of the literature on parenting practices and their outcomes, adolescents who grow up in authoritative homes score higher on indices of psychological development and mental health, virtually however defined. Much of the work on the benefits of authoritative parenting, however, has been conducted on samples of white, middle-class youngsters growing up in two-parent households. Whether these same principles apply to other populations of adolescents and parents is an exceedingly important question.

A handful of studies have examined parent-adolescent relations from the parent's point of view. These studies have found that parents of adolescents are likely to feel less adequate and more anxious about parenting than parents with younger children; that reports of parental stress are highest in early adolescence and related to youngsters' demands for more autonomy and, presumably, to conflicts that arise over autonomy-related issues; and that distance between parents and adolescents may diminish marital satisfaction and provoke midlife reappraisal and self-reevaluation (e.g., Silverberg & Steinberg, 1988). However, several studies point to the very different roles played by mothers and fathers in the adolescent's family, and the overall picture suggests that the four parent-adolescent dyads may be characterized by quite different types of relations (Youniss & Smollar, 1985).

Although researchers have searched for fundamental principles that characterize the family's transition into adolescence, the nature of the family's transition into this era is not likely to be universal across families. Among the most important factors likely to moderate the pattern of this relational transformation are the affective quality of the parent-child relationship prior to adolescence, the structure of the family (i.e., intact, divorced, remarried), and the expectations about adolescence held by parents, teenagers, and the society in which they live. Unfortunately, we know very little about the ways in which childhood attachments, family structure, and individual expectations affect the family's transition into adolescence. Given the very reasonable hypothesis suggesting that parental expectations prior to adolescence may influence the quality and nature of parent-adolescent relations, more research on the sources of information sought and used by parents of preadolescents and young adolescents, and the impact of this information on parenting practices, is needed.

References

Barnes, G. (1984). Adolescent alcohol abuse and other problem behaviors: Their relationship and common parental influences. *Journal of Youth and Adolescence, 13*, 329–348.

Baumrind, D. (1967). Child care practices anteceding three patterns of preschool behavior. *Genetic Psychology Monographs, 75*, 43–88.

Collins, W. A. (1988). Research on the transition to adolescence: Continuity in the study of developmental processes. In M. Gunnar (Ed.), *21st Minnesota symposium on child psychology* (pp. 1–15). Hillsdale, NJ: Lawrence Erlbaum Associates.

Conger, J. (1981). Freedom and commitment: Families, youth, and social change. *American Psychologist, 36*, 1475–1484.

Cooper, C. (1988). Commentary: The role of conflict in adolescent parent relationships. In M. Gunnar (Ed.), *21st Minnesota symposium on child psychology* (pp. 181–187). Hillsdale, NJ: Lawrence Erlbaum Associates.

Freud, A. (1958). Adolescence. *Psychoanalytic Study of the Child, 13*, 255–278.

Grotevant, H., & Cooper, C. (1986). Individuation in family relationships: A perspective on individual differences in the development of identity and role-taking skill in adolescence. *Human Development, 29*, 82–100.

Hill, J. P. (1980). The family. In M. Johnson (Ed.), *Toward adolescence: The middle school years. The seventy-ninth yearbook of the National Society for the Study of Education* (pp. 32–55). Chicago: University of Chicago Press.

Hill, J., & Holmbeck, G. (1986). Attachment and autonomy during adolescence. In G. Whitehurst (Ed.), *Annals of child development* (Vol. 3, pp. 145–189). Greenwich, CT: JAI Press.

Kandel, D., & Lesser, G. (1972). *Youth in two worlds.* San Francisco: Jossey-Bass.

Maccoby, E., & Martin, J. (1983). Socialization in the context of the family: Parent-child interaction. In E. M. Hetherington (Ed.), *Handbook of child psychology; Socialization, personality, and social development* (Vol. 4, pp. 1–101). New York: Wiley.

Montemayor, R. (1986). Family variation in parent-adolescent storm and stress. *Journal of Adolescent Research, 1*, 15–31.

Offer, D. (1969). *The psychological world of the teenager.* New York: Basic Books.

Rutter, M., Graham, P., Chadwick, F., & Yule, W. (1976). Adolescent turmoil: Fact or fiction? *Journal of Child Psychology and Psychiatry, 17*, 35–56.

Silverberg, S., & Steinberg, L. (in press). Psychological well-being of parents at midlife: The impact of early adolescent children. *Developmental Psychology.*

Smetana, J. (1988). Concepts of self and social convention: Adolescents' and parents' reasoning about hypothetical and actual family conflicts. In M. Gunnar (Ed.), *21st Minnesota symposium on child psychology* (pp. 79–122). Hillsdale, NJ: Lawrence Erlbaum Associates.

Steinberg, L. (1987). The impact of puberty on family relations: Effects of pubertal status and pubertal timing. *Developmental Psychology, 23*, 451–460.

Steinberg, L. (1988). Pubertal maturation and parent-adolescent distance: An evolutionary perspective. In G. Adams, R. Montemayor, & T. Gullotta (Eds.), *Advances in adolescent development* (Vol. 1, pp. 71–97). Beverly Hills, CA: Sage.

Youniss, J., & Smollar, J. (1985). *Adolescent relations with mothers, fathers, and friends.* Chicago: University of Chicago Press.

See Also

Conflict, Adolescent-Parent: A Model and a Method; Divorce, Effects on Adolescents; Divorce, Parental during Late Adolescence; Family Interaction, Gender Differences in; Family Life Education; Family Structure; Generation Gap; Generational Continuity and Change; Grandparent-Grandchild Relations; Parent-Adolescent Relations in Mid and Late Adolescence; Parental Influence; Parenting Styles and Adolescent Development; Sibling Relationships in Adolescence.

Parent-Adolescent Relations in Middle and Late Adolescence

Raymond Montemayor
Daniel J. Flannery
Department of Psychology
The Ohio State University

A primary issue for parents and adolescents during middle and late adolescence, the period between about 15 and 19 years of age, is the negotiation of *independence* and *togetherness* (Gould, 1978; Grotevant & Cooper, 1985, 1986; Youniss & Ketterlinus, 1987). These two dimensions have been described with a plethora of terms that have not been clearly distinguished from each other. Terms to describe independence include autonomy, individuation, separation, and disengagement; terms to describe togetherness include attachment, connectedness, and dependence. In this entry we examine the development of parent-adolescent independence and togetherness. Further, we examine conflict between parents and adolescents since many have argued that the root cause of much parent-adolescent disagreement is negotiation about independence and togetherness. Finally, we look at the impact of parent-adolescent relations on what is considered to be the most important achievement during late adolescence: establishing an identity.

Changes in who children and adolescents spend time with and turn to for support and guidance reveal a developmental increase in adolescent independence. In general, middle and late adolescents associate less with their parents and more with peers than do children and early adolescents (Berndt, 1982; Blyth, Hill, & Thiel, 1982; Montemayor & Brownlee, 1987; Steinberg & Silverberg, 1986). This pattern reveals a growing physical and psychological separation between parents and adolescents, although throughout adolescence parents continue to influence their adolescents (Rutter, 1980) and adolescents maintain a high degree of love, loyalty, and respect for their parents (Greenberg, Siegel, & Leitch, 1983; Josselson, 1980; Troll & Bengston, 1982).

Traditional theoretical views of adolescence have stressed the importance to adolescents of achieving independence from parents (Blos, 1962, 1979; Freud, 1958). More recently, however, it has become evident that increased autonomy, defined as greater freedom from parental influence and emotional disengagement from the family of origin (Montemayor, 1986), is not the adolescent norm (Hill & Holmbeck, 1986). On the contrary, for most adolescents, autonomy develops within an atmosphere of continued connectedness to parents and family (Hill, 1980).

Psychoanalytic theorists have been especially interested in the development of autonomy during adolescence. Peter Blos argues that the primary psychological task for adolescents is to transform childhood emotional dependence on parents to a relationship of mature independence (Blos, 1979). According to Blos, adolescence is a time when a "second individuation process" occurs. As a result of unacceptable sexual feelings initiated by puberty, adolescents turn away from parents and turn toward peers, especially opposite-sex peers. One shortcoming of Blos's approach is that it focuses on the adolescent and largely ignores parents. Stierlin (1981) extends Blos's ideas by considering the needs of both adolescents and parents. According to Stierlin, adolescents and parents are not single-minded in their respective desires for autonomy and togetherness. Instead, both seek to balance those needs, although adolescents want more autonomy, while parents desire more togetherness.

Hauser and his colleagues (Hauser, Powers, Noam, Jacobson, Weiss, & Follansbee, 1984; Powers, Hauser, Schwartz, Noam, & Jacobson, 1983) have used Stierlin's theory as a framework to examine parents' contribution to adolescent ego development, an aspect of autonomy. Specifically Hauser proposes that parents may either "enable" or "constrain" adolescent ego development. In one study Hauser and his colleagues reported that parents who encouraged their adolescents to express their own feelings and ideas during interactions with them (enabling) had adolescents

with high levels of ego development (Hauser et al., 1984).

Although parents may encourage adolescent autonomy, many theorists and clinicians argue that parents and adolescents frequently disagree about how much freedom an adolescent should have (Montemayor, 1983). According to this view, adolescents' desires for independence collide with parents' desires for continued connection, which leads to a breakdown of the parent-child relationship and frequent arguments and squabbles about mundane daily issues (Montemayor, 1982). Some have suggested that mild conflict may contribute to the development of adolescent autonomy (Greenberger, 1984; Grotevant & Cooper, 1985; Kandel & Lesser, 1972; Stierlin, 1981). The relationship between parent-adolescent conflict and autonomy is not well understood, however (Silverberg & Steinberg, 1987). Conflict between parents and children increases during adolescence, especially during early adolescence, then declines during late adolescence (Montemayor, 1983). It is not known at this time why conflict decreases during late adolescence, although the simple fact that many older adolescents move away from home does lead to some decrease in face-to-face arguments (Sullivan & Sullivan, 1980).

Going to college is the most common circumstance under which American adolescents first leave home for an extended period of time; it is also an event that affects individual adolescent functioning, at least temporarily, and transforms the parent-adolescent relationship (Montemayor, 1986). For adolescents, one important source of difficulty in adapting to leaving home is separation distress (Hansburg, 1972). Many adolescents experience a temporary period of homesickness, manifested by feelings of grief, depression, and a sense of loss (Aldous, 1978; Bloom, 1980; Haley, 1980). In fact, most college freshmen report some degree of loneliness during their first months away from home (Cutrona, 1982). Homesickness and loneliness may contribute to the poor academic performance of some college freshmen (Bloom, 1971; Margolis, 1981). For most adolescents, however, leaving home to attend college is a positive step toward maturity and leads to increases in personal control, self-reliance, and maturity (Greenberger & Sorensen, 1984; Moore & Hotch, 1981, 1983).

Leaving home to attend college also transforms the parent-adolescent relationship, generally improving it—at least according to adolescents. Sullivan and Sullivan (1980) studied the impact of attending college on parent-son relations. Students who went away to college reported increases in affection and independence and better communication with their parents after they left home. Students were also more satisfied with their degree of independence. These changes were not found for sons who continued to live at home while attending college. Mothers generally perceived their relationship with their sons as improved after the sons moved away, while separation was more problematic for fathers, many of whom experienced some difficulty adjusting to their son's independence. Other researchers have also reported increases in adolescent feelings of affection and intimacy toward parents, especially fathers, after leaving home to attend college (Offer & Offer, 1975; Shaver, Furman, & Buhrmester, 1984). The experience of leaving home, entering college, and adjusting to new living circumstances appears to more profoundly affect the views adolescents have about their parents than the complementary experience of an adolescent leaving home affects the views parents have about their adolescents.

Although older adolescents are engaged in the process of separation from parents, recent work has begun to examine the continuing effects of attachment to parents on adolescents. Specifically, attachment to parents during infancy appears to be a critical context within which children learn styles of emotional regulation in response to distress (Kobak & Sceery, 1988). Presumably these patterns endure into adolescence and perhaps beyond. In fact college students who were classified as securely attached perceived their parents as highly supportive and had low levels of anxiety and hostility, according to peers. In contrast, students whose attachment to parents was less secure viewed their parents as more distant and less supportive and were rated by peers as more anxious and hostile (Kobak & Sceery, 1988). These results are consistent with the idea that adjustment during late adolescence is related to memories of attachment during childhood and, perhaps, to actual attachment.

Establishing a coherent and integrated sense of identity is a major psychological accomplishment during late adolescence (Erikson, 1968). Relations between parents and adolescents play an important part in the process of identity exploration during adolescence and in its outcome. Adolescents who have achieved an identity are more assertive in conversations with their parents, talk more, and interrupt their parents more often than do adolescents who have not achieved an identity. Further, identity-achieved adolescents have parents who encourage and facilitate dialogue and the exploration of differences of opinion between themselves and their adolescents (Bosma & Gerrits, 1985; Grotevant & Cooper, 1985; Hauser et al., 1984). Correlational investigations reveal that adolescents who have not achieved an identity perceive their parents as highly controlling, not encouraging independence, and somewhat more affectionate and less communicative than adolescents who have achieved an identity (Adams & Jones, 1983; Campbell, Adams, & Dobson, 1984).

These findings reveal two contrasting family contexts in which adolescent identity development is either facilitated or retarded. High parent-adolescent affection and companionship, coupled with low encouragement for independence, may bind the adolescent to early childhood identifications and discourage identity exploration. In contrast, adolescent identity formation is facilitated by a family context in which members express moderate affection toward each other, independence and separation are encouraged, and rules are neither absent nor overly rigid. This characterization is consistent with Cooper, Grotevant, and Condon's (1983) empirically based conclusion that adolescent psychosocial development is facilitated by a family environment with a balance between the expression of individuality and the maintenance of a moderate degree of connectedness. In these identity-facilitative families parents encourage independence and self-assertive expression, tolerate a certain degree of conflict, and maintain an affectionate and supportive relationship that does not overly enmesh or emotionally bind the adolescent to the family.

In general, during middle and late adolescence parents and children are engaged in the process of establishing acceptable limits on adolescent independence and family togetherness. Both parents and adolescents want and need lives apart from each other, while at the same time both desire some degree of continuing connection. Severe conflict about these and other issues is rare, although occasional disagreements are common, which may reflect, and even facilitate, the development of adolescent identity formation. Leaving home is a major milestone for older adolescents and their parents. It is a life event with opportunities for personal growth and failure. In general, moving away from home improves relations between adolescents and their parents who, although living apart, maintain ties that bind. The task for older adolescents and their parents is more than successfully separating, however. It is to develop familial interdependence and differentiation in which emotional bonds with parents are maintained at the same time that adolescents become more independent (Greene & Boxer, 1986).

References

Adams, G. R., & Jones, R. M. (1983). Female adolescents' identity development: Age comparisons and perceived childrearing experiences. *Developmental Psychology*, *19*, 249-256.

Aldous, J. (1978). *Family careers: Developmental change in families*. New York: Wiley.

Berndt, T. (1982). The features and effects of friendship in early adolescence. *Child Development*, *53*, 1447-1460.

Bloom, B. L. (1971). A university freshman preventive intervention program: Report of a pilot project. *Journal of Consulting and Clinical Psychology*, *37*, 235-242.

Bloom, M. V. (1980). *Adolescent-parent separation*. New York: Gardner.

Blos, P. (1962). *On adolescence: A psychoanalytic interpretation*. New York: Free Press.

Blos, P. (1979). *The adolescent passage*. New York: International Universities Press.

Blyth, D., Hill, J. P., & Thiel, K. S. (1982). Early adolescents' significant others: Grade and gender differences in perceived relationships with familial and nonfamilial adults and young people. *Journal of Youth and Adolescence*, *11*, 425-450.

Bosma, H. A., & Gerrits, R. S. (1985). Family functioning and identity status in adolescence. *Journal of Early Adolescence*, *5*, 69-80.

Campbell, E., Adams, G. R., & Dodson, W. R. (1984). Familial correlates of identity formation in late adolescence: A study of the predictive utility of connectedness and individuality in family relations. *Journal of Youth and Adolescence, 13,* 509–525.

Cooper, C. R., Grotevant, H. D., & Condon, S. M. (1983). Individuality and connectedness in the family as a context for adolescent identity formation and role-taking skill. In H. D. Grotevant & C. R. Cooper (Eds.), *Adolescent development in the family* (pp. 43–59). San Francisco: Jossey-Bass.

Cutrona, C. E. (1982). Transition to college: Loneliness and the process of social adjustment. In L. A. Peplau & D. Perlman (Eds.), *Loneliness: A sourcebook of current theory, research, and therapy* (pp. 291–309). New York: Wiley.

Erikson, E. H. (1968). *Identity: Youth and crisis.* New York: Norton.

Freud, A. (1958). Adolescence. *Psychoanalytic Study of the Child, 13,* 255–278.

Gould, R. L. (1978). *Transformations.* New York: Touchstone.

Greenberg, M. T., Siegel, J. M., & Leitch, C. J. (1983). The nature and importance of attachment relationships to parents and peers during adolescence. *Journal of Youth and Adolescence, 12,* 373–386.

Greenberger, E. (1984). Defining psychosocial maturity in adolescence. In P. Karoly & J. J. Steffen (Eds.), *Adolescent behavior disorders: Foundations and contemporary concerns* (pp. 3–37). Lexington, MA: D. C. Heath.

Greenberger, E., & Sorensen, A. B. (1984). Toward a concept of psychosocial maturity. *Journal of Youth and Adolescence, 3,* 329–358.

Greene, A. L., & Boxer, A. W. (1986). Daughters and sons as young adults: Restructuring the ties that bind. In N. Datan, A. Greene, & H. Reese (Eds.), *Life-span developmental psychology: Intergenerational relations* (pp. 125–150). Hillsdale, NJ: Lawrence Erlbaum Associates.

Grotevant, H. D., & Cooper, C. R. (1985). Patterns of interaction in family relationships and the development of identity explora-

tion in adolescence. *Child Development, 56,* 415–428.

Grotevant, H. D., & Cooper, C. R. (1986). Individuation in family relationships. *Human Development, 29,* 82–100.

Haley, J. (1980). *Leaving home: The therapy of disturbed young people.* New York: McGraw-Hill.

Hansburg, H. G. (1972). *Adolescent separation anxiety.* Springfield, MA: C. C. Thomas.

Hauser, S. T., Powers, S. I., Noam, G. G., Jacobson, A. M., Weiss, B., & Follansbee, D. J. (1984). Familial contexts of adolescent ego development. *Child Development, 55,* 195–213.

Hill, J. P. (1980). The family. In M. Johnson (Ed.), *Toward adolescence: The middle school years. The seventy-ninth yearbook of the National Society for the Study of Education* (pp. 32–55). Chicago: University of Chicago Press.

Hill, J., & Holmbeck, G. N. (1986). Attachment and autonomy during adolescence. In G. Whitehurst (Ed.), *Annals of child development* (Vol. 3, pp. 145–189). Greenwich, CT: JAI Press.

Josselson, R. (1980). Ego development in adolescence. In J. Adelson (Ed.), *Handbook of adolescent psychology* (pp. 188–210). New York: Wiley.

Kandel, D., & Lesser, G. S. (1972). *Youth in two worlds.* San Francisco: Jossey-Bass.

Kobak, R. R., & Sceery, A. (1988). Attachment in late adolescence: Working models, affect regulation, and representations of self and others. *Child Development, 59,* 135–146.

Margolis, G. (1981). Moving away: Perspectives on counseling anxious freshmen. *Adolescence, 16,* 633–640.

Montemayor, R. (1982). The relationship between parent-adolescent conflict and the amount of time adolescents spend alone and with parents and peers. *Child Development, 53,* 1512–1519.

Montemayor, R. (1983). Parents and adolescents in conflict: All families some of the time and some families most of the time. *Journal of Early Adolescence, 3*, 83–103.

Montemayor, R. (1986). Developing autonomy: The transition of youth into adulthood. In G. K. Leigh & G. W. Peterson (Eds.), *Adolescents in families* (pp. 205–225). Cincinnati, OH: South-Western.

Montemayor, R., & Brownlee, J. (1987). Fathers, mothers, and adolescents: Gender-based differences in parental roles during adolescence. *Journal of Youth and Adolescence, 16*, 281–291.

Moore, D., & Hotch, D. F. (1981). Late adolescents' conceptualizations of home-leaving. *Journal of Youth and Adolescence, 10*, 1–10.

Moore, D., & Hotch, D. F. (1983). The importance of different home-leaving strategies to late adolescents. *Adolescence, 18*, 413–416.

Offer, D., & Offer, J. (1975). *From teenage to young manhood.* New York: Basic Books.

Powers, S. I., Hauser, S. T., Schwartz, J. M., Noam, G. G., & Jacobson, A. M. (1983). Adolescent ego development and family interaction: A structural-developmental perspective. In H. D. Grotevant & C. R. Cooper (Eds.), *Adolescent development in the family* (pp. 5–25). San Francisco: Jossey-Bass.

Rutter, M. (1980). *Changing youth in a changing world.* Cambridge: Harvard University Press.

Shaver, P., Furman, W., & Buhrmester, D. (1984). Aspects of a life transition: Network changes, social skills, and loneliness. In S. Duck & D. Perlman (Eds.), *Understanding personal relationships* (pp. 193–220). Beverly Hills, CA: Sage.

Silverberg, S. B., & Steinberg, L. (1987). Adolescent autonomy, parent-adolescent conflict, and parental well-being. *Journal of Youth and Adolescence, 16*, 293–312.

Steinberg, L., & Silverberg, S. B. (1986). The vicissitudes of autonomy in early adolescence. *Child Development, 57*, 841–851.

Stierlin, H. (1981). *Separating parents and adolescents.* New York: Aronson.

Sullivan, K., & Sullivan, A. (1980). Adolescent-parent separation. *Developmental Psychology, 16*, 93–99.

Troll, L., & Bengston, V. (1982). Intergenerational relations throughout the life span. In B. Wolman (Ed.), *Handbook of developmental psychology* (pp. 890–911). Englewood Cliffs, NJ: Prentice-Hall.

Youniss, J., & Ketterlinus, R. D. (1987). Communication and connectedness in mother- and father-adolescent relationships. *Journal of Youth and Adolescence, 16*, 265–280.

See Also

Conflict, Adolescent-Parent: A Model and a Method; Divorce, Effects on Adolescents; Divorce, Parental during Late Adolescence; Family Interaction, Gender Differences in; Family Life Education; Family Structure; Generation Gap; Generational Continuity and Change; Grandparent-Grandchild Relations; Parent-Adolescent Relations; Parental Influence; Parenting Styles and Adolescent Development; Sibling Relationships in Adolescence.

Parental Behavior, Adolescent

Michael E. Lamb
Robert D. Ketterlinus
National Institute of Child Health and Human Development

Because of the adolescent's age and because of the stressful events that frequently accompany youthful pregnancy and parenthood, clinicians and researchers have long questioned the ability of adolescent parents to care for their children in ways that promote optimal child development. Specifically, they have suggested that adolescents may be deficient with respect to parental behavior, knowledge, and attitudes or perceptions.

Several researchers have focused on the sensitivity or appropriateness of maternal behavior. Compared to older women, younger women have been found to be less sensitive and responsive to their young infants (e.g., Landy, 1981); these results obtain after controlling for demographic and background variables such as race, socioeconomic status, and marital status (Crnic, Greenberg, & Ragozin, 1981; Jones, Green, & Krauss, 1980; Ragozin, Basham, Crnic, Greenberg, & Robinson, 1982). Also, Lawrence, McAnarney, Aten, Iker, Baldwin, and Baldwin (1981) substantiated their clinical impressions that adolescents' interactions with their infants were marked by aggressive behaviors such as picking, poking, and pinching. Unfortunately, these researchers did not compare the behaviors of adolescents and adults, and in two studies that did compare adolescents and adults the same research team obtained inconsistent results concerning the incidence of touching, speaking with a higher pitch, maintaining proximity, and the exhibition of synchronicity (McAnarney, Lawrence, & Aten, 1979; McAnarney, Lawrence, Aten, & Iker, 1984).

In another study teen mothers exhibited less positive affect in face-to-face interactions with their infants, and in a teaching context they verbalized less, exhibited less affect, and demonstrated skills less often than the adult mothers did; maternal age was unrelated to mutual gaze and contingent responding in the face-to-face interactions (Levine, Garcia-Coll, & Oh, 1985). These findings are difficult to interpret, however, because of the large group differences in marital status, family status, and educational attainment. In a study that controlled for these factors, older Hispanic mothers exhibited more effective eye, verbal, and physical contact than did their 14-year-old counterparts. The finding that the

735 ∎

infants of adolescent mothers are more likely to be avoidantly attached than are the infants of older mothers (Lamb, Hopps, & Elster, 1987) may thus be attributed to adolescents' inappropriate or ineffective interactions with their infants.

A consistent finding regarding adolescent parenting is that younger mothers usually provide low levels of *verbal* stimulation, a deficiency sometimes compensated for by an emphasis on interactions marked by *physical* behaviors (Osofsky & Osofsky, 1970; Sandler, Vietze, & O'Connor, 1981). Nonverbal communication, then, is the most common mode of interaction in adolescent mother-infant dyads; this is particularly the case with the youngest teens and those who underestimate their infants' needs and abilities (Epstein, 1980).

Epstein's findings are important when considering studies that suggest that adolescent parents do not understand childrearing and child development. Both DeLissovoy (1973) and Epstein (1980) reported that adolescents were ignorant regarding developmental schedules and appropriate childrearing techniques. DeLissovoy found that adolescent mothers and fathers *overestimated* their children's rate of development, whereas Epstein found underestimates to be more common. Field, Widmayer, Stringer, and Ignatoff (1980) found that older black mothers whose infants were born prematurely had more realistic expectations concerning the achievement of developmental milestones; the results of this study, however, must be qualified because the authors did not control for parity and marital status. The importance of a realistic knowledge base was highlighted by Chamberlain, Szumoski, and Zastowny (1979) who suggested that a gain in knowledge accompanied improvements in the quality of maternal behavior.

It is plausible that adolescents' knowledge of childrearing and child development is influenced by attitudes about and perceptions of their children and their parental roles. Although Green, Sandler, Altemeier, and O'Connor (1981) found that young mothers held less appropriate attitudes toward childrearing than did older mothers, Mercer, Hackley, and Bostrom (1984) reported that 15- to 19-year-old mothers and 20- to 29-year-old mothers did not differ in their feelings about and love for their infants. On the other hand, the younger mothers felt most gratified as parents earlier than the older mothers did. It may be that adolescents initially adjust positively to their new roles, but as the reality and stresses of parenthood become apparent their coping abilities fail. Zuckerman, Winesmore, and Alpert (1979), for example, found that both adult and adolescent mothers perceived their newborns as temperamentally easy, and both expressed high levels of enjoyment in their parental roles. By the third month, however, the adolescents perceived their infants as more greedy and expressed insecurity about their maternal roles. Young mothers who give birth prematurely appear to enter this maladaptive phase soon after their infants' births. Field et al. (1980) found that young, unmarried mothers had more punitive childrearing attitudes at 2 days, 4 months, and 8 months than did older, mostly married mothers. (Note again the possible confounding of maternal age, parity, and marital status in this study.)

In summary, there is some evidence that adolescent mothers provide less appropriate forms of stimulation and care for their children, although there is no evidence that adolescent mothers are more likely than adult mothers to neglect or abuse their offspring (Bolton & Belsky, 1986). Deficits in parenting might be rooted in inaccurate knowledge and inappropriate attitudes concerning childrearing and child development. The suggestions that adolescent parents exhibit inappropriate behaviors, lack an accurate knowledge base, and hold inappropriate attitudes is not altogether suprising given their developmental status. Adolescence, particularly early adolescence, is marked by egocentrism (Elkind, 1967) and preformal operational thinking. In addition, adolescents often create a personal fable in which they perceive themselves as invincible when challenged by the vicissitudes of life (Elkind & Bowen, 1979). Thus, deficient parental behavior might be rooted in either the inability to recognize means-ends relationships or the reluctance to sacrifice personal comfort for the benefit of others.

Finally, because most research on adolescent parenting involves *maternal* functioning, we do not know whether adolescent fathers tend to behave similarly. In some respects it appears that adolescent maternal and paternal roles differ from one another in the same ways that adult maternal and paternal roles differ, and in both cases, there is great variability within groups (Elster & Lamb, 1986; Lamb & Elster, 1985).

References

Bolton, F. G., & Belsky, J. (1986). The adolescent father and child maltreatment. In A. B. Elster & M. E. Lamb (Eds.), *Adolescent fatherhood* (pp. 122–140). Hillsdale, NJ: Lawrence Erlbaum Associates.

Chamberlain, R. W., Szumoski, E. K., & Zastowny, T. T. (1979). An evaluation of efforts to educate mothers about child development in pediatric office practices. *American Journal of Public Health, 69,* 875–885.

Crnic, K. A., Greenberg, M. T., & Ragozin, A. S. (1981, April). *The effects of stress and social support on maternal attitude and the mother-infant relationship.* Paper presented at the biennial meeting of the Society for Research in Child Development, Boston.

DeLissovoy, V. (1973). Child care by adolescent parents. *Child Today, 2,* 23–25.

Elkind, D. (1967). Egocentrism in adolescence. *Child Development, 38,* 1025–1034.

Elkind, D., & Bowen, R. (1979). Imaginary audience behavior in children and adolescents. *Developmental Psychology, 15,* 38–44.

Elster, A. B., & Lamb, M. E. (Eds.). (1986). *Adolescent fatherhood.* Hillsdale, NJ: Lawrence Erlbaum Associates.

Epstein, A. A. (1980). *Assessing the child development information needed by adolescent parents with very young children* (Final Report, U.S. Department of Health, Education, and Welfare.) Washington, D.C.

Field, T. M., Widmayer, S. M., Stringer, S., & Ignatoff, E. (1980). Teenage, lower-class, black mothers and their preterm infants: An intervention and developmental follow-up. *Child Development, 51,* 426–436.

Green, J. W., Sandler, H. M., Altemeier, W. A., & O'Connor, S. M. (1981). Child rearing attitudes, observed behavior, and perception of infant temperament in adolescent versus older mothers. *Pediatric Research, 15,* 442.

Jones, F. A., Green, V., & Krauss, D. R. (1980). Maternal responsiveness of primiparous mothers during the postpartum period: Age differences. *Pediatrics, 65,* 579–584.

Lamb, M. E., & Elster, A. B. (1985). Adolescent mother-infant-father relationships. *Developmental Psychology, 21,* 768–773.

Lamb, M. E., Hopps, K., & Elster, A. B. (1987). Strange situation behavior of infants with adolescent mothers. *Infant Behavior and Development, 10,* 39–48.

Landy, S. (1981). *An investigation of teenage mothers, their infants, and the resulting mother-infant dyads.* Unpublished doctoral dissertation, University of Regina, Regina, Saskatchewan.

Lawrence, R. A., McAnarney, E. R., Aten, M. J., Iker, H. P., Baldwin, C. P., & Baldwin, A. L. (1981). Aggressive behaviors in young mothers: Markers of future morbidity? *Pediatric Research, 15*, 443.

Levine, L., Garcia-Coll, C. T., & Oh, W. (1985). Determinants of mother-infant interaction in adolescent mothers. *Pediatrics, 75*, 23–29.

McAnarney, E. R., Lawrence, R. A., & Aten, M. J. (1979). Premature parenthood: A preliminary report of adolescent mother-infant interaction. *Pediatric Research, 13*, 328.

McAnarney, E. R., Lawrence, R. A., Aten, J. M., & Iker, H. P. (1984). Adolescent mothers and their infants. *Pediatrics, 73*, 358–362.

Mercer, R. T., Hackley, K. C., & Bostrom, A. (1984). Adolescent motherhood: Comparison of outcome with older mothers. *Journal of Adolescent Health Care, 5*, 7–13.

Osofsky, H. J., & Osofsky, J. D. (1970). Adolescents as mothers: Results of a program for low-income pregnant teenagers with some emphasis upon infants' development. *American Journal of Orthopsychiatry, 40*, 825–834.

Ragozin, A. S., Basham, R. B., Crnic, K. A., Greenberg, M. T., & Robinson, N. M. (1982). Effects of maternal age on parenting role. *Developmental Psychology, 18*, 627–634.

Sandler, H. M., Vietze, P. M., & O'Conner, S. (1981). Obstetric and neonatal outcomes following intervention with pregnant teenagers. In K. G. Scott, T. Field, & E. Robertson (Eds.), *Teenage parents and their offspring* (pp. 249–263). New York: Grune & Stratton.

Zuckerman, B., Winesmore, G., Alpert, J. J. (1979). A study of attitudes and support systems of inner-city adolescent mothers. *Journal of Pediatrics, 95*, 122–125.

See Also

Childbearing, Adolescent: Obstetric and Filial Outcomes; Childbearing, Teenage: Effects on Children; Childbirth and Marriage, Adolescent: Associations with Long-Term Marital Stability; Fathers, Adolescent; Fathers, Teenage; Mothers, Adolescent and Their Young Children; Parenthood and Marriage in Adolescence: Associations with Educational and Occupational Attainment; Pregnancy and Childbearing: Effects on Teen Mothers; Pregnancy in Adolescence, Interventions to Prevent.

Parental Influence

Roseann Giarrusso
Vern L. Bengtson
University of Southern California

Parental influence is, according to both folk wisdom and early behavioral science, the traditional vehicle by which older generations transmit attitudes, values, and behaviors to succeeding generations. Yet the mechanisms of such influence have proven difficult to trace. Moreover, the role of intentional parental influence attempts in the socialization of offspring has received only weak empirical support in the social psychological literature.

Four issues appear important in evaluating the research in this area (Smith, 1983). One area relevant to the identification of parental influence is the work relating parental childrearing practices to child personality and behavior. Rollins and Thomas (1979) conclude that parental nurturance and parental use of induction (reasoning) lead to "socially competent behaviors" such as cognitive development and high self-esteem, whereas parental punishment leads to socially incompetent behaviors such as aggression. Although these findings may appear to support the role of parental influence in intergenerational transmission, they do so only indirectly, if it is assumed that parental influence is an intentional activity. Parents are not necessarily aware of the effects of the different childrearing practices they employ.

A second body of research investigates the extent to which adolescents *feel* they are influenced by their parents. In general, studies in this area have found that adolescents do believe they are influenced by their parents in their decision making, at least for the major decisions they face. For example, Sebald (1968) found that although adolescents reported reliance on their peer group when deciding about clothing styles and leisure activities, they reported reliance on their parents' views when making long-range decisions about money, education, and occupations. But this existing research provides only weak evidence of parental influence since the reports of adolescents may be based on misperceptions of their parents' attitudes.

A third area examines the correspondence between adolescents' attitudes and adolescents' *perceptions* of their parents' attitudes. Most of this research deals with educational goals, the most notable among them being the classic Wisconsin Study by Sewell and his colleagues (Sewell & Shah, 1968; Sewell, Haller, & Portes, 1969). Results suggest a high correlation between the educational aspirations of adolescents and what they perceive to be their parents' aspirations for them. That is, adolescents who report that their parents expect them to attend college also report personal plans for college attendance. Thus, this type of research is also limited by the possibility of adolescents' misperceptions of parental attitudes. Agreement with incorrectly attributed attitudes of parents may be indicative of adolescent motivation to comply with parental goals. However, it does not provide support for intentional parental influence.

A fourth area of research examines the similarity of adolescents' attitudes and parents' *actual* attitudes. Overall, these results show a low level of correspondence between adolescents' attitudes and the actual attitudes of their parents. In fact, Acock and Bengtson (1980) found that, for political and religious attitudes, what children think their parents think is a better predictor of youths' orientations than what their parents actually think. However, Jennings and Niemi (1974) found that attitudes that are concrete and specific and are made salient for an extended period of time are more likely to be transmitted from parents to adolescents than those that are abstract or not consistently held as important. For example, adolescents are more likely to be influenced by their parents' political party identification (a concrete attitude) than they are by their parents' views of such basic values as humanism or materialism (abstract concepts).

However, similarity does not necessarily mean influence: a high degree of similarity between adolescents' attitudes and parents' actual attitudes does not necessarily indicate that parents influence the orientation of their children. An alternative explanation is that attitude similarity between parents and children results from the influence of children on their parents (Bengtson & Troll, 1979; Lerner & Spanier, 1978). Contrary to traditional theories of socialization that have ignored this reverse pattern of influence, developmental aging theories acknowledge that children and parents are engaged in an exchange over time that can change with developmental changes in the cognitive skills, social standing, and health of parents as well as children (Glass, Bengtson, & Dunham, 1986).

In addition, attitude similarity or continuity between generations may result not from parental influence but rather from the inheritance of class, race, religion, and other types of social statuses. As youth age and assume the same social statuses as their parents, these common experiences are likely to replace direct parental influence in generating attitude similarity (Acock, 1984).

Finally, attitude similarity may be confounded with "period effects" in which contemporaneous generations may be exposed to the same social or historical events (Bengtson, 1989). For example, those family generations who lived through the Great Depression may have formed similar attitudes about issues of economic stability and risk taking. Thus, similarity in attitudes can also be the result of living through the same sociohistorical events rather than the direct influence attempts of parents.

In conclusion, viewing intergenerational transmission of attitudes, values, and behaviors as a unidirectional process that occurs only during the early years of a child's life as a direct result of intentional parental influence is misleading. Future research should continue to examine intergenerational attitude similarity across the life span, taking into account the developmental changes in parents and children and possible confounding factors such as period effects.

References

Acock, A. C. (1984). Parents and their children: The study of inter-generation influence. *Sociology and Social Research, 68,* 151–171.

Acock, A. C., & Bengtson, V. L. (1980). Socialization and attribution processes: Actual versus perceived similarity among parents and youth. *Journal of Marriage and the Family, 42* (3): 501–515.

Bengtson, V. L. (1989). The problem of generations: Age group contrasts, continuities, and social change. In V. L. Bengtson & K. W. Schaie (Eds.), *The course of later life: Research and reflections* (pp. 25–52). New York: Springer Publishing Co.

Glass, J., Bengtson, V. L., & Dunham, C. C. (1986). Attitude similarity in three-generation families: Socialization status inheritance, or reciprocal influence? *American Sociological Review, 51,* 685–698.

Jennings, M. K., & Niemi, R. G. (1974). *The political character of adolescence: The influence of families and schools.* Princeton, NJ: Princeton University Press.

Lerner, R. M., & Spanier, G. B. (1978). *Child influence on marital and family interaction.* New York: Academic Press.

Rollins, B. C., & Thomas, D. L. (1979). Parental support, power, and control techniques in the socialization of children. In W. Burr, R. Hill, R. I. Nye, & I. L. Reiss (Eds.), *Contemporary theories about the family* (Vol. 1, pp. 317–364). New York: Free Press.

Sebald, H. (1968). *Adolescence: A sociological analysis.* New York: Appleton.

Sewell, W. H., & Shah, V. P. (1968). Parents' educational aspirations and achievements. *American Sociological Review, 33,* 191–209.

Sewell, W. H., Haller, A. O., & Portes, A. (1969). The educational and early occupational attainment process. *American Sociological Review, 34,* 82–91.

Smith, T. E. (1983). Parental influence: A review of the evidence of influence and a theoretical model of the parental influence process. In A. Kerkhoff (Ed.), *Research in sociology of education and socialization* (Vol. 4, pp. 13–45). Greenwich, CT: JAI Press.

Troll, L. & Bengtson, V. L. (1979). Generations in the family. In W. Burr, R. Hill, I. Reiss, & I. Nye (Eds.), *Theories about the family* (Vol. 1, pp. 127–161). New York: Free Press.

See Also

Conflict, Adolescent-Parent: A Model and a Method; Divorce, Effects on Adolescents; Divorce, Parental during Late Adolescence; Family Interaction, Gender Differences in; Family Life Education; Family Structure; Generation Gap; Generational Continuity and Change; Grandparent-Grandchild Relations; Parent-Adolescent Relations; Parent-Adolescent Relations in Mid and Late Adolescence; Parenting Styles and Adolescent Development; Sibling Relationships in Adolescence.

Parenthood and Marriage in Adolescence: Associations with Educational and Occupational Attainment

Michael E. Lamb
National Institute of Child Health and Human Development

Douglas M. Teti
University of Maryland at Baltimore County

Researchers have repeatedly demonstrated that women who give birth and men who become fathers in adolescence complete fewer years of schooling, hold less prestigious jobs, and earn less than women and men who postpone parenting until adulthood (Card & Wise, 1978; Furstenberg, 1976; Haggstrom, Kanouse, & Morrison, 1986; Hofferth & Moore, 1979; Marini, 1984; Moore & Waite, 1977; Mott & Marsiglio, 1985; Teti & Lamb, 1989). Card and Wise (1978), for example, found that mothers and fathers who had their first child in adolescence obtained less education and held lower-status jobs 11 years after high school than did parents who postponed becoming parents until adulthood. These negative sequelae may occur because the abrupt transition to parenthood compels parents to abandon educational pursuits in favor of full-time and lower-status employment, and this in turn has adverse effects on socioeconomic status.

For many adolescents, furthermore, pregnancy and childbirth are also associated with adolescent marriage. Adolescent marriage in itself may bring abrupt stresses (due to the rapid assumption of marital and other "adult" responsibilities) that are independent of those associated with parenthood but have similarly disruptive effects on the resolution of adolescent developmental tasks. Like those who have studied adolescent childbirth, researchers report that adolescent marriage (without regard to the potential co-occurrence of adolescent childbirth) is associated with short- and long-term reductions in socioeconomic status: adults who marry prior to 19 years of age earn less, accumulate fewer assets, and receive less education than individuals who marry as adults (Bartz & Nye, 1970; Bayer, 1968; Burchinal, 1965; De Lissovoy, 1973; Folger, Astin, & Bayer, 1970; Haggstrom et al., 1986; Kerchoff & Parrow, 1979; Lowe & Witt, 1984; Marini, 1978, 1984; Nye & Berardo, 1973; Teti, Lamb, & Elster, 1987). Freedman and Thornton (1979) reported that, over a 15-year period, couples who had been premaritally pregnant appeared to rebound somewhat from the initial effects of early marriage and parenthood, although by their mid-30s, permaritally pregnant couples still earned 12% less income and had 22% fewer assets than their postmaritally pregnant peers. Most other researchers have examined relatively short-term effects, but Teti et al. (1987) reported that males who married as adolescents did not catch up—educationally, financially, or occupationally—with their same-aged, same-race peers who married as adults, even after periods of 30 to 40 years.

The common association between adolescent childbirth and adolescent marriage makes it possible that their "effects" may be confounded, rendering unclear the degree of risk associated with each separately and with both when they occur together. Presumably, the rapid, unexpected transition to both parental and marital roles during adolescence creates more stress and adjustment difficulties than the premature transition to either the parental or spousal role alone. Consequently, individuals who give birth and marry in adolescence might be expected to have a poorer long-term prognosis than those who give birth as adolescents but never marry and those who give birth as adolescents but postpone marriage until adulthood. In addition, individuals who give birth and marry as adolescents might

be expected to fare worse than those who marry as adolescents but never give birth and those who marry as adolescents but who postpone childbirth until adulthood. Haggstrom et al. (1986) reported that women who gave birth and married by late adolescence completed about a year of schooling less than childless, single peers and about half a year of schooling less than women who married in adolescence but had no children. These differences, which could not be explained by initial differences in the socioeconomic status of the women's families of origin, suggest that the combination of adolescent marriage and adolescent childbirth is associated with poorer educational outcomes than the occurrence of adolescent marriage alone.

In a subsequent study of women aged from 30 to 55, Teti and Lamb (1989) found that the co-occurrence of adolescent marriage and adolescent childbirth is associated with different degrees of socioeconomic risk than the occurrence of either event alone. The best socioeconomic outcomes were obtained by those women who did not experience transitions to either the spousal or parental roles in adolescence. By contrast, women who married in adolescence without giving birth in adolescence had a poorer socioeconomic status at survey time than women who did not experience childbirth and marriage in adolescence, and the combination of adolescent marriage and adolescent childbirth was associated with worse socioeconomic outcomes than the occurrence of adolescent marriage alone. Importantly, however, equally poor socioeconomic outcomes were linked to adolescent childbirth *regardless* of the presence or timing of marriage. By contrast, long-term risks associated with adolescent marriage unaccompanied by an adolescent birth were not quite so profound.

The timing of childbirth and marriage may not only serve as "causes" but also as "consequences" of socioeconomic conditions. That is, marriage and childbirth may be consciously postponed as individuals pursue educational and career aspirations or may occur early in the life course if men and women place little importance on educational and career achievements. In longitudinal studies, researchers (Card & Wise, 1978; Haggstrom et al., 1986; Hofferth & Moore, 1979; Marini, 1978, 1984; Michael & Tuma, 1985; Waite & Spitze, 1981) have demonstrated that early childbirth and early marriage are more common among individuals from socioeconomically disadvantaged backgrounds. Moreover, those who give birth and/or marry as adolescents are more likely to come from environments that are less supportive of educational pursuits and have more modest educational and career goals than those who postpone childbirth and/or marriage. Thus, many who give birth and/or marry as adolescents may already be on a different trajectory than those who postpone these events until adulthood, and this may have as much (or more) to do with long-term socioeconomic crises as the discrete occurrences of adolescent marriage and pregnancy. We do know, however, that early marriage is associated with reductions in educational attainment, even after initial differences in the socioeconomic status of the families of origin are taken into account (Kerckhoff & Parrow, 1979; Lowe & Witt, 1984). Presumably, therefore, the two patterns of causality work together to suppress the long-term vocational and educational attainments of those who marry or become parents in adolescence.

References

Bartz, K. W., & Nye, F. I. (1970). Early marriage: A propositional formulation. *Journal of Marriage and the Family, 32*, 258–268.

Bayer, A. E. (1968). The college dropout: Factors affecting senior college completion. *Sociology of Education, 41*, 305–316.

Burchinal, L. G. (1965). Trends and prospects for young marriages in the United States. *Journal of Marriage and the Family, 27*, 243–254.

Card, J. J., & Wise, L. L. (1978). Teenage mothers and teenage fathers: The impact of early childbearing on the parents' personal and professional lives. *Family Planning Perspectives, 10*, 199–205.

De Lissovoy, V. (1973). High school marriages: A longitudinal study. *Journal of Marriage and the Family, 35*, 245–255.

Folger, J. K., Astin, H. S., & Bayer, A. E. (1970). *Human resources and higher education.* New York: Russell Sage Foundation.

Freedman, D. S., & Thornton, A. (1979). The long-term impact of pregnancy at marriage on the family's economic circumstances. *Family Planning Perspectives, 11*, 6–21.

Furstenberg, F. F. (1976). The social consequences of teenage parenthood. *Family Planning Perspectives, 8*, 148–164.

Haggstrom, G. W., Kanouse, D. E., & Morrison, P. A. (1986). Accounting for the educational shortfalls of mothers. *Journal of Marriage and the Family, 48*, 175–186.

Hofferth, S. L., & Moore, K. A. (1979). Early childbearing and later economic well-being. *American Sociological Review, 44*, 784–815.

Kerckhoff, A. C., & Parrow, A. A. (1979). The effect of early marriage on the educational attainment of young men. *Journal of Marriage and the Family, 41*, 97–107.

Lowe, G. D., & Witt, D. D. (1984). Early marriage as a career contingency: The prediction of educational attainment. *Journal of Marriage and the Family, 46*, 689–698.

Marini, M. D. (1978). The transition to adulthood: Sex differences in educational attainment and age at marriage. *American Sociological Review, 43*, 483–507.

Marini, M. D. (1984). Women's educational attainment and the timing of entry into parenthood. *American Sociological Review, 49,* 491–511.

Michael, R. T., & Tuma, N. B. (1985). Entry into marriage and parenthood by young men and women: The influence of family background. *Demography, 22,* 515–544.

Moore, K. A., & Waite, L. J. (1977). Early childbearing and educational attainment. *Family Planning Perspectives, 9,* 220–225.

Mott, F. L., & Marsiglio, W. (1985). Early childbearing and completion of high school. *Family Planning Perspectives, 17,* 234–237.

Nye, F. I., & Berardo, F. M. (1973). *The family: Its structure and interaction.* New York: Macmillan.

Teti, D. M., & Lamb, M. E. (1989). Socioeconomic and marital outcomes of adolescent marriage, adolescent childbirth, and their co-occurrence. *Journal of Marriage and the Family, 51,* 203–212.

Teti, D. M., Lamb, M. E., & Elster, A. B. (1987). Long-range socioeconomic and marital consequences of adolescent marriage in three cohorts of adult males. *Journal of Marriage and the Family, 49,* 499–506.

Waite, L. J., & Spitze, G. D. (1981). Young women's transition to marriage. *Demography, 18,* 681–694.

See Also

Childbearing, Adolescent: Obstetric and Filial Outcomes; Childbearing, Teenage: Effects on Children; Childbirth and Marriage, Adolescent: Associations with Long-Term Marital Stability; Fathers, Adolescent; Fathers, Teenage; Mothers, Adolescent and Their Young Children; Parental Behavior, Adolescent; Pregnancy and Childbearing: Effects on Teen Mothers; Pregnancy in Adolescence, Interventions to Prevent.

Parenting Styles and Adolescent Development

Diana Baumrind

University of California, Berkeley

During the past decade conceptually and methodologically sophisticated research linked to the distinctive features of middle-class Caucasian adolescents and their families has increased dramatically both in quantity and quality. The results of cross-fertilization and replication promise consensual validation based upon cumulative knowledge. Unfortunately, as Hill (1987) emphasized, similar high-quality research for ethnic families of color is virtually absent. Information on the effects of parenting styles on adolescents in separated and nontraditional families is sparse (see Hetherington and colleagues, 1984, 1985; Springer & Wallerstein, 1983). In this brief review I will focus upon a few studies, including preliminary data from my own, that are conceptually guided, use focused observation and/or intensive interview data, and employ multidimensional, multisituational assessments of individuals rather than survey questionnaires.

Adolescent Development

Human development as a process is characterized by alternating periods of rela-tive disequilibrium and equilibrium, in which the global and diffuse organization of ontogenetically primitive discrete schemes of action become increasingly differentiated, coherent, and better adapted to specific demand characteristics of the environment. The normative adolescent stage-transition in our society from "child" to "adult" includes major role changes in the individual's position relative to others, a shift in loyalties toward peers—if not away from family—and a different mix of entitlements and obligations within the family and the larger society. An adolescent's personal commitment to courses of thought and action that depart from early, more stable and secure patterns is facilitated by commensurate accommodations to his or her changing status by parents and other significant adults.

Greenberger (1984) defines *psychosocial maturity* during adolescence as the integration of agency and communion. In the psychological literature (for example, Bakan, 1966), *communion* refers to the need to be of service and to be included and connected, whereas *agency* refers to the drive for independence, individuality, and self-aggrandizement. The social dimensions of status (dominance, power) and love (solidarity, affiliation) that emerge as the two orthogonal axes from almost all factor analyses of human behavior (for example, Baumrind & Black, 1967; Leary, 1957; Lonner, 1980; Wiggins, 1979) are manifestations of agency and communion.

A differentiated and integrated understanding of *identity formation* that accords personal agency and communion equal value defines it as conservation of a sense of continuity through the act of validating *simultaneously* the interests of personal emancipation and individuation, and the claims of other individuals and mutually shared social norms.

Psychoanalytically oriented theorists (e.g., Marcia, 1980) have traditionally recommended disengagement from parents to facilitate identity formation. According to critics (Bellah, Madson, Sullivan, Swidler, & Tipton, 1985; Gilligan, 1982, 1987; Lasch, 1978; Sampson, 1988), agency is emphasized by these theorists at the expense of communion and connectedness. As a subordinate minority, blacks' collective identity is achieved in opposition to the perceived social identity of the dominant group (Ogbu, 1988). Therefore, black ghetto culture, like white middle-class culture, also promotes agency and independence (Harrison, Serafica, & McAdoo, 1984; Silverstein & Krate, 1975). By contrast, two ethnic groups of color, Asian-Americans and Hispanic Americans, classified by Ogbu (1988) as immigrant minorities because they bring with them their primary cultural differences, have traditionally attempted to instill in children a sense of collectivity and cooperation (Ramirez & Castenada, 1974; Steward & Steward, 1973; Suzuki, 1980). Identity formation in ethnic adolescents is complicated and enriched by biculturalism, or the individual's ability to function adaptively in two cultural contexts, drawing from a repertoire of behaviors appropriate to each (Laosa, 1977).

Classic, Transition-Prone, and Contemporary Views of Parent-Adolescent Relationship

According to the *classic view* based on psychoanalytic formulations (Blos, 1979; Erikson, 1959; A. Freud, 1969), and Piagetian stage theory (Kohlberg, 1969; Piaget 1932/1965), identity formation during adolescence is achieved by emotional separation from family and a transfer of affection to peers, resulting in negation of the child's heteronomous view of authority as unilateral and role-bound in favor of an autonomous view of authority arising from symmetrical and reciprocal relationships established among peers; adolescents who remain emotionally attached to parents and respectful of their authority are said to suffer from a "foreclosed identity."

The classic view contrasts sharply with its antithesis, the *transition-proneness view*, put forth by contemporary researchers concerned with the prevention of "problem behavior" (e.g., Jessor & Jessor, 1978). By "transition-proneness" they refer to a set of behaviors that emerges in early adolescence: higher value on independence, increased social activism, decreased religiosity, perceived relaxation of parental standards, and increased reliance on friends relative to parents. Middle-class adolescents value self-reliance and the ability to make their own decisions extremely highly (Feather, 1980; Greenberger, 1984). These developmentally appropriate behaviors are viewed as problematic because they are often (but not typically) accompanied by lowered achievement, early sexual experience, and substance use. Researchers or practitioners concerned with preventing such undesirable behavior advocate traditional values and restrictive practices in order to postpone or avert the problems sometimes associated with movement toward independence and intensification of peer relations. Their advice conflicts with that of classic Freudian or Piagetian stage theorists to "let go."

Parents are caught on the horns of a dilemma—adolescents, in order to become self-regulated, individuated, competent individuals, require both freedom to explore and experiment, and protection from experiences that are clearly dangerous. The classic view emphasizes the importance of the former; its antithesis, the importance of the latter.

What I call the *contemporary view* has sought to resolve this dilemma. It fosters interdependence rather than emotional autonomy or continued dependence, emphasizing, as in another transitional period—infancy—the role of security of attachment in facilitating adolescent individuation and exploratory behavior (Hartup, 1979; Hill, 1980; Hill & Holmbeck, 1986). In place of the "classic" emphasis on emotional detachment from parents or the "transition-proneness" emphasis on delaying psychosocial maturity to minimize problem behaviors, these contemporary investigators stress the *balance* between agency and communion, between separation and connection, and between conflict and harmony in family relationships as the sine qua non that defines adolescent maturity. A substantial body of empirical literature is accumulating that supports a contemporary synthesis, in contrast to the classic view or its antithesis.

Cooper, Grotevant, and Condon (1982, 1983) describe the effective family system as one that avoids both enmeshment, in which individuality is discouraged in favor of exaggerated family harmony, and disengagement, in which family members are so separate that they have little effect on each other. They refer to the *individuated* adolescent or the effective parent as one who achieves a *balance* between individuality (clear, differentiated presentation of one's own point of view) and connectedness (responsiveness to, and respect for, the views of others). Similarly, Steinberg and Silverberg (1986) claim that, for boys, a subjective sense of self-reliance develops out of family relations that are neither very close nor very distant, and that resistance to peer pressure is facilitated by close but not enmeshed family ties.

Reiss, Oliveri, and Curd (1983) use a systems approach to group families into a four-category typology based on high or low scores on two problem-solving dimensions: *configuration* or cognitive integration of parts into a complex, patterned whole; and *coordination* or interpersonal integration of each family's contribution into a harmonious whole. Their ideal (*environment-sensitive*) families are organized optimally to investigate both the cognitive and social dimensions of the environment because they are high on both dimensions. By contrast, the *consensus-sensitive* family and the *achievement-sensitive* family are both unbalanced, the former, high on coordination but low on configuration, is interpersonally oriented, seeking harmony at the expense of information; and the latter, low on coordination and high on configuration, is individualistically oriented at the expense of group processes. *Distance-sensitive* families, low on both dimensions, explore neither the inner nor the outer world. Both the ideal (environment-sensitive) and the least competent (distance-sensitive) family types generated adolescents who were highly autonomous; autonomy is reflected in the environment-sensitive home as prosocial assertiveness, and in the distance-sensitive home as depressed alienation. Thus, adolescent autonomy, and the socialization patterns that encourage it, have ambivalent implications for mental health, contributing to both healthy individuation and to problem behaviors (see also Baumrind, in press).

The importance to adolescents of parental support is underscored by data from Hauser, Powers, Noam, Jacobson, Weiss, and Follansbee (1984) and Powers, Hauser, Schwartz, Noam, and Jacobson (1983). These investigators hypothesized that adolescent ego development would be enhanced by exposure to conflicting points of view within the family as well as by opportunities to share one's own perspective and take the role of others. They expected to find that cognitive conflicts would accelerate adolescents' ego development by disequilibrating their expectations. Instead, they found that adolescent ego development was related not to parent behaviors hypothesized to be cognitively stimulating (challenging and focusing), but instead to acknowledgment and support of the adolescent's perspective. They concluded that challenging behaviors have a salutary effect, primarily within a context of acceptance and support. In our own study, parents' responsiveness—that is, encouragement of independence, individuality, and verbal give-and-take together with warmth and support—correlated highly with all aspects of adolescents' competence, and with love and respect for parents (Baumrind, in press).

Theorists have divided adolescence into two or three phases that differ in the extent of adolescent-parent conflict. Josselson (1973) differentiates the process of individuation into two phases. The first, called the *practicing* phase, is characterized by an unambivalent assertion of will as adolescents define themselves oppositionally to their parents and other authority figures. Power relations between adolescents and their parents in the "practicing" phase are typically still asymmetrical, and parents may appropriately continue to make be-

havioral demands while allowing psychological freedom. Decrease in mutual support and regard may occur at this time, accompanied by avoidance or escalation of conflict rather than confrontation and resolution (Hill & Holmbeck, 1987). This period can be especially difficult for mothers and daughters (Hill & Holmbeck, 1987; Josselson, 1973; Montemayor, 1982; Smetana, in press). But in the second, *rapprochement* phase, feeling safer from regressive childhood impulses, midadolescents attempt to reestablish amicable bonds with parents, provided that their parents give them room to grow. Most adolescents at this time report feeling "close" or "very close" to their parents (80% to their mothers, according to Greenberger, 1984).

Beatrix Hamburg (1974) delineated adolescence into early, mid, and late phases, with each phase differing in the optimal balance of parental authority and adolescent autonomy. In *early adolescence*, coinciding with junior high school, the pubescent youth assumes a pseudoindependent stance as part of the process of de-idealizing parents (Smollar & Youniss, 1985; Steinberg & Silverberg, 1986). Early adolescence corresponds to Turiel's (1978) fourth level of social-conventional reasoning in which children typically come to question parental authority and social expectations as bases for following convention. Unlike themselves as children, early adolescents can differentiate between legitimate and illegitimate authority and justify their claim to greater participation in decisions that affect them; they are likely to regard issues as personal that their parents regard as important conventional matters still under adult jurisdiction, a mismatch that may result in generational conflict. *Midadolescence*, coinciding with the high school years, brings forth cognitive and social gains associated with Turiel's fifth level in which systematic concepts of social structure emerge and adult-supported conventions are once again affirmed so that parents can increase both responsibilities and entitlements in the domains of money management and individual liberty, allowing more events to fall under adolescents' personal jurisdiction. A second period of estrangement can occur toward *late adolescence* with level 6 negation of convention as "nothing but" arbitrary nonfunctional societal standards. For example, in Smetana's study (in press) both boys and girls reported poorer (but not poor) relations with their mothers at around 18 than at any previous period. A truly symmetrical intellectual relationship is not experienced as genuinely appropriate by most parents or their adolescents until at least graduation from high school.

In sum, interdependence rather than independence or emotional detachment from significant adults facilitates adolescent individuation and exploration. As the child matures through the phases of adolescence the appropriate ratio of autonomy to control increases, particularly in domains that adolescents regard as under their personal jurisdiction. Only in late adolescence, sometimes with an intervening "moratorium" in the form of college or apprenticeship, does emancipation become the central developmental issue.

Effective Parenting Styles

Typological analyses often provide more meaningful information about individuals and relationships than linear analyses (Hinde & Dennis, 1986). Factor analyses of parents' behavior typically yield two dimensions, which are manifestations in parents of demandingness and responsiveness (see Maccoby & Martin, 1983, for a review). Baumrind has used these dimensions to derive a fourfold classification of parenting behavior that describes how parents reconcile the joint needs of children for nurturance and limit-setting.

The operational definitions of these four prototypes—Authoritative, Authoritarian, Permissive, and Rejecting-Neglecting—differ somewhat depending upon social context, developmental period, and method of assessment, but share certain essential features. *Authoritative* parents are both demanding and responsive. They monitor and impart clear standards for their children's conduct. They are assertive, but not intrusive or restrictive. Their disciplinary methods are supportive rather than punitive. They want their children to be assertive as well as socially responsible, and self-regulated as well as cooperative. *Permissive* or nondirective parents are more responsive than they are demanding. They are nontraditional and lenient, do not require mature behavior, allow considerable self-regulation, and avoid confrontation. *Authoritarian* parents are demanding and directive, but not responsive. They are obedience- and status-oriented and expect their orders to be obeyed without explanation. They provide an orderly environment and a clear set of regulations and monitor their children's activities carefully. Not all traditional parents are authoritarian. *Rejecting-Neglecting* or disengaged parents are neither demanding nor responsive. They do not structure and monitor, and are not supportive, but may be actively rejecting or else neglect their childrearing responsibilities altogether.

The consequences for children prior to adolescence in the *Family Socialization and Developmental Competence Project* (*FSP*) of these four parental styles may be summarized as follows. Children from *authoritative* homes have consistently been found to be more instrumentally competent—agentic, communal, and cognitively competent—than other children (for an overview see Hill, 1980, and Maccoby & Martin, 1983; for examples of empirical studies see Baumrind, 1987; Clark, 1983; Ritter, Dornbusch, Leiderman, Roberts, & Fraleigh, 1987). The effects of *authoritarian* upbringing in early childhood have been found to be more harmful for (middle-class) boys than girls (Baumrind, 1971, 1989), preschool white girls than black (Baumrind, 1972), and white than Hispanic boys (Dornbusch et al., 1987). Preschool and primary school girls from *permissive* homes, compared to those from authoritative homes, were markedly less self-assertive (Baumrind, 1971, 1989), and preschool children of both sexes were less cognitively competent. Generally speaking, children from *rejecting-neglecting* homes tended to be the least competent of all.

When their children were adolescents, parents in the FSP were jointly classified by two psychologists into six types with one of these types further subdivided (for a total of 7 groups). Index of agreement (kappa) is .89. Three parent behavior scales were used to define the six types, with a fourth scale used to subdivide the "directive" type. The three major scales are *Directive/Conventional Control (D/C C)*, containing items that assess restrictive control and conventional values; *Assertive Control (AC)*, assessing firm, clear, nonrestrictive monitoring of adolescents' life-style and activities, confrontation and enforcement of rules; and *Supportive Control (SC)*, assessing considerateness, responsive discipline, principled use of rational explanations to influence adolescent, intellectual stimulation, and encouragement of individuation. The fourth scale, *Intrusive (I)*, assesses officiousness, subversion of the child's independence, and overcontrol. A small group of Directive families were not intrusive (I not high).

There were 48 single families and 81 intact families with data on both adolescents and their parents. Parents in the same families were classified separately, and then combined. One single and 4 intact families could not be classified because either (1) an extrinsic stressor, such as a developmental anomaly resulting in retarded growth, or a recent family death had a prepotent effect, or (2) parents' scores diverged too much to evaluate their joint effect. For the 124 families who could be classified, percentage exact agreement for mothers and fathers in the same family was 76%. When there was slight to moderate divergence, precedence was given to the mother's scores because (1) we knew from correlational analyses (Baumrind, in press) that mothers were more influential than fathers in affecting adolescents' (especially their daughters') behavior.

Adolescents grouped by parent type were contrasted on six attributes (three competence and three problem behavior item composites): *Overall Competence* (comparison of adolescent's rating with average of ten psychologists' Q-sort ratings of the "ideal" fifteen year old); *Autonomous* (emancipated from adult control, courageous, exploratory, poised); *Prosocial* (self-regulated, considerate, friendly, reciprocal); *Internalizing Problem Behavior* (socially withdrawn, anxious, depressed); *Externalizing Problem Behavior* (overactive, inattentive, aggressive); and *Substance User Types* (5-point scale: 1, virtual nonusers of alcohol and drugs; 2, recreational user of alcohol; 3, casual user of cannabis; 4, heavy user of alcohol or drugs; 5, dependent user of alcohol or drugs). Mean interrater reliability across items for the adolescent ratings is .91 and for the parent ratings is .85.

Results of the ANOVA comparisons were highly significant on all six adolescent attributes across the parent types. In the definitions of parent types that follow, "high" and "low" pertain to one-half standard deviation from the total mean for *each* family, rather than for the average of parents placed in the parent type.

Adolescents from (21) *Authoritative* families (high on *AC* and *SC*) were outstandingly competent and prosocial. They manifested the lowest incidence of internalizing problem behavior and also had a lower incidence of drug use than all other groups of adolescents (except those from Nonauthoritarian-Directive families). Authoritative parents are characterized by their rational, agentic style of control. Authoritative parents successfully model commitment, reciprocity between obligations and entitlements, and integration of agentic and communal qualities. Because authoritative parents are nurturant, both their approval and their withdrawal of approval are likely to be highly effective reinforcers.

Adolescents from (25) *Democratic* homes (medium on *AC*, high on *SC*, not-high on *D/C C*) compared to those from Authoritative homes were not significantly less competent, prosocial, and autonomous. However, compared to Authoritative families, they used more drugs. Democratic parents are more responsive than demanding, are agentic but not officious, and set limits when necessary, although their preference is to be lenient. The slight imbalance in favor of responsiveness over demandingness did not enhance or detract from adolescents' competence but it did affect drug use.

Adolescents from (13) *"Good-Enough"* homes (see Winnicott, 1965) (medium-low to medium-high on the three major definers) were, as the name suggests, adequately but not outstandingly, competent and without serious problem manifestations.

Adolescents from (28) *Directive* homes (medium-high or high on *D/C C* and *AC* with each parent high on at least one; medium-low or low on *SC*) were less generally competent and prosocial than adolescents from either Democratic or Authoritative homes. They used less drugs than adolescents from Democratic homes. Using correlational analyses we found that Directive/Conventional control, the distinctive feature of Directive parents, was associated with low externalizing problem behavior such as drug use, and with behavioral conformity, but not with internalization of prosocial values, mature ego development, individuation, or secure attachment to parents (Baumrind, in press). Hauser & colleagues (1984) have linked *constraining* discourse (e.g., withholding, indifference, devaluing) to lower adolescent ego development, and *enabling* discourse (e.g., problem solving, explaining, acceptance, and empathy) to higher development. *Directive* parents were subdivided into those (21) who were *Authoritarian* (high or medium high on *I*) and those (7) who were *Nonauthoritarian* (medium on *I*; none were low). Authoritarian control, by contrast to authoritative or democratic control, is status-oriented, nonnegotiated, and constraining. Adolescents from Authoritarian-Directive homes differed from those from Nonauthoritarian-Directive homes in that they (girls especially) used more drugs and exhibited more internalizing problem behavior. Thus, when Directive parents are intrusive, they become less effective.

Adolescents from (7) *Nondirective* homes (low *D/C C* and *AC*; medium-high or high *SC*) were medium-low in competence, but manifested more internalizing problem behavior than any group of adolescents except those whose parents were Unengaged. Children from Nondirective homes used more marijuana and other illicit drugs than those from Authoritative or Directive homes, but not more than those from Democratic or Unengaged homes. Nondirective families do not set limits and are permissive because they are unwilling to engage in conflict, in contrast to Democratic families where leniency during adolescence reflects a commitment to democratic ideology and respect for adolescents' autonomy. The reason we called these families "nondirective" rather than "permissive" was because mothers were not in fact highly supportive.

Adolescents from (30) *Unengaged* homes (low or medium-low on *SC* and *AC*) were the least prosocial and individuated, and suffered most from internalizing and externalizing problem behavior. Adolescents with unengaged parents were heavy drug users and autonomous. Indeed many were functionally emancipated. Compared to those from Democratic homes, girls from Unengaged homes were less prosocial and competent.

When the parent types were contrasted on levels of adolescent drug use, the results were highly significant. Adolescents with the highest use came from Unengaged families; adolescents with the lowest use came from Nonauthoritarian-Directive homes, followed closely by those from Authoritative homes. An important finding is that Authoritative parents were at least as effective as Authoritarian parents in deterring adolescent drug use, and that significantly more heavy drug users, i.e. Types 4 and 5, came from Democratic than from Authoritative homes. However, heavy users (Types 4 and 5) from Democratic families were much more competent than heavy users from other families, reinforcing the importance of parenting style as a protective factor, even for drug abusers.

In sum, adolescents' developmental progress is held back by directive, officious, or unengaged practices and facilitated by reciprocal, balanced interaction characteristic of both Authoritative and Democratic parents. Directive parents who are authoritarian generate internalizing problem behaviors and are less successful at curtailing drug use. Directive parents who are not authoritarian effectively curtail adolescents' drug use but do not promote positive competence. These generalizations apply to both sexes and to intact and separated families. It should be noted, however, that family types differed by structure and by sex of targeted adolescent.

Disproportionately more girls were reared by Authoritative parents, and disproportionately fewer by Authoritarian-Directive and Disengaged parents. However, there were no sex differences in the total sample, even in expected directions (e.g., higher Autonomy for boys and higher Prosocial behavior for girls) and none that were significant within types.

For girls, but not for boys, those from intact families were significantly more prosocial and manifested less problem behavior and drug use. Family pattern and structure were related for adolescents. Disproportionately fewer single families of both sexes were Authoritative or Directive, and disproportionately more were Unengaged. Sample size was not adequate to disentangle statistically the effects of family type and family structure, or to examine the single families separately. However, the generalizations above also held when only the intact families were evaluated. Visual inspection of the means indicate that when single versus intact families were compared, there were no differences for Authoritative families. Adolescents from single Democratic families were as competent but used more drugs than their peers from intact homes. Sons of single Authoritarian-Directive parents were less competent than their counterparts from intact homes. Children from intact Unengaged homes were as incompetent as their counterparts from single homes, but the girls used less drugs. Thus, the problems caused by marital separation are not inevitable and appear to differ by family type, in general increasing

753 ▪

problems already apparent in the intact families of that type.

Ethnic Families of Color

Families of color differ between and within ethnic groups but share common concerns about bicultural identity and assimilation that are not shared with the dominant culture. An emic description of behavior from within each culture is preferable to a purely etic approach that imposes a measurement or explanation external to the culture being studied (Berry, 1980). Such studies should: (1) reflect the unique survival strategies that determine the socialization goals of each ethnic group in addition to those that each shares with other cultures; (2) consider issues of bicultural identity and assimiliation; (3) control for socioeconomic status and geographical location; (4) match ethnic origin of subject with examiner; and (5) evaluate subcultural variations within the Afro-American, Asian-American, and Hispanic ethnic groups.

It is necessary to understand the special survival problems and strategies adopted by each subculture to cope with its environment and ethnic status (Ogbu, 1981). For example, the continued importance of a network of kin, especially of the adolescent mother's own mother to her daughter, as well as to her grandchild, has been documented in the black community (Furstenberg, 1976; Silverstein & Krate, 1975; Stevens, 1984). Socialization methods which by middle-class white standards appear authoritarian, punitive, or seductive are typically intended to prepare black adolescents to cope with the hazards of contemporary ghetto life. In lower-class families, strategies that appear authoritarian from a middle-class perspective may be used to inculcate obedience and conformity (Kohn, 1977). "Constricted" rather than "elaborated" codes of communication are employed that foreclose verbal give-and-take in authority-subordinate relationships (Bernstein, 1970). Parental practices that would be overly restrictive in a benign middle-class environment may provide optimum supervision in an urban ghetto (Baldwin, Baldwin, & Cole, in press; Baumrind, 1972). The early shift from adult to peer orientation seen as necessary by many black ghetto parents encourages a linguistic pattern, identification, and socialization process antithetical to the middle-class school culture, despite its richness, complexity, and coherence within the poor black culture (Young, 1974). Young identified a style of "contest" interaction in which black school age children are teased into exhibiting independence and assertiveness toward their mothers in order to break the dependent tie and to foster the idea that the interpersonal, if not the work, environment is negotiable. Sroufe and Ward (1980) identified a similar pattern of maternal-toddler interaction that they called "seductive" and conducive to insecure attachment and psychopathology, thus offering a deficit interpretation from an etic or universalist perspective that is a difference from Young's emic or relativist perspective. According to Harrison, Serafica, and McAdoo (1984), bicultural adaptation is the overriding socialization goal of black families. However, the two studies with ethnic families of color that have compared authoritative with other parenting styles (Clark, 1983; Dornbusch et al., 1987) do not examine bicultural identity.

In their large-sample study using questionnaire data obtained from adolescents to assess both their competencies and their parents' styles, Dornbusch and colleagues concluded that for the population as a whole, grades were associated negatively with both authoritarian and permissive parenting practices, and positively with authoritative practices. Prediction, however, was best among white students, and the negative effects of authoritarianism were absent for Hispanic males and Asians.

Using a small sample, ethnographic approach, Reginald Clark, an "insider," concluded that the authoritative style of mutual empowerment, high support, high expectations, close supervision, and respect for their child's intellectual achievement characterizes poor black parents of high achievers, whereas authoritarian or permissive styles characterize parents of low achievers. His description of these parent styles (1983, pp. 2–3, 200) provide excellent processual descriptions that are applicable equally to any cultural group. Clark argues that these processual variables take precedence over structural factors such as ethnicity or family intactness in generating competence.

At present, as Hill concluded, we lack definitive information on adolescence in ethnic families of color (but see reviews on the values and socialization goals of Asian-American and black families by Harrison et al., 1984; and on Hispanic families by Ramirez & Castenada, 1974). Although some family processes and dynamics have been found to determine success or failure across subcultures, Procrustean assumptions are unwarranted when life realities vary the indigenous competencies parents attempt to generate in adolescents in order that they can master their particular cultural tasks.

References

Bakan, D. (1966). *The duality of existence: Isolation and communion in western man.* Boston: Beacon Press.

Baldwin, A. L., Baldwin, C., & Cole, R. E. (in press). Stress-resistant families and stress-resistant children. To appear in J. Rolf, A. Masten, D. Cicchetti, K. Neuchtherlin, & S. Weintraub (Eds.), *Risk and protective factors in the development of psychopathology.*

Baumrind, D. (1971). Current patterns of parental authority. *Developmental Psychology Monographs, 4* (1, part 2).

Baumrind, D. (1972). An exploratory study of socialization effects on black children: Some black-white comparisons. *Child Development, 43,* 261–267.

Baumrind, D. (1987). A developmental perspective on adolescent risk-taking behavior in contemporary America. In W. Damon (Ed.), *New directions for child development: Adolescent health and social behavior* (Vol. 37, pp. 92–126). San Francisco: Jossey-Bass.

Baumrind, D. (1989). Rearing competent children. In W. Damon (Ed.), *Child development today and tomorrow* (pp. 349–378). San Francisco: Jossey-Bass.

Baumrind, D. (in press). Effective parenting during the early adolescent transition. To be published in P. A. Cowan & E. M. Hetherington (Eds.), *Advances in family research* (Vol. 2). Hillsdale, NJ: Lawrence Erlbaum Associates.

Baumrind, D., & Black, A. E. (1967). Socialization practices associated with dimensions of competence in preschool boys and girls. *Child Development, 38,* 291–327.

Bellah, R. N., Madsen, R., Sullivan, W. M., Swidler, A., & Tipton, S. M. (1985). *Habits of the heart: Individualism and commitment in American life.* Berkeley and Los Angeles: University of California Press.

Bernstein, B. (1970). Elaborated and restricted codes: Their social origins and some consequences. In K. Danziger (Ed.), *Readings in child socialization* (pp. 165–186). New York: Pergamon Press.

Berry, J. W. (1980). Introduction to methodology. In H. C. Triandis & J. W. Berry (Eds.), *Handbook of cross-cultural psychology* (Vol. 2, pp. 1–28). Boston: Allyn & Bacon.

Blos, P. (1979). The second individuation process. In P. Blos (Ed.), *The adolescent passage: Developmental issues of adolescence* (pp. 141–170). New York: International University Press.

Clark, R. (1983). *Family life and school achievement: Why poor black children succeed or fail.* Chicago: University of Chicago Press.

Cooper, C. R., Grotevant, H. D., & Condon, S. M. (1982). Methodological challenges of selectivity in family interaction: Addressing temporal patterns of individuation. *Journal of Marriage and the Family, 44,* 749–754.

Cooper, C. R., Grotevant, H. D., & Condon, S. M. (1983). Individuality and connectedness in the family as a context for adolescent identity formation and role-taking skill. In H. D. Grotevant & C. R. Cooper (Eds.), *New directions for child development: Vol. 22. Adolescent development in the family* (pp. 43–59). San Francisco: Jossey-Bass.

Dornbusch, S. M., Ritter, P. L., Leiderman, P. H., Roberts, D. F., & Fraleigh, M. J. (1987). The relation of parenting style to adolescent performance. *Child Development, 58,* 1244–1257.

Erikson, E. H. (1959). Identity and the life cycle: Selected papers. *Psychological Issues, 1*(1).

Feather, N. (1980). Values in adolescence. In J. Adelson (Ed.), *Handbook of adolescent psychology* (pp. 247–294). New York: John Wiley.

Freud, A. (1969). Adolescence as a developmental disturbance. In G. Kaplan & S. Lebovici (Eds.), *Adolescence: Psychosocial perspectives* (pp. 5–10). New York: Basic Books.

Furstenberg, F. (1976). *Unplanned parenthood: The social consequences of teenage childbearing.* New York: Free Press.

Gilligan, C. (1982). *In a different voice: Psychological theory and women's development.* Cambridge: Harvard University Press.

Gilligan, C. (1987). Adolescent development reconsidered. In C. E. Irwin, Jr. (Ed.), *New directions for child development,* (Vol. 37, pp. 63–92). San Francisco: Jossey-Bass.

Greenberger, E. (1984). Defining psychosocial maturity in adolescence. In P. Karoly & J. J. Steffen (Eds.), *Adolescent behavior disorders: Foundations and contemporary concerns* (rev. ed., pp. 3–39). Lexington, MA: D. C. Heath.

Hamburg, B. A. (1974). Coping in early adolescence: The special challenges of the junior high school period. In Gerald Caplan (Ed.), S. Arieti (Series Ed.), *American handbook of psychiatry: Vol. 2. Child and adolescent psychiatry, sociocultural and community psychiatry* (2nd ed., pp. 385–397). New York: Basic Books.

Harrison, A., Serafica, F., & McAdoo, H. (1984). Ethnic families of color. In R. D. Parke (Ed.), *Review of child development research: Vol. 7. The family* (pp. 329–371). Chicago: University of Chicago Press.

Hartup, W. W. (1979). The social worlds of childhood. *American Psychologist, 34,* 944–950.

Hauser, S. T., Powers, S. I., Noam, G. G., Jacobson, A. M., Weiss, B., & Follansbee, D. J. (1984). Familial contexts of adolescent ego development. *Child Development, 55,* 195–213.

Hetherington, E. M., & Camara, K. A. (1984). Families in transition: The processes of dissolution and reconstitution. In R. D. Parke (Ed.), *Review of child development research: Vol. 7. The family* (pp. 398–440). Chicago: University of Chicago Press.

Hetherington, E. M., Cox, M., & Cox, R. (1985). Long-term effects of divorce and remarriage on the adjustment of children. *Journal of the American Academy of Child Psychiatry, 24,* 518–530.

Hill, J. P. (1980). The early adolescent and the family. In M. Johnson (Ed.), *The seventy-ninth yearbook of the National Society for the Study of Education* (pp. 32–55). Chicago: University of Chicago Press.

Hill, J. P. (1987). Research on adolescents and their families: Past and prospect. In C. E. Irwin (Ed.), *New directions for child development* (Vol. 37, pp. 13–31). San Francisco: Jossey-Bass.

Hill, J. P., & Holmbeck, G. N. (1986). Attachment and autonomy during adolescence. In G. Whitehurst (Ed.), *Annals of child development* (Vol. 3, pp. 145–189). Greenwich, CT: JAI Press.

Hill, J. P., & Holmbeck, G. N. (1987). Familial adaptation to biological change during adolescence. In R. M. Lerner & T. T. Foch (Eds.), *Biological-psychosocial interactions in early adolescence* (pp. 207–233). Hillsdale, NJ: Lawrence Erlbaum Associates.

Hinde, R. A., & Dennis, A. (1986). Categorizing individuals: An alternative to linear analysis. *International Journal of Behavioral Development*, 105–119.

Jessor, R., & Jessor, S. L. (1978). Theory testing in longitudinal research on marijuana use. In D. B. Kandel (Ed.), *Longitudinal research on drug use: Empirical findings and methodological issues* (pp. 41–71). Washington, DC: Hemisphere.

Josselson, R. L. (1973). Psychodynamic aspects of identity formation in college women. *Journal of Youth and Adolescence*, 2, 3–52.

Kohlberg, L. (1969). Stage and sequence: The cognitive-developmental approach to socialization. In D. A. Goslin (Ed.), *Handbook of socialization theory and research* (pp. 347–480). Chicago: Rand McNally.

Kohn, M. L. (1977). *Class and conformity: A study in values* (2nd ed.). Chicago: University of Chicago Press.

Laosa, L. M. (1977). Cognitive styles and learning strategies research: Some of the areas in which psychology can contribute to personalized instruction in multi-cultural education. *Journal of Teacher Education*, 28, 26–30.

Lasch, C. (1978). *The culture of narcissism: American life in an age of diminishing expectations*. New York: Norton.

Leary, T. (1957). *Interpersonal diagnosis of personality: A functional theory and methodology for personality evaluation*. New York: Ronald Press.

Lonner, W. J. (1980). The search for psychological universals. In H. C. Triandis & W. W. Lambert (Eds.), *Handbook of cross-cultural psychology* (Vol. 1, pp. 143–204). Boston: Allyn & Bacon.

Maccoby, E. E., & Martin, J. A. (1983). Socialization in the context of the family. Parent-child interaction. In E. M. Hetherington (Ed.), P. H. Mussen (Series Ed.), *Handbook of child psychology: Vol. 4. Socialization, personality, and social development* (pp. 1–101). New York: Wiley.

Marcia, J. E. (1980). Identity in adolescence. In J. Adelson (Ed.), *Handbook of adolescent psychology* (pp. 159–187). New York: Wiley.

Montemayor, R. (1982). The relationship between parent-adolescent conflict and the amount of time adolescents spend alone and with parents and peers. *Child Development*, 53, 1512–1519.

Ogbu, J. U. (1981). Origins of human competence: A cultural-ecological perspective. *Child Development*, 52, 413–429.

Ogbu, J. U. (1988). Culture, development, and education. In A. D. Pelligrini (Ed.), *Psychological bases of early education* (pp. 245–273). London: Wiley.

Piaget, J. (1965). *Moral judgment of the child*. New York: Free Press. (Original work published 1932.)

Powers, S. I., Hauser, S. T., Schwartz, J. M., Noam, G. G., & Jacobson, A. M. (1983). Adolescent ego development and family interaction: A structural-developmental perspective. In H. D. Grotevant & C. R. Cooper (Eds.), *Adolescent development in the family* (pp. 5–26). San Francisco: Jossey-Bass.

Ramirez, M., & Castenada, A. (1974). *Cultural democracy, bicognitive development, and education*. San Francisco: Academic Press.

Reiss, D., Oliveri, M. E., & Curd, K. (1983).

Family paradigm and adolescent social behavior. In H. D. Grotevant & C. R. Cooper (Eds.), *New directions for child development: Adolescent development in the family* (pp. 77–92). San Francisco: Jossey-Bass.

Sampson, E. E. (1988). The debate on individualism: Indigenous psychologies of the individual and their role in personal and societal functioning. *American Psychologist, 43*(1), 15–22.

Silverstein, B., & Krate, R. (1975). *Children of the dark ghetto: A developmental psychology.* New York: Praeger.

Smetana, J. G. (in press). Concepts of self and social convention: Adolescents' and parents' reasoning about hypothetical and actual family conflicts. In M. R. Gunnar (Ed.), *21st Minnesota symposium on child psychology.* Hillsdale, NJ: Lawrence Erlbaum Associates.

Smollar, J., & Youniss, J. (1985, April). Transformations in adolescents' perceptions of parents. Paper presented at the Biennial Meetings of the Society for Research in Child Development, Toronto.

Springer, C., & Wallerstein, J. S. (1983). Young adolescents' responses to their parents' divorces. In L. A. Kurdek (Ed.), *New directions for child development: Vol. 19. Children and divorce* (pp. 15–28). San Francisco: Jossey-Bass.

Sroufe, L. A., & Ward, M. J. (1980). Seductive behavior of mothers of toddlers: Occurrences, correlates, and family origins. *Child Development, 51,* 1222–1229.

Steinberg, L., & Silverberg, S. B. (1986). The vicissitudes of autonomy in early adolescence. *Child Development, 57,* 841–851.

Stevens, J. H., Jr. (1984). Black grandmothers' and black adolescent mothers' knowledge about parenting. *Developmental Psychology, 20*(6), 1017–1025.

Steward, M., & Steward, D. (1973). The observation of Anglo-, Mexican-, and Chinese-American mothers teaching their children. *Child Development, 44,* 329–337.

Suzuki, H. H. (1980). The Asian-American family. In M. D. Fantine & R. Cardenas (Eds.), *Parenting in a multicultural society* (pp. 74–102). New York: Longman.

Turiel, E. (1978). Social regulations and domains of social concepts. In W. Damon (Ed.), *Directions for child development: Social cognition* (pp. 45–74). San Francisco: Jossey-Bass.

Wiggins, J. S. (1979). A psychological taxonomy of trait-descriptive terms: The interpersonal domain. *Journal of Personality and Social Psychology, 37,* 395–412.

Winnicott, D. W. (1965). *The maturational processes and the facilitating environment: Studies in the theory of emotional development.* New York: International Universities Press.

Young, V. H. (1974). A black American socialization pattern. *American Ethnologist, 1,* 405–413.

See Also

Conflict, Adolescent-Parent: A Model and a Method; Divorce, Effects on Adolescents; Divorce, Parental during Late Adolescence; Family Interaction, Gender Differences in; Family Life Education; Family Structure; Generation Gap; Generational Continuity and Change; Grandparent-Grandchild Relations; Parent-Adolescent Relations; Parent-Adolescent Relations in Mid and Late Adolescence; Parental Influence; Sibling Relationships in Adolescence.

During the preparation of this paper, the author was supported by a Research Scientist Award (#1-K05-MH00485) and a research grant (#1-RO1-MH38343) from the National Institute of Mental Health. During the adolescent phase of the research, the project was supported by a research grant (#1-RO1-DA01919) from the National Institute on Drug Abuse, and by one from the John D. and Catherine T. MacArthur Foundation. The William T. Grant Foundation has provided consistent and generous support of this longitudinal program of research including the present phase of analysis of the early adolescent data (supported by grant #84044973).

Peer Counseling: A Human Resource Program

Barbara B. Varenhorst

Palo Alto Peer Counseling Program

From observations of the trend of adolescent problems throughout the 1980s, one can conclude that youth are substituting drugs and technology (i.e., computers and video-games) for human interaction. It has been said that we live in an age of indifference that will become a permanent part of society unless significant changes are made. Peer Counseling is a human resource program that is proving to be an effective intervention tool for addressing these issues in homes, schools, churches, and communities throughout the nation. The essence of the concept is the training of nonprofessionals to provide help, support, and friendship to a defined peer group. Since the first school-based adolescent program was started in the Palo Alto, California, school district in 1970, the concept has expanded to various populations, ranging from elementary students to senior citizens and to such diverse "peer" groups as cancer patients, disabled people, prisoners, battered women, and single parents. However, the power and effectiveness of peer counseling is best demonstrated with adolescents, and the majority of existing programs are designed for youth from grades 7–12.

A natural part of adolescent development is the gradual movement away from parents and family and toward the peer group for further socialization, identity, friendship, and help. During adolescence peers carry more credibility, authority, power, and influence than at any other time of life. Acceptance or rejection by the peer group leaves a permanent imprinting on an adolescent's life; the inability to relate to peers can create problems in relationships throughout life. However, because of the power and influence of peers, youth represent a vast human resource that can be mobilized to provide friendship and constructive help with normal problems. By creating caring and cooperative school atmospheres for example, peers can reduce the cruelty and isolation that many youth experience in their schools. In fact, as young people learn how to be helping friends to their peers, provided opportunities to utilize these skills in service to others, they gradually acquire abilities and attitudes that assist them with coping with their own developmental tasks. These experiences and challenges powerfully affect their self-worth, achievement and efficacy.

Basic Structure

Implementing an effective peer counseling program involves attention to and implementation of five basic components. These are: (1) a defined *purpose*, (2) task-oriented *training*, (3) assigned *service* activities, (4) *supervision*, and (5) *evaluation*.

PURPOSE ▪ An essential element in the success of peer counseling programs is the focus on serving others rather than getting help for oneself. Therefore the target population to be served must be defined clearly, and for what purpose. The population and need define the content of training given to peer counselors and the service activities that follow. Typical examples are reducing drug use, truancy, or drop-outs; creating a warmer school atmosphere; reducing fights and conflicts on campus; or integrating non-English speaking students into the life and culture of the school.

TRAINING ▪ Desire and willingness to help is not sufficient to be an effective peer counselor. The quality of service youth can provide is directly related to the kind of training they receive, as well as their commitment to the program. The commitment is tested through voluntary enrollment or through a carefully screened process. Providing open enrollment instead of screening often attracts students who come for training seeking personal help, as well as students who themselves understand what it is like to have problems; these students often turn out to be the most effective peer counselors.

The training must be task-oriented, involving the teaching of skills, attitudes, and information that a student will employ to perform the needed services. Most training courses include basic interpersonal skills, such as how to initiate conversations with shy peers, listening and questioning, wel-

coming someone to a group, decision making, counseling versus advice giving, and how and when to make referrals. As part of their training students practice helping a peer with such problems as family concerns, peer relationships, health and drug issues, sexuality, and death and dying.

Training can be offered in a variety of settings, including elective classes during regular school hours, after-school weekly sessions, and summer or weekend retreats.

SERVICE ▪ A peer counseling *program* provides for training, personal growth and *service*. Often the service component is neglected in light of the personal growth that is a result of training, or due to difficulties in identifying appropriate service assignments. However, for the training to become a permanent part of their lives, peer counselors must be given opportunities to apply their training to appropriate and genuine tasks of helping others.

Most programs use students to work on an individual basis with peers assigned to them who do not have friends, or who lack social skills; special education students who need contacts with mainstream school life; students who need tutoring; or students entering the middle or high school who will benefit from upperclass buddies. Some students work with elementary students identified as needing an older student's help. Peer counselors can serve as group leaders, conflict management teams, or as coleaders of training groups. One of the most significant services students can perform is being a bridge between a troubled peer and a professional in such cases as potential suicide, drug abuse, or child abuse. Through peer-counseling referrals, situations have been identified that have saved lives.

Students may get credit for training, but normally do not receive pay or credit for service activities performed. Most peer counselors meet and work with their assigned counselee outside of class, on their own time, and often meet several times per week. Beyond the assigned activities, students are urged to make peer counseling a way of life, which involves giving care and help to anyone with whom they come in contact, whether assigned or merely encountered.

SUPERVISION ■ Supervision is critical both in terms of liability issues and a peer counselor's achievement and learning. A weekly practicum for active peer counselors where problems encountered can be discussed and work can be monitored is a very effective means of supervision.

EVALUATION ■ Periodic evaluations need to be conducted on the effectiveness of the training and on the results of the program with respect to the defined purpose or goal. This is done by collecting before and after data related to the target problem; through use of questionnaires collected from students and teachers; and by means of standardized surveys and instruments.

Benefits

The benefits of peer counseling as a human resource program have been only partially documented through hard research or evaluations. Anecdotal evidence is overwhelming, of principals demanding to know how their counterparts in other schools have made such dramatic changes in school climate; of teachers initially skeptical of the program becoming reliant on its services for their most at-risk students; of students themselves experiencing turnarounds in their self-regard, academic performance, and sense of personal direction and purpose.

Of the research evidence that does exist, Nancy Tobler's "meta-analysis" of 143 drug abuse prevention programs, published in the *Journal of Drug Issues* is very convincing. She found that unlike programs that primarily emphasized knowledge about drugs or personal growth, "peer programs were found to show a definite superiority" in effectiveness, and were especially useful with school-based populations. Benard's 1988 survey of the literature in *Prevention Forum* concludes that "there is no better way to ensure that prevention is empowerment than to make peer programs—in their truest sense of providing opportunities for meaningful participation and responsibility—the major approach in prevention programs for children and youth."

In a national study on early adolescents conducted by Search Institute involving 8,000 5th-9th graders and 10,000 of their parents, the youth were asked to rank the kinds of programs they would be interested in, if available to them. The three top-ranked programs were: (1) finding out how to do something good for others, (2) learning how to make friends and be a friend, and (3) finding out what is special about me. Peer counseling encompasses all three. The rapid growth of these programs over the last five years and the expansion of the concept into churches as peer ministry is another indication that peer counseling is meeting real needs.

Many starting programs have chosen the name of Peer Helping or Peer Facilitating, rather than Peer Counseling, feeling that the word "counseling" implies more expertise and training than is realistic for this type of program. When the national organization was started in 1987, it chose the name of the National Peer Helpers Association. This association now has over 1500 members and is serving as a network for all state and local programs in a variety of settings. A code of ethics and standards has been developed to monitor programs, and a quarterly journal keeps members informed of work being done nationally and in Canada, and provides up-to-date information on ideas and resources.

More information on peer counseling can be obtained by writing to Barbara B. Varenhorst, 350 Grove Drive, Portola Valley, California 94028.

References

Benard, Bonnie. (1988, January). Peer programs: The lodestone to prevention. *Prevention Forum.*

Search Institute. (1984). *Young adolescents and their parents: Summary of finding.* Minneapolis, MN (no author).

Tobler, Nancy. (1986). Meta-analysis of 143 adolescent drug prevention programs: Quantitative outcome results of program participants compared to a control or comparison group. *Journal of Drug Issues 16*(4), 537–567.

See Also

Dating during Adolescence; Friendships; Peer Relations and Influences; Peer Status Groups.

Peer Status Groups

Patricia L. East
University of California, San Diego

Sociometric groups were first recognized in the early 1930s in Moreno's (1934) classic study of group structure and relationships among institutionalized individuals. Sociometric methods, which assess the degree to which an individual is liked or disliked by other group members, have since been widely used to describe status hierarchy and friendship structure in children's and adolescents' peer groups. Particularly over the past decade, sociometric studies have enjoyed a renewed popularity due to the increasing awareness of the importance of peer relations in adolescent psychological, emotional, and cognitive development, and to evidence that a poor peer status in childhood is predictive of a variety of maladaptive outcomes in adulthood. Measures of sociometric status are currently being used to select children and adolescents for preventive intervention programs and to assess the success of those programs.

The most common assessment of peer status is the sociometric nomination procedure, which requires respondents to nominate a group member who satisfies a particular criterion, such as "whom do you like most?" or "whom do you like least?" Rating-scale methods, in which respondents rate each group member on a Likert-type scale according to a specified criterion, are also used to assess social status. The average rating received is a person's score. In comparing these methods, nomination procedures typically assess high-choice companions and high-impact individuals, whereas rating scales measure an individual's overall acceptability or likability in the peer group. Moreover, the stability of peer status varies depending on the sociometric device employed with nomination procedures yielding more variable and less stable scores than the peer-rating method (Gresham, 1981).

Beginning in the late 1970s, attention shifted from an emphasis on status hierarchy along social acceptance and rejection continuums (e.g., Moore & Updegraff, 1964) to a more categorical orientation in which specific *types* of individuals could be identified based on their shared social status within a group. By simultaneously analyzing positive and negative sociometric nomination scores, Peery (1979) introduced two new dimensions of social status, *social impact* and *social preference*. Social impact refers to the prominence of a child's negative and positive behaviors and is operationalized as the number of positive nominations *plus* the number of negative nominations. Social preference refers to the predominance of favorable peer evaluations and is indexed by the number of positive nominations *minus* the number of negative nominations.

Based on these two social dimensions, four peer status groups can be identified: (1) *popular* (both high impact and highly preferred); (2) *amiable* (low impact but preferred); (3) *isolated* (low impact and nonpreferred); and (4) *rejected* (high impact but highly nonpreferred). More recently, Coie, Dodge, and Coppotelli (1982) identified a fifth sociometric group of *controversial* children who receive many positive nominations *and* many negative nominations. This pattern of sociometric scores suggests that by exhibiting highly salient behaviors of both a negative and positive valence, these children are very visible members of the peer group.

Using Peery's conceptual model of sociometric status it becomes possible to distinguish between two types of individuals who lack friends: those who exhibit excessive aggressive-disruptive behavior and consequently are actively disliked by their peers (rejectees); and those who are shy and withdrawn and as a result are simply not nominated by their classmates (isolates). By discriminating between children whose histories involve different interpersonal problems, clinicians are able to design and implement more tailored and effective social skills intervention programs.

In general, the peer status groups comprise the following percentages of a sample: 48% average status, 17% rejected, 16% popular, 11% neglected, and 8% controversial. Generally, there is a high degree of stability of membership in a sociometric group, with the rejected group having the highest long-term stability and membership in a neglected status group showing the lowest stability (Bukowski & Newcomb, 1984). When rejectees' status does shift, it is to the neglected or average-status groups with very few rejectees achieving a popular status. Those in the neglected group eventually move toward more positive social status categories (i.e., average or popular) and almost never become rejected or controversial (Coie & Dodge, 1983).

Various methods are used to assign individuals to sociometric groups. The most common procedure uses nomination scores and involves the following criterion: (1) individuals receiving positive nomination scores at least .5 standard deviation (SD) *above* the mean for positive scores and negative nominations at least .5 SD *below* the mean for negative scores are classified as popular; (2) the rejected group scores at least .5 SD *above* the mean on negative and .5 SD *below* the mean on positive nominations; (3) the neglected group receives scores .5 SD *below* the mean on both positive and negative nominations; (4) individuals who comprise the controversial group receive nominations .5 SD *above* the mean on both positive and negative nominations; and (5) those who do not satisfy the criteria for inclusion into the above four groups are classified as average.

Observational research has yielded much descriptive information on the behavioral concomitants of the five above-noted sociometric groups. Correlates of peer popularity include physical attractiveness, intelligence, athletic success, cooperation, ability to lead others, and sociability. Individuals identified as controversial are observed to be disruptive and aggressive but with good leadership and assertiveness skills. The peer-rejected group is characterized as physically and verbally aggressive, off-task, highly disruptive in the classroom, and not performing well scholastically. In addition, rejected youngsters tend to interact with companions who are also unpopular and spend a majority of their time in younger and smaller groups than popular or average-status group members (Ladd, 1983). Neglected or peer-withdrawn adolescents have conflicting behavioral profiles, with some researchers characterizing neglectees as shy, anxious, passive, and exhibiting signs of depression and emotional detachment, while other investigators have found that neglected youngsters show no more behavioral problems than average-status or popular children. The inconsistency across studies is thought to reflect the internalizing nature of neglectees' problems that may cause them to go undetected. Only the rejected and neglected status groups are associated with a variety of concurrent disorders and the risk for later adult adjustment problems. The peer-neglected status is most often related to later internalizing problems such as anxiousness, low self-esteem, and mental health difficulties (Ledingham, 1981), while peer-rejection is often predictive of externalizing problems such as delinquency and adult conduct disorders (Roff & Sells, 1968).

One limitation of sociometric methods is that, while they are useful for identifying youngsters with interpersonal problems and in isolating those in need of intervention, they fail to provide information on the behavioral antecedents that contribute to a particular sociometric status. The recent use of experimental strategies that examine a newcomer's attempt to assimilate into an already formed group has brought researchers closer to understanding the evolution of social status positions. Several studies that examine the behavioral styles associated with a group-entry situation (e.g., Coie & Kupersmidt, 1983; Dodge, 1983; Putallaz, 1983) have highlighted three key dimensions of group acceptance and social competence: (1) the *ability to adapt* one's behavior to the ongoing flow of interaction; (2) appropriate and positive *responsiveness* to the initiations of others; and (3) *social knowledge* or the general understanding of prosocial behaviors and how to implement them. Thus, children who are successful at gaining entry into an ongoing interaction and who later achieve a high status in a peer group seem to have the ability to read the social situation appropriately and to monitor their behavior as a function of the feedback from others.

Many advances have recently taken place in sociometry, including the development of more appropriate research designs and more powerful statistical techniques to aid in analyzing sociometric data. In addition, recent attempts to conceptualize the interactional processes underlying social competence have restored the vitality of sociometry methods. As a result, the nature and scope of sociometric studies have expanded considerably. While the quality of sociometric studies has generally improved over the past few years, many shortcomings still persist. For example, few studies have focused on developmental issues in addressing whether behaviors predictive of peer popularity, rejection, and neglect remain similar at different points in development. It is likely that these limitations will be the focus of future sociometric research.

References

Bukowski, W., & Newcomb, A. (1984). Stability and determinants of sociometric status and friendship choice: A longitudinal study. *Developmental Psychology, 20,* 941–952.

Coie, J., & Dodge, K. (1983). Continuities and changes in children's social status: A five-year longitudinal study. *Merrill-Palmer Quarterly, 29,* 261–282.

Coie, J., Dodge, K., & Coppotelli, H. (1982). Dimensions and types of social status: A cross-age perspective. *Developmental Psychology, 18,* 557–570.

Coie, J., & Kupersmidt, J. (1983). A behavioral analysis of emerging social status in boys' groups. *Child Development, 54,* 1400–1416.

Dodge, K. (1983). Behavioral antecedents of peer social status. *Child Development, 54,* 1386–1399.

Gresham, F. (1981). Validity of social skills measures for assessing social competence in low-status children: A multivariate investigation. *Developmental Psychology, 17,* 390–398.

Ladd, G. (1983). Social networks of popular, average, and rejected children in school settings. *Merrill-Palmer Quarterly, 29,* 283–307.

Ledingham, J. E. (1981). Developmental patterns of aggressive and withdrawn behavior in childhood: A possible method for identifying preschizophrenics. *Journal of Abnormal Child Psychology, 9,* 1–22.

Moore, S., & Updegraff, R. (1964). Sociometric status of preschool children related to age, sex, nurturance-giving, and dependency. *Child Development, 35,* 519–524.

Moreno, J. L. (1934). *Who shall survive?: A new approach to the problem of human interrelations.* Washington, DC: Nervous and Mental Disease Publishing.

Peery, J. C. (1979). Popular, amiable, isolated, rejected: A reconceptualization of sociometric status in preschool children. *Child Development, 50,* 1231–1234.

Putallaz, M. (1983). Predicting children's sociometric status from their behavior. *Child Development, 54,* 1417–1426.

Roff, M., & Sells, S. (1968). Juvenile delinquency in relation to peer acceptance-rejection and socioeconomic status. *Psychology in the Schools, 5,* 3–18.

See Also

Dating during Adolescence; Friendships; Peer Counseling: A Human Resource Program; Peer Relations and Influences.

The work of the author was supported by a Research Service Award from the National Institute of Mental Health (2-F32-MH-9619).

Peer Relations and Influences

Frederick S. Foster-Clark
Millersville University

Dale A. Blyth
American Medical Association

Among the most fundamental of changes occurring during adolescence is the restructuring of social relationships including the increased importance of peer relations and their influence over the adolescent's behavior and development. This entry reviews theoretical perspectives on this restructuring and the roles peers play in the socialization of adolescents, and then goes on to delineate the mechanisms of peer influence, the domains in which peers are influential, and factors that may moderate the nature and extent of peer influence.

Theories of development based largely upon psychoanalytic traditions have viewed the restructuring of adolescent social relations as a giving up of childhood dependencies. Blos (1979) conceptualizes a "second individuation process" wherein the final severing of the psychological dependency upon parents takes place and autonomous adult functioning can proceed. Erikson's psychosocial theory of development (1968) views the establishment of a separate ego identity as the fundamental task of adolescence, and its successful establishment as the base for continued psychosocial growth during adulthood. But Blos's theory recognized the vital role of the adolescent peer group in the transition from parental dependency to autonomous selfhood, as a source of both emotional refuge and socialization. Similarly, Newman and Newman (1976) expanded upon Erikson's treatment of adolescence to identify a distinct stage of early adolescence in which the fundamental developmental tension is peer-focused, a tension between group identity and alienation from peers. Youniss (1980) has recently reconceptualized the structure and function of childhood and adolescent peer relations based upon the theories of Piaget and Sullivan (see below). The psychological importance of peer relations and a sense of group belongingness, and the shift in orientation from parents to peers are thus explicitly recognized in developmental theories of adolescence.

The restructuring of the adolescent's social world is evident in empirical work as well. The social networks of adolescents become more peer dominated from preadolescence to later adolescence. (Peer networks also increasingly come to include opposite-sex peers.) The intimacy of peer relationships also increase over adolescence, coming to match or even exceed the intimacy typical of relations with parents (especially for girls). These changes are paralleled by decreasing trends in parental conformity and increasing levels of conformity to peers. Peer relations thus become more pervasive, more intense, and carry greater psychological importance during the adolescent period, especially during early adolescence. In addition, peers come to be an important influence on adolescent behavior patterns.

The Role of Peers in Adolescent Socialization

The peer culture as part of the normal adolescent experience became an important focus of social science research beginning around the time of Coleman's (1961) classic study, *Adolescent Society*. Coleman introduced the notion of a peer culture separate and largely antithetical to adult society, a notion whose grip on the field has only recently loosened. The negative influence of the adolescent peer culture has been further supported by decades of research on social deviance, which has consistently found linkages between antisocial behaviors such as delinquency and drug use and the behavior and attitudes of the adolescent's peers.

But recent studies have led to a more moderate view of peer influence by suggesting a high degree of overlap between parental and peer values and standards for behavior. Part of this congruence between parents and peers derives from a recognition that parents play an important role in

shaping the adolescent's peer environment. This is not to suggest that peers do not play an important role in modeling and encouraging antisocial and antiauthority behavior, but simply that the negative influence is not as omnipresent and one-sided as earlier thinking seemed to suggest.

There has also been a recent emphasis on the positive, constructive role that adolescent peers may play in development. This owes largely to two forces. One is Youniss's reinterpretation and synthesis of social development based on the writings of Sullivan and Piaget. Youniss (1980) argues that the nature of peer relations is fundamentally different from adult-child relations. Reciprocity and cooperation are features largely unique to peer relations that are necessary to certain aspects of social development such as sensitivity and mutuality in social relationships and the transformation of relations with adults from authority-based to more egalitarian interactions. Close friendships during childhood and adolescence have also been associated with the development of prosocial behavior. As others have noted, though, the *processes* by which friends or larger peer groups influence the adolescent's behavior and the course of development are not well studied.

Mechanisms of Peer Influence

So how is it that peers come to exert influence over the adolescent's behavior? That is, what are the mechanisms of peer influence? First, peers increasingly become a reference point for behavior during adolescence; they provide a standard by which adolescents measure their own behavior. Peers also take a more active role in shaping behavior by exerting explicit pressures for conformity. Classic studies using the Asch conformity paradigm generally gave rise to the view that conformity to peers peaks in early adolescence. More contemporary research yields a similar but more differential and complex picture of conformity than that based on these earlier studies.

Berndt (1979), building upon earlier work by Bronfenbrenner (1967) and Devereux (1970), studied developmental trends in peer conformity by examining what respondents would do in response to hypothetical situations involving active pressure from peers. Indeed, early to middle adolescents were found to be more susceptible to the influence of peers, especially regarding antisocial behavior, than were younger or older respondents. Brown and his associates (Brown, Clasen, & Eicher, 1986; Brown, Lohr, & McClenahan, 1986) have replicated many of Berndt's specific findings and have extended Berndt's work by incorporating perceived explicit peer pressures in various domains and actual self-reported behaviors along with peer conformity dispositions. Not only do explicit perceived pressures contribute additively with conformity dispositions in the explanation of actual behavior, but these two factors interact such that perceived peer pressures have their strongest effects for those individuals having a propensity toward conformity to peers.

Siman's (1977) model of peer group influence adds another way in which normative pressures from peers influence adolescent behavior. Siman sees the peer group as a filter through which the adolescent interprets parental norms. His research suggests that the general peer group norm (i.e., mean rating among actual peer group as to their parents' approval or disapproval of certain activities) was actually more influential in explaining the adolescent's own behavior than was the adolescent's specific perception of his/her own parents' norm. Peer influence can also take the form of social reinforcement, specific rewards and punishments disbursed by peers in response to adolescent behavior. For example, Magnusson's research with adolescent girls in Sweden (Magnusson, Stattin, & Allen, 1986) has implicated peers' sanctioning responses as a factor that can either limit or encourage antisocial activities.

A final mechanism whereby peers can exert control over adolescent behavior is through the provision of social support, specific emotional or practical resources that peers can provide in times of need. Despite recent increased scientific concern with coping and social support processes, including attention focused specifically on children and adolescents, our knowledge about peers as providers of social or emotional support in times of stress is limited.

Arenas of Influence

Early research on peer conformity and the influence of peer group pressure often pitted parents against peers to assess which of the two was the dominant source of influence. With the publication of Brittain's study in 1963 and subsequent work, most notably that of Kandel (e.g., Kandel & Andrews, 1987), research has generally recognized that the relative importance of peers versus parental influence varies by issue, with peers more influential in life-style considerations and certain aspects of behavior (e.g., fashion, drug use), while parents remain more influential in the more difficult and value-laden concerns (e.g., educational goals). Recent research has also recognized greater congruence between the influence of parents and peers than has traditionally been assumed.

One area where peer influence appears to be strong, at least in this country, is antisocial behavior. Developmentally, peer conformity in antisocial situations has been found to increase through middle adolescence before declining toward late adolescence. Brown's research also suggests a closer link between peer pressures/conformity and actual behaviors in the antisocial domain than in other domains of behavior. Despite peers being influential in the antisocial domain, it should be noted that, on balance, peer pressure weighs against misconduct, and peer conformity is generally stronger in neutral or prosocial situations than in antisocial ones.

Clearly then, peer influence, both relative to parental influence and in absolute terms, varies by the situational context. In addition to these variations, characteristics of the individual also affect the extent and nature of peer influence.

Factors Affecting the Influence of Peers

The effect of one factor, age, has already been discussed: conformity to peers generally increases up to middle adolescence and then declines. Gender also relates to peer influence in a relatively consistent way across studies. Boys tend to be more susceptible to the influence of their peers, but this difference holds only for antisocial situations. The notion of susceptibility, or having a disposition to be conforming, underlies much of the research on peer influence. Greater conceptual clarity regarding such a personality disposition, including its relationship to related constructs such as autonomy, is needed.

Parenting style and other factors in the family context have been related to susceptibility to antisocial influences from peers. Permissive parenting styles appear to encourage, and authoritative parenting to discourage, negative influences from peers. An authoritarian parenting style, meanwhile, can increase youth's dependence on peers. Lack of adult supervision and parental monitoring of adolescent activities also contribute to greater susceptibility to peer influence.

A last factor that may condition peer influences is the nature of the peers themselves. Magnusson's research suggests that, at least among girls, having peers who are older serves to alter the normative context for behavior, thereby encouraging higher rates of deviant activity. Similar effects have been noted in studies of marijuana use in the U.S.

Since cultural or societal differences in patterns of peer conformity have been noted in the limited cross-cultural research that has been conducted to date, it is important to caution that the generalizations made throughout this article are drawn from research conducted principally in modernized Western cultures. Even within these cultures, subcultural variations (e.g., racial differences) have largely gone unstudied.

References

Berndt, T. J. (1979). Developmental changes in conformity to peers and parents. *Developmental Psychology, 15*, 608–616.

Blos, P. (1979). *The adolescent passage: Developmental issues.* New York: International Universities Press.

Brittain, C. V. (1963). Adolescent choices and parent-peer cross-pressures. *American Sociological Review, 28*, 385–391.

Bronfenbrenner, U. (1967). Response to pressure from peers versus adults among Soviet and American school children. *International Journal of Psychology, 2*, 199–207.

Brown, B. B., Clasen, D. R., & Eicher, S. A. (1986). Perceptions of peer pressure, peer conformity dispositions, and self-reported behavior among adolescents. *Developmental Psychology, 22*, 521–530.

Brown, B. B., Lohr, M. J., & McClenahan, E. L.

(1986). Early adolescent's perceptions of peer pressure. *Journal of Early Adolescence*, *6*, 139–154.

Coleman, J. S. (1961). *The adolescent society.* New York: Free Press.

Devereux, E. (1970). The role of the peer group experience in moral development. In J. Hill (Ed.), *Minnesota Symposium on child psychology* (Vol. 4, pp. 94–140). Minneapolis: University of Minnesota Press.

Erikson, E. H. (1968). *Identity: Youth and crisis.* New York: W. W. Norton.

Kandel, D. B., & Andrews, K. (1987). Processes of adolescent socialization by parents and peers. *International Journal of the Addictions*, *22*, 319–342.

Magnusson, D., Stattin, H., & Allen, V. L. (1986). Differential maturation among girls and its relations to social adjustment: A longitudinal perspective. In D. L. Featherman & R. M. Lerner (Eds.), *Life-span development and behavior* (Vol. 7, pp. 135–172). New York: Academic Press.

Newman, P. R., & Newman, B. M. (1976). Early adolescence and its conflict: Group identity vs. alienation. *Adolescence*, *11*, 261–274.

Siman, M. L. (1977). Application of a new model of peer group influence to naturally existing adolescent friendship groups. *Child Development*, *48*, 270–274.

Youniss, J. (1980). *Parents and peers in social development.* Chicago: University of Chicago Press.

See Also

Dating during Adolescence; Friendships; Peer Counseling: A Human Resource Program; Peer Status Groups.

Pharmacology, Developmental

Karen Hein

Albert Einstein College of Medicine
Montefiore Medical Center

When one considers the total amount of medication that is prescribed or taken therapeutically plus the nontherapeutic or illegal substances consumed, it behooves the health care provider to know the action and interaction of these agents in order to provide optimal care for teenagers.

The reasons for including a special entry on therapeutics in adolescence are as follows. Growth during puberty of body tissues and organs that absorb, distribute, metabolize, and excrete drugs affects the amount of drug needed and the frequency of drug administration (Hein, 1987). Behavioral and psychological changes in adolescence require a different "contract" between patient and health provider (Friedman & Litt, 1987). Certain biochemical properties of a drug may have special importance during the teenage years. Examples include the lipid solubility of a compound, the extent of protein binding, and the degree of competition with endogenous substances (e.g, sex steroids) for common metabolizing enzyme systems.

This entry includes a review of the changes in the body and environment of the adolescent that have particular relevance for the type, amount, and frequency of drug use. For most classes of drugs, the dose and dose interval differs between childhood and adulthood.

Virtually every youngster will use a prescribed, over-the-counter (OTC) and/or illicit drug during their teenage years. The dose, response, and side effects of these medications when taken by teenagers may be very different from those noted in childhood and adulthood. Even among different teenagers, a wide range of doses are required. Some of the factors that are known to influence the dose-response relationship are reviewed (Vessell, 1980). More importantly, some of the special factors that must be considered in caring for adolescent patients are highlighted.

Types of Drugs

Teenagers certainly take much more medication than that prescribed by a physician, but rarely do doctors consider the effects of the interaction of OTC drugs or illicit drugs on the adolescent. The exact amounts of medications consumed by American adolescents over the decade of the teenager years is unknown (Pente,

1984). Most surveys focus on illicit drug use by young people. There are no comparable data about the extent of OTC or prescribed medications.

PRESCRIBED AND OVER-THE-COUNTER MEDICATIONS ∎

There are only two surveys of the use of OTC and prescribed medication by youngsters under the age of 17. An annual survey of high school students includes the use of psychoactive medications among high school students (Johnston, O'Malley, & Bachman, in press). In the other survey of OTC and prescribed medications other than psychoactive medications (Sharpe & Smith, 1983), the authors grouped children and adolescents under the age of 17 years together. During the two-week period of the survey, 13% had taken one prescribed medication and 21.5% had taken one OTC medication. The most frequently used OTC categories were analgesics (29.4%), cold/cough remedies (19.2%), vitamins (15.7%), and anti-infectious agents (12.4%). These four categories accounted for three-fourths of the instances of drug use. Although most of the prescribed medications taken were new prescriptions as opposed to refills, the majority (63%) of the OTC medications taken were already in the household. It is not known if the amount, types, or frequency of use of prescribed or OTC medications differs between childhood and adolescence. If these data are used to estimate yearly consumption of medications by youngsters under the age of 17 years, an average of three prescriptions and five OTC medications would be consumed per child per year.

ERGOGENIC AIDS ∎ Ergogenic aids

are substances used by adolescents to improve their athletic performance. Examples of such drugs include psychomotor stimulants, anabolic steroids, nutritional aids, narcotic analgesics, local anesthetics, illicit drugs, and anti-inflammatory agents.

These drugs are commonly used and available outside the health care delivery network. The balance of benefits versus risks, the side effects, and the drug interactions are rarely considered by the teenage athlete because the consensus among young people is that these agents are safe and effective (Dyment, 1987).

Since most teenage athletes know that the use of some of the ergogenic aids, such as amphetamines and anabolic steroids, is not permitted, adolescents will not reveal use to a physician unless confidentiality is assured. Despite the fact that the use of over 50 specific stimulants, sympathomimetic amines, narcotic analgesics, and anabolic steroids was banned at the Olympics and by other competitive athletic organizations for youth, use of ergogenic aids continues to be common among teenage athletes.

ILLICIT DRUGS ∎ Current data (Johnston et al., in press) regarding illicit drug

use by high school students demonstrates that the epidemic that appeared in the 1960s and 1970s has declined among American high school students. The proportion of students reporting any illicit drug use declined by approximately one-fourth between 1979 and 1984. However, the rates are still the highest among all industrialized nations. In 1987 over half (57%) of all high school seniors polled had tried an illicit drug and over one-third had tried a drug other than marijuana.

The vast majority of students had tried alcohol (over 90%) and cigarettes (over 60%) by their senior year. Of concern is the persistence of a small subgroup of heavy users over the last 5 of the 13 years of the annual survey. For cigarettes there is a higher percent of female daily users (>20%) and half a pack per day smokers (about 15%) than males. In addition, roughly 10%

of males and 5% of females reported daily use of alcohol and 3.3% reported daily use of marijuana. Cocaine use had risen to nearly 13% of students in 1986. However, the most recent survey in 1987 showed a decline by one-fifth in "ever use" as well as "frequent use" among students in the past year. The principal investigators of the Monitoring the Future Project concluded that "the kinds of young people most at risk remain much the same although the types and amounts of substances they use shift somewhat from year to year."

Longitudinal studies provide invaluable information about trends among high school students. However, a subgroup of adolescents who are not living at home and are not attending school account for some of the heavier drug users and abusers during adolescence. Inner-city institutionalized youngsters are a group with a high percent of teenage runaways and truants. A survey of drug use patterns in this group helps complete the picture of the usage patterns among teenagers in the past two decades (Hein, Cohen, & Litt, 1979). Although no systematic surveys of cocaine use by disenfranchised youth (runaways, incarcerated youth, or school dropouts) have been conducted, it is evident that many of the more troubled youth are now heavy users of "crack," the smokeable form of cocaine.

Brunswick and Josefson (1972) surveyed a representative sample of Harlem youths twice, first when they were 12–17 years old and again when they were 18–23 years old. Although this was a household survey, the data are helpful because they were gathered from a population whose truancy rate is higher than average. Lifetime prevalence for three or more episodes of use of alcohol (80%), marijuana (79%), cocaine (33%), and heroin (15%) were higher than those reported in a national probability sample in 1977.

Finally, the nontherapeutic use of psychoactive drugs has increased dramatically in the past decades (Nicholi, 1983). In summary, four categories of medications are consumed by American youths: prescribed, over-the-counter, ergogenic, and illicit. An appropriate evaluation of the teenager means that each category must be considered by the health professional at all stages of evaluation and treatment of an adolescent.

Age-Related Changes in Drug Disposition

Variation in drug disposition between subjects ranges from three- to fortyfold. Factors accounting for the variation include age, sex, and genetic constitution as well as environmental influences (Aranda & Stern, 1983). Reviews of age-related differences in dose requirements, toxicity, and effectiveness of many therapeutic agents have elucidated changes in drug-absorption distribution, metabolism, and excretion principally during four stages of development: neonates, children, adults, and the elderly (Morselli, 1979). Studies of sex-related differences in drug metabolism for many classes of drugs (anesthetics, narcotics, alcohol, analgesics, anticonvulsants, and stimulants) (Goble, 1975) demonstrate that the drug effect may be more pronounced or persist longer in adult females as compared to males or younger children (Steger, 1982). It is assumed that puberty is a time when certain alterations in drug-utilization patterns appear. Few studies have determined the exact time or nature of the alterations in adolescence (Hein, Dell, Pesce, Coupolos, & Miller, 1983; Hein, Dell, Puig-Antich, & Cooper, 1983).

Three ways of defining the age-related changes between childhood and adulthood are (1) the decrease in dose (mg/kg);

(2) the increase in half-life (minutes or hours); and (3) the increase in ratio of concentration/dose.

CHANGES IN BODY COMPOSITION ■

Because drugs are differentially distributed into body tissues depending on their solubility characteristics, knowing the amount of fat or water in a given patient may be a key factor in understanding why that patient requires a certain amount of a given drug. As an individual enters puberty, the amount of fat, water, and lean body mass changes. Drugs will be distributed in a new way based on these body compositional factors (Butler & Richie, 1960).

The effect of puberty on drug disposition is graphically displayed in Figures 1 and 2. In Figure 1 the teenager's body is viewed as a "tank" with various compartments. Drugs that are put into the tank exit by one of two outflow tracts, either metabolism or excretion. During puberty the rise in sex steroids predominantly affects two parts of this system. First, it affects the composition of the tank by influencing body composition. Second, it affects metabolism largely through alterations in liver function.

In Figure 1 the schematic diagram shows a simplified version of the potential effect of the rise in sex steroids on drug disposition. As a drug or medication enters the adolescent's body, it is distributed according to its solubility characteristics and transport features into various body compartments. The composition of the tank will influence the distribution and extent of storage in each compartment. For example, a given dose of a water-soluble drug will be distributed very differently into the tissues of two normal 14-year-old teenagers if one is a male (Tanner V) with 60% of his body weight composed of water as compared to a female (Tanner V), who may have only

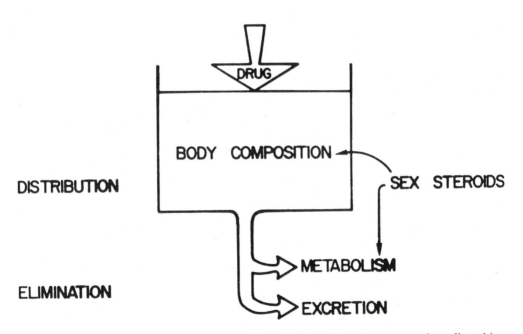

FIGURE 1   Schematic representation of the effect of pubertal development on drug disposition. Model showing the potential effects of the rise of sex steroids on the body composition and organ function of an adolescent, which then influence drug disposition.

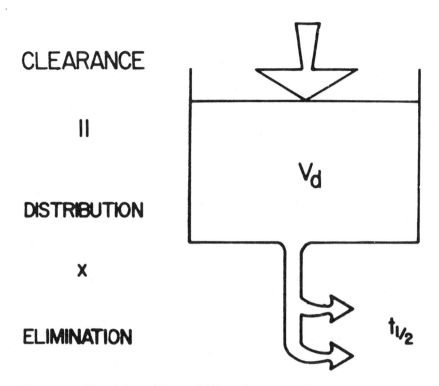

CLEARANCE

=

DISTRIBUTION

x

ELIMINATION

Figure 2   Translation of the model into pharmacologic terms.

45% of her total body weight composed of water. Once distributed, there may be a difference in rates of metabolism and excretion. These differences are to a large extent due to genetic factors. However, there are also differences in rates of elimination documented between males and females.

In Figure 2 the system is translated into simplified pharmacologic terms. The size of the tank into which the drug is distributed is described by the volume of distribution. The process of drug elimination, simply stated, is a combination of drug metabolism and excretion. These processes are described by drug half-life. Clearance is a function of both volume of distribution as well as changes in organs (such as the liver) on subsequent changes in drug metabolism. By investigating these two aspects of drug disposition, a clearer understanding of the differences in drug

clearance between childhood and adulthood will emerge and can form the basis of a more rational dose schedule for rapidly growing teenagers.

CHANGES IN ORGAN FUNCTION ■

Understanding hepatic changes is the key to explaining the alterations in drug utilization that occur during puberty (Blizzard, 1968). Several structural and functional changes occur during puberty. The rate of enzyme activity is usually low in the fetus, higher in the neonate, and, in some cases, peak in preadolescence (Schmucker, Mooney, & Jones, 1977).

In summary, the changes in body composition affect the way a given drug is distributed within the body. Changes in organ structure and function, specifically those in the liver, affect the rate of metabolism and, therefore, the excretion of the drug. These two factors may account for some of the variability in drug dose and drug response noted among pubertal individuals and noted between children and adults for almost all classes of drugs.

Conclusion

Despite growing interest in developmental pharmacology, specific information about adolescence is relatively scanty. Studies of the dose-concentration-effect relationship over the life cycle tend to emphasize the neonate, child, adult, or elderly patient, excluding specific information about teenagers. In many cases errors in management would be made if physicians were to treat teenagers either as big children requiring a high milligram/kilogram dose or as little adults.

UNEXPECTED TOXICITY OR INEFFECTIVENESS ▪ Low blood levels in adolescents should not necessarily be equated with noncompliance. Many factors work synergistically to raise levels or antagonistically to lower levels so that the net effect may be difficult to predict for a given teenager taking a given drug at a given time. Therefore, if an unexpected clinical finding is observed, multiple blood levels are necessary in addition to knowledge of the dose to understand the balance of individual dispositional factors.

When range and dose requirements vary widely among individuals, therapeutic drug monitoring is usually indicated. For example, a phenobarbital dose of 1 mg/kg may be sufficient for providing hypnotic effects in adults whereas in very young children, 5, 8, or 10 mg/kg may be required. Similarly, the imipramine dose in adults may be 1 mg/kg whereas for children 7 mg/kg may be required (FDA's current recommendation for children is not to exceed 5 mg/kg). For a given teenager, it is imperative to monitor level to know how the majority of factors (genetic, distributional, excretory, etc.) will balance out.

Information about drug safety and efficacy in children is still quite limited. In 1975 70% of the drugs listed in the *Physicians Desk Reference* contained some form of disclaimer or lacked specific dose information for youth and children. The term "therapeutic orphans," refers not only to children but also to adolescents. Adolescence is a time of exposure to illicit, nontherapeutic, and environmental chemical agents as well as prescribed and OTC medications. Studies of the pharmacodynamics of alcohol, marijuana, methaqualone, etc., are usually based on adults as the study population. Understanding the dose-response relationship of these agents in teenagers requires knowledge of the chemical properties of the drugs and physiologic changes in body composition and organ function. Finally, the clinician must possess a balanced view between those behavioral factors likely to affect compliance and the physiologic factors that have been described in this entry.

EMERGING ISSUES IN MEDICATION USE FOR ADOLESCENTS ▪ Adolescents are not big children, nor are they small adults. Their unique physical, psychological, and social status renders extrapolation from younger or older age groups inappropriate. One of the latest examples of adolescents "falling through the cracks" has been the history of the clinical trials program for the development and evaluation of treatments for HIV infection and AIDS. After the first protocols were developed for adults, special protocols for children under the age of 13 followed. However, adults were defined as persons over the age of 18 years.

Therefore, teenagers 13–17 were initially excluded. As discussion ensued about the appropriate place to include teenagers, it became evident that the unique physiologic status of the adolescent made inclusion in either age group inappropriate without some modification to take into account the diversity in body size and organ function, the effect of endocrinologic changes during puberty, and the cofactors that would influence the natural history of HIV infection or drug disposition in this age group. This most recent example epitomizes the special needs of adolescents regarding the use of medications.

References

Aranda, J. V., & Stern, L. (1983). Clinical aspects of developmental pharmacology and toxicology. *Pharmacology and Therapeutics, 20*, 1–51.

Blizzard, R. M. (1968). Differentiation, morphogenesis, and growth. In D. Cheek (Ed.), *Human growth* (pp. 48–50). Philadelphia: Lea and Febinger.

Brunswick, A., & Josefson, E. (1972). Adolescent health in Harlem. *American Journal of Public Health* (Suppl.)

Butler, A., & Richie, R. (1960). Simplification and improvement in estimating drug dosage and fluid and dietary allowances for patients of varying sizes. *New England Journal of Medicine, 262*, 903–908.

Dyment, P. G. (1987). The adolescent athlete and ergogenic aids. *Journal of Adolescent Health Care, 8*, 68–73.

Friedman, I., & Litt, I. (1987). Adolescents' compliance with therapeutic regimens. *Journal of Adolescent Health Care, 8*, 52–67.

Goble, F. A. (1975). Sex as a factor in metabolism, toxicity, and efficacy of pharmacodynamic and chemotherapeutic agents. *Advances in Pharmacology and Chemotherapy, 13*, 173–252.

Hein, K. (1987). Use of therapeutics in adolescence. *Journal of Adolescent Health Care, 8*, 8–35.

Hein, K., Cohen, M. I., & Litt, I. (1979). Illicit drug use among urban adolescents. *American Journal of Diseases of Children, 133*, 38–40.

Hein, K., Dell, R., Pesce, M., Copoulos, E., & Miller, M. (1985). Effects of adolescent development on theophylline half-life. *Pediatric Research, 19*, 173.

Hein, K., Dell, R., Puig-Antich, K., & Cooper, T. (1983). Effect of adolescent development on imipramine disposition. *Pediatric Research, 17*, 89A.

Johnston, L., O'Malley, P., & Bachman, J. (1989 in press). Illicit drug use, smoking, and drinking by America's high school students, college students, and young adults, 1975–1987. National Institute on Drug Abuse.

Morselli, P. L. (1979). Drug disposition during development. *Spectrum* (pp. 1–150).

Nicholi, A. M., Jr. (1983). The nontherapeutic use of psychoactive drugs: A modern epidemic. *New England Journal of Medicine, 308*, 925–933.

Pente, P. (1984). Toxicity of over-the-counter stimulants. *Journal of the American Medical Association, 252*, 1898–1903.

Schmucker, D., Mooney, J., & Jones, A. (1977). Age related changes in the hepatic endoplasmic reticulum: A quantitative analysis. *Science, 197*, 1005–1008.

Sharpe, T. R., & Smith, M. C. (1983). Patterns of medication use among children in households enrolled in the Aid to Families with Dependent Children Program. *Pediatric Research, 17*, 617–619.

Steger, R. W. (1982). Age-dependent changes in the responsiveness of the reproductive system to pharmacological agents. *Pharmacology and Therapeutics, 17*, 1–64.

Vessell, E. S. (1980). Why are toxic reactions to drugs so often undetected initially? *New England Journal of Medicine, 303*, 1027–1029.

See Also

Anabolic-Androgenic Steroids, the Nonmedical Use by Adolescents; Cocaine Use among Adolescents and Young Adults, Antecedents/Predictors of; Drug Use, Adolescent; Drug Use, Epidemiology and Developmental Stages of Involvement; Drug Use, Minority Youth and; Drug Use, Predictors and Correlates of Adolescent; Hallucinogens; Health and Substance Abuse in Adolescence: Ethnic and Gender Perspectives; Smokeless Tobacco Use among Adolescents; Smoking and Drug Prevention with Early Adolescents, Programs for; Stimulants.

Physical Abuse of Adolescents

Penelope K. Trickett
Robert J. Weinstein
The Chesapeake Institute

Although the physical abuse of children has a long history, it was not until the early 1960s, when the first description of the "battered child syndrome" was published (Kempe, Silverman, Steele, Droegenmueller, & Silver, 1962), that some public awareness of the magnitude of this problem began to surface. This "syndrome" was characterized by the physical injury of infants and young children by parents or other caregivers (Gil, 1970). In these initial publications there was little or no recognition that adolescents could also be or were victims of parental abuse. In fact, adolescents are frequently abused. Although estimates vary, one recent national survey concluded that adolescent maltreatment accounts for 47% of all child abuse, although teenagers account for only 38% of the population under 18 years of age (Burgdorf, 1980; Garbarino, Sebes, & Schellenbach, 1984). Other estimates are lower but still substantial (e.g., 33%—Powers & Echenrode, in press; 25%—American Humane Association, 1989; or 42%—Blum & Runyan, 1980). The most recent national incidence study (National Center on Child Abuse and Neglect

[NCCAN], 1988) also confirms a higher rate of physical abuse of adolescents as compared with younger children. This study also reports a considerable rise in the incidence of physical abuse of adolescents since the previous national incidence study (in 1980) and attributes this rise to the recent increase in *recognition* of the problem.

The slow recognition of the abuse of adolescents has been caused by a number of factors. First, child abuse is commonly discovered in hospital emergency rooms or other medical settings where infants and small children are treated for broken bones or other physical injuries that have been inexplicably sustained. Since small children are more vulnerable to injury than larger ones, this way of identifying abuse victims leads to the misperception that younger children are more often abused. This increased vulnerability of the youngest victims of abuse is supported by the most recent national incidence study (NCCAN, 1988), which found that there were more fatalities and a greater likelihood of serious injuries among younger abused children than among older abused children.

Second, adolescent abuse is less likely to be reported to protective service agencies than is the abuse of younger children. Often the abuse is not what initially brings these youths and their families to the attention of professionals. Rather, it may be the teenager's school problems, delinquency, or running away. Ironically, Garbarino and Gilliam (1980) have reported that 20% of adolescent abuse cases first come to the attention of the authorities when the abusive parent charges the child with assault.

A third reason for the lack of attention to adolescent abuse may stem from society's ambivalent feelings toward adolescents, who do not evoke as much concern or sympathy as do infants and young children. Fisher and Berdie (1978) describe a "threshold shift" that occurs in society, in which, due to both the physical size of the adolescent and the assumption that the adolescent should bear some responsibility for his or her behavior, the distinction between acceptable parenting and abusive parenting becomes less clear.

How else does the abuse of adolescents differ from that of young children? First, it is the only age period when girls are more likely to be physically abused than boys. Boys are most likely to be abused as toddlers or preschoolers while girls suffer more abuse at midadolescence (Burgdorff, 1980). Also, it seems that the older the victim of physical abuse, the greater the likelihood that the father rather than the mother is the abuser. Garbarino and Gilliam (1980) report data from one survey showing that, for victims up to age six, the mother is 50% more likely than the father to be the abuser; for children ages 6 to 13, mothers and fathers are equally likely to be the abuser; and for victims 13 and above, the father is more likely than the mother to be the abuser. Another difference is that families in which adolescent abuse occurs are more likely to be of higher socioeconomic status than families in which physical abuse of preadolescents occurs (Garbarino & Gilliam, 1980).

Garbarino and Gilliam (1980) have posited that the abuse of adolescents can be viewed as being of two basically different types; those in which the abuse is just a continuation of child abuse into adolescence, and those in which abuse begins during adolescence. They suggest that cases of adolescent abuse are about equally divided between these two types. The etiologies of these two types of abuse may be quite different. Garbarino and Gilliam suggest that poverty and concomitant stresses are a more important causative factor in the abuse of children (and thus of children who continue to be abused during adolescence) than they are of abuse that begins during adolescence, which they consider to be more interpersonal in nature.

There is, however, a growing body of evidence that interpersonal and interactional factors are also important in the abuse of younger children. Recent research examining abusive families in which the child victim is 11 years old or younger has found that abusive parents as a group differ in a number of important ways from nonabusive parents in their childrearing approaches. In particular, the abusive parents are not only more punitive in their discipline style, but they also make less use of reasoning and other more educative types of discipline; they are less flexible or adaptive in their use of discipline; they are less open to new experiences and less encouraging of the development of autonomy and independence in their children; they report more anger and conflict in the family in general and in their reaction to the abused child in particular; they express more dissatisfaction with their child and the parenting role; they report smaller social networks, especially of the type that provides support for childrearing; and they report greater isolation from the wider community (Corse, Schmid, & Trickett, in press; Disbrow, Doerr, & Caulfield, 1977; Reid, 1986; Trickett & Kuczynski, 1986; Trickett & Susman, 1988, 1989; Wolfe, 1985).

Abuse that begins during adolescence is probably related to factors associated with the developmental tasks of adolescence. Thus the growing need and desire for independence and autonomy in children entering adolescence cause stress and conflict in many families and may result in abuse in some. Similarly, issues arising about the child's sexual maturation and growing interest in heterosexual relationships can produce intense stress. It may well be that one of the reasons that girls are more at risk for abuse during adolescence is that sexual acting out is less tolerated in female adolescents than male adolescents, especially by fathers. (There is also some indication that girls who have been sexually abused by their fathers as preadolescents may refuse to cooperate actively when they become adolescents and that this lack of cooperation, coupled with a growing interest in normal peer and heterosexual relationships, leads to their being physically abused by these same fathers at this age.) The stress that is a concomitant of these developmental changes in the adolescent, combined with the developmental tasks of the parents as they enter middle-age (Lourie, 1979), contribute to an atmosphere that can foster physical abuse.

Since, as previously stated, adolescent physical abuse is often discovered as a result of attention to other mental health conditions (e.g., delinquency, running away, school problems), an understanding of its impact on the victim has been obtained indirectly. That is, much of our knowledge about the impact of adolescent abuse has accrued while studying adolescents identified for other problems. In the early 1970s Butler (1974) estimated that 5% of all teenage runaways were physically abused or neglected in their homes. Since that time the estimates have increased considerably. In a recent study of 199 adolescent runaways residing in a youth shelter, 78% reported serious physical abuse by a parent during the year prior to leaving home (Farber, Kinast, McCoard, & Falkner, 1984).

Garbarino and Gilliam (1980) found gender differences in adolescents' reactions to abuse: abused males were described as aggressive, delinquent, and acting out, while abused females showed behavior that was directed inward, in the form of depression and self-destructive behavior. Overall, many of the children manifested low self-esteem, high anxiety, depression, suicidal tendencies, substance abuse, and school problems. As this type of antisocial behavior continues, these adolescents become increasingly socially isolated (Garbarino, 1978).

Galambos and Dixon (1984) found that a maltreated adolescent's sense of locus of control (as it develops in an abusive home situation) is an important factor in determining his/her psychosocial functioning. Their results indicated that adolescents who were abused for a long period of time (i.e., throughout childhood) manifested a more external locus of control. The authors suggest that an external locus of control is related to feelings of helplessness, hopelessness, and an overall sense of powerlessness, which can result in problems such as delinquency, depression, or suicide in these children.

Now that the nature of adolescent physical abuse is becoming better understood, it is important to apply this knowledge to treatment and prevention issues. First, there must be an increase in awareness that adolescents are, in fact, physically abused, and that this type of abuse may come to light first in schools, psychiatric clinics, the juvenile court system, or runaway shelters, rather than in reports to protective service agencies. It is essential that such institutions acknowledge this reality and develop systematic procedures both to identify such abuse and then to deal appropriately with it. Better coordination between such institutions and protective service agencies is one need.

Also, treatment programs at such sites as runaway shelters should be tailored to the needs of victims of adolescent abuse. This parallels the overarching need for better treatment of child abuse victims in general. Such treatment needs to focus explicitly on the mental health needs of children and adolescents with attention to the varying needs of children at different developmental stages. Also, where feasible, such treatment must focus not only on stopping the abuse, but also on modifying dysfunctional family interaction patterns in order to enhance the development of the child who is growing up in that family.

In the specific case of adolescent abuse, the education of parents about adolescence is essential. By teaching parents early about the timing and normative course of adolescence, and teaching them appropriate and functional ways in which to deal with the difficulties inherent in that stage of development, much of the physical abuse that develops in adolescence could be controlled. This type of intervention can be implemented in the school system. Through primary prevention techniques such as this, a major problem could potentially be brought under control.

References

American Humane Association. (March 1989). Personal communication.

Blum, R., & Runyan, C. (1980). Adolescent abuse: The dimensions of the problem. *Journal of Adolescent Health Care*, *1*, 121–126.

Burgdorff, K. (1980). *Recognition and reporting of child maltreatment: Findings from the National Incidence and Severity of Child Abuse and Neglect*. Washington, DC: National Center on Child Abuse and Neglect.

Butler, D. (1974). *Runaway House: A Youth-run project*. Washington, DC: U.S. Government Printing Office.

Corse, S. J., Schmid, K., & Trickett, P. K. (in press). Social network characteristics of mothers in abusing and nonabusing families and their relationships to parenting beliefs. *Journal of Community Psychology*.

Disbrow, M. A., Doerr, H., & Caulfield, C. (1977). Measuring the components of parents' potential for child abuse and neglect. *Child Abuse and Neglect*, *1*, 279–296.

Farber, E. D., Kinast, C., McCoard, W. D., & Falkner, D. (1984). Violence in families of adolescent runaways. *Child Abuse and Neglect*, *8*, 295–299.

Fisher, B., & Berdie, J. (1978). Adolescent abuse and neglect. *Child Abuse and Neglect*, *2*, 173–192.

Galambos, N. L., & Dixon, R. A. (1984). Adolescent abuse and the development of personal sense of control. *Child Abuse and Neglect*, *8*, 285–293.

Garbarino, J. (1978). Child abuse and juvenile delinquency: The developmental impact of isolation. In Y. Walker (Ed.), *Exploring the relationship between child abuse and delinquency* (pp. 189–203). Seattle, WA: Northwest Institute for Human Services.

Garbarino, J., & Gilliam, G. (1980). *Understanding abusive families*. Lexington, MA: Lexington Books.

Garbarino, J., Sebes, J., & Schellenbach, C. (1984). Families at risk for destructive parent-child relations in adolescence. *Child Development*, *55*, 174–183.

Gil, D. G. (1970). *Violence against children: Physical child abuse in the United States*. Cambridge: Harvard University Press.

Kempe, C. H., Silverman, F. N., Steele, B. F., Droegenmueller, W., & Silver, H. K.

(1962). The battered child syndrome. *Journal of the American Medical Association, 181*, 17–24.

Lourie, I. (1979). Family dynamics and the abuse of adolescents: A case for a developmental phase specific model of child abuse. *Child Abuse and Neglect, 3*, 967–974.

National Center on Child Abuse and Neglect, Office of Human Development Services, Department of Health and Human Services. (1988). *Study findings: Study of national incidence and prevalence of child abuse and neglect.* Washington, DC: U.S. Government Printing Office.

Powers, J., & Eckenrode, J. (in press). The substantiation of adolescent maltreatment. *Child Abuse and Neglect.*

Reid, J. B. (1986). Social-interaction patterns in families of abused and nonabused children. In C. Zahn-Waxler, E. M. Cummings, & R. Iannotti (Eds.), *Altruism and aggression: Social and biological origins* (pp. 238–255). New York: Cambridge University Press.

Trickett, P. K., & Kuczynski, L. (1986). Children's misbehaviors and parental discipline strategies in abusive and nonabusive families. *Developmental Psychology, 22*, 115–123.

Trickett, P. K., & Susman, E. J. (1988). Parental perceptions of childrearing practices in physically abusive and nonabusive families. *Developmental Psychology, 24*, 270–276.

Trickett, P. K., & Susman, E. J. (1989). Perceived similarities and disagreement about childrearing practices in abusive and nonabusive families: Intergenerational and concurrent family processes. In D. Cicchetti & V. Carlson (Eds.), *Child maltreatment: Theory and research on the causes and consequences of child abuse* (pp. 280–301). New York: Cambridge University Press.

Wolfe, D. A. (1985). Child abusive parents: An empirical review and analysis. *Psychological Bulletin, 97*, 462–482.

See Also

At-Risk Youth, State Policies for; Black Adolescents At-Risk: Approaches to Prevention; Injury during Adolescence, Risk Factors for.

Physical Attractiveness and Adolescent Development

Gerald R. Adams
University of Guelph

While early theoretical analyses of adolescence have included some discussion of the role of physical attractiveness for understanding adolescent development, contemporary scholars have given considerably more attention to the function of physical attractiveness for adolescent development. Based upon the belief that an individual not only reacts to and is shaped by environmental factors, but also produces or shapes others' reactions (e.g., Lerner & Busch-Rossnagel, 1981; Lerner & Foch, 1987), theroetical perspectives referred to as dynamic interaction, dialectic, developmental contextual, and probabilistic epigenesis (see Lerner, Lerner & Tubman, 1989) have been advanced.

Early scholars (e.g., Erikson, 1968; Freud, 1969; McCandless, 1970) have noted the importance of pubescence, biological change, and physical appearance for psychological development during adolescence. Some have argued that anatomy is destiny. Others have argued that the body is the foundation upon which self-development emerges. Clearly, maturational changes affect how young adolescents feel about themselves. For example, Brooks-Gunn (1986) notes that menarche (as the hallmark of puberty and physical growth) heralds increasing social maturity, perceived and real peer prestige, higher self-esteem, heightened self-awareness of one's body, and increased self-consciousness.

The impact of physical appearance on adolescent behavior and development can be conceptualized through a social perception process. Figure 1 synthesizes the basic elements of the social perception process. As individuals we can and do evaluate differences between various degrees of physical attractiveness. Attractive persons, in comparison to their unattractive peers, are expected to possess more socially desirable characteristics. Further, this social stereotyping process can actually evolve into a social reality. That is, due to our impressions that attractive others are expected to have desirable personal and social characteristics, we engage in positive social interactions with attractive individuals that result in the individual internalizing the "desirable" social message. In turn, the attractive person internalizes the message in his or her personality and manifests the message in positive social behaviors. When the individual shows the very behaviors we expected of them, based on stereotypic impressions, we have a confirmation of our stereotype. This confirmation process is

FIGURE 1   A conceptualization of the social perception process underlying the effects of physical attractiveness.

thought to account for why stereotypic impressions and expectations are so highly resistant to change.

Several extensive reviews confirm the process (e.g., Adams, 1982; Berscheid & Walster, 1974) and suggest that the influence of physical attractiveness on individual development begins with basic perceptions of physical attractiveness. Physically attractive youths are perceived by their peers and others to possess more desirable characteristics and are expected to be more successful in their social behaviors. In turn, people interact with physically attractive youths in more supportive and constructive ways that encourage attractive adolescents to internalize the expectations and impressions of others. Further, as attractive adolescents develop personality styles and engage in corresponding behavioral manifestations of what has been expected of them, they reflect the very stereotyped behaviors that are associated with attractiveness. In turn, such behaviors confirm the original impressions and expectations that are affiliated with the original, physical attractiveness–based, social-perception stereotype.

The research on physical attractiveness and its social and psychological impact is voluminous. Several excellent references can be read for detail (e.g., Hatfield, 1985; MacGregor, 1974; Miller, 1982; Patzer, 1985). However, the role of physical attractiveness for adolescent development can be highlighted through recent research emerging from the Pennsylvania Early Adolescent Transition Study. In a series of

investigations conducted by Richard M. Lerner and associates the role of physical appearance in predicting an adolescent's level of adaptation, adjustment, and social development has been examined. For example, in one investigation, Lerner, Jovanovic, Delaney, Hess, and von Eye (1987) examined the role of physical attractiveness in predicting teachers' expectations and their influences on academic competence. As predicted, physically attractive youths had teachers who held higher expectations of performance. Further, these expectations were associated with higher levels of academic performance. However, comparisons from the beginning, middle, and end of the sixth grade revealed that the effects of physical attractiveness dissipated with the amount of time in the setting. These authors therefore conclude that the effects of attractiveness are strongest upon entering a new setting and diminish with familiarity and exposure. Investigations such as these and others (e.g., Blyth, Simmons, & Zakin, 1985; Zakin, Blyth, & Simmons, 1984) illustrate the importance of contextualism in understanding the role and impact of physical attractiveness on individual behavior and development.

Social scientists have clearly established that people generally hold a "beauty-is-good" hypothesis (Dion, Berscheid & Walster, 1972) where attractive individuals are seen in more favorable ways than their lesser attractive peers. Attractive adolescents are more likely than their unattractive counterparts to be judged as possessing better character, to be seen as more poised, viewed as more self-confident, kind, flexible, and sexually responsive, while being perceived as having greater control of their own destiny (see Adams, 1977 for a review). Other evidence indicates that attractive adolescents are viewed as having greater source credibility (Patzer, 1983) and are more effective in persuading others to agree with their viewpoint (e.g., Chaiken, 1979).

Some evidence suggests physically unattractive youths may be at greater risk for psychopathology. For example, Krebs and Adinolfi (1975) have shown that physically unattractive adolescents are likely to have a highly constrained, asocial personality, while Mathes and Kahn (1975) provide evidence suggesting unattractiveness is associated with neuroticism. Adams and Read (1983), in an experimental laboratory study, have shown that unattractive late adolescents enage in significantly more undesirable social influence behaviors than attractive comparisons. In a social influence context, unattractive females were more demanding, interrupting, opinionated, hostile and antagonistic.

Considerable evidence establishes that attractiveness plays a substantial role in adolescent dating behavior. Clearly, attractive individuals are preferred in dating selection, regardless of their other characteristics (see Walster, Aronson, Abrahams & Rottmann, 1966; Mathes, 1975). Other evidence also suggests that attractive youths are more likely to engage in and experience fulfilling premarital social and/or sexual relations (MacCorquodale & DeLamanter, 1979; Curran & Lippold, 1975). Likewise, Elder (1969) and Taylor and Glenn (1976) have shown that marital selection is based, in part, on the level of attractiveness of the female. While Udry (1977) argues that education is a more influential factor than attractiveness in determining social mobility through marriage, Taylor and Glenn

(1976) find, for lower class females, that attractiveness is a primary determinant of marriage to a higher status husband.

As adolescents enter the work force attractiveness may influence employability (e.g., see Cash, Gillen & Burns, 1977). Attractive job candidates are judged as having better employee potential than unattractive applicants. Further, when hired and under evaluation, attractive persons are judged to have higher task performance than unattractive peers, even when the performance is poor (Landy & Sigall, 1974). Unfortunately, attractive adolescents may not then know when their performance is being properly and appropriately evaluated. Indeed, some research findings suggest that attractive females may not readily accept the sincerity of praise for performance by an evaluator in a face-to-face encounter (Sigall & Michela, 1976). That is, they may be uncertain whether they are being praised because of their pleasing looks or their actual performance or ability.

In summary, the evidence suggests a perception-based mechanism operates around a beauty-is-good principle. This mechanism includes the reinforcement of certain social behaviors and attitudes where attractive individuals are both expected to manifest and are reinforced for emitting certain social behaviors. Attractive adolescents, in contrast to their unattractive peers, are more likely to reflect greater confidence and positive mental health. However, attractive youths are also likely to question whether their performance and behavior is being reinforced due to their appearance or their actual ability.

References

Adams, G. R. (1977). Physical attractiveness: toward a developmental social psychology of beauty. *Human Development, 20,* 217–239.

Adams, G. R. (1982). Physical attractiveness. In A. G. Miller (Ed.), *In the eye of the beholder: Contemporary issues in stereotyping* (pp. 253–304). New York: Praeger.

Adams, G. R., & Read, D. (1983). Personality and social influence styles of attractive and unattractive college women. *Journal of Psychology, 114,* 151–157.

Berscheid, E., & Walster, E. (1974). Physical attractiveness. In L. Berkowitz (Ed.), *Advances in experimental social psychology* (Vol. 7, pp. 157–215). New York: Academic Press.

Blyth, D. A., Simmons, R. G., & Zakin, D. F. (1985). Satisfaction with body image for early adolescent females: The impact of pubertal timing within different school environments. *Journal of Youth and Adolescence, 14,* 207–226.

Brooks-Gunn, J. (1986). Pubertal processes and girls' psychological adaptation. In R. M. Lerner & T. T. Foch (Eds.), *Biological psychosocial interactions in early adolescence: A life-span perspective* (pp. 123–153). Hillsdale, NJ: Lawrence Erlbaum Associates.

Cash, T. F., Gillen, B., & Burns, D. S. (1977). Sexism and "beautyism" in personal consultant decision making. *Journal of Applied Psychology, 62,* 301–310.

Chaiken, S. (1979). Communicator physical attractiveness and persuasion. *Journal of Personality and Social Psychology, 37,* 1387–1397.

Dion, K., Berscheid, E., & Walster, E. (1972). What is beautiful is good. *Journal of Personality and Social Psychology, 24,* 285–290.

Elder, G. H. (1969). Appearance and education in marriage mobility. *American Sociological Review, 34,* 519–533.

Erikson, E. H. (1968). *Identity: Youth and crisis.* New York: Norton.

Freud, A. (1969). Adolescence as a developmental disturbance. In G. Caplan & S. Lebovici (Eds.), *Adolescence* (pp. 5–10). New York: Basic Books.

Hatfield, E. (1985). Physical attractiveness in social interaction. In J. A. Graham & A. M. Kligman (Eds.), *The psychology of cosmetic treatment* (pp. 77–92). New York: Praeger.

Krebs, E. & Adinolfi, A. A. (1975). Physical attractiveness, social relations, and personality style. *Journal of Personality and Social Psychology, 31,* 245–253.

Landy, D., & Sigall, H. (1974). Beauty is talent: Task evaluation as a function of the performer's physical attractiveness. *Journal of Personality and Social Psychology, 29,* 299–304.

Lerner, R. M., & Busch-Rossnagel, N. A. (1981). Individuals as producers of their development: Conceptual and empirical bases. In R. M. Lerner & N. A. Busch-Rossnagel (Eds.), *Individuals as producers of their development: A life-span perspective* (pp. 1–36). New York: Academic Press.

Lerner, R. M., & Foch, T. T. (Eds.). (1987). *Biological-psychosocial interactions in early adolescence.* Hillsdale, NJ: Lawrence Erlbaum Associates.

Lerner, R. M., Jovanovic, J., Delaney, M., Hess, L. E., & von Eye, A. (1987). Early adolescent physical attractiveness and academic competence. Unpublished manuscript. (Cited in R. M. Lerner, J. V. Lerner, & J. Tubman, 1989.)

Lerner, R. M., Lerner, J. V., & Tubman, J. (1989). Organismic and contextual bases of development in adolescence: A developmental-contextual view. In G. R. Adams, T. Gullotta, & R. Montemayor (Eds.), *Advances in adolescent development: The biological connection to adolescent behavior and development* (Vol. 1, pp. 11–37). Newbury Park, CA: Sage.

MacCorquodale, P., & DeLamanter, J. (1979). Self-image and premarital sexuality. *Journal of Marriage and the Family, 41,* 327–339.

MacGregor, F. C. (1974). *Transformation and identity: The face and plastic surgery.* New York: Quadrangle Press.

McCandless, B. R. (1970). *Adolescents.* Hinsdale, IL: Dryden Press.

Mathes, E. W. (1975). The effects of physical attractiveness and anxiety on heterosexual attraction over a series of five encounters. *Journal of Marriage and the Family, 37,* 769–774.

Mathes, E. W., & Kahn, A. (1975). Physical attractiveness, happiness, neuroticism, and self-esteem. *Journal of Psychology, 90,* 27–30.

Miller, A. G. (Ed.). (1982). *In the eye of the beholder: Contemporary issues in stereotyping.* New York: Praeger.

Patzer, G. L. (1985). *The physical attractiveness phenomena.* New York: Plenum Press.

Sigall, H., & Michela, J. (1976). I'll bet you say that to all the girls: Physical attractiveness and reactions to praise. *Journal of Personality, 44,* 611–626.

Taylor, P. A., & Glenn, N. D. (1976). The utility of education and attractiveness for females' status attainment through marriage. *American Sociological Review, 41,* 484–497.

Udry, J. R. (1977). The importance of being beautiful: A reexamination and racial comparison. *American Journal of Sociology, 83,* 154–160.

Walster, E., Aronson, V., Abrahams, D., & Rottmann, L. (1966). Importance of physical attractiveness in dating behavior. *Journal of Personality and Social Psychology, 4,* 508–516.

Zakin, D. F., Blyth, D. A., & Simmons, R. G. (1984). Physical attractiveness as a mediator of the impact of early pubertal changes for girls. *Journal of Youth and Adolescence, 13,* 439–450.

See Also

Body Image; Menarche and Body Image.

Piaget, Jean

Willis F. Overton
Temple University

Jacques Montangero
University of Geneva

Jean Piaget was a Swiss psychologist whose hundreds of theoretical and empirical books and papers framed the context for psychology's understanding of cognitive development during the second half of the twentieth century (see Piaget 1952, 1954, 1962). Piaget was born in 1896 and died in 1980. His theory of cognitive development was often called "genetic epistemology." The term "genetic" means development, and "epistemology" refers to forms of knowing.

Piaget's theory is grounded in several organismic assumptions. First, meaning is understood as being ultimately rooted in the activity of the organism. This led to Piaget's famous constructivist position that maintains all knowledge is the product of the organism's activity as it makes contact with the world. Second, development proceeds according to principles of integration and differentiation, and these are understood as being basically the processes or activities of assimilation and accommodation. Thus, development is not explained as the product of endogenous neural activity, nor the product of exogenous environmental activity. Development is a process explained by the assimilation/accommodation equilibration system. Finally, development is understood as proceeding through a series of levels of organization or levels of system, where later systems integrate and subsume earlier systems and later systems exhibit systemic properties that are not characteristic of the earlier systems.

Given these basic assumptions, Piaget presented a specific theory that described two subsystems at each level of development (see Piaget, 1987; Piaget & Garcia, 1986). One subsystem describes the competence or understanding of the world that is available at that particular level, the other describes the procedures or strategies designed to successfully access and implement that competence. At the earliest level, the competence is organized biological activity, and procedures develop out of this activity as it encounters the world. Early procedural activity results in a competence at the level of psychological processes. This competence is termed sensorimotor knowledge and it is not clearly differentiated initially from its procedural aspect (know how). At the next level, a representational competence develops that permits thinking, along with procedures appropriate to this level. At the following level, which extends through the preadolescent period (see Inhelder & Piaget, 1964), thinking becomes organized into systems of thought that permit knowing in terms of a fragmentary logic that is tightly connected to the observational world. Then, in adolescence (see Inhelder & Piaget, 1958), the individual's knowing system becomes organized as a unified system of thought that permits systematic and logical reasoning on elements of the previous fragmentary logic. This adolescent form of knowing Piaget called formal operational thought or formal reasoning. It is an area of investigation that has had a major impact on the way psychology understands the nature of adolescent cognition, thinking, and reasoning, as these processes are applied across a wide variety of domains from deductive reasoning to investigations of morality, identity, self, social relationship, and many life issues.

References

Inhelder, B. & Piaget, J. (1958). *The growth of logical thinking from childhood to adolescence.* New York: Wiley.

Inhelder, B. & Piaget, J. (1964). *The early growth of logic in the child.* New York: Harper and Row.

Piaget, J. (1952). *The origins of intelligence in children.* New York: Norton.

Piaget, J. (1954). *The construction of reality in the child.* New York: Basic Books.

Piaget, J. (1962). *Play, dreams and imitation in childhood.* New York: Norton.

Piaget, J. (1987). *Possibility and necessity. Volume 1. The role of possibility in cognitive development. Volume 2. The role of necessity in cognitive development.* Minneapolis: Univ. of Minnesota Press.

Piaget, J. & Garcia, R. (1986). *Vers une logique de signification.* Geneva, Switzerland: Editions Murionde.

See Also

Blos, Peter; Erikson, Erik Homburger; Freud, Anna; Freud, Sigmund; Havighurst, Robert J.; Inhelder, Barbel.

Political Development

Joseph Adelson
University of Michigan

Most research on adolescent politics stems from two separate sources: political science and developmental psychology. At one time there was reason to expect some confluence of these tributaries, but it has not yet taken place, and likely will not in the foreseeable future. Work in political science has from its beginnings emphasized attitudes and affiliations—how they are acquired, and their stability or change over time. The earliest work concentrated on knowledge alone—what youngsters knew about the political system and its actors. The results were discouraging (as they continue to be) in that information about government and politics seemed inadequate; in the fullness of time, however, it became clear that the weakness was not limited to the young, nor limited to politics, but was part of a more general pattern of educational mediocrity (e.g., as in the findings reported by Ravitch & Finn, 1988).

The first work in the political science tradition that was analytic in nature—that went beyond the descriptive—can be placed under the rubric of "political socialization." How do children become educated to the political? Who influences them—parents, teachers, peers—and how and when, and in which domains? This has proved to be an extraordinarily difficult set of questions to answer. What may be the leading work in this area, Jennings and Niemi's *Generations and Politics* (1981) has its hands full simply explicating the remarkably dense texture of relationships they uncover. They find, for example, that youngsters do "inherit" parental politics, but only to a limited degree. There are generational differences, but no gap. Within a generation one will find stability in positions taken, but also change. If children depart from their parents' politics over time, so do the parents depart from their own (earlier) politics. And so it goes. It is no wonder that the authors' final chapter is titled: "Interpretation of a Half-empty Glass." Perhaps the most important single suggestion to come out of the larger body of work is that the views developed in adolescence tend to persist into later life.

We may note that these rich and complex findings do not, and cannot, address the questions likely to be of central interest to most psychologists: how political thinking develops, or what intrapsychic processes are involved in adolescent political sentiment. On the latter question, one has the sense of opportunities missed. Much of the work was done in the late 1960s and tended to celebrate the youth politics of the moment. It concentrated on demographic extremes—highly politicized youngsters of elite background—and overused "clinical" (i.e., anecdotal) approaches. A meticulous critique of the canon, by Rothman and Lichter (1982) did not have the impact it merited, having been published after interest had subsided.

Studies of adolescent political thinking were inspired by the Piagetian tradition that dominated postwar developmental psychology. This approach centers on the growth of cognitive capacity, seen as an outcome of the interaction between biological maturation and the stimulation provided by learning and experience. These studies are less interested in content—in attitudes and beliefs—than in the quality of thinking as it changes during the adolescent years.

A representative set of researches in this area were carried out by Adelson and his associates (Adelson, 1986). Youngsters ranging in age from eleven to eighteen were asked to imagine a group of a thousand people migrating to a Pacific island to build a new society. The specific interview questions asked the youngsters to make decisions as the islanders might, on a wide range of issues: government, law, justice, the balance between rights and responsibilities, and the balance between personal liberty and the common good. The findings demonstrate a fundamental change in cognition, with the years between thirteen and fifteen appearing to be pivotal. First, children achieve abstractness, and as a result can grasp principles (e.g., freedom of speech or religion) that are merely catchphrases up to that point. They are also able to understand such terms as "community," and can judge issues with respect to the overall needs of the social order. Second, they achieve a longer time perspective, taking into account effects in the distant future. Third, they are more aware of complexity, both in human psychology and in their appraisal of social institutions. Fourth, they are far less authoritarian and punitive, less likely to glorify the state and its power,

or to propose Draconian punishment for trivial offenses. Fifth, they are less idealistic, less willing to believe in utopian outcomes, and more cautious about the frailties of "human nature." These findings hold up in cross-national study (U.S., Great Britain, and W. Germany) and in middle- and working-class samples, both black and white.

The topic is at the moment moribund, a sub-Sahara in a domain—adolescent psychology in general—which is itself underdeveloped. An informal survey of psychological journals for the last few years finds little new work being published. It may well be that the topic is suffering from its mixed ancestry, psychologists perhaps perceiving it as "belonging" to political science. Or it may be that the strong interest in moral psychology has entirely captured the attention of those scholars who might otherwise study the parallel processes in political thinking. Be that as it may, the topic survives, does not thrive, and waits to be revived.

References

Adelson, J. (1986). Inventing Adolescence. *Transaction*.

Jennings, M. K. & Niemi, R. G. (1981). *Generations and Politics*. Princeton: Princeton University Press.

Ravitch, D. and Finn, C. E. (1987). *What Do Our 17-Year-Olds Know?* New York: Harper and Row.

Rothman, S. & Lichter, S. R. (1982). *Roots of Radicalism*. New York: Oxford University Press.

See Also

Conformity in Adolescence; Intimacy; Introspectiveness, Adolescent; Rites of Passage; Self-Regulation; Temperament during Adolescence; Temperament in Adolescence and Its Functional Significance.

Pregnancy in Adolescence

Deborah L. Coates
Brigit Van Widenfelt
Department of Psychology
The Catholic University of America

Pregnancy and parenthood during adolescence is an undesirable social phenomenon and is largely an unintended consequence of adolescent sexual behavior. Adolescent pregnancy has received significant national attention because of the moral, legal, health, and social issues that it raises. The National Research Council (NRC) of the National Academy of Sciences, in a comprehensive report titled *Risking the Future*, identifies three perspectives associated with adolescent pregnancy. Adolescent pregnancy can be viewed as (1) an indicator of early, nonmarital sexual activity among adolescents; (2) a problem created by the availability of contraception and particularly of abortion services; or (3) a social burden resulting from serious social and economic consequences of adolescent parenting (National Research Council [NRC], 1987).

Trends: The Extent of the Phenomenon

A noticeable increase in births to adolescent mothers began in 1960. From 1960 to 1975 there was a 50% increase in the number of births to adolescent mothers. The proportion of adolescents becoming pregnant each year, or the teen pregnancy rate, rose steadily in the 1970s, but this rate has remained fairly stable in the 1980s. Currently about 11% of adolescents (approximately 1 million) become pregnant each year. Twenty-five percent of young women who were age 18 in 1981 are estimated to have been pregnant at least once and 44% of the young women who were 20 years old in 1981 had been pregnant at least once. Using 1985 trends, it is estimated that 8.7% of adolescents will have at least one live birth and 8.8% will have one or more abortions by age twenty.

Births to teens have declined steadily since 1970. Births to 15- to 19-year-olds declined in 1986 to 51 births per 1,000 from 68 per 1,000 in 1970. In 1987 there were 472, 623 adolescent births representing a 100,000 births decline since 1979. This decline is expected to continue somewhat for the next several years. It has been attributed to a decline in the adolescent population, to a slight decline in the birth rate, and to an increase in adolescent abortions. About 44% of adolescents who become pregnant choose to abort their pregnancies according to data collected in 1987. Few choose to place their infants in adoptive homes. The most dramatic declines in recent birth rates have occurred for older rather than younger adolescents and for African-Americans (classified as "black" in the U.S. Census). Despite these declines, adolescent pregnancy occurs at a notably greater rate in the United States than in other Western nations. The NRC (1987) notes that this difference is most noticeable among younger adolescents. Girls 15 and younger are five times more likely to give birth in the United States than in other Western nations.

Sixty-five percent of all adolescent mothers were unmarried in 1987. The rate of unmarried adolescent births has increased fourfold since 1960. Younger and African-American mothers are more likely to be unmarried at a birth. The birth rate for African-American adolescents in 1985 was 18.6% and was twice as high as the 9.3% rate for European-American adolescents. Both groups of adolescents are equally likely to have an abortion once pregnant. However, African-American adolescents are more likely to have births and abortions because of their higher pregnancy rates.

These pregnancy rate trends are based on data reported in several sources (Adams, Adams-Taylor, & Pittman, 1989; Henshaw, Kenney, Somberg, & Van Vort, 1989; Hughes, Johnson, Rosenbaum, Butler, & Simmons, 1988; Moore, 1989; NRC, 1987). More detailed data on pregnancy trends are available in published annual summaries of national data (see end of this entry) and state and local vital statistics offices or state health departments. Primary sources for these reports are general population surveys conducted by the U.S. Census Bureau, The National Center for Health Statistics, and other federal agencies, including the National Survey of Family Growth, The National Natality Survey, and the Health and Nutrition Examination. Each collects ongoing data and has been in progress between 5 and 44 years.

Why Adolescents Become Pregnant and Choose to Parent

Sexual activity obviously may lead to pregnancy; thus adolescents who are more sexually active are more likely to become pregnant. Once an adolescent has decided to become sexually active she must also decide: (1) whether to use contraceptives; (2) if pregnant, whether to deliver or abort; and (3) if a child is delivered, whether to parent or give that responsibility to someone else (Flick, 1986). If adolescents come from single-parent or low-income families, or are male or African-American, then they are more likely to be sexually active at an earlier age than are other adolescents. Early physical development is strongly associated with the early beginning of sexual activity. However, social influences, such as parental communication and church attendance, have been found to curtail the initiation of sexual activity (NRC, 1987). Some adolescents without sex education begin sexual activity earlier, but sex education in itself does not seem to result in either an increase or a decrease of sexual activity. Adolescents who become pregnant are more likely to have mothers who were pregnant or who became a parent as an adolescent (Flick, 1986; NRC, 1987). This appears to be less true for a sample of adolescents followed longitudinally in the Furstenberg (1987) Baltimore study. Adolescent girls seeking approval and acceptance may turn to sexual behavior, in many instances without considering contraceptive options, to gratify these needs (Dash, 1989).

Permissive attitudes toward sexuality, cultural mores that value children and accept childbearing without marriage, and the demotivating persistence of severe economic hardship have all been suggested as reasons why pregnancy and parenting occur at high rates for some youngsters. Racism and poverty have been identified as factors leading to higher rates of pregnancy among African-American adolescents. These conditions create perceptions that marriage and family formation are unavailable and that prospects for obtaining valued educational and career goals are limited (Franklin, 1987). This means that the typical personal and economic incentives that often help to motivate one to delay pregnancy are not available to these youngsters (Johnson, Lay, & Wilbrandt, 1988). There are no data available that help us to understand how economic factors affect pregnancy rates independently of ethnic group classification.

Evidence also suggests that African-American and Hispanic families value children to a greater extent than some other cultural groups and that African-American adolescents are more accepting of sexual intercourse and childbirth outside of marriage (Furstenberg, 1987; Ortiz & Nuttall, 1987). Adolescent girls who tend to have poor self-esteem have been found to become pregnant and, once becoming pregnant, to keep their infants, at a higher rate than other girls (Dash, 1989). Girls who become pregnant are also more likely to come from low-income families; to be older and to be Mexican-American, rather than African-American or European-American; to have had a sibling who was pregnant as a teen; and to have poorer school performance (Flick, 1986).

Adolescents who decide to abort are usually younger, are in school, highly mo-tivated to perform well in school, and are self-confident. Those adolescents choosing to deliver are likely to come from single-parent homes; to have a longer, stable relationship with a boyfriend; and to have had a sibling or mother who was pregnant as a teen (Flick, 1986). There is little research available that explores the differences between adolescents who choose to parent and those who give their child up to an adoptive family, either formally or informally. One study, however, found no differences in the emotional stability of these two groups of pregnant adolescents (Flick, 1986).

Adolescents' perceptions of family, community, social opportunities, and future vocational and marital prospects are central to understanding the complex patterns of factors resulting in adolescent pregnancy. These self-perceptions are influenced by the adolescent's family, neighborhood, and social environment, which often includes racial discrimination, poverty, and other negative social influences. Understanding why adolescents risk pregnancy may lead to effective prevention of pregnancy.

Consequences of Adolescent Pregnancy and Characteristics of Adolescent Parents

Pregnancy and parenting during adolescence results in medical, social, and economic problems for the adolescents and/or their offspring. Few negative medical or social consequences have been associated with abortion or adoption placement, although some minor risks are associated with these choices (McLaughlin, Pearce, Manninen, & Winges, 1988). Most pregnant adolescents experience few medical problems, although they are more likely to occur if the mother is living in poverty or is very young.

Adolescents more frequently spontaneously abort a pregnancy than older women (NRC, 1987). Very young adolescents have higher rates than older mothers of medical complications during pregnancy, pregnancy-related maternal and infant death, and babies who are born too small (NRC, Volume II, 1987). Medical problems experienced by adolescent mothers are likely to be the result of poor weight gain due to inadequate diet before and during pregnancy (Heidiger, School, Belsky, Ances, & Salamon, 1989). In addition, many adolescent mothers do not receive early and adequate prenatal care, which increases the likelihood of an unhealthy newborn (Osofsky, Culp, & Ware, 1988). This is more likely to be the case for African-American adolescent mothers living in poverty. The health risks associated with adolescent pregnancy are greatly reduced with adequate prenatal care and good nutrition intake (Institute of Medicine, 1985).

Use of drugs during pregnancy may pose the most serious maternal and child health risks for adolescents. Drug use may be a key factor in determining which adolescents mothers and infants are likely to experience medical problems. Drug use and pregnancy outcomes have been examined among African-American adolescents and have been associated with a number of other social and health problems (Amaro, Zuckerman, & Cabral, 1989).

A number of studies conclude that adolescents who give birth are less likely to complete high school or to attain other educational goals as compared to women who delay childbirth until their twenties. The NRC (1987) concludes that women who give birth between ages 16 and 18 are less likely to finish high school than mothers who give birth at a younger age. These differences in education attainment be-

tween adolescent and older mothers diminish several years after the birth and are less prevalent for African-American as compared to European-American adolescents (Furstenberg, Brooks-Gunn, & Morgan, 1987).

About one-third of the marriages among adolescents occur after pregnancy although the majority of pregnant adolescents do not marry (NRC, 1987). Marriage after pregnancy is more likely to occur for older and for European-American adolescents and these marriages are highly unstable, as are most adolescent marriages (Furstenberg, 1976). Adolescent mothers often have more children, on average one more child, and their children are closer in age than children of women who delay childbearing until their twenties (Moore & Hofferth, 1987). This is less true for recent trends and has not been noted for African-American adolescent mothers (Furstenberg, et al., 1987).

Lack of educational achievement and many other factors make it difficult for adolescent parents to obtain adequate employment and this leads to income instability. This is especially true for European-American adolescent mothers, perhaps because they have fewer work expectations and less work experience than their African-American counterparts (Koo & Bilsborrow, 1979, as cited in NRC, 1987). European-American adolescent mothers, when compared to European-American older mothers, are less educated, have a lower standard of living, and often require public assistance (Furstenberg, 1976; Garcia-Coll, Hoffman, Van Houten, & Oh, 1987; Moore & Burt, 1982). The cost of providing this public assistance has been estimated to be about $16.6 billion dollars annually; other cost estimates are provided by Burt (1986).

The problems of an adolescent mother change over the family life cycle. Early in the parenting experience adolescent mothers have lower status occupations and incomes and also experience less satisfaction with work than do women who become parents at older ages. However, much later in life these differences decline (Trussel & Abowd, 1979, as cited in NRC, 1987). This may be due to the diversity of outcomes which result after long periods of time and because older women who give birth often decline to work or work part-time during the early childhood period (Furstenberg et al., 1987; Koo & Bilsborrow, 1979, as cited in NRC, 1987).

The social support system and coping mechanisms of adolescent mothers have been described extensively (Barth, 1988; Colletta, 1983; Panzarine, 1988; Reis & Herz, 1987; Stevens, 1988). Pregnant African-American adolescents seem to experience a martialing of social relationships that provide considerable material and emotional support during and following pregnancy. This support usually occurs after some period of disapproval and mild rejection of the pregnancy by parents. Adolescent mothers and pregnant adolescents experience less depression and anxiety than has typically been assumed. They do not seem to worry about the issues raised by a pregnancy to any greater extent than their nonpregnant peers worry about other matters (Barth, 1988).

Offspring of adolescents have been found to be less likely to have adequate early development and physical health, and to be less successful at school than those born to adult mothers (Furstenberg et al., 1987; Hofferth, 1981, as cited in NRC, Volume II, 1987). These differences are long term and consistent for African-American and European-American mothers and for boy and girl offspring, although they are more prevalent among boys (Brooks-Gunn & Furstenberg, 1986). These children of children tend to (1) do

more poorly on standard tests of intellectual ability and achievement; (2) have poorer grades; (3) have higher rates of behavior problems and school suspension; (4) be less socially secure and skilled; (5) be more likely to abuse harmful substances (e.g., alcohol, drugs, cigarettes); and (6) be more likely to engage in sexual behavior (NRC, 1987). Early work has shown that children of adolescent mothers are also more likely to be hospitalized by age five and to become pregnant during adolescence than those born to adult mothers (Furstenberg & Brooks-Gunn, 1985; Taylor, Wadsworth, & Butler, 1983, as cited in NRC, 1987). These consequences do not appear to be directly related to adolescent pregnancy but occur as a result of the social and economic difficulties that pregnancy and parenting present.

Adolescent fathers are less affected by pregnancy than adolescent mothers of their children, but do experience stress. Little is known about how adolescent fathers experience this stress because this problem has been examined in a limited way (see Furstenberg, Brooks-Gunn, & Chase-Landsdale, 1989).

Prevention of Pregnancy and Intervention with Parenting Adolescents

The NRC (1987) has identified five types of adolescent pregnancy interventions: abortion services, prenatal and perinatal health care services, economic support programs, services to improve the social, emotional, and cognitive development of adolescent mothers, and programs that enhance the life options of adolescent parents. Many theories and service programs have been offered to prevent pregnancy or to reduce its negative consequences once it has occurred. Detailed information about this is widely available (Allen-Meares & Shore, 1986; Barth, 1988; Herz, Olson, & Reis, 1988; Polit, Quint, & Riccio, 1988; Quinn, 1986; Roosa, 1986; Schinke, Barth, Gilchrist, & Maxwell, 1986; Zabin & Hirsch, 1988).

Most interventions attempt to prevent a first pregnancy; others are designed to intervene with pregnant adolescents to prevent a subsequent pregnancy or birth to an adolescent. Most schools now have sex education programs in their curriculum but these programs vary widely in content. These efforts focus on the causes of sexual activity and pregnancy and have attempted to educate adolescents about reproduction and contraception. Other programs have focused on interpersonal planning and decision-making skills, and attempt to help adolescents have a greater sense of control over their life options. Some of these programs have resulted in increased use of contraceptives. These programs sometimes include the use of adult role models. Family-focused prevention has found that the mother plays a significant role in delaying sexual activity and encouraging contraception use (Quinn, 1986). Family planning clinics have offered prevention services by providing easily available contraceptive information and products. These services have been controversial because it has been argued that they encourage sexual activity among adolescents. But no current research supports this view (NRC, 1987).

Pregnancy prevention efforts have not been extensively evaluated; reported results are mixed, unclear, or short term. Determining the impact of these efforts on pregnancy rates is complicated because it is difficult to obtain accurate information about who is becoming pregnant and when and how a pregnancy ends. However, many programs are successful in meeting interim program goals such as improving knowledge about contraception, fostering family communication, teaching problem-solving skills, and improving educational and job aspirations and attainment. Access to contraceptive abortion services increases contraception use and decreases childbearing (NRC, 1987). The Johns Hopkins Adolescent Pregnancy Prevention Program is a primary pregnancy prevention program that has been carefully evaluated. Moderate prevention success has been reported; this program provides a model and methods that allow for replication. This program provided extensive services to adolescents, was school and off-campus based, and used professional nurses and social workers to provide services during and after school hours (see Zabin and Hirsch, 1988, for detailed description).

Supportive services during pregnancy, such as nutrition counseling and expanded prenatal care, improve the birth outcomes for adolescent mothers. Supportive services for adolescent parents include: income support, child care services, and education about parenting skills, life options, and work skills. Moderate effects on parenting, life choices, aspirations, and the attainment of economic security have been found. Interventions with children of young mothers have also been moderately successful. All of these intervention approaches are costly, complex to administer and offer, and have short-term rather than long-term benefits. The Manpower Demonstration Research Corporation has provided a detailed evaluation of four moderately successful interventions offered in Boston, Harlem, Phoenix, and Riverside, California. They evaluated Project Redirection, a multisite effort to offer and test the effectiveness of services to adolescent parents. This report provides a detailed example of information on the complexities of such interventions and the most promising outcomes related to the services offered (Polit et al., 1988).

Adolescent Pregnancy, Parenting Policy, and Future Research

A number of suggestions have been offered regarding what should be done both nationally and locally to address the problem of adolescent pregnancy (see Adams et al., 1989; Furstenberg et al., 1987; Furstenberg et al., 1989; NRC, 1987; Ooms, 1981). The Children's Defense Fund, a child advocacy organization, has suggested that to prevent early parenthood adolescents need access to every resource that would prevent pregnancy and compelling reasons or incentives to delay pregnancy. They suggest that pregnant and parenting adolescents need extensive education in parenting skills, employment training, and friendly support assistance so that self-sufficiency can be obtained. The NRC (1987) generally concurs with these recommendations. It offers detailed suggestions that support these general guiding policies. The NRC (1987) also supports the development of national data sets to collect ongoing data on adolescent fertility and childbearing and on the costs of support and prevention services. A notable lack of data is available on abortion and adoption. Extensive research in service settings is required to address this data deficiency. More information is needed about the role of families, communities, the media, public policies, and societal influences on adolescent pregnancy.

Sources of Information on Adolescent Pregnancy

A number of organizations and published articles are excellent sources of information about adolescent pregnancy. Adams et al. (1989) have provided a compendium of organizations and materials on adolescent pregnancy. Child Trends, the Alan Guttmacher Institute, and The Children's Defense Fund, all located in Washington, D.C., compile summary data on the incidence of adolescent fertility and parenting nationally and for each state, major city, region of the country, and major ethnic group. The Ford Foundation, the Robert Wood Johnson Foundation, and the Charles Stewart Mott Foundation have funded major research projects exploring aspects of adolescent pregnancy. The Mott Foundation maintains a "Too Early Childbearing Network" of organizations whose goals are to prevent adolescent pregnancy, to expand life options for adolescent mothers, and to enhance the lives of children born to adolescents. A directory is available from Mott.

References

Adams, G., Adams-Taylor, S., & Pittman, K. (1989). Adolescent pregnancy and parenthood: A review of the problem, solutions, and consequences. *Family Relations, 38,* 223–229.

Allen-Meares, P., & Shore, D. (1986). A transactional framework for working with adolescents and their sexualities. *Journal of Social Work and Human Sexuality, 5,* 71–80.

Amaro, H., Zuckerman, B., & Cabral, H. (1989). Drug use among adolescent mothers: Profile of risk. *Pediatrics, 84,* 144–151.

Barth, R. (1988). Social skill and social support among young mothers. *Journal of Community Psychology, 16,* 132–143.

Brooks-Gunn, J., & Furstenberg, F. (1986). The children of adolescent mothers: Physical, academic, and psychological outcomes. *Developmental Review, 6,* 224–251.

Burt, M. R. (1986). *Estimates of public costs for teenage childbearing.* Washington, DC: Urban Institute.

Colletta, N. (1983). At risk for depression: A

study of young mothers. *Journal of Genetic Psychology, 142*, 301–310.

Dash, L. (1989). *When children want children: The urban crisis of teenage childbearing.* New York: William Morrow.

Flick, L. (1986). Paths to adolescent parenthood: Implications for prevention. *Public Health Reports, 101*, 132–147.

Franklin, D. (1987). Black adolescent pregnancy: A literature review. *Child and Youth Services, 9*, 15–39.

Furstenberg, F. (1976). *Unplanned parenthood: The social consequences of teenage childbearing.* New York: Free Press.

Furstenberg, F. (1987). Race differences in teenage sexuality, pregnancy, and adolescent childbearing. *Milbank Quarterly, 65*, 381–403.

Furstenberg, F., & Brooks-Gunn, J. (1985). Adolescent fertility: Causes, consequences, and remedies. In L. Aiken & D. Mechanic (Eds.), *Applications of social science to medicine and health policy* (pp. 307–334). New Brunswick: Rutgers University Press.

Furstenberg, F., Brooks-Gunn, J., & Chase-Landsdale, L. (1989). Teenaged pregnancy and childbearing. *American Psychologist, 44*, 313–320.

Furstenberg, F., Brooks-Gunn, J., & Morgan, S. (1987). *Adolescent mothers in later life.* Cambridge: Cambridge University Press.

Garcia-Coll, C., Hoffman, J., Van Houten, L., & Oh, W. (1987). The social context of teenage childbearing: Effects on the infant's care-giving environment. *Journal of Youth and Adolescence, 16*, 345–360.

Heidiger, M., School, T., Belsky, D., Ances, I., & Salamon, R. (1989). Patterns of weight gain in adolescent pregnancy: Effects on birth weight and preterm delivery. *Obstetrics and Gynecology, 74*, 6–12.

Henshaw, S., Kenney, A., Somberg, D., & Van Vort, J. (1989). *Teenage pregnancy in the United States: The scope of the problem and state responses.* Washington, DC: Alan Guttmacher Institute.

Herz, E., Olson, L., & Reis, J. (1988). Family planning for teens: Strategies for improving outreach and service delivery in public health settings. *Public Health Reports, 103*, 422–430.

Hofferth, S. L. (1981). "Effects of Number and Timing of Births on Family Well-Being Over the Life Cycle." Final Report to National Institute of Child Health and Human Development. Contract #NO1-HD-82850. Washington, DC: Urban Institute.

Hughes, D., Johnson, K., Rosenbaum, S., Butler, E., & Simmons, J. (1988). *The health of America's children: Maternal and child health data book.* Washington, DC: Children's Defense Fund.

Institute of Medicine (1985). *Preventing low birth weight.* Washington, DC: National Academy of Sciences Press.

Johnson, F., Lay, P., & Wilbrandt, M. (1988). Teenage pregnancy: Interventions and direction. *Journal of the National Medical Association, 80*, 145–152.

Koo, H. P., & Bilsborrow, R. E. (1979). Multivariate analyses of effects of age at first birth: Results from the 1973 National Survey of Family Growth and 1975 Current Population Survey. Research Triangle, NC: Research Triangle Institute.

McLaughlin, S., Pearce, S., Manninen, D., & Winges, L. (1988). To parent or relinquish: Consequences for adolescent mothers. *Social Work, 33*, 320–324.

Moore, K. A., & Burt, M. R. (1982). *Private crisis public cost: Policy perspectives on teenage childbearing.* Washington, DC: Urban Institute.

Moore, K. (1989). *Facts at a glance.* Washington, DC: Child Trends.

Moore, K., & Hofferth, S. (1987). The consequences of age at first childbirth: Family size (Working Paper 1146-02). Washington, DC: Urban Institute.

National Research Council. (1987). *Risking the future: Adolescent sexuality and childbearing:*

(Vol. 1). *Working Papers* (Vol. 2). Washington, DC: National Academy of Sciences Press.

Ooms, T. (Ed.). (1981). *Teen pregnancy in a family context: Implications for policy.* Philadelphia: Temple University Press.

Ortiz, C., & Nuttall, E. (1987). Adolescent pregnancy: Effects of family support, education, and religion on the decision to carry or terminate among Puerto Rican teenagers. *Adolescence, 22,* 897–917.

Osofsky, J., Culp, A., & Ware, L. (1988). Intervention challenges with adolescent mothers and their infants. *Psychiatry, 51,* 236–241.

Panzarine, S. (1988). Teen mothering: Behaviors and interventions. *Journal of Adolescent Health Care, 9,* 443–448.

Polit, D., Quint, J., & Riccio, J. (1988). *The challenge of serving teenage mothers: Lessons from Project Redirection.* New York: Manpower Demonstration Research Corporation.

Quinn, J. (1986). Rooted in research: Effective adolescent pregnancy prevention programs. *Journal of Social Work and Human Sexuality, 5,* 99–110.

Reis, J., & Herz, E. (1987). Correlates of adolescent parenting. *Adolescence, 22,* 599–609.

Roosa, M. (1986). Adolescent mothers, school drop-outs, and school-based intervention programs. *Family Relations, 35,* 313–317.

Schinke, S., Barth, R., Gilchrist, L., & Maxwell, J. (1986). Adolescent mothers, stress, and prevention. *Journal of Human Stress, 12,* 162–167.

Stevens, J. (1988). Social support, locus of control, and parenting in three low-income groups of mothers: Black teenagers, black adults, and white adults. *Child Development, 59,* 635–642.

Taylor, I. B., Wadsworth, J., & Butler, N. R. (1983). "Teenage mothering, admission to hospital, and accidents during the first five years." *Archives of Disease in Childhood. 58,* (6).

Trussell, T. J., & Abowd, J. (1979, April). *Teenage mothers, labor force participation and wage rates.* Paper presented at the Annual Meeting of the Population Association of America, Philadelphia.

Zabin, L., & Hirsch, M. (1988). *Evaluation of pregnancy prevention in the school context.* Lexington, MA: Lexington Books.

See Also

Childbearing, Adolescent: Obstetric and Filial Outcomes; Childbearing, Teenage: Effects on Children; Childbirth and Marriage, Adolescent: Associations with Long-Term Marital Stability; Fathers, Adolescent; Fathers, Teenage; Mothers, Adolescent and Their Young Children; Parental Behavior, Adolescent; Parenthood and Marriage in Adolescence: Associations with Educational and Occupational Attainment; Pregnancy and Childbearing: Effects on Teen Mothers; Pregnancy in Adolescence, Interventions to Prevent.

Pregnancy and Childbearing: Effects on Teen Mothers

Frank F. Furstenberg, Jr.

University of Pennsylvania

Each year about one million teenagers in the United States become pregnant. Because fewer teens are marrying today, a growing proportion of adolescent births are to single mothers (Hofferth & Hayes, 1987). The U.S. rate of teenage pregnancy and childbearing is among the highest of any Western nation including those with comparable levels of sexual activity. For example, teens in the U.S. are twice as likely to become pregnant and have children as Canadian adolescents and three times as likely as Swedish youth. Birth rates among adolescents ages 15-19 declined only moderately in the U.S. during the period from the early 1970s to the early 1980s while they plummeted in almost all other Western nations. Teenage childbearing has emerged as a major social problem in the U. S. while adolescent parenthood has become a rare event in most other Western nations (Jones et al., 1986).

These cross-national differences are not easily explained. True, blacks contribute disproportionately to high rates of early childbearing in the U.S. But even when blacks are removed from the comparisons, the cross-national differential is only slightly reduced. Indeed, in the past decade black rates of nonmarital teen parenthood have remained relatively stable while white rates have been steadily rising. In 1960 the rate of nonmarital childbearing was 12 times as high for black adolescents as for whites; in 1970, this ratio had dropped to about nine times; by 1985, the ratio had declined to about four. It appears that white youth in the U.S. are increasingly resembling blacks in their pattern of teen sexuality, pregnancy, and childbearing (Furstenberg, 1987; Moore, Simms, & Betsey, 1986).

How are we to account for the unusually high rate of pegnancy and early childbearing among U.S. youth? The explanation can be traced in part to the transformation that occurred in family formation after the mid-1960s when the postwar pattern of early marriage and childbearing came to a screeching halt. A greater number of adolescents postponed marriage in order to improve their long-term economic prospects, especially as the supply of well-paying unskilled jobs declined sharply. As marriage age rose, the link between onset of sexual relations and matrimony was severed. Youth were no longer willing to wait to initiate sex until they were married or about to marry. No doubt, the greater openness about sex in the 1960s and the availability of the contraceptive pill also contributed to the rapid shift in sexual standards (Chilman, 1983).

Prior to the 1970s, only incomplete information exists on the level of sexual activity among U.S. teenagers. The much publicized 1971 survey by Zelnik and Kantner of teenage females revealed surprisingly high rates of sexual experience (Zelnik, Kantner, & Ford, 1981). Moreover, two subsequent studies by the same team of researchers demonstrated that teenage females sharply increased their rates of sexual initiation throughout the 1970s (Zelnik & Kantner, 1980). Evidence from the National Survey of Family Growth suggests that teenage sexual activity may have reached a plateau in the early 1980s, but at very high levels. By 1982 45% of all females aged 15-19 had ever had premarital intercourse, up from 32% in 1971. At age 19 73% of teens were sexually active (72% of whites and 83% of blacks).

Despite the prevalence of sexual activity among teens, American society—unlike Europe or even Canada—has remained strongly disapproving of premarital sex, at least at an official level. Unwilling to adopt a pragmatic view about sex, contraceptive services are generally regarded in American society as a controversial and rather clandestine activity. Only recently, as the fear of AIDS has spread, has the government, media, educational institutions, and voluntary organizations been willing to treat sexual behavior among American teens as a reality, rather than a moral issue.

Official disapproval of premarital sex and the related unwillingness to support and promote contraceptive services may explain why sexually active American teenagers often fail to use contraception. Most teens know about contraception, most even know where and how to obtain it, but a relatively small fraction use birth control at first intercourse or practice contraception regularly after they initiate sexual relations (Zabin, 1981). Moreover, many American teenagers seem reluctant to plan for sexual behavior or to acknowledge the risks involved. The result is an extraordinarily high rate of unintended pregnancy. In 1984 almost one sexually active teen in four became pregnant (Hofferth & Hayes, 1987).

Of the one million pregnancies to teens in 1984, 134,000 ended in miscarriage and about 400,000 (or two out of five) were terminated by abortion. Abortion rates among American teens (as well as adults) are extremely high by international standards, another sign indicating the difficulty young women have in using contraception in this country.

Because legal restrictions on abortion have begun to tighten, abortion may begin to decline; however, as yet, the incidence of abortion has remained fairly stable (Henshaw & Van Vort, 1989). Relatively few teens are inclined to place their children for adoption, perhaps no more than 5% of the nearly half million who bring the pregnancy to term. The incidence of adoption has been largely unaffected by the active policy of the Reagan and Bush Administrations to discourage abortion by encouraging adoption.

A shrinking fraction of births to teenage mothers occur within marriage (Hofferth & Hayes, 1987). In 1960 only 15% of births to teenage mothers were to unmarried mothers; by 1985 this figure had jumped to 58% (45% of whites and 90% of blacks). Among teen mothers under age

18 marriage has all but disappeared among blacks (96% are single at delivery) and is rapidly declining among whites (60% are single at delivery).

Much has been written about the consequences of teen childbearing for young mothers. There is strong and consistent evidence that premature parenthood creates lasting disadvantages by increasing rates of school dropout, truncating women's training for economic careers, elevating their chances of marital instability, and magnifying their chances of having more children than they intend (Chilman, 1983; Hofferth & Hayes, 1987; McAnarney & Schreider, 1984; Trussel, 1988).

The data on the social consequences of early childbearing on school achievement are compelling. A number of studies have shown that teen mothers are much less likely to graduate from high school or to attend college. Some of the apparent effect of early childbearing on educational attainment, to be sure, actually may be traced to factors that precede the pregnancy (Furstenberg, 1976; Geronimus, 1987; Upchurch & McCarthy, 1989). Girls who are poor students, disaffected from school, and who are experiencing behavior problems are prone to becoming pregnant. After they do, they may also be more likely to bring the pregnancy to term. Thus, teen parenthood may not have a large independent effect on educational attainment when these selection factors are taken into account. Nevertheless, it seems likely that early parenthood itself complicates the process of schooling and reduces a teen mother's chances of completing high school.

Similarly, teen mothers fare less well in the labor market, in part because of poor skills and low education. Consequently, they are more likely to enter the welfare rolls and have a greater likelihood of becoming chronic welfare recipients. A study carried out by the Urban Institute calculated that teen parents added over 16 billion dollars in 1985 to the public costs of welfare and social programs (Burt & Levy, 1987).

Teen mothers are economically vulnerable in large measure because they are far more likely to be heads of households, living as single parents. Most young mothers reside with their parents during the transition to parenthood, but eventually the large majority set up independent households (Furstenberg & Crawford, 1978). While most teen mothers move out of their parents' household to enter marriage or a cohabiting relationship, the stability of such dyadic unions is low. Several studies have shown that teen mothers have much higher rates of marital instability. A recent study reveals that teen marriages were twice as likely to dissolve as marriages contracted by women in their late 20s. About a third of teen marriages ended within five years (Castro & Bumpass, 1989). And a growing proportion of teen mothers are electing to remain unmarried indefinitely. While not all of these women will remain single throughout their lives, their probability of entering a stable relationship (whether a formal or informal marriage) is relatively low. Lacking the benefit of a joint income, teen parents are more likely to live below or near the poverty line during their childrearing years.

Despite this rather grim portrait, a recent longitudinal study of mostly black teen mothers in Baltimore revealed that eventually many women are able to find their way out of poverty. The Baltimore results were replicated using data from several national surveys. These different data sets revealed a common result, a considerable variation in the economic and social well-being of teen mothers in their later life. Although many had dropped out of high school and sought public assistance, eventually most went back to school and got off welfare. By their early thirties the majority were economically self-sufficient. Only a quarter were still on welfare. In short, there appears to be more fluidity in the life course than is suggested by the results of short-term studies of teen parenthood (Furstenberg, Brooks-Gunn, & Morgan, 1987).

Economic success largely depends on continued schooling and the ability to regulate further fertility. Thus, programs directed at keeping teens in school or helping them to return to school are likely to have a high payoff in the long run. Similarly, efforts to provide intensive family planning information and services to teen mothers may be cost-effective. The Baltimore study revealed that participation in a special school program during pregnancy and a family planning clinic after delivery reduced the likelihood of being on welfare in life by more than two-thirds.

Even though recent research shows that the life course of the teenage mother is far from predetermined, it would be wrong to conclude that early childbearing is a benign event. For many women and their offspring, it has an aversive and, frequently, permanent impact on the shape of their lives. Premature parenthood limits individuals' chances of economic and marital success and therefore affects the well-being of their children. While ameliorative programs may mitigate the deleterious effects of early childbearing, prevention is a more cost-effective and socially acceptable strategy. A recent report (Hayes, 1987) issued by the National Research Council of the National Academy of Sciences, identified three general strategies for implementing this goal: enhancing the life options of disadvantaged youth; encouraging younger teens to delay sexual activity; and providing effective contraceptive sevices to sexually active youth.

References

Burt, M. R., & Levy, F. (1987). Estimates of public costs for teenage childbearing: A review of recent studies and estimates of 1985 public costs. In S. L. Hofferth & C. D. Hayes (Eds.), *Risking the Future* Vol. 2 (pp. 264–293). Washington, DC: National Academy Press.

Castro, T., & Bumpass, L. (1989). Recent trends in marital disruption. *Demography, 26*(1), 37–51.

Chilman, C. S. (Ed.). (1983). *Adolescent sexuality in a changing American society: Social and psychological perspectives for the human services professions* (2nd ed.). New York: John Wiley & Sons.

Furstenberg, F. F., Jr. (1976). *Unplanned parenthood: The social consequences of teenage childbearing*. New York: Free Press.

Furstenberg, F. F., Jr., & Crawford, A. G. (1978). Family support: Helping teenage mothers to cope. *Family Planning Perspectives, 10*(6), 322–333.

Furstenberg, F. F., Jr., Brooks-Gunn, J., & Morgan, S. P. (1987). *Adolescent mothers in later life*. New York: Cambridge University Press.

Furstenberg, F. F., Jr. (1987). Race differences in teenage sexuality, pregnancy, and adolescent childbearing. *Milbank Quarterly, 65*(2), 381–403.

Geronimus, A. (1987). On teenage childbearing and neonatal mortality in the United States. *Population and Development Review, 13*(2), 245–279.

Hayes, C. D. (Ed.). (1987). *Risking the future* (Vol. 1). Washington, DC: National Academy Press.

Henshaw, S. K., & Van Vort, J. (1989). Teenage abortion, birth, and pregnancy statistics: An update. *Family Planning Perspectives, 21*(2), 85–88.

Hofferth, S. L., & Hayes, C. D. (Eds.). (1987). *Risking the future* (Vol. 2). Washington, DC: National Academy Press.

Jones, E. F., Forrest, J. D., Goldman, N., Henshaw, S., Lincoln, R., Rosoff, J. I., Westoff, C. F., & Wulf, D. (1986). *Teenage pregnancy in Westernized countries*. New Haven: Yale University Press.

McAnarney, E. R., & Schreider, C. (1984). *Identifying social and psychological antecedents of adolescent pregnancy: The contribution of research to concepts of prevention*. New York: William T. Grant Foundation.

Moore, K. A., Simms, M. C., & Betsey, C. L. (1986). *Choice and circumstance*. New Brunswick, NJ: Transaction Books.

Trussell, J. (1988). Teenage pregnancy in the United States. *Family Planning Perspectives*, *20*(6), 262–272.

Upchurch, D. M., & McCarthy, J. (1989). Adolescent childbearing and high school completion in the 1980s: Have things changed? *Family Planning Perspectives*, *21*(5), 199–202.

Zabin, L. S. (1981). The impact of early use of prescription contraceptives on reducing premarital teenage pregnancies. *Family Planning Perspectives*, *13*(1), 72–74.

Zelnik, M., & Kantner, J. F. (1980). Sexual activity, contraceptive use and pregnancy among metropolitan-area teenagers: 1971–1979. *Family Planning Perspectives*, 12:230–237.

Zelnik, M., Kantner, J. F., & Ford, K. (1981). *Sex and pregnancy in adolescence*. Beverly Hills, CA: Sage Publications.

See Also

Childbearing, Adolescent: Obstetric and Filial Outcomes; Childbearing, Teenage: Effects on Children; Childbirth and Marriage, Adolescent: Associations with Long-Term Marital Stability; Fathers, Adolescent; Fathers, Teenage; Mothers, Adolescent and Their Young Children; Parental Behavior, Adolescent; Parenthood and Marriage in Adolescence: Associations with Educational and Occupational Attainment; Pregnancy in Adolescence, Interventions to Prevent.

Pregnancy, Interventions to Prevent

Roberta L. Paikoff
Jeanne Brooks-Gunn
Educational Testing Service

While teenage pregnancy and parenthood have always existed, little attention was paid to them until the last 25 years. Heightened concern is due in part to the rapid rise in the number of teenage girls in the United States engaging in sexual activity, the striking increase in babies born to single teenage mothers, and the often devastating consequences to the teenager as well as to her children (Brooks-Gunn & Furstenberg, 1989; Hofferth & Hayes, 1987; Moore, 1985). The National Academy of Sciences (NAS) report, *Risking the Future* (Hayes, 1987) was written in response to this situation. Three overarching policy goals were spelled out by the NAS panel: (1) to reduce the rate and incidence of unintended pregnancy among adolescents, especially among school-age teens; (2) to provide alternatives to adolescent childbearing and parenting; and (3) to promote positive social, economic, health, and developmental outcomes for adolescent parents and their children. We have reviewed programs that address the first two of these objectives.

Pregnancy Prevention Programs

Most programs undertaken to prevent teen pregnancy have focused on either a school or a community level, and have attempted to aid teenagers in delaying sexual initiation and avoiding pregnancy through a wide variety of means. Within the school system, traditional sex education, affective or value education programs, problem-solving skills training programs, and health clinics have all been used. In general, traditional sex education and school-based clinics have not been found to increase or decrease sexual behavior, but may increase knowledge (Kirby, 1984; Stout & Rivara, 1989). Additionally, school-based clinics have been found to meet the goal of providing a wide range of health-related services for adolescents (Kirby, 1988). One community-based clinic with strong school links, however, reported substantial increases in contraceptive knowledge, as well as a delay in sexual initiation and a decrease in sexual activity among female program participants (after one year's involvement with the program—see Zabin, Hirsch, Smith, Streett, & Hardy, 1986).

Affective or value education and problem-solving skills training have both been found to alter beliefs and values related to health and delay of sexual onset in immediate post-testing. Long-term follow-up data (e.g., over 6 months) for these programs are not yet available, and short-term follow-ups (3–4 months) provide contradictory results. It appears more likely that problem-solving skills training will affect sexual behavior than the values or affective education approach.

When programs are based in the community rather than the school, family planning clinics, community-wide information programs, and continuing education/enhancing life options approaches have been tried. While the majority of sexually active adolescents who use birth control procure it through community family planning clinics, the effects of these clinics on fertility, birth, and abortion rates remain unclear and controversial (Hofferth & Miller, 1989; Paikoff & Brooks-Gunn, in press). Community-wide information programs and life options approaches have produced some exciting initial results, but since they are relatively new, long-term follow-up behavioral data on these approaches are not yet available.

A major impediment to designing, implementing, and evaluating programs aimed at preventing teen pregnancy is the relative dearth of basic research integrating the study of teenage sexuality into the framework of adolescent development. Instead, we find a literature consisting of fairly static descriptions of age at first intercourse, number of partners, contraceptive use at first and last intercourse, and, if we are lucky, information on relationship to partner(s), sequencing of sexual behaviors

(i.e., kissing, petting, intercourse), links between contraceptive attitudes and behavior, and use of drugs and alcohol during sexual encounters. Several aspects of the adolescent experience, however, may be germane to an understanding of teenage sexual behavior. We will review three general areas where development during adolescence could affect the design and implementation of future prevention programs: (1) socialization and social influences; (2) social cognitive processes; and (3) situational influences.

Social Influences

PEERS ■ Teenagers rely on peers for much of their sexual information and are influenced by their peers' sexual behavior (or at least by their perceptions of peers' behavior). For some subgroups, friendship choices may be influenced by sexual activity as well (Billy & Udry, 1985; Hofferth & Hayes, 1987). We know very little, however, about how friends influence one another's sexual behavior. Individual variation in friendship and peer groups may be important; perhaps peers are more salient when the behavior in question is less common or has acquired less "normative" status in a particular group.

The importance of peer relationships could be used effectively in designing pregnancy prevention programs by having peers serve as "opinion leaders" (Turner, Miller, & Moses, 1989). Individuals may listen more to peers than to experts when contemplating a behavior change (Turner et. al., 1989); thus involving peers in intervention programs may be particularly effective in promoting change. Indeed, the Postponing Sexual Involvement Program (PSI) (Howard & McCabe, 1990) has used peer group leaders in its intervention program with some very promising initial results.

PARENTS ▪ Parent-child discussions about sex and reproduction occur more frequently than is commonly thought. For example, in a 1982 survey, about two-thirds of 15-year-old girls had talked about intercourse and one-half about contraception with their parents; similar percentages were reported by 18-year-olds (Dawson, 1986). Such discussions may be rarer between parents and their sons (although little information regarding such discussions is available): almost no boys talk to their mother or father prior to or following the occurrence of first ejaculation, and only a few do so after the event (Gaddis & Brooks-Gunn, 1985; Shipman, 1971). Additionally, large discrepancies exist between what parents and their teenagers think they have communicated to one another regarding sex and birth control (Newcomer & Udry, 1985). Although parent-child communication about sex and birth control has been associated with later age of intercourse and better contraceptive use (Morrison, 1985), almost no process-oriented research has been directed at how parents may influence their teens' sexual behavior (Brooks-Gunn & Furstenberg, 1989). It may be possible to enhance discussions regarding sex and birth control either through intervention approaches conducted jointly with parents and their children, or with special programs targeted at parent and child's individual needs and perceptions of one another. Such approaches thus far have presented mixed results, and also present a challenge to the program evaluator, since need for multiple participants within the same family creates a nonrandom program participant sample.

MEDIA ▪ We need to know much more about the effects of media portrayals of sexuality upon adolescent attitudes, knowledge, and behavior (Brown, Childers, & Waszak, in press). American youth are bombarded with media messages about attractiveness and sexuality, but not with information about contraception. In 1985 the average teenage viewer had seen almost 2000 sexual references on television. In stark contrast, references to birth control or to sexually transmitted diseases are almost nonexistent (L. Harris & Associates, 1987). We have surprisingly little information regarding how this sexually charged environment affects our youth, and most of it comes from college samples. We recommend that the following topics be put on the research agenda: (1) how television viewing may influence younger and older adolescents differently; (2) how perceptions differ as a function of cognitive reasoning abilities; (3) how such viewing influences perceptions of the future consequences of sex; (4) how content of television shows are interpreted by different groups; and (5) whether alternative portrayals of sexuality affect teenagers' attitudes or behaviors (see Brown et al., in press).

Social Cognitive Processes

Individuals underestimate personal risks for undesirable outcomes and tend to believe they are at less risk than are their peers (Turner et al., 1989). At least one study suggests that lower- to lower-middle-class adolescents generally perceive adolescent pregnancy as undesirable, at least relative to postponing pregnancy till later adult life (Paikoff, in press). Risk-taking behavior may occur in many behavioral domains more frequently during adolescence than at other ages (Irwin & Millstein, 1986) and developmental processes such as cognitive difficulties in assessing personal risk, lack of experience with the consequences of risk, ignorance, and denial may underlie this phenomena. A number of studies have cited the problem adolescents have in assessing the probability of pregnancy (Morrison, 1985), and cited the fact that teenagers' initial reaction to an unwanted pregnancy is most often surprise ("it couldn't happen to me") as evidence that teenagers underestimate pregnancy probability, perhaps due to their lack of experience with undefined probability situations such as pregnancy (Brooks-Gunn & Furstenberg, 1989; Paikoff, in press). While misinformation or ignorance (especially about the relation of fertility to the menstrual cycle) may account for some teens' undesired pregnancies, our reading of the literature suggests that the majority of teens hold fairly accurate beliefs about pregnancy possibility, and that myths may be invoked as post-hoc explanations for an undesired pregnancy, rather than representing the teen's actual knowledge base. Finally, the fact that pregnant teenagers often report that they procrastinated or forgot to use birth control is suggestive of denial of personal responsibility for sexual behavior (Zabin & Clark, 1981). We know very little about whether and in what ways teenagers differ from adults and from each other with respect to dimensions of risk assessment. Such knowledge could enhance prevention efforts.

Situational Influences

USE OF ALCOHOL AND DRUGS ■ Alcohol and drug use may reduce the likelihood that contraceptives are used in any one sexual encounter. Since substance use may have disinhibitory effects on behavior, programs may need to teach teenagers explicitly how to handle sex in situations where they have been drinking or doing drugs. To our knowledge, no information exists on how often sex occurs in such contexts. Such findings could be relevant to prevention; teenagers may benefit from knowing in what situations they are less likely to be responsible contraceptors, and from learning techniques for managing sexual interchanges when under the influence of alcohol or drugs.

MEANING OF SEXUALITY ■ We know very little about the meaning and importance of sexuality in the adolescent's life. The frequency of intercourse in adolescents is fairly low, but it is not clear whether this is due to lack of opportunity, concerns about other developmental tasks, worries about getting pregnant, or ambivalent feelings regarding sexual activity. In addition, individual variation in importance or frequency of adolescent intercourse has not been systematically studied, and the demographic and psychological correlates of such differences are not known. Such information is the key to designing and implementing programs that will speak to the needs and concerns of youth regarding sexual activity and pregnancy.

Conclusions

A number of very promising pregnancy prevention programs have been initiated over the past few years, and many have reported initial evaluation data that are fairly positive. In the spirit of speculation from the small data base that currently exists, we suggest that programs providing life options or continuing education, as well as those that attempt to explore and teach problem-solving skills and value education may be the most effective in helping adolescents delay sexual initiation, or prevent pregnancy once they are already sexually active. We further suggest that continued integration of the basic developmental literature on the adolescent experience with the program design and evaluation literature will provide even greater opportunities for fruitful dialogue and for assisting our youth in their decision making regarding sexuality.

References

Billy, J. O., & Udry, J. R. (1985). *The effects of age and pubertal development on adolescent sexual behavior.* Unpublished manuscript, University of North Carolina.

Brooks-Gunn, J., & Furstenberg, F. F., Jr. (1989). Adolescent sexual behavior. *American Psychologist, 44,* 249–257.

Brown, J. D., Childers, K. W., & Waszak, C. S. (in press). Television and adolescent sexuality. *Journal of Adolescent Health Care.*

Dawson, D. A. (1986). The effects of sex education on adolescent behavior. *Family Planning Perspectives, 18*(4), 162–170.

Gaddis, A., & Brooks-Gunn, J. (1985). The male experience of pubertal change. *Journal of Youth and Adolescence, 14*(1), 61–69.

Harris, L., & Associates. (1987). Sexual material on American network television during the 1987–1988 season. New York: Author.

Hayes, C. D. (Ed.). (1987). *Risking the future: Adolescent sexuality, pregnancy, and childbearing* (Vol. 1). Washington, DC: National Academy of Sciences Press.

Hofferth, S. L., & Hayes, C. D. (Eds.). (1987). *Risking the future: Adolescent sexuality, pregnancy, and childbearing* (Vol. 2). Washington, DC: National Academy of Sciences Press.

Hofferth, S. L., & Miller, B. C. (1989). An overview of adolescent pregnancy prevention programs and their evaluations. In J. J. Card (Ed.), *Evaluation program aimed at preventing teenage pregnancies* (pp. 25–40). Palo Alto: Sociometrics Corporation.

Howard, M. & McCabe, J. (1990). Helping teenagers postpone sexual involvement. *Family Planning Perspectives, 22*(1), 21–26.

Irwin, C. E., & Millstein, S. G. (1986). Biopsychosocial correlates of risk taking behaviors during adolescence. *Journal of Adolescent Health Care, 7,* 82S–96S.

Kirby, D. (1984). *Sexuality education: An evaluation of programs and their effects.* Santa Cruz, CA: Network Publications.

Kirby, D. (1988). *The effectiveness of educational programs to help prevent school-age youth from contracting HIV: A review of relevant research.* Washington, DC: Center for Population Options.

Moore, K. A. (1985). *Facts at a glance.* Unpublished manuscript, Washington, DC, Child Trends, Inc.

Morrison, D. M. (1985). Adolescent contraceptive behavior: A review. *Psychological Bulletin, 98, 538–568.*

Newcomer, S. F., & Udry, J. R. (1985). Parent-child communication and adolescent sexual behavior. *Family Planning and Perspectives, 17*(4), 169–174.

Paikoff, R. L. (in press). Attitudes towards consequences of pregnancy in young women attending a family planning clinic. *Journal of Adolescent Research.*

Paikoff, R. L., & Brooks-Gunn, J. (in press). Taking fewer chances: Teenage pregnancy prevention programs. *American Psychologist.*

Shipman, G. (1971). The psychodynamics of sex education. In R. E. Muuss (Ed.), *Adolescent behavior and society: A book of readings* (pp. 326–336). New York: Random House.

Stout, J. W., & Rivara, F. P. (1989). Schools and sex education: Does it work? *Pediatrics, 83,* 375–379.

Turner, C. F., Miller, H. G., & Moses, L. E. (Eds.). (1989). *AIDS: Sexual behavior and intravenous drug use.* Washington, DC: National Academy Press.

Zabin, L. S., & Clark, S. D., Jr. (1981). Why they delay: A study of teenage family planning clinic patients. *Family Planning Perspectives, 13*(5), 205–217.

Zabin, L. S., Hirsch, M. B., Smith, E. A., Streett, R., & Hardy, J. B. (1986). Evaluation of pregnancy prevention programs for urban teenagers. *Family Planning Perspectives, 18*(3), 119–126.

See Also

Black Adolescents At-Risk, Approaches to Prevention; Family Planning Clinics: Efficacy for Adolescents; Peer Counseling: A Human Resource Program; Psychotherapeutic Interventions for Adolescents; Puberty, Precocious, Treatment of; Smoking and Drug Prevention with Early Adolescents, Programs for.

Preindustrial World, Adolescence In

Beatrice B. Whiting
John W. M. Whiting
Harvard University

Contrasting the experience of modern adolescents with that of their peers growing up in preindustrial societies identifies the constraints that are imposed by being born into a society that is a member of the world economy. The advanced technology of this world requires literacy and schooling. Thus, particularly in the case of girls, reproduction may be postponed to allow for an extended period devoted to education. Occupational specialization that enables individuals to choose a style of life different from that of their parents requires technological training. In the preindustrial world an individual could expect to live in a manner similar, if not identical to, that of his/her forebears. Roles were learned by apprenticeship; in the majority of societies there were no institutions whose primary function was to teach literacy or the skills required for earning a living.

There are few, if any, cultures left that have not been changed radically by the introduction of new religious beliefs, schools, national governments, and international trade. There are, however, some universal aspects of adolescent life as defined here

that occur in all societies. All individuals undergo dramatic physiological changes as they become mature and capable of reproduction. In all societies individuals must adjust to their increased size, the development of secondary sex characteristics and associated hormonal changes with strong motivational components. All societies recognize the physiological changes and respond to the new potentials of the developing young boys and girls. The ethnographic accounts indicate that the responses of the parental generation to the signs of sexual maturity, and the timing of celebrations and rituals at puberty, differ markedly for boys and girls.

Since most preindustrial societies lack calendars, our knowledge of the chronological age for developmental events is scanty. A survey of the literature by Eveleth & Tanner (1976) reported that the age of menarche, the developmental marker for the onset of the adolescent period most frequently reported, varied between 14 and 18 years. The median age of 12.2 years for middle-class American girls (Eveleth & Tanner, 1976) does not fall within this distribution. The common explanation for this difference, that modern societies have better nutrition, has little evidential support. Two alternative hypotheses are more strongly supported by the cross-cultural data. The first attributes the so-called secular trend in the age of menarche to an increase in medical care and the consequent decline in the incidence of infant mortality. Since there is evidence that fast-growing infants are more highly at risk (Ellison, 1981a, 1981b), they tend to be selected out and genes for slow-maturing infants are favored. This hypothesis was supported when tested on two different cross-cultural samples. There is also evidence that infants who are stressed in infancy grow faster and menstruate earlier than those who are not stressed (Landauer & Whiting, 1981). Many preindustrial societies scrupulously protect their infants from stressful events by carrying them in their arms, or in a shawl on the back or hip. By contrast, in nearly all postindustrial societies infants spend most of their time in cribs, cradles, and playpens and have less of the comfort and safety of close body contact with the mother or other caretaker (J. Whiting, 1981).

Girls in preindustrial societies begin their reproductive careers before boys. For the majority of these girls the period between menarche and the birth of the first child was of short duration (Whiting, Burbank, & Ratner, 1986). In many of these societies a girl was married at or before menarche. A comparable study has not been made of the duration of bachelorhood, but the ethnographic evidence indicates that it was considerably longer. In some societies, particularly where polygyny is common, the grooms are as much as ten to fifteen years older than their brides. As will be indicated below, the discrepancy in age that is typical of a great many societies reflects the fact that adolescent males of the same chronological age as the girls are less prepared to take on the responsibilities of adult males.

The appearance of the bodily changes that mark the approach of puberty signals societal recognition of sex differences and the associated culturally defined roles expected of males and females. Although there are no universal cultural patterns that characterize the life-style of pubescent girls and boys, some customs have wide distribution. It is not uncommon for societies to encourage the separation of girls and boys at the beginning of the growth spurt (adrenarche) and the appearance of secondary sex characteristics, and to assign them to new settings with new responsibilities and prescriptions for approved behavior. Boys spend more time away from their mothers and sisters. A cross-cultural study of children's behavior indicates, however, that the separation would probably occur around seven years of age without the encouragement of the parental generation. As early as four and five children begin to prefer to interact with same-sex companions (Whiting & Edwards, 1988), and when they are allowed to leave the environs of the home, around six years of age, seek same-sex peers. Although the data is scanty, it is probable that in many societies cross-sex interaction is infrequent until a year or two into adolescence, and even then will be significantly less frequent than same-sex interaction.

At around adrenarche, boys frequently experience changes in sleeping arrangements and task assignment. If housing allows, boys move their sleeping quarters from the parental bedroom, if they have not already done so. Particularly in the tropics, where houses are easily constructed, boys move into separate men's or boys' houses (e.g., Kenyatta, 1965), or even into separate villages, as among the Nyakyusa (Wilson, 1951). Mothers recognize the physical changes in their sons by taking into consideration the division of labor by sex when assigning tasks. Those who have expected boys to help with housework, child care, and other tasks considered by the culture to be women's work, around the beginning of the growth spurt no longer assign these tasks if a girl or woman can be found as an alternate (see Whiting & Edwards, 1988). All societies have norms for the division of labor between the sexes (Murdock, 1935; D'Andrade, 1966). There is variation, however, in the exclusiveness of the allocation of types of work to one sex, and in the stigma attached to deviation from the norm. The cross-cultural evidence suggests that the clarity of the separate roles of adult males and females is greatest in societies in which it is necessary for young men to be trained as warriors, who are responsible for protecting the property of the community (Whiting & Whiting, 1975).

Concern for gender differences may be postponed until the beginning of the development of secondary sex characteristics. In some preindustrial societies distinctive terms of reference for males and females are not used until the beginning of the growth spurt and the appearance of secondary sex characteristics. Previous to these physiological changes there may be few differences in the clothing and hairstyles of girls and boys. But there are societies that from birth make a clear distinction between the sexes, using hairstyles, jewelry, and type of clothing as markers.

Female Adolescents

Ritual recognition of changes in status associated with physiological changes occur in some societies, with different ceremonies for girls and boys. (For early cross-cultural study of puberty, see Ford & Beach, 1951). Since both the rituals and the life experience of the sexes differ, we will divide our presentation accordingly. The timing of the ceremonies for girls varies: some ceremonies are held at the first budding of the breasts, others are postponed until menarche, and still others, especially in societies with infant betrothal or other forms of arranged marriage, are postponed until the girl is entering into marriage and incorporated into the wedding ceremony (cf. Brown, 1981, for cross-cultural review of female life cycle).

Wedgewood (1933) describes a community celebration of a girl's first menstruation on the island of Manam off the coast of New Guinea. In this culture stages in the development of secondary sex characteristics are noted by changes in the terms for describing girls and also changes in their apparel. Up until the time when the first physiological changes are noted, girls and boys are both referred to by the same term and do not wear clothes. At eleven or twelve a girl dons her first petticoat, one that is very short, just long enough to hide her genitals and cover her buttocks. When her breasts begin to develop she is given a longer petticoat. At the time of the celebration of her first period she is given the type of skirt worn by adult women. It should be noted that the pubescent girl during the ritual celebration of her first period is waited on by her younger sisters and cousins and that there is no secrecy about menstruation.

Ritual recognition of menarche is the most frequent ceremony for girls. In a recent study of a sample of 108 preindustrial societies, Paige and Paige (1981) reported that, for exactly half of the 88 societies for which data was available, the onset of menstruation was associated with a rite of passage from childhood to a new status. Since in small local groups that are the common settlement pattern for preindustrial societies it is unlikely for more than one girl to reach menarche at the same time, ceremonies that occur at this time are primarily for individuals rather than for groups, the latter type being more characteristic of ceremonies for boys. In societies with named age grades there may be a ceremony celebrating a girl's menarche and later a ceremony for a group of girls initiating them into an age grade. These ceremonies occur at the time boys are being initiated. Schlegel and Barry (1979) report that ceremonies for groups of girls occur in less than 15% of a sample of 84 preindustrial societies.

Participants in individual rites are frequently limited to family members. In many of the hunting and gathering societies of North and South America, for example, at menarche a girl moved into a menstrual hut for the duration of her period. During her isolation in the hut certain rituals were required to ensure that the girl developed the characteristics valued as womanly. Among the Wadadika Paiute of Harney Valley, Oregon (Whiting, 1950), during her first period a girl was isolated in a menstrual hut for a month. Her mother or grandmother instructed her about menstrual taboos, hygiene, and the development of beauty and other valued physical and social traits. A sagebrush bark band was placed around the girl's head so that her hair would grow long. Girls were instructed only to scratch themselves with sticks, to brush their hair every day, and to bathe. They were required to get up early, to quickly make their own fire, and cook for themselves. Both men and women could visit them, but only young children could sleep in the menstrual hut with them. When the month was over the girl took a bath, put on a new dress, painted her face with red paint, and returned home. The seclusion of women in the menstrual hut during their monthly periods continued until menopause. In Wadadika society, as in many societies that live on game and wild vege-

table products, menstrual blood is considered dangerous to men when they are planning a hunting expedition or preparing for war (Whiting, 1950, p. 106).

Schlegel and Barry (1979, 1980) report that 64% of the societies coded in the standard sample of societies (Murdock & White, 1969) had ceremonies that included the seclusion of the girls at first menstruation and associated taboos. They note that since the seclusion occurs most frequently in societies that obtain some of their food from hunting, it may have some basis in reality, the odor of menstrual blood being easily detected by such animals as deer (March, 1980). There is some evidence also that menstrual blood will wilt or kill plants (see also Ford & Beach, 1951).

Child and Child (1985) take issue with anthropologists who report that seclusion during menstruation is necessarily demeaning to women. They quote from Buckley's (1982) article on the Yurok women, that they consider menstruating women to be at the height of their power. Seclusion enables them, free from mundane tasks and worldly concerns, to concentrate their thoughts on the nature of their lives, allowing them time to go "into yourself and make yourself stronger." It may be considered a time when women have special spiritual power (LaFontaine, 1985). The longer seclusion at menarche is a time when young girls think about becoming young women. More elaborate ceremonies at menarche are reported for societies that fear first menstruation, menstrual blood, and pollution, and require the ritual purification of girls.

A central theme of group rituals for girls is the public announcement and celebration of sexual maturity and fertility. Unlike American middle-class communities that are unsure of how to handle teenage sexuality, the rites celebrate fertility and sexuality. A girl is now considered ready for reproduction. Her new status is that of a nubile girl ready to assume the responsibilities of an adult woman. Changes in hairstyle, type of clothing, and cosmetic adornment announce the new status. There is instruction in values, appropriate social behavior, and the character traits that are expected of adult females. Brown (1981) has noted the importance of training for responsibility and the proper attitude toward work, especially in societies where women play a major role in the subsistence economy. She notes that Richards (1956) in her detailed monograph on the "Chisungu" ceremony among the Bemba of Central Africa stresses the importance of the tests of competence that the adolescent girls must pass. Although they already have the skills necessary for their adult roles they are now expected to perform them "with a new spirit and a new sense of responsibility" (Richards, 1956, p. 128). This is also a theme of the Wadadika ceremony reported above and of many of the rituals at first menstruation reported for North and South America.

In the rituals that include specific instruction in sexual behavior, the instructor is rarely the mother; grandmothers or special women are designated as teachers. In many of the rituals the initiators pantomine or in other ways describe coitus and symbolically present the cultural script for the sexual relations of males and females. For example, during the Gusii initiation ceremonies that take place in western Kenya around adrenarche and include a genital operation—clitoridectomy (the excision of the tip of the clitoris)—the women of the community engage in lewd behavior, use obscene language, talk and sing about the sex act and its mechanics, and demonstrate pelvic movements. They hold sticks that represent phalluses, sing songs of sex from the man's point of view, and engage in mock military combat. LeVine and LeVine comment that the behavior suggests the aggressive interpretation of sexuality prevalent in the community (LeVine and LeVine, 1966, pp. 183–194). In the bush schools of the Mende in Sierra Leone and Liberia girls are isolated for several months and instructed in sexual matters as well as in all womanly behavior (Little, 1951).

Girls' group initiation rites at puberty with some type of genital operation are found primarily in societies where there are genital operations for boys (Brown, 1963). These rites are most frequent in sub-Saharan Africa but are reported in isolated cases in Macronesia and South America. Clitoridectomy is the most common type of genital operation. As will be discussed below, the rites have been interpreted as ceremonies that affirm appropriate gender identity, with the clitoris considered similar to the penis and therefore to be removed from adult females. The operation on girls' genitals has also been variously interpreted as necessary for reducing the sex drive of women, for ensuring the fidelity of wives, and/or for ensuring easy delivery in childbirth. Recent interpretations have stressed the fact that the clitoris is an important organ of sexual pleasure and its excision is a way of reducing the sexual desires of women (Hrdy, 1981).

Other types of operations that make changes in the adolescent girl's body include scarification, tattooing, tooth filing, and the piercing of the ear lobes. These painful and permanent changes in physical appearance are thought to enhance a girl's beauty as well as to announce her new status. The drama of these ceremonies that include painful operations emphasizes the importance of gender, changes of status, and the values associated with womanhood. Rituals that include groups of girls foster solidarity and sisterhood between initiates.

It is the belief in some societies that sexual fondling or even intercourse is necessary for the pubertal development of girls. Among the Kenyan Maasai prepubertal girls spend time in the camps of the junior warriors, where they are decorated and fondled by the young bachelors on whom they wait. At menarche these girls will be married to older men (Llewleyn-Davies, 1978, 1981). Burbank (1988, p. 227) reports the statement of an Australian Aboriginal woman in the Darwin area: "Sometimes breasts don't come out until a man touches them." Other accounts report that menstrual blood will not flow until a girl has had sexual intercourse. Ritual defloration by an older, designated man was reported among the Australian Aborigines (Kaberry, 1939).

A universal problem for all nubile girls is the selection of an appropriate mate. In some societies, especially those with low-density populations, children are betrothed, sometimes at birth. In societies that practice infant and child betrothal the ceremonies at menarche are often the first rituals of the arranged marriages. The girl goes directly from childhood into marriage.

In a recent cross-cultural study of the adolescent period in preindustrial cultures (Whiting, Burbank, & Ratner, 1986), menarche was taken as an index of the end of childhood, and marriage as the marker for the beginning of adulthood. To avoid confusion with other definitions of adolescence, the interval between these two events was labeled "maidenhood." Perhaps the most striking finding of the study was the difference between preindustrial and modern cultures in the duration of the maidenhood period. Of the 46 preindustrial societies representing Africa, Eurasia, the Insular Pacific, and North and South America, twenty cases—nearly half—had no period of maidenhood at all. Girls were expected to marry at or immediately after menarche. Many of these girls were betrothed in childhood and some moved into their future husband's residence before menarche. For the remainder, ten had a maidenhood period of approximately two years, fourteen of approximately three years, and in only two was marriage delayed for four years after first menstruation. This is in sharp contrast to a sample of 24 modern, postindustrial cultures for whom the median duration of maidenhood was 8.7 years with a range of 5.2 to 11.8.

How does one explain this discrepancy in the length of maidenhood and the age of marriage? One clear difference between pre- and postindustrial societies is the complexity of the technology and social culture that must be learned before a girl or a boy is ready to undertake the responsibilities of raising a family. Unlike her modern peers, by the end of maidenhood, when a girl in a preindustrial society takes on the responsibilities of a wife and mother, she has learned most of the skills required of the new status as defined by the culture into which she is born. As a young girl she has served as a child nurse for younger siblings or cousins in extended families. She will have nurtured infants and helped to train toddlers in the social roles that she has so recently learned. She has worked with her mother and sisters, preparing food, cooking, and cleaning. She has learned the rudiments of gathering wild plants, agriculture, and animal husbandry, and has helped in all the adult women's work. However, she may not have had prepubertal sexual experience or learned how to relate to a husband. If she has lived on an isolated homestead or in a small lineage community, she may never have interacted with young males who are not kin. It is these latter skills that form an important central theme of the indoctrination that takes place in the ceremonies at puberty or marriage.

For young girls betrothed before menarche, the wedding ceremony serves as an initiation into womanhood. Both the bride and groom are instructed in the behavior expected of adults. In rare cases defloration rituals occur before the betrothed cohabits with her husband (e.g., Kaberry, 1938). It is usual in the societies where girls are married at the end of childhood for the young married couple to live with the family of either the bride or the groom at least until the birth of the first child. The mother, mother-in-law, or senior wife—in the case of polygynous marriages—advises the young bride and continues her training in wifely and maternal behavior. Thus the girl has the support of adult women during the period of initiation into the pleasures and pains of adult life. In societies where marriage occurs at or before menarche and the groom is not required to pay a bride price, divorce is easy and frequent, first marriages are often dissolved before the birth of the first child, and can be considered trial marriages (for a case study of !Kung San, see Shostak, 1981).

For those girls who are not betrothed in childhood, finding a suitable mate is a task that must be accomplished during the maidenhood period. If maidenhood is absent or brief, this problem is usually solved by the girl's parents or other relatives. If the girl is living in a nomadic hunter-gatherer culture where the population density is very sparse and all the young men in her band are close relatives, and therefore tabooed by incest rules, betrothal arrangements are very helpful.

In many of the preindustrial cultures in which maidenhood lasts for from two to four years, the period may be used as an occasion for sexual experimentation and for seeking a compatible mate. This is carried out in a variety of ways. In Ifugao, in the Philippines, maidens slept in a girls' dormitory where it was expected that they would be visited by young men from neighboring villages, or they arranged trysts in the houses of some young married couple (Barton, 1930). If pregnancy occurred, a maiden chose the lover with whom she was most compatible and they were officially married. In the Trobriand Islands, according to Malinowski (1922, p. 53), "Chastity is an unknown virtue. . . . At an incredibly early age they (girls and boys) become initiated into sexual life. . . . As they grow up, they live in promiscuous free love, which gradually develops into more permanent attachments, one of which ends in marriage." Here, as in numerous other societies, lovers are considered married when they are seen eating breakfast together.

It is a folk belief in many cultures, including our own, that menarche marks the beginning of female fecundity. The evidence indicates that this belief is only approximately true. A period of up to five years following first menstruation ensues before full fecundity is attained (Reiter, 1968, Whiting et al., 1986). The preindustrial societies that lack contraceptive devices but permit lovemaking as a part of courtship have unwittingly taken advantage of this phenomenon. Ethnographers report that premarital pregnancy is not common even though sexual intercourse is frequent. Trobriand elders told Malinowski that the white man's theory that pregnancy is the result of sexual intercourse was clearly wrong as attested by the fact that Trobriand maidens rarely became pregnant although they frequently engaged in sexual intercourse (Malinowski, 1929, pp. 179–186).

Reports of early explorers in the South Pacific (Oliver, 1974) suggest that a sexually free maidenhood was also not uncommon in the area. Some of these Pacific islands, however, were socially stratified, and there were different rules for nobles and commoners. This was the case in Samoa, a fact which may well be responsible for the controversy between Mead (1928, 1930, p. 94) who had described the sexual freedom of Samoan maidens, and Freeman (1983) who claimed that Samoan girls were expected to be virgins when they married.

Permission for a period of sexual exploration usually occurs in ethnically homogeneous, unstratified societies where all available lovers (excluding those tabooed by incest regulations) would be considered suitable mates (see Broude, 1981; Goethals, 1971; Murdock, 1964, for discussion of the social structure and economic variables associated with premarital sexual permissiveness). In case pregnancy does occur, a marriage may be arranged by the parents of the girl and the boy purported to be the father. If the genitor of the child does not wish to marry, in some societies he may pay a fine to the girl's family, and the mother's parents will incorporate the baby into the family. In extended family households and kin-based communities, this can be done without causing too much stress. In societies where children are highly valued, as among the Ijo of Nigeria, the genitor pays for the rituals surrounding the first childbirth of a girl, thus claiming his rights to the child (Hollos & Leis, 1989). It is unthinkable in this culture for a child to have no identified father, and unless he is named, it is believed the baby cannot be delivered.

Infanticide of illegitimate children is permitted in some societies. In a cross-cultural study of 94 preindustrial societies, about one-third were reported to permit the killing of illegitimate infants (Whiting, 1977).

Some of the cultures of East Africa who prolong the period of maidenhood for up to four years have adopted a method of contraception rather than depending on subfecundity. This is described by Kenyatta (1938). The practice of "ngweko" (interfemoral intercourse) is taught to girls during their initiation. Older girls instruct the young initiates on how to arrange their clothing and how to lie with young men so as to avoid full intercourse. Young boys are similarly instructed by older girls. In these societies the groom, when his bride moves into the homestead of his father, pays a "brideprice" to the family of the girl, reimbursing them for the care they have taken of the girl and the labor they lose when she leaves her natal home. This payment finalizes the groom's claim to all the children his bride bears. In these societies the brideprice may be reclaimed if the wife proves barren.

Virginity is seldom a major concern in preindustrial societies. In many cases the fact that a girl has already borne a child indicates that she is fertile and will produce children for her husband. Where infant mortality is high and children are an asset as workers, and where the sons grow up to be warriors who protect the property of the kin group while daughters bring bridewealth, men are anxious to have many children. Polygyny is common and virginity is not considered essential in a bride. Among the Kikuyu of Kenya, men and women desired many children and a man preferred to know that a woman was capable of bearing his offspring. Although the payment of a brideprice was necessary to finalize the marriage, the lovers often had intercourse once small initial payments of the brideprice had been paid (Worthman & Whiting, 1987). However, in some of these societies young virgins may demand a higher brideprice.

In those societies where virginity is considered essential in selecting a bride, the parents of a girl must either arrange to marry their daughter before there is a risk of pregnancy, or isolate her from boys who are not tabooed by incest rules. In many of the Mediterranean Islamic societies the brothers of a young girl are responsible for guarding her virginity (Davis & Davis,

1990). Displays of blood on the nuptial sheet indicate to the wedding guests, and sometimes to the entire community, that the hymen of the bride was pierced for the first time by the groom.

In sum, by menarche in most preindustrial societies girls had learned the skills they needed as adult women. They had cared for infants and trained younger siblings in appropriate behavior; they had learned to garden and take care of animals; and they had learned to gather wild plants and hunt small animals. Where there are reports of specific instruction in approved sexual behavior, it was initiated at the time of menarche, taught overtly in ceremonies by older initiates, or specially appointed women, not by the mothers of the girls. In those societies that did not have special rituals involving sexual instruction, grandmothers or older female siblings were most often mentioned as the teachers. It appears that mothers very seldom gave their daughters explicit information about coitus.

Male Adolescents

As a boy approaches puberty he is behind his female age mate in being prepared to enter the adult world. When a boy is young he spends his time in the company of women and young children. Until he is old enough to leave the environs of the family compound he has little opportunity to participate in the daily life and work of his father and older brothers. He has had limited contact with adult male role models. Unlike his sisters, he enters puberty with little or no practice in the activities that are the work of adult males. Many of these require the attainment of full growth and strength. Although in late childhood he avoids women and girls, he still is excluded from the adult male world. The beginning of the adolescent growth spurt is a signal to the adults that he is ready to begin to learn the adult male role. Size rather than sexual maturity is the criterion for membership in this world.

At adrenarche, a boy is permitted to join the adult males on hunting or trapping expeditions or to go with the herd when it is moved to winter pastures rather than staying at home with his mother and grandfather and caring for the calves. He also may be permitted to go on a cattle-stealing raid or be called upon to help protect family herds and gardens from predation by animals or humans. Since as a child he has not been permitted to do these things, he is eager to participate and this form of apprentice training is very effective. There are fewer specialized occupations in preindustrial societies than in the modern world. In the least complex societies they are limited to the shaman or curer, and perhaps a blacksmith. Such specialized skills are passed from father to son, or an expert is persuaded to take on the boy as an apprentice.

The privilege of participating in the activities associated with the adult male role is often marked by a ceremony or "rite of passage." In some cases these ceremonies simply announce an accomplishment. In societies whose subsistence base is hunting there are rituals celebrating a boy's first kill of a large animal. Among the Harney Valley Pauite (Whiting, 1950), when a boy killed his first deer or antelope he ran home and summoned his father, who skinned the animal and carried the meat to the camp. The boy stood on the skin with the meat. The father lowered a hoop, made from a willow branch wrapped with the intestines of the animal, over the boy many times, mentioning all the land and water game. The boy wore sagebrush bands around his ankles, knees, waist, and wrists for five days, thus announcing his new status. He abstained from eating the flesh of the animal he had killed to ensure that he would have endurance in later life and would be a good hunter (Whiting, 1950, p. 106). Similar ceremonies are reported for other societies where hunting is an important source of food (e.g., the Inuit of Northern Canada [Condon, 1987], and the Bushman of the Kalahari Desert in south Africa [Marshall, 1976]).

In many Indian tribes of North America, a young male was expected to have a dream or vision in which some animal appeared to become a spirit helper, offering supernatural power to aid the boy in becoming a good hunter, a brave warrior, or a successful shaman. To ensure that the boy attained such power, he was told that he must fast and remember his dreams but keep the source of his power secret. If a boy had not had a vision by the time he reached puberty, he was sent on a vision quest which involved fasting and sleeping away from home until he was blessed by a vision. Crashing Thunder, a Winnebago, describes in his autobiography the role his father played in preparing him for adulthood: "My father would wake us up early in the morning and, seated around the fireplace, speak to us. 'My son, when you grow up, see to it that you are some benefit to your fellow men. There is only one way you can aid them and that is by fasting. . . . Try to have one of the spirits created by Earthmaker take pity on you. Whatever he says will come about. If you do not possess one of the spirits from whom to obtain strength and power, you will be of no consequence socially and those around you will show you little respect'" (Radin, 1926, p. 56). The lesson continues with a long sermon listing the qualities that a good Winnebago man should have. (For discussion of the vision quest and guardian spirits see also Benedict, 1923; Pettit, 1946.)

These cultural practices focus on the attainment of skills and, like the celebration of menarche in girls, are an individual matter, but they depend on size, strength, and skill rather than the attainment of reproductive maturity. They are more common in food collecting rather than food producing societies (Schlegel & Barry, 1980, p. 697). In the latter case, where there are gardens or herds, cooperative groups organize to protect families and their possessions from human or animal predation (Whiting & Whiting, 1975). In societies that do not have the schools and team sports that characterize the industrial world, prepubertal boys seldom have experience in cooperation in male peer groups. Initiation ceremonies, timed around puberty, organized groups of boys into male sodalities and trained them as warriors (Young, 1965).

The Kikuyu of Kenya accomplished this by organizing regiments of warriors. The heads of the patrilineages, corporate groups that owned land and animals, set a time after the fall rains for initiation rites for all the boys of Kikuyuland. Although the rites were held at many different locations, all the boys initiated at the same time were formed into an age set named after some event that coincided with their year of initiation. All the boys of an age set were supposed to behave toward one another as though they were siblings. Mutual support was emphasized rather than individual achievement. Every eight years there were two years during which no rites were held and the previous eight age sets were formed into a regiment of junior warriors. The regiment together with the previously formed regiment, who had just been advanced to senior warriors, were charged with the duties of defending Kikuyuland and property from enemy attack (Kenyatta, 1938/1965; Leakey, 1977).

Similar types of groups are found in sub-Saharan Africa, Melanesia, and New Guinea. Entrance into these fraternities of men takes place in initiation ceremonies that vary in duration and elaboration. In the majority of these ceremonies the boys are secluded from women and undergo some form of painful hazing and operation on the body. These activities emphasize the solidarity of males and the values associated with manliness. Paige and Paige (1981) and Young (1965) have discussed the formation and rituals of these "fraternal interest groups."

More often than to celebrate a fait accompli, initiation ceremonies are a rite of passage from childhood to some higher status on the way to adult manhood. Van Gennep in an insightful early publication, *Les Rites de Passage* (1909/1960), noted that ceremonies for males at the time of puberty celebrated a transition in status consisting of a ritual of entrance into a liminal period of isolation from the settings of childhood, and a ritual terminating the transitional period and celebrating reentry into society as an adult. Death and rebirth is often used as a metaphor in the ceremonies, and is sometimes dramatized. There may be more than one transition rite marking increasing maturity. (See Turner, 1964, 1967 for detailed accounts of rites de passage.)

A genital operation is a focal feature of male initiation rites at puberty in some preindustrial societies, particularly those situated in Africa, Australia, and the islands of the Pacific. There have been many theories to account for this practice. Freud (1939) offered a psychoanalytic theory of the meaning of those male puberty rites that involved circumcision. He assumed that such rites symbolized the threat of castration by the jealous father induced by rivalry over the boy's mother. Paige and Paige (1981) accept the castration theme and argue that a father consolidates his position in his patrilineage and at the same time tests the loyalty of his classificatory

brothers by "risking his son's penis" in the circumcision ceremony organized by the patrilineage.

Bettelheim (1954) rejects the Freudian interpretation that circumcision is a castration threat imposed by the father, claiming that it is a product of gender ambivalence stemming from the initiate himself. Kikuyu informants in Kenya, who included genital operations in puberty ceremonies for both males and females, had formulated a theory that explicitly recognized the concern of the ceremonies for establishing appropriate sex and gender identity. They explained that both sexes are born with inappropriate genitals, girls having a "masculine" clitoris and boys a "feminine" prepuce. Before reaching adulthood, these errors must be redressed by slitting or removing the prepuce and removing the tip of the clitoris (Worthman & Whiting, 1987). These rites have been interpreted as a way of assuring girls and boys that they have the appropriate gender role as they enter their adult years (Munroe, Munroe, & Whiting, 1981).

Rites that involve superincision or subincision of the penis, or ritualized forms of male blood-letting such as nose-bleeding (Herdt, 1987) are also interpreted as indications of gender ambivalence, in this case indicating an envy of the power of women to give birth, and the belief that ridding the body of old, bad blood, as in menstruation, is part of the essence of female power (Bettelheim, 1954; Whiting, 1941). Mead (1949, pp. 78–104) discussed a similar interpretation of this type of rite, interpreting the ceremonies as an indication of womb envy and the men's attempts to compensate for their basic inferiority. The Kwoma of New Guinea (Whiting, 1941) respond to the envy by ritually acquiring female power. They cut the penis so that it bleeds like a menstruating woman. After the initial operation that occurs as part of the initiation rite, boys were instructed to bleed their penises once a month. They were told that females remain healthy as a consequence of menstruation which automatically occurs to remove the blood that has deteriorated and must be renewed. Similar practices occur elsewhere in New Guinea and other Pacific Islands (see Hogbin, 1934, p. 330). Herdt's (1981, 1987) recent analysis of rites involving ritual homosexuality and the ingestion of semen by young males who engage in fellatio with older males also suggests an analogy to the female, in this case feeding the young a substance considered similar to breast milk. The semen is fed from the body of the older males when it is time to make boys into men.

The interpretation of gender ambivalence suggests that these rites occur in societies with strong cross-gender identity conflicts that must be resolved. This is supported by the fact that such rites occur most frequently in societies where there is a close and exclusive relationship between mother and infant together with corporate patrilineages that enhance the power of males. In societies with these characteristics, the theory holds, a male child initially envies the female role and identifies with women since his mother is perceived to control all the important resources. In middle childhood, however, since males wield the power in the adult world, he sees that his infantile perceptions were distorted. For this reason he must be assured of his masculine identity. Adult males wish to help their sons resolve this gender identity conflict by removing all signs of gender ambiguity. (For cross-cultural evidence supporting this theory, see Munroe, Munroe, & Whiting, 1981).

Regardless of what functional interpretation one favors, it is evident that the parental generation uses the anxiety and strong emotions engendered by the antici-

pation of the pain of genital or other operations, and the boys' elation when they have successfully conquered fear, to dramatize the teaching of cult secrets as well as codes of morality and appropriate behavior. Participating through one or a series of rituals announces to the community that a boy has become a man.

Sexual knowledge appears to be shared more easily among male than among female adolescents. The detailed data on sexual behavior in the monographs is meager, but there is more information on adolescent boys' practices than on those of girls (Ford & Beach, 1951). There are reports of group masturbation, bestiality, and homosexuality. In some societies it is assumed that boys will go through a period of homosexuality before marriage (Herdt, 1981). It is probably safe to say that in most preindustrial societies young males have had more sexual experience than girls before marriage. In some societies it is expected that an adolescent boy's first heterosexual experience will be with an older woman, either a widow or an adulterous wife.

Parents and kin play a role in mate selection for boys as well as for girls. Control is probably strongest in societies organized into corporate patrilineages. In these societies it is customary for the groom's father to arrange for his son's children to belong to his lineage. He must compensate the parents of the bride for relinquishing the right to the offspring of their daughters by paying a so-called bride price. This usually entails a substantial transfer of property, often cattle.

Conclusions

There are few places left in the world where it is possible to study the life of preindustrial societies. The research of the Harvard Adolescent Project in 1980 indicated that adopting Western-style schooling and joining the modern industrial world have revolutionized the type of societies discussed here. The adolescent's concern with individual achievement and securing a wage-earning job in the national economy has replaced in primacy the concern for status in the extended family, lineage, or clan. Traditional rites of passage have been replaced by state examinations and high school graduation exercises. Often the values transmitted as part of traditional rites of passage are omitted from the socialization process. For example, the teaching of appropriate sexual behavior that had been part of the initiation ceremonies in Kikuyuland have not been replaced by a new type of teaching since the ceremonies were discontinued. The age of the marriage of girls is postponed as they work to complete their education. The length of time between a girl's attainment of sexual maturity and the birth of her first child is extended. This has the consequence of greatly increasing the incidence of unwanted pregnancy (Worthman & Whiting, 1987). In societies that had segregated girls and boys during adolescence and had arranged marriages for their girls, coeducational classrooms introduced new settings for which no realistic rules for the interaction of adolescents had been devised (cf. Burbank, 1988; Condon, 1987; Davis & Davis, 1989; Hollos & Leis, 1989).

Menarche for girls and the attainment of full physical size for boys are less important markers of status change in the life cycle of adolescents in the modern world. Adolescents in the industrial world are faced with many choices both of career and marriage mates. The rules governing the division of labor by sex have been altered. Most occupations are open to both sexes. Parents can no longer monitor the individuals who are the companions of adolescents and their potential marriage partners. In many communities there have been marked discontinuities in the life cycle. Parents have not known how to prepare their children for the modern world. There have been false promises as to the benefits of schooling, with the job market unable to absorb the number of high school and university students who seek white-collar employment. Many new life-styles are possible in the industrial world, offering both benefits and liabilities.

The selected bibliographic references presented below serve only as an introduction to the relevant ethnographic and theoretical publications on adolescence in the preindustrial world. Extensive bibliographies can be found in these publications to guide researchers. The Human Relations Area Files to be found in some libraries have bibliographies and ethnographic indices to a large sample of societies.

References

Barton, R. F. (1930). *The half-way sun: Life among the headhunters of the Philippines.* New York: Brewer & Warren.

Benedict, R. (1923). The concept of the guardian spirit in North America. *Memoir of the American Anthropological Association, 29.*

Bettelheim, B. (1954). *Symbolic wounds: Puberty rites and the envious male.* Glencoe, IL: Free Press of Glencoe.

Broude, G. J. (1981). The cultural management of sexuality. In R. H. Munroe, R. L. Munroe, & B. B. Whiting (Eds.), *Handbook of cross-cultural human development* (pp. 633–674). New York: Garland Publishing.

Brown, J. K. (1963). A cross-cultural study of female initiation rites. *American Anthropologist, 65,* 837–853.

Brown, J. K. (1973). The recruitment of a female labor force. *Anthropos, 73,* 41–48.

Brown, J. K. (1981). Cross-cultural perspectives on the female life cycle. In R. H. Munroe, R. L. Munroe, & B. Whiting (Eds.),

Handbook of cross-cultural human development (pp. 581–610). New York: Garland Publishing.

Buckley, T. (1982). Menstruation and the power of women: Methods in cultural reconstruction. *American Ethnologist, 9,* 47–60.

Burbank, V. (1988). *Aboriginal adolescence: Maidenhood in an Australian community.* New Brunswick, NJ: Rutgers University Press.

Child, A. B., & Child, I. L. (1985). Biology, ethnocentrism, and sex differences. *American Anthropologist, 87,* 125–128.

Condon, R. (1987). *Inuit youth: Growth and change in the Canadian Arctic.* New Brunswick, NJ: Rutgers University Press.

D'Andrade, R. G. (1966). Sex differences and cultural institutions. In E. E. Maccoby (Ed.), *The development of sex differences* (pp. 173–204). Stanford: Stanford University Press.

Davis, D., & Davis, S. (1990). *Presenting the self: Adolescence in a Moroccan town.* New Brunswick, NJ: Rutgers University Press.

Ellison, P. T. (1981a). Threshold hypotheses, developmental age, and menstrual function. *American Journal of Anthropology, 54,* 337–340.

Ellison, P. T. (1981b). Morbidity, mortality, and menarche. *Human Biology, 53,* 635–643.

Eveleth, P., & Tanner, J. M. (1976). *Worldwide variations in human growth.* Cambridge: Cambridge University Press.

Ford, C., & Beach, F. (1951). *Patterns of sexual behavior.* New York: Harper & Brothers.

Freeman, D. (1983). *Margaret Mead and Samoa: The making and unmaking of an anthropological myth.* Cambridge: Harvard University Press.

Freud, S. (1939). *Moses and monotheism.* New York: Alfred A. Knopf.

Gennep, A. Van (1960). *The rites of passage.* Chicago: University of Chicago Press. (Originally published in 1909.)

Goethals, G. W. (1971). Factors affecting permissive and nonpermissive rules regarding premarital sex. In J. M. Henslin (Ed.), *Sociology of sex: A book of readings* (pp. 9–26). New York: Appleton-Century-Croft.

Herdt, G. (1981). *Guardians of the flute: Idioms of masculinity.* New York: McGraw-Hill.

Herdt, G. (Ed.). (1982). *Rituals of manhood: Male initiation in Papua New Guinea.* Berkeley and Los Angeles: University of California Press.

Herdt, G. (1987). *The Sambia: Ritual and gender in New Guinea.* New York: Holt, Rinehart & Winston.

Hogbin, H. I. (1934). Native culture of Wogeos. *Oceania, 5*(3), 330.

Hollos, M., & Leis, P. (1989). *Becoming Nigerian in Ijo society.* New Brunswick, NJ: Rutgers University Press.

Hrdy, S. B. (1981). *The woman who never evolved.* Cambridge: Harvard University Press.

Kaberry, P. (1939). *Aboriginal woman: Sacred and profane.* New York: Gordon Press.

Kenyatta, J. (1965). *Facing Mt. Kenya.* New York: Vintage Books. (Originally published 1938.)

LaFontaine, J. S. (1985). *Initiation.* Manchester, England: Manchester University Press.

Landauer, T. K., & Whiting, J. W. M. (1981). Correlates and consequences of stress in infancy. In R. H. Munroe, R. L. Munroe, & B. Whiting (Eds.), *Handbook of cross-cultural human development* (pp. 355–402). New York: Garland Publishing.

Leakey, L. S. B. (1977). *The Southern Kikuyu before 1903.* New York: Academic Press.

LeVine, R., & LeVine, B. (1977). *Nyansongo: A Gusii community.* New York: Robert Krieger Publishing. (Originally published 1966.)

Little, K. (1951). *The Mende of Sierra Leone.* London: Routledge & Kegan Paul.

Llewelyn-Davies, M. (1978). Two contexts of solidarity. In P. Caplan & J. Bujra (Eds.), *Women united and women divided: Cross-cultural perspectives on female solidarity* (pp. 206–237). London: Tavistock Publications.

Llewelyn-Davies, M. (1981). *Women, warriors, and patriarchs.* In S. Ortner & H. Whitehead (Eds.), *Sexual meanings: The cultural construction of gender and sexuality* (pp. 330–358). Cambridge: Cambridge University Press.

Malinowski, B. (1922). *Argonauts of the western Pacific.* London: George Routledge & Sons.

Malinowski, B. (1929). *The sexual life of the savages of North-Western Melanesia.* New York: Halcyon House.

March, K. S. (1980). Deers, bears, and blood: A note on nonhuman animal response to menstrual odor. *American Anthropologist, 82,* 125–127.

Marshall, L. (1976). *The !Kung of Nyae Nyae.* Cambridge: Harvard University Press.

Mead, M. (1928). *Coming of age in Samoa: A study of adolescence and sex in primitive society.* New York: William Morrow.

Mead, M. (1930). *Social organization of Manua.* Honolulu, Hawaii: Bishop Museum.

Mead, M. (1949). *Male and female: A study of the sexes in a changing world.* New York: William Morrow.

Munroe, R. L., Munroe, R. H., & Whiting, J. W. (1981). Male sex-role resolutions. In R. H. Munroe, R. L. Munroe, & B. Whiting (Eds.), *Handbook of cross-cultural human development* (pp. 611–632). New York: Garland Publishing.

Murdock, G. P. (1935). Comparative data on the division of labor by sex. *Social Forces, 15,* 551–553.

Murdock, G. P. (1964). Cultural correlates of the regulation of premarital sex behavior. In R. A. Manners (Ed.), *Process and pattern in culture* (pp. 399–410). Chicago: Aldine.

Murdock, G. P., & White, D. R. (1969). Standard cross-cultural sample. *Ethnology, 8,* 329–369.

Oliver, D. (1974). *Ancient Tahitian society* (Vol. 1). Honolulu: University of Hawaii Press.

Paige, K., & Paige, J. (1981). *The politics of reproductive ritual.* Berkeley and Los Angeles: University of California Press.

Pettit, G. (1946). *Primitive education in North America.* University of California Publications in American Archaeology and Ethnology.

Radin, P. (1926). *Crashing Thunder: The autobiography of a Winnebago Indian.* New York: D. Appleton.

Ratner, M. (in press). *Adolescence in a Romanian village.* New Brunswick, NJ: Rutgers University Press.

Reiter, E. (1986). Neuroendocrine regulation of pubertal onset. In J. Lancaster & B. Hamburg (Eds.), *School-age pregnancy and parenthood: Biosocial dimensions* (pp. 53–78). New York: Aldine.

Richards, A. (1956). *Chisungu: A girl's initiation ceremony among the Bemba of northern Rhodesia.* New York: Grove Press.

Schlegel, A., & Barry, H. (1979). Adolescent initiation ceremonies: A cross-cultural code. *Ethnology, 18,* 199–210.

Schlegel, A., & Barry, H. (1980). The evolutionary significance of adolescent initiation ceremonies. *American Ethnologist, 7,* 695–715.

Shostak, M. (1981). *Nisa: The life and words of a !Kung woman.* Cambridge: Harvard University Press.

Turner, V. (1964). Betwixt and between: The liminal period in rites de passage. In J. Helm (Ed.), *Symposium on new approaches to the study of religion* (pp. 4–20). Proceedings of the American Ethnological Society. Seattle: University of Washington Press.

Turner, V. (1967). *The forest of symbols: Aspects of Ndembu ritual.* Ithaca, NY: Cornell University Press.

Wedgewood, C. (1933). Girls' puberty rites in Manaam Island, New Guinea. *Oceania, 4*(2), 132–155.

Whiting, B. B. (1950). *Paiute sorcery.* New York: Viking Fund.

Whiting, B. B., & Edwards, C. (1988). *Children of different worlds: The formation of social behavior.* Cambridge: Harvard University Press.

Whiting, J. W. M. (1941). *Becoming a Kwoma.* New Haven: Yale University Press.

Whiting, J. W. M. (1977). Euthanasia, family planning, and female infanticide. Paper presented at the Society for Cross Cultural Research.

Whiting, J. W. M. (1981). Environmental constraints on infant care practices. In R. H. Munroe, R. L. Munroe, & B. B. Whiting (Eds.), *Handbook of cross-cultural human development* (pp. 155–180). New York: Garland Publishing.

Whiting, J., Burbank, V., & Ratner, M. (1986). The duration of maidenhood across cultures. In J. Lancaster & B. Hamburg (Eds.), *School-age pregnancy and parenthood: Biosocial dimensions* (pp. 273–302). New York: Aldine.

Whiting, J., & Whiting, B. (1975). Aloofness and intimacy of husbands and wives: A cross-cultural study. *Ethos, 3,* 183–207.

Wilson, M. (1951). *Good company: A study of Nyakyusa age-villages.* London & New York: Oxford University Press.

Worthman, C. (1986). Developmental dysynchrony as normative experience: Kikuyu adolescents. In J. Lancaster & B. Hamburg (Eds.), *School-age pregnancy and parenthood: Biosocial dimensions* (pp. 95–112). New York: Aldine.

Worthman, C., & Whiting, J. W. (1987). Social change in adolescent sexual behavior, mate selection, and premarital pregnancy rates in a Kikuyu community. *Ethos, 15*(2), 145–165.

Young, F. (1965). *Initiation ceremonies: A cross-cultural study of status dramatization.* Indianapolis: Bobbs-Merrill.

See Also

Colonial America, Adolescence in; History of Research on Adolescence; Menarche, Secular Trend in Age of; Nineteenth-Century America, Adolescence in; Twentieth-Century America, Adolescence in.

Premenstrual Syndrome (PMS)

Kathryn E. Hood

The Pennsylvania State University

The belief that women's feelings and behaviors change each month, with heightened depression or irritability or appetite during the week just before menstruation, is the basis of current stereotypes about premenstrual syndrome (PMS). Whether the stereotype actually fits women's experiences and behaviors is a focus of controversy. Early studies of PMS used clinical samples and investigative techniques that have now been surpassed (Rubinow & Roy-Byrne, 1984). More recent studies of normal women consistently find that when women are not aware of the purpose of the study, their daily self-reports of mood and their actual behaviors do not show PMS (Abplanalp, Donnelly, & Rose, 1979; Golub & Harrington, 1981; Hood, 1990; Lahmeyer, Miller, & De-Leon-Jones, 1982; Sanders, Warner, Backstrom, & Bancroft, 1983; for a comprehensive review, see Parlee, 1982). The inconsistency between previous and current findings may result from women's own stereotypes about behavior and the menstrual cycle. Experimental studies have explicitly demonstrated that women's beliefs about PMS alter their self-reports of mood changes. For example, Ruble (1977) used scientific hocus-pocus to persuade women that they were in a stage of the menstrual cycle other than their own actual cycle stage. When these women reported on their present mood state, they showed the patterns corresponding to the stereotype of PMS, and not to their actual cycle stage. (Also see AuBuchon & Calhoun, 1985; Brooks-Gunn & Ruble, 1982; Englander-Golden, Whitmore, & Dienstbier, 1978; Koeske & Koeske, 1975; Koeske, 1983; Olasov & Jackson, 1987; Parlee, 1974; Rodin, 1976; Ruble & Brooks-Gunn, 1979, 1982). Several intensive longitudinal investigations of normal women and men have shown that women's moods do not change more often than men's, and that the degree of change associated with the menstrual cycle is not greater than the change associated with social events like the weekday cycle (McFarlane, Martin, & Williams, 1988; Mansfield, Hood, & Henderson, 1989; Rossi & Rossi, 1977; Wilcoxon, Schrader, & Sherif, 1976; Woods, Dery, & Most, 1982). In cross-cultural studies of 5,000 women from 10 nations, only the women from Western cultures showed PMS (Snowden & Christian, 1984). Taken together, these studies imply that while some women may experience some degree of change in mood or behavior during some of their menstrual cycles, this change is modest compared to the inflated stereotype of PMS. Changes in behaviors and abilities have not been reliably found (Sommer, 1982).

These research findings contradict the view that PMS constitutes "a serious mental and public health problem" (Janowsky & Rausch, 1985; see Brooks-Gunn, 1986; Laws, 1983; Ginsburg & Carter, 1987, for discussions of these issues). In particular, the experimental use of progesterone as a treatment for PMS has not been shown to be safe or effective. In a special issue, the *Journal of Reproductive Medicine* (1983, vol. 28, no. 8) reviews a variety of medical treatments for PMS. Despite ongoing controversy about the extent of scientific support for PMS as a prevalent condition, the American Psychiatric Association included "Periluteal Phase Dysphoric Disorder" in the Appendix to the revised third edition of the clinical *Diagnostic and Statistical Manual*.

References

Abplanalp, J. J., Donnelly, B. A., & Rose, R. M. (1979). Psychoendocrinology of the menstrual cycle: 1. Enjoyment of daily activities and moods. *Psychosomatic Medicine, 41*, 587-604.

AuBuchon, P. B., & Calhoun, K. S. (1985). Menstrual cycle symptomatology: The role of social expectancy and experimental demand characteristics. *Psychosomatic Medicine, 47*, 35-45.

Brooks-Gunn, J. (1986). Differentiating premenstrual symptoms and syndromes. *Psychosomatic Medicine, 48*, 385-387.

Brooks-Gunn, J., & Ruble, D. (1982). The development of menstrual-related beliefs and behaviors during early adolescence. *Child Development, 53*, 1567-1577.

Englander-Golden, P., Whitmore, M. R., & Dienstbier, R. A. (1978). Menstrual cycle as focus of study and self-reports of moods and behaviors. *Motivation and Emotion, 2*, 75-86.

Ginsburg, B. E., & Carter, B. F. (1987). *Premenstrual syndrome: Ethical and legal implications in a biomedical perspective*. New York: Plenum.

Golub, S., & Harrington, D. M. (1981). Premenstrual and menstrual mood changes in adolescent women. *Journal of Personality and Social Psychology, 41*, 961-965.

Hood, K. E. (1990a). Contextual determinants of menstrual cycle effects in observations of social interactions. In A. J. Dan & L. Lewis (Eds.), *Menstrual health in women's lives*. Chicago: University of Illinois Press.

Hood, K. E. (1990b). Menstrual behavioral changes depend on social context in observations of women's interactions. Submitted for publication.

Janowsky, D. S., & Rausch, J. (1985). Biochemical hypotheses of premenstrual tension syndrome. *Psychological Medicine, 15*, 3-8.

Koeske, R. D., & Koeske, G. F. (1975). An attributional approach to moods and the menstrual cycle. *Journal of Personality and Social Psychology, 31*, 473-478.

Koeske, R. H. (1983). Lifting the curse of menstruation: Toward a feminist perspective on the menstrual cycle. In S. Golub (Ed.), *Lifting the curse of menstruation* (pp. 1-16). New York: Haworth Press.

Lahmeyer, H. W., Miller, M., & DeLeon-Jones, F. (1982). Anxiety and mood fluctuation during the normal menstrual cycle. *Psychosomatic Medicine, 44*, 183-194.

Laws, S. (1983). The sexual politics of premenstrual tension. *Women's Studies International Forum, 6*, 19-31.

Mansfield, P. K., Hood, K. E., & Henderson, J. (1989). Women and their husbands: Mood and arousal fluctuations across the menstrual cycle and days of the week. *Psychosomatic Medicine, 51*, 66-80.

McFarlane, J., Martin, C. L., & Williams, T. M. (1988). Mood fluctuations: Women versus men and menstrual versus other cycles. *Psychology of Women Quarterly, 12,* 201–224.

Olasov, B., & Jackson, J. (1987). Effects of expectancies on women's reports of moods during the menstrual cycle. *Psychosomatic Medicine, 49,* 65–78.

Parlee, M. B. (1974). Stereotypic beliefs about menstruation: A methodological note on the Moos Menstrual Distress Questionnaire and some new data. *Psychosomatic Medicine, 36,* 229–240.

Parlee, M. B. (1982). The psychology of the menstrual cycle: Biological and psychological perspectives. In R. C. Freeman (Ed.), *Behavior and the menstrual cycle* (pp. 77–99). New York: Dekker.

Rodin, J. (1976). Menstruation, reattribution, and competence. *Journal of Personality and Social Psychology, 33,* 345–353.

Rossi, A. S., & Rossi, P. E. (1977). Body time and social time: Mood patterns by menstrual cycle phase and day of week. *Social Science Research, 6,* 273–308. (Reprinted in J. E. Parsons [Ed.]. [1980]. *The psychobiology of sex differences and sex roles,* [pp. 269–304]. New York: McGraw-Hill).

Rubinow, D. R., & Roy-Byrne, P. (1984). Premenstrual syndromes: Overview from a methodologic perspective. *American Journal of Psychiatry, 41,* 163–172.

Ruble, D. N. (1977). Premenstrual symptoms: A reinterpretation. *Science, 197,* 291–292.

Ruble, D. N., & Brooks-Gunn, J. (1979). Menstrual symptoms: A social cognition analysis. *Behavioral Medicine, 2,* 171–194.

Ruble, D. N., & Brooks-Gunn, J. (1982). A developmental analysis of menstrual distress in adolescence. In R. C. Friedman, *Behavior and the menstrual cycle* (pp. 177–198). New York: Dekker.

Sanders, D., Warner, P., Backstrom, T., & Bancroft, J. (1983). Mood, sexuality, hormones, and the menstrual cycle: 1. Changes in mood and physical state: Description of subjects and method. *Psychosomatic Medicine, 45,* 487–581.

Snowden, R., & Christian, B. (1984). *Patterns and perceptions of menstruation.* New York: St. Martin's Press.

Sommer, B. (1982). Cognitive behavior and the menstrual cycle. In R. C. Friedman (Ed.), *Behavior and the menstrual cycle* (pp. 101–128). New York: Dekker.

Wilcoxon, L. A., Schrader, S. J., & Sherif, C. W. (1976). Daily self-reports on activities, life-events, moods, and somatic changes during the menstrual cycle. *Psychosomatic Medicine, 38,* 399–417.

Woods, N. F., Dery, E. K., & Most, A. (1982). Stressful life events and perimenstrual symptoms. *Journal of Human Stress, 8,* 23–31.

See Also

Adrenarche; Androgens, Adrenal; Androgens, Gonadal; Hormone-Behavior Links at Puberty, Menstrual Cycle, Methodological Issues in the Study of Hormones and Behavior in Adolescence; Puberty, Endocrine Changes at; Puberty, Hypothalamic-Pituitary Changes of.

Preschool Programs, The Impact on Adolescent Development

Valora Washington
W. K. Kellogg Foundation

In the early 1960s the U.S. government rediscovered what Michael Harrington (1962) called "the other America," the nearly one-quarter of the U.S. population who lived in poverty. Outraged, and buoyed by a relatively strong economy, President John F. Kennedy suggested that "the prevention of adult poverty and dependency must begin with the case of dependent children." Following this view, President Lyndon Johnson declared an "unconditional war on poverty" that was intended "not only to relieve the symptoms of poverty but to cure it; and above all, to prevent it." The major weapon in this war, the Office of Economic Opportunity, was directed to pay special attention to the needs of young people (Zigler & Anderson, 1979).

Although the original proposal for a community action program did not target preschool children, hope existed that a focus on youth would be an effective means to achieve equal opportunity for the poor. Indeed, Project Head Start, the nation's preeminent preschool program, was invented six months after enactment of the Economic Opportunity Act, presumably with the hope of developing a more comprehensive program and one that would show quick results (Steiner, 1976). Quick results—results that would influence adolescence and adult behavior positively—were viewed as practical and realistic expectations by both the public and the policymakers. With these implied promises, preschool programs found their way into the national consciousness and budget. Project Head Start, still the only federally sponsored comprehensive preschool program, was immediately popular, serving 561,359 children in 11,068 centers during the summer of 1965.

Underlying the excitement associated with Head Start were beliefs in education as the solution to poverty (Zigler & Anderson, 1979) and in the preschool years as a "critical period," especially for the development of verbal ability and general school achievement (Steiner, 1976). Two classic volumes were influential in redirecting empirical thought about child development and its role in shaping life outcomes. In the first, J. McVicker Hunt's *Intelligence and*

Experience (1961), Hunt concluded that experience programs the development of the human brain and affects the rate of early development in human infants. Benjamin Bloom's classic work, *Stability and Change in Human Characteristics* (1964), concluded that the important human characteristics showed a pattern of very rapid growth in the early years, followed by a steady decline. For general intelligence, Bloom surmised that about 50% of the variation possible for any particular child was established by age four. In sharp contrast to the notion of predetermined and fixed development formerly prevalent, these works set the stage for a decade of vigorous insistence on the predominate role of the environment in development, and therefore social responsibility for the disadvantaged (Steiner, 1976).

In this atmosphere child development experts readily acquiesced as preschool programs moved quickly from experiment to institution without wide-ranging debate about reasonable expectations, likely cost, benefits, or alternatives. From President Johnson's October 1965 education message to President Nixon's February 1969 message on the reorganization of the antipoverty program, the investment value of preschool experiences generally was not questioned (Slaughter, 1982; Steiner, 1976).

Middle-class parents were not oblivious to the new perspectives on the importance of the early years of development. These parents also believed they could give their children a "head start" through their private resources. While early experiences for the poor were expected to mitigate the presumed deleterious effects of the home and social environments (Zigler & Valentine, 1979), schooling for affluent children apparently sought to extend and augment existing advantages. Middle-class parents expressed concern and anxiety about preparing their children to compete in later

life. "We finally found a good nursery school" one mother tells another as they watch their children playing. "It's the only one where they start cramming for the SAT" (cartoon in *Phi Delta Kappa*, September 1984, p. 64).

How realistic are these parental and political expectations for preschool programs? What is the investment value of preschool programs on later development? Since the premier preschool programs are nearly 25 years old, it is now possible to examine critically their lasting effects through adolescence and early adulthood.

Early (1960s) accounts of the impact of preschool programs quickly dampened the high expectations about their role in promoting significant social change. In the first large-scale national study to evaluate the impact of Head Start participation on later school achievement, the Westinghouse Learning Corporation (1969) concluded that the modest immediate gains "faded out" after a few years of elementary school. This "fade out" assessment, widely accepted by 1975, put a brake on planning new children's programs; experts began to speak publicly about the "naive environmentalism" that caused Head Start to be oversold in the early days (see Steiner, 1976, p. 29). Although researchers produced several volumes of criticisms about the Westinghouse study methods and findings, research conducted throughout the 1970s generally supported its basic findings (see Washington & Oyemade, 1987). These assessments basically agreed that Head Start graduates: (1) enter primary school close to or at national norms on measures of school readiness; (2) maintain this advantage during the first year of school; and (3) fail to show substantially better performance in comparison with non-Head Start participants in grades two and three.

Nevertheless, Head Start was staunchly defended and it remained popular among participants and acceptable in Congress. The failure of children to have continued academic success was now viewed as reflecting deficiencies of the elementary schools rather than inadequacies of the preschool programs. Zigler and Valentine (1979) argued that the idea that a one-shot preschool intervention can counterbalance the debilitating effects of inadequate inner-city school systems and the associated conditions of living in poverty must be subjected to intense scrutiny. Slaughter (1982) argued that the causes of low academic achievement did not lie solely with the children's families, as was originally implied by Head Start. Rather, these causes are multiply determined and shared by all of the children's caregivers.

Results from longitudinal studies, including the Consortium on Developmental Continuity, which began to appear around 1979, showed that graduates of various preschool programs were less likely to be placed in special education classes or kept back in a grade. The General Accounting Office (1979) concluded that preschool programs that reach children during their first four years help them to "perform significantly better in school" and produce "lasting, significant gains." Zigler and Valentine (1979) showed that there were "sleeper effects" on attitudes and achievement measures, relative to non-Head Start comparison groups, but final levels of test performance for both groups were still woefully low.

By the 1980s there had been numerous evaluations of the impact of preschool programs on later development. However, these studies generally lacked coherence or consistency in the evaluation effort (Zigler & Rescorla, 1985). The broad conceptual objectives emphasizing the development of the "whole child" were generally obscured by the focus on preschool *education*. Indeed, it is the unrealized expectation and focus of

Head Start's educational objectives that has resulted in the severest criticism of the program (Zigler & Anderson, 1979).

Studies on the impact of preschool programs on later development generally can be criticized along at least three dimensions. First, there is the problem of possible selection biases in who attends preschool programs. The issue of selection bias is important in interpreting evaluation results where randomly selected control groups are not available. For example, if one assumes that Head Start served the neediest children first, the Westinghouse data reveal reliable and important value-added effects of Project Head Start on later achievement.

Second, there is the question of program continuity. The issue here is whether the special attention received by preschool children, such as those in Head Start, is carried through to the primary, middle, and high school settings. For example, Head Start children who continued in Project Follow Through in elementary school had steadier and higher performance on the Mathematics Achievement Test from kindergarten through third grade than those who did not continue (Weisberg & Haney, 1977). Further, it is likely that children from middle-class families are better able to sustain a continuous level and quality of experience following the preschool programs.

Third, there is the problem of the narrowness of outcome measures. Assessment of preschool effectiveness has been concentrated in the cognitive and academic achievement domains, with particular focus on IQ. Weikart (1982) argues that standardized tests simply are approximations of real-world goals, and that it is unclear what early grade achievement correlates mean in terms of actual performance later in life. Comprehensive preschool programs, such as Head Start, are optimally designed to influence a broad array of factors, including children's physical well-being, formal cognitive development, more circumscribed academic achievement, and socioemotional development. Zigler and Valentine (1979) warn that no one of these factors should be judged as preeminent; rather, all should be viewed as interacting in order to enhance social competence.

Recent studies on the impact of preschool programs on adolescent development generally offer positive assessments of these effects. For example, in 1984, the Perry Preschool Project reported several long-term beneficial effects of preschool programs for 123 poor black children who were then age 19, including: improved scholastic placement and achievement during the school years; decreased delinquency, crime, use of public assistance, and adolescent pregnancy rates; and increased high school graduation rates, enrollment in postsecondary programs, and employment. Similarly, a synthesis study of Head Start research conducted by CSR, Inc. in 1985 concluded that Head Start has had immediate positive effects on children's cognitive ability; appears to affect the long-term school achievement of participants in terms of being retained in grade or assigned to special education classes; promotes immediate socioemotional gains in the areas of self-esteem, achievement motivation, and social behavior, with mixed results in the persistence of these gains over the long term; improves child health, motor development, nutrition and dental care; and generates increased use of education, health, and social services. It was unclear whether parents' involvement in Head Start is related to their children's cognitive test scores or whether Head Start improves parental childrearing practices.

Although the CSR study findings were generally positive, they again raised questions about the persistence of the cognitive and socioemotional gains over the long term. Child advocates pointed to the Perry Study as evidence of long-term gains, but it is important to note that the Perry Study dealt with long-term impact on school success, socioeconomic success, and social responsibility, *not* with cognitive and socioemotional gains.

While there has been a wealth of longitudinal data on the impact of preschool experiences on poor children, relatively little is known about the effects of preschool on educationally/economically advantaged children. Contrary to the assumption that home and family experiences are sufficient to enhance development and learning for advantaged children, studies tend to indicate that social competence is enhanced by preschool participation (Larsen, Hite, & Hart, 1983). Preschool experiences for advantaged boys have also been found to have a significant effect on later (2nd and 3rd grade) school achievement scores, particularly in the area of language development (Larsen & Robinson, 1987). In general, however, math and reading comprehension scores for educationally advantaged children are not greatly influenced by preschool participation. Nevertheless, given limited literature on the lasting effects of early intervention on middle-class and upper-class children, the value of preschool for these children cannot be fully determined.

Recognizing that studies on poor children may not be generalizable to the middle-class, evidence of the impact of preschool programs on adolescents can be summarized as follows. The evidence for short-term effects are represented by CSR and by Larsen and her colleagues. Evidence for mid-term effect comes from the Consortium on Developmental Continuity. Long-term effects are illustrated by the Perry Preschool project. We do not know if all programs produce short-, mid-, and long-term effect, "but we do know that all these effects are possible" (Schweinhart & Weikart, 1986, p. 23). Preschool programs for the disadvantaged, they add, help our nation to provide equal educational opportunity for those children whose parents cannot afford to provide nonpublic schooling for their children (also see Slaughter, 1982).

Based on these findings, Schweinhart and Weikart assert that three levels of probability can be used in claims about preschool effects: "Good preschool programs for children at risk of school failure do better prepare them for school both intellectually and socially, probably help them to achieve greater school success, and can lead to greater life success in adolescence and adulthood" (Schweinhart & Weikart, 1986, p. 23).

In the future, preschool programs are likely to place less emphasis on the preschool years as a "critical period" that establishes an irreversible trajectory leading to the child's future success or failure. This is partly due to the growing recognition of the importance of other phases of the life cycle, including adolescence and old age. The realization that education alone cannot solve the complexities of poverty has also reduced emphasis on the preschool years as a critical period. This "life-span" approach to human development assumes that predictions about development from childhood to later periods of life are always inconclusive or partial for the individual (Baltes & Brim, 1978–1982).

Presently, preschool programs, including Project Head Start, continue to enjoy public confidence within both the poor and middle-class communities. The present popularity is no doubt largely due to the fact that credible program data and favorable evaluation studies about preschool programs are now available and widely publicized (e.g., Berrueta-Clement, Schweinhart, Barnett, Epstein, & Weikart, 1984).

Greater predictability between childhood and adolescence could be achieved if there is a means to assure continuity in the years following preschool. There should be more effective planning of classroom activities; closer partnerships between parents and teachers; greater emphasis on school readiness skills, and closer linkages between preschools and elementary schools to assure continuation of the growth that children demonstrate while in preschool programs (Washington & Oyemade, 1987).

References

Baltes, P., & Brim, O. (1978–1982). *Lifespan development and behavior* (Vol. 1–4). New York: Academic Press.

Berrueta-Clement, J. R., Schweinhart, L. J., Barnett, W. S., Epstein, R. S., Weikart, D. P. (1984). *Changed lives—The effects of the Perry Preschool Program on Youths through age 19.* Ypsilanti, MI: High/Scope Educational Research Foundation.

Bloom, B. (1964). *Stability and change in human characteristics.* New York: Wiley and Sons.

General Accounting Office. (1979). *Early childhood and family development programs improve the quality of life for low-income families.* (GAO, Report #HRD-79-40). Washington, DC: GAO.

Harrington, M. (1962). *The other America: Poverty in the United States.* New York: Macmillan.

Hunt, J. M. (1961). *Intelligence and experience.* New York: Ronald Press.

Larsen, J. M., Hite, S. J., & Hart, C. J. (1983). The effects of preschool on educationally advantaged children: First phases of a longitudinal study. *Intelligence, 7,* 345–452.

Larsen, J. M., & Robinson, C. C. (1987, April). Later effects of preschool on low-risk children. Paper presented at the biennial meeting of the Society for Research in Child Development, Baltimore, MD.

Schweinhart, L. J., & Weikart, D. P. (1986).

What do we know so far? Do Head Start programs work? *High Scope Resource Magazine, 5,* 1, 20, 22–23.

Slaughter, D. T. (1982, March). What is the future of Head Start? *Young Children,* pp. 3–9.

Steiner, G. Y. (1976). *The children's cause.* Washington, DC: The Brookings Institution.

Washington, V. & Oyemade, U. J. (1987). *Project Head Start: Past, present, and future trends in the context of family needs.* New York: Garland Publishing.

Weikart, D. P. (1982). Preschool education for disadvantaged children. In J. R. Travers & R. J. Light (Eds.), *Learning from experience: Evaluating early childhood demonstration programs.* Washington, DC: National Academy Press.

Weisberg, H. I. & Haney, W. (1977). *Longitudinal evaluation of Head Start planned variation and follow through.* Cambridge, MA: Huron Institute.

Westinghouse Learning Corporation. (1969). *The impact of Head Start: An evaluation of the effects of Head Start on children's cognitive and affective development* (Vols. 1–2 and Executive Summary). Athens, OH: Ohio University.

Zigler, E., & Rescorla, L. (1975). Social science and social policy: The case of social competence as a goal of intervention programs. In R. A. Kassochau, L. P. Rehmm, & L. P. Ullman (Eds.), *Psychology research, public policy and practice: Toward a productive partnership* (pp. 62–94). New York: Praeger.

Zigler, E., & Valentine, J. (Eds.). (1979). *Project Head Start: A legacy of the war on poverty.* New York: Free Press.

Zigler, E., & Anderson, K. (1982). An idea whose time had come: The intellectual and political climate for Head Start. In E. Zigler & J. Valentine (Eds.), *Project Head Start* (pp. 3–19). New York: Free Press.

See Also

Academic Achievement; Achievement: Evidence from High School and Beyond; Dropouts, High School; Issues of Race and Sex; Dropouts, School; Educational Achievement and Tracking in High School; Educational Achievement, Tracking and; Family Life Education; Gifted Adolescents; Graduate School Attendance, Barriers to: Access and Equity along the Education Pipeline; Learning Disabilities in Adolescents: Description, Assessment, and Management; Minority and Female Participation in Math and Science, Increase in: The Importance of the Middle School Years; Parenthood and Marriage in Adolescence: Associations with Educational and Occupational Attainment; Puberty Education; School Programs, Evaluation of; School Transition, Secondary; Schooling; School-Linked Programs, Potential of; Sex Education; Underachievers and Dropouts.

Problem Behavior in Adolescence

Michael Windle
Research Institute on Alcoholism

Early conceptions of adolescent development often portrayed adolescence as a period of "storm and stress," implying that some problem behavior during this stage of development may be quite common, though not necessarily desirable for those parties involved. More recent conceptions, influenced in part by a range of empirical studies, have greatly modified this view of adolescent development. Investigators have proposed that while there are a number of age-specific events, changes, and challenges during adolescence, the "storm and stress" metaphor is not apt. Further, as is discussed subsequently, *serious*, traitlike problem behavior among adolescents, which is nonnormative, must be distinguished from *experimental*, statelike problem behavior, which in some instances, indeed may be considered normative. The material regarding problem behavior in adolescence is presented in three sections. First, the heterogeneous behaviors used to refer to problem behavior in adolescence are presented. Second, prominent antecedents and correlates of adolescent problem behavior are identified, with a primary focus on parental and peer influences. Third, adulthood consequences of adolescent problem behavior are presented and related to a life-span, developmental tasks framework.

Problem Behavior in Adolescence

Two major approaches have been used to describe problem behaviors in adolescence. The first, originating and developed principally within the clinical psychiatric literature (e.g., American Psychiatric Association, 1987), has emphasized heterogeneity in the etiology, developmental course, treatment, and probable outcome of diagnostically labeled disorders. Subject populations often have consisted of clinical treatment groups and psychiatric cases identified in clinical epidemiological studies. The second approach stems from developmental and psychosocial research and has focused on normative and nonnormative life events and processes associated with "normal" development. Subject populations often have consisted of nonclinical high school and general population samples. While these two approaches are not incompatible, professional training and research traditions often have restricted integrated perspectives, though recent efforts toward a constructive synthesis have been proposed (e.g., Sroufe & Rutter, 1984). Research related to the first approach (i.e., the clinical research literature) is reviewed in detail in several other places within this volume and is referred to peripherally only in this entry. Research related to the second approach (i.e., the developmental-psychosocial) is emphasized here with respect to findings of problem behaviors in adolescence.

Although high school and general population studies include some evidence supporting the heterogeneity of developmental pathways leading toward dysfunctional behavior in adolescence (e.g., Kellam, Brown, Rubin, & Ensminger, 1983; Parker & Asher, 1987), a corpus of data suggests that adolescent problem behaviors tend to be highly intercorrelated. Some researchers (e.g., Jessor & Jessor, 1977) have referred to this unitary pattern of covariation among problem behaviors as the *problem behavior syndrome*. Similarly, others have suggested that this pattern of covariation among problem behaviors reflects a personality style of behavioral undercontrol or "deviance proneness." In defining the unitary, problem behavior syndrome, the following behaviors generally have been shown to manifest a pattern of moderate-to-high covariation: precocious sexual activity, alcohol and illicit drug use and abuse, cigarette use, poor academic performance, a lower value on academic achievements, conflict with parents and teachers, rebelliousness, unconventionality, low self-esteem, delinquency, low religiosity, more external locus of control and more negative life events (e.g., Barnes & Welte, 1986; Donovan & Jessor, 1985; Jessor & Jessor, 1977). Additionally, this unitary pattern of covariation has been found not only for white, middle-class samples, but also for different ethnic/racial groups (e.g., Barnes & Welte, 1986; Jessor, Graves, Hanson, &

Jessor, 1968) and for males and females (Windle & Barnes, 1988).

Antecedents and Correlates of Adolescent Problem Behavior

Some research has implicated genetic factors and associated dysfunctional familial influences as antecedents and correlates of some specific problem behaviors in adolescence. For example, Chassin, Mann, and Sher (1988) have suggested that a family history of alcoholism may contribute to a stressful family environment for adolescents, as well as provide the adolescents with parental role models who use alcohol as a way of coping to reduce stress (e.g., Newcomb & Harlow, 1986). As such, this combination of a genetic diathesis for alcoholism, a stressful home environment, and the adoption of alcohol consumption as a preferred coping strategy may foster activity likely to enhance the range and intensity of problem behaviors for adolescents.

However, most research concerned with antecedents and correlates of adolescent problem behavior has focused on the respective socialization influences of parents and peers (e.g., Huba & Bentler, 1980; Kandel & Andrews, 1987). The research findings clearly suggest that both parental and peer influences are salient for adolescents. Research regarding parental influences has indicated that high parental nurturance, or support, is inversely associated with problem behaviors in adolescence (e.g., Barnes & Windle, 1987), and that strong parent-child social bonding may be a protective influence with regard to the initiation of alcohol and drug use (e.g., Brook, Whiteman, Gordon, & Cohen, 1986). Parental disciplinary practices also have been associated with adolescent problem behavior, suggesting that both too little control (perhaps reflecting parental neglect and disinterest) and cruel, harsh, violent punishment may increase the risk for problem behaviors. Research regarding peer influences has indicated that alcohol and illicit drug use, cigarette use, and delinquent activity often takes place within the peer context; it has been proposed that peers become more influential reference sources than parents during the adolescent years.

A more precisely articulated perspective on parent and peer influences on adolescent development has been proffered by Kandel and her associates. Kandel and Lesser (1972) have suggested that peer relations are more important for issues related to immediate life-style, such as clothing, music, and use of drugs, whereas parental relations are important for issues related to future life goals, such as educational and occupational aspirations. Therefore, specificity of the arena, or content domain, is posed as necessary to differentiate the impact of parents and peers on adolescent development. In addition to the specificity of the content domain, Kandel, Margulies, and Davies (1978) have indicated that degree of parental and peer influence depends on the phase, or stage, of the content domains as well. For example, in reference to stages of substance use, Kandel et al. (1978) found that parental modeling influences and attitudes regarding drug use were strongest *prior to* adolescent initiation into drug involvement. Once drug experimentation had begun, parental influences were restricted to indirect effects only, by influencing the friends selected by their adolescents. Once initiated and involved in substance use, the peer context becomes more prominent in terms of influence with respect to quantity, frequency, and variety of drug usage and other deviant behaviors.

Adult Consequences of Adolescent Problem Behavior

There have been a large number of longitudinal studies of early and late adulthood consequences associated with problem behaviors in adolescence. In general, these studies have focused on a specific adolescent problem behavior (e.g., drug involvement) rather than the problem behavior syndrome, and outcome variables have ranged from family and occupational functioning to alcoholism, illicit drug abuse, and criminality. It is beyond the scope of this entry to review all of these studies. Rather, a selective sampling of these studies is presented and implications are drawn with regard to the constancy and change of problem behaviors across the life span from adolescence through adulthood.

Perhaps the strongest support for the constancy, or continuity, of problem behavior from adolescence to adulthood has been reported for aggressive, antisocial behavior. Robins (1978) has suggested that antisocial behavior in adulthood is highly predicted by *all* types of antisocial behavior in childhood. Similarly, Huesmann, Lefkowitz, Eron, and Walder (1984) reported a high level of stability for aggressive behavior over a 22-year period (subjects were age 8 years at the first occasion of measurement, and age 30 years at the last occasion of measurement). Further, the findings of Huesmann et al. indicated that early aggressiveness was predictive of subsequent criminal behavior, spouse abuse, traffic violations, and physical aggression. The pervasive influence of adolescent problem behaviors associated with illicit drug use have been reported with regard to undermining major developmental tasks of early adulthood. Kandel, Davies, Karus, and Yamaguchi (1986) found that illicit drug use in adolescence and young adulthood was predictive of higher rates of delinquency, greater unemployment, increases in the number of divorces, and a higher rate of abortions in adulthood. Likewise, Kandel, Raveis, and Kandel (1984) reported that school dropouts had more difficulties in adjusting to the major life tasks of early adulthood, such as the establishment of and maintenance of a stable job and family. Additionally, dropouts tended to engage in more delinquent activity and to consume more illicit drugs. With a 7–9 year interval between occasions of measurement, Donovan, Jessor, and Jessor (1983) found that 51% of those adolescents classified as problem drinkers at the first occasion of measurement were similarly classified at the second occasion of measurement, and that these stable problem drinkers continued to engage in higher rates of other problem behaviors (e.g., marijuana use, deviant activity) in young adulthood.

While the longitudinal studies cited above may suggest considerable continuity in problem behaviors from adolescence to early adulthood, there is also much research that supports the discontinuity of the various problem behaviors across these phases of the life span. For instance, a common finding of nonclinical high school and general population studies with respect to delinquency, alcohol use, and illicit substance use is that adolescents tend to "mature out" of these problem behaviors as they engage in tasks of early adulthood (e.g., marriage, stable occupation) and assume adult social roles (e.g., husband, father, employee). That is, as many adolescents assume more responsible adult social roles, there often is a corresponding reduction in problem behaviors. Robins (1978) also has noted that while adult antisocial behavior is almost universally associated with childhood antisocial behavior, most antisocial children do not become antisocial

adults. Similarly, based on a review of longitudinal studies predicting criminal behavior from juvenile delinquency, Cline (1980) concluded that only a small core of individuals manifest a pattern of continuity in predicting adult criminal behaviors.

Therefore, rather than being an issue of continuity *versus* discontinuity of problem behaviors from adolescence to early adulthood, the empirical evidence suggests that both patterns are quite common. There does appear to be a period, or phase, in adolescence when some problem behaviors (e.g., alcohol consumption, marijuana usage, minor delinquency) are manifested at some level for a large percentage of adolescents. However, a pattern of statelike experimentation needs to be differentiated from a pattern of chronic, traitlike problem behaviors. It is the chronic, traitlike pattern that is more likely to persist into early adulthood and to interfere with the successful resolution of the developmental tasks of early adulthood and beyond.

References

American Psychiatric Association (1987). *Diagnostic and Statistical Manual of Mental Disorders (DSM-III-R)*. Washington, DC: Author.

Barnes, G. M., & Welte, J. W. (1986). Patterns and predictors of alcohol use among 7th–12th grade students in New York State. *Journal of Studies on Alcohol, 47*, 53–62.

Barnes, G. M., & Windle, M. (1987). Family factors in adolescent alcohol and drug abuse. *Pediatrician, 14*, 13–18.

Brook, J. S., Whiteman, M., Gordon, A. S., & Cohen, P. (1986). Some models and mechanisms for explaining the impact of maternal and adolescent characteristics on adolescent stage of drug use. *Developmental Psychology, 22*, 460–467.

Chassin, L., Mann, L. M., & Sher, K. J. (1988).

Self-awareness theory, family history of alcoholism, and adolescent alcohol involvement. *Journal of Abnormal Psychology, 97*, 206–217.

Cline, H. F. (1980). Criminal behavior over the life span. In O. G. Brim & J. Kagan (Eds.), *Constancy and change in human development* (pp. 641–674). Cambridge: Harvard University Press.

Donovan, J. E., & Jessor, R. (1985). Structure of problem behavior in adolescence and young adulthood. *Journal of Consulting and Clinical Psychology, 53*, 890–904.

Donovan, J. E., Jessor, R., & Jessor, S. L. (1983). Problem drinking in adolescence and young adulthood: A follow-up study. *Journal of Studies on Alcohol, 44*, 109–137.

Huba, G., & Bentler, P. M. (1980). The role of peer and adult models for drug taking at different stages in adolescence. *Journal of Youth and Adolescence, 9*, 449–465.

Huesmann, L. R., Lefkowitz, M. M., Eron, L. D., & Walder, L. O. (1984). Stability of aggression over time and generations. *Developmental Psychology, 20*, 1120–1134.

Jessor, R., Graves, T. D., Hanson, R. C., & Jessor, S. L. (1968). *Society, personality, and deviant behavior: A study of a tri-ethnic community.* New York: Holt, Rinehart & Winston.

Jessor, R., & Jessor, S. L. (1977). *Problem behavior and psychosocial development: A longitudinal study of youth.* New York: Academic Press.

Kandel, D. B., & Andrews, K. (1987). Processes of adolescent socialization by parents and peers. *International Journal of the Addictions, 22*, 319–342.

Kandel, D. B., Davies, M., Karus, D., & Yamaguchi, K. (1986). The consequences in young adulthood of adolescent drug involvement. *Archives of General Psychiatry, 43*, 746–754.

Kandel, D. B., & Lesser, G. I. (1972). *Youth in two orlds.* San Francisco: Jossey-Bass.

Kandel, D. B., Margulies, R. Z., & Davies, M. (1978). Analytical strategies for studying transitions into developmental stages. *Sociology of Education, 51*, 162–176.

Kandel, D. B., Raveis, V. H., & Kandel, P. I. (1984). Continuity in discontinuities: Adjustment in young adulthood of former school absentees. *Youth and Society, 15*, 325–352.

Kellam, S. G., Brown, C. H., Rubin, B. R., & Ensminger, M. E. (1983). Paths leading to teenage psychiatric symptoms and substance use: Developmental epidemiological studies in Woodlawn. In S. B. Guze, F. J. Earls, & J. E. Barrett (Eds.), *Childhood psychopathology and development* (pp. 17–51). New York: Raven Press.

Newcomb, M. D., & Harlow, L. L. (1986). Life events and substance use among adolescents: Mediating effects of perceived loss of control and meaninglessness in life. *Journal of Personality and Social Psychology, 51*, 564–578.

Parker, J. G., & Asher, S. R. (1987). Peer relations and later personal adjustment: Are low-accepted children at risk? *Psychological Bulletin, 102*, 357–389.

Robins, L. N. (1978). Sturdy childhood predictors of adult antisocial behavior: Replications from longitudinal studies. *Psychological Medicine, 8*, 611–622.

Sroufe, L. A., & Rutter, M. (1984). The domain of developmental psychopathology. *Child Development, 55*, 17–29.

Windle, M., & Barnes, G. M. (1988). Similarities and differences in correlates of alcohol consumption and problem behaviors among male and female adolescents. *International Journal of the Addictions, 23*, 707–728.

See Also

Aggressive Behavior in Adolescence; Attention Deficit Disorder and Hyperactivity; Bulimia

Nervosa in Adolescence; Conflict, Adolescent-Parent: A Model and a Method; Delinquency; Handicapped Adolescents, Providing Services for; Learning Disabilities in Adolescents: Description, Assessment, and Management; Psychophysiological/Psychosomatic Problems; Runaways, Negative Consequences for; Self-Destructiveness, Chronic, Role of in Adolescence; Stress and the Adolescent; Stress and Coping in the Adolescent; Suicide, Adolescent; Suicides, Cluster; Type A and Teenagers.

Prosocial Development in Adolescence

Nancy Eisenberg

Arizona State University

In the last 20 years psychologists and educators have done much research concerning the development of prosocial behavior (i.e., voluntary behavior intended to benefit another, such as helping, sharing, and comforting). Nonetheless, as was noted by Hoffman in 1980, there has been surprisingly little research on adolescents' moral development, including their prosocial development. Similarly, in a recent review of research concerning adolescents' social competence, Hill (1987) noted that the "capability for relatedness, connectedness, communion, and for what Gilligan has termed 'caring mortality' have . . . been little studied" (p. 24).

Although there is relatively little research on prosocial development in adolescence, there is reason to expect development during the adolescent years. Behaviors such as helping, sharing, and comforting have been linked both conceptually and empirically with perspective-taking skills (Eisenberg, 1986; Underwood & Moore, 1982b); empathic and sympathetic responding, or the tendency to experience vicariously another's emotional state or condition and to sympathize (Batson, 1987; Eisenberg & Miller, 1987; Hoffman, 1984); and level of moral reasoning (Blasi,

1980; Eisenberg, 1986; Underwood & Moore, 1982b). All of these skills appear to develop into adolescence (Hill & Palmquist, 1978). Moreover, there is a large data base indicating that individuals' moral reasoning about issues other than prosocial behaviors becomes more sophisticated during adolescence (see, for example, Colby, Kohlberg, Gibbs, & Lieberman, 1983; Rest, 1983). Thus, moral reasoning about moral dilemmas concerning conflicts between two people's needs, or prosocial moral reasoning (see Eisenberg, 1986; Higgins, Power, & Kohlberg, 1984), could be expected to change during adolescence. In addition, because higher-level moral reasoning tends to be positively related to quantity and quality of individuals' prosocial behaviors (the amount of the behavior and the motivational basis for the behavior; Bar-Tal, Korenfeld, & Raviv, 1985; Blasi, 1980), a trend toward more altruistic, other-oriented behavior can be expected during adolescence.

In this short review, research on adolescents' prosocial behaviors and cognitions about prosocial behavior (i.e., moral reasoning) is summarized. The focus is on research conducted with children in late elementary school (i.e., sixth grade) and

845 ∎

high school, not college students (for a review of work on college-aged activists, see Hoffman, 1980). Data on adolescents' prosocial behaviors are reviewed, and issues such as age-related change in the role of socialization, personality, and sociocognitive variables in prosocial development are considered briefly. In addition, research on adolescents' prosocial moral reasoning is summarized.

Age-Related Changes in Prosocial Behavior

There is relatively little research available concerning changes with age in the frequency and quality of prosocial behaviors during the preadolescent and adolescent years. Moreover, the results of the limited extant work sometimes are inconsistent across studies.

HELPING ▪ Some investigators have found that helping increases with age during adolescence (Berndt, 1985), whereas others have noted little change with age (Collins & Getz, 1976; Green & Schneider, 1974; Lowe & Ritchey, 1973; Midlarsky & Hannah, 1985) or a decrease with age (Bar-Tal & Nissim, 1984). In studies with preadolescents, mixed results also have been obtained (Payne, 1980; Peterson, 1983a, 1983b; Staub, 1970).

Apparently, adolescents are not necessarily more helpful than younger children. Nonetheless, they do help more on tasks that involve age-related knowledge and skills (Midlarsky & Hannah, 1985; Peterson, 1983a). Moreover, adolescents' failures to help frequently may be due to factors different from those affecting younger children. For example, in a study of helping in an emergency, adolescents, in comparison to elementary school children, reported

being more hesitant to help because of fear of disapproval from the recipient and fear that the recipient would be embarrassed or feel that the help was condescending (Midlarsky & Hannah, 1985). Younger children were more likely to report not helping because of perceptions of their own incompetence. Similarly, in another study in which adolescents were asked about times when they had failed to help others, they frequently cited the desire not to interfere in another's personal situation or/and the desire not to violate internalized values, laws, or rules. In contrast, elementary school children were more likely to cite perceived incompetence (Barnett, Thompson, & Schroff, 1987).

DONATING AND SHARING ▪ The findings with regard to sharing and donating behavior are somewhat more consistent than are those pertaining to helping. Donating and sharing have been found to increase with age into preadolescence (i.e., sixth grade) or early adolescence in several, although not all, studies (e.g., Dreman, 1976; Emler & Rushton, 1974; Green & Schneider, 1974; Levin & Bekerman-Greenberg, 1980; Payne, 1980; also see Radke-Yarrow, Zahn-Waxler, & Chapman, 1983). In only one of these studies (Ugurel-Semin, 1952) were any high-school–aged subjects included, so it is impossible to determine change from early to middle adolescence in donating or sharing. Moreover, whether the pattern of findings is due to differences in the value of the commodity across age groups or in willingness to deny oneself of a desirable commodity has not been tested adequately.

COMFORTING ▪ There is little research regarding age differences in comforting behavior. Berndt and Perry (1986) interviewed 2nd, 4th, 6th, and 8th graders about their perceptions of social support provided by friends. Reports that friends and acquaintances provided emotional support increased markedly from 2nd to 4th grade but not thereafter. Reports of emotional support from acquaintances increased nonsignificantly from 2nd to 8th grade. However, in other research, adolescents appeared to be more effective in their comforting behavior than were younger children (Burleson, 1982; Feldman, Nash, & Cutrona, 1977).

Consistency in Prosocial Responding

An important issue in the study of personality is the consistency of personality traits. Thus, it is not surprising that a number of researchers have sought to determine whether there is an altruistic personality, that is, whether some people are consistently more prosocial than others.

Although consistency has not always been observed (e.g., Eisenberg, Cialdini, McCreath, & Shell, 1987; Payne, 1980), individual differences in level of prosocial responding are somewhat stable across situations and time during preadolescence and adolescence (Bar-Tal & Raviv, 1979; Dlugokinski & Firestone, 1973; Hampson, 1981). For example, adolescents at summer camping outings over periods of weeks (at wilderness travel programs and travel camp programs) recognized individual differences in peers' prosocial behaviors after only four days, and their perceptions of peers' altruism remained stable for weeks (Small, Zeldin, & Savin Williams, 1983; Zeldin, Small, & Savin-Williams, 1982). Moreover, their prosocial behavior, as observed by trained coders, was consistent across time and different settings (Zeldin et al., 1982; also see Savin-Williams, 1987).

Personal Characteristics

A variety of adolescents' personal characteristics have been examined in relation to interindividual differences in typical level of prosocial behavior. A few of those examined most frequently are now reviewed.

SEX ■ The limited research on gender differences in adolescents' prosocial behavior is not consistent (see Eisenberg, 1990). This pattern of findings is not surprising given the lack of consistent gender differences in childhood (see Radke-Yarrow et al., 1983; Shigetomi, Hartmann, & Gelfand, 1981; Underwood & Moore, 1982a). Among adults, however, males appear to engage in more instrumental acts of helping, especially those that involve an audience and might be perceived as dangerous (Eagly & Crowley, 1986). In contrast, females may provide more emotional support (Bem, Martyna, & Watson, 1976; Johnson & Aries, 1983; also see Eagly & Crowley, 1986). Thus, although adolescent males and females differ relatively little in their overall level of prosocial behavior, it is possible that females provide more emotional support whereas males provide more instrumental aid. The finding by Zeldin et al. (1982) that male adolescents displayed more physical assistance behaviors (such as setting up a tent) whereas females offered more verbal support is consistent with this hypothesis.

SOCIOECONOMIC STATUS, RACE, AND ETHNIC BACKGROUND ■ There are relatively few studies concerning the relation of socioeconomic class, race, or ethnic group to adolescents' prosocial behavior. In several involving samples of preadoles-

cents or adolescents, higher parental education and/or socioeconomic status have been associated with higher levels of helpfulness or sensitivity to others' needs (Loban, 1953, for males only; Lowe & Ritchey, 1973; Payne, 1980; Raviv & Bar-Tal, 1981), although boys from entrepreneurial middle-class families appear to assist others primarily on the basis of reciprocity (Berkowitz, 1968; Berkowitz & Friedman, 1967; also see Dreman, 1976).

In contrast, the limited research concerning the relation of race and ethnic group to adolescents' prosocial behavior is not consistent across studies (Cox, 1974; Loban, 1953; Raviv & Bar-Tal, 1981), especially if the effects of socioeconomic status are controlled.

PERSONALITY CHARACTERISTICS

Among adolescents, lack of popularity and loneliness appear to be associated with relatively low levels of prosocial behavior (Hampson, 1984; Loban, 1953; Yarcheski & Mahon, 1984). This pattern may be due, in part, to the fact that the less popular children seem to be less adept than other children at selecting helping strategies valued by their peers (Ladd & Oden, 1979). In addition, although McGuire and Weisz (1982) did not find a relation between popularity and altruism, they did find that fifth and sixth graders who had a chum exhibited more prosocial behaviors in the classroom (but having a chum was unrelated to donating behavior or teachers' ratings of altruism).

Increments in self-worth (Jarymowicz, 1977) also have been related to self report of prosocial sensitivity. Moreover, there is modest support for the conclusion that socially competent adolescents who are concerned about others and their own responsibilities are more prosocial than are other youth (Loban, 1953). Adolescents who are more prosocial also score relatively high on measures of sympathy and empathy (e.g., Barnett, Howard, King, & Dino, 1981; Eisenberg-Berg, & Mussen, 1978) and moral judgment (Dreman, 1976; Eisenberg-Berg, 1979b; Emler & Rushton, 1974; see Blasi, 1980, and Eisenberg, 1986, for general reviews). Thus, it appears that prosocial adolescents are socially competent, empathic, and relatively advanced in their moral reasoning, although firm conclusions cannot be drawn because of the limited relevant data.

Adolescents' personal characteristics also seem to interact with aspects of the helping context in their effect on prosocial behavior. For example, Hampson (1984) found popular eighth graders preferred to engage in peer-related helping tasks (such as talking to peers in distress and spending time with them) whereas less popular students preferred to help in less direct, behind-the-scenes ways (e.g., by returning permission slips on time or volunteering by telephone to help younger children). More popular adolescents are likely to feel more comfortable being sociable and asserting themselves with peers, perhaps because their peers respond more positively to their attempts to assist.

Socialization Correlates

Many researchers have examined the relation of socializers' childrearing practices to children's prosocial behaviors (see Eisenberg & Mussen, 1989; Moore & Eisenberg, 1984; Radke-Yarrow et al., 1983). In general, they have found that high levels of prosocial behavior are associated with supportive parenting accompanied by the use of reasoning (i.e., inductions), but not overly punitive techniques in disciplinary contexts. Additional socialization practices linked with children's prosocial behavior include socializers' modeling of prosocial behaviors, the provision of opportunities for children to engage in prosocial actions, socializers' verbalizations indicating the value of prosocial behavior, and the setting of high standards for children.

The limited data from studies involving adolescents are, in general, consistent with the pattern obtained for children. Adolescents' prosocial behavior seems to be enhanced by supportive parenting combined with procedures (such as the use of reasoning) that focus the individual's attention on others rather than on themselves and implicitly provide positive modeling— in other words, supportive parents are themselves models of caring behavior (Bar-Tal, Nadler, & Blechman, 1980; Dlugokinski & Firestone, 1974; Hoffman & Saltzstein, 1967; Karylowski, 1982). Additionally, social responsibility in adolescence has been linked with authoritative child rearing practices (supportive parenting involving clear standards, the use of inductions, and sensitivity to the child's perspective) (Baumrind, 1987). Whether these relations are due solely to patterns established before adolescence or to a continuing relation between socializers' practices and children's prosocial behaviors (during childhood and adolescence) is unknown, although it is likely that the latter is true.

Extrafamilial socialization may also play a role in prosocial development. For example, encouragement to engage in extracurricular helping activities may be associated with enhanced prosocial behavior because participation in such activities is related to relatively high levels of prosocial behavior in adolescence (Cox, 1974; also see Eisenberg, Cialdini, McCreath, & Shell, 1987, and Staub, 1979, for discussion of socializers' encouragement of participation in prosocial activities). In contrast, ado-

lescents' participation in the working world seems to have relatively little effect on levels of social responsibility (Steinberg, Greenberger, Garduque, Ruggiero, & Vaux, 1982).

Moral Reasoning About Prosocial Dilemmas

People's reasoning about why one should or should not assist others is of relevance to understanding prosocial development because such reasoning provides insights into the values and motives that underlie prosocial behavior. In research on prosocial moral reasoning, people are asked to resolve moral dilemmas (real or hypothetical), and then are asked to explain their reasoning. Based on research of this sort, it appears that cognitions about prosocial dilemmas and behaviors change during preadolescence and adolescence, and that there are some gender differences in these cognitions (at least in the United States).

For example, Eisenberg and her colleagues and students found that there are increases in prosocial moral reasoning reflecting concern about others' approval and the quality of one's interactions with others during the late elementary school years. During this same age span stereotypic conceptions of good and bad behavior and concerns about direct reciprocity are also verbalized with increasing frequency. For girls only, increases in reasoning reflecting role-taking and a sympathetic orientation were also found from age 9–10 to 11–12 years of age (Eisenberg, Shell, Pasternack, Lennon, Beller, & Mathy, 1987; Eisenberg-Berg, 1979a; also see Eisenberg, 1986).

In addition, high school students, in comparison to elementary school students, verbalize more reasoning reflecting internalized norms and values, positive and negative affect related to either the consequences of one's behavior for others or self-respect and living up to one's own values, and concern for the rights of others and the condition of society (Eisenberg, 1977; Eisenberg-Berg, 1979a). Approval/interpersonally oriented and stereotypic reasoning appear to peak in or prior to ninth grade, and then decrease in usage. Similarly, in other research with adolescents from Germany, Italy, Poland, and the United States, adolescents preferred other-oriented or task-oriented motives for assisting another, and there was some indication that conformity and hedonistic motives were less preferred with age (Boehnke, Silbereisen, Eisenberg, Reykowski, & Palmonari, 1989; also see Eisenberg, 1986). Finally, consistent with the aforementioned findings for sixth graders, high school females and males in America appear to use somewhat different reasoning. Specifically, when discussing reasons for assisting or not assisting a needy other, males tend to be more concerned than females with direct reciprocity, hedonistic concerns, and the helper's affective tie to the needy other (i.e., if they were a friend, relative, or disliked). In contrast, females express more other-oriented, empathic concerns (Eisenberg, 1977).

Gilligan and her colleagues (e.g., Gilligan, 1977, 1982; Gilligan & Attanucci, 1988; Lyons, 1983) also have studied adolescents' and adults' moral reasoning, and have found gender differences in reasoning. Specifically, they have found that males tend to resolve moral dilemmas by referring to principles of justice and fairness whereas females are more likely to focus on issues related to caring and a connection between people. Gilligan has argued that males and females tend to exhibit two different moral orientations (although they can use either or both orientations): males favor a justice perspective, in which the core notion is not to treat others unfairly whereas females favor a care orientation, in which the focus is not to turn away from others. Although several researchers have obtained findings similar to those of Gilligan and her colleagues (Ford & Lowery, 1986; Gibbs, Arnold, & Burkhart, 1984), others have not (e.g., Walker, 1989; Walker, deVries, & Trevethan, 1987; see Brabeck, 1983, and Walker, 1984, for reviews of relevant research). In particular, there is relatively little evidence of a gender difference in justice-oriented moral reasoning. However, gender differences in care-related reasoning may be most obvious when individuals discuss moral dilemmas focusing on prosocial rather than prohibition- or justice-related issues (which has not been the case in many studies).

Gilligan (1982) outlined a sequence for the development of an ethic of caring (analogous to Kohlberg's [1976] stages of moral reasoning). At the first level, the individual's focus is on caring for the self, and relationships are conceptualized in self-serving terms. This period is followed by a transitional stage in which such self-oriented concerns are criticized as being selfish. At the second level, good is equated with caring for other people, and one's own needs often are subjugated. At this level, concern with one's own needs tends to be viewed as selfish. In the second transitional state, women start to see that a morality of care includes care for the self as well as others. Thus, one must strive to consider the needs of the self as well as others and be responsible for oneself as well as others. Finally, at the third level, the individual focuses on the dynamics of relationships, and the interconnectedness of self and other. One is responsible for relationships, the quality of which depends on meeting the needs of all participants. Moral equality between self and other is accomplished by applying an injunction against hurting anyone.

Unfortunately, Gilligan has not systematically studied the emergence of her stages of caring orientation using sizable samples of adolescents (although some adolescents have been involved in her studies). However, based on her anecdotal examples of reasoning, it would appear that adolescents typically reason at Gilligan's first level or first transitional stage, although some may be at the second level or higher.

In other research involving elementary school children, adolescents, and their parents, care reasoning appeared to increase somewhat with age, but at a very slow rate (Walker, 1989). Thus, it appears that care-oriented reasoning, as conceptualized by Gilligan, does increase with age, although changes within the period of adolescence may be small.

Summary

Unfortunately, we know relatively little about the development of prosocial behaviors and reasoning in adolescence. This is due to numerous factors. First, there is relatively little theoretical work on prosocial development—or, indeed, moral development—during adolescence. Kohlberg's theoretical work (1969, 1976, 1984; Colby et al., 1983) is the most comprehensive concerning adolescent moral development; however, his focus has not been on the positive aspects of morality. Some writers such as Hoffman (1980, 1984) have touched briefly on issues related to prosocial development during adolescence, but none have focused primarily on this issue.

A second reason for the dearth of information concerning adolescents' prosocial development is the lack of focus in the empirical work on moral development during adolescence per se. In most studies involving adolescence, adolescents were included because they were a convenient sample to obtain or because the sample ranged in age from children to adults. In many of these studies the investigators have not specifically examined change for a given index of moral development into or during adolescence. If adolescence per se is not a period of interest to investigators, they are not likely to calculate the statistical tests that would directly address questions related to moral development in adolescence.

If we are to obtain a better understanding of prosocial development in adolescence, it would seem worthwhile to examine the relation of prosocial behavior to some of the variables of particular conceptual importance in current work concerning adolescence. For example, in their research concerning prosocial development, investigators might focus on the role of family processes related to the degree of individuality and connectedness in family relationships (Grotevant & Cooper, 1986), ego and identity development (Loevinger & Wessler, 1970; Waterman, 1982), or changes in adolescents' self-concepts (Damon & Hart, 1982). In doing so, investigators might be able to tie more general theories regarding adolescent development to the study of prosocial behavior, and discover influences on prosocial development that are unique to the adolescent period.

References

Barnett, M. A., Howard, J. A., King, L. M., & Dino, G. A. (1981). Helping behavior and the transfer of empathy. *Journal of Social Psychology*, *115*, 125–132.

Barnett, M., Thompson, M. A., & Schroff, J. (1987). Reasons for not helping. *Journal of Genetic Psychology*, *148*, 489–498.

Bar-Tal, D., Korenfeld, D., & Raviv, A. (1985). Relationships between the development of helping behavior and the development of cognition, social perspective, and moral judgment. *Genetic, Social, and General Psychology Monographs, 11*, 23–40.

Bar-Tal, D., Nadler, A., & Blechman, N. (1980). The relationship between Israeli children's helping behavior and their perception of parents' socialization practices. *Journal of Social Psychology, 111*, 159–167.

Bar-Tal, D., & Nissim, R. (1984). Helping behavior and moral judgment among adolescents. *British Journal of Developmental Psychology, 2*, 329–336.

Bar-Tal, D., & Raviv, A. (1979). Consistency in helping-behavior measures. *Child Development, 50*, 1235–1238.

Batson, C. D. (1987). Prosocial motivation: Is it ever truly altruistic? In L. Berkowitz (Ed.), *Advances in experimental social psychology* (Vol. 20, pp. 65–122). New York: Academic Press.

Bem, S. L., Martyna, W., & Watson, C. (1976). Sex typing and androgyny: Further explorations of the expressive domain. *Journal of Personality and Social Psychology, 34*, 1016–1023.

Berkowitz, L. (1968). Responsibility, reciprocity, and social distance in help giving: An experimental investigation of English social class differences. *Journal of Experimental Social Psychology, 4*, 46–63.

Berkowitz, L., & Friedman, P. (1967). Some social class differences in helping behavior. *Journal of Personality and Social Psychology, 5*, 217–225.

Berndt, T. J. (1985). Prosocial behavior between friends in middle childhood and early adolescence. *Journal of Early Adolescence, 5*, 307–317.

Berndt, T. J., & Perry, T. B. (1986). Children's perceptions of friendships as supportive relationships. *Developmental Psychology, 22*, 640–648.

Blasi, A. (1980). Bridging moral cognition and moral action: A critical review of the literature. *Psychological Bulletin, 88*, 1–45.

Boehnke, K., Silbereisen, R. K., Eisenberg, N., Reykowski, J., & Palmonari, A. (1989). The development of prosocial motivation: A cross-national study. *Journal of Cross Cultural Psychology, 20*, 219–243.

Brabeck, M. (1983). Moral judgement: Theory and research in differences between males and females. *Developmental Review, 3*, 274–291.

Burleson, B. R. (1982). The development of comforting strategies in childhood and adolescence. *Child Development, 53*, 1578–1588.

Colby, A., Kohlberg, L., Gibbs, J., & Lieberman, M. (1983). A longitudinal study of moral judgement. *Monographs of the Society for Research in Child Development, 48*(Serial No. 200), 1–124.

Collins, W. A., & Getz, S. K. (1976). Children's social responses following modeled reactions to provocation: Prosocial effects of a television drama. *Journal of Personality, 44*, 488–500.

Cox, N. (1974). Prior help, ego development, and helping behavior. *Child Development, 75*, 594–603.

Damon, W., & Hart, D. (1982). The development of self-understanding from infancy through adolescence. *Child Development, 53*, 841–864.

Dlugokinski, E., & Firestone, I. J. (1973). Congruence among four methods of measuring other-centeredness. *Child Development, 44*, 304–308.

Dlugokinski, E. L., & Firestone, I. J. (1974). Other-centeredness and susceptibility to charitable appeals: Effects of perceived discipline. *Developmental Psychology, 10*, 21–28.

Dreman, S. B. (1976). Sharing behavior in Israeli school children: Cognitive and social learning factors. *Child Development, 47*, 186–194.

Eagly, A. M., & Crowley, M. (1986). Gender and helping behavior: A meta-analytic review of the social psychological literature. *Psychological Bulletin, 100*, 283–308.

Eisenberg, N. (1977). The development of prosocial moral judgment and its correlates.

Dissertation Abstracts International, 37, 4753B. (University Microfilms No. 77–444)

Eisenberg, N. (1990). Prosocial development in early and mid-adolescence. In R. Montemayor, G. R. Adams, T. P Gullotta (eds.), *From childhood to adolescence: A transitional period? Advances in adolescence.* Vol. 2 (pp. 240–269). Newbury Park, CA: Sage.

Eisenberg, N., Cialdini, R. B., McCreath, H., & Shell, R. (1987). Consistency-based compliance: When and why do children become vulnerable? *Journal of Personality and Social Psychology, 52,* 1174–1181.

Eisenberg, N., & Miller, P. (1987). The relation of empathy to prosocial and related behaviors. *Psychological Bulletin, 101,* 91–119.

Eisenberg, N., & Mussen, P. H. (1989). *The roots of prosocial behavior in children.* Cambridge: Cambridge University Press.

Eisenberg, N., Shell, R., Pasternack, J., Lennon, R., Beller, R., & Mathy, R. M. (1987). Prosocial development in middle childhood: A longitudinal study. *Developmental Psychology, 23,* 712–718.

Eisenberg-Berg, N. (1979a). Development of children's prosocial moral judgment. *Developmental Psychology, 15,* 128–137.

Eisenberg-Berg, N. (1979b). The relationship of prosocial moral reasoning to altruism, political liberalism, and intelligence. *Developmental Psychology, 15,* 87–89.

Eisenberg-Berg, N., & Mussen, P. (1978). Empathy and moral development in adolescence. *Developmental Psychology, 14,* 185–186.

Emler, N. P., & Rushton, J. P. (1974). Cognitive-developmental factors in children's generosity. *British Journal of Social and Clinical Psychology, 13,* 277–281.

Feldman, S. S., Nash, S. C., & Cutrona, C. (1977). The influence of age and sex on responsiveness to babies. *Developmental Psychology, 13,* 675–676.

Ford, M. R., & Lowery, C. R. (1986). Gender differences in moral reasoning: A comparison of the use of justice and care orientations. *Journal of Personality and Social Psychology, 50,* 777–783.

Gibbs, J. C., Arnold, K. D., & Burkhart, J. E. (1984). Sex differences in the expression of moral judgment. *Child Development, 55,* 1040–1043.

Gilligan, C. (1977). In a different voice: Women's conceptions of self and of morality. *Harvard Educational Review, 47,* 481–517.

Gilligan, C. (1982). *In a different voice: Psychological theory and women's development.* Cambridge: Harvard University Press.

Gilligan, C. (1987). Adolescent development reconsidered. *New Directions in Child Development, 37,* 63–92.

Gilligan, C., & Attanucci, J. (1988). Two moral orientations: Gender differences and similarities. *Merrill Palmer Quarterly, 34,* 223–237.

Green, F. P., & Schneider, F. W. (1974). Age differences in the behavior of boys on three measures of altruism. *Child Development, 45,* 248–251.

Grotevant, H. D., & Cooper, C. R. (1986). Individuation in family relationships. *Human Development, 29,* 82–100.

Hampson, R. B. (1981). Helping behavior in children: Addressing the interaction of a person-situation model. *Developmental Review, 1,* 93–112.

Hampson, R. B. (1984). Adolescent prosocial behavior: Peer group and situational factors associated with helping. *Journal of Personality and Social Psychology, 46,* 153–162.

Higgins, A., Power, C., & Kohlberg, L. (1984). The relationship of moral atmosphere to judgments of responsibility. In W. M. Kurtines & J. L. Gewirtz (Eds.), *Morality, moral behavior, and moral development* (pp. 74–106). New York: Wiley & Sons.

Hill, J. P. (1987). Research on adolescents and their families: Past and prospects. *New Directions in Child Development, 37,* 13–31.

Hill, J. P., & Palmquist, W. J. (1978). Social cognition and social relations in early adolescence. *International Journal of Behavioral Development, 1,* 1–38.

Hoffman, M. L. (1980). Moral development in adolescence. In J. Adelson (Ed.), *Handbook of adolescent psychology* (pp. 295–343). New York: Wiley.

Hoffman, M. L. (1984). Interaction of affect and cognition on empathy. In C. E. Izard, J. Kagan, & R. B. Zajonc (Eds.), *Emotions, cognition, and behavior* (pp. 103–131). Cambridge: Cambridge University Press.

Hoffman, M. L., & Saltzstein, H. D. (1967). Parent discipline and the child's moral development. *Journal of Personality and Social Psychology, 5,* 45–57.

Jarymowicz, M. (1977). Modification of self-worth and increment of prosocial sensitivity. *Polish Psychological Bulletin, 8,* 45–53.

Johnson, F. L., & Aries, E. J. (1983). Conversational patterns among same-sex pairs of late adolescent close friends. *Journal of Genetic Psychology, 142,* 225–238.

Karylowski, J. (1982). Doing good to feel good vs. doing good to make others feel good: Some child-rearing antecedents. *School Psychology International, 3,* 149–156.

Kohlberg, L. (1969). Stage and sequence: The cognitive-developmental approach to socialization. In D. A. Goslin (Ed.), *Handbook of socialization theory and research* (pp. 325–480). New York: Rand McNally.

Kohlberg, L. (1976). Moral stage and moralization: The cognitive-developmental approach. In T. Lickona (Ed.), *Moral development and behavior: Theory, research, and social issues* (pp. 84–107). New York: Holt, Rinehart, & Winston.

Kohlberg, L. (1984). *Essays on moral development:* Vol. 2. *The psychology of moral development.* San Francisco: Harper & Row.

Ladd, G., & Oden, S. (1979). The relationship between peer acceptance and children's ideas about helpfulness. *Child Development, 50,* 402–408.

Levin, I., & Bekerman-Greenberg, R. (1980). Moral judgment and moral reasoning in

sharing: A developmental analysis. *Genetic Psychological Monographs, 101,* 215–230.

Loban, W. (1953). A study of social sensitivity (sympathy) among adolescents. *Journal of Educational Psychology, 44,* 102–112.

Loevinger, J., & Wessler, R. (1970). *Measuring ego development* (Vol. 1). San Francisco: Jossey-Bass.

Lowe, R., & Ritchey, G. (1973). Relation of altruism to age, social class, and ethnic identity. *Psychological Reports, 33,* 567–572.

Lyons, N. P. (1983). Two perspectives: On self, relationships, and morality. *Harvard Educational Review, 53,* 125–145.

McGuire, K. D., & Weisz, J. R. (1982). Social cognition and behavior correlates of preadolescent chumship. *Child Development, 53,* 1478–1484.

Midlarsky, E., & Hannah, M. E. (1985). Competence, reticence, and helping by children and adolescents. *Developmental Psychology, 21,* 534–541.

Moore, B. S., & Eisenberg, N. (1984). The development of altruism. In G. Whitehurst (Ed.), *Annals of child development* (pp. 107–174). Greenwich, JAI Press.

Payne, F. D. (1980). Children's prosocial conduct in structured situations and as viewed by others: Consistency, convergence, and relationships with person variables. *Child Development, 51,* 1252–1259.

Peterson, L. (1983a). Influence of age, task competence, and responsibility focus on children's altruism. *Developmental Psychology, 19,* 141–148.

Peterson, L. (1983b). Role of donor competence, donor age, and peer presence on helping on an emergency. *Developmental Psychology, 19,* 873–880.

Radke-Yarrow, M., Zahn-Waxler, C., & Chapman, M. (1983). Prosocial dispositions and behavior. In E. M. Hetherington (Ed.) & P. Mussen (General Ed.), *Manual of child psychology: Vol. 4. Socialization, personality, and social development* (pp. 469–545). New York: John Wiley & Sons.

Raviv, A., & Bar-Tal, D. (1981). Demographic correlates of adolescents' helping behavior. *Journal of Youth and Adolescence, 10*, 45–53.

Rest, J. R. (1979). *Development in judging moral issues.* Minneapolis: University of Minnesota Press.

Rest, J. R. (1983). Morality. In P. Mussen (Ed.), *Handbook of child psychology: Vol. 3. Cognitive development* (pp. 556–629). New York: John Wiley & Sons.

Savin-Williams, R. C. (1987). *Adolescence: An ethological perspective.* New York: Springer-Verlag.

Shigetomi, C. C., Hartmann, D. P., & Gelfand, D. M. (1981). Sex differences in children's altruistic behaviors and reputations for helpfulness. *Developmental Psychology, 17*, 434–437.

Small, S. A., Zeldin, R. S., & Savin-Williams, R. C. (1983). In search of personality traits: A multimethod analysis of naturally occurring prosocial and dominance behaviors. *Journal of Personality, 51*, 1–16.

Staub, E. (1970). A child in distress: The influence of age and number of witnesses on children's attempts to help. *Journal of Personality and Social Psychology, 14*, 130–140.

Staub, E. (1978). *Positive social behavior and morality: Vol. 1. Social and personal influences.* New York: Academic Press.

Staub, E. (1979). *Positive social behavior and morality: Vol. 2. Socialization and development.* New York: Academic Press.

Steinberg, L. D., Greenberger, E., Garduque, L., Ruggiero, M., & Vaux, A. (1982). Effects of working on adolescent development. *Developmental Psychology, 18*, 385–395.

Ugurel-Semin, R. (1952). Moral behavior and moral judgment of children. *Journal of Abnormal and Social Psychology, 47*, 463–474.

Underwood, B., & Moore, B. S. (1982a). The generality of altruism in children. In N. Eisenberg (Ed.), *The development of prosocial behavior* (pp. 25–52). New York: Academic Press.

Underwood, B., & Moore, B. (1982b). Perspective-taking and altruism. *Psychological Bulletin, 91*, 143–173.

Walker, L. J. (1984). Sex differences in the development of moral reasoning: A critical review. *Child Development, 55*, 677–691.

Walker, L. J. (1989). A longitudinal study of moral orientation. *Child Development, 60*, 157–166.

Walker, L. J., deVries, B., & Trevethan, S. D. (1987). Moral stages and moral orientations in real life and hypothetical dilemmas. *Child Development, 58*, 842–858.

Waterman, A. S. (1982). Identity development from adolescence to adulthood: An extension of theory and a review of research. *Developmental Psychology, 18*, 341–358.

Yarcheski, A., & Mahon, N. E. (1984). Chumship relationships, altruistic behavior, and loneliness in early adolescents. *Adolescence, 19*, 913–924.

Zeldin, R. S., Small, S. A., & Savin-Williams, R. C. (1982). Prosocial interactions in two mixed-sex adolescent groups. *Child Development, 53*, 1492–1498.

See Also

Cults, Adolescence and; Moral Development in Adolescence; Religion and Adolescence.

Preparation of this entry was supported by grants from the National Science Foundation (BNS-8509223 and BNS-8807784) and the National Institute of Child Health and Development (KO4 HD00717).

Protective and Risk Factors

Barton J. Hirsch
Northwestern University

This entry addresses risk and protective factors as these pertain to mental health. Research interest in this area has increased markedly during the past decade. Although certain trends in the findings are clear, few studies have been longitudinal. Claims for causal relations on the basis of existing cross-sectional data must therefore be viewed with some caution.

Risk factors may generally be classified as to whether they involve situations that have recently developed or, instead, are ongoing. A major focus of attention has been on the amount of recent life change or "life events" (e.g., Johnson, 1986). These are typically assessed via self-report checklists on which adolescents indicate which events (e.g., parental divorce) have occurred in their lives over a specified time period (typically six months or one year). The events that are checked are then summed to give an overall index of life change. Initial studies tended to weigh events differentially according to their potential impact, but a simple summary score has been shown to be sufficient.

Findings from these life-event studies consistently reveal that negative or undesirable changes are linked to poorer mental health. The occurrence of positive or neutral changes have also been linked with symptomatology, but the direction of the relation has been inconsistent across studies.

A specific major life change that has received considerable attention has been the transition from elementary school to junior high or middle school. Most of these studies have been longitudinal, with the principal dependent variable being self-esteem. An early study in Milwaukee public schools found that girls who changed school suffered impaired global self-esteem as compared to girls who did not change schools (they were attending a K–8 school) or boys (see recent summary by Simmons & Blyth, 1987). More recent studies have generally failed to replicate this result. Many of these studies have found a mixture of positive and negative changes across a wider array of outcomes (e.g., Hirsch & Rapkin, 1987). However, none of the more recent studies have been of urban samples.

In considering ongoing stressors that put adolescents at risk, the primary concern has focused on family variables. Family conflict and poor communication styles consistently emerge as the most serious risk factors for adolescents. Mental health outcomes include depressive symptoms as well as schizophrenia (e.g., Rodnick, Goldstein, Lewis, & Doane, 1984). The presence of a clinically disturbed parent has also been related to poorer mental health among adolescent offspring (e.g., Hirsch, Moos, & Reischl, 1985).

Research on protective factors has been less extensive. The primary thrust has been to consider how family and friends can serve as a social support system (e.g., Belle, 1989). Supports are hypothesized to provide emotional sustenance, identity validation, and problem-solving resources that serve protective functions when under stress. Supportive family members and friends have each been linked to better mental health. Longitudinal studies are particularly sparse in this area.

Only a handful of investigators have examined how secondary schools may serve protective functions. The social climate and organizational design of schools have been related to outcomes such as delinquency and self-esteem (e.g., Rutter, Maughan, Mortimore, Ouston, & Smith, 1979). For example, one experimental study found that grouping students together across classes to provide a more stable peer group and assigning teachers counseling responsibilities protected students from lowered self-esteem during the first year in high school (Felner, Ginter, & Primavera, 1982).

A number of investigators are currently involved in longitudinal research in these areas, utilizing increasingly sophisticated conceptual frameworks and research methodologies. Ensuing findings should clarify the nature and causal role of risk and protective factors.

References

Belle, D. (Ed.). (1989). *Children's social networks and social supports.* New York: Wiley.

Felner, R., Ginter, M., & Primavera, J. (1982). Primary prevention during school transitions: Social support and environmental structure. *American Journal of Community Psychology, 10,* 277–290.

Hirsch, B. J., Moos, R., & Reischl, T. (1985). Psychosocial adjustment of adolescent children of a depressed, arthritic, or normal parent. *Journal of Abnormal Psychology, 94,* 154–164.

Hirsch, B. J., & Rapkin, B. (1987). The transition from elementary school to junior high school: A longitudinal study of self-esteem, psychological symptomatology, school life, and social support. *Child Development, 58,* 1235–1243.

Johnson, J. (1986). *Life events as stressors in childhood and adolescence.* Newbury Park, CA: Sage.

Rodnick, E., Goldstein, M., Lewis, J., & Doane, J. (1984). Parental communication style, affect, and role as precursors of offspring schizophrenia-spectrum disorders. In N. Watt, E. J. Anthony, & L. Wynne (Eds.), *Children at risk for schizophrenia: A longitudinal perspective* (pp. 81–92). New York: Cambridge University Press.

Rutter, M., Maughan, B., Mortimore, P., Ouston, J., with Smith, A. (1979). *Fifteen thousand hours: Secondary schools and their effects on children.* Cambridge: Harvard University Press.

Simmons, R., & Blyth, D. (1987). *Moving into adolescence: The impact of pubertal change and school context.* Hawthorne, NY: Aldine de Gruyter.

See Also

Psychoanalytic Theory

Juris G. Draguns

The Pennsylvania State University

Psychoanalytic theory is the explanatory account of human behavior and motivation, as developed by Sigmund Freud and his collaborators. The principal feature of this theory is the importance of *unconscious motivation* as a mainspring of human behavior. Unconscious motives pervade all complex and socially significant human acts and codetermine all significant human decisions. Psychopathological symptoms have an unconscious purpose and meaning. Dreams and slips of the tongue and the pen (Freud, 1938a, 1938b) are expressions of unconscious impulses. In symbolic disguise, the unconscious is expressed in all of the arts. Outlets for unconscious motives are provided in sports, other recreational activities, and leisure pursuits.

Freud (1949) pioneered the development of techniques by which the unconscious could be reached. The most prominent of these is *free association*, which plays a pivotal role in clinical psychoanalysis. The patient is asked to say anything and everything that comes to mind and to do so without considering the rationality, appropriateness, or logic of his or her utterances. In this manner, a bridge is built between the conscious and the unconscious. As free associations proceed, references to the remote past replace statements about the present. Concerns with the current reality situation recede into the background and the experiences and feelings originated in the past assume prominence. Logic gives way to communication based on fantasy, wish, and feeling. Communications of patients in analysis based on free association constitute the principal source of the empirical "raw material" on which psychoanalytic theory is based.

A major tenet of this theory is that the basic source of energy for human action and conduct is sexual in nature (Freud, 1953, 1957). All human acts and relationships are fueled by the reservoir of this energy, which is referred to as *libido*. Portions of the libido are attached to various persons, activities, and things, collectively called objects. As a result of libidinal investment, or cathexis, various objects in the external environment assume importance for the person. According to Freud (1963, 1965), human beings are endowed with sexual energy and are capable of experiencing sexual pleasure from birth. *Infantile sexuality* is of paramount importance for the development of human relationships, modes of controlling impulses, and the experience of any psychopathological symptoms. The clash between the child's need for sexual gratification and the restrictions placed by society upon such gratification result in the formation of a person's unique

■ 858

personality. The experience of infantile sexuality is divided into three *stages of psychosexual development: oral*, roughly extending over the first one and a half years of life; *anal*, lasting from the age of 1½ to 3½; and *phallic*, lasting from age 3½ to 5 or 6 years of age. The names of these three stages refer to the respective principal sites of experiencing sexual pleasure: the mouth, the anus, and the primary sex organ for either gender.

The phallic stage overlaps with the experience of the *Oedipal conflict* in which love for the parent of the opposite sex is accompanied by feelings of jealousy, rivalry, and rage directed at the parent of the same sex. The female version of this experience is named the *Electra complex*, although this term has partially fallen into disuse in clinical psychoanalysis. The nature of fixations at or regressions to any of these three stages influences personality formation and the development of symptoms, if any. The Oedipal conflict and its resolution are of crucial importance for the development of sexual orientation and identity and constitute the point of origin for all the neuroses or, in current terminology, the anxiety, somatoform, and dissociative disorders. The temporary suppression and the partial resolution of the Oedipal conflict ushers in the experience of *latency* during which the attention of the child is directed toward the mastery of the external world and the development of coping skills.

Remarkably, Freud had relatively little to say about the experience of adolescence, even though many of his patients were young and some were late adolescents. In traditional psychoanalysis, adolescence is viewed as a period in which the sexual impulses, repressed during latency after the experience of the Oedipal conflict, reassert themselves. With the revival of sexuality, the unresolved conflicts of the three psychosexual stages of development are reactivated. The result of this development is the emotional turbulence of adolescence. It remained for modern psychoanalysts, Peter Blos, Erik Erikson, and Anna Freud, to describe and conceptualize adolescent experience in more specific terms and to capture the experience of adolescence in its uniqueness.

Late in life, Freud (1955, 1962) turned his attention to aggression as a source of energy coequal in importance to sexuality. He conceived of aggression as an externalization of an inherent biological drive toward death or the *death instinct*. Neither Freud nor any other psychoanalyst elaborated the stages of development for aggression with anything approaching the specificity of the psychoanalytic account of the psychosexual stages of development. The manifestations of the death instinct in normal and abnormal experience have not been described in sufficient detail to be clinically useful. What remains is the assertion of the psychoanalytic view that aggression is a basic drive and a biological characteristic of the human species. As such, it defies being reduced to such experiences as frustration or the imitation of aggressive models, which nonpsychoanalytic theorists have proposed as sources of aggressive behavior.

One of Freud's best known contributions is the *structural model* of the human psyche consisting of the *id, ego*, and *superego* (Freud, 1962). These three structures differ in goals, purposes, and modes of operation. The id is the oldest of these; it constitutes the repository of sexual and aggressive impulses. The ego emerges gradually beginning in the first year of life. It is concerned with adaptation to reality as it attempts to balance the demands of, in Freud's words, its three harsh masters: the id, the superego, and the external environment. The superego is concerned with moral evaluation; it roughly corresponds to conscience in everyday speech, except that it can make its judgment felt both consciously and unconsciously. Conflicts between these structures are inevitable; they constitute the point of departure for the development of many psychological disorders, especially the neuroses.

The subjective form of this conflict is *anxiety*, which Freud termed the danger signal of the ego (Freud, 1936). Depending on the structures involved in this conflict, anxiety assumes the form of reality anxiety, or fear in the presence of external dangers threatening the ego; it acquires the characteristics of moral anxiety, or anticipatory guilt in conflicts in which superego is involved; and is experienced in the form of neurotic anxiety in those cases where the id and/or the superego imperil the integrity of the ego. In modern usage, the term anxiety has been largely restricted to neurotic anxiety. Anxiety is an unpleasant experience which human beings attempt to reduce at whatever cost. They also strive to prevent its reoccurrence. These objectives are accomplished, with varying degrees of success, by the *defense mechanisms* of the ego, such as repression, projection, denial, isolation, intellectualization, rationalization, regression, displacement, and others. Of these, *repression* is of fundamental importance; other defenses rest on the base of purposeful and motivated forgetting of the experience of a conflictual and anxiety-generating impulse or a personally threatening experience. The repressed material does not disappear, but is submerged in the unconscious. It can be recaptured in psychoanalysis, mainly by means of free association.

All of the above formulations represent Freud's attempt to describe the results of his observations and to communicate them meaningfully to the public. As a theorist, he was almost exclusively concerned with explanation of psychological phenomena and minimally concerned, if at all, with prediction of behavior. His formulations are entirely based on clinical evidence; the unit of his observation was the case study and the corpus of the writings by Freud and other psychoanalytic pioneers does not contain even rudimentary quantitative data. Neither was Freud engaged in experimentation. His theories have been criticized as being uneconomical and nonfalsifiable. Many of his explanatory concepts are so far removed from the observables as to defy operationalization. Consequently, they remain nontestable. Other components of his theoretical structure (e.g., the several defense mechanisms) are more amenable to observation, measurement, and experimental manipulation. Over the years numerous attempts have been made to test psychoanalytic propositions by objective, systematic, and public means. This effort has led to mixed results and different conclusions. (See H. J. Eysenck & G. D. Wilson, *The Experimental Study of Freudian Theories* [1973]; P. Kline, *Fact and Fantasy in Freudian Theory* [1972]; I. Sarnoff, *Testing Freudian Concepts* [1971]; S. Fisher & R. P. Greenberg, *The Scientific Credibility of Freud's Theories and Therapy* [1977].) At this time, psychoanalysis survives as one of the several competing psychological theories of development, personality, and psychopathology. Its adherents are attracted by its subtlety, complexity, and sensitivity; its critics decry its speculative and unparsimonious nature.

References

Eysenck, H. J., & Wilson, G. D. (1973). *The experimental study of Freudian theories.* London: Methuen.

Fisher, S., & Greenberg, R. P. (1977). *The scientific credibility of Freud's theories and therapy.* New York: Bosie Books.

Freud, S. (1936). *The problem of anxiety.* (H. A. Bunker, Trans.) New York: Norton (originally published in 1926).

Freud, S. (1938a). Psychopathology of everyday life. In A. A. Brill (Ed. & Trans.) *The basic writings of Sigmund Freud*. New York: Modern Library (originally published in 1901).

Freud, S. (1938b). The interpretation of dreams. In A. A. Brill (Ed. & Trans.) *The basic writings of Sigmund Freud*. New York: Modern Library (originally published in 1900).

Freud, S. (1949). *An outline of psychoanalysis*. (J. Strachey, Trans.) New York: Norton (originally published in 1940).

Freud, S. (1953). *Three essays on sexuality*. (J. Strachey, Trans.) London: Hogarth (originally published in 1905).

Freud, S. (1955). Beyond the pleasure principle. In J. Strachey (Ed. and Trans.) *The standard edition of the complete psychological works of Sigmund Freud, Vol. 18* (pp. 3–64). London: Hogarth (originally published in 1920).

Freud, S. (1957). Instincts and their vicissitudes. In J. Strachey (Ed. and Trans.) *The standard edition of the complete psychological works of Sigmund Freud, Vol. 14*. London: Hogarth (originally published in 1915).

Freud, S. (1962). *Civilization and its discontents*. (J. Strachey, Ed. & Trans.) New York: Norton (originally published in 1932).

Freud, S. (1963). Introductory lectures on psycho-analysis. In J. Strachey (Ed. and Trans.) *The standard edition of the complete psychological works of Sigmund Freud, Vols. 15 & 16*. London: Hogarth (originally published in 1917).

Freud, S. (1965). *New introductory lectures in psycho-analysis*. (J. Strachey, Ed. & Trans.) New York: Norton (originally published in 1933).

Kline, P. (1972). *Fact and fiction in Freudian theory*. London: Methuen.

Sarnoff, I. (1971). *Testing Freudian concepts*. New York: Springer Publishing Company.

See Also

Blos, Peter; Erikson, Erik Homburger; Freud, Anna; Freud, Sigmund.

Psychophysiological/ Psychosomatic Problems

Michael W. Vasey
William J. Ray
The Pennsylvania State University

The study of the involvement of psychological factors within adolescent health and illness reflects the changing intellectual foci and paradigmatic shifts of an emerging field. Initially, psychosomatic/psychophysiological disorders were viewed within the context of psychodynamic theory under the name "psychosomatic medicine." Within this frame of reference, specific medical disorders were viewed as maladaptive responses to internal conflict (Alexander, 1950). Contained within this formulation was the understanding that specific emotions or conflicts might be expressed in different physiological systems. Thus, it would be suggested that particular types of conflicts (e.g., guilt) would influence people with particular types of personalities (e.g., passive) to result in a particular disorder. In the psychosomatic approach seven main disorders were emphasized. These were bronchial asthma, rheumatoid arthritis, ulcerative colitis, essential hypertension, duodenal peptic ulcer, neurodermatitis, and thyrotoxicosis. Problems with this approach were the inability to describe specific psychophysiological mechanisms relating internal conflict to pathology as well as a lack of empirical data.

Following the psychosomatic approach, a theoretical shift was instituted that emphasized illness more as a response to environmental stress and less as a reflection of internal psychological conflicts (e.g., Hinkel, 1967; Lipowski, 1977). Within this tradition came the behavioral medicine movement and its recognition of the changing nature of Western mortality and longevity over the century with the transition from germ-orientated disorders (e.g., tuberculosis) to environmentally influenced ones (e.g., smoking and cancer or diet and hypertension). Likewise the list of disorders was expanded. This theoretical overview has continued to expand with the introduction of pediatric psychology (e.g., Routh, 1988; Tuma, 1982) and the study of children's knowledge concerning their bodies, their illness, and their health (e.g., Eiser, 1985). Clinical studies have increased to include cancer, diabetes mellitus, eating disorders, cardiovascular problems, as well as the traditional seven of psychosomatic medicine. The present view also emphasizes the multicausation of pathology across a variety of levels.

As has been true of the field of adolescent development in general (e.g., Petersen, 1988), there is little research concerning psychophysiological disorders in adolescence. Thus, estimates of the prevalence of such problems among adolescents are difficult to obtain. When available, such estimates are dependent on population and cohort factors such as age, setting, and type of symptom.

It appears that as many as 25% of adolescents will at some time show some form of chronic pain such as headache, limb, or abdominal pain (Oster, 1972; Shapiro & Rosenfeld, 1987). In a random sample of Danish adolescents, 14.4% reported recurrent abdominal pain, 20% reported chronic headache, and 15.5% reported chronic limb pain. Prevalence appears to be roughly 7% for severe tension (Bille, 1962) and 4%–15% for migraines (Bille, 1962; Sillanpa, 1976). As many as 60% of adolescent migraine sufferers will show considerable improvement or remission by age 18 (Sillanpa, 1976). According to Alexander (1980), asthma appears to occur in about 5% of children. By adolescence, however, 40% or more of these children show remission, though recurrence in adulthood is not uncommon. Prevalence figures for other disorders come mainly from clinic and hospital samples. In a survey of 47,145 children and adolescents, roughly 10% of adolescents referred for treatment suffered a psychosomatic disorder (Starfield et al., 1980). Recurrent abdominal pain, asthma, and headache accounted for the majority of these cases. Rauste-von Wright and von Wright (1981) similarly found that the most common disorders among 14- to 16-year-olds were headache and limb pain.

In general, a greater proportion of adolescents present for treatment of most psychophysiological disorders than do child populations. This fact has prompted several researchers to suggest that adolescence is a period of risk for such problems (Aro, 1987; Hoffman, 1983; Humphries, 1982; Mechanic, 1983). Adolescence is a time of increased stress due to social and physical changes and, with increasing introspective ability, many adolescents become preoccupied with physical changes and bodily appearance and function. Such stress appears to predispose adolescents to increased risk for psychophysiological symptoms (Brunswick & Merzel, 1986; Mechanic, 1983).

Recent research indicates that the key risk factor associated with adolescent problems is puberty. For example, somatic complaints have been shown to increase significantly after puberty in a sample of 90 normal individuals (Rauste-von Wright & von Wright, 1981). Hamburg (1974) has argued that because of psychophysiological pubertal changes, early adolescence is more stressful than later adolescence. This may account for the fact that when assessed again at ages 15 and 18, such complaints had decreased significantly from their height at age 13.

Other attempts have been made to link these findings specifically to the stress of pubertal changes. Aro and Taipale (1987) tested the hypothesis that those girls who experience early puberty may be especially prone to such disorders due to the stressful nature of early puberty in females (Brooks-Gunn & Petersen, 1983). However, their results merely confirmed the previous finding of increased psychophysiological complaints following puberty in females. Thus, while the specific mechanism remains unclear, some aspect of pubertal change is associated with increased somatic complaints.

Additional indications of changes in somatic complaints related to puberty appear in the sex-ratio for such complaints. Prior to puberty, most studies suggest that such symptoms are equally prevalent among boys and girls (Rauste-von Wright & von Wright, 1981; Shapiro & Rosenfeld, 1987). Following puberty, the rates for males either decrease or continue unchanged while females report such symptoms much more frequently. This pattern and these rates are similar to those found in adult populations. In one review of 13 studies of various psychophysiological disorders, it was found that adolescent females are four times as likely to report such problems (Shapiro & Rosenfeld, 1986). For example, Bille (1962) found that both tension and migraine headaches were more prevalent in boys prior to age 10. After this, girls caught up, and by puberty had surpassed the boys. In addition, females appeared to show greater constancy in symptoms over the period from age 11 to 18 (Rauste-von Wright & von Right, 1981).

This gender difference appears to be related to greater life stress perceived by girls (Aro, 1987). In general, a high level of perceived stress is associated with more frequent psychophysiological problems. Walker and Greene (1987) have shown that more frequent negative life events were associated with increased psychophysiological symptoms in male and female adolescents. However, females report higher levels of perceived life stress (Aro, 1987). Significantly, when equated for levels of perceived life stress and relationship problems, boys report as many somatic symptoms as do girls.

Since life stress appears related to psychophysiological symptoms, several researchers have explored the importance of peer and family support during adolescence in reducing such symptoms. Walker and Greene (1987) demonstrated that peer support is especially important. As negative life events increased, males with low peer support reported more symptoms while males with high peer support appeared to be unaffected. Among females, those with low peer support reported high levels of symptoms regardless of current life stress. Walker and Greene (1987) speculate that lack of peer support may constitute a significant stressor in its own right. Thus, peer support appears to act as a buffer against psychophysiological problems. Similar results were obtained for family cohesion.

Overall, the trend is to view psychosomatic/psychophysiological disorders within a broad context of health and behavior involving a theoretical orientation based on a variety of disciplines. One consistent trend is an emphasis on environmental and stress-related factors as well as emotional responding, including interpersonal relationships. However, neither a unified theoretical approach nor a disorder-related classification system designed specifically for adolescents has yet to emerge.

References

Alexander, A. B. (1980). The treatment of psychosomatic disorders: Bronchial asthma in children. In B. B. Lahey & A. E. Kazdin (Eds.), *Advances in child clinical psychology* (Vol. 3, pp. 265–310). New York: Plenum.

Alexander, F. (1950). *Psychosomatic medicine*. New York: Norton.

Aro, H. (1987). Life stress and psychosomatic symptoms among 14- to 16-year old Finnish adolescents. *Psychological Medicine, 17*, 191–201.

Aro, H., & Taipale, V. (1987). The impact of timing of puberty on psychosomatic symptoms among fourteen- to sixteen-year-old Finnish girls. *Child Development, 58*, 261–268.

Bille, B. (1962). Migraine in school children. *Acta Paediatrica Scandinavica* (Suppl. B6), 1–152.

Brooks-Gunn, J., & Petersen, A. (Eds.). (1983). *Girls at puberty: Biological and psychosocial perspectives*. New York: Plenum.

Brunswick, A. F., & Merzel, C. R. (1980). Biopsychosocial and epidemiologic perspectives on adolescent health. In N. A. Krasnegor, J. D. Arasteh, & M. R. Cataldo (Eds.), *Child health behavior: A behavioral pediatrics perspective.* (pp. 94–112). New York: Wiley.

Eiser, C. (1985). *The psychology of childhood illness.* New York: Springer-Verlag.

Hamburg, B. C. (1974). Early adolescence: A specific and stressful stage of the life cycle. In G. Coelho, D. Hamburg, & J. Adams (Eds.), *Coping and adaptation* (pp. 101–124). New York: Basic Books.

Hinkel, L. E. (1967). Ecological observations of the relations of physical illness, mental illness, and the social environment. *Psychosomatic Medicine, 23,* 298.

Hoffman, A. (1983). *Adolescent medicine.* Menlo Park, CA: Addison-Wesley.

Humphries, C. L. (1982). Psychosomatic problems in adolescent medicine. In R. Blum (Ed.), *Adolescent health care: Clinical issues* (pp. 267–270). New York: Academic Press.

Lipowski, Z. J. (1977). Psychosomatic medicine: Current trends and clinical applications. In Z. Lipowski, D. Lipsitt, & P. Whybrow (Eds.) *Psychosomatic medicine: Current trends and clinical applications.* New York: Oxford University Press.

Mechanic, D. (1983). Adolescent health and illness behavior: Review of the literature and a new hypothesis for the study of stress. *Journal of Human Stress 9,* 4–13.

Oster, J. (1972). Recurrent abdominal pain, headache, and limb pain in children and adolescents. *Pediatrics, 50,* 429–436.

Petersen, A. (1988). Adolescent development. *Annual Review of Psychology, 39,* 583–607.

Rauste-von Wright, M., & von Wright, J. (1981). A longitudinal study of psychosomatic symptoms in healthy 11–18-year-old girls and boys. *Journal of Psychosomatic Research, 25,* 525–534.

Routh, D. (Ed.). (1988). *Handbook of pediatric psychology.* New York: Guilford Press.

Shapiro, E. G., & Rosenfeld, A. A. (1987). *The somatizing child: Diagnosis and treatment of conversion and somatization disorders.* New York: Springer-Verlag.

Sillanpa, M. (1976). Prevalence of migraine and other headaches in Finnish children starting school. *Headache, 16,* 288–290.

Starfield, B., Gross, E., Wood, M., Pantell, R., Allen, C., Gordon, B., Moffatt, P., Drachman, R., & Katz, H. (1980). Psychosocial and psychosomatic diagnoses in primary care of children. *Pediatrics, 66,* 159–167.

Tuma, J. M. (Ed.). (1982). *Handbook for the practice of pediatric psychology.* New York: Wiley-Interscience.

Walker, L. S., & Greene, J. W. (1987). Negative life events, psychosocial resources, and psychophysiological symptoms in adolescence. *Journal of Clinical Child Psychology, 16,* 29–36.

See Also

Affective Disorders; Depression in Adolescence, Gender Differences in; Developmental Psychopathology and the Adolescent; Fears and Phobias in Adolescence; Moodiness, Adolescent; Schizophrenia in Adolescence and Young Adulthood, Antecedents/Predictors of; Turmoil, Adolescent.

Psychotherapeutic Interventions for Adolescents

Philip C. Kendall

Temple University

Grayson N. Holmbeck

Loyola University of Chicago

Although some (Blos, 1962, 1979; Erikson, 1968; A. Freud, 1958; Hall, 1904) have viewed adolescence as a period of normative storm, stress, and disturbance, epidemiological and developmental research has not supported these early notions (e.g., Douvan & Adelson, 1966; Kandel & Lesser, 1972; Lerner, Shroeder, Rewitzer, & Weinstock, 1972; Montemayor, 1983; Offer & Offer, 1975; Offer, Ostrov, & Howard, 1981; Petersen, 1988; Rutter, 1980; Rutter, Graham, Chadwick, & Yule, 1976; see Hill & Holmbeck, 1986, for a review). For most adolescents, parent-adolescent relationships remain harmonious and most adolescents do not develop psychiatric symptoms. The myth of storm and stress is probably perpetuated because of an exclusive focus, by some theorists and certainly by the media (see Bandura, 1964), on disturbed adolescents, and because there appear to be increases in moodiness ("inner turmoil"; Rutter, 1980) during adolescence and altercations between parents and adolescents over *minor issues* (Rutter, 1980).

Given that the period of adolescence is frequently misunderstood, it is critical that the therapist who works with adolescents be quite familiar with the developmental tasks typical of this period. Although there are several uniformity myths (Kiesler, 1966), child-clinical psychologists may be guilty of endorsing what Kendall called the "developmental uniformity myth" (Kendall, 1984). That is, therapists may implicitly believe that children aged 8 to 13 are a homogeneous group and that treatments for latency-aged children, for example, should have direct applicability to early adolescents. Unfortunately, such applicability has not been demonstrated (e.g., Kendall, Lerner, & Craighead, 1984). Thus, one purpose of this entry[1] is to

---

1. Other, more complete, reviews are available: see Adelson, 1980; Van Hasselt & Hersen, 1987; and other entries in this volume.

briefly present an overview of the critical developmental tasks of adolescence that should be taken into account when designing empirical investigations, treatment studies, or intervention programs involving this age group. Adolescence is marked by "change" and such change must also be taken into account.

Despite the lack of support for storm and stress theory, a meaningful proportion of adolescents have psychological problems. It is this group to which we will turn our attention in this chapter. It seems clear that adolescence is a period during which there are important changes in the pattern and rate of certain disorders (Rutter, 1980). Various disorders reach their peak during this developmental period (e.g., anorexia nervosa, parasuicide) and there are shifts in the sex ratios of various disorders (e.g., depression is now more common among females). There are both continuities and discontinuities for adolescent psychopathology with respect to child and adult pathology (Rutter, 1980).

Distressed adolescents are not known for their willingness to listen to adults, authorities, or tradition. To the adolescent, psychotherapists may present themselves as middle-aged power-figures advocating the merits of more than the present moment. There exists a naturally occurring barrier to therapeutic gain. But whether or not they realize it, adolescents and therapists have a common goal. Adolescents, in transition from the instruction-following state of childhood to the instruction-giving status of adulthood, are on their normal developmental trajectory toward autonomous/ independent functioning. The goal of psychotherapy of all persuasions is also to have the individual move from being controlled by certain forces toward more self-directed, autonomous, and healthy functioning (Kendall & Norton-Ford, 1982).

The present coverage of therapy with adolescents will first consider the status of adolescents' physical and cognitive changes and the development of a sense of self as well as the implications that these changes have for psychotherapy. The last section highlights several areas of intervention that focus on adolescent issues and their respective outcomes.

Developmental Changes of Adolescence and Implications for Psychotherapy

PHYSICAL CHANGES ▪ More than any other stage of life except the fetal/ neonatal period, adolescence is a time of substantial physical growth and change. Tanner (1962) has charted most of the characteristics of these changes in males and females. Changes in body proportions, facial characteristics, voice, body hair, strength, and coordination are found in males and changes in body proportions, body hair, and menarcheal status are found in girls. Crucial to the understanding of this process is the knowledge that the peak of pubertal development occurs two years earlier in the modal female than in the modal male and that there are substantial variations between individuals in the time of onset, the duration, and the termination of the pubertal cycle. Thus, not only is there intraindividual variation in terms of the onset of the different pubertal changes but there is interindividual variation in the many parameters of these changes as well. Both pubertal status (an individual's placement in the sequence of predictable pubertal changes) and pubertal timing (timing of changes relative to one's age peers) should be taken into account (Petersen, 1988).

Unlike the newborn, adolescents are

aware of these changes and this awareness may be pleasing or horrifying; lack of information about puberty/sexuality can contribute to emotional upset (Ruble & Brooks-Gunn, 1982). Most of the psychological effects of pubertal changes are probably not direct, but rather are mediated by the responses of the individual or significant others to such changes (Petersen, 1988; Petersen & Taylor, 1980; Richards & Petersen, 1987). Significant others may assume, for example, that physical changes indicate development in psychological areas. This is, of course, not the case.

COGNITIVE CHANGES ■

Reviews of the literature on cognitive changes during adolescence have been provided by Hill and Palmquist (1978) and Keating (1980). Though less overtly observable, cognitive changes in adolescence are probably as dramatic as the physical changes. Piaget (1970, 1972) is credited with the identification of adolescence as the period of formal operational thinking where adult-level reasoning can take place. Some adolescents can, for example, begin to think about their own thinking (metacognition). However, this new skill is not without potential difficulties. Elkind (1967) suggested that the adolescent may become obsessed with this new ability. Even if not obsessed, the adolescent is not fully developed in a social cognitive sense and may misperceive others as equally interested in his/her own thoughts and actions (i.e., the imaginary audience) and yet perceive them as unable to understand his/her emotional experiences. Other changes associated with the advent of formal operations and the implications such changes have for adolescent psychopathology and psychotherapy have been detailed by Gordon (1988), Hains (Hains & Miller, 1980; Hains & Ryan, 1983) and Russo (1986).

SENSE OF SELF AND IDENTITY FORMATION ■

A major psychological task of adolescence is believed to be the development of an identity (Erikson, 1968; Sprinthall & Collins, 1984). Although the notion that all adolescents experience identity crises appears to be a myth (Rutter, 1980), identity development is recognized as an adolescent issue. A related issue is the development of a sense of self-governance and a feeling of autonomy—however defined (Douvan & Adelson, 1966; Steinberg & Silverberg, 1986). Research with healthy adolescents (e.g., Kandel & Lesser, 1972) suggests that autonomy from parents does not develop at the expense of relationships with parents and that the values of parents and the values of one's peer group are usually more alike than different (Hartup, 1970). The therapist should be aware, however, that continued development of independence can progress at a rapid rate and there may be a need for adolescents to make personal decisions even if these decisions are at variance with adults/therapists.

IMPLICATIONS FOR THERAPY ■

Developmental psychology has a number of implications for treatment of the adolescent. Informed therapists can use their knowledge of developmental transitions to facilitate prevention and remediation efforts. A knowledge of developmental predictors of outcomes (e.g., a life-span perspective) can enable the therapist to separate developmental change from therapeutic change. A knowledge of developmental psychopathology, as it applies to adolescents (Masten, 1988), is also useful for the adolescent therapist insofar as the therapist understands more fully the changes in the types, patterns, and rates of various psychopathologies (also see Rutter, 1980). Development can also have moderating effects on treatment. Finally, and given the importance of developmental tasks during adolescence, we can develop therapy approaches that "treat" the individual's developmental level. For example, treatments have been devised that foster the development of social cognitive skills (e.g., Gordon, 1988).

Therapists who work with adolescents should be aware of the diversity of changes that occur during this portion of the life span. Therapists should not assume that adolescents welcome their physical changes and should not use physical growth as an indicator of cognitive abilities or psychological maturity (Steinberg & Hill, 1978). Discussion and information provision about physical changes facilitate both the therapist-adolescent relationship and the adolescent's later adjustment. An understanding of cognitive changes in adolescence is especially important for therapists. Adolescent thinking may work against therapy, if the therapist tries to convince an adolescent that he/she "understands," or if the therapist, like some parents, fails to accept the adolescent's increased need for privacy.

Several behavioral and cognitive-behavioral treatment strategies (see Kendall, 1991) may be particularly appropriate for adolescents, given identity issues (Kendall & Williams, 1986). Self-monitoring procedures can facilitate the adolescent's self-understanding. Being sensitive to an adolescent's need to not be controlled, self-monitoring can be introduced as something the adolescent does for his/herself. Therapists can help with the development of autonomy by reinforcing an adolescent's independent behavior. Seeing an older adolescent alone in therapy, rather than in the family, may be more commensurate with natural developmental changes and may foster skill in facing the task of separating from the family. Lastly, adolescents with problems in need of therapy are not typically self-identified—they are referred by others. Therapists and treatment outcomes

will benefit from allowing adolescents to participate in treatment decisions.

A cognitive-behavioral problem-solving model (Kendall, 1985) appears promising for the therapist who works with adolescent clients. In this model, the role of each individual's cognitive functioning, behavioral learning history, and present environment are integrated. Cognitive functioning is viewed from an information-processing perspective (Ingram & Kendall, 1986), where the cognitive content (what a person says to him/herself), cognitive processes (how information is operated on), cognitive products (such as causal attributions), and cognitive structures (a social scheme or template for viewing the world in a certain manner) interact and are implicated in adjustment. An environmental event may be designed and intended to produce a positive outcome, but it is the manner in which the event is cognitively processed by the adolescent that will bear on its eventual effects. Cognitive appraisal processes are influential in client construals of therapists' "programs."

Also part of the cognitive-behavioral problem-solving model is a reliance on behavioral procedures to influence change. Strategies such as self-monitoring, modeling, reinforcement, role-plays, and other performance-based efforts are used to faciliate cognitive change.

The problem-solving emphasis is seen in the nature of the therapeutic interaction. The therapist does not "know" or "have" the answer. Rather, the therapist helps the adolescent to recognize a problem early on (problem identification), to generate possible alternative solutions, to consider the likely behavioral and emotional consequences of each alternative for each party involved, and to come to a reasonable plan. The therapist is a consultant who helps to examine issues, to devise ways to test assumptions, and to steer a realistic course in the processing of relevant personal and social information. A therapist following this model would be concerned with: (1) both the learning process and the influence of the contingencies and models in the environment, while (2) underscoring the centrality of mediating/information-processing factors (Kendall, 1985, 1991).

Relatedly, the therapist asks about the client's assumptions/beliefs and orchestrates, in a collaborative empiricism, tests to determine if the belief/assumption holds true. The cognitive-behavioral problem-solving model strives to be consistent with developmental theory in order to maximize long-term therapeutic gain.

Adolescent Problems and Promising Treatments

Personal struggle, such as with identity, depression, and suicide, conflict with authorities, such as parent-adolescent conflict, academic challenges, such as school attendance, and a range of health-related matters, such as smoking, unwanted pregnancy, and drug/alcohol problems, are illustrative of the psychological problems facing adolescents. These potential problems are important in adolescence because starting to work, trying alcohol/drugs, becoming a nonvirgin, etc. occur for the first time in adolescence and can have far-reaching effects on later adjustment. Adolescence is a time of risk; it is a time when new risk behaviors are learned and risk-taking aspects of personality are acquired. Hopefully, it is also an important time for the learning of strategies to reduce risk. Accordingly, adolescence is a potent period in life-span development in terms of the potential long-term effect of psychological interventions (Jessor, 1984). While there are promising interventions in several of these areas, others have received minimal re-

search and are in need of greater attention. Several volumes are available on treatment for adolescents (e.g., Barth, 1986; Mirkin & Koman, 1985; Mishne, 1986; Stein & Davis, 1982; also see Magrab, 1987). Therefore, the following review is far from complete. We chose to focus on interventions for health-related matters and parent-adolescent conflict.

HEALTH-RELATED MATTERS ▪
Adolescence is a period of special importance for the development of healthy behavior (Coates, Petersen, & Perry, 1982; Jessor, 1984). Illustrative psychological interventions in the area of smoking will be described. Other examples also could have been discussed (e.g., unwanted pregnancy; see Schinke, Blythe, & Gilchrist, 1981).

Promising programs for smoking prevention among adolescent teenagers include the Counseling Leadership Against Smoking Pressure (CLASP) program in which students are exposed to situations where they will experience social pressure to smoke and are taught skills for dealing with such pressures. High school students are involved in teaching junior high students. Behavioral methods including modeling, role playing, practice, and homework are part of the program, the goal of which is a smoke-free environment. According to Telch, Killen, McAlister, Perry, and Maccoby (1982), CLASP produced a 5.1% smoking rate follow-up as opposed to a national rate of 12%. A factor that we consider to be important in the success of this and related programs is the incorporation of peer influences (see also Howard & Kendall, 1988). Peers, rather than adults, take charge, and some developmental issues are thereby properly addressed.

PARENT-ADOLESCENT CONFLICT ▪ Emerging from a problem-solving, communication skill building

background, a program for the remediation of parent-adolescent conflict (Robin & Foster, 1988) has been developed that includes three distinct components: (1) interpersonal problem-solving and communication skills training, (2) identifying and altering irrational beliefs about the family, and (3) facilitating structural changes in the family (Koepke & Robin, 1988). The program does not target the adolescent or the parent(s) as the "case," instead focusing on the skills of self-expression, negotiation, reaching an agreement, and follow-through. While it may not be accurate to label adolescence as the period of storm and stress, adolescence is a crucial period for the emergence, refinement, and establishment of adultlike problem-solving habits.

In one illustrative study, Robin (1981) treated 33 families with adolescents aged 11 to 16. They were reporting rule and responsibility disagreements and were provided with the problem-solving therapy or family therapy, or placed in the waiting list control condition. During the 2-month treatment subjects received seven one-hour sessions.

Those families given the cognitive-behavioral problem-solving program were taught a problem-solving model that included 4 steps: defining the problem without accusations, generating alternatives, determining a naturally satisfactory solution, and laying out a plan for implementation. To foster these skills and buttress the learning of this pattern of interacting, provision of positive and negative feedback, modeling, and opportunities for behavioral rehearsal were employed. Cognitive restructuring procedures were used to modify unreasonable beliefs held by the client(s). The program integrated cognitive and behavioral procedures. The alternative treatment, family therapy, was provided by experienced clinicians using their respective theoretical models (e.g., family systems, psychodynamic).

Both treatment conditions resulted in significant gains on self-report measures of disputes and conflictual communication in the home. Only the specialized problem-solving approach, however, resulted in significant gains in problem-solving communication behavior objectively coded from family discussions. Some evidence of maintenance was provided by 10-week follow-up data. One potentially potent aspect of the Robin approach is that the adolescent is not told what to do or how to do it, but is given the opportunity to participate in adult-like discussions of alternative actions, likely consequences, and the decision-making and plan-enactment phases of problem solving. The family is involved, but the strategies of the intervention do not assume that parent or child is necessarily the patient, necessarily right, or necessarily wrong.

Conclusion

As noted by Petersen (1988) in a recent review of the adolescent development literature, the quantity of research on adolescence has increased dramatically. There is a new research society, the Society for Research on Adolescence, there are new journals, and more researchers are involved. This quantitative increase in productivity has also been accompanied by an increase in the quality of the research. Increases in the developmental area have been accompanied by increases in the area of adolescent clinical psychology, though to a lesser extent. Most of the empirically evaluated treatments have involved group therapy with delinquents and many other disorders await specific treatments. Community-based treatments exist but few have been evaluated rigorously and the best of these treatments are sometimes being applied to those least in need (e.g., drug programs being used in suburban areas with predominantly white middle-class adolescents). Peer involvement in treatment shows promise (Howard & Kendall, 1988) as do programs designed to facilitate cognitive development (Gordon, 1988). For the betterment of therapy with adolescents, it is recommended that: (1) a full curriculum of developmental psychology coursework be incorporated into child/adolescent clinical training programs, (2) a subdiscipline of adolescent clinical psychology be developed and promoted with training programs that produce clinicians who specialize in this area, and (3) pathology-specific treatments be developed and evaluated whereby factors associated with improvement are investigated.

References

Adelson, J. (Ed.). (1980). *Handbook of adolescent psychology.* New York: Wiley.

Bandura, A. (1964). The stormy decade: Fact or fiction? *Psychology in the Schools, 1,* 224–231.

Barth, R. P. (1986). *Social and cognitive treatment of children and adolescents: Practical strategies for problem behaviors.* San Francisco: Jossey-Bass.

Blos, P. (1962). *On adolescence.* New York: Free Press.

Blos, P. (1979). *The adolescent passage.* New York: International Universities Press.

Coates, T. J., Petersen, A. C., & Perry, C. L. (Eds.). (1982). *Promoting adolescent health: A dialogue on research and practice.* New York: Academic Press.

Douvan, E., & Adelson, J. (1966). *The adolescent experience.* New York: Wiley.

Elkind, D. (1967). Egocentrism in adolescence. *Child Development, 38,* 1025–1034.

Erikson, E. (1968). *Identity: Youth and crisis.* New York: Norton.

Freud, A. (1958). Adolescence. *Psychoanalytic Study of the Child, 13,* 231–258.

Gordon, D. E. (1988). Formal operations and

interpersonal and affective disturbances in adolescents. In E. D. Nannis & P. A. Cowan (Eds.), *Developmental psychopathology and its treatment* (pp. 51–74). (In *New Directions for Child Development,* no. 39, W. Damon, Ed.). San Francisco: Jossey-Bass.

Hains, A., & Miller, D. (1980). Moral and cognitive development in delinquent and nondelinquent children and adolescents. *Journal of Genetic Psychology, 137,* 21–35.

Hains, A., & Ryan, E. (1983). The development of social cognitive processes among juvenile delinquents and nondelinquent peers. *Child Development, 54,* 1536–1544.

Hall, G. S. (1904). *Adolescence: Its psychology and its relations to physiology, anthropology, sociology, sex, crime, religion, and education.* New York: Appleton-Croft.

Hartup, W. W. (1970). Peer interaction and social organization. In P. H. Mussen (Ed.), *Manual of child psychology* (3rd ed., pp. 361–456). New York: Wiley.

Hill, J. P., & Holmbeck, G. N. (1986). Attachment and autonomy during adolescence. In G. J. Whitehurst (Ed.), *Annals of Child Development* (Vol. 3, pp. 145–189). Greenwich, CT: JAI Press.

Hill, J. P., & Palmquist, W. (1978). Social cognition and social relations in early adolescence. *International Journal of Behavioral Development, 1,* 1–36.

Howard, B. L., & Kendall, P. C. (1988). *Child interventions: Having no peers?* Unpublished manuscript, Temple University, Philadelphia, PA.

Ingram, R. E., & Kendall, P. C. (1986). Cognitive clinical psychology: Implications of an information processing perspective. In R. E. Ingram (Ed.), *Information processing approaches to clinical psychology* (pp. 1–22). Orlando, FL: Academic Press.

Jessor, R. (1984). Adolescent development and behavioral health. In J. D. Matarazzo, S. M. Weiss, J. Herd, N. Miller, & S. Weiss (Eds.), *Behavioral health: A handbook of health enhancement and disease prevention.* New York: Wiley.

Kandel, D., & Lesser, G. S. (1972). *Youth in two worlds.* San Francisco: Jossey-Bass.

Keating, D. P. (1980). Thinking processes in adolescence. In J. Adelson (Ed.), *Handbook of adolescent psychology* (pp. 211–246). New York: Wiley.

Kendall, P. C. (1984). Social cognition and problem solving: A developmental and child-clinical interface. In B. Gholson & T. L. Rosenthal (Eds.), *Applications of cognitive-developmental theory* (pp. 115–149). New York: Academic Press.

Kendall, P. C. (1985). Toward a cognitive-behavioral model of child psychopathology and a critique of related interventions. *Journal of Abnormal Child Psychology, 13,* 357–372.

Kendall, P. C. (1991). *Child and adolescent therapy: Cognitive-behavioral procedures.* New York: Guilford.

Kendall, P. C., Lerner, R. M., & Craighead, W. E. (1984). Human development and intervention in childhood psychopathology. *Child Development, 55,* 71–82.

Kendall, P. C., & Norton-Ford, J. D. (1982). *Clinical psychology: Scientific and professional dimensions.* New York: Wiley.

Kendall, P. C., & Williams, C. L. (1986). Therapy with adolescents: Treating the "Marginal Man." *Behavior Therapy, 17,* 522–537.

Kiesler, D. J. (1966). Some myths of psychotherapy research and the search for a paradigm. *Psychological Bulletin, 65,* 110–136.

Koepke, T., & Robin, A. L. (1988, March). Treatment of parent-adolescent conflict. In G. N. Holmbeck & D. R. Papini (Co-chairs), *Advances in research on parent-adolescent conflict.* Symposium presented at the biennial meeting of the Society for Research on Adolescence, Alexandria, Virginia.

Lerner, R. M., Schroeder, C., Rewitzer, M., & Weinstock, A. (1972). Attitudes of high school students and their parents toward contemporary issues. *Psychological Reports, 31,* 255–258.

Magrab, P. R. (Ed.). (1987). Adolescent mental health issues. *Clinical Psychologist, 40,* 84–93.

Masten, A. S. (1988). Toward a developmental psychopathology of early adolescence. In M. D. Levine & E. R. McAnarney (Eds.), *Early adolescent transitions* (pp. 261–278). Lexington, MA: Lexington Books.

Mirkin, M. P., & Koman, S. L. (Eds.). (1985). *Handbook of adolescents and family therapy.* New York: Gardner Press.

Mishne, J. M. (1986). *Clinical work with adolescents.* New York: Free Press.

Montemayor, R. (1983). Parents and adolescents in conflict: All families some of the time and some families most of the time. *Journal of Early Adolescence, 3,* 83–103.

Offer, D., & Offer, J. B. (1975). *From teenage to young manhood: A psychological study.* New York: Basic Books.

Offer, D., Ostrov, E., & Howard, K. I. (1981). *The adolescent: A psychological self-portrait.* New York: Basic Books.

Petersen, A. C. (1988). Adolescent development. In M. R. Rosenzweig & L. W. Porter (Eds.), *Annual Review of Psychology* (Vol. 39, pp. 583–608). Palo Alto, CA: Annual Reviews.

Petersen, A. C., & Taylor, B. (1980). The biological approach to adolescence: Biological change and psychosocial adaptation. In J. Adelson (Ed.), *Handbook of adolescent psychology* (pp. 117–155). New York: Wiley.

Piaget, J. (1970). Piaget's theory. In P. H. Mussen (Ed.), *Manual of child psychology* (3rd ed., pp. 703–732). New York: Wiley.

Piaget, J. (1972). Intellectual evolution from adolescence to adulthood. *Human Development, 15,* 1–12.

Richards, M., & Petersen, A. C. (1987). Biological theoretical models of adolescent development. In V. B. Van Hasselt & M. Hersen (Eds.), *Handbook of adolescent psychology* (pp. 34–52). New York: Pergamon Press.

Robin, A. L. (1981). A controlled evaluation of problem-solving communication training with parent-adolescent conflict. *Behavior Therapy, 12,* 593–609.

Robin, A. L., & Foster, S. (1988). *Negotiating adolescence: A behavioral family systems approach.* New York: Guilford.

Ruble, D. N., & Brooks-Gunn, J. (1982). The experience of menarche. *Child Development, 53,* 1557–1566.

Russo, T. J. (1986). Cognitive counseling for adolescents. *Journal of Child and Adolescent Psychotherapy, 3,* 194–198.

Rutter, M. (1980). *Changing youth in a changing society: Patterns of adolescent development and disorder.* Cambridge: Harvard University Press.

Rutter, M., Graham, P., Chadwick, O., & Yule, W. (1976). Adolescent turmoil: Fact or fiction? *Journal of Child Psychology and Psychiatry, 17,* 35–56.

Schinke, S. P., Blythe, B. J., & Gilchrist, L. D. (1981). Cognitive-behavioral prevention of adolescent pregnancy. *Journal of Counseling Psychology, 28,* 451–454.

Sprinthall, N. A., & Collins, W. A. (1984). *Adolescent psychology: A developmental view.* Reading, MA: Addison-Wesley.

Stein, M. D., & Davis, J. K. (1982). *Therapies for adolescents: Current treatments for problem behaviors.* San Francisco: Jossey-Bass.

Steinberg, L. D., & Hill, J. P. (1978). Patterns of family interaction as a function of age, the onset of puberty, and formal thinking. *Developmental Psychology, 14,* 683–684.

Steinberg, L. D., & Silverberg, S. B. (1986). The vicissitudes of autonomy in early adolescence. *Child Development, 57,* 841–852.

Tanner, J. (1962). *Growth at adolescence* (2nd ed.). Springfield, IL: Charles C. Thomas.

Telch, M. J., Killen, J. D., McAlister, A. L., Perry, C. L., & Maccoby, N. (1982). Long-term follow-up of a pilot project on smoking prevention with adolescents. *Journal of Behavioral Medicine, 5,* 1–8.

Van Hasselt, V. B., & Hersen, M. (1987). *Handbook of adolescent psychology.* New York: Pergamon.

See Also

Black Adolescents At-Risk, Approaches to Prevention; Family Planning Clinics: Efficacy for Adolescents; Peer Counseling: A Human Resource Program; Pregnancy in Adolescence, Interventions to Prevent; Puberty, Precocious, Treatment of; Smoking and Drug Prevention with Early Adolescents, Programs for.

Pubertal Development, Assessment of

Christy Miller Buchanan
Stanford University

Although its meaning may differ across contexts, pubertal change is inarguably a universal marker in the transition from childhood to adulthood, and thus a central set of events by which adolescence is defined. Understanding puberty is, therefore, of concern to clinicians and researchers working with adolescents. In order to be able to understand puberty, one needs to be able to measure it.

One of the challenging things about measuring puberty is that it is not an event but a process involving many dimensions. Both sexual and nonsexual body changes occur, and although the general progression of these changes has been charted, the rate and sequence of development in any individual may differ from the general pattern.

This summary of what we know about measuring puberty will have the following foci: (1) general issues in planning the assessment of puberty; (2) dimensions of pubertal development that can be assessed and measures available for assessing them; and (3) correspondence between information gained from different instruments and different sources.

General Issues

It has been said that *puberty is a process* and not an event. Maintaining that perspective is crucial as one approaches assessment. One event, such as first menarche, or the status of pubic hair development at one point in time, may not tell you about an individual's pubertal *experience*. Ideally, assessment of the pubertal experience is multidimensional and occurs over time. Where time or resources constrain the ideal, one must try to understand how specific events fit into the entire process, as well as be very explicit about the limitations of the measures used.

Secondly, one must decide if *actual* or *perceived* measures of puberty are desired. Pubertal assessment will produce somewhat different results depending on the source (doctor, parent, adolescent, teacher, researcher) used to gain information. Assessment aimed at measuring such things as timing and/or sequence of pubertal events, correspondence between hormonal and morphological changes, or abnormal patterns of development require "objective" and well-trained sources such as doctors or nurses. However, if assessment is aimed at understanding the meaning of pubertal development to the individual experiencing puberty, or to those around him/her, assessment based on "subjective" sources is not only acceptable but preferable. In cases where information about actual development is preferred, but resources do not permit a doctor or nurse's assessment, measures that can be administered to adolescents themselves, or their parents, and that offer an adequate degree of congruence with more objective sources, are available. These measures, and their strengths and limitations, will be discussed later.

Thirdly, an important consideration in choosing a method of assessment is the *age of the adolescent* being considered. Different pubertal events are salient at different ages. For example, using the occurrence of menarche as a measure of whether young pubertal girls have entered puberty or not is inappropriate, since girls experience pubertal events such as breast development, pubic hair growth, or changes in height earlier than they experience menarche. For late adolescent girls, menarche may be a good measure of the occurrence and general timing of puberty since it is a salient and fairly well-remembered event.

Dimensions of Pubertal Development: What Changes and How Can It Be Measured?

Extensive and detailed discussion of the progression of pubertal change (e.g., Doering, 1980; Faust, 1983; Grumbach, 1980; Harlan, Grillo, Cornoni-Huntley, & Leaverton, 1979; Harlan, Harlan, & Grillo, 1980; Johnson & Everitt, 1984; Marshall & Tanner, 1969; Tanner & Whitehouse, 1976) and measurement of pubertal events (e.g., Brooks-Gunn, 1987; Brooks-Gunn

& Petersen, 1984; Brooks-Gunn, Petersen, & Eichorn, 1985; Brooks-Gunn & Warren, 1985; Petersen, Crockett, Richards, & Boxer, 1988; Tanner, 1966) are available. The reader is referred to these original articles for more detailed information. The dimensions of puberty covered here are the ones commonly measured and certainly not the only ones potentially of interest (see above references for discussion of others).

SKELETAL AGE ■ Bone age is a more accurate measure of physical maturation than chronological age. Bone development, measured by X-ray, has often been used to assess pubertal stage and timing (see Garn, 1980; Tanner, 1966). This type of measurement is appropriate if the intent of measurement is to obtain actual stage or timing, rather than that perceived by the adolescent, and if facilities are available for this purpose.

GROWTH IN HEIGHT ■ The most dramatic growth in height except for the first years after birth occurs during adolescence. Actual height, compared to norms for age and pubertal status, or peak height velocity, are often used as measures of pubertal development (e.g., Petersen & Crockett, 1985; Simmons & Blyth, 1987), especially for boys. Actual height can be measured reliably with a standard measuring instrument, taking the average of two or more readings, at a standard time of day. Peak height velocity can be calculated (see Bock, Wainer, Petersen, Thissen, Murray, & Roche, 1973; Petersen & Crockett, 1985; Simmons & Blyth 1987; Tanner, 1966) if one collects or has access to information about growth in height over the appropriate years (starting as young as 8 years for girls and 9 years for boys).

CHANGES IN BODY FAT AND MUSCLE ■ Body fat increases for girls at puberty, and body fat is related to the occurrence of menarche. For boys, muscle cells multiply dramatically and body fat drops. Thus, indices of body fat, and changes in body fat over time, are potentially valuable in assessing pubertal development. Body fat can be measured directly or estimated based on height and weight, and, as with height, can be compared with norms for development (see Brooks-Gunn & Warren, 1985).

MENARCHE ■ For girls, menarche is a late, but clear, pubertal event. Whether or not menarche has occurred, and when it occurred for the first time, are useful pieces of knowledge for general assessments of pubertal status and pubertal timing. For work with young adolescent girls, or where more detailed knowledge of the entire pubertal process is desired, occurrence and/or timing of menarche is not the measure of choice.

SECONDARY SEXUAL CHARACTERISTICS ■ A range of secondary sexual developments are potentially important in understanding puberty. These include pubic hair growth, breast and genital development, voice changes, and growth of underarm and facial hair. Tanner (1966) described five stages of development for pubic hair (for girls and boys), breast development (for girls) and genital development (for boys). Doctors use these descriptions to assess growth in their examinations of adolescents. Photographs (Tanner, 1966) and schematic drawings (developed by Morris & Udry, 1980; see Figures 1 through 4) depicting these stages are often used to obtain self- and parent reports of development.

Resistance (among parents or school administrators) to adolescents undergoing doctors' Tanner assessments, or to rating themselves using Tanner pictures, spurred Petersen, Crockett, Richards, and Boxer

(1988) to develop an instrument (the Pubertal Development Scale, or PDS) for gathering information about puberty without requiring that the adolescent undress or view pictures. The PDS describes aspects of pubertal growth relevant to each sex, and asks the adolescent whether growth has "not begun," "barely begun," "definitely begun," or "been completed" on those aspects. A mean pubertal score, as well as a stage classification comparable to Tanner staging, can be computed. The PDS was developed for an interview format, but has also been modified for use as a questionnaire (Brooks-Gunn, Warren, Rosso, & Gargiulo, 1987; Miller, Tucker, Pasch & Eccles, 1988).

PUBERTAL TIMING ■ Timing of puberty in comparison to a reference group is often of interest apart from pubertal stage. Perceptions of timing can be assessed by asking the adolescent (or parent, doctor, etc.) if they feel bodily changes are happening (or happened) earlier than, the same as, or later than a reference group (e.g., "your friends," "kids your age," "your classmates"). Timing can also be defined based on criteria established by the investigator: the occurrence of some aspect(s) of pubertal development in comparison to national norms or the norms of a large sample for which one has collected data, or the occurrence of pubertal change by a certain age or grade. See Brooks-Gunn and Petersen (1984) for a discussion of some of the criteria researchers in the field of adolescence have used.

Correspondence Between Measures and Sources

To better understand the information one obtains using various measures and/or

FIGURE 1 The Drawings on this page show different stages of development of the breasts. A female passes through each of the five stages shown by these sets of drawings. Please look at each set of drawings and read the sentences under the drawing. Then choose the set of drawings closest to your stage of breast development and mark it 1. Then choose the drawing that is the next closest and mark it 2.

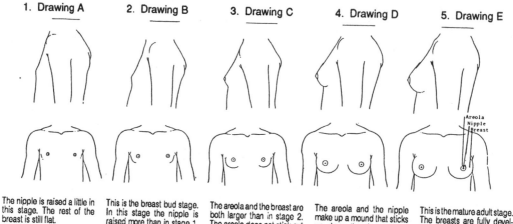

1. Drawing A   2. Drawing B   3. Drawing C   4. Drawing D   5. Drawing E

The nipple is raised a little in this stage. The rest of the breast is still flat.

This is the breast bud stage. In this stage the nipple is raised more than in stage 1. The breast is still a small mound. The areola is larger than in stage 1.

The areola and the breast are both larger than in stage 2. The areola does not stick out from the breast.

The areola and the nipple make up a mound that sticks up above the shape of the breast. (Note: This stage may not happen at all for some girls. Some girls develop from stage 3 to stage 5, with no stage 4.)

This is the mature adult stage. The breasts are fully developed. Only the nipple sticks out in this stage. The areola has moved back to the general shape of the breast.

FIGURE 2 The drawings on this page show different amounts of female pubic hair. A girl passes through each of the five stages shown by these drawings. Please look at each drawing and read the sentences under the drawings. Then choose the drawing closest to your stage of hair development and mark it 1. Then choose the drawing that is next closest and mark it 2.

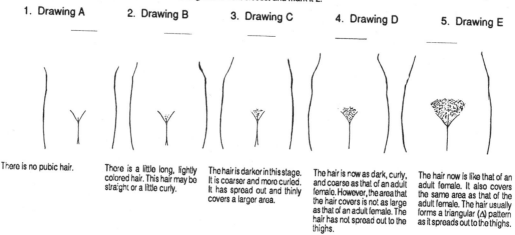

1. Drawing A   2. Drawing B   3. Drawing C   4. Drawing D   5. Drawing E

There is no pubic hair.

There is a little long, lightly colored hair. This hair may be straight or a little curly.

The hair is darker in this stage. It is coarser and more curled. It has spread out and thinly covers a larger area.

The hair is now as dark, curly, and coarse as that of an adult female. However, the area that the hair covers is not as large as that of an adult female. The hair has not spread out to the thighs.

The hair now is like that of an adult female. It also covers the same area as that of the adult female. The hair usually forms a triangular (Δ) pattern as it spreads out to the thighs.

Reprinted with permission from Morris, N. M., & Udry, J. R. (1980). Validation of a self-administered instrument to assess stage of adolescent development. *Journal of Youth and Adolescence, 9,* 271–280.

sources, it is useful to know how different measures of puberty compare to one another, and how reports of puberty from one source (e.g., doctors) compare to reports of puberty from another source (e.g., the adolescent) on the same measure.

HEIGHT AND WEIGHT ■ Self-reported height is highly correlated with actual height (Brooks-Gunn et al., 1987; Petersen & Crockett, 1985). Self-reports of weight are also fairly accurate among girls (boys have not been studied), although

FIGURE 3 The drawings on this page show different amounts of male pubic hair. A boy passes through each of the five stages shown by these drawings. Please look at each of the erasing and read the sentences under the drawing. Then choose the drawing closest to your stage of hair development and mark it 2. In choosing the right picture, look only at the <u>pubic hair</u> and not at the size of the testes, scrotum and penis.

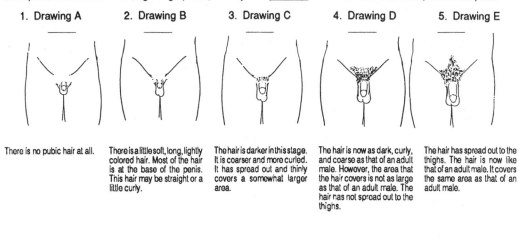

1. Drawing A	2. Drawing B	3. Drawing C	4. Drawing D	5. Drawing E
There is no pubic hair at all.	There is a little soft, long, lightly colored hair. Most of the hair is at the base of the penis. This hair may be straight or a little curly.	The hair is darker in this stage. It is coarser and more curled. It has spread out and thinly covers a somewhat larger area.	The hair is now as dark, curly, and coarse as that of an adult male. However, the area that the hair covers is not as large as that of an adult male. The hair has not spread out to the thighs.	The hair has spread out to the thighs. The hair is now like that of an adult male. It covers the same area as that of an adult male.

FIGURE 4 The drawings of this page show <u>Different stages of development of the testes, scrotum, and penis.</u> A boy passes through each of the five stages shown by these drawings. Please look at each of the drawings and read the sentences under the drawing. Then choose the drawing closest to your stage of development. Mark a "1" on the line above that drawing. Then choose the drawing that is the next closest to your stage of development and mark it "2." In choosing the right picture, look only at the stage of development, not at pubic hair.

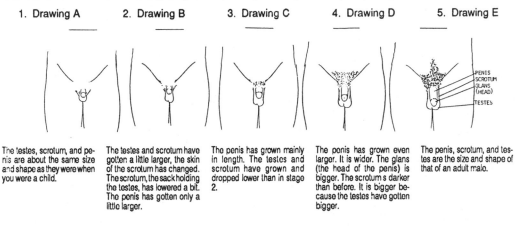

1. Drawing A	2. Drawing B	3. Drawing C	4. Drawing D	5. Drawing E
The testes, scrotum, and penis are about the same size and shape as they were when you were a child.	The testes and scrotum have gotten a little larger, the skin of the scrotum has changed. The scrotum, the sack holding the testes, has lowered a bit. The penis has gotten only a little larger.	The penis has grown mainly in length. The testes and scrotum have grown and dropped lower than in stage 2.	The penis has grown even larger. It is wider. The glans (the head of the penis) is bigger. The scrotum is darker than before. It is bigger because the testes have gotten bigger.	The penis, scrotum, and testes are the size and shape of that of an adult male.

Reprinted with permission from Morris, N. M., & Udry, J. R. (1980). Validation of a self-administered instrument to assess stage of adolescent development. *Journal of Youth and Adolescence*, 9, 271–280.

there is a tendency toward underreporting (Brooks-Gunn et al., 1987).

MENARCHE ▪ Self-reports of menarche by girls across the adolescent years are mostly accurate, with the following qualifications: (1) right around the time of first menarche, there may be confusion for a small number of girls over whether or not menarche has occurred (Brooks-Gunn & Ruble, 1982); and (2) accuracy of self-reports seems to increase if information is obtained in an interview format with a clinician as opposed to use of a paper and pencil measure (Dorn & Nottelmann, 1988). Research also suggests that women recall time of menarche with a fairly high degree of accuracy (e.g., Damon, Damon, Reed, & Valadian, 1969).

SECONDARY SEXUAL CHARACTERISTICS ▪ Since the most commonly used "perceived" measures of secondary sexual development are ratings using photographs or schematic drawings of the Tanner stages, or the PDS, the data summarized here compare doctor, parent, and adolescent ratings of pubertal development within and across these measures. Data summarized are from Brooks-Gunn et al. (1987), Duke, Litt, and Gross (1980), Miller, Tucker, Pasch, and Eccles (1988), and Morris and Udry (1980).

Agreement among child, parent (usually the mother), and doctor on these scales is generally good, but not perfect. Agreement is worse for boys than girls, and may be lower in the early stages of puberty, especially for boys. Initial pubertal changes may be the hardest to assess, regardless of who is the respondent.

On the PDS, a parent's report of their child's pubertal development more closely approximates an "objective" report (using a doctor as the standard) than the child's own self-report *if* that child is a girl and *if* the girl is young (8 to 9 years old). Girls older than eleven are likely to be equally as good or better raters of their own pubertal status than their parents.

Boys agree more closely with doctors about their pubertal status on the PDS than their parents do (although this may be due to the fact that the parent represented in this research is usually the mother; fathers may be more accurate reporters of sons' development than mothers, but research has not addressed this question).

Where differences occur for girls on the PDS, young girls (aged 8–9) tend to say they are less developed than their parents or doctors do, whereas girls 10 and older tend to rate themselves as more mature than parents or doctors rate them. Boys of all ages systematically rate themselves as more mature than parents or doctors rate them.

Using Tanner schematic drawings, both girls and boys tend to rate themselves as more mature than parents rate them. For girls, self- and mother reports using Tanner schematics correlate highly with a doctor's assigned Tanner stage; where differences occur, the self- and mother ratings are more advanced.

Doctors' ratings on the PDS are in fairly high agreement with their own Tanner stage assignments for girls, although for girls over age 11 the PDS often results in ratings that are more advanced (no matter who fills out the PDS) than the doctors' Tanner classifications. For boys, differences between doctor's assigned Tanner stage and doctors' PDS ratings are not systematic. However, as with their PDS ratings, doctors' Tanner staging of boys is less advanced than boys' self-ratings using the PDS.

As for comparisons between the PDS and Tanner schematics, the two measures give similar information if parents are the respondents. However, as compared to the Tanner drawings, girls tend to rate themselves as more mature, and boys as less mature (at least in the early stages of puberty) on the PDS. Thus, for girls, Tanner schematic self-ratings may be more accurate reflections of actual pubertal growth given the findings that self-ratings on the PDS tend to result in more mature pubertal classifications than doctors' Tanner stage assignments. In fact, one study that compared girls' schematic ratings *and* PDS ratings to a doctor's assessment indicated that the Tanner ratings compared more closely to the doctor's ratings (Brooks-Gunn et al., 1987).

Unlike for girls, boys' self-ratings on Tanner pictures may be *less* accurate reflections of pubertal development than the PDS. Boys tend to rate themselves as more advanced than doctors do, and they tend to be classified as even more advanced on Tanner picture self-ratings than the PDS. Potentially, the Tanner drawings result in extreme "overestimations" of development for boys.

Ratings on the PDS correlate moderately with age at peak height velocity. Adolescents rated as more mature on the PDS had earlier peak height velocities, indicating that the more advanced children were more likely to have experienced their peak height growth at a younger age (Petersen et al., 1988).

Because the data summarized here suggest that reports across sources and instruments are correlated, but not in perfect agreement, self or parent assessments are most appropriate for situations where (1) perceptions of pubertal development are of more interest than actual development or (2) relative differences in pubertal status are of more interest than actual differences.

In addition, methods for assessing secondary sexual development in boys are not as advanced or accurate as those for girls. Pubertal markers for boys are not as visible nor as easily measured, and less work has been done to discern the meaning of different pubertal changes for boys than girls. One retrospective study of college males suggests that pubic hair development, changes in height and weight, the development of facial hair, and increasing sex interest are the most significant markers of puberty for adolescent boys (Sheldon, 1988).

PUBERTAL TIMING ■

Parent (usually mother) and adolescent perceptions of timing have been compared for a pre- and early pubertal sample (Miller, 1988). In general, young adolescents expect that puberty should be occurring earlier than their parents do. Over 40% of the girls (at each of three times of measurement) rated themselves as later in timing than their parents. Agreement on a timing category was higher for boys and parents, but about 30% of boys at each wave also said they were one category of timing later than their parents rated them.

References

Bock, R. D., Wainer, H., Petersen, A., Thissen, D., Murray, J., & Roche, A. (1973). A parameterization for individual human growth curves. *Human Biology, 45*(1), 63–80.

Brooks-Gunn, J. (1987). Pubertal processes and girls' psychological adaptation. In R. M. Lerner & T. T. Foch (Eds.), *Biological-psychosocial interactions in early adolescence* (pp. 123–154). Hillsdale, NJ: Lawrence Erlbaum Associates.

Brooks-Gunn, J., & Petersen, A. C. (1984). Problems in studying and defining pubertal events. *Journal of Youth and Adolescence, 13*(3), 181–196.

Brooks-Gunn, J., Petersen, A. C., & Eichorn, D. (1985). The study of maturational timing effects in adolescence. *Journal of Youth and Adolescence, 14*(3), 149–161.

Brooks-Gunn, J., & Ruble, D. N. (1982). The development of menstrual-related beliefs and behaviors during early adolescence. *Child Development, 53*, 1567–1577.

Brooks-Gunn, J., & Warren, M. P. (1985). Measuring physical status and timing in early adolescence: A developmental perspective. *Journal of Youth and Adolescence, 14*(3), 163–189.

Brooks-Gunn, J., Warren, M. P., Rosso, J., & Gargiulo, J. (1987). Validity of self-report measures of girls' pubertal status. *Child Development*, *58*, 829–841.

Damon, A., Damon, S. T., Reed, R. B., & Valadian, I. (1969). Age at menarche of mothers and daughters with a note on accuracy of recall. *Human Biology*, *41*, 161–175.

Doering, C. H. (1980). The endocrine system. In O. G. Brim, Jr. & J. Kagan (Eds.), *Constancy and change in human development* (pp. 229–271). Cambridge: Harvard University Press.

Dorn, L. D., & Nottelmann, E. D. (1988, March). *Variability in self-report menstrual histories and hormone levels in young adolescents.* Paper presented at the bienniel meetings of the Society for Research in Child Development, Alexandria, VA.

Duke, P. M., Litt, I. F., & Gross, R. T. (1980). Adolescents' self-assessment of sexual maturation. *Pediatrics*, *66*, 918–920.

Faust, M. S. (1983). Alternative constructions of adolescent growth. In J. Brooks-Gunn & A. C. Petersen (Eds.), *Girls at puberty: Biological and psychosocial perspectives* (pp. 105–126). New York: Plenum Press.

Garn, S. M. (1980). Continuities and change in maturational timing. In O. G. Brim, Jr. & J. Kagan (Eds.), *Constancy and change in human development* (pp. 113–162). Cambridge: Harvard University Press.

Grumbach, M. M. (1980). The neuroendocrinology of puberty. In D. T. Krieger & J. C. Hughes (Eds.), *Neuroendocrinology* (pp. 249–258). Sunderland, MA: Sinauer Associates.

Harlan, W. R., Grillo, G. P., Cornoni-Huntley, J., & Leaverton, P. E. (1979). Secondary sex characteristics of boys 12 to 17 years of age: U.S. Health Examination Survey. *Journal of Pediatrics*, *95*, 293–297.

Harlan, W. R., Harlan, E. A., & Grillo, G. P. (1980). Secondary sex characteristics of girls 12 to 17 years of age: The U.S. Health Examination Survey. *Journal of Pediatrics*, *96*, 1074–1078.

Johnson, M., & Everitt, B. (1984). *Essential reproduction* (2nd ed.). Oxford: Blackwell Scientific Publications.

Marshall, W. A., & Tanner, J. M. (1969). Variations in pattern of pubertal change in girls. *Archives of Disease in Childhood*, *44*, 291–303.

Miller, C. L. (1988). Pubertal development in early adolescent girls: Relationships to mood, energy, restlessness, and certainty about self. *Dissertation Abstracts International*, *49*(5), 1967-B.

Miller, C. L., Tucker, M. L., Pasch, L., & Eccles, J. S. (1988, March). *Measuring pubertal development: A comparison of different scales and different sources.* Paper presented at the bienniel meeting of the Society for Research in Child Development, Alexandria, VA.

Morris, N. M., & Udry, J. R. (1980). Validation of a self-administered instrument to assess stage of adolescent development. *Journal of Youth and Adolescence*, *9*(3), 271–280.

Petersen, A. C., & Crockett, L. (1985). Pubertal timing and grade effects on adjustment. *Journal of Youth and Adolescence*, *14*(3), 191–206.

Petersen, A. C., Crockett, L., Richards, M., & Boxer, A. (1988). A self-report measure of pubertal status: Reliability, validity, and initial norms. *Journal of Youth and Adolescence*, *17*(2), 117–133.

Sheldon, J. (1988). *The pubertal experience.* Unpublished manuscript, University of Michigan.

Simmons, R. G., & Blyth, D. A. (1987). *Moving into adolescence: The impact of pubertal change and school context.* New York: Aldine-DeGruyter.

Tanner, J. M. (1966). *Growth at adolescence* (2nd ed.). Oxford: Blackwell Scientific Publications.

Tanner, J. M., & Whitehouse, R. H. (1976). Clinical longitudinal standards for height, weight, height velocity, weight velocity, and the stages of puberty. *Archives of Disease in Childhood*, *51*, 170–179.

See Also

Cognitive Abilities and Physical Maturation; Growth Spurt, Adolescent; Maturational Timing, Antecedents of in Girls; Maturational Timing Variations in Adolescent Girls, Consequences of; Menarche and Body Image; Menarche, Secular Trend in Age of; Menstrual Cycle; Physical Status and Timing in Early Adolescence, Measurement of; Puberty, Body Fat and; Puberty Education; Puberty, Endocrine Changes at; Puberty, Hypothalamic-Pituitary Changes of; Puberty, Precocious, Treatment of; Puberty, Sport and; Spatial Ability and Maturation in Adolescence; Spermarche.

Puberty and Body Fat

Rose E. Frisch
Harvard Center for Population Studies

Many young girls who diet excessively, or who are well-trained athletes or dancers, have a delayed menarche (primary amenorrhea). Menarche may be delayed until as late as age 19 or 20 years. If excessive dieting or strenuous training begins after menarche, girls may have anovulatory menstrual cycles, irregular cycles, or a complete absence of cycles (secondary amenorrhea). In addition to these extreme effects of weight loss and athletic training on the menstrual cycle, girls who train moderately, or who are regaining weight into the normal range, may have a menstrual cycle that appears to be normal, but that actually has a shortened luteal phase or is anovulatory.

All these disruptions of reproductive ability are usually reversible, after varying periods of time, following weight gain, decreased athletic training, or both.

Secondary amenorrhea occurs in dieting girls and women, or in athletes and dancers, when weight loss is in the range of 10 to 15% of normal weight for height; this total weight loss is equivalent to a loss of about one-third of body fat. Primary amenorrhea (absence of menarche at age 16 years or older) also occurs in association with excessive thinness. These data suggest that a minimum level of body fat (i.e., stored, easily mobilized energy) in relation to the lean body mass is necessary for the onset and maintenance of regular ovulatory menstrual cycles. Both the absolute and relative amounts of fat are important, since the lean mass and the fat must be within a particular absolute range, as well as within a relative range (i.e., the individual must be big enough to reproduce successfully).

WHY FAT? ■ Reproduction costs calories; a pregnancy requires about 50,000 calories over and above normal metabolic requirements. Lactation requires an extra 1,000 calories a day. In premodern times lactation was an essential part of reproduction. Fat storage when food supplies are uncertain, as they were in our prehistory, would therefore be of selective advantage to the female.

Whatever the reason, during the adolescent growth spurt, which precedes menarche, girls increase their body fat by 120%, compared to a 44% increase in lean body mass. Changes in body composition can be monitored by direct measurements of body water. Since fat contains only about 10% water, compared to about 80% water in muscle and viscera, an increase in fat results in a decrease in the body water as a percentage of body weight. Direct measurements of the body water of girls from birth to completion of growth show a continuous decline in the proportion of body water because of the large relative increase in body fat. At menarche girls averaged about 24% of their body weight as fat (11 kg, or 24 lb). At the completion of growth, between ages 16 to 18 years, the body of a well-nourished young girl in the U.S. contains, on average, about 26% to 28% fat (16 kg, or 35 lb) and about 52% water. In contrast, the body of a boy of the same height and weight contains about 12% fat and about 63% water (Table 1). At the completion of growth men are about 15% fat, and about 61% water.

The main function of the 16kg of stored female fat, which is equivalent to 144,000 calories, may be to provide energy for a pregnancy and for about three months' lactation.

IS THE AMENORRHEA OF ATHLETES AND UNDERWEIGHT GIRLS ADAPTIVE? ■

Infant survival is correlated with birth weight, and birth weight is correlated with the prepregnancy weight of the mother and, independently, with her weight gain during pregnancy. An underweight woman therefore is at high risk for an unsuccessful pregnancy. As Dr. J. M. Duncan (1871) observed over a century ago, if a seriously undernourished woman could get pregnant, the chance of her giving birth to a viable infant, or herself surviving the pregnancy, is small. Therefore, the amenorrhea of underweight girls and women can be considered adaptive.

HOW BODY FAT MAY REGULATE FEMALE REPRODUCTION ■

There are at least four mechanisms by which body fat (adipose tissue) may directly effect ovulation and the menstrual cycle, and, through both, fertility. First, because conversion of androgen to estrogen takes place in adipose tissue of the breast and abdomen, the omentum, and the fatty marrow of the long bones, adipose tissue is a significant extragonadal source of estrogen. Second, body weight, and thus degree of fatness, influences the direction of estrogen metabolism to the most potent or least potent forms. Third, fatter girls and women have a diminished capacity to bind

TABLE 1
TOTAL WATER/BODY WEIGHT PERCENT AS AN INDEX OF FATNESS: COMPARISON OF GIRL AGE 18 YEARS AND BOY AGE 15 YEARS OF SAME HEIGHT AND WEIGHT

	GIRL: AGE 18 YR.	BOY: AGE 15 YR.
Height (cm)	165.0	165.0
Weight (kg)	57.0	57.0
Total body water:TBW (liters)	29.5	36.0
Lean body weight:TBW/0.72 (kg)	41.0	50.0
Fat (kg)	16.0	7.0
Fat/body wt %	28.0	12.0
Total body water/Body wt %	51.8	63.0

Fat/body wt % = 100 − [(TW/BWt%/)0.72]

From Frisch, R. E. What's below the surface? *New England Journal of Medicine* 305:1019, 1981.

serum sex hormone binding globulin (SHBG), which results in an elevated percentage of free serum estradiol. Fourth, adipose tissue stores steroid hormones.

Changes in relative fatness might also affect reproductive ability indirectly, through disturbance of the regulation of body temperature and energy balance by the hypothalamus. Lean amenorrheic women, both anorectic and nonanorectic, display abnormalities of temperature regulation, at the same time that they have delayed response, or lack of response, to exogenous luteinizing hormone releasing hormone (LHRH).

HYPOTHALAMIC DYSFUNCTION, GONADOTROPIN SECRETION, AND WEIGHT LOSS ■ It is now known that the amenorrhea of underweight and excessively lean girls and women is due to hypothalamic dysfunction. Consistent with the view that this type of amenorrhea is adaptive, the pituitary-ovarian axis is apparently intact and functions when exogenous luteinizing hormone releasing hormone (LHRH) is administered in pulsatile form or as a single injection.

Girls and women with this type of hypothalamic amenorrhea display both quantitative and qualitative changes in the secretion of gonadotropins, luteinizing hormone (LH), and follicle-stimulating hormone (FSH). First, LH and FSH are low; estradiol levels are also low. Second, the secretion of LH and the response to luteinizing hormone (LHRH) (which is secreted by the hypothalamus) are reduced in direct correlation with the amount of weight loss. Third, underweight patients respond to exogenous LHRH with a pattern of secretion similar to that of prepubertal children; the FSH response is greater than the LH response. The return of LH responsiveness is correlated with weight gain. Fourth, the maturity of the 24 hour LH secretory pattern and body weight are related; weight loss results in an age-inappropriate secretory pattern resembling that of prepubertal or early pubertal children. Weight gain restores the postmenarcheal secretory pattern. Fifth, a reduced response, or absence of response, to clomiphene is correlated with the degree of the loss of body weight, hence fat.

INITIAL FINDINGS: WEIGHT AT PUBERTY ■ The idea that relative fatness is important for female reproductive ability followed from our first findings that the events of the adolescent growth spurt, particularly menarche in girls, were each closely related to an average critical body weight. The mean weight at menarche for United States' girls was $47.8 + 0.5$ kg, at the mean height of $158.5 + 0.5$ cm, and at the mean age of $12.9 + 0.1$ years. (This mean age included girls from Denver, who have a slightly later age of menarche than the rest of the population due to the slowing effect of altitude on growth rate.)

Since individual girls have menarche at all different weights and height, the notion of an average critical weight of 47 kg for early- and late-maturing girls at menarche was analyzed in terms of the components of body weight at menarche. Body composition was investigated because total body water (TW) and lean body weight (LBW, TW/0.72) are more closely correlated with metabolic rate than is body weight, since they represent the metabolic mass as a first approximation. Metabolic rate was considered important since a food intake–lipostat–metabolic signal was hypothesized by G. C. Kennedy (1963) to explain his elegant findings on weight and puberty in the rat.

FATNESS AS A DETERMINANT OF MINIMAL WEIGHTS FOR MENARCHE AND THE RESTORATION OF MENSTRUAL CYCLES ■ Figure 1 is a nomogram that has been found useful clinically in the

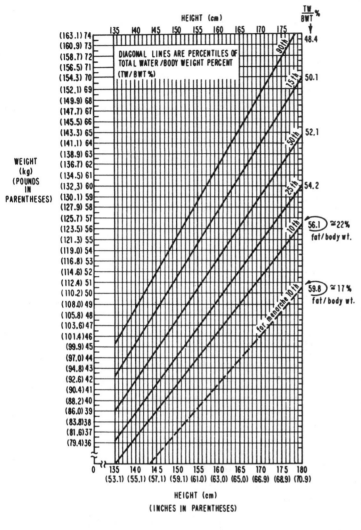

FIGURE 1 The minimal weight necessary for a particular height for restoration of menstrual cycles in amenorrhea due to weight loss is indicated on the weight scale by the 10th percentile diagonal line of total water/body weight percent, 56.1% as it crosses the vertical height line. For example, a 20-year-old woman whose height is 160 cm (63 inches) should weigh at least 43.6 kg (102 lb) before menstrual cycles would be expected to resume.

The minimal weight necessary for a particular height for onset of menstrual cycles is indicated on the weight scale by the 10th percentile diagonal line of total water/body weight percentage 59.8% (dashed line), as it crosses the vertical height lines. Height growth of girls must be completed, or approaching completion. For example, a 15-year-old girl whose completed height is 160 cm (63 in) should weigh at least 41.4 kg (91 lb) before menstrual cycles can be expected to start. No prediction can be made *above* the minimum weights for menarche or resumption of cycles.

(Adapted from Frisch, R. E., & McArthur, J. W., *Science*, *185*, 949–951, 1974. Reprinted with permission.)

evaluation and treatment of young girls and women with primary or secondary amenorrhea due to weight loss. The nomogram was developed from data on the relative fatness of normal girls at menarche and at the completion of growth of the same girls at age 18 years. Total water as percent of body weight, the diagonal lines on the nomogram, is a fatness index since fat has relatively little water (Table 1).

The minimum weight necessary for a point where the diagonal 10th percentile line of total water as percent of body particular height for *restoration* of menstrual cycles is indicated on the weight scale at the weight (56.1%) crosses the appropriate vertical height line. This percentile of TW/BWT% is equivalent to about 22% fat of body weight. For example, a 20-year-old woman whose height is 160 cm (63 inches) should weigh at least 46.3 kg (102 lbs) before menstrual cycles would be expected to resume.

The minimal weight necessary for a particular height for the *onset* of menstrual cycles (menarche) is indicated at the point where the dashed line, representing the 10th percentile of total water/body weight percentage at menarche (59.8%) crosses the appropriate vertical height line. This percentile is equivalent to about 17% fat of body weight.

Height growth of girls must be completed, or nearing completion, for use of the nomogram for menarche. For example, a 15-year-old girl whose completed height is 160 cm (63 inches) should weigh at least 41.4 kg (91 lbs) before menstrual cycles can be expected to start.

The minimal weights for menarche (indicated by the dashed line) would be used also for girls who become amenorrheic as a result of weight loss shortly after menarche, as is often found in cases of anorexia nervosa.

Table 2 presents the minimal weights for menarche and for resumption of cycles for each height in the nomogram.

Other factors, such as emotional stress, affect the maintenance or onset of menstrual cycles. Therefore, menstrual cycles may cease without weight loss and may not resume in girls and women even though the minimal weight-for-height has been achieved. Also, these minimal weight standards apply thus far only to Caucasian women in the United States and Europe. Different races have different critical weights at menarche, and it is not yet known whether the different critical weights represent the same critical body composition of fatness.

Some amenorrheic athletes, such as shotputters, oarswomen, and some swimmers, are not lightweight; they are already above the minimal weight for their height because they are very muscular, and muscles are heavy. The cause of their amenorrhea is, nevertheless, most probably the increased lean mass and reduced fat content of their bodies. Again, gaining body fatness or ceasing exercise usually restores menstrual cycles. However, at present, their minimal weight for height for restored cycles cannot be predicted.

In relation to athletic amenorrhea, it is also important to note that body composition may change without any change in body weight. Muscle is heavy, since it contains 80% water, compared to 10% water in fat. A woman may increase muscle mass by increasing training, and at the same time lose fat, without a perceptible change in body weight. Nevertheless the change in lean/fat ratio could affect her ovulatory function.

Measuring body fat by skin folds or underwater weighing can lead to inaccurate estimations of body fat, particularly of female subjects, because of variations in the skeletel mass, which is considered part of the lean body mass.

DELAYED MENARCHE OF ATHLETES

Many studies have reported that young athletes and dancers have a delayed age of menarche, averaging 14 to 15 years. But one may ask, did the exercise delay menarche, or did late-maturing girls choose to be athletes or dancers? When athletes were classified according to whether their training had begun before or after menarche, we found that the average age of menarche of runners and swimmers whose training began before menarche was 15.1 yr, whereas the average age of those whose training began *after* menarche, was 12.7 yr. The latter age was the same as the controls in the study and the general population (Figure 2). In this sample of runners and swimmers each year of training delayed menarche by 5 months (0.4 yr).

TABLE 2

MINIMAL WEIGHT FOR PARTICULAR HEIGHT NECESSARY FOR THE ONSET OR RESTORATION OF MENSTRUAL CYCLES

		MENARCHE OR PRIMARY AMENORRHEA			SECONDARY AMENORRHEA		
		MINIMAL[a] WEIGHT		AVER-AGE WEIGHT	MINIMAL[b] WEIGHT		AVER-AGE WEIGHT
(inches)	Height (cm)	(10th percentile) (lb)	(kg)	(50th percentile) (kg)	(10th percentile) (lb)	(kg)	(50th percentile) (kg)
53.1	135	66.7	30.3	34.9	74.6	33.9	38.9
53.9	137	68.6	31.2	36.0	76.8	34.9	40.1
54.7	139	70.6	32.1	37.0	79.0	35.9	41.2
55.5	141	72.6	33.0	38.0	81.2	36.9	42.4
56.3	143	74.4	33.8	39.0	83.4	37.9	43.5
57.1	145	76.3	34.7	40.1	85.6	38.9	44.7
57.9	147	78.3	35.6	41.1	87.8	39.9	45.8
58.7	149	80.3	36.5	42.1	90.0	40.9	47.0
59.4	151	82.3	37.4	43.1	92.2	41.9	48.1
60.2	153	84.3	38.3	44.2	94.4	42.9	49.3
61.0	155	86.2	39.2	45.2	96.6	43.9	50.4
61.8	157	88.2	40.1	46.2	98.8	44.9	51.5
62.6	159	90.2	41.0	47.2	101.0	45.9	52.7
63.4	161	92.2	41.9	48.3	103.2	46.9	53.8
64.2	163	93.9	42.7	49.3	105.4	47.9	55.0
65.0	165	95.9	43.6	50.3	107.6	48.9	56.1
65.7	167	97.9	44.5	51.4	109.8	49.9	57.3
66.5	169	99.9	45.4	52.4	112.0	50.9	58.4
67.3	171	101.9	46.3	53.4	114.0	51.8	59.6
68.1	173	103.8	47.2	54.4	116.2	52.8	60.7
68.9	175	105.8	48.1	55.5	118.4	53.8	61.8
69.7	177	107.8	49.0	56.5	120.6	54.8	63.0
70.5	179	109.6	49.8	57.5	122.8	55.8	64.1
71.3	181	111.8	50.8	58.5	125.2	56.9	65.3

[a]Equivalent to 17% fat/body weight. Height Growth must be completed or approaching completion.
[b]Equivalent to 22% fat/body weight

PUBLIC HEALTH NOTE ■ A positive way to lower risk of teen-age pregnancy may be to have girls begin regular, team training in elementary school. Regular ovulatory cycles do not begin in late maturers until about 3 years after menarche. Athletic training also increases self-esteem and provides the comraderie of teammates and coach. In addition, as discussed below, early, regular, moderate athletic training is associated later in life with a lower risk of the serious diseases of women in the menopausal years.

One caveat: young adolescent athletes

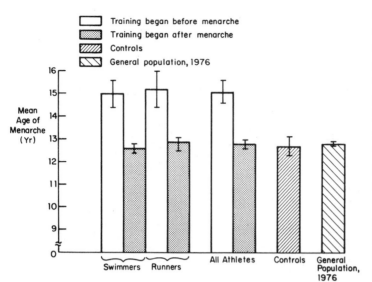

FIGURE 2   Mean (±SEM) ages at menarche of swimmers, runners, and all athletes according to whether training began before or after menarche, compared with the mean menarcheal age of the controls and the general population, in 1976.

(Reprinted with permission from *Journal of the American Medical Association, 246, 1559, 1981.*)

should not be pressured to lose weight for competition, as, for example, gymnasts or body wrestlers are sometimes advised. Loss of weight at critical periods in the adolescent growth spurt can result in stunting of final height.

THE LONG-TERM TREND TO AN EARLIER AGE OF MENARCHE ▪ In addition to the delaying effects of exercise on menarche, other delaying factors include undernutrition and diseases such as cystic fibrosis, juvenile onset diabetes, Crohn's disease, and sickle-cell anemia. All these environmental factors slow the rate of weight growth and affect the normal increase in body fatness of girls during the adolescent growth preceding sexual maturation. An extreme example is the sexual maturation

of two females and one developmentally disabled male who matured at ages 24, 33, and 29 years respectively, after nutritional rehabilitation by enteral (tube feeding). Sexual maturation was confirmed by hormonal assays. Maturation occurred after rapid weight gain, but without catch-up growth in height, even though the heights were still in the prepubertal range.

In addition to environmental factors, age of menarche is, of course, affected by genetic factors, which most probably include inheritance of rate of growth. The long-term (secular) trend to an earlier age of menarche in the United States and Europe (Figure 3) is correlated with more rapid growth in height and weight in the last century. The average age of menarche a century ago was 16 years. The average age of menarche in the United States, at present, for normal nonathletic girls, is 12.6 years. The adolescent growth spurt in US girls now begins at about 9.5 years.

LONG-TERM EXERCISE LOWERS THE RISKS OF SEX HORMONE SENSITIVE CANCERS ▪
The amenorrhea and delayed menarche of athletes raised the question, are there differences in the long-term reproductive health of athletes compared to nonathletes?

A study of 5,398 college alumnae, 2,622 of whom were former athletes, and 2,776 of whom were nonathletes, showed that the former athletes had a significantly lower lifetime occurrence of breast cancer and cancers of the reproductive system

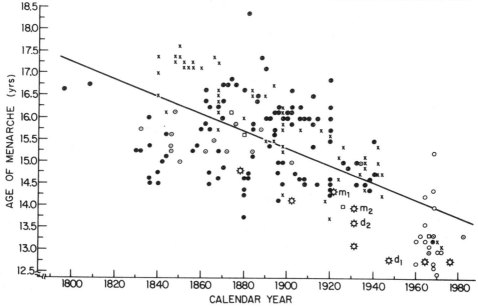

FIGURE 3   Mean or Median Age of Menarche as a Function of Calendar Year from 1790 to 1980. The symbols refer to England (⊙); France (•); Germany (⊗); Holland (□); Scandinavia (x) (Denmark, Finland, Norway, and Sweden); Belgium, Czechoslovakia, Hungary, Italy, Poland (rural), Rumania (urban and rural), Russia (15.2 years at an altitude of 2500 m and 14.4 years at 700 m), Spain, and Switzerland (all labeled o); and the United States (☆; data not included in the regression line). Twenty-seven points for Europe were identical and do not appear on the graph. The regression line cannot, of course, be extended indefinitely.

The age of menarche has already leveled off in some European countries, as it has in the United States.

(Reprinted from the *New England Journal of Medicine*, *306*, 1982 with permission.)

compared to nonathletes. Over 82% of the athletes began their training in high school or earlier. The analysis controlled for potential confounding factors including age, age of menarche, age of first birth, smoking, cancer family history, etc. The former college athletes also had a lower lifetime occurrence of benign tumors of the breast and reproductive system, and lower prevalence of diabetes, particularly after age 40, compared to the nonathletes. No greater risk of bone fractures was found for the former athletes, including risk of wrist and hip fractures, in the menopausal period compared to nonathletes.

These data indicate that long-term exercise begun in high school or earlier, which is not Olympic or marathon level, but is regu-lar, in energy-intensive sports such as tennis, swimming, track, basketball, and hockey reduce the risk of the serious diseases of women later in life. The data suggest that exercise programs for young girls have potential for improved public health.

References

Duncan, J. M. (1871). *Fecundity, fertility and allied topics* (2d ed.). Edinburgh: Adam & Charles Black.

Feigelman, T., Frisch, R. E., MacBurney, M., Schiff, I., & Wilmore, D. (1987). Sexual maturation in the third and fourth decades, after nutritional rehabilitation by enteral feeding. *Journal of Pediatrics, 3*, 620–623.

Fishman, J., Boyar, R. M., & Hellman, L. (1975). Influence of body weight on estradiol metabolism in young women. *Journal of Clinical Endocrinology and Metabolism, 41*, 989–991.

Frisch, R. E. (1985). Fatness, menarche, and female fertility. *Perspectives in Biology and Medicine, 28*, 611–633.

Frisch, R. E. (1988). Fatness and fertility. *Scientific American, 258*, 88–95.

Frisch, R. E., & McArthur, J. (1974). Menstrual cycles: Fatness as a determinant of minimum weight for height necessary for their maintenance or onset. *Science, 185*, 949–951.

Frisch, R. E., Welbergen, A. V., McArthur, J. W., Albright, T., Witschi, J., Bullen, B., Birnholz, J., Reed, R. B., & Hermann, H. (1981). Delayed menarche and amenorrhea of college athletes in relation to age of onset of training. *Journal of the American Medical Association, 246*, 1559–1563.

Frisch, R. E., Wyshak, G., Albright, N. L., Albright, T. E., Schiff, I., Jones, K. P., Witschi, J., Shiang, E., Koff, E., & Marguglio, M. (1985). Lower prevalence of breast cancer and cancers of the reproductive system among former college athletes compared to non-athletes. *British Journal of Cancer, 52*, 885–981.

Frisch, R. E., Wyshak, G., & Vincent, L. (1980). Delayed menarche and amenorrhea of ballet dancers. *New England Journal of Medicine, 303*, 17–19.

Kennedy, G. D., & Mitra, J. (1963). Body weight and food intake as initiation factors for puberty in the rat. *Journal of Physiology, 166*, 408–418.

Pugliese, M. T., Lifshitz, F., Grad, G., Fort, P., & Marks-Katz, M. (1983). Fear of obesity: A cause of short stature and delayed puberty. *New England Journal of Medicine, 309*, 513–518.

Vigersky, R. A., Andersen, A. E., Thompson, R. H., & Loriaux, D. L. (1977). Hypothalamic dysfunction in secondary amenorrhea associated with simple weight loss. *New England Journal of Medicine, 297*, 1141–1145.

Wyshak, G., & Frisch, R. E. (1982). Evidence for a secular trend in age of menarche. *New England Journal of Medicine, 306*, 1033–1035.

See Also

Cognitive Abilities and Physical Maturation; Growth Spurt, Adolescent; Maturational Timing, Antecedents of in Girls; Maturational Timing Variations in Adolescent Girls, Consequences of; Menarche and Body Image; Menarche, Secular Trend in Age of; Menstrual Cycle; Physical Status and Timing in Early Adolescence, Measurement of; Pubertal Development, Assessment of; Puberty Education; Puberty, Endocrine Changes at; Puberty, Hypothalamic-Pituitary Changes of; Puberty, Precocious, Treatment of; Puberty, Sport and; Spatial Ability and Maturation in Adolescence; Spermarche.

Puberty Education

Paula Duke-Duncan

Clinical Assistant Professor of Pediatrics
University of Vermont School of Medicine

Information about puberty helps children and early adolescents understand and view positively physical and emotional changes that accompany this important development stage. Puberty education prepares young people for this experience by presenting not only the facts concerning physical change, but the wide range of normal variation as well.

Chronological age and developmental stage are both important determinants of the physical changes. The chronologic age of puberty onset varies widely. Girls begin puberty as early as 8 or as late as 13, with the average onset of breast development being 10 to 11. Boys start puberty between 9 and 14 years with the average being 11. The five stages of sexual maturation (SMS) are defined by a standard set of drawings/photographs of five stages each of female breast and pubic hair development, and male genital and pubic hair development (Tanner, 1962).

For girls the pubertal events (changes in the ovaries, uterus, clitoris and vagina, height and weight increase, appearance of underarm hair, vaginal discharge and menarche) follow a fairly predictable sequence and are each linked to one of the five stages.

Boys have their own SMS associated developmental sequence consisting of the testes and sperm production, ejaculation, growth of underarm and facial hair, voice change, and height and weight increase. Many will also have some degree of temporary breast enlargement (Slap, 1986).

An adolescent's stage of sexual maturation is thus a much more accurate marker than chronological age of the degree of pubertal development and physical changes. Since it has been demonstrated that adolescents can accurately identify their own SMS (Duke, Litt, & Gross, 1980; Morris & Udrey, 1980) this concept can be used effectively with students.

The emotional changes that accompany pubertal maturation occur in the cognitive, affective, and behavioral realms. Although the precise relationships between hormone levels and psychological changes are only beginning to be delineated, children and their parents can be advised of feelings commonly experienced during puberty (e.g., moodiness, self-consciousness about physical appearance, and a sense of invulnerability). By the end of adolescence most young people will achieve positive self-esteem, independence from parents, meaningful work or study, and the ability to form satisfying relationships. The feelings and behaviors common in puberty must be viewed in the context of these expected outcomes.

Much of our understanding about the importance of puberty education comes from research on menarche. Brooks-Gunn and Ruble (1983) have demonstrated the importance of preparation for menarche. Girls who had knowledge concerning menstruation prior to menarche experienced fewer cramps and generally had more positive attitudes toward menstruation. These authors also found that the adequacy of menarche preparation influenced the degree of menstrual distress, i.e., girls who felt more prepared at menarche reported less pain. Negative feelings about menstruation are still common among young teens and instructional programs need to incorporate affective as well as factual information (Kuff, 1982; Morse & Dorn, 1987; Stubbs, 1988).

Young people have many questions regarding sexual development (Taussig, 1982) and it is felt that adequate preparation should be done about other changes of puberty. In order to ensure that children receive education about puberty before they begin the changes, education will have to begin by 8 or 9 years of age for some children. Parents may certainly want to start discussing some of these changes even earlier as their children raise questions about adult body shapes, breast, or muscles. By age 10 or 11 even if the child has not shown any signs of pubertal change, he/she needs to understand what is happening to their classmates and what will be happening to them.

Parents, teachers, physicians, nurses, peers, and the media have all been considered puberty educators. Retrospectively college students reported that they had received most of their education about selected pubertal topics (e.g., seminal emissions and ejaculations) from their peers and literature (Thornburg, 1972). The only exception was menstruation, with mothers being the primary source of information. Almost all girls learn about menstruation in part from their mother (Brooks-Gunn & Ruble, 1980; Dunham 1979). Two-thirds of the girls who had older sisters received information from them and 75% received facts from female friends (Brooks-Gunn & Ruble, 1980). Fathers played a minimal role in this area with 75% of the girls reporting that they would not or did not tell their fathers when they began to menstruate. In families where the fathers did know about their daughters' menarche, the girls reported less severe menstrual symptoms. High school girls reported learning more about menstruation from media sources than did girls in earlier grades.

Physicians provide education about puberty during well child visits. Beginning around age 9 or 10, the focus for anticipatory guidance shifts somewhat to include the child more directly while continuing to provide information to parents. Physicians can easily build on earlier discussions of development and sexuality issues often related to younger children (Montauk & Clasen, 1989). Using the Tanner stages, the child's stage of sexual maturation, family history regarding pubertal development, and expectations for other growth parameters can be easily combined with an outline of the more common emotional developmental occurrences. This not only provides parents and children with important information, but also identifies the physician as a knowledgeable and willing resource for future queries. This pre-or-early adolescent well visit is valuable on several levels, but most importantly it provides the child with the assurance that his/her individual pattern of growth and development is perfectly normal, even though it may be quite different than that of a best friend.

Many schools include the topic of pubertal changes in their curriculum (Orr, 1982). The amounts of information provided and the grades when taught vary widely among states and communities. This information is most effective when included as an integrated part of a comprehensive health education curriculum. These discussions can be part of growth and development, anatomy, physiology, family life, emotional changes and well-being, consumer health (e.g., acne products), science and physical education. In addition to comprehensive health education textbook sections, instructional materials including pamphlets, books, filmstrips, and videos are available for students and parents.

Education about puberty is an ideal area for parents and teachers to work together. School-based programs need not only to inform parents of the content of the program but also to actively enlist their support as coeducators of their children about these important topics. This approach must involve parental education, since in many cases their knowledge is incomplete and limited to their own pubertal experiences. In a California study (Cohen, Adler, Beck, & Irwin, 1986) parents from varied ethnic and SES groups had mixed positive and negative perceptions of changes in their early adolescent children. Single parents perceived positive changes in their adolescents more frequently than other parents. Parents younger than 38 perceived more negative changes and experienced more negative and anxious feelings toward their children. First-born children generated more negative feelings for their parents. These findings suggest that older parents and later siblings probably benefit from increased knowledge and experience. Physician-parent discussion during well child care visits, school-sponsored parent sessions, and reading material are all appropriate vehicles for increasing parental knowledge about puberty (McCoy & Wibbleman, 1986; Madaras, 1987). Courses in which children 9–12 and their parents participate together have also been implemented (Henschke, 1984). Community agencies such as Girls' Clubs and Scouting organizations have become active in helping parents provide education about puberty.

A group of California 10 to 12 year olds most often chose their parents as the persons from whom they would most like to hear about puberty (Duke-Duncan, Jones & Morgan, 1986). Efforts designed to support parents in this task should continue to be developed in this field.

Familial adaptation to pubertal change also needs to be considered in designing puberty education strategies. For example, a period of increased conflict between mothers and sons at the apex of the son's puberty has been reported (Steinberg, 1981). The son's influence over family decision making increases and mother's influence declines linearly over the pubertal period. Fathers on the other hand become more dominant and sons more submissive to them in the early pubertal period. For girls, a temporary period of perturbations occurs in family relationships shortly after menarche (Hill & Holmbeck, 1987). As more is understood about these family reactions and changes at puberty, puberty education interventions can be even more effective.

References

Brooks-Gunn, J., & Ruble, D. (1980). Menarche: The interaction of physiology, cultural, and social factors. In J. J. Dan, E. Graham, & C. P. Beecher (Eds.), *The menstrual cycle* (pp. 132–144). New York: Springer.

Brooks-Gunn, J., & Ruble, D. (1983). The experience of menarche from a developmental perspective. In J. Brooks-Gunn & A. Peterson (Eds.), *Girls at puberty* (pp. 155–179). New York: Plenum.

Cohen, M., Adler, N., Beck, A., & Irwin, D. E. (1986). Parental reactions to the onset of adolescence. *Journal of Adolescent Health Care, 7*(2), 101–105.

Duke-Duncan, P., Jones, L. A., & Morgan, L. (1985, May). *Evaluation of puberty education intervention.* Paper presented at the Ambulatory Pediatrics Association Meeting, Washington D.C.

Duke, P. M., Litt, I. F., & Gross, R. T. (1980). Adolescents' self-assessment of sexual maturation. *Pediatrics, 66*, 918.

Dunham, G. (1979). Timing and sources of information about and attitudes toward menstruation among college females. *Journal of Genetic Psychology, 117*, 205–207.

Henschke, J. (1984). *New directions in facilitating the teaching role of parents in the sex education of their children.* Paper presented at the Adult Education Conference, Louisville, KY.

Hill, J. P., & Holmbeck, G. N. (1987). Familial adaptation to biological change during adolescence. In R. M. Lerner & T. T. Foch (Eds.), *Biological-psychosocial interactions in early adolescence* (pp. 207–223). Hillsdale, NJ: Lawrence Erlbaum Associates.

Kuff, E. (1982). Memories of menarche. *Journal of Youth and Adolescence, 11*(1), 1–9.

Madaras, L. (1987). *What's happening to my body?* New York: Newmarket Press.

McCoy, K., & Wibblesman, C. (1986). *Growing, and changing.* New York: Putnam.

Montauk, S., & Clasen, M. (1989). Sex education in primary care: infancy to puberty. *Medical Aspects of Human Sexuality, 10*, 22–33.

Morris, N. M., & Udrey, J. R. (1980). Validation of a self-administered instrument of assess stage of adolescent development. *Journal of Youth and Adolescence, 9*, 271–280.

Morse, J. M., & Doan, H. M. (1987). Adolescents' response to menarche. *Journal of School Health, 57*, 385–387.

Orr, M. T. (1982). Sex education and contraceptive education in U.S. public schools. *Family Planning Perspectives, 17*, 169–174.

Slap, G. (1986). Normal physiological and psychosocial growth in the adolescent. *Journal of Adolescent Health Care, 7*, 13S–23S.

Steinberg, L. (1981). Transformations in family relations at puberty. *Developmental Psychology, 17*, 833–840.

Stubbs, M. L. (1988). Becoming a woman: Considerations in educating adolescents about menstruation. Wellesley, Mass: Wellesley College Center for Research on Woman.

Tanner, J. M. (1962). *Growth at adolescence.* Oxford: Blackwell, Scientific Publishing.

Taussig, W. C. (1982). Sixth grade children's questions regarding sex. *Journal of School Health, 52*, 412–416.

Thornburg, H. D. (1972). A comparative study of sex information sources. *Journal of School Health, 42*, 88–91.

See Also

Cognitive Abilities and Physical Maturation; Growth Spurt, Adolescent; Maturational Timing, Antecedents of in Girls; Maturational Timing Variations in Adolescent Girls, Consequences of; Menarche and Body Image; Menarche, Secular Trend in Age of; Menstural Cycle; Physical Status and Timing in Early Adolescence, Measurement of; Pubertal Development, Assessment of; Puberty, Body Fat and; Puberty, Endocrine Changes at; Puberty, Hypothalamic-Pituitary Changes of; Puberty, Precocious, Treatment of; Puberty, Sport and; Spatial Ability and Maturation in Adolescence; Spermarche.

Puberty, Endocrine Changes at

Howard E. Kulin

*The Pennsylvania State University
College of Medicine*

Although the secretory products of the hypothalamic-pituitary-gonadal axis are the primary modulators of the somatic changes that appear during puberty, other hormones also play a role. In particular, growth hormone appears to be necessary to realize the full growth-promoting effects of certain gonadal steroids. Boys deficient in growth hormone exhibit a growth spurt when exposed to testosterone, but to a far lesser degree than in the presence of somatotropin. Changes in growth hormone production with age have been described, but the exact dependence of the adolescent growth spurt on such fluxes remains unclear.

The growth-promoting effects of somatotropin are mediated by somatomedins, particularly somatomedin-C. During late puberty this polypeptide reaches a peak nearly three times the adult level. Current evidence suggests that the pubertal change in somatomedin-C is secondary to rising sex steroid levels and to increased amounts of growth hormone.

Thyroxine levels do not change with puberty but provide a permissive action in terms of maximal linear growth. Thyroid hormone appears to act as a primary stimulant to skeletal maturation; the delayed bone age resulting from thyroxine deficiency may also be associated with abnormalities in neuroregulation of pubertal onset.

The increase in adrenal production of weakly androgenic substances, as represented by an increase in circulating dehydroepiandrosterone (DHEA) and its sulfate and the excretion of urinary 17-ketosteroids (adrenarche), usually occurs before the pubertal activation of gonadal sex steroid secretion. Adrenal androgens are not required for the pubertal growth spurt; however, they have an effect on the development of pubic and axillary hair in girls. An as yet unidentified pituitary hormone is probably the cause of the rise in adrenal androgens at age 6 to 8 years, well before the onset of gonadarche. Increments in lean body mass and height acceleration, that precede by a year or more the appearance of secondary sexual characteristics, could be the result of a subliminal increase in production of gonadal hormone or possibly adrenal androgens.

Mineralocorticoid and glucocorticoid secretion from the adrenal gland do not change during puberty. Glucocorticoid excess, either endogenous or exogenous, is almost invariably associated with a decrease in rate of growth and a delay in pubertal onset. These effects appear to be mediated at end-organ sites as part of the catabolic effects of these steroids. When glucocorticoids are used in the therapy of disease states that in themselves may delay growth, the delay in the pubertal process may be marked and prolonged.

The exact hormonal determinants of the pubertal growth spurt in each sex remain unclear. Estrogens in low dose are growth promoters and probably provide a significant stimulus in girls; in boys estrogens may also be involved in the spurt along with testosterone. Somatotropin and thyroxine are important modulators, perhaps working through somatomedin generation to maximize the rate of height gain. Sex steroids serve to limit the duration of pubertal growth by their effects on bone maturation.

Gonadal Function

Although the testis increases significantly in size in the several years before the onset of puberty, testosterone levels appear to remain constant at less than 20 ng/dl (in boys and girls) throughout childhood; testicular size may increase beyond the prepubertal range without a significant change in measurable testosterone. A testicular length of more than 2.5 cm is consistent with early pubertal development, the change being primarily due to the tublar constituents of the gonad. Studies of the onset of spermatogenesis in boys are few, but this process may occur at a relatively early stage of sexual maturation. By age 14 sperm may be found in the urine of most boys who are appropriately studied.

Once testosterone levels begin to rise in boys, they do so relatively rapidly over approximately 10 months. This is usually the time associated with the pubertal growth spurt. There is a great variability between pubic hair development and plasma testosterone, and even with advanced stages of pubic hair development in boys testosterone measurements may be within the range of those in adult women. During puberty in boys circulating testosterone increases more than twentyfold.

The prepubertal testis may be easily stimulated when exposed to the appropriate tropin. Human chorionic gonadotropin (hCG), a luteinizing hormone–like substance, causes a prompt increase in measurable testosterone; administration of hCG can aid in assessing testicular function even before the onset of puberty. The maturing testis is highly responsive to hCG stimulation within 24 to 48 hours. The capacity to secrete testicular androgen is not a limiting factor in the onset of male puberty.

Although the prepubertal ovary exhibits rather dramatic changes in terms of histologic development (presumably gonadotropin-induced), measurable differences in circulating 17β-estradiol (E_2) between boys and girls are not detectable before 7 or 8 years of age; blood levels of this most active gonadal estrogen are less than 10 pg/ml before the onset of puberty. Uterine size increases at about age 7, clearly before the onset of breast development. By age 10 years levels of E_2 in girls exceed those in boys by approximately twofold. Then there is a steady rise in estradiol concentration throughout female puberty with wide individual fluctuations manifest by the time of menarche. A small but significant increment in estradiol also occurs during male puberty as a result of both testicular secretion and the peripheral conversion of other hormones (e.g., testosterone) to estrogens. The prepubertal ovary, like the testis, can be stimulated when exposed to the appropriate stimulus, and ovulation can be induced by exogenous gonadotropin.

Pituitary Secretion

Prolactin levels change little during childhood and adolescence, and prolactin probably plays no role in the onset of sexual maturation. The gonadotropins, however, are key hormones in this regard. There are no sex differences in the levels of gonadotropins during much of childhood, although follicle-stimuluating hormone (FSH) measurements do appear greater in girls than boys in the first 2 years. Gonadotropin secretion reaches a nadir at 3 to 5 years of age, after which levels increase steadily. As puberty approaches, FSH appears to increase more rapidly than does luteinizing hormone (LH) and attains adult levels before LH.

Levels of serum gonadotropins (by radioimmunoassays) in the adult are only two- to fivefold greater than in the child, with considerable variation reported between laboratories. On the other hand, striking increments in urinary excretion of FSH and LH have been detected during puberty, so that adults excrete about 30 times as much LH and 10 times as much FSH as do prepubertal children; if related to body size, this difference is reduced to fifteenfold for LH and fivefold for FSH. Newly developed assay systems applied to blood have shown pubertal changes which may exceed the urinary gonadotropin changes.

The pituitary gland responds to gonadotropin-releasing hormone (GnRH) with a prompt release of LH and FSH, indicating that hypophyseal function is not a limiting factor in the onset of puberty. During much of childhood girls have a greater FSH response than do boys to the hypothalamic tropin. It remains unclear whether different molecular species of LH—as detected by different assay systems—may be secreted during the process of sexual maturation.

References

Bourguignon, J. P. (1988). Linear growth as a function of age at onset of puberty and sex steroid dosage: Therapeutic implications. *Endocrine Reviews, 9,* 467–488.

Delemarre-van de Waal, H., Plant, T. M., Van Rees, J., & Schoemaker, J. (Eds.). (1989). *Control of the onset of puberty, III.* Amsterdam: Elsevier.

Givens, J. R., Venturoli, S., & Flamigni, C. (Eds.). (1985). *Adolescence in females.* Chicago: Yearbook.

Gupta, D., Attanasio, A., & Raaf, S. (1975). Plasma estrogen and androgen concentrations in children during adolescence. *Journal of Clinical Endocrinology and Metabolism, 40,* 636–643.

Reiter, E. O. (1987). Neuroendocrine control processes. *Journal of Adolescent Health Care, 8,* 479–491.

See Also

Adrenarche; Androgens, Adrenal; Androgens, Gonadal; Hormone-Behavior Links at Puberty, Methodological Issues in the Study of Hormones and Behavior in Adolescence; Premenstrual Syndrome (PMS); Puberty, Hypothalamic-Pituitary Changes of; Spermarche.

Puberty, Hypothalamic-Pituitary Changes of

Howard E. Kulin

The Pennsylvania State University College of Medicine

Hypothalamic Function

Although the precise neurochemical process leading to the onset of puberty remains unknown, several physiologic events relating to gonadotropin control mechanisms have been recognized. Luteinizing hormone (LH) and follicle-stimulating hormone (FSH) secretion are episodic at all ages because of the pulsatile release of endogenous gonadotropin-releasing hormone (GnRH). The activity of the hypothalamic pulse generator at various ages has been the subject of intense research. Attention to the frequency of sampling, duration of sampling, timing of sampling, age of patients, and sensitivity of assays must be borne in mind.

Current evidence points to an increase in amplitude as well as frequency in LH pulses with age. The pulsatility of GnRH is greatly affected by the ambient steroid milieu. The consequent release of an LH pulse in the adult male and female in the early follicular phase occurs approximately every 90 minutes. Sustained exposure of the gonadotroph to GnRH will cause desensitization or down-regulation of pituitary receptors and result in cessation of LH and FSH secretion.

Increased amounts of LH during sleep have been detected in the blood and urine of pubertal children. The sleep-associated LH secretion also elevates nocturnal testosterone levels in boys; this elevation may in turn cause the first visible somatic change of puberty. Circadian rhythms of gonadotropin production occur in prepubertal and pubertal children but not in adults.

Efforts to discern the neural trigger for puberty continue. Current views have focused on a central restraining influence of gonadotropin production because FSH and LH decrease during midchildhood from relatively elevated levels in infancy. A search for endogenous opiate-mediated mechanisms during puberty has not been productive, nor is there agreement that significant changes with age occur in the pineal gland secretion of melatonin. Though metabolic signals have been proposed as important factors—based on known weight and energy expenditure effects on LH secretion—critical amounts of particular body constituents have not been substantiated to produce pubertal onset.

Feedback Relationships

The adult hypothalamic-pituitary axis is very sensitive to fluctuations in the sex steroid environment. The ability of certain hormones to suppress gonadotropin production is referred to as negative feedback; in such a system removal of gonadal secretory products causes an elevation in FSH and LH. Several lines of evidence suggest the existence of such a phenomenon in the prepubertal child. Most important is that elevated levels of gonadotropins have been detected in children without gonads—clinically useful information in evaluating patients suspect for gonadal dysgenesis.

A change in the sensitivity of this negative feedback system occurs during sexual maturation in humans. The adult-type interaction is attained only in mid- or late puberty as levels of gonadotropins and gonadal steroids increase. Negative feedback control occurs at the hypothalamic and pituitary level. An appropriate setpoint between gonadal steroids and gonadotropins may be necessary to initiate the ovulatory events of the menstrual cycle, particularly the rise in FSH in the early follicular phase.

A second important interaction between gonad, hypothalamus, and pituitary gland is referred to as positive feedback, when gonadal hormones further stimulate the hypothalamic-pituitary axis to secrete additional amounts of gonadotropins, especially LH. This form of feedback is integral to the ovulatory process in normal menstruating women, in whom rising levels of estrogen precede the sharp midcycle burst of LH that causes the release of the ovum from the appropriately ripened follicle. The rise in estrogen from the maturing follicle is the trigger for ovulation and induces the required LH surge by means of positive feedback. This phenomenon does not become manifest until late in the process of sexual maturation; regular ovulatory cycles in the adolescent girl may not occur for several years after the onset of menarche. Positive feedback also exists in the adult male.

Tests That Assess Maturity of the Hypothalamic-Pituitary-Gonadal Axis

No available tests can supplant a careful history and physical examination, coupled with knowledge of the normal pattern and progression of secondary sex characteristics. Although a great deal may be learned from measuring the concentrations of serum FSH, LH, testosterone, and estradiol, a single set of such measures has limited value in an ongoing process like puberty. Significant hormonal increments over several months are the most reassuring laboratory evidence of normal pubertal progression. Frequent sampling to assess the nature of periodic LH release or to detect circadian rhythms is useful but difficult to perform in children. Timed urine collections, which allow the kidney to integrate pulsatile secretion, provide a convenient means to obtaining specimens for gonadotropin radioimmunoassay.

There is no specific provocative test for endogenous GnRH release in children. In adults, clomiphene citrate can be used for such a purpose, but a stimulatory response to this drug does not become manifest until midpuberty. At present, GnRH stimulation may be one of the most useful tests for pubertal staging; the magnitude of rise in LH seems to reflect the level of endogenous releasing hormone. Furthermore, there is a maturity-related change in FSH release after GnRH with more of this gonadotropin produced by prepubertal girls than pubertal girls, prepubertal males, or pubertal males.

References

Delemarre-van de Waal, H., Plant. T. M., Van Rees, J., Schoemaker, J. (Eds.). (1989). *Control of the onset of puberty, III.* Amsterdam: Elsevier.

Hale, P. M., Khoury, S., Foster, C. M., Beitins, I. Z., Hopwood, N. J., Marshall, J. C., & Kelch, R. P. (1988). Increased luteinizing hormone pulse frequency during sleep in early to midpubertal boys: Effects of testosterone infusion. *Journal of Clinical Endocrinology and Metabolism 66*, 785–791.

Petraglia, F., Larizza, D., Maghnie, M., Facchinetti, F., Volpe, A., Bernasconi, S., Genazzani, A. R., & Severi, F. (1988). Impairment of the opioidergic control of luteinizing hormone secretion in Turner's Syndrome: Lack of effect of gonadal steroid therapy. *Journal of Clinical Endocrinology and Metabolism 66*, 1024–1028.

Plant, T. M. (1988). Puberty in primates. In E. Knobil & J. Neil (Eds.), *Physiology of reproduction* (pp. 1763–1788). New York: Raven Press.

See Also

Cognitive Abilities and Physical Maturation; Growth Spurt, Adolescent; Maturational Timing, Antecedents of in Girls; Maturational Timing Variations in Adolescent Girls, Consequences of; Menarche and Body Image; Menarche, Secular Trend in Age of; Menstrual Cycle; Physical Status and Timing in Early Adolescence, Measurement of; Pubertal Development, Assessment of; Puberty, Body Fat and; Puberty Education; Puberty, Endocrine Changes at; Puberty, Precocious, Treatment of; Puberty, Sport and; Spatial Ability and Maturation in Adolescence; Spermarche.

Puberty, Precocious, Treatment of

Gordon B. Cutler, Jr.

National Institute of Child Health and Human Development

Definition of Precocious Puberty

Puberty is considered precocious when it begins before the age of 8 years in a girl or before the age of 9 years in a boy (Cutler, 1988). The initial sign of puberty is usually breast budding or pubic hair development in girls and genital enlargement or pubic hair development in boys.

Precocious puberty triggers a pubertal growth spurt and increases the rate of bone maturation in both girls and boys. Although children with precocious puberty are tall for their age because of an earlier adolescent growth spurt, they are short as adults because their increased rate of bone maturation causes an early fusion of the bone growth plates and hence an early cessation of growth (Cutler et al., 1986). In extreme cases growth can stop as early as 8 or 9 years of age compared to the median normal ages of 16 in girls and 18 in boys. As a general rule, children with precocious puberty lose one inch (2.5 cm) of adult height for each year that their puberty precedes age 8 in a girl or age 9 in a boy.

The goal of precocious puberty treatment is to restore growth and development to the normal pattern in order to avoid the behavioral, psychosocial, and growth consequences of early puberty (Sonis et al., 1985). Achievement of this goal, however, requires accurate diagnosis of the cause of the premature sexual development and selection of treatment that is appropriate to the underlying mechanism.

Diagnosis of Premature Sexual Development

Classification of the causes of early sexual maturation includes four major categories (Table 1). Premature thelarche refers to isolated breast development without a growth spurt or pubic hair development. It occurs only in girls, usually before age 3. Premature adrenarche refers to the early occurrence of the normal maturational increase of adrenal androgen secretion ("adrenarche"), which causes isolated pubic hair development in either girls or boys without increased growth rate or bone maturation in most cases. Both premature

TABLE 1

CLASSIFICATION OF THE CAUSES OF PREMATURE SEXUAL DEVELOPMENT

DISORDER

Premature thelarche
Premature adrenarche
LHRH-dependent* precocious puberty:
  Idiopathic
  Central nervous system lesion
  Secondary to LHRH-independent precocious
    puberty
LHRH-independent precocious puberty:
  Adrenal:
    21-Hydroxylase deficiency
    11-Hydroxylase deficiency
    Tumor
  Gonadal:
    McCune-Albright syndrome+
    Familial male precocious puberty†
    Tumor
  Ectopic human chorionic gonadotropin-
    secreting tumor
  Hypothyroidism
  Massive extraglandular aromatization
  Factitious

*LHRH, luteinizing hormone-releasing hormone
+The unexplained association of hyperpigmented skin spots, polyostotic fibrous dysplasia, and precocious puberty
†An autosomal dominant disorder that is expressed only in males.

thelarche and premature adrenarche are relatively benign disorders of unknown cause that have little or no effect on the later onset of the normal pubertal mechanism. There is currently no treatment for either disorder.

Luteinizing hormone-releasing hormone (LHRH)–dependent precocious puberty (also termed central or true precocious puberty) denotes the premature activation of the normal pubertal mechanism. The normal pubertal mechanism causes the increased secretion of LHRH from the hypothalamus, a region of the brain located just above the pituitary gland. LHRH stimulates the pituitary gland to release luteinizing hormone (LH) and follicle-stimulating hormone (FSH). In boys, LH and FSH cause the testes to produce the male hormone testosterone. In girls these same pituitary hormones stimulate the ovaries to make the female hormone estradiol. The sex steroid hormones testosterone and estradiol produce the secondary sexual changes of puberty.

LHRH-dependent precocious puberty subsumes three major categories. First, there may be no apparent explanation for the precocious puberty, which is termed idiopathic. Second, there may be a central nervous system abnormality, such as a developmental anomaly or brain tumor. Third, there may be an overall acceleration of the tempo of development because of an LHRH-independent form of precocious puberty such as congenital adrenal hyperplasia or gonadal disorder (see Table 1 and below). In this situation the normal pubertal mechanism seems to be influenced more by the child's advanced body and bone development than by his or her inappropriately young chronologic age. Thus, a LHRH-independent form of precocious puberty may lead to the secondary development of LHRH-dependent precocious puberty.

LHRH-independent precocious puberty refers to premature secondary sexual development that is independent of the normal pubertal mechanism. The two major categories comprise inherited or neoplastic disorders of the adrenal glands or gonads (Table 1). Less frequent causes include activation of the testis by human chorionic gonadotropin (hCG)-secreting tumors, severe hypothyroidism, an inborn error causing increased androgen-to-estrogen conversion (massive extraglandular aromatization), and factitious exposure to androgens or estrogens.

The clinical, laboratory, and radiographic steps to obtain a specific diagnosis in the child with premature sexual development are beyond the scope of this entry and can be found in medical textbooks (Cutler, 1988; Ross, 1985; Styne & Grumbach, 1986).

Treatment of Precocious Puberty

LHRH-DEPENDENT PRECOCIOUS PUBERTY ■ Children with LHRH-dependent precocious puberty respond dramatically to treatment with long-acting agonist analogues of LHRH. The molecular basis for the effectiveness of these analogues is not fully understood. Their resistance to metabolism and long duration of action appears to superimpose continuous stimulation of the pituitary LHRH receptors upon the normal physiologic pattern of pulsatile LHRH secretion. Continuous LHRH stimulation appears to uncouple occupancy of the LHRH receptor from the normal pituitary response, so that the hypothalamic LHRH signals can no longer be received by the pituitary. Thus, LH, FSH, and sex steroid levels decrease to normal or nearly normal prepubertal levels. The progression of secondary sexual development is arrested and regression of secondary sexual development may occur in some children. Growth rate and bone maturation decrease to normal or less than normal rates, and predicted adult height increases progressively with duration of treatment (Comite et al., 1986; Cutler et al., 1986; Manasco et al., 1989).

LHRH analogue treatment of precocious puberty was first introduced in 1979. Although the results thus far have been favorable, it is too soon to know the adult height and reproductive function of treated children. Thus, further research studies are needed before reaching definite conclusions about the long-term safety and effectiveness of this form of treatment.

LHRH-INDEPENDENT PRECOCIOUS PUBERTY ■ Whereas each type of LHRH-dependent precocious puberty can be treated with long-acting agonist analogues of LHRH, each of the LHRH-independent forms of precocious puberty has unique features that require a specific treatment for each diagnostic category. For example, treatment of adrenal, gonadal, and hCG-secreting tumors is aimed at eradicating the underlying tumor through surgery, chemotherapy, or radiation. Treatment of virilizing congenital adrenal hyperplasia due to 21-hydroxylase or 11-hydroxylase deficiency works through suppression of the hyperplastic adrenal gland by administration of adrenal steroid hormone. Treatment of the McCune-Albright syndrome and familial male precocious puberty is directed either at blocking sex steroid secretion by the gonad or at inhibiting sex steroid action at the target organ, as described below.

The precocious puberty of McCune-Albright syndrome occurs primarily in girls and results from the secretion of estrogen from ovarian cysts, which appear and disappear cyclically in an apparently autonomous fashion. To treat the precocious puberty testolactone, an inhibitor of androgen-to-estrogen conversion (the last enzymatic step of estrogen biosynthesis), was given to block estrogen synthesis (Feuillan et al., 1986). This treatment was highly effective in 50%, moderately effective in 40%, and ineffective in 10% of patients. More potent inhibitors of androgen-to-estrogen conversion, which are currently being tested in adults, offer promise of improving these results.

Familial male precocious puberty can be treated by ketoconazole, a drug that inhibits the synthesis of testosterone (Holland, Fishman, Bailey, & Fazekas, 1985) or by the combination of an antiandrogen, a drug that blocks the action of testosterone at its target tissues, and testolactone, an inhibitor of androgen-to-estrogen conversion (Laue et al., 1989). Blockade of estrogen formation is important in familial male precocious puberty because estrogen (derived by conversion from the male hormone testosterone) plays an important role in the male pubertal growth spurt. Blockade of androgen action alone is not sufficient to restore growth and development to the normal prepubertal pattern unless estrogen formation is also inhibited.

Summary

Despite similar manifestations, the different disorders that cause precocious puberty have different mechanisms that require different treatments. The LHRH-dependent forms of precocious puberty can be treated by long-acting analogues of LHRH that intercept and block the endogenous LHRH signal. The LHRH-independent forms of precocious puberty have many underlying mechanisms; treatment must be tailored to each particular diagnosis.

Most of the treatments of precocious puberty are relatively new. The long-term safety and effectiveness of these treatments are still being established, and further improvements in treatment are likely.

References

Comite, F., Cassorla, F., Barnes, K. M., Hench, K. D., Dwyer, A., Skerda, M. C., Loriaux, D. L., Cutler, G. B., Jr., & Pescovitz, O. H. (1986). Luteinizing hormone-releasing hormone analogue therapy of central precocious puberty: Long-term effect on somatic growth, bone maturation, and predicted height. *Journal of the American Medical Association, 255*, 2613–2616.

Cutler, G. B., Jr. (1988). Precocious puberty. In J. W. Hurst (Ed.), *Medicine for the practicing physician* (2nd ed., pp. 526–530). Boston: Butterworths.

Cutler, G. B., Jr., Cassorla, F. G., Ross, J. L., Pescovitz, O. H., Barnes, K. M., Comite, F., Feuillan, P. P., Laue, L., Foster, C. M., Kenigsberg, D., Caruso-Nicoletti, M., Garcia, H. B., Uriarte, M. M., Hench, K. D., Skerda, M. C., Long, L. M., & Loriaux, D. L. (1986). Pubertal growth: Physiology and pathophysiology. *Recent Progress in Hormone Research, 42*, 443–470.

Feuillan, P. P., Foster, C. M., Pescovitz, O. H., Hench, K. D., Shawker, T. H., Loriaux, D. L., & Cutler, G. B., Jr. (1986). Treatment of precocious puberty in McCune-Albright syndrome with the aromatase inhibitor testolactone. *New England Journal of Medicine, 315*, 1115–1119.

Holland, F. J., Fishman, L., Bailey, J. D., & Fazekas, A. T. A. (1985). Ketoconazole in the management of precocious puberty not responsive to LHRH-analogue therapy. *New England Journal of Medicine, 312*, 1023–1028.

Laue, L., Kenigsberg, D., Pescovitz, O. H., Hench, K. D., Barnes, K. M., Loriaux, D. L., & Cutler, G. B., Jr. (1989). Treatment of familial male precocious puberty with spironolactone and testolactone. *New England Journal of Medicine, 320*, 496–502.

Manasco, P. K., Pescovitz, O. H., Hill, S. C., Jones, J. M., Barnes, K. M., Hench, K. D., Loriaux, D. L., & Cutler, G. B., Jr. (1989). Six-year results of luteinizing hormone-releasing hormone (LHRH) agonist treatment in children with LHRH-dependent precocious puberty. *Journal of Pediatrics, 115*, 105–108.

Ross, G. T. (1985). Disorders of the ovary and female reproductive tract. In J. D. Wilson & D. W. Foster (Eds.), *Textbook of endocrinol-*

ogy (7th ed., pp. 206–258). Philadelphia: Saunders.

Sonis, W. A., Comite, F., Blue, J., Pescovitz, O. H., Rahn, C. W., Hench, K. D., Cutler, G. B., Jr., Loriaux, D. L., & Klein, R. P. (1985). Behavior problems and social competence in girls with precocious puberty. *Journal of Pediatrics, 106*, 156–160.

Styne, D. M., & Grumbach, M. M. (1986). Puberty in the male and female: Its physiology and disorders. In S. S. C. Yen & R. B. Jaffe (Eds.), *Reproductive endocrinology: Physiology, pathophysiology, and clinical management* (2nd ed., pp. 313–384). Philadelphia: Saunders.

See Also

Cognitive Abilities and Physical Maturation; Growth Spurt, Adolescent; Maturational Timing, Antecedents of in Girls; Maturational Timing Variations in Adolescent Girls, Consequences of; Menarche and Body Image; Menarche, Secular Trend in Age of; Menstrual Cycle; Physical Status and Timing in Early Adolescence, Measurement of; Pubertal Development, Assessment of; Puberty, Body Fat and; Puberty Education; Puberty, Endocrine Changes at; Puberty, Hypothalamic-Pituitary Changes of; Puberty, Sport and; Spatial Ability and Maturation in Adolescence; Spermarche.

Puberty, Sport and

Robert M. Malina
University of Texas at Austin

Competitive sports have an important role not only in the adolescent's own world, but also in the broader sociocultural complex within which the adolescent lives. Most communities provide some form of agency-sponsored athletic competition for boys and girls, often beginning at 5–6 years of age. Interscholastic athletic competition for boys at the junior and senior high school levels is an established feature of the American way of life and is rapidly attaining salience for many junior and senior high school girls as well.

The number of children who occasionally and regularly participate in organized sports generally reaches a maximum between 11 and 13 years of age. The decline in participants after these ages is related in part to changing interests and preferences, to variation in the timing of the adolescent growth spurt and sexual maturation, to the social demands of adolescence, and to the quest for independence. Further, the demands and selection criteria for specific sports, and the level of competition for all sports, ordinarily become more rigorous as the age of participants increases. Those who persist in sport are often labeled as elite athletes, many of whom compete internationally in sports such as gymnastics and swimming.

Given the relatively widespread participation and the relatively young ages at which adolescents begin systematically training for sport, concern is often expressed about the effects of rigorous training and competition on the growth and maturation of the young athletes. Concern is often specifically expressed about possible effects of regular training for sport on the timing and tempo of the adolescent growth spurt and sexual maturation.

Need for a Biosocial Perspective

Although the focus of this entry is on the role of regular training for sport as a possible influence on growth and maturation during adolescence, it must be noted that training is only one of many factors that may modify these biological processes. There are many other factors which may influence these processes, and they are often in or mediated through the social environments of the developing individual. Hence, growth and maturation, though they are biological processes, should not be approached in a solely biological manner. A biosocial perspective is essential.

When environmental conditions are optimal, growth and maturation are regulated primarily by genetic factors. Genotype-environment interactions mediate the responsiveness of individuals to various stresses. Many stresses that can affect growth and maturation are either directly or indirectly influenced by social environments. For example, energy and nutrient intake are to a large extent directed by the family, especially the mother; participation in sport, including training, is influenced by home, school, and community environments; family size is related to the age at menarche, but the mechanism of this relationship is not known. Growth and maturation are thus outcomes of multiple interactions between the individual and his/her environments. Given the complexity of environmental sources of stress, a single stress, such as regular training for sport, operating over a significant period of a child's life, will not by itself determine the individual's growth and maturation.

Training for Sport

Training refers to regular, systematic practice of physical activities such as running, swimming, and games/sports at specific intensities and for specific periods of time, often with competition as the objective. Physical activity is not necessarily the same as regular training, although physical activities comprise such programs. Training programs vary in kind (e.g., endurance, strength, and sports skill training) but may include a variety of training stimuli (e.g., both strength and endurance training in swimming, or endurance and skill training in soccer). Training is thus not a single entity; rather, it can be viewed as a continuum from relatively mild to severely stressing physical work.

Young Athletes

Young athletes are usually defined in terms of success on agency or interscholas-

tic teams, in selected club and age-group competitions, and in national and international competitions. They tend to be a highly selected group who often differ in size, physique, and maturity status relative to the general population of children and youth. Selection is ordinarily based on skill, but size and physique are also criteria. Variation in size and physique is in part related to the maturity status of the individual. Within a given chronological age group, children advanced in biological maturity status are, on average, taller and heavier, and have a larger fat-free mass and fat mass than those who are delayed. The maturity-associated differences are most pronounced during midadolescence. Late maturing children generally catch up in stature as they experience their growth spurts, but the differences in body weight and composition tend to persist. Variation in maturity status also influences physical performance, but does so differentially in boys and girls. Among boys, those advanced in maturity status within a given age group tend to be stronger and to perform better on tests of motor performance. Those differences relate in part to the size advantage of early maturing boys. Among girls, early maturers tend to be slightly stronger in early adolescence, but as adolescence continues, the differences between girls in contrasting maturity groups are reduced considerably. There is little consistent difference in the motor performance of early and late maturing girls, and the latter are often included among the good performers.

Successful young male athletes in several team and individual sports (American football, baseball, swimming, track and field, cycling) during early adolescence, in general, tend to be early maturing (i.e., advanced in skeletal and sexual maturation). But young ice hockey players, gymnasts, and distance runners tend to be somewhat delayed in maturity status. However, as maturity-associated differences in size are reduced with the catch-up of late maturing boys, the size and maturity status of young male athletes is of less significance, so that the pool of successful athletes in late adolescence may be different from that in early adolescence.

In contrast to boys, successful young female athletes tend to be delayed in skeletal and sexual maturation. The data are derived largely from individual sports such as gymnastics, figure skating, and ballet, with a noticeable lack of data for participants in team sports. Age-group swimmers in late childhood and early adolescence are often an exception in that many are advanced or average in maturity status. However, retrospective data for the age at menarche in late adolescent and young adult athletes in a variety of individual and team sports almost invariably indicate later mean ages at menarche compared to nonathletes.

Training, Growth, and Maturation of Young Athletes

Given the nature of the data on young athletes, which are largely cross-sectional, and selection practices in youth sports, especially as competitive levels increase, it is difficult to make inferences about the role of regular training as a factor influencing the growth and maturation of young athletes. Regular training has no apparent effect on statural growth. But training for sport *is* an important factor in the regulation of body weight. Regular training often results in a decrease in fatness and an increase in fat-free mass in adolescent boys. Short-term observations on girls, which are limited to gymnasts and swimmers, suggest similar trends, especially for fatness. Sex differences in the responses of fat-free mass

and fat mass to intensive training during growth perhaps merit further consideration.

There does not appear to be a significant effect of regular training on physique during growth. Some forms of training, however, may result in muscular hypertrophy of the body parts specifically exercised (e.g., thoracic and arm musculature in male gymnasts or shoulder musculature in young swimmers).

Regular training does not influence the timing of the adolescent growth spurt. Mean ages at peak height velocity are quite similar in boys classified as active and inactive, or regularly active and normally active. Corresponding data for girls are not presently available.

Regular training does not influence skeletal maturation of the hand and wrist, which is the area of the body used most often in growth studies as an indicator of skeletal maturity. The presently available data are consistent for adolescent athletes of both sexes.

Longitudinal data on the sexual maturation of either girls or boys undergoing regular training are not extensive. Discussions of training and sexual maturation most often focus on later mean ages at menarche in athletes and intensive training is suggested as the factor that delays menarche. Data dealing with the inferred relationship between training and menarche are, however, associational and retrospective. Other factors such as dietary restriction and family size, which are known to influence menarche, are ordinarily not considered. Selection for physical characteristics in some sports is an additional factor. A linear physique, which is valued among young ballet dancers and gymnasts, is also a physique associated with delayed maturation.

In contrast to concern for training and menarche, little is said about the effects of training on the sexual maturation of boys. Given the logic used relating training to delayed menarche, and given the advanced maturity status of many young male athletes, should it be concluded that training accelerates their maturation? Definitely not! Association does not imply a cause-effect sequence.

Overview

Young athletes of both sexes grow as well as nonathletes (i.e., the experience of training for sport does not have harmful effects on growth and maturation). Regular training does not influence stature, skeletal maturation, age at peak height velocity, and sexual maturation. The young trained athlete, however, is generally leaner, having a lesser percentage of body weight as fat. Maturity relationships are not entirely consistent across sports. Male athletes often tend to be advanced in maturation compared to nonathletes. These differences seem more apparent in sports where size is a factor. On the other hand, female athletes tend to be delayed in maturity status. There is a need for prospective studies in which young athletes are followed from the prepubertal state through puberty, in which several indicators of growth and maturity are monitored, and in which training as well as other factors known to influence growth and maturation are considered.

References

Malina, R. M. (1983a). Menarche in athletes: A synthesis and hypothesis. *Annals of Human Biology, 10*, 1–24.

Malina, R. M. (1983b). Human growth, maturation, and regular physical activity. *Acta Medica Auxologica, 15*, 5–27.

Malina, R. M. (1988a). Biological maturity status of young athletes. In R. M. Malina (Ed.), *Young athletes: Biological, psychological, and educational perspectives* (pp. 121–140). Champaign, IL: Human Kinetics.

Malina, R. M. (1988b). Competitive youth sports and biological maturation. In E. W. Brown & C. F. Brant (Eds.), *Competitive sports for children and youth* (pp. 227–245). Champaign, IL: Human Kinetics.

Malina, R. M. (1989). Growth and maturation: Normal variation and the effects of training. In C. V. Gisolfi & D. R. Lamb (Eds.), *Perspectives in exercise science and sports medicine: Vol. 2. Youth, exercise, and sport* (pp. 223–265). Indianapolis, IN: Benchmark Press.

See Also

Cognitive Abilities and Physical Maturation; Growth Spurt, Adolescent; Maturational Timing, Antecedents of in Girls; Maturational Timing Variations in Adolescent Girls, Consequences of; Menarche and Body Image; Menarche, Secular Trend in Age of; Menstrual Cycle; Physical Status and Timing in Early Adolescence, Measurement of; Pubertal Development, Assessment of; Puberty, Body Fat and; Puberty Education; Puberty, Endocrine Changes at; Puberty, Precocious, Treatment of; Spatial Ability and Maturation in Adolescence; Spermarche.

Reasoning in the Adolescent

Willis F. Overton
Temple University

If adolescence is a time of transitions, the change from childhood to adolescent reasoning represents perhaps the most central and basic of these transitions. Changes in the reasoning process have profound influences on changes in the way the adolescent reasons about many specific contents, including the nature of self, identity, gender, morality, social relations, friendship, knowing, science, as well as other life issues.

Reasoning is itself a set of processes that composes part of a more general set of processes known as cognition. Cognitive processes are all those that concern the construction, acquisition, maintenance, and utilization of knowledge. Thus, cognitive processes include, at least, perception, thinking, language, memory, and problem solving. Thinking is the construction and manipulation of symbols, and reasoning is a particular type of thinking. Reasoning is thinking that involves inference, that is, the process where one proposition (the conclusion) is arrived at and accepted on the basis of other propositions (the premises) that were originally accepted. Premises provide the evidence from which inferences are made to lead to a conclusion. Reasoning, then, is distinguished from other types of thinking such as associative thinking, fantasy thinking, productive thinking, and creative thinking that do not directly involve the inference process.

Reasoning is a specific type of thinking, but there are also several types of reasoning. Usually, these are divided into inductive reasoning processes and deductive reasoning processes. Induction involves inference that moves from the particular to the general. For example, to reason from having seen several white swans that "All swans are white" is to reason inductively. Examples of inductive reasoning include pragmatic reasoning—where inferences are based on evidence drawn from the context—and statistical reasoning—where inferences are made on the basis of probabilities. In these, and all other cases of inductive processes, the premises provide probable, but not certain or necessary, evidence for the conclusions. No matter how many white swans one sees (premises), it may still be the case that some unseen swans are not white.

Deductive reasoning is unique because it is the only reasoning where the inference process leads from general to particular statements. Deductive reasoning is also the only reasoning where the premises provide absolutely conclusive (*"necessary"*) evidence for the truth of the conclusions. Reasoning "If computers are used for business, then the cost of a computer merits a tax deduction," "This computer is used for business," therefore "The cost of this computer merits a tax deduction," is deductive reasoning. If the premises are true, they provide absolute certainty that the conclusion is true.

Although deductive reasoning is also referred to as formal logical reasoning, there are important distinctions between logic and deductive reasoning. Logic is a discipline that is concerned with establishing the rules of valid arguments and argument forms. For example, a simple argument form (the one used in the above computer example) is called *Modus Ponens*. Modus Ponens asserts "If p then q," "p is the case," "therefore, q is the case." The discipline of logic produces systems of such rules and these are called logics. Neither the discipline of logic, nor the logic systems are concerned with the human processes of reasoning that produce valid and invalid arguments. Deductive reasoning refers to inference processes that lead to behavior that is consistent with a logic system. Deductive reasoning is the domain of cognitive and cognitive developmental psychologists. These psychologists use logic systems as models or standards against which to judge the reasoning processes of individuals.

Psychology's understanding of the way cognitive processes develop, and particularly the way thinking and reasoning develop, continues to be shaped in the context of Jean Piaget's theory. This is especially true for understanding transitions to, and the nature of, adolescent reasoning. From this Piagetian context, adolescence is understood as one of several major life periods at which the cognitive system becomes differentiated and reintegrated in such a way that novel forms of reasoning become available to the individual (see Piaget, 1987; Piaget & Garcia, 1986). The infant begins the journey initially as an organized activity system. Early interactions with the actual world lead—through processes of assimilation and accommodation—to reorganization of this activity at a *level of sensorimotor coordinations of actions.* Here a fragmented and action-embedded logic is ultimately achieved. That is, the young child comes to behave in ways that the psychologist describes as very roughly matching a very primitive logic system. However, neither thought nor reasoning are available as processes at this level due to the absence of mobile symbols. The achievement of a logic, primitive as it is, is action based and not based on thought or reasoning.

In the next major period the cognitive system becomes reintegrated and differentiated at the *level of representational knowing.* Here the child develops the capacity to construct and acquire symbols and symbol systems. This period extends from early toddlerhood through middle childhood and covers what Piaget termed preoperational and concrete operational thought. During this period thinking and reasoning processes gradually differentiate out of the matrix of symbolic cognitive processes. Further, the action logic of the sensorimotor period forms the context for the acquisition of a symbolic logic of classes and relations. Both inductive and deductive reasoning are in evidence, but deductive reasoning is fragmented, and highly embedded in concrete contexts. The child may be able to reason about some real or imagined events, but the child is unable to reason in a systematic way about a system of reason. For example, when told, "If you mow the lawn, you will receive five dollars," the child may well reason that mowing the lawn will lead to receiving five dollars. This is reasoning about a specific event. However, the child at

913 ∎

this level is less likely to understand that there is a whole system of interrelated outcomes that are relevant to this statement. For example, it is doubtful that the child at this level would understand that the logic of the situation does not prevent the possibility of receiving five dollars even if he does not mow the lawn.

It is during adolescence that cognitive processes become reintegrated at the *level of self-reflective representational knowing*. The key novelty that emerges from this reintegration is a system of symbolic knowing that permits systematic representational knowing of systematic representational knowing. With this development, the adolescent attains what Piaget termed the level of formal reasoning. Formal reasoning refers to the idea that the person can reason deductively with the form of the argument rather that reason with just the argument itself. Sometimes this is termed second order reasoning because it is reasoning about reasoning about events, real or imaginary. From another viewpoint it can be said that a formal logic has been achieved. That is, the adolescent demonstrates the capacity to behave in ways that may be described as matching a formal predicate logic system.

Formal reasoning or—to use an equivalent Piagetian term—formal operational thought, is the unique cognitive acquisition of adolescence. There are several points about this reasoning that deserve emphasis. The first of these points has to do with the specific nature of this acquisition. In Inhelder and Piaget's (1958) seminal work on the development of adolescent reasoning, a series of physics-type problems were used to assess formal reasoning. These tasks, however, confounded inductive reasoning processes, involving the isolation of variables and the generation of testable hypotheses, and deductive reasoning processes, involving the deductive testing of hypotheses. It is quite clear that only the latter processes directly implicate formal reasoning. As a consequence, most of the contemporary work that attempts to examine the transition to adolescent reasoning has turned directly to deductive reasoning tasks (see Overton, 1990a). These tasks more adequately capture the meaning of formal reasoning than do the original Piagetian tasks.

A second point about formal reasoning concerns the relation between its availability and its expression. Quite simply, there is no one-to-one relationship between these. Individuals who have developed, and who thus have this type of reasoning available in their cognitive repertoire, may, in fact, prefer to reason on a concrete level, or not to reason at all in many situations. The evaluation of formal reasoning requires the use of tasks that demand its expressions rather than tasks that allow preferred modes of thought to emerge. Further, it may be the case that although an individual has developed the competence to reason formally, the individual may not have developed the appropriate strategies or procedures to best access and apply this competence (Overton, 1990b). Reasoning competence involves adequate understanding, and reasoning procedures involve successful strategies for accessing this competence. They are interrelated and necessary components for a complete analysis of formal reasoning.

As a final point concerning formal reasoning, it should be mentioned that although it is abstract reasoning, this does not mean that formal reasoning can successfully operate without content. For a time it was believed that formal reasoning was reasoning in terms of abstract symbols completely divorced from any content. It is now generally recognized, however, that form and content can never be entirely separated (Overton, Ward, Noveck, Black, &

O'Brien, 1987; Ward & Overton, 1990). Tasks involving only abstract symbols seem to put too heavy a requirement on memory to serve as an adequate evaluative tool for reasoning (Overton, 1990b; Overton et al., 1987).

As suggested earlier, the acquisition of formal reasoning competence has widespread effects across a broad range of cognitive activities. Most closely related to the deductive nature of the formal reasoning process itself is the adolescent's emerging capacity to test scientific hypotheses in a systematic fashion. Prior to adolescence hypothesis testing is fragmented and the child frequently fails to understand that a system of interrelated possibilities must be kept constant while one possibility is tested in the actual world. Systematic hypotheis testing, in turn, implies that the adolescent is now capable of beginning reasoning from systems of possibilities rather than from actual events. Thus, the adolescent can begin with universal ideas and move to particular events. This, in itself, represents a major advance over the child whose ideas tend to be highly sensitive to contextual constraints of the actual world.

To be capable of beginning from universals rather than from particulars opens a whole new world for the adolescent. In general terms, it permits systematic thinking about systems of thought. For example, the adolescent becomes capable of consciously asserting a metaphysical position such as idealism, with its emphasis on the primacy of the abstract, or materialism, with its emphasis on the primacy of the particular. Further, such systems can be compared and evaluated in terms of such abstract systemic features as coherence, consistency, and scope. On a more pragmatic level, systematic planning for the future becomes possible. While even the young child can "plan" to become a doctor, it is only at the level of formal reason-

ing that this plan becomes a system of possibilities that extends into the future and is realized in an ordered pattern of actual events.

Beginning from universals rather than particulars also has the potential to influence each of the topical areas upon which the adolescent focuses attention. For example, in the area of moral reasoning the adolescent, in contrast to the child, can make judgments in the context of universal principles of morality. Understandings of the nature of self and identity, and the other topics mentioned at the beginning of this entry, are similarly influenced by the adolescent's new-found ability to generate universal and coordinated systems of ideas and to reason systematically within these systems.

References

Inhelder, B., & Piaget, J. (1958). *The growth of logical thinking from childhood to adolescence.* New York: Wiley.

Overton, W. F. (Ed.), (1990a). *Reasoning, necessity, and logic: Developmental perspectives.* Hillsdale, NJ: Lawrence Erlbaum Associates.

Overton, W. F. (1990b). Competence and procedures: Constraints on the development of logical reasoning. In W. F. Overton (Ed.), *Reasoning, necessity, and logic: Developmental perspectives* (pp. 1–32). Hillsdale, NJ: Lawrence Erlbaum Associates.

Overton, W. F., Ward, S. L., Noveck, I. A., Black, J., & O'Brien, D. P. (1987). Form and content in the development of deductive reasoning. *Developmental Psychology, 23,* 22–30.

Piaget, J. (1987). *Possibility and necessity. Volume 1. The role of possibility in cognitive development. Volume 2. The role of necessity in cognitive development.* Minneapolis: University of Minnesota Press.

Piaget, J. & Garcia, R. (1986). *Vers une logique*

de signification. Geneva, Switzerland: Editions Murionde.

Ward, S. H., & Overton, W. F. (1990). Semantic familiarity, relevance, and the development of deductive reasoning. *Developmental Psychology, 26,* 488–493.

See Also

Cognition, Adolescent; Cognition and Health; Cognitive Abilities and Physical Maturation; Cognitive and Psychosocial Gender Differences, Trends in; Cognitive Development; Egocentrism Theory and the "New Look" at the Imaginary Audience and Personal Fable in Adolescence; Formal Operational Thinking and Identity Resolution; Illness, Adolescents' Conceptualization of; Inhelder, Barbel; Introspectiveness, Adolescent; Memory; Piaget, Jean; Relativistic Thinking in Adolescence; Reasoning, Higher-Order, in Adolescence; Scientific Reasoning, Adolescent; Social Intelligence in Adolescence; Spatial Ability and Maturation in Adolescence.

Reasoning, Higher-Order, in Adolescence

Deanna Kuhn
Columbia University

Do adolescents develop new ways of thinking they did not possess as children? Though it has often been suggested that with increasing age thought develops in certain broad respects such as abstractness (Werner, 1948), Piaget and Inhelder were the first to propose that a major reorganization in the structure of thought occurs during the period of early to middle adolescence (Inhelder & Piaget, 1958). Their theory has played a dominating role in the investigation of adolescent thinking over the last 25 years.

With the emergence of the cognitive stage of formal operations, Piaget and Inhelder claimed, adolescents assume new thought capacities, created by the reorganization of the concrete operations that characterize childhood thought into a new, more comprehensive structure. Formal operations are second-order "operations on operations," that is, cognitive operations on the elementary operations of classification and relation that comprise concrete operations. The adolescent becomes able, for example, not only to categorize animals' species and habitats but also to operate on these categorizations—to put *them* into categories and on this basis to draw inferences regarding relations that hold among species and habitats. Derivative of this second-order operatory structure is the hypothetico-deductive "scientific method": all possible relations and combinations of factors are considered, and the adolescent is able to conduct a controlled experiment, in which one factor is varied systematically to assess its effect while all others are held constant to remove their influence.

Piaget and Inhelder themselves, and other researchers following them, have suggested that these developments at adolescence extend beyond the purely cognitive into domains of personal-social cognition and behavior. The shift in focus from observing what is concretely present to contemplating possibilities, it is suggested, contributes to adolescents' increased focus on their own future and possible identities. Other researchers have noted developmental changes in self-concept (Damon & Hart, 1988), interpersonal understanding (Selman, 1980), and moral judgment (Colby & Kohlberg, 1987), and suggested their cognitive underpinnings.

Subsequent research has both supported and refuted aspects of Piaget and Inhelder's theory of formal operations. In problems in which subjects are asked to engage in scientific exploration of a phenomenon, children below adolescence perform in the unsystematic ways Inhelder and Piaget (1958) described: observations accumulate but the subject cannot isolate causal relations among variables, and invalid inferences are frequent. However, further research has shown that the performance of many adolescents and adults is far from optimum in this respect. Moreover, modest instruction or simply exercise in engaging such problems improves the performance of adults, adolescents, and children as young as 8 or 9. Both of these sets of research findings have served to cast doubt on the model of formal operations as a "structured whole" that emerges as an integrated entity within the fairly narrow age period of early adolescence.

Another characteristic of the pioneering work of Piaget and Inhelder that has led to a diminishment of its influence is its dependence on a model of formal propositional logic to portray the organization underlying adolescent thought. Recently, compelling arguments have been made against the utility of formal logic as a model of human thought (Cheng & Holyoak, 1985). Yet another factor contributing to this diminshed influence is a growing awareness that thinking occurs in a context that significantly shapes its form and expression, and these contextual factors are not ones that formal structural theories of development readily accommodate (Rogoff, 1982). In particular, with respect to simple cognitive operations such as classification and concept formation, cognitive psychologists now recognize that strictly logical criteria such as similarity cannot by themselves account for concept formation (Neisser, 1987). Instead, peoples' specific theories regarding themselves and their physical and social environments both derive from and guide their interpretation of their experience and hence the categories they form. Likewise, then, higher-order

reasoning needs to be examined within the specific meaningful contexts in which individuals use it. This is especially true during adolescence when interests are dominated by concerns of relevance to the self.

The response of some theorists and researchers to these developments has been to question whether there in fact exist broad changes in forms of reasoning with development. Instead, proponents of a domain-specific approach claim, conceptual understanding develops in terms of a succession of partially correct theories within specific content domains; *modes* of reasoning and understanding, however, remain constant (Carey, 1985).

Other recent work, however, indicates strong restructuring with development in the instruments, not just the products, of thinking. Kuhn, Amsel, and O'Loughlin (1988) have taken the child, adolescent, and adult's own theories about familiar phenomena as the starting point of their investigations and then examined how their subjects coordinate these theories with evidence. Their results indicate that this coordination process does not operate in an identical way in children, adolescents, adults, and professional scientists. In this sense, then, the metaphor of child or adolescent as scientist may be fundamentally misleading (Kuhn, 1989).

Like Piaget and Inhelder, Kuhn et al. (1988) examine the ability to execute the second-order operations of thinking *about* a theory, rather than merely *with* it. Similarly, they examine ability to think about evidence (and how it bears on a theory), rather than merely be influenced by it. Prior to adolescence, their results show, children conceive of both theories and evidence in very restricted senses, showing limited ability to differentiate and hence construct relations between the two. When theory and evidence are compatible, they often are melded into a single representation of "the way things are." Instances of this script are confused with evidence for its correctness. When theory and evidence are discrepant, their alignment is maintained either by adjusting the theory or "adjusting" the evidence, by ignoring it, or by attending to it in a selective, distorting manner. As a result, identical evidence is interpreted one way in relation to a favored theory and differently in relation to a theory not favored. The evidence thus does not retain its identity, its constancy of meaning, across a range of theories to which it relates.

In scientific exploration activities, lack of differentiation and coordination of theory and evidence is likely to lead to uncontrolled domination of one over the other. Exploration is either so theory-bound that the subject has difficulty "seeing" the evidence or is so data-bound that the subject is confined to local interpretation of isolated results, without benefit of a theoretical representation that would allow the subject to make sense of the data.

At the other end of this developmental continuum is the full differentiation and coordination of theories and evidence and the elevation of theory/evidence interaction to the level of conscious control. Consistent with earlier research is the developmental change along this continuum between middle childhood and adolescence. As important as this change, however, are the limited reasoning abilities shown by many adolescents and adults.

These results suggest the significance of the study of higher-order reasoning from a practical as well as a theoretical perspective, a significance missing in the case of less advanced forms of reasoning that develop in all individuals of normal and mental ability. What are the experiences and contexts that determine the extent to which higher-order reasoning will develop? There may be a potential during the adolescent period of the life span for facilitating development of ways of thinking about theories and evidence and ways of achieving control of their interaction in one's own thought, a potential that is absent before this period and diminished afterward. This possibility deserves the serious attention of educators.

References

Carey, S. (1985). *Conceptual change in childhood.* Cambridge: MIT Press.

Cheng, P., & Holyoak, K. (1985). Pragmatic reasoning schemas. *Cognitive Psychology,* *17*, 391–416.

Colby, A., & Kohlberg, L. (1987). *The measurement of moral judgment: Vol. 1. Theoretical foundations and research validation.* Cambridge: Cambridge University Press.

Damon, W., & Hart, D. (1988). *Self-understanding in childhood and adolescence.* Cambridge: Cambridge University Press.

Inhelder, B., & Piaget, J. (1958). *The growth of logical thinking from childhood to adolescence.* New York: Basic Books.

Kuhn, D. (1989). Children and adults as intuitive scientists. *Psychological Review, 96,* 674–689.

Kuhn, D., Amsel, E., & O'Loughlin, M. (1988). *The development of scientific thinking skills.* Orlando, FL: Academic Press.

Neisser, U. (Ed.). (1987). *Concepts and conceptual development: Ecological and intellectual factors in categorization.* Cambridge: Cambridge University Press.

Rogoff, B. (1982). Integrating context and cognitive development. In M. Lamb & A. Brown (Eds.), *Advances in developmental psychology* (Vol. 2). Hillsdale, NJ: Lawrence Erlbaum Associates.

Selman, R. (1980). *The growth of interpersonal understanding.* New York: Academic Press.

Werner, H. (1948). *Comparative psychology of mental development.*

See Also

Cognition, Adolescent; Cognition and Health; Cognitive Abilities and Physical Maturation; Cognitive and Psychosocial Gender Differences, Trends in; Cognitive Development; Egocentrism Theory and the "New Look" at the Imaginary Audience and Personal Fable in Adolescence; Formal Operational Thinking and Identity Resolution; Illness, Adolescents' Conceptualization of; Inhelder, Barbel; Introspectiveness, Adolescent; Memory; Piaget, Jean; Relativistic Thinking in Adolescence; Reasoning in the Adolescent; Scientific Reasoning, Adolescent; Social Intelligence in Adolescence; Spatial Ability and Maturation in Adolescence.

Relativistic Thinking in Adolescence

Bonnie Leadbeater

Yale University

Since the translation of Inhelder and Piaget's work *The Growth of Logical Thinking from Childhood to Adolescence* in 1958, adolescent thinking has been characterized as exhibiting mental structures or schema modeled after formal logic or hypothetico-deductive reasoning. Inhelder and Piaget (1958, p. 335) argued that formal operational schema are "like a center from which radiate the various more visible modifications of thinking which take place in adolescence." The modifications comprehended developing capacities to think abstractly about possibilities, including those contrary to the individual's beliefs; to generate hypotheses deductively and then empirically test them; to use planning strategies for future problem solving; to consider abstract concepts like humanity or social justice; and to engage in reflective thinking or thinking about thinking. At first idealistic and egocentric, the adolescent's thinking gradually becomes more objective. According to Inhelder and Piaget (1958, p. 345), "egocentrism . . . is the undifferentiated state prior to multiple perspectives, whereas objectivity implies both differentiation and coordination of the points of view which have been differentiated."

Inhelder and Piaget, however, leave unstated the relations between the development of mental structures characterized by formal logic or hypothetico-deductive reasoning and the development of reasoning involving the differentiation and coordination of multiple perspectives. They suggest instead that the adolescent discovers the fragility of his or her theories in discussions among friends and when he or she undertakes a real adult job; that is, through acting in the social world. How adolescents come to recognize and reconcile the subjectivity of knowledge resulting from the acknowledgment of multiple perspectives is the central problem studied by investigators of relativistic thinking in adolescence.

Piaget's formal operational model of adolescent thinking has generated widespread criticisms. Empirical challenges to the validity of the model include findings that only 40–60% of adults from Western cultures are successful at formal tasks. Cross-cultural research has also not demonstrated the universal development of formal thinking. Task performance has been found to be content specific, and other cognitive components (such as memory, familiarity with the materials, instructions given, etc.) have been found to influence performance (see reviews by Keating, 1980; 1990). Theoretically, the model has been charged with the reduction of thought to the scientific method at the expense of other models of thinking (e.g., interpretation, information processing, etc.); with the alienation of subjectivity from objective thought; with cultural and sexual biases; and with vagueness in the use of such terminology as formal logic and reflective thinking (Blasi & Hoeffel, 1974; Broughton, 1978, 1983). Piaget (1972) himself suggested that formal operational schema may not develop in unfavorable environments or that they may characterize the thinking only of individuals engaged in specialized modes of thinking such as mathematics and science.

Stimulated by this debate, research into adolescent and adult cognitive development has taken one of two directions. The first continues to investigate the belief that formal operational structures of mind are fundamental to adolescent thinking, while adult thought is seen as becoming more relativistic, contextual, open, dialectical, related to content and experience, pragmatic, etc. (see reviews by Broughton, 1983, and Leadbeater, 1986). The second has begun to explore the nature, development, and role of relativistic thinking in adolescents.

The Meaning of Relativism

The idea of relativistic thinking in its colloquial and philosophical usages carries with it a recognition of the subjective character of human knowledge, a recognition that "other minds" may not interpret the same events or facts in the same way. Expressions like "it all depends," "it's all relative," or "everyone has a right to their own opinion" acknowledge the uncertainty of knowledge inherent in multiple perspec-

tives. However, except for the radical skeptic who affirms the paradoxical belief that no one knows anything with absolute certainty, relativistic thinking is qualified by a context of interpretation. The platitudes become "it depends on . . ." or "it's all relative to . . ." (Leadbeater, 1986, 1987). Assertions may, for example, be interpreted in relation to an individual's own personal beliefs and attitudes (subjective relativism); or to the individual's spatial, temporal, or paradigmatic focus (objective relativism); or to the intellectual or conceptual background that the individual brings to the assertion from his or her cultural, historical, and ideological context (conceptual relativism) (Mandelbaum, 1982).

The Development of Relativistic Thinking

Studying the intellectual and ethical development of Harvard College students longitudinally over four years of undergraduate study, Perry (1970) describes a progression from dualism to multiplicity (skepticism) to relativism. The dualist is embedded in the facts; absolute right answers exist for everything and are known by an authority. The multiplicity position is that of the radical relativist or skeptic, who emphasizes the subjectivity of all perception and sees no possibilities for judging among these opinions. The relativist believes that reasonable, valid differences in the interpretation of facts exist and that these stem from differences in points of view, value systems, or interpretations.

Subsequent research has generally accepted Perry's findings for college students (Basseches, 1980; Broughton, 1978; Kitchener & King, 1981). However, considerable controversy exists concerning the meaning of relativism in this research (Leadbeater, 1986), and methodological problems hamper conclusions about the development of relativistic thinking in adolescents (Chandler, 1987; Kramer & Woodruff, 1986). The almost exclusive use of college student populations limits generalization of findings to younger adolescents. Researchers typically have asked subjects to describe and justify their epistemological beliefs when provided with controversial issues, relying heavily on the self-reflection and verbal abilities of subjects. Efforts to score protocols using multidimensional scoring systems that assess broad philosophical concepts such as reflective judgment; views of mind, self, and others, and dialectical thinking have interfered with both the establishment of adequate inter-rater agreement and with widespread use of the measures. Finally, few longitudinal assessments of the development of relativistic thinking have been conducted.

Based on cross-sectional studies, however, researchers have begun to converge on a theoretical description of a sequence of tacit epistemologies thought to mark the "developmental stations of doubt" (Chandler, 1987) in the evolution and resolution of relativistic thinking. These "stations" are generally regarded as positions or stances of tacit epistemologies rather than universal, invarient, developmental stages of thought. Collecting together the work of several researchers (Broughton, 1978; Chandler, 1987; Kitchener & King, 1981, 1985; Kuhn, Pennington, & Leadbeater, 1983; Leadbeater & Kuhn, 1988; Perry, 1968) the following sequence of development is suggested.[1] The prerelativistic position of the naive realist assumes that everyone shares the same meanings because reality is perceived by everyone in the same way. Differences in interpretation of the same facts are not acknowledged. This view is seen to be succeeded by the predualistic recognition that differences in perspectives are possible but that these are due to factual discrepanices originating in errors of omission, oversights, inadequate information, not seeing the same thing, etc. The idea that two persons with the same facts could disagree continues to be inconceivable.

In all subsequent positions there is a recognition of the subjective construction of knowledge and of the possibility of differences in the interpretation of the same facts. This change is seen to be fueled by the developing ability to take the perspective of another, not only in terms of seeing what the other sees but also in thinking about what the other thinks about. However, there are differences in how the recognition of multiple perspectives is seen to effect the possibility of knowing with certainty.

Initially, differences of perspectives are dualistically attributed to efforts of individuals to prejudice, bias, or distort the real facts for their own personal gain or subjective interests. In the case of two discrepant interpretations, one must be wrong. This view preserves a dualism between objective facts that are knowable and subjective interpretations that are correctable. Once the idea of a subjective domain of knowledge is acknowledged, however, it becomes increasingly difficult to preserve an independent domain of absolutely certain facts. As Chandler (1987, p. 141) puts it, the "well is poisoned" and the prospect that diversity of opinion and uncertainty is fundamental to all knowledge looms large.

At the next position, the individual skeptic or radical relativist holds that all

1. Titles given to each level in the suggested sequences of relativistic thinking have varied from author to author. Those used here (naive realist, predualist, dualist, etc.) are meant to suggest the underlying philosophical stance of the position.

knowledge is subjectively constructed in the mind of the knower. Thus, no one knows anything with absolute certainty and everyone-has-a-right-to-their-own-opinion. What is known depends on the eye of the beholder. Alternately, the skeptic can avoid the disequilibrium of skepticism through a commitment in faith to a transpersonal authority (science or God), who alone is acknowledged as having privileged access to truth (dogmatism). Continuing the developmental sequence, tacit epistemologies leading away from skepticism offer standards or grounds for making better decisions, or for distinguishing between more or less rational arguments (postskeptical rationalism). In the case of discrepant viewpoints, underlying facts can be detected through appeal to methods of critical inquiry like hypothesis testing, elimination of contradictions, etc. (objective relativist) or through open discussion of all interpretations (hermeneuticist).

Avenues for Future Research

While early studies suggested that relativistic thinking developed late in adolescence, recent research shows evidence of relativistic thinking in the majority of high school students, and gives some support to age-linked differences compatible with the above sequence of epistemological positions (Chandler, Ball, & Boyes, 1988; Clinchy, Lief, & Young, 1977; Clinchy & Mansfield, 1985; Kramer & Woodruff, 1986; Leadbeater & Kuhn, 1988). It remains unclear, however, what motivates developmental changes in relativistic thinking. Little research has been conducted, but many factors have been suggested as influencing the development of relativistic thinking, including the growth of interpersonal understanding or role-taking abilities,

the development of formal thinking, the growth in the legitimation of or tolerance for others' opinions in peer discussions, and the availability of opportunities for the discussion of discrepant viewpoints. Detecting whether development is in the direction of the sequence described or takes an alternative route reflecting skips or even reversals in this sequence also awaits further longitudinal research. Finally, implications of developmental differences in relativistic thinking have also not been widely studied. Some adolescent behaviors and problems (for example, cliquishness and the press toward conformity, prejudice or stereotypy, joining of dogmatic cults or advocating an exclusive set of religious or secular beliefs, as well as suicide attempts) may reflect efforts of adolescents to cope with the "vertigo" or "epistemological loneliness" stemming from the realization of the relativistic nature of knowledge (Chandler, 1975; Chandler et al., 1988).

References

Basseches, M. (1980). Dialectical schemata: A framework for the empirical study of the development of dialectical thinking. *Human Development, 23,* 400–421.

Blasi, A., & Hoeffel, E. C. (1974). Adolescence and formal operations. *Human Development, 17,* 344–363.

Broughton, J. (1978). The development of concepts of self, mind, reality, and knowledge. In W. Damon (Ed.), *New directions in psychology: Social cognition* (pp. 75–100). San Francisco: Jossey-Bass.

Broughton, J. (1983). Not beyond formal operations but beyond Piaget. In M. Commons, R. Richardson, & C. Armon (Eds.), *Beyond formal operations in late adolescent and adult cognitive development* (pp. 395–411). New York: Praeger.

Chandler, M. (1975). Relativism and the problem of epistemological loneliness. *Human Development, 18*, 171–180.

Chandler, M. (1987). The Othello effect: Essay on the emergence and eclipse of skeptical doubt. *Human Development, 30*, 137–159.

Chandler, M., Ball, L., & Boyes, M. (1988, March). *Relativism and stations of epistemic doubt.* Paper presented at the second biennial meeting of the Society for Adolescent Development, Alexandria, VA.

Clinchy, B., Lief, J., & Young, P. (1977). Epistemological and moral development in girls from a traditional and a progressive high school. *Journal of Educational Psychology, 69*, 337–343.

Inhelder, B., & Piaget, J. (1958). *The growth of logical thinking from childhood to adolescence.* New York: Basic Books.

Keating, D. (1980). Thinking processes in adolescents. In J. Adelson (Ed.), *Handbook of adolescent psychology* (pp. 211–246). New York: John Wiley and Sons.

Keating, D. (1990). Structuralism, deconstruction, reconstruction: The limits of reasoning (pp. 299–319). In W. F. Overton (Ed.), *Reasoning, necessity, and logic: Developmental perspectives.* Hillsdale, NJ: Lawrence Erlbaum Associates.

Kitchener, K., & King, P. (1981). Reflective judgment: Concepts of justification and their relationships to age and education. *Journal of Appled Developmental Psychology, 2*, 106–116.

Kitchener, K., & King, P. (1985). The reflective judgment model: Ten years of research. In M. Commons, R. Richardson, & C. Armon (Eds.), *Beyond formal operations in late adolescent and adult cognitive development* (pp. 395–411). New York: Praeger.

Kramer, D. A., & Woodruff, D. S. (1986). Relativistic and dialectical thought in three adult age-groups. *Human Development, 29*, 280–290.

Kuhn, D., Pennington, N., & Leadbeater, B. (1983). Adult reasoning in developmental perspective: The sample case of juror reasoning. In P. Baltes & O. Brim (Eds.), *Lifespan development and behavior* (Vol. 5, pp. 157–195). New York: Academic Press.

Leadbeater, B. (1986). The resolution of relativism in adult thinking: Subjective, objective, or conceptual? *Human Development, 29*, 291–300.

Leadbeater, B., & Kuhn, D. (1988). Interpreting discrepant narratives: Hermeneutics in adult cognition. In J. Sinnott (Ed.), *Everyday problem solving* (pp. 175–190). New York: Praeger.

Mandelbaum, M. (1982). Subjective, objective, and conceptual relativism. In J. W. Meiland & M. Krausz (Eds.), *Relativism, cognitive and moral* (pp. 34–61). Notre Dame, IN: University of Notre Dame Press.

Perry, W. (1970). *Forms of intellectual and ethical development in the college years.* New York: Holt, Rinehart & Winston.

Piaget, J. (1972). Intellectual evolution from adolescence to adulthood. *Human Development, 15*, 1–12.

Selman, R. L. (1980). *The growth of interpersonal understanding.* New York: Academic Press.

See Also

Cognition, Adolescent; Cognition and Health; Cognitive Abilities and Physical Maturation; Cognitive and Psychosocial Gender Differences, Trends in; Cognitive Development; Egocentrism Theory and the "New Look" at the Imaginary Audience and Personal Fable in Adolescence; Formal Operational Thinking and Identity Resolution; Illness, Adolescents' Conceptualization of; Inhelder, Barbel; Introspectiveness, Adolescent; Memory; Piaget, Jean; Reasoning, Higher-Order, in Adolescence; Reasoning in the Adolescent; Scientific Reasoning, Adolescent; Social Intelligence in Adolescence; Spatial Ability and Maturation in Adolescence.

Religion and Adolescence

Bernard Spilka
University of Denver

For over a century theoretical definitions of religion have occasioned more criticism than agreement. The prevailing view is that such definitions are likely to be satisfactory only to their authors (Yinger, 1967). The only alternative is to rely on operational measures of religious content such as behaviors, measured beliefs, or reports of religious experience. With few exceptions attention has focused on attendance at services, ceremonial activity, questionnaire responses, and interviews (Spilka, Hood, & Gorsuch, 1985).

The Piagetian interview method has been utilized to understand adolescent religious ideation as an aspect of cognitive development. Concepts of God, prayer, and faith identification have been explored in this manner (Elkind, 1971; Fowler, 1981; Goldman, 1964; Havighurst & Keating, 1971). This work has resulted in various characterizations of the faith of youth as (1) individualistic (Harms, 1944); (2) stressing a practical idealism (Smith, 1941); (3) deconcretized and abstract (McCann, 1955); and (4) private, abstract, and differentiated (Long, Elkind, & Spilka, 1967). Cognitively abstruse and highly personalized images and ideas dominate during the teen years. Such views are said to be the outcome of formal operational thinking in which self-reflection plays a central role (Fowler, 1981). Spiritual reflective reference, however, seems to be part of a larger process of self- and other-understanding, and consists of intellectually and emotionally making comparisons and relationships. Adolescent religion is therefore one aspect of a more general effort by youth to locate themselves in the scheme of things, to establish meanings that involve self, others, and ultimates (Fowler, 1981). The idea of an immanent boundless deity with unlimited knowledge and power has also been theorized to be a normal and natural result of cognitive development (Elkind, 1970).

American youth are basically a religious group, but it is a group that evidences much variation and conflict. Orthodoxy, liberalism, and individual experimentation are easily found (Damrell, 1978; Strommen, 1974). Ninety-five percent of 13–18 year-olds profess a belief in God, and this is comparable to adults. Though 90% express some degree of confidence in organized religion, and about 75% claim that their religious beliefs are fairly to very important to them, the same proportion feel that one can be a good Christian or Jew without attending a church or synagogue (Gallup & Poling, 1980). Most adolescents take their faith seriously, but they frequently find themselves caught between institutional religion and their personal spiritual views (Gallup & Poling, 1980).

Concurrently, many signs of lessening

religious commitment are also evident as conservatism transforms into liberalism. For example, the view that "only good people go to heaven" declines from 72% to 33%; and belief in "the literal truth of the Bible" reduces from 79% to 34%. In addition, weekly church attendance drops from 70% to 42% (Argyle & Beit-Hallahmi, 1975).

Since adolescence is a period in which the establishment of identity involves significant questions about personal meaning, religion is often of great significance (Strommen, 1974). Frequently, such concerns are manifested through affiliation with a religious body or doctrine. Adolescence has thus been considered *the* time of conversion. Studies comprising over 15,000 people reveal an average age for conversion of 15.2 years (Johnson, 1959). Overwhelmingly, these commitments are to the system in which the convert was reared (Wilson, 1978). Where attachment occurs to a different group, whether cult, sect, or church, the long term propensity is to return to the original fold (Mauss & Peterson, 1973; Wright, 1987).

Conversion may or may not involve intense personal spiritual experiences, but acute and vivid encounters with God have been reported by the majority of high school youth (Elkind & Elkind, 1962; Remmers & Radler, 1957). A picture thus emerges of a rich adolescent religion that involves ideological, experiential, and behavioral concerns (Strommen, 1974).

Adolescence is, however, also a time of challenge with considerable opposition to formal church doctrine plus frequent rejection of family religious traditions. Invariably, efforts are still made to cope with spiritual issues, often in a very personalized, idiosyncratic manner (Rosen, 1965; Stewart, 1967). High conversion rates and lowering overall commitment imply a paradox, but these simply reflect the adolescent decision-making process. Some youth identify strongly with their faith; most move toward a liberal stance, and others may come to oppose all institutional forms.

Generally, parental religious involvement relates positively to that of youth, but the latter's participation in church programs is mostly a function of peer relations (Hoge & Petrillo, 1978). As a rule, when familial considerations are accounted for, very little is left to other sources of influence (Erickson, 1962; Greeley & Rossi, 1966; Himmelfarb, 1977). Religious schooling, however, has its greatest influence on formal religious knowledge, but demonstrates little effect on religious beliefs and actions. Even though secular education, especially in college, is said to counter religious commitment, such influence is dependent on the nature of the institution and its students (Feldman, 1969). Where change occurs, it is primarily among the more liberal religious students (Hunsberger, 1976, 1978).

The religion of adolescence is far from other-worldly. Whether its expressions are individualized or conventional, the faith of youth is concerned with issues of social morality and personal aggrandizement (Havighurst & Keating, 1971; Strommen, 1963, 1974; Strommen, Brekke, Underwager, & Johnson, 1972). This picture is quite complex. At least two distinctly different religious orientations have been identified among adolescents, and a third is in contention. These have been termed intrinsic or committed, extrinsic or consensual, and finally a controversial Quest faith has been proposed (Allport, 1966; Batson & Ventis, 1982; Hunt & King, 1971; Spilka, Hood, & Gorsuch, 1985).

Youth who embrace a committed-intrinsic faith emphasize moral principle and a search for truth. They evidence an altruistic-humanitarian, world-minded viewpoint, and oppose prejudice and other forms of social injustice (Allen & Spilka, 1967; Strommen, 1963, 1974). This kind of personal religion also counters the use of drugs, alcohol, and premarital sexual activity (Ernsberger & Manaster, 1981; Spilka, Hood, & Gorsuch, 1985). In essence, intrinsic faith basically is a salient moral referent for everyday behavior.

An extrinsic-consensual orientation treats faith as a utilitarian avenue for achieving personal goals. Extrinsics employ their religion opportunistically for security and personal advantage. Concerns with morality and justice are largely irrelevant to this position. This is a religion of convenience to be called upon when it serves some immediate purpose, particularly confrontation with crisis.

Recently, a Quest form of personal faith has been proposed that seems especially appropriate to adolescence. It stresses an open-minded, questioning outlook in which doubt and conflict often prevail (Batson & Ventis, 1982; Kojetin, McIntosh, Bridges, & Spilka, 1987).

In sum, religion is an important aspect of adolescent life and culture. Adolescence is a period of religious concern, search, and awakening. Faith seems to be an integral part of youth's struggle for maturity. It offers young people meanings that buttress their sense of control and esteem as they move from the protection of childhood to the independence of adulthood. By late adolescence these conflicts are usually being resolved (Hanawalt, 1963; Strommen, 1974).

References

Allen, R. O., & Spilka, B. (1967). Committed and consensual religion: A specification of religion-prejudice relationships. *Journal for the Scientific Study of Religion, 6,* 191–206.

Allport, G. W. (1966). The religious context of prejudice. *Journal for the Scientific Study of Religion, 5,* 447–457.

Argyle, M., & Beit-Hallahmi, B. (1975). *The social psychology of religion.* London: Routledge & Kegan Paul.

Batson, C. D., & Ventis, W. L. (1982). *The religious experience: A social-psychological perspective.* New York: Oxford University Press.

Damrell, J. (1978). *Search for identity: Youth, religion, and culture.* Beverly Hills, CA: Sage.

Elkind, D. (1970). The origins of religion in the child. *Review of Religious Research, 12,* 35–42.

Elkind, D. (1971). The development of religious understanding in children and adolescents. In M. P. Strommen (Ed.), *Research on religious development: A comprehensive handbook* (pp. 655–685). New York: Hawthorn.

Elkind, D., & Elkind, S. (1962). Varieties of religious experience in young adolescents. *Journal for the Scientific Study of Religion, 2,* 102–112.

Erickson, D. (1962). *Differential effects of public and sectarian schooling on the religiousness of the child.* Unpublished doctoral dissertation, University of Chicago.

Ernsberger, D. J., & Manaster, G. J. (1981). Moral development, intrinsic/extrinsic religious orientation, and denominational teachings. *Genetic Psychology Monographs, 104,* 23–41.

Feldman, K. A. (1969). Change and stability of religious orientations during college. *Review of Religious Research, 11,* 40–60, 103–128.

Fowler, J. W. (1981). *Stages of faith: The psychology of human development and the quest for meaning.* New York: Harper & Row.

Gallup, G., Jr., & Poling, D. (1980). *The search for America's faith.* Nashville, TN: Abingdon.

Goldman, R. (1964). *Religious thinking from childhood to adolescence.* London: Routledge & Kegan Paul.

Greeley, A. M., & Rossi, P. H. (1966). *The education of Catholic Americans.* Chicago: Aldine.

Hanawalt, N. G. (1963). Feelings of security and self-esteem in relation to religious belief. *Journal of Social Psychology, 59,* 347–353.

Harms, E. (1944). The development of religious experience in children. *American Journal of Sociology, 50,* 112–122.

Havighurst, R. J., & Keating, B. (1971). The religion of youth. In M. P. Strommen (Ed.), *Research on religious development: A comprehensive handbook* (pp. 688–723). New York: Hawthorn.

Himmelfarb, H. S. (1977). The interaction effects of parents, spouse, and schooling: Comparing the impact of Jewish and Catholic schools. *Sociological Quarterly, 18,* 464–477.

Hoge, D. R., & Petrillo, G. H. (1978). Determinants of church participation and attitudes among high school youth. *Journal for the Scientific Study of Religion, 17,* 359–379.

Hunsberger, B. (1976). Background religious denomination, parental emphasis, and the religious orientation of college students. *Journal for the Scientific Study of Religion, 15,* 251–255.

Hunsberger, B. (1978). The religiosity of college students: Stability and change over years at university. *Journal for the Scientific Study of Religion, 17,* 159–164.

Hunt, R. A., & King, M. B. (1971). The intrinsic-extrinsic concept: A review and evaluation. *Journal for the Scientific Study of Religion, 10,* 339–356.

Johnson, P. E. (1959). *Psychology of religion.* New York: Abingdon.

Kojetin, B. A., McIntosh, D. N., Bridges, R. A., & Spilka, B. (1987). Quest: Constructive search or religious conflict. *Journal for the Scientific Study of Religion, 26,* 111–115.

Long, D. G., Elkind, D., & Spilka, B. (1967). The child's conception of prayer. *Journal for the Scientific Study of Religion, 6,* 101–109.

Mauss, A. L., & Peterson, D. M. (1973, October). *Prodigals as preachers: Jesus freaks and the return to respectability.* Paper presented at the 1973 Convention of the Society for the Scientific Study of Religion, San Francisco, CA.

McCann, R. V. (1955). Developmental factors in the growth of a mature faith. *Religious Education, 50,* 147–155.

Remmers, H. H., & Radler, D. H. (1957). *The American teenager.* Indianapolis, IN: Bobbs-Merrill.

Rosen, B. C. (1965). *Adolescence and religion: The Jewish teenager in American society.* Cambridge, MA: Schenkman.

Smith, J. J. (1941). The religious development of children. In C. E. Skinner & P. L. Harriman (Eds.), *Child psychology* (pp. 273–298). New York: Prentice-Hall.

Spilka, B., Hood, R. W., Jr., & Gorsuch, R. L. (1985). *The psychology of religion: An empirical approach.* Englewood Cliffs, NJ: Prentice-Hall.

Stewart, C. W. (1967). *Adolescent religion: A developmental study of the religion of youth.* Nashville, TN: Abingdon.

Strommen, M. P. (1963). *Profiles of church youth.* St. Louis, MO: Concordia.

Strommen, M. P. (1974). *Five cries of youth.* New York: Harper & Row.

Strommen, M. P., Brekke, M. L., Underwager, R. C., & Johnson, A. L. (1972). *A study of generations.* Minneapolis, MN: Augsburg.

Wilson, J. (1978). *Religion in American society.* Englewood Cliffs, NJ: Prentice-Hall.

Wright, S. A. (1987). Leaving cults: The dynamics of defection. *Monographs of the Society for the Scientific Study of Religion, Monograph.* (Serial No. 7).

Yinger, J. M. (1967). Pluralism, religion, and secularism. *Journal for the Scientific Study of Religion, 6,* 17–28.

See Also

Cults, Adolescence and; Moral Development in Adolescence; Prosocial Development in Adolescence.

Rights of Adolescents

Gary B. Melton
University of Nebraska-Lincoln

Until relatively recently, even an encyclopedic review of phenomena related to adolescence would have been unlikely to include a chapter on adolescents' rights. Such an omission would have been unsurprising for two reasons. First, adolescence historically has been a concept foreign to law. A 17-year-old, like a 17-day-old, is a legal "infant." In general, the law provides for no transition between infancy and adulthood. Second, the U.S. Supreme Court did not hold that minors are "persons" under the Constitution until the landmark case of *In re Gault*, decided in 1967. Therefore, a discussion of adolescents' rights had little practical meaning until the late 1960s.

Gault spawned a plethora of Supreme Court cases about the limits of minors' rights. Although *Gault* and its progeny typically are labeled as cases about "*children's* rights," the parties involved typically have been adolescents. In one line of cases, the court has considered the rights of respondents in delinquency proceedings. Because preadolescent juveniles rarely are charged with delinquent offenses, such cases unsurprisingly have focused primarily on adolescent respondents. In that line of cases, the court has held that juvenile respondents are entitled to the procedural rights necessary for "fundamental fairness." In effect, juveniles charged with delinquent offenses have been accorded most of the due-process rights owed criminal defendants. Thus, juvenile respondents have constitutionally based rights to counsel, notice of the charges, the privilege against self-incrimination, and confrontation and cross-examination of witnesses (*In re Gault*, 1967). Analogous to criminal trials, a finding of delinquency requires proof beyond a reasonable doubt (*In re Winship*, 1970), and juveniles cannot be subjected to double jeopardy through application of both juvenile and criminal proceedings (*Breed v. Jones*, 1975).

The Supreme Court has stopped short, though, of holding that juvenile respondents have the same rights as criminal defendants. For example, juveniles do not possess a federal constitutional right to a jury trial, in part because of uncertainty about the meaning of trial by peers when juveniles are involved (*McKeiver v. Pennsylvania*, 1971).

At the same time, the Court has been reluctant to recognize special protections for juveniles under the Constitution. Despite evidence that juveniles are more likely than adult defendants to fail to appreciate their rights under the fifth and sixth amendments (Grisso, 1981), the Court rejected an argument that a juvenile respondent's request for his or her probation officer should be treated as an invocation of the privilege against self-incrimination, akin to an adult defendant's request for an attorney (*Fare v. Michael C.*, 1979). Although the Court has recognized youthfulness as a mitigating circumstance, it has failed thus far even to hold that the eighth amendment bars capital punishment of all juveniles (*Eddings v. Oklahoma*, 1982; *Penry v. Lynaugh*, 1989; *Stanford v. Kentucky*, 1989; *Thompson v. Oklahoma*, 1988; *Wilkins v. Missouri*, 1989). Resurrecting the argument that infringements on juveniles' liberty are trivial because they always are in some form of custody, the Court also has upheld preventive detention of juveniles accused of delinquent offenses not yet adjudicated (*Schall v. Martin*, 1984).

The second line of post-*Gault* cases has examined the limits of minors' rights to autonomy and privacy. The Court has considered a remarkably diverse range of specific contexts in which such rights might be expressed: access to contraceptives (*Carey v. Population Services International*, 1976); admission to mental hospitals (*Parham v. J. R.*, 1979); access to pornography (*Ginsberg v. New York*, 1968); school disciplinary proceedings (*Goss v. Lopez*, 1975), including use of corporal punishment (*Ingraham v. Wright*, 1977); school searches (*New Jersey v. T. L. O.*, 1985); political expression in public schools (*Tinker v. Des Moines Independent School District*, 1969), including student campaign speeches that include sexual innuendo (*Bethel School District No. 403 v. Fraser*, 1986); censorship of student newspapers (*Hazelwood School District v. Kuhlmeier*, 1988) and school library collections (*Board of Education v. Pico*, 1982); religious expression in public schools (*Bender v. Williamsport Area School District*, 1986)—even access to video arcades (*City of Mesquite v. Aladdin's Castle*, 1982)!

The general trends in the Supreme Court's approach to these issues are best illustrated by its ambivalent decision making in a lengthy series of cases on the limits that states may place on minors' right to privacy in abortion decisions (*Bellotti v. Baird I*, 1976; *Bellotti v. Baird II*, 1979; *City of Akron v. Akron Center for Reproductive Health, Inc.*, 1983; *H. L. v. Matheson*, 1981; *Hartigan v. Zbaraz*, 1987; *Hodgson v. Minnesota*, 1990; *Ohio v. Akron Center for Reproductive Health*, 1990; *Planned Parenthood of Central Missouri v. Danforth*, 1976; *Planned Parenthood of Kansas City, Missouri v. Ashcroft*, 1983; *Thornburgh v. American College of Obstetricians and Gynecologists*, 1986). Although the Court has recognized minors' right to privacy, it has permitted states to require a choice of parental consent or judicial review, and it has upheld parental notice statutes, as applied to immature minors. Moreover, the Court has permitted states to limit minors' privacy rights whenever *significant* state interests can be demonstrated (rather than *compelling* state interests, as normally are required whenever a constitutional right is infringed). Such limitations on adolescents' rights have been premised on unsupportable assumptions about adolescents' competence as decision makers, the vulnerability of adolescents, and the effects of various procedural alternatives (see, e.g., Interdivisional Committee, 1987; Melton, 1986, 1987b). Indeed, the common practice of the Supreme Court in cases involving expressions of autonomy and privacy by adolescents has been to recognize that a constitutionally protected interest exists, but then to discuss at great length, usually without appropriate references to social-science authority, why the interest is unimportant (Melton, 1987c).

The conflict common in Supreme Court opinions reflects to some extent the inconsistencies among youth advocates themselves (see Melton, 1983). Some youth advocates are concerned primarily with promotion of special entitlements (e.g., the right to education) designed to protect children and adolescents; others emphasize "liberation" of youth so that they can exercise greater autonomy through, for example, freedom of expression. Each perspective is informed more by underlying a priori assumptions about the nature of childhood and adolescence than by empirical data about such matters (Melton, 1987c). Each school of youth advocates also frames its agenda in the language of "rights."

In part as a result of the attention more to symbolism than to practical policy dilemmas, youth policy is largely unplanned and apparently on a collision course with itself (Melton, 1987a). At the same time that there has been unprecedented attention to the personal autonomy of adolescents, there also has been unprecedented deference to family privacy and parental autonomy. These conflicting trends have been further confused by removal of children and adolescents from their biological families at a greater pace than ever before, apparently as an expression of a "get-tough" policy on wayward adolescents and ineffective parents. The "new paternalism" in public health policy also has promoted greater intrusion on the liberty and privacy of adolescents and their families, as the state has attempted to foster healthier life-styles through selective coercion intended to reduce risky behavior by youth.

References

Bellotti v. Baird I, 428 U.S. 132 (1976).

Bellotti v. Baird II, 443 U.S. 622 (1979).

Bender v. Williamsport School District, 475 U.S. 534, *reh'g denied*, 476 U.S. 1132 (1986).

Bethel School District No. 403 v. Fraser, 478 U.S. 675 (1986).

Board of Education v. Pico, 457 U.S. 853 (1982).

Breed v. Jones, 421 U.S. 519 (1975).

Carey v. Population Services International, 431 U.S. 678 (1977).

City of Akron v. Akron Center for Reproductive Health, 462 U.S. 416 (1983).

City of Mesquite v. Aladdin's Castle, 455 U.S. 283 (1981).

Eddings v. Oklahoma, 455 U.S. 104 (1982).

Fare v. Michael C., 442 U.S. 707 (1979).

Ginsberg v. New York, 390 U.S. 629 (1968).

Goss v. Lopez, 419 U.S. 565 (1975).

Grisso, T. (1981). *Juveniles' waiver of rights*. New York: Plenum.

Hartigan v. Zbaraz, 108 S.Ct. 479 (1987), *reh'g denied*, 108 S.Ct. 1064 (1988).

H. L. v. Matheson, 450 U.S. 398 (1981).

Hazelwood School District v. Kuhlmeier, 108 S.Ct. 562 (1988).

Hodgson v. Minnesota, ___ S. Ct. ___ (1990).

In re Gault, 387 U.S. 1 (1967).

In re Winship, 397 U.S. 358 (1970).

Ingraham v. Wright, 430 U.S. 651 (1977).

Interdivisional Committee on Adolescent Abortion. (1987). Adolescent Abortion: Psychological and legal issues. *American Psychologist, 42,* 73–78.

McKeiver v. Pennsylvania, 403 U.S. 528 (1971).

Melton, G. B. (1983). *Child advocacy: Psychological issues and interventions*. New York: Plenum.

Melton, G. B. (Ed.) (1986). *Adolescent abortion: Psychological and legal issues*. Lincoln: University of Nebraska Press.

Melton, G. B. (1987a). Law and random events: The state of child mental health policy. *International Journal of Law and Psychiatry, 10,* 81–90.

Melton, G. B. (1987b). Legal regulation of adolescent abortion: Unintended effects. *American Psychologist, 42,* 79–83.

Melton, G. B. (1987c). The clashing of symbols: Prelude to child and family policy. *American Psychologist, 42,* 345–354.

New Jersey v. T. L. O., 469 U.S. 325 (1985).

Ohio v. Akron Center for Reproductive Health, __ S. Ct. __ (1990).

Parham v. J. R., 442 U.S. 584 (1979).

Penry v. Lynaugh, 109 S.Ct. 2934 (1989).

Planned Parenthood of Central Missouri v. Danforth, 428 U.S. 52 (1976).

Planned Parenthood of Kansas City, Missouri, v. Ashcroft, 462 U.S. 476 (1983).

Schall v. Martin, 467 U.S. 253 (1984).

Stanford v. Kentucky, 109 S.Ct. 2969 (1989).

Thompson v. Oklahoma, 108 S.Ct. 2687 (1988).

Thornburgh v. American College of Obstetricians and Gynecologists, 476 U.S. 747 (1986).

Tinker v. Des Moines Independent School District, 393 U.S. 503 (1969).

Wilkins v. Missouri, 109 S.Ct. 2969 (1989).

See Also

At-Risk Youth, State Policies for; Black Adolescents, the Impact of Federal Income Assistance Policies on; Carnegie Council on Adolescent Development; Handicapped Adolescents, Providing Services for; Health Services for Adolescents, Barriers to; Health Services for Adolescents in the United States, the Financing of; Health Services for Older Adolescents; Health Services to Adolescents, Delivery of; Legal Rights for Adolescents as Research Subjects; School Linked Programs, Potential of.

Risk-Taking Behaviors During Adolescence

Charles E. Irwin, Jr.
University of California, San Francisco

Susan G. Millstein
University of California

During the past decade the term *risk taking* has often been used to describe some of the behaviors and their associated negative outcomes occurring during adolescence. Homicide, suicide, eating disorders and other psychiatric disorders, vehicle use, sexual activity, and substance use have all been included under this generic construct of risk taking. A careful review of these presumed risk-taking behaviors and their outcomes leads to a classification of behavior that is more consistent with the etiologic factors of the behaviors. This classification establishes three categories of behaviors: (1) behaviors that are inherently pathogenic (e.g., psychiatric disorders, including suicide); (2) behaviors that are primarily a result of the environment and/or sociological forces (e.g., violent behaviors, including homicide); and (3) behaviors that result from an interaction of the biopsychosocial processes of adolescence and the environment (Irwin, in press; Irwin & Millstein, 1986). We purposely restrict our definition of risk taking to the last category of behaviors.

This brief review will focus on the similarities of the behaviors included under this more restricted generic construct and highlight the importance of the interaction of the biopsychosocial and environmental forces.

Behaviors associated with some of the major mortalities and morbidities of adolescents share a common theme: risk taking. Our definition of risk taking includes only volitional behaviors in which the outcomes remain uncertain. Risk-taking behavior must have a potentially noninjurious outcome as well as an outcome that may result in harm. Young people with limited experience engage in behaviors, with expectation of benefit and/or without understanding the immediate or long-term harmful consequences of their actions (Irwin, 1989).

Three behaviors fit our definition: substance use, sexual activity, and vehicle use. These behaviors have their onset in early adolescence, are prevalent in all socioeconomic groups, and account for greater than 50% of the morbidity occurring during the

■ 934

second decade of life (Irwin & Millstein, 1986). In addition, recreational vehicle use (with or without substance use) accounts for approximately 50% of the mortality during the second decade of life (Bass, Gallagher, & Mehta, 1985, National Center for Health Services Research, 1988, 1989). Over the last decade the prevalence of these three risk behaviors has either increased or remained at high levels, leading to an assumption that these behaviors are normative in spite of their well-recognized negative health outcomes (Irwin, 1987). In addition, these three behaviors are often interrelated (Irwin & Millstein, 1986; Jessor & Jessor, 1977).

Specific Risk Behaviors

SUBSTANCE USE AND ABUSE ▪

High rates of substance use have been documented in national surveys since 1975 (Johnston, O'Malley, & Bachman, 1988; National Institue on Drug Abuse, 1987). The 1988 lifetime prevalence rates of marijuana and cocaine use are 47.2% and 12.1%, respectively. These rates have declined markedly since the peak for marijuana use in 1979 and cocaine use in 1985. But it is important to note that the use of crack and cocaine as reported by the High School Survey probably underestimates the frequency of use because adolescents not in school may have higher rates of use. The 1988 rates of alcohol and cigarette use continue to remain high at 92% and 66.4% respectively.

The 1987 daily use of cigarettes is reported by 18.1% of high school seniors. Females have consistently reported greater daily use than males since 1978 (Johnston et al., 1988). In addition to the high prevalence of daily smoking for high school seniors, there is evidence to suggest that boys are using smokeless tobacco as an al-ternative to cigarettes (Connolly Winn, Hecht, Henningfield, Walker, Hoffman, 1986; Hunter, Croft & Burke, 1986). Age 12 is the mean self-reported age of onset (Centers for Disease Control, 1987).

Alcohol remains the most commonly used substance. Daily use of alcohol in 1988 remains high at 4.2%, with 34.7% of high school seniors stating that they had five or more drinks in a row sometime in the last two weeks (Johnston, O'Malley & Bachman, 1988). Alcohol consumption begins early in adolescence, with a mean age of onset of 12.6 years (National Institute on Drug Abuse, 1987). Males consistently reported more frequent and heavier use by a factor of 2 to 1.

MOTOR/RECREATIONAL VEHICLE USE ▪

Sixty percent of deaths during adolescence are caused by unintentional injuries (Mayhew, Donelson, Beirness, Simpson, 1986; National Center for Health Services Research, 1989). Hospital discharge surveys document the role of injuries, with trauma being the most common discharge diagnosis—even when one includes pregnancy-related diagnoses. Sixteen percent of all outpatient visits to doctor's office are categorized as secondary to vehicle use (Irwin, 1986). The peak time for these injuries is at night when life-style factors appear to have a greater influence on behavior (Millstein & Irwin, 1988).

SEXUAL BEHAVIOR ▪

Sexual activity described as sexual intercourse has increased dramatically from 1971 to the early 1980s (Hofferth & Hayes, 1987). In the most recent survey (1983), 77.9% of males and 62.9% of females had ever experienced intercourse by 19 years of age. These percentages run higher for blacks (92.2% for males and 77.0% for females) than for whites (75.0% for males and 60.8% for females) or Hispanics (78.5%

for males and 58.6% for females) (Hofferth & Hayes, 1987). Recent reports concerning coital activity of adolescents younger than 15 years range from 12% to 55% (Irwin & Millstein, 1986; Orr, Wilbrandt, Brack, Rauch & Ingersoll, 1989; Zelnick & Shah, 1983). Little is known about sexual behaviors other than coitus, including homosexual activity (Brooks-Gunn & Furstenberg, 1989; Weddle, McKenry, & Leigh, 1988).

Interrelationships of Risk Behaviors

Risk-taking behaviors do not exist in isolation: they tend to be associated with each other in predictable ways (Irwin & Millstein, 1986). Recently a number of investigators have been focusing on interrelationships of specific behaviors and the mechanisms responsible for their interactions (Baumrind, 1987; Irwin & Millstein, 1986; Jessor & Jessor, 1977; Mott & Haurin, 1987; Udry, 1988).

The close association between alcohol use and accidental injury is well established. Alcohol-related motor vehicle accidents remain the leading cause of mortality for 15- to 24-year-olds (National Center for Health Services Research, 1988, 1989). Alcohol has also been implicated in a large number of other unintentional injuries, including drownings, and death or injury by fires, falls, accidents associated with non-motorized vehicles (e.g., bicycles and skateboards) (Friedman, 1985; Mayhew Donelson, Beirness, Simpson, 1986; National Center for Health Services Research, 1988, 1989). The definitive role of other substances in unintentional injuries remains to be established.

Substance use is positively correlated with early sexual activity (see Ensminger, 1987, for extensive discussion). Several studies have now documented the relationship of substance use and sexual activity. Jessor and Jessor (1977) documented the association between use of marijuana cigarettes and alcohol and early sexual activity. Using drinking status as a marker for at-risk youth, they found 80% were marijuana users and better than 50% had initiated coitus (Jessor & Jessor, 1977). Zabin has documented the association of early sexual activity, ineffective contraceptive use, and cigarette use (Zabin, 1984). Analyses of the National Longitudinal Survey of Youth have attempted to further understand the relationship of substance use and sexual activity. Their results tend to indicate that early alcohol use in females is more predictive than use in males of early sexual activity (Mott & Haurin, 1987). From our longitudinal analyses of our own data, we have found that the number of risk behaviors (e.g., substance use, dangerous vehicle use, etc.) reported by white females correlates positively with their intention to become sexually active (Irwin & Millstein, in press; Kegeles, Millstein, Adler, Irwin, Cohn, & Dolcini, 1987).

Beyond the association of substance use with other risk behaviors, substances themselves are associated in predictable ways. For example, increasingly, alcohol and/or tobacco use portend the use of illicit substances. Kandel and her colleagues have documented the typical progression in a cohort of adolescents followed through young adulthood (Yamaguchi & Kandel, 1984). The sequence of progression is as follows: alcohol, cigarettes and marijuana, other illicit substances (including psychedelics, cocaine, heroin, and other nonprescribed stimulants, sedatives, and tranquilizers), and prescribed psychoactive drugs. For females, it appears that cigarettes are the drug of choice for initiation. Recently, a five-year longitudinal study has chronicled the initiation of cocaine use and its association with other substances. Alcohol use in the preceding year was an important predictor of marijuana use. And marijuana use in the preceding year was an important predictor of cocaine use in the following year (Newcomb & Bentler, 1986).

Adolescence and Risk Taking

Adolescence is a developmental period during which significant changes occur in biological, cognitive, psychological, and social processes. Major environmental changes interact with these maturational processes. There is increasing evidence that sex hormones (e.g., testosterone) play a significant independent and interdependent role in the onset of sexual behavior and other risk behaviors in males (Udry, 1988; Udry & Billy, 1987). With the onset of these maturational changes, risk-taking behavior emerges as a component of normal adolescent development (Baumrind, 1987). Experimentation with a variety of behaviors is necessary for the healthy development of the young person, but it is critical to distinguish between normal transitional risk-taking behaviors that are developmentally enhancing and those same behaviors that by their frequency or intensity are pathological expressions for which there is little evidence of secondary gain for the teenager (Baumrind, 1987; Irwin, 1987; Irwin & Ryan, 1989).

Biosocial Modes of Risk Behaviors

Several models (Irwin & Millstein, 1986; Jessor & Jessor, 1977; Udry, 1988) have been proposed that integrate adolescent developmental principles with risk factors for the development of risk-taking behaviors. Jessor and Jessor have proposed a problem behavior framework that arises from an interaction of factors that arise within and between the personality system, the perceived environment systems, and the behavior system (Jessor, 1984; Jessor & Jessor, 1977). More recently, Udry has proposed a model for males that includes the effects of sex hormones. Specifically, in looking at a factor of five behaviors (got drunk, smoked cigarettes, cut school, had sex, and used marijuana), levels of free testosterone added significant variance to a social model (Udry, 1988). In girls, there were no specific biological effects. Other models utilize the concept of sensation seeking as a personality trait that correlates with risk behaviors (Daitzman & Zuckerman, 1989; Zuckerman, 1986) and risk perception constructs (Slovic, 1987).

Our own model draws heavily upon the previous work of Jessor and Jessor, and the biological effects demonstrated by Udry, and integrates what we know about the psychosocial effects of timing of pubertal maturation. The impact of timing of puberty appears to have its greatest effect in the areas of self-conceptions (body image and self-esteem), developmental needs (heterosexual relationships, peer affiliation, family independence), performance in school (academic performance and problem behaviors), and environmental responses (peer, parental, and teacher expectations). These effects vary as a function of gender, the relationship of the adolescent's pubertal status to that of his or her peers, definitions of early and late timing, and the specific risk behavior under investigation. (For extensive discussion, see Brooks-Gunn, 1989; Brooks-Gunn, Petersen, & Eichorn, 1985; Irwin & Millstein, 1986.) In general, the most negative effects have been reported for early maturing females (Brooks-Gunn, 1988). Some recent work has shown that the effects of early maturation may be detrimental for both sexes, with early maturation in males being associated with the early initiation of sexual activity (Irwin, Millstein & Turner, 1989; Westney, Jenkins, Butt & Williams, 1984).

Figure 1 depicts our causal model of risk-taking behavior. The model maintains that timing of biological maturation affects cognitive scope, self-perceptions, perceptions of the social environment, and personal values. These four variables are hypothesized to predict adolescent risk-taking behavior via the mediating effects of risk-perception and peer-group characteristics. In a series of studies being conducted in our division at the present time, we are analyzing the strength of the various components of the model in a heterogeneous urban sample of adolescents. At present, we have found that early timing of pubertal maturation for both females and males is a good

predictor of several risk behaviors, including sexual activity, substance use, and physical fights (Irwin, Millstein & Turner, 1989; Irwin & Millstein, 1988). Several of our early analyses have focused on the relationship between onset of risk behaviors and the attributions assigned to risk behaviors. We have found that positive attributions regarding sexual activity and fighting predict their onset, whereas less negative attributions predict substance-abuse behaviors (Irwin, Millstein & Adler, 1988). Preliminary analyses of the social environment point out that adolescents in nontraditional families have a greater tendency to initiate substance-use–related behaviors earlier; however, the effects of emotional detachment (Steinberg & Silverberg, 1986; Ryan & Lynch, 1989) are powerful predictors of initiation and maintenance of risk behav-

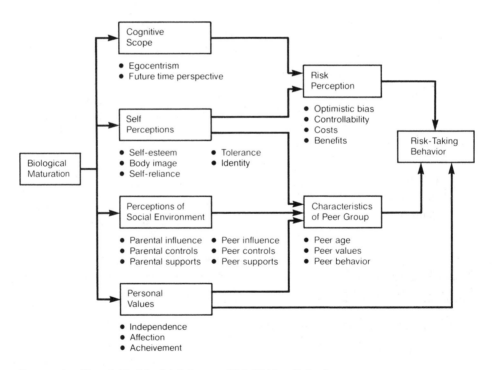

FIGURE 1   Causal Model of Adolescent Risk-Taking Behavior

Modified and adapted from: Irwin C. E. Jr. Millstein S. G. (1986). Biophysical correlates of risk-taking behaviors during adolescence. *Journal of Adolescent Health Care 6* 89S. Nov. Suppl.

iors (Turner, Irwin, & Millstein, 1989). Throughout our studies, intention to initiate a behavior remains the most critical factor in determining whether adolescents will engage in a behavior in the following year (Irwin, Millstein & Adler, 1988) which further confirms the volitional nature of these behaviors.

Figure 2 integrates our causal model with the other associated factors described in the literature (Billy & Udry, 1985; Bijur, Golding, & Haslum, 1988; Kline, Canter, & Robin, 1987; Lewis & Lewis, 1984; Newcomer & Udry, 1987; Richardson, Dwyer, McGuigan, Hansen, Dent, Johnson, et al., 1987; Schuckit, 1985) (see Irwin & Ryan, 1988, for extensive discussion of model). The model highlights the importance of biopsychosocial factors that are primarily endogenous and environmental factors that are primarily exogenous. The model further delineates the importance of predisposing factors that increase the vulnerability of the adolescent and precipitating factors that are more immediate and may be the final pathway causing the adolescent to initiate the behavior.

BIOPSYCHOSOCIAL FACTORS ■

Biopsychosocial factors that are primary include male gender, attitudes and beliefs about consequences, role modeling, affective states—including sensation seeking, aggressiveness, self-esteem, and developmental drives. Attitudes, perceptions, motivations, and, most importantly, intentions—all predict the onset of behaviors. Personality factors that have been identified include high values on independence, decreased expectation for academic performance, and less involvement in conventional activities such as religiosity.

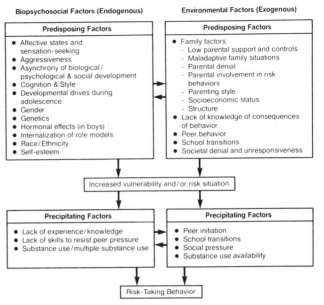

FIGURE 2   Principal Factors in Risk-Taking Behaviors

Modified and adapted from: Irwin, C. E., Jr., Millstein, S. G. (1986). Biophysical correlates of risk-taking behaviors during adolescence. *Journal of Adolescence Health Care 6* 935 and Irwin, C. E., Jr., Ryan S. (1989). Problem Behavior of Adolescents, *Pediatrics in Review 10* 235-46.

Generally decreased cognitive competence has been associated with onset of behavior, but Baumrind has demonstrated the risk of increased competence and the onset of risk behaviors (Baumrind, 1987). Precipitating factors in the biopsychosocial area include substance use, lack of experience and knowledge, and lack of skills to resist peer pressure (Scott & Cabral, 1988).

ENVIRONMENTAL FACTORS ■

The role of the environment remains an important predictor in the onset of risk behavior. The protective role of supportive environments must be acknowledged during adolescence (Irwin, 1987; Simmons & Blyth, 1987). Family and peer factors remain crucial, with parental behavior and style being important correlates of onset.

Increased parental involvement not only prevents the onset of risk behaviors but also mitigates the most negative outcomes.

Precipitating factors include substance use availability, peer onset, and multiple social transitions, including school.

Conclusion

A decade ago investigators—with a few exceptions—were attempting to understand the mechanisms involved in the initiation and maintenance of single behaviors. Over the past decade there has been considerable movement in attempting to understand the interrelationships of risk behaviors. In spite of this movement, limited attention has been devoted to understanding the mechanisms responsible for the initiation, maintenance, meaning, and natural history of the specific behaviors and how the behaviors covary. Adolescent developmental theory maintains that risk taking is functional, yet little work has been done to explore the functional nature that risk taking may actually serve (Baumrind, 1987; Jessor, 1984; Millstein, 1989; Petersen, 1988).

References

Bass, J. L., Gallagher, S. S., & Mehta, K. A. (1985). Injuries to adolescents and young adults. *Pediatric Clinics in North America, 32,* 31–39.

Baumrind, D. (1987). A developmental perspective on risk taking in contemporary America. In C. E. Irwin, Jr. (Ed.), *Adolescent social behavior and health* (pp. 91–126). *New Directions for Child Development* (No. 37). San Francisco: Jossey-Bass.

Baumrind, D. (1989). Rearing competent children. In W. Damon (Ed.), *Child development today and tomorrow* (pp. 349–378). San Francisco: Jossey-Bass.

Bijur, R., Golding, J., & Haslum, M. (1988). Behavioral predictors of injury in school-age children. *American Journal of Diseases in Children, 142,* 1307–1312.

Billy, J. O., & Udry, J. R. (1985). Patterns of adolescent friendship and effects on sexual behavior. *Psychology Quarterly, 48,* 27–41.

Brooks-Gunn, J. (1988). Antecedents to and consequences of variations in girls maturational timing. *Journal of Adolescent Health Care, 9,* 1–9.

Brooks-Gunn, J. (1989). Pubertal processes and the early adolescent transition. In W. Damon (Ed.), *Child development today and tomorrow* (pp. 155–176). San Francisco: Jossey-Bass.

Brooks-Gunn, J., & Furstenberg, F. F., Jr. (1989). Adolescent sexual behavior. *American Psychologist, 44,* 249–257.

Brooks-Gunn, J., Petersen, A. C., & Eichorn, D. (1985). The timing of maturation and psychosocial functioning in adolescence. *Journal of Youth and Adolescence, 14* (3 & 4): entire.

Centers for Disease Control. (1987). Psychosocial predictors of smoking among adolescents. *Morbidity and Mortality Weekly Report, 45,* 1S–45S.

Connolly, G. N., Winn, D. M., Hecht, S. S., Henningfield J. E., Walker, B., Jr., & Hoffmann, D. (1986). The reemergence of smokeless tobacco. *New England Journal of Medicine, 314,* 1020–1027.

Daitzman, R., & Zuckerman, M. (1980). Disinhibitory sensation seeking, personality, and gonadal hormones. *Personality and Individual Differences, 1,* 103–110.

Ensminger, M. E. (1987). Adolescent sexual behavior as it relates to other transition behaviors in youth. In S. L. Hofferth & C. D. Hayes (Eds.), *Risking the future: Adolescent sexuality, pregnancy, and childbearing* (Vol. 2, pp. 36–55). Washington DC: National Academy Press.

Friedman, I. M. (1985). Alcohol and unnatural deaths in San Francisco youths. *Pediatrics, 76,* 191–193.

Hayes, C. D. (Ed.). (1987). *Risking the future: Adolescent sexuality, pregnancy, and childbearing* (Vol. 1). Washington DC: National Academy Press.

Hofferth, S. L., & Hayes, C. D. (Eds.). (1987). *Risking the future: Adolescent sexuality, pregnancy, and childbearing* (Vol. 2). Washington DC: National Academy Press.

Hunter, S. M., Croft, J. B., & Burke, G. L. (1986). Longitudinal patterns of cigarette smoking and smokeless tobacco use in youth: The Bogalusa heart study. *American Journal of Public Health, 76,* 193–195.

Irwin, C. E., Jr. (1987) *Adolescent social behavior and health. New Directions for Child Development* (No. 37). San Francisco: Jossey-Bass.

Irwin, C. E., Jr. (1989). Risk-taking behaviors in the adolescent patient: Are they impulsive? *Pediatric Annals, 18,* 122–134.

Irwin, C. E., Jr. (in press). Risk taking during adolescence. In M. Green & R. J. Haggerty (Eds.), *Ambulatory pediatrics* (Vol. 3). Philadelphia: W. B. Saunders.

Irwin, C. E., Jr., & Millstein, S. G. (1986). Biopsychosocial correlates of risk-taking behaviors during adolescence: Can the physician intervene. *Journal of Adolescent Health Care,* 7(suppl.), 82S–96S.

Irwin, C. E., Jr., & Millstein, S. G. (in press). Correlates and predictors of risk-taking behaviors during adolescence. In L. Lipsitt & L. Mitnick (Eds.), *Self Regulating & Risk Taking Behavior: Causes & Consequences.* Norwood, New Jersey: Ablex Inc.

Irwin, C. E., Jr., Millstein, S. G., & Adler, N. E. (1988). Predictors of risk-taking behaviors in early adolescents. *Pediatric Research, 23,* 201A.

Irwin, C. E., Jr., Millstein, S. G., & Turner, R. (1989). Pubertal timing and adolescent risk taking: Are they correlated? *Pediatric Research, 25,* 8A.

Irwin, C. E., Jr., & Ryan, S. A. (1989). Problem behaviors of adolescence. *Pediatrics in Review, 10,* 235–246.

Jessor, R. (1984). Adolescent development and behavioral health. In J. D. Matarazzo, S. M. Weiss, J. A. Herd, N. E. Miller & S. M. Weiss (Eds.), *Behavioral health: A handbook of health enhancement and disease prevention* (pp. 69–90). New York: Wiley.

Jessor, R., & Jessor, S. L. (1977). *Problem behavior and psychosocial development: A longitudinal study of youth.* New York: Academic Press.

Johnston, L. D., O'Malley, P. M., & Bachman, J. G. (1988). *Illicit drug use, smoking, and drinking by America's high school students, college students, and young adults.* (DHHS Publication N. (ADM) 89-1602). Washington DC. U.S. Government Printing Office.

Kegeles, S., Millstein, S. G., Adler, N. E., Irwin, C. E., Jr., Cohn, L., & Dolcini, P. (1987). The transition to sexual activity and its relationship to other risk behaviors. *Journal of Adolescent Health, 8,* 303.

Kline, R. B., Canter, W. A., & Robin, A., (1987). Parameters of teenage alcohol use: A path analytic conceptual model. *Journal of Consulting and Clinical Psychology, 55,* 521–528.

Lewis, C. L., & Lewis, M. A. (1984). Peer pressure and risk-taking behaviors in children. *American Journal of Public Health, 74,* 580–584.

Mayhew, D. R., Donelson, A. C., Beirness, D. J., Simpson, H. (1986). Youth, alcohol, and relative risk of crash involvement. *Accident Annals and Prevention, 18,* 273–287.

Millstein, S. G. (1989). Adolescent health: Challenges for behavioral scientists. *American Psychologist, 44,* 837–842.

Millstein, S. G., & Irwin, C. E., Jr. (1988). Accident-related behavior in adolescents: A biopsychosocial view. *Alcohol, Drugs, and Driving, 4,* 1–9.

Mott, F. L., & Haurin, R. J. (1987, April/May). *The inter-relatedness of age at first intercourse, early pregnancy, and drug use among American adolescents: Preliminary re-*

sults from the National Longitudinal Survey of Youth Labor Market Experience. Paper presented at Annual Meeting of the Population Association of America, Chicago, Illinois.

National Institute on Drug Abuse. (1989). National Household Survey on Drug Abuse, 1985 and 1988, NIDA Capsules. Washington DC: U.S. Government Printing Office.

National Center for Health Services Research (1988). Vital statistics for the United States, 1985 (Vol. 1, DHHS Publication No. (DHS) 88-1113 Public Health Service). Washington DC: U.S. Government Printing Office.

National Center for Health Services Research (1989). Health United States, 1988 (DHHS Publication No. (DHS) 89-1232). Washington DC: U.S. Government Printing Office.

National Institute on Drug Abuse (1987). National Household Survey on Drug Abuse 1985 Population Estimates (DHHS Publication No. (ADM) 87-1539). Rockville, MD: Division of Epidemiology & Statistical Analysis, National Institute on Drug Abuse.

Newcomb, M. D., & Bentler, P. M. (1986). Cocaine use among adolescents: Longitudinal associates with social context, psychopathology, and use of other substances. Addictive Behaviors, 11, 263-273.

Newcomer, S. F., & Udry, J. R. (1987). Parental marital status effects on adolescent sexual behavior. Journal of Marriage and Family Counseling, 49, 235-240.

Orr, D. P., Wilbrandt, M. L., Brack, C. J., Rauch, S. P., & Ingersoll G. M. (1989). Reported sexual behaviors and self esteem among young adolescents. American Journal of Diseases of Children, 143, 86-90.

Petersen, A. C. (1988). Adolescent development. In M. R. Rosenzweig, & L. W. Porter (Eds.), Annual review of psychology (Vol. 39, pp. 583-607). Palo Alto: Annual Reviews Inc.

Richardson, J. L., Dwyer, K., McGuigan, K., Hansen, W. B., Dent, C., Johnson, C. A, et al. (1989). Substance use among eighth-

grade students who take care of themselves after school. Pediatrics, 84, 556-566.

Ryan, R. M., & Lynch, J. H. (1989). Emotional autonomy versus detachment: Revisiting the vicissitudes of adolescence and young adulthood. Child Development, 60, 340-356.

Schuckit, M. A. (1985). Genetics and the risk for alcoholism. Journal of the American Medical Association, 18, 2614-2617.

Scott, H. D., & Cabral, R. M. (1988). Predicting hazardous life-styles among adolescents based on health-risk assessment data. American Journal of Health Promotion, 2, 23-28.

Simmons, R. G., & Blyth, D. A. (1987). Moving into adolescence: The impact of pubertal change and school context. New York: Aldive Press.

Slovic, P. (1987). Perceptions of risk. Science, 236, 280-285.

Smith, E. A., Udry, J. R., & Morris, N. M. (1985). Pubertal development and friends: A biosocial explanation of adolescent sexual behavior. Journal of Health and Social Behavior, 26, 183-192.

Steinberg, L., & Silverberg, S. B. (1986). The vicissitudes of autonomy in early adolescence. Child Development, 57, 841-851.

Turner, R., Irwin, C. E., Jr., & Millstein, S. G. (1989). Effects of family structure, emotional autonomy, and parental permissiveness on adolescent risk behaviors. Journal of Adolescent Health Care, 10, 250.

Udry, J. R. (1985). Serum androgenic hormones motivate sexual behavior in boys. Fertility and Sterility, 43, 90-94.

Udry, J. R. (1988). Biological predispositions and social control in adolescent sexual behavior. American Sociological Review, 53, 709-722.

Udry, J. R., & Billy, J. O. (1987). Initiation of coitus in early adolescence. American Sociological Review, 52, 841-855.

Weddle, K. D., McKenry, P. C., & Leigh, G. K. (1988). Adolescent sexual behavior:

Trends and issues in research. *Journal of Adolescent Research, 3*, 245–257.

Westney, Q. E., Jenkins, R. R., Butts, J. D., & Williams, I. (1984). Sexual development and behavior in black adolescents. *Adolescence, 19*, 558–568.

Yamaguchi, K., & Kandel, D. B. (1984). Patterns of drug use from adolescence to young adulthood: 3. Predictors of progression. *American Journal of Public Health, 74*, 673–681.

Zabin, L. S. (1984). The association between smoking and sexual behavior among teens in U.S. contraceptive clinics. *American Journal of Public Health, 74*, 261–263.

Zelnik, M., & Shah, F. K. (1983). First intercourse among young Americans. *Family Planning Perspectives, 15*, 64–72.

Zuckerman, M. (1986). Sensation seeking and the endogenous deficit theory of drug abuse. In S. I. Szara (Ed.), *Neurobiology of behavioral control in drug abuse. National Institute on Drug Abuse Research Monograph 74* (DHHS Publication No. ADM 87–1506). Washington DC: U.S. Government Printing Office.

See Also

At-Risk Youth, State Policies for; Black Adolescents At-Risk: Approaches to Prevention; Injury during Adolescence, Risk Factors for; Physical Abuse of Adolescents.

During the preparation of this manuscript, Dr. Irwin was supported in part by the Bureau of Maternal and Child Health and Resources Development (MCJ000978 and MCJ060564) and the William T. Grant Foundation.

Rites of Passage

Kevin MacDonald
California State University-Long Beach

Although far from being a universal practice, a great many human societies have developed rituals at or near the time of puberty. These rites of passage often involve the participation of large segments of the community and tend to be highly sex-differentiated. Rites of passage are often a time of feasting and celebration and include practices such as the genital mutilation and hazing of boys and the seclusion of girls.

The ubiquity of these rituals as well as their cross-cultural diversity has resulted in attempts to find patterns of associations between the characteristics of these rituals and other theoretically important societal characteristics. Regarding the rites of males, Whiting (1964) has noted associations between polygyny, partrilocality, patrilineality, exclusive mother-son sleeping arrangements, genital mutilation, a postpartum sex taboo, and a tropical environment. Whiting proposes a causal chain beginning with a low-protein tropical environment leading to a postpartum sexual taboo (necessary to ensure adequate nutrition for the child) and polygyny (a result of the husband's desire for sexual satisfaction during the period of sexual taboo). Polygynous societies tend to be patrilocal in order for males to more easily control their co-wives. Polygyny also gives rise to exclusive mother-son sleeping arrangements and therefore a difficulty in developing a strong male identity. Highly salient male initiation rites, including practices such as circumcision, serve the psychodynamic function of producing a strong male identity by focusing the child's attention on his role as a male.

Other theorists have emphasized an association between intensive male initiation practices and the introduction of the boy into a larger kinship group. In societies ranging from low to intermediate levels of economic production there are positive associations between the level of economic production, the presence of large solidary groups of related males, and the presence of dramatic male initiation rites (Young, 1965; Paige & Paige, 1981). The initiation rites are thus proposed to function to introduce the boy to the larger male kinship (see also Cohen, 1964). Paige and Paige (1981) note the common appearance of circumcision in these rites and suggest that the danger and aversiveness of this procedure function to indicate allegiance to tribal elders in societies based on solidary groups of males, which are particularly prone to conflicting allegiances and fissioning. Finally, MacDonald (1987) proposes an evolutionary-ecological theory that emphasizes the associations between level of economic production, polygyny, and solidary groups of related males. Deriving from basic evolutionary theory, it is proposed that sexual competition among males, typified by polygyny, increases as societies become more economically productive. In addition, solidary groups of males are required to defend important resources; cooperation and competition among these males as well as patterns of fission and fusion are theorized to depend on the extent to which the males are genetically related. Male initiation rites then function, as noted by several of the above theorists, to integrate the boy into the larger male society. Their hostile and dangerous character reflects the lack of social cohesion of societies which have no centralized means of social control but which have high levels of sexual competition and low levels of common genetic interest among the males.

Regarding the puberty rites of girls, it has often been noted that these rites tend to occur around the time of menarche (e.g., Paige & Paige, 1981). Transition-rite theories (van Gennep, 1961) emphasize the ceremony as an initiation into adulthood. Brown (1963) proposes that such rites are particularly important in societies where the girl continues to live with the people she grew up with; in societies where the girl must leave her native group when she becomes an adult (i.e., patrilocal or bilocal societies), there is no need for such a ceremony because leaving in itself is a sufficient demarcation of the event. Paige and Paige (1981) propose that ceremonies surrounding menarche perform important political functions in societies with relatively low economic production. Fathers in such societies are unable to rely on extensive kinship groups to ensure their interest in their daughter's marriage but instead use the ceremony in order to form a temporary coalition within the community to perform this function. At intermediate levels of economic production menarcheal ceremonies

are unnecessary since large solidary male kinship groups operate to ensure the marriage value of the daughter. MacDonald (1987) has noted that this theory is consistent with a modern evolutionary approach, since it emphasizes the interrelationships between variation in economic production, male sexual competition, extensive male kinship relationships, and the value of females as reproductive resources.

Although the presence of a variety of theories of puberty rites suggests a fundamental lack of agreement, these theories tend to agree on the empirical correlates of these rites. The theories focus on a set of highly intercorrelated societal characteristics, some of which are then singled out as more basic and causally important than others depending on the theoretical predispositions of the author. At present there is no consensus on which of these theoretical perspectives provides the most plausible conceptualization of the underlying forces responsible for these intercorrelations.

References

Brown, J. K. (1963). A cross-cultural study of female initiation rites. *American Anthropologist*, *65*, 837–853.

Cohen, Y. A. (1964). The establishment of identity in a social nexus: The special case of initiation ceremonies and their relation to value and legal systems. *American Anthropologist*, *60*, 529–552.

MacDonald, K. B. (1987). Biological and psychosocial interactions in early adolescence: A sociobiological perspective. In R. M. Lerner & T. T. Foch (Eds.), *Biological and psychosocial interactions in early adolescence: A life-span perspective* (pp. 95–120). Hillsdale, NJ: Lawrence Erlbaum Associates.

Paige, K. E., & Paige, J. M. (1981). *The politics of reproductive ritual.* Berkeley and Los Angeles: University of California Press.

van Gennep, A. (1961). *Rites of passage.* Chicago: University of Chicago Press.

Whiting, J. W. M. (1964). The effects of climate on certain cultural practices. In W. H. Goodenough (Ed.), *Explorations in cultural anthropology* (pp. 511–544). New York: McGraw-Hill.

Young, F. W. (1965). *The function of male initiation ceremonies: A cross-cultural test of status dramatization.* New York: Bobbs-Merrill.

See Also

Conformity in Adolescence; Intimacy; Introspectiveness, Adolescent; Political Development; Self-Regulation; Temperament during Adolescence; Temperament in Adolescence and Its Functional Significance.

Runaways, Negative Consequences for

Gerald R. Adams
University of Guelph

According to a national survey of households (Opinion Research Corporation, 1976), between 750,000 and one million youths run away from home annually. While considerable debate exists regarding the definition of runaway behavior (Young, Godfrey, Matthews, & Adams, 1983), agreement exists regarding the potential for negative consequences during runaway episodes.

Runaways appear to leave home (or are thrown out) for a variety of reasons. Various observers have suggested that runaway behavior is due to the loss of authority and structure in American institutions, parental rejection, alcoholism, the diminishing value of work, peer group problems, or social change (Hardy & Cull, 1974; Leavy, 1975). Others recognize runaway behavior not as an unbalanced or delinquent act, but as a daring, courageous, yet somewhat impulsive risk-taking behavior (Chapman, 1976).

At the very core of our contemporary problem of homeless adolescents is the family. Poor home environments reflecting rejection, neglect, disinterest, hostile control, parent-adolescent conflict, poor supervision, and disorganization are consistently observed to be associated with runaway behaviors (e.g., Adams, Gullotta, & Clancy, 1986; Blood & D'Angelo, 1974; Brandon, 1974; English, 1973; Gottlieb & Chafetz, 1977; Hildebrande, 1963; Matsumoto & Suzuki, 1974; Tobias, 1970; Wattenberg, 1956). However, the impact of poor family environments on runaway children may vary for males and females. For example, Wolk and Brandon (1977) report that while runaway boys view their parents as unsupportive and punitive in their parenting practices, runaway girls view their parents as more controlling and punitive of their behaviors. These and other findings suggest that running away may be associated with low levels of control that results in immature and nonadaptive behaviors in general. Further, the findings on runaways suggest they receive limited and poor supervision, seldom obtaining assistance in school work, and live in a home environment that provides little emotional support or open communication. Therefore, the very crux of the runaway problem in North America likely begins with a dysfunctional family. Hence, intervention efforts must begin with the recognition that the runaway problem is at its core a family systems problem.

Several reviews (e.g., Adams & Adams, 1987; Nye & Edelbrock, 1980; Young, Godfrey, Matthews, & Adams, 1983) have delineated a number of substantial negative consequences associated with running away. Such consequences can be broadly categorized under the headings of home environment, juvenile justice, substance abuse, sexual behavior, academic and vocational potential, and parenting.

A major paradox of adolescence is the quest for independence while maintaining positive family relationships. Given the common strain between adolescent and parents prior to running away, it is not surprising that returning adolescents find parental controls more stringent and communications more strained (e.g., Gottlieb & Chafetz, 1977). Therefore, while negative home conditions may motivate an adolescent to run, increased stress and tension following the runaway event can create a vicious cycle of increased tension and predispositional environmental presses that enhance the chances of running again. Such findings clearly indicate that intervention programs must include efforts at effectively reintegrating the adolescent into his or her home. Merely returning the runaway, without a program that reduces tension and hostility, is unlikely to deter further runaway incidents.

Further, runaways, on the average, receive poor treatment when confronted by the legal system (Adams, 1980). In particular, girls who encounter the legal system find more problems than males (Libertoff, 1980). Evidence suggests that girls are held in detention longer than are boys and are less likely to be given the option of community program placement, which offers educational training and guidance (National Institute for Juvenile Justice and Delinquency Prevention, 1977). Thus, treatment itself is generally poor for adolescent runaways, and the stigmatizing effects of

juvenile justice action is likely to have as yet undetermined and continuing negative effects into the future on these adolescents' lives.

Brennan, Hulzinga, and Elliott (1978) report that drug use is common among runaways prior to and during a runaway episode. Further, runaways often sell drugs to support themselves. Other evidence indicates that runaways tend to drink frequently and consume large quantities of liquor (Van Houten & Golembiewski, 1978). While some experimentation with substance use is expected of most contemporary adolescents, runaways appear to be at greater risk with few parental or societal sanctions that might limit or inhibit such behavior.

Many runaways support themselves by selling sex for favors (Baizerman, Thompson, & Stafford-White, 1979; Chapman, 1976; Perlman, 1980). Girls, in particular, are at considerable risk for turning to prostitution for a living. According to Boyer and James (1981), there are 600,000 prostitutes between 6 and 16 years of age, the majority of whom emerge from runaway and throwaway backgrounds. Unfortunately, experience in such sexual deviance appears to result in a high probability of a permanent adoption of such a life-style.

While runaways appear to have more school problems than their nonrunaway peers (e.g., see Shellow, Schamp, Liebow, & Unger, 1967), running away furthers this problem by disrupting formal schooling and academic progress (Opinion Research Corporation, 1976). Further, at least one study indicates that both vocational and training difficulties continue into adulthood due to school disruption associated with runaway episodes (Olson, Lievow, Mannino, & Shore, 1980). We can speculate that the relation between less education, poor academic success, and vocational difficulties is likely to result in employability problems, less income potential, and chronic unemployment well into adulthood.

Finally, running away can result in premature pregnancy and early parenting. Perlman (1980) notes that for many runaways a sense of failure in parent-child relations stimulates many runaways toward imitating intentional pregnancies. The runaway seeks a child to love who will make her existence purposeful and meaningful. However, the quality of runaways' parenting and its implications for positive child-rearing have been questioned by several social scientists (Young et al., 1983).

Collectively, the facts as we know them today indicate that running away from home is associated with numerous negative personal and social consequences. Further, the adolescent and family appear to be at risk both prior to and following runaway episodes. The runaway problem must be viewed as both an adolescent and family problem. Runaways are at risk of not completing the normal process of development during adolescence, and are likely to have numerous negative consequences due to running away. The family of the adolescent runaway is at risk as a dysfunctional structure, and is unlikely to readily adjust to the runaway incidence. Therefore, a broad based intervention that includes individual, educational, and family therapy is needed.

References

Adams, G. R. (1980). Runaway youth projects: Comments on care programs for runaways and throwaways. *Journal of Adolescence, 3*, 321–334.

Adams, P. R., & Adams, G. R. (1987). Intervention with runaway youth and their families: Theory and practice. In J. C. Coleman (Ed.), *Working with troubled adolescents* (pp. 281–300). London: Academic Press.

Adams, G. R., Gullotta, T. P., & Clancy, M. A. (1985). Homeless adolescents: A descriptive study of similarities and differences between runaways and throwaways. *Adolescence, 20*, 715–724.

Adams, G. R., & Munro, G. (1979). Portrait of the North American runaway: A critical review. *Journal of Youth and Adolescence, 8*, 359–373.

Baizerman, M., Thompson, M. J., & Stafford-White, K. (1979). Adolescent prostitution. *Children Today, 8*, 20–24.

Blood, L., & D'Angelo, R. (1974). A progress research report on values issues in conflict between runaway and their parents. *Journal of Marriage and the Family, 36*, 486–491.

Boyer, D., & James, J. (1981). Easy money: Adolescent involvement in prostitution. In K. Weisberg (Ed.), *Women and the law: The interdisciplinary perspective* (pp. 46–59). Cambridge, MA: Schuckman.

Brandon, J. (1974). The relationship of runaways' behavior in adolescence to the individual's perceptions of self, the environment, and parental antecedents. Unpublished doctoral dissertation, University of Maryland.

Brennan, T., Hulzinga, D., & Elliott, D. S. (1978). *The social psychology of runaways.* Boston: D. C. Heath.

Chapman, C. (1976). *America's runaways.* New York: Morrow.

English, C. (1973). Leaving home: A typology of runaways. *Society, 10*, 22–24.

Gottlieb, D., & Chafetz, J. S. (1977). Dynamics of familial generational conflict and reconciliation: A research note. *Youth and Society, 9*, 283–294.

Hardy, R., & Cull, J. (1974). Runaway youth: Causes for runaway behavior. In R. Hardy (Ed.), *Psychological and vocational rehabilitation of the youthful delinquent* (pp. 69–83). Springfield, IL: Charles C. Thomas.

Hildebrand, J. (1963). Why runaways leave home. *Journal of Criminal Law, Criminology, and Police Science, 54*, 211–216.

Leavy, P. (1975). The runaways—Who are they, why do they run? *Keynote, 4*, 31.

Libertoff, K. (1980). The runaway child in America. *Journal of Family Issues, 1*, 151–164.

Matsumoto, I., & Suzuki, S. (1974). Parent-child relations and runaway behavior in first and repeated instances of running away from home. *Reports of the National Research Institute for Police Science, 15*, 99–104.

National Institute of Juvenile Justice and Delinquency Prevention. (1977). *Little sisters and the law.* Washington, DC: Department of Justice.

Nye, I. F., & Edelbrock, C. (1980). Some social characteristics of runaways. *Journal of Family Issues, 1*, 147–150.

Olson, L., Liebow, E., Mannino, F. V., & Shore, M. F. (1980). Runaway children twelve years later: A follow-up. *Journal of Family Issues, 1*, 165–188.

Opinion Research Corporation. (1976). National statistical survey on runaway youth. Part 1 (Report prepared for the Office of the Secretary, Department of Health, Education and Welfare). Princeton, NJ: Opinion Research Corporation.

Perlman, S. B. (1980). Pregnancy and parenting among runaway girls. *Journal of Family Issues, 1*, 262–272.

Shellow, R., Schamp, J., & Liebow, E., & Unger, E. (1967). Suburban runaways of the 1960's. *Monograph of the Society for Research in Child Development, 32*, 1–51.

Tobias, J. (1970). The affluent suburban male delinquent. *Crime and Delinquency, 16*, 273–279.

Van Houten, T., & Golembiewski, G. (1978). *Adolescent life stress as a predictor of alcohol abuse and/or runaway behavior.* Boulder, CO: Behavioral Research and Evaluation Corporation.

Young, R. L., Godfrey, W., Matthews, B., & Adams, G. R. (1983). Runaways: A review of negative consequences. *Family Relations, 32*, 275–281.

Wattenberg, W. (1956). Boys who run away from home. *Journal of Educational Psychology, 47*, 335–343.

Wolk, S., & Brandon, J. (1977). Runaway adolescents' perceptions of parents and self. *Adolescence, 12*, 175–188.

See Also

Aggressive Behavior in Adolescence; Attention Deficit Disorder and Hyperactivity; Bulimia Nervosa in Adolescence; Conflict, Adolescent-Parent: A Model and a Method; Delinquency; Handicapped Adolescents, Providing Services for; Learning Disabilities in Adolescents: Description, Assessment, and Management; Problem Behavior in Adolescence; Psychophysiological/Psychosomatic Problems; Self-Destructiveness, Chronic, Role of in Adolescence; Stress and the Adolescent; Stress and Coping in the Adolescent; Suicide, Adolescent; Suicides, Cluster; Type A and Teenagers.

Safer Sex and Adolescence

Mary Jane Rotheram-Borus
Cheryl Koopman

HIV Center for Clinical and Behavioral Studies
New York State Psychiatric Institute
Columbia-Presbyterian Medical Center
Columbia University

Most persons become sexually active during adolescence. The exact percentages of sexually active adolescents vary by ethnicity and gender. Black adolescents initiate sexual intercourse earlier than white or Hispanic adolescents. Males report earlier sexual activity than females (Center for Human Resource Research, cited in Hayes, 1987; Zelnik & Kantner, 1980). Seventy-eight percent of white females have experienced sexual intercourse by age 18 (Wyatt, Peters, & Gutherie, 1988). There is evidence that poor adolescents living in social service care become sexually experienced at earlier ages than other adolescents (Hein, Cohen, Marks, Schonberg, Meyer, & McBride, 1978). However, white females are increasingly initiating sexual intercourse at earlier ages (Wyatt et al., 1988; Zelnick & Kantner, 1980). While youth are sexually active, they fail to engage in safer sex (e.g., sex with a condom or erotic substitutes for intercourse), thus establishing the primary behaviors for contracting AIDS, STDs, and pregnancy during adolescence (Brooks-Gunn, Boyer, & Hein, 1988; Centers for Disease Control, 1987; Hein & Hurst, 1988).

Once a behavior has been initiated, it is more difficult to change than it would be prior to its commencement (Flora & Thoresen, 1988). Therefore, prevention approaches should be tailored to whether the adolescents are sexually active (DiClemente, Zorn, & Temoshok, 1986). Interventions using education alone are not fully effective; more comprehensive approaches are needed (DiClemente et al., 1986; Rotheram-Borus, Koopman, & Bradley, 1989). The appropriate strategy to encourage in an AIDS prevention program is unclear. Abstinence effectively prevents transmission through sexual intercourse, but the feasibility of persuading the majority of adolescents to implement this strategy is questionable. There are several other controversial strategies receiving consideration: encouraging monogamous sexual relationships, screening partners, HIV testing, and explicit discussion about sex. These issues are discussed below.

The Threat of Unsafe Sexual Activities to Adolescents

Evidence of the high incidence of unsafe adolescent sexual behavior is derived from behavioral AIDS research, research on pregnancy and the use of birth control among adolescents, and research on sexually transmitted diseases (STDs) among adolescents.

Behavioral AIDS research demonstrates that while adolescents are sexually active, they are failing to respond to the AIDS epidemic with effective changes in their sexual behavior. Recent evidence demonstrates that general knowledge of AIDS is high (DiClemente, Zorn & Temoshok, 1987), particularly the importance of using condoms (Association for the Advancement of Health Education, 1988). Yet adolescents are not worried about contracting AIDS (Price, Desmond, & Kukulka, 1985) and have not incorporated this knowledge into practice. Among adolescents at a health clinic, only 8.2% of the males and 2.1% of the females consistently used condoms (Kegeles, Adler, & Irwin, 1988); 60% of those targeted in a media prevention campaign plan to use a condom "some of the time" or less (Yankelovich, Skelly, & White/Clancy, Shulman, Inc. poll, cited in Fineberg, 1988a); most feel unable to discuss condoms and "know" intuitively which partners are at risk (Caron, Bertran, & McMullen, 1987). Only 3% reported intending to behave in a manner that could potentially lower their risk of contracting AIDS (Strunin & Hingson, 1987).

Evidence about risk taking with sex also comes from research showing that adolescents' use of birth control methods is low. Kisker (1984) found that adolescents did not seek contraceptive information for over a year after beginning to have sexual intercourse. Thirty-three percent of all sexually active, unmarried teenagers (15–19 years old) have been pregnant (Zelnick & Kantner, 1980), resulting in approximately 850,000 unplanned teenage pregnancies each year in the U.S. (Alan Guttmacher Institute, 1981)—a high figure relative to other developed countries (Dryfoos, 1985).

The prevalence of STDs among adolescents is another source of alarming evidence regarding adolescent risk taking. Among sexually active persons, adolescents have higher rates of gonorrhea, pelvic inflammatory disease, syphilis, and chlamydia than young adults (Hein, 1987). The number of cases of gonorrhea in teenagers exceeds 200,000 annually (Centers for Disease Control, 1988). When the high prevalence of asymptomatic venereal disease, such as asymptomatic gonorrhea, is considered, these figures become even more alarming because adolescents are known to underuse the health care system (Hein, 1987).

Some adolescents are at particular risk; these include gay youth, adolescents with multiproblem behavior syndrome, partners of IV drug users, and sex offenders. It is important to understand that it is the high-risk behaviors of these youths, not membership in a high-risk group, that increases the risk of HIV transmission. Adolescents engaging in these behaviors engage in more high-risk sexual behavior than other adolescents (Rotheram-Borus & Koopman, 1990), increasing the opportunities for HIV infection to spread throughout the adolescent population.

Prevention Approaches

Several issues must be resolved prior to the design and implementation of any AIDS prevention program. The goals of AIDS prevention programs for adolescents differ in several significant characteristics: taking a moralist versus a rationalist approach; choice of the population served; emphasis on a message of fear versus one of developing a positive attitude toward sexuality and sex-role behavior that reduces risk; and targeting comprehensive versus specific changes in behavior.

Whether to take a moralist or a rationalist view underlies the debate regarding which interventions are appropriate for adolescents (Fineberg, 1988a). The moralist stance holds that it is wrong to even discuss topics such as sex outside of marriage, because such discussions condone sexual behavior (Schlafly, cited in Tatum, 1982; Welbourne-Moglia & Edwards, 1986). The rationalist perspective is that "just say no" is an ineffective intervention (Botvin & Tortu, 1988; Wallack & Corbett, 1987), and it is only realistic to try to modify sexual behavior, not to eliminate it. Support for the rationalist position comes from surveys of adolescents in which adolescents approve of sexual relations among their peers (Association for the Advancement of Health Education, 1988).

AIDS prevention goals differ according to the needs of the population served. The major distinguishing factor is whether the youth are sexually active or inactive (Rotheram-Borus et al., 1989). For the sexually active, the goal is reduction or elimination of risky behavior by substitution of safer behaviors. For the sexually inactive, the goal is to slow down or prevent the onset of high-risk sexual behavior, perhaps by encouraging the youth to proceed through the sexual milestones other than sexual intercourse. For example, among some adolescents, holding hands or kissing may have rarely, if ever, occurred, even though they engage in sexual intercourse (Rotheram-Borus et al., 1989).

Cultural norms regarding sexuality are also relevant when considering alternatives

to high-risk sexual behavior. White females are likely to experience a series of graduated sexual milestones: dating, kissing, breast petting, genital petting, and then sexual intercourse (Vener & Stewart, 1974). This norm delays the onset of the higher-risk activity of sexual intercourse to a later age for this group. This sequence does not accurately portray the sexual development of black adolescents, who engage in sexual intercourse at earlier ages, often before they have experienced other sexual milestones (Belcastro, 1985; Hayes, 1987). Furthermore, low-risk sexual activities, such as masturbation and genital petting, are valued differently by various cultures (Asayama, 1975; Gregersen, 1986; Klausner, 1964; Money & Musaph, 1977). One potential implication of these cultural differences is that interventions could try to encourage the adoption of sexual norms for low-risk behavior, such as encouring masturbation or genital petting to delay the onset of sexual intercourse. However, this raises questions about the effects of trying to encourage different norms regarding sexuality on the youth's ethnic identity (Rotheram-Borus et al., 1989).

The threat of AIDS also requires a shift in sex roles. Males feel pressured to identify themselves with their genital activity, and "some see in it the answer to all problems" (Basow, 1986, p. 92). Traditionally, males have been encouraged to have sex, while females were encouraged to abstain. Simultaneously, females are primarily responsible for ensuring protection from the negative consequences of sexuality (e.g., unwanted pregnancy). Because condoms are the primary means of protection from HIV transmission during sexual intercourse, the female is more dependent than ever on the male's cooperation for protecting both partners (Rotheram-Borus & Bradley, in press). Adolescents need help to develop positive sexual-role behaviors that help protect them from contracting AIDS.

An important decision in goal setting for AIDS prevention is how to increase perceived threat of AIDS (usually with fear messages) and simultaneously transmit positive attitudes toward sexuality. In Australia and Britain the Grim Reaper is the symbol used in AIDS campaigns. In the 18th century this symbol was used to signify the plague (Fineberg, 1988b). Fear messages associating sex with AIDS and death have also been used in the U.S. For example, one AIDS prevention poster shows an attractive couple in bed with the caption, "Bang. You're dead!" A recent movie was titled *Suddenly Sex Is Very Dangerous* (Haffner, 1988). Fear arousal to reduce adolescents' high-risk sexual activity is of questionable effectiveness (Brooks-Gunn et al., 1988). Many females have enough difficulty already achieving satisfactory sexual relations, having learned to associate their sexuality with guilt, shame, and fear (Tevlin & Leiblum, 1983). The fear of contracting AIDS could exacerbate these negative associations. Its potential for negatively influencing positive attitudes toward sexuality has not been examined.

Evidence from earlier smoking and drug prevention programs would suggest that fear messages are inadequate for promoting sexual behavior change. Earlier in the twentieth century public campaigns to prevent syphilis and gonorrhea used fear to try to promote abstinence among youth, but fear messages failed to significantly reduce these diseases (Haffner, 1988). Such admonitions do not consider the social context in which high-risk behavior occurs (Wallack & Corbett, 1987); furthermore, they fail to provide alternatives for satisfying the powerful needs met by high-risk sexual behavior.

Social learning theory (Bandura, 1977) would suggest that observing role models deriving satisfaction from safe behaviors would promote behavior change in the observer. Powerful reinforcers must become associated with the behavior intended to supplant the high-risk behavior. Therefore, highly attractive role models of both sexes might be presented in messages demonstrating how satisfaction can result from safe behavior. One example is to show young men and women dressing attractively, having fun on a date, and abstaining from sex. Another example, illustrated in the 1987 movie, *Broadcast News*, is the portrayal of the heroine's carrying a condom in her purse as sexy behavior.

A crucial decision in goal setting for AIDS prevention is whether to use an intervention approach that targets comprehensive or specific goals. A specific goal is to increase condom use among sexually active youth. A more comprehensive approach has multiple goals (e.g., promoting abstinence, decreasing anal intercourse, and reducing the number of sexual partners, in addition to increasing condom use). It may be more appropriate to target a specific change with adolescent populations with relatively few high-risk behaviors. However, among youth with many high-risk behaviors, such as runaway youth who are homeless, depressed, using drugs, and sexually active, a more comprehensive approach seems necessary (Rotheram-Borus et al., 1989).

In addition to the question of comprehensive versus specific goals for AIDS prevention, it is necessary to question whether the content of prevention programs should be focused specifically on information about AIDS or whether the content should be more comprehensive. Prevention research to curb drug and alcohol abuse (Botvin & Tortu, 1988; Wallack & Corbett, 1987) and prevent pregnancy (Eisen, Zellman, & McAlister, 1985; Schinke & Gilchrist, 1978) have demonstrated that education is not as effective as more comprehensive approaches. Similarly, in AIDS prevention efforts with adolescents, two- to three-hour educational interventions have proven to be insufficient for promoting behavior change (DiClemente et al., 1986; Downer, 1987). Among gay males, education efforts alone have not substantially reduced high-risk behavior, although knowledge does appear to be one prerequisite to such reduction (Calabrese, Harris, & Easley, 1987; St. Lawrence, Kelly, Hood, & Brasfield, 1987; Stall, Coates, & Hoff, 1988). Prevention researchers with IV drug users have found that, in addition to general knowledge, behavior change depends on other factors such as socioeconomic status and sense of power (Mondanaro, 1987; Stein, with Jones & Fischer, 1988).

Therefore, comprehensive AIDS prevention programs appear necessary, ones which target all components thought to be critical to behavior change. Four components that mediate high-risk sexual behavior can be identified: general knowledge, personalized knowledge, coping skills, and access to comprehensive health care services (Rotheram-Borus & Bradley, in press).

Controversial Tactics for AIDS Prevention with Adolescents

SEXUAL ABSTINENCE ∎

Abstinence, the safest means for preventing the sexual transmission of HIV infection, does not encounter the adult community opposition often directed at alternative approaches. However, the results of pregnancy-prevention efforts suggest that sexual abstinence is not perceived as an acceptable solution for AIDS prevention by all adolescents, and fails as an effective strategy (Hayes, 1987).

MONOGAMY ∎

Encouraging a monogamous sexual relationship is controversial because it implicitly accepts adolescent sexuality. It is also likely to be unfeasible for many adolescents. In a study by Sorensen (1973), two kinds of sexual patterns were found among sexually active adolescents: serially monogamous and sexually adventurous. The latter pattern describes 41% of male and 13% of female adolescents, who averaged 3.2 sexual partners in the previous month.

Serial monogamy, as opposed to absolute monogamy for life, is inadequate for protecting individuals from HIV infection, especially if the monogamous relationship endures for only one month. In a sexual relationship where at least one partner's HIV status is unknown, monogamy does not eliminate the risk of HIV infection. The possibility remains for one of the partners to be seropositive (Kutchinsky, 1988; Peto, 1986).

SCREENING PARTNERS ∎

The rationale for screening partners is to determine the likelihood of their being HIV-infected due to prior or ongoing high-risk sex or drug behavior. The implication is that sex with high-risk partners would either be avoided altogether, or, at minimum, safer sex practices would be strictly employed.

A major problem with screening partners to determine their likelihood of being HIV infected is that people lie in order to have sex. In a recent survey of college students (Keeling, 1988), the majority of males and females reported that they lie in order to have sex. Even if potential sex partners were not likely to lie, asking them the necessary questions to elicit others' sex and drug history is problematic. Adolescents, in general, may not be so different from high-risk youth; when participating in focus groups on AIDS, these adolescents would stare open-mouthed when asked to role-play asking about their partner's sexual history (Rotheram-Borus et al., 1988).

HIV TESTING PROGRAMS ▪

HIV testing programs have been promoted by legislators as a means of stopping AIDS transmission. However, the data do not support this hypothesis. Changing high-risk behavior is critical to stem the tide of infection. Testing programs do not, in themselves, accomplish this change (Coates, Stall, Kegeles, Lo, Morin, & McKusick, 1988; Fox, Odaka, Brookmeyer, & Polk, 1987; McCusker, Stoddard, Mayer, Zapka, Morrison, & Haltzman, 1988; Ostrow, Joseph, Kessler, Soucy, Tarl, Eller, Chmiel, & Phair, 1989).

Particularly with adolescents, HIV testing does not appear promising as a prevention strategy for several reasons. First, HIV testing for those involved in brief serial monogamous relations is not a viable alternative. By the time the couple had waited the necessary 6 months for reliable results, the relationship would have ended. Second, if it is questionable whether adults have changed their behaviors when informed of HIV status (e.g., Ostrow et al., 1989), it is even less likely that adolescents would permanently change their behavior. Finally, there appears to be a heightened risk of suicide among persons diagnosed with AIDS (Marzuk, Tierney, Tarfidd, Gross, Morgan, Hsu, & Mann, 1988), raising concerns about the effects of informing adolescents of positive test results.

EXPLICIT DISCUSSION ABOUT SAFER SEXUAL BEHAVIOR ▪

This is perhaps the most controversial approach to AIDS prevention for adolescents. There is much reliable information about sexual acts that reduce risk for AIDS (e.g., it is clear that wearing a condom is better

than no protection while engaging in vaginal or anal intercourse) (Tovey, 1987). The exact risk of contracting AIDS due to condom slippage, breakage, and/or leakage is not yet known, although it is suggested by the various estimates of women who get pregnant each year (0.8–4.8% [Thiery, 1987] or 13–15% [Kelly, 1987]) while relying solely on condom use for contraception. Using condoms and avoiding specific high-risk sexual practices are often encouraged under the rubric of *safe sex*. These activities are more accurately designated *safer* rather than safe because they are not absolutely effective in preventing individuals from contracting AIDS (Goedert, 1987). Still, the use of condoms could significantly slow the spread of the infection (Fineberg, 1988a). Encouraging safer sex is most likely to effectively change sexual behavior when a person does not have a steady partner. It is not realistic to expect most persons to continue to practice safer sex with a steady partner over time, unless they know that at least one of them is seropositive (Kutchinsky, 1988).

In trying to modify adolescents' sexual behavior, it is important that they understand that a partial cutback in high-risk sexual behavior is insufficient. For example, if condom use is to be relied upon for protection, it is insufficient to use condoms most of the time (Fineberg, 1988a). Advice to make consistent condom use more likely provides explicit details such as the importance of using condoms that are of the appropriate size (Ross, 1987), and when and how to put on a condom.

SUMMARY ▪

Each of these strategies for reducing adolescents' risk from sexual activity has shortcomings. There is no one answer, and recommendations are controversial. A mixed strategy would appear to be the best approach for achieving safer behavior by tailoring its recommendations to the adolescent's situation. Adolescents who have not yet engaged in sexual intercourse are encouraged to remain sexually abstinent. It is less clear whether one wants to encourage such acts as kissing or fondling as means of delaying the onset of sexual intercourse. Adolescents who have partners of unknown HIV status are encouraged, by explicit discussion, to engage only in safer sex with condoms. Some researchers suggest that adolescents who are in monogamous sexual relationships be encouraged to get their partners and themselves HIV tested, but only when testing is accompanied by counseling and other services ensuring that adolescents are prepared to cope with the knowledge of their test results (Kutchinsky, 1988).

Sensitivity to community norms is critical to designing an AIDS prevention program that encourages safer sex, as is consideration of government regulations regarding consent, confidentiality, and content of programs pertaining to adolescent sexuality (English, 1988). Experience with efforts to provide sex education suggests that community opposition, while stemming from a small minority (Scales, 1982), has two major concerns that should be addressed by efforts to promote safer sex in adolescence: (1) the need for community participation in the decision-making planning process and (2) care to avoid community fears that its moral authority over its children is being undermined (Chethik, 1981). Developing community support is an important prerequisite for establishing AIDS prevention efforts meeting the needs of the community.

References

Alan Guttmacher Institute. (1981). *Teenage pregnancy: The problem that hasn't gone away.* New York: Author.

Asayama, S. (1975). Adolescent sex develop-ment and adult sex behavior in Japan. *The Journal of Sex Research, 11,* 91–112.

Association for the Advancement of Health Education. (1988). *National Adolescent Student Health Survey.* Reston, VA: Author.

Bandura, A. (1977). *Social learning theory.* New York: Prentice-Hall.

Basow, S. A. (1986). *Gender stereotypes: Traditions and alternatives.* Monterey, CA: Brooks Cole.

Becker, M. H. (Ed.). (1974). *The health belief model and personal health behavior.* Thorofare, NJ: Slack.

Belcastro, P. A. (1985). Sexual behavior differences between black and white students. *Journal of Sex Research, 21,* 56–67.

Botvin, G. J., & Tortu, S. (1988). Preventing adolescent substance abuse through life-skills training. In R. H. Price, E. L. Cowen, R. P. Lorion, & J. Ramos-McKay (Eds.), *Fourteen ounces of prevention: A casebook for practitioners.* Washington, DC: American Psychological Association.

Brooks-Gunn, J., Boyer, C., & Hein, K. (1988). Preventing HIV infection and AIDS in children and adolescents: Behavioral research and intervention strategies. *American Psychologist, 43,* 958–964.

Calabrese, L. H., Harris, B., & Easley, K. (1987, June). *Analysis of variables impacting on safe sexual behavior among homosexual men in an area of low incidence for AIDS.* Paper presented at the Third International Conference on AIDS, Washington, DC.

Caron, S. L., Bertran, R. M., & McMullen, T. (1987, July–August). AIDS and the college student: The need for sex education. *SIECUS Report,* 6–7.

Centers for Disease Control. (1987). Human immunodeficiency virus in the United States. *Morbidity and Mortality Weekly Report, 36,* 801–804.

Centers for Disease Control. (1988). *Sexually transmitted diseases: Statistics for 1987.* Atlanta, GA: Centers for Disease Control.

Chethik, B. B. (1981). Developing community

support: A first step toward a school sex education program. *Journal of School Health, 51*, 266–270.

Coates, T. J., Stall, R. D., Kegeles, S. M., Lo, B., Morin, S. F., & McKusick, L. (1988). AIDS antibody testing. Will it stop the AIDS epidemic? Will it help people infected with HIV? *American Psychologist, 43*, 859–864.

DiClemente, R. J., Zorn, J., & Temoshok, L. (1986). Adolescents and AIDS: A survey of knowledge, attitudes, and beliefs about AIDS in San Francisco. *American Journal of Public Health, 76*, 1443–1445.

DiClemente, R. J., Zorn, J., & Temoshok, L. (1987). The association of gender, ethnicity, and length of residence in the Bay Area to adolescents' knowledge and attitudes about Acquired Immunodeficiency Syndrome. *Journal of Applied Social Psychology, 17*, 216–230.

Downer, A. (1987, June). *AIDS: What you need to know. A teaching unit for secondary schools.* Presented at the International AIDS Conference, Washington, DC.

Dryfoos, J. (1985). What the United States can learn about prevention of teenage pregnancy from other developed countries. *SIECUS Report, 14*, 1–7.

Eisen, M., Zellman, G. L., & McAlister, A. L. (1985). A health belief model approach to adolescents' fertility control: Some pilot program findings. *Health Education Quarterly, 12*, 185–210.

English, A. (1988). Adolescents and AIDS: Legal and ethical questions multiply. In M. Nelson with K. Clark, *The AIDS challenge: Prevention and education for young people* (pp. 255–271). Santa Cruz, CA: Network Publications.

Fineberg, H. V. (1988a). Education to prevent AIDS: Prospects and obstacles. *Science, 239*, 592–596.

Fineberg, H. V. (1988b, October). The social dimensions of AIDS. *Scientific American, 259*, 128–134.

Flora, J. A., & Thoresen, C. E. (1988). Reducing the risk of AIDS in adolescents. *American Psychologist, 43*, 965–970.

Fox, R., Odaka, N. J., Brookmeyer, R., & Polk, B. F. (1987). Effect of HIV antibody disclosure on subsequent sexual activity in homosexual men. *AIDS, 1*, 241–246.

Goedert, J. J. (1987). What is safe sex? *New England Journal of Medicine, 316*, 1339–1342.

Gregersen, E. (1986). Human sexuality in cross-cultural perspective. In D. Byrne & K. Kelley (Eds.), *Alternative approaches to th study of sexual behavior* (pp. 87–102). Hillsdale, NJ: Lawrence Erlbaum Associates.

Haffner, D. W. (1988). The AIDS epidemic: Implications for the sexuality education of our youth. *SIECUS Reports, 16*, 1–5.

Hayes, C. D. (1987). *Risking the future: Adolescent sexuality, pregnancy, and childbearing.* Washington, DC: National Academy Press.

Hein, K. (1987). AIDS in adolescents: A rationale for concern. *New York State Journal of Medicine, 87*, 290–295.

Hein, K., Cohen, M. I., Marks, A., Schonberg, S. K., Meyer, M., & McBride, A. (1978). Age at first intercourse among homeless adolescent females. *Journal of Pediatrics, 93*, 147–148.

Hein, K., & Hurst, M. (1988). Human immunodeficiency virus infection in adolescence: A rationale for action. *Adolescent Pediatric Gynecology, 1*, 73–82.

Keeling, R. P. (1988, November). *Beyond AIDS 101.* Paper presented at the AIDS Education Symposium, Boston, MA.

Kegeles, S. M., Adler, N. E., & Iwin, C. E., Jr. (1988). Sexually active adolescents and condoms: Changes over one year in knowledge, attitudes, and use. *American Journal of Public Health, 78*, 460–461.

Kelly, J. A. (1987). Cautions about condoms in prevention of AIDS. [Letter]. *Lancet, 3*, 323–324.

Kisker, E. E. (1984). The effectiveness of family planning clinics in serving adolescents. *Family Planning Perspectives, 16*, 117–128.

Klausner, S. (1964). Inferential visibility and sex norms in the Middle East. *Journal of Social Psychology, 63*, 1–29.

Kutchinsky, B. (1988). *The role of HIV testing in AIDS prevention.* Copenhagen: University of Copenhagen.

Marzuk, P. M., Tierney, H., Tarfidd, K., Gross, E. M., Morgan, E. B., Hsu, M. A., & Mann, J. G. (1988). Increased risk of suicide in persons with AIDS. *Journal of the American Medical Association, 259*, 1332–1333.

McCusker, J., Stoddard, A. M., Mayer, K. H., Zapka, J., Morrison, C., & Haltzman, S. P. (1988). Effects of HIV antibody test knowledge on subsequent sexual behaviors in a cohort of sexually active men. *American Journal of Public Health, 78*, 462–467.

Mondanaro, J. (1987). Strategies for AIDS prevention: Motivating health behavior in drug dependent women. *Journal of Psychoactive Drugs, 19*, 143–149.

Money, J., & Musaph, H. (1977). *Handbook of sexology.* Amsterdam: Northern Holland Biomedical Press.

Ostrow, D. G., Joseph, J. G., Kessler, R., Soucy, J., Tarl, M., Eller, M., Chmiel, J., & Phair, J. T. (1989). Disclosure of HIV antibody status: Behavioral and mental health correlates. *AIDS Education and Prevention, 1*, 1–11.

Peto, J. (1986). AIDS and promiscuity. *Lancet, 2*, 979.

Price, J. H., Desmond, S., & Kukulka, G. (1985). High school students' perceptions and misperceptions of AIDS. *Journal of School Health, 55*, 107–109.

Ross, M. W. (1987). Problems associated with condom use in homosexual men. *American Journal of Public Health, 77*, 877–878.

Rotheram-Borus, M. J., & Bradley J. (in press). AIDS prevention among youth at high risk. In S. Blumenthal, A. Eichler, & G. Weissman, *Women and AIDS: Promoting Healthy Behaviors.* Washington, DC: American Psychiatric Press.

Rotheram-Borus, M. J., & Koopman, C. (1990). AIDS and adolescents. In R. Lerner, A. Peterson, & J. Brooks-Gunn (Eds.), *Encyclopedia of Adolescence* (this volume). New York: Garland Publishing.

Rotheram-Borus, M. J., Koopman, C., & Bradley, J. (1989). Barriers to successful AIDS prevention programs with runaway youth. In J. O. Woodruff, D. Doherty, & T. G. Athey (Eds.), *Troubled Adolescents and HIV Infection: Issues in Prevention and Treatment* (pp. 37–55). Washington, DC: Georgetown University.

St. Lawrence, J. S., Kelly, J. A., Hood, H. V., & Brasfield, T. L. (1987, June). *The relationship of AIDS risk knowledge to actual risk behavior among homosexually-active men.* Paper presented at the Third International Conference on AIDS, Washington, DC.

Scales, P. (1982). Sex education update: Community action that works. *Journal of Sex Education and Therapy, 8*, 17–20.

Schinke, S. P., & Gilchrist, L. D. (1978). Adolescent pregnancy: An interpersonal skills training approach to prevention. *Social Work in Health Care, 3*, 159–167.

Sorensen, R. E. (1973). *Adolescent sexuality in contemporary America: Personal values and sexual behavior.* New York: Abrams.

Stall, R. D. Coates, T. J., & Hoff, C. (1988). Behavioral risk reduction for HIV infection among gay and bisexual men. *American psychologist, 43*, 878–885.

Stein, J. B., with Jones, S. J., & Fischer, G. (1988). AIDS and IV drug use: Prevention strategies for youth. In M. Quackenbush & M. Nelson, with K. Clark (Eds.), *The AIDS challenge: Prevention education for young people* (pp. 273–295). Santa Cruz, CA: Network Publications.

Strunin, L., & Hingson, R. (1987). Acquired immunodeficiency syndrome and adolescents: Knowledge, beliefs, attitudes, and behaviors. *Pediatrics, 79*, 825–828.

Tatum, M. L. (1982). *Speaker in conference: Winning the battle for sex education.* New York: SIECUS.

Tevlin, H. E., & Leiblum, S. R. (1983). Sex-role stereotypes and female sexual dysfunction. In V. Franks & E. D. Rothblum (Eds.), *The stereotyping of women: Its effects on mental health* (pp. 129–150). New York: Springer.

Thiery, M. (1987). Condoms and AIDS prevention. [Letter]. *Lancet, 3,* 979.

Tovey, S. J. (1987). Condoms and AIDS prevention. [Letter]. *Lancet, 3,* 979.

Vener, A. M., & Stewart, C. S. (1974). Adolescent sexual behavior in middle America revisited: 1970–1973. *Journal of Marriage and the Family, 36,* 728–735.

Wallack, L., & Corbett, K. (1987). Alcohol, tobacco, and marijuana use among youth: An overview of epidemiological, program, and policy trends. *Health Education Quarterly, 14,* 223–249.

Welbourne-Moglia, A., & Edwards, S. R. (1986). Sex education must be stopped! *SIECUS Reports, 15,* 1–3.

Wyatt, G. E., Peters, S. D., & Gutherie, D. (1988). Kinsey revisited, Part 1: Comparisons of the sexual socialization and sexual behavior of white women over 33 years. *Archives of Sexual Behavior, 17,* 201–239.

Zelnick, M., & Kantner, J. F. (1980). Sexual activity, contraceptive use, and pregnancy among metropolitan-area teenagers, 1971–1979. *Family Planning Perspectives, 12,* 230–237.

See Also

AIDS and Adolescents; Contraceptive Behavior as a Process; Dating during Adolescence; Family Planning Clinics: Efficacy for Adolescents; Gay and Lesbian Youth; Homosexuality, Adolescent; Sex Education; Sexual Behavior in Black Adolescents, Initiation of; Sexual Onset, Early; Sexual Behavior, Sexual Attitudes and Contraceptive Use, Age Differences in Adolescent; Sexually Transmitted Diseases in Adolescence.

This work was supported by Grant 1P50 MH 43520 to the HIV Center for Clinical and Behavioral Studies from the National Institute of Mental Health and the National Institute of Drug Abuse.

Schizophrenia in Adolescence and Young Adulthood, Antecedents/ Predictors of

L. Erlenmeyer-Kimling
Barbara Cornblatt
New York State Psychiatric Institute
Columbia University

Schizophrenia, probably the most devastating of the psychiatric disorders, usually makes its first appearance in adolescence or young adulthood, a fact reflected in the name by which the illness initially was called: *dementia praecox*, or insanity of youth. Despite its commonly early emergence, however, schizophrenia is most appropriately viewed as a lifetime disorder, for, once begun, it afflicts more than 50% of its victims through the remainder of their lives, with periods of remission varying in length from individual to individual. Schizophrenia affects approximately 1% of the adult population in the United States and Europe and has been found to occur in all known societies. The disorder occurs equally frequently in men and women, but onset is usually earlier and prognosis is often poorer in men (Gottesman & Shields, 1982).

Although there have been, and continue to be, various schools of thought about the clinical features of schizophrenia, and although schizophrenic patients show considerable diversity in symptom pictures and course of the illness, several characteristics are generally agreed upon as being core to the definition of schizophrenia. These are: psychotic symptoms (delusions or hallucinations) during an active phase of the illness; characteristic disturbances in thought processes and in affect; a marked decrease in functional level in work, social relations, and/or self-care; and a duration of at least several months. Additional clinical features frequently present include social isolation or withdrawal, disturbances in psychomotor activity, ritualistic or stereotyped behavior, odd ideation, unusual perceptions, loss of drive, restrictions in spontaneous speech, flattened affect, dysphoric mood, and loss of sense of self.

This entry concerns antecedents and predictors of schizophrenia in adolescence and young adulthood. Both terms, antecedents and predictors, are used in several different ways in the literature and, indeed, distinctions between the terms are sometimes blurred. Here, *antecedent* is used to refer to etiological or causative factors underlying the development of schizophrenia, whereas *predictor* is used to refer to factors that identify groups of people or individuals as being at elevated risk for developing this disorder. The predictors considered here are *specific* predictors, which identify individuals at risk. Studies of both antecedents and predictors may help to clarify the basic pathophysiology and pathopsychology of schizophrenia, with valuable implications for treatment and preventive intervention strategies.

Almost every possible "cause" that can be imagined has been hypothesized at some time as being an antecedent of schizophrenia, and the array of variables proposed as being predictors is similarly wide. In the present entry, only those hypotheses that remain viable in the late 1980s are considered.

Antecedents

Although the role of genetic factors in schizophrenia was vigorously debated for many years, most workers in schizophrenia research now believe that the disorder has a genetic basis, with only a small portion of cases being attributable solely to nongenetic causes (Gottesman & Shields, 1982). Whatever gene or genes may be implicated, however, they are not thought to act alone but, rather, to interact with other biological or environmental factors in the development of schizophrenia. The fact that schizophrenia rarely appears before adolescence is compatible with the theory of genetic involvement, as many genes are known to be unexpressed at birth and in childhood, only to "switch on" and to reveal their effects at later ages. The nature of the genetic factors in schizophrenia is unknown, as is the primary pathophysiology that the genes produce. Three genetic models are currently considered to be possible: a single, probably dominant, autosomal gene with low penetrance; a heterogeneous situation, with different genes being associated with different forms of the disorder; or a multifactoral, polygenic mode of transmission, in which several or many genes act together. Hypotheses about the primary pathophysiology are numerous but are centered increasingly around the neurotransmitters—especially dopamine—and their receptor systems and/or around structural defects of the brain. Along with other suggestions, both autoimmune processes and alterations in the endorphin (endogenous morphine) system have been proposed as causing dopaminergic hyperactivity, which in turn is hypothesized to be responsible for the symptoms of schizophrenia.

Other biological factors have been postulated as antecedents of schizophrenia, frequently as interacting with or resulting from genetic factors underlying the illness, but not necessarily so. These include pre- and perinatal complications resulting in hypoxia; viruses, especially those such as the herpes group, which are known to have an affinity for nerve cells and to remain latent for long periods of time; a nutritional intolerance, such as that involved in celiac disease, which some researchers believe shares genes with schizophrenia; and vitamin deficiencies, vitamins B and C in particular. Whereas empirical support appears to be increasing only for the first of these hypotheses, none of the hypotheses has been refuted entirely, and it remains possible that some or all of these biological factors are antecedents of some forms of schizophrenia.

Psychosocial hypotheses, often focused on family dynamics with a psychoanalytic orientation and often centering blame on the mother—as in the "schizophrenogenic mother"—dominated thinking about the antecedents of schizophrenia for many years. Such hypotheses are no longer prominent, although it is clear that family attitudes toward the patient (often called *expressed emotion* [EE]) may influence the probability of relapse in schizophrenic and other psychiatric disorders, and it is possible that, for some individuals, EE plays an antecedent role in interaction with genetic factors. Deviant communication patterns in some of the parents of schizophrenic patients, once thought to be causes of the illness, may be expressions of thought disorder and may reflect the fact that these parents carry some of the schizophrenia genes themselves. Other types of nonbiological factors, including several types of specific life events, have also been suggested as antecedents of schizophrenia. No specific environmental events or circumstances have been found in the backgrounds of all schizophrenic patients, however, and a current conjecture is that the cumulative experience of ordinary stresses of living may result in the occurrence of schizophrenia in individuals who are prone to the illness. In addition to the cumulation of nonspecific stresses by adolescence and young adulthood, use of street drugs or alcohol, which is frequently started at these ages, may act as a potent trigger of a first episode, and subsequently of relapse, in persons with a genetic predisposition to this disorder.

Predictors

One of the most active areas of study in schizophrenia research in recent years has concerned the detection of biological and biobehavioral indicators, or "markers," that may identify individuals carrying genes for schizophrenia. Usually, the variables under investigation are ones that are known to be deviant in many schizophrenic patients, and the research subjects are drawn from groups classified as being at elevated statistical risk for developing schizophrenia, compared to the general population risk of about 1% (Goldstein & Tuma, 1987). When the goal is to use the "markers" as predictors of schizophrenia in adolescence or young adulthood, the research subjects are most commonly offspring of schizophrenic parents; based on follow-up studies in adulthood, such offspring are known to have schizophrenia risks of 10 to 15% if one parent is affected (35 to 45% if both parents are affected), whether they are reared by their biological parents or away from them. Other groups examined in the search for "markers" are parents and siblings of schizophrenic patients, and individuals who share some psychological or biological trait that is thought to be characteristic of schizophrenic patients.

Among the categories of variables examined in risk groups as possible "markers" for the schizophrenia "genotype" are: (1) attention and information processing (AIP), measured by several research paradigms, including reaction time, sustained and selective attention, and short-term memory; (2) neurological signs and motor behavior; (3) psychophysiological functioning, assessed by electrodermal responses for the autonomic nervous system and by cortical event-related potential recordings for the central nervous system; (4) smooth pursuit eye movements (SPEM); (5) structural brain abnormalities, measured in brain imaging studies, which frequently have focused on the size of the cerebral ventricles; (6) associations with the human leukocyte antigens (HLA), that are concerned with immune responses; and (7) blood platelet activity of monoamine oxidase (MAO), the enzyme that catabolizes dopamine and other neurotransmitters. All seven of these categories have been studied in some types of relatives of schizophrenic patients as potential biological markers, although only the first three have been examined prospectively in offspring of schizophrenic parents as possible predictors of later schizophrenia. Initially promising, electrodermal activity, HLA associations, and MAO activity levels do not now appear to be useful as markers or predictors. Conclusions cannot be drawn at present about neurological signs and motor behavior, cortical event-related potentials, or cerebral ventricular size, as the research literatures on each of them are currently troubled by inconsistent results. However, with further research, any or all of these areas may prove to be predictors of some forms of schizophrenia or, at least, of mental disorders in general (Erlenmeyer-Kimling, 1987).

Certain types of AIP deficits and disturbances in SPEM are strongly supported in the research literature as comprising biological markers for schizophrenia. Follow-up studies on children of schizophrenic parents suggest that AIP deficits seen at young ages in some of these children may be predictors of later schizophrenic disorders. Most prominent are deficiencies in sustained attention to complex visual displays (although auditory attention, which has been less well-studied, may be disturbed also), distractibility, and ability to attend to different stimuli simultaneously. SPEM dysfunctions, which are seen in about 50% of the first-degree relatives of schizophrenic patients, are possibly biological markers for identifying individuals carrying genes for schizophrenia, but they are not necessarily predictors, as many of the relatives with poor SPEM do not develop schizophrenia.

Among individuals identified by a global predictor as being at risk for schizo-phrenia (such as the offspring of schizophrenic parents), below-average IQ, lower Verbal than Performance IQ, increasing difficulties in school and deteriorating social relations as the child moves into adolescence may be signals that a schizophrenic disorder is developing. Extreme shyness, supersensitivity to noise or light, or abrasive, acting-out behavior may also be seen in some preschizophrenic individuals during childhood and early adolescence. It is important to point out, however, that not all high-risk children who later become schizophrenic show any of these characteristics. Equally important, it must be noted that many children and young adolescents in the general population—that is, children who are not known to be at risk for schizophrenia—may display some of the aforementioned characteristics without going on to develop schizophrenia.

To the extent that the theory of schizophrenia as a genetic disorder is correct, the ultimate search for a predictor will focus on identification and localization of the responsible gene or genes through modern strategies of molecular genetics and genetic linkage analyses (McGue & Gottesman, 1989). Advances in recombinant DNA technology and in gene mapping have led to the recent localization of genes for a number of disorders. If schizophrenia is attributable to a single major gene, or if each of several forms of schizophrenia depends on a single gene, it is likely that the gene or genes will be discovered relatively soon. If, as is more probable, schizophrenia involves several or many genes acting together, the search will take longer but eventually should be resolvable.

References

Erlenmeyer-Kimling, L. (1987). Biological markers for the liability to schizophrenia. In H. Helmchen & F. A. Henn (Eds.),

Biological perspectives of schizophrenia. New York: John Wiley & Sons.

Goldstein, M. J., & Tuma, A. H. (Eds.). (1987). High-risk research (entire issue). *Schizophrenia Bulletin, 13*(3).

Gottesman, I. I., & Shields, J. (1982). *Schizophrenia, the epigenetic puzzle.* New York: Cambridge University Press.

McGue, M., & Gottesman, I. I. (1989). Genetic linkage in schizophrenia. *Schizophrenia Bulletin, 15*(3), 453–464.

See Also

Affective Disorders; Depression in Adolescence, Gender Differences in; Developmental Psychopathology and the Adolescent; Fears and Phobias in Adolescence; Moodiness, Adolescent; Psychophysiological/Psychosomatic Problems; Turmoil, Adolescent.

School Programs, Evaluation of

Laurie Schwab Zabin
The Johns Hopkins University

It has become increasingly clear that clusters of high-risk behaviors are affecting the present and future well-being of adolescents in the United States. Premature sexuality, pregnancy and childbearing, drug and alcohol use, among other behaviors, are not isolated problems but are often related. Simultaneously, there has been a growing recognition of the many health needs of youthful Americans, needs often unmet by their usual medical care, which tends to be of a crisis nature. The perceived need to reach teenagers before their educations and health are endangered, and an increased appreciation of the comprehensive nature of their problems, has led to the establishment of preventive health programs in many of the nation's schools. Some of these represent purely medical interventions, while others are part of larger educational and/or counseling initiatives. There is a growing need to subject these programs to rigorous evaluation in order to (1) establish their efficacy in reducing the health problems of adolescents; (2) justify the investment they require; (3) upgrade the services themselves; and (4) influence those who make policy and design programs in these areas of social and medical concern.

Problems in assessing the contribution of school-based or school-linked programs fall generally into three categories: (1) definition of goals and components; (2) access and data collection; and (3) analytic issues. These problems are both political and scientific, complicated by the perceived sensitivity of some components of these programs, and by the challenge of designing evaluation models for initiatives among transient samples of students, differentially exposed to a range of competing or loosely-defined interventions.

1. Definition of Goals and Components

Not all programs are appropriate for academic evaluation because not all are designed with clear objectives and measurable components. Many programs are unable to collect the information required for impartial assessment. Laying down the bases on which evaluation will proceed can be a creative exercise for program managers if they are committed to the process. It can help them define their programs' long- and short-term goals and understand the relationship between objectives and projected services.

Some level of agreement about program goals is essential; a recurrent problem in school-related research has been the lack of such consensus. For example, whereas a program may be funded to reduce substance abuse or unintended pregnancy, the staff may see themselves as general health care providers, not equipped to render categoric care related to those goals. Or, high-level planners might stress a reduction in drop-out or absentee rates; if health is not the major cause of poor attendance, and if the program addresses only medical conditions without strong counseling components, projected goals and actual services may be ill-matched. Evaluation can only proceed in the light of defined objectives that suggest appropriate outcome measures. Some agreement between planners, funders and program staff on the effects they seek is therefore a necessary precondition for responsible evaluation. Similarly, some correspondence between objectives and program components is required. In its absence, some redefinition of goals or redesign of services is probably indicated before an evaluation is undertaken.

Another problem in choosing appropriate sites for evaluation is the presence of confounding influences. School systems tend to introduce many initiatives, sometimes system-wide and sometimes in specific schools, making the impact of a particular program difficult to isolate. Matched schools, required as controls in a responsible study, are not always easy to find; schools tend to differ in their economic, geographic, racial, gender, and curriculum mixes, and matched schools which do not share the same programs may be hard to locate within a system. A focus on *change* between pre- and post-program characteristics, rather than on characteristics of students at any one point in time, may reduce the confounding effects of baseline differences.

It is important that schools in which serious evaluation is undertaken be committed to the endeavor; to that end, it is important that evaluation be an integral part of the program offering. Pressures upon school staffs are great but, because of financial constraints, they are often open to new interventions that can be undertaken without straining the school's budget. If evaluation is included as a precondition of service, it is more likely to be acceptable than if imposed upon programs already in place.

2. Access and Data Collection

Similarly, the process of data collection will be strengthened if school administrators are strongly committed to evaluation. Problems often arise when evaluators fail to understand the role of the principal as guardian of the school's reputation and surrogate parent of each of his or her students. School systems are answerable to the entire community and to political jurisdictions, as well. The principal is required to protect his school from exposure to adverse publicity, and to maintain a position of trust within the school family. Whatever evaluation is undertaken in any school should have the explicit support of the principal, and, in turn, his faculty, staff, parents, and students.

There are three basic kinds of data available to the evaluator of school projects, all described in greater detail in Zabin and Hirsch, "Evaluation of Pregnancy Prevention Programs in the School Context" (1988).

Aggregate Survey Data Collected from the Entire Student Body. This is generally anonymous, although some attempts at identifiable, longitudinal interviews have been successful. The use of anonymous surveys probably permits the most honest response on the part of the students, who must be asked extremely personal questions which might place them at some risk (i.e., drug use, parenting, etc.). Collected before the program begins, after a predetermined follow-up period, and if possible at some intermediate points in time, these data permit one to assess program impacts on the entire school, not merely the self-selected subset of students who utilize services. Because the prime argument for placing programs in schools is their potential impact on persons who might not otherwise use them, assessment of school-wide effects is important. Models for survey instruments are in the public domain; one set is published in the appendix of the aforementioned text, where the derivation of its questions and methods of survey administration are discussed.

An important issue in collecting school-wide data is the question of parental notification. Requiring written consent is prohibitive, biasing samples so as to destroy their usefulness. However, some notification procedure is essential. Parents should be able to obtain information, examine the instrument if they wish, and/or withdraw their offspring from the study. (The role of a parent-teacher organization can be explored.) Thoughtful notification procedures, building on trust between principal and parents, have been highly successful in the past. Diminishingly few parents exercise their option to limit children's participation, but the omission of such a procedure can put an entire project at risk.

Service Records for Each School-Based Service, Including Staff Logs, Clinic Records, Counselors' Records, and Referrals. Access to these records must be negotiated with appropriate authorities. They give a close-up picture of services rendered, but reflect only effects on those who utilize the program. Procedures to amplify their usefulness include: clear definition of program eligibility; specified criteria for defining "enrollment"; specification of services included in the program; careful design of registration forms, medical and social records, and clear protocols for their maintenance; and a predetermined period of study.

Public Access Data from Schools, Health Departments, etc. These include materials the school system can provide such as rolling enrollment records; attendance, drop-out and promotion figures for individual schools, classrooms, or homerooms; and birth records. All of these have been used successfully (the usefulness of birth certificates is limited because they do not include the school attended at the time of conception).

In addition, special surveys can be utilized; for example, community or parent surveys, surveys of dropouts, and questionnaires addressed to users of particular services.

3. Analytic Issues

Differentials in age, grade, and program exposure plague school-centered evaluation. Measurement focuses on students at a time of life when age brings about change in the absence of interventions. Grades are differentially exposed to programs, and individuals move in, out, and through the schools. Methods of handling these complications are proposed in the aforementioned text; in brief, all data should be compiled and analyzed by grade, controlling for differences in years of potential exposure; then an appropriate statistical method can be used to sum across exposure groups. It should be noted that longer exposure to a program generally implies older ages, which invalidates comparisons of age-related behaviors unless such techniques are used. Grades not available in certain exposure groups in posttest data must be omitted from baseline data, as well.

Establishing a denominator for schoolwide studies presents a challenge. A maximal denominator includes all students ever registered during the study period, derived from monthly or weekly enrollment rosters. A minimal estimate might sum only students registered in homerooms. One compromise is the use of a single enrollment roster, preferably the school's November rolls. Evaluated against this total of persons eligible for service will be the numbers served, collected from records maintained by the program staff.

References

Zabin, L. S., & Hirsch, M. B. (1988). *Evaluation of pregnancy prevention programs in the school context*. Lexington, MA: D. C. Heath.

See Also

Academic Achievement; Achievement: Evidence from High School and Beyond; Dropouts, High School: Issues of Race and Sex; Dropouts, School; Educational Achievement and Tracking in High School; Educational Achievement, Tracking and; Family Life Education; Gifted Adolescents; Graduate School Attendance, Barriers to: Access and Equity along the Education Pipeline; Learning Disabilities in Adolescents: Description, Assessment, and Management; Minority and Female Participation in Math and Science, Increase in: The Importance of the Middle School Years; Parenthood and Marriage in Adolescence: Associations with Educational and Occupational Attainment; Preschool Programs, Impact of on Adolescent Development; Puberty Education; Schooling; School-Linked Programs, Potential of; School Transitions, Secondary; Sex Education; Underachievers and Dropouts.

School Transitions, Secondary

L. Mickey Fenzel
Loyola College in Maryland

Dale A. Blyth
American Medical Association

Roberta G. Simmons
University of Pittsburgh

The history of secondary education in the United States during the twentieth century indicates that youth have experienced earlier and sometimes more frequent school transitions over time. Both phenomena were evidenced when school structures changed from an 8/4 grade configuration of building units to the 6/3/3 alignment that created the junior high school at the beginning of the century. As the middle school movement gathered a large following in the 1960s, another realignment of school units occurred that moved both secondary school transitions to earlier grade levels in most cases. The transition to middle school now typically occurs in sixth grade, and sometimes fifth, while high school tends to begin at ninth grade. Junior high schools, on the other hand, generally house students in grades seven to nine.

The transition to middle, junior high, or high school for adolescents often drastically alters the roles, activities, and interpersonal interactions in which they participate. Such changes may be beneficial or detrimental to adolescents' personal growth and development. The success or failure to adjust to a secondary school transition depends on many school factors and characteristics of the adolescents and their families.

Research shows that school transitions during early and middle adolescence can have short-term, intermediate-term, and long-term effects on individuals because of the adjustments required. The effects that have been investigated include changes in self-concept, participation in extracurricular activities, perceptions of school as threatening or as a source of anonymity, motivation, grade point average, perceptions of academic competence, and somatic symptoms.

The middle level school transition has been shown to be generally more difficult than the later high school transition, especially for girls. Reasons cited by researchers for the earlier transition difficulty include the presence of additional changes such as early pubertal development, disrupted peer networks, and increased school and parent demands. The cumulative effect of these demands which occur simultaneously may put the early adolescent on overload (see Simmons & Blyth, 1987). The middle level school program may differ more from the elementary school program than the later high school program, thereby providing greater discontinuity of school experience during the transition to junior high or middle school.

During the middle grades school transition students are usually exposed to a school which, compared to the elementary school, is larger and more compartmentalized. With students changing classes frequently, the student is usually faced with several teachers in a less personalized and less intimate setting. At a time when early adolescents are capable of and require greater intimacy or closeness with peers and adults, frequent movement between classes tends to provide fewer opportunities to develop close relationships and promotes greater anonymity.

The research of Eccles and Midgley (1989) and of Eccles, Midgley, and Adler (1984) has shown that middle schools often fail to provide a program that "fits" the social and cognitive developmental needs of early adolescents, who require increased behavioral autonomy and more opportunities to demonstrate higher ordered thinking and problem solving. They found, for example, that teachers in junior high schools tend to exert more control over student behavior and allow less student input than do most elementary school teachers. In addition, students are placed in tracked classes in some subjects for the first time and are faced with increased work demands and different and often stricter grading policies than before. The increased work load may not, unfortunately, be accompanied by opportunities to utilize higher level cognitive skills appropriate for this age group. However, a marked discrepancy between an elementary school program that demands little independent work and a middle school that demands much outside work has been shown to contribute to transition stress (see Fenzel, 1988).

The extent to which the elementary school environment differs from the new secondary school environment may affect adjustment during the early weeks of middle level schooling. Some research shows that students', especially boys', grades tend to decline and participation in school activities often drops off. Students may also feel more anonymous and experience an increase in psychological distress and a decrease in self-concept when they move to the new school setting (see Simmons & Blyth, 1987; Hawkins & Berndt, 1985).

Research on the junior high school transition conducted in the 1970s suggests two characteristics associated with urban school districts that may contribute to transition difficulties: heterogeneity and unfamiliarity with the student body. When students from a relatively small neighborhood elementary school enter a large junior high school, containing students from several elementary schools, they are likely to experience increased heterogeneity and interactions with a large number of strangers among the student body in the new setting. The increased anonymity that results when one faces both a larger setting and one that contains many unknown students with different ethnic backgrounds and neighborhood experiences is likely to contribute to increased stress (Simmons & Blyth, 1987).

Many studies, however, have shown that the middle level school transition can be relatively free of difficulty. When elementary and middle level schools anticipate the transition, short-term effects can be more positive. A "team" or "house" organization is one such innovation that has been implemented in many middle schools to help ease the transition. Team organization, which makes use of a school-within-a-school philosophy, helps reduce the size of a student's reference group to allow for closer relationships among pupils and between pupil and teacher (see Fenzel, 1988; Hawkins & Berndt, 1985; Lipsitz, 1984). In addition, characteristics of the student such as initial self-esteem level, friendship and peer group stability, and physical appearance, as well as family characteristics, most notably high parental expectations and involvement, may reduce the adverse effects of school transitions. Recent work has shown that the transition may be beneficial for boys, who experience more strain in elementary school than do girls (Fenzel, 1989).

Certain student behaviors and perceptions may persist beyond a normal adjustment period of a few weeks. Students who face a school situation markedly different from their elementary school in achievement demands and peer support, or who face difficulties or changes in other aspects of their lives at this time, are likely to experience adjustment effects for the duration of the school year or longer. For example, early pubertal development and dating demands made of girls concurrent with the junior high transition may present young people with a number of simultaneous changes and thereby contribute to longer lasting behavioral difficulties and a lower self-image. In addition, the adverse effects of the first transition on the self tend to predict more difficulties during a subsequent transition to senior high school (Simmons & Blyth, 1987).

Certain qualities of the learning environment may also contribute to long-term adjustment difficulties to the school transition. The developing early adolescent experiences a need for greater autonomy and control over schooling and appropriate cognitive challenge and may become more frustrated as the months, or middle level school years, progress if such needs are not met. Research that has examined the effects of open and traditional school structures has shown that classrooms in which teachers allow students to share control over selecting assignments and monitoring their progress are associated with greater school satisfaction among students (see Epstein & McPartland, 1976).

Although the middle level school transition is one shared by the great majority of American young people, it appears to take many forms. Successful transitions tend to occur, it seems, when secondary school environments provide early and middle adolescents with opportunities to exhibit developmentally appropriate behaviors in an environment that supports and challenges. Such school environments are difficult to create when students vary greatly in levels of physical, cognitive, and social development, yet they must be constructed to meet these needs at an individual level.

Research also suggests that stress may be minimized when the transition occurs in a community setting wherein elementary and secondary schools are similar in the degree of heterogeneity of student background characteristics and in the level of academic demands placed on students (see Fenzel, 1988).

Generalizations about the nature and effects of school transitions are difficult to make because of the considerable variability found in personality and family characteristics of students and the characteristics of the schools and communities in which they are located. Efforts aimed at investigating school transitions among a variety of diverse ethnic and racial groups and of youth in other cultures is badly needed. Further research and program development is needed before we will be able to optimize the challenges and opportunities this transition presents for development, prevention, and education.

References

Eccles, J. S., & Midgley, C. (1989). Stage environment fit: Developmentally appropriate classrooms for young adolescents. In R. E Ames & C. Ames (Eds.), *Research in motivation in education* (Vol. 3, pp. 139–186). New York: Academic Press.

Eccles, J., Midgley, C., & Adler, T. F. (1984). Grade-related changes in the school environment: Effects on achievement motivation. In J. Nicholls & M. L. Maehr (Eds.), *Advances in motivation and achievement* (Vol. 3, pp. 283–331). Greenwich, CT: JAI Press.

Epstein, J. L., & McPartland, J. M. (1976). *Classroom organization and the quality of school life* (Report No. 216). Baltimore: Johns Hopkins University, Center for Social Organization of Schools.

Fenzel, L. (1988). *The transition to middle school: An ecological study of student role strains and their effects on self-esteem and school performance.* Unpublished doctoral dissertation, Cornell University.

Fenzel, L. M. (1989). Role strains and the transition to middle school: Longitudinal trends and sex differences. *Journal of Early Adolescence, 9,* 211–226.

Hawkins, J. A., & Berndt, T. J. (1985). Adjustment following the transition to junior high school. In G. R. Adams (Chair), *School transitions: Positive and negative associations for social, emotional, and academic development.* Symposium presented at the Biennial Meeting of the Society for Research in Child Development, Toronto, Canada.

Lipsitz, J. (1984). *Successful schools for young adolescents.* New Brunswick, NJ: Transaction Books.

Simmons, R. G., & Blyth, D. A. (1987). *Moving into adolescence: The impact of pubertal change and school context.* New York: Aldine.

See Also

Academic Achievement; Achievement: Evidence from High School and Beyond; Dropouts, High School: Issues of Race and Sex; Dropouts, School; Educational Achievement and Tracking in High School; Educational Achievement, Tracking and; Family Life Education; Gifted Adolescents; Graduate School Attendance, Barriers to: Access and Equity along the Education Pipeline; Learning Disabilities in Adolescents: Description, Assessment, and Management; Minority and Female Participation in Math and Science, Increase in: The Importance of the Middle School Years; Parenthood and Marriage in Adolescence: Associations with Educational and Occupational Attainment; Preschool Programs, Impact of on Adolescent Development; Puberty Education; Schooling; School-Linked Programs, Potential of; School Programs, Evalution of; Sex Education; Underachievers and Dropouts.

Schooling

L. Mickey Fenzel
Loyola College in Maryland

Dale A. Blyth
American Medical Association

Schools for adolescents, including middle, junior high, and senior high schools, function primarily to socialize young people to meet the expectations of the dominant culture and to select and train individuals for productive adult roles in society. Specifically, schools are expected to foster intellectual and social growth in students. The past decade has brought to bear considerable criticism of the effectiveness of secondary schools from national blue ribbon committees (e.g., National Commission on Excellence in Education [NCEE], 1983) and university-based researchers (e.g., Goodlad, 1984). At the same time many researchers conclude that schools do make—and have made—a difference in meeting the intellectual and social needs of younger and older adolescents. Both criticisms and successes of schools will be examined in this entry.

Many school researchers and critics have demonstrated that secondary schools vary little in their teacher-lecturer format, reward system for individual achievement, and division of the school day into subjects and periods that provides a segmented view of knowledge (see Goodlad, 1984).

Schools have recently been criticized for failing students intellectually as suggested by low standardized test scores and high illiteracy rates (see NCEE, 1983). Equity is another critical issue. Schools have been called to task for providing lower-quality education for minorities, although recent reports suggest educational services for minority students are improving. Other critics have argued that the "unspecial" student who is designated neither gifted nor handicapped is largely ignored in schools (Powell, Farrar, & Cohen, 1985).

Despite the criticisms of secondary schools, many researchers acknowledge school successes. There are exemplary schools that appear to do an excellent job of educating young people even under extremely adverse conditions. Michael Rutter and his colleagues (1979), for example, found that a certain school "ethos" characterized London secondary schools that evidenced comparatively better student behavior and academic achievement. These effective schools demonstrated a strong academic emphasis, high levels of reward and praise for good work, opportunities for students to take meaningful responsibility in the school, and teachers united on expectations for academic and social behaviors. Strong leadership provided by the school principal, who serves as a critical link in the process of creating a productive school climate, has also been associated with effective schools (see also Brookover & Erickson, 1975; Lipsitz, 1984).

Many psychologists cite the importance of schools as contexts for adolescent development. As young people enter and progress through adolescence they require opportunities for expressing growing needs for autonomy, achieving a sense of identity, and intimate sharing with adults and peers in addition to academic challenges in line with developing cognitive abilities (see Hill, 1980). School structures and processes can and should exist to promote such development. Small secondary schools, for example, appear to facilitate adolescent social and cognitive development by providing more opportunities for participation and leadership by students, than in large schools (e.g., Barker & Gump, 1964; Mergendoller, 1982).

Middle level schools should differ from senior high schools because of the different developmental needs of early and middle adolescents (Alexander & George, 1981; Lipsitz, 1984). For example, early adolescents require the availability of many different kinds of academic and nonacademic offerings in school in order to help them identify potential areas of interest and ability and experience academic challenges appropriate to their developing cognitive abilities. Middle level schools must also provide opportunities for social interaction to help meet early adolescents' growing needs for increased closeness in interpersonal relations. Interdisciplinary team teaching is one approach used to address such early adolescent needs.

In order to better prepare students for life after high school, researchers and critics have called for more effective experience-based educational opportunities, including apprenticeships and community service (Goodlad, 1984; Youth and America's Future, 1988). A curriculum taught using a variety of strategies and made relevant to students' life experiences and conducive to their intellectual competencies may keep more adolescents in school and better prepare them for their adult roles.

References

Alexander, W. M., & George, P. S. (1981). *The exemplary middle school*. New York: Holt, Rinehart and Winston.

Barker, R. G., & Gump, P. V. (1964). *Big school, small school: High school size and student behavior*. Stanford, CA: Stanford University Press.

Boyer, E. L. (1983). *High school: A report on secondary education in America*. New York: Harper & Row.

Brookover, W. B., & Erickson, E. L. (1975). *Sociology of education*. Homewood, IL: Dorsey Press.

Coleman, J. S. (1961). *The adolescent society: The social life of the teenager and its impact on education*. New York: Free Press.

Goodlad, J. I. (1984). *A place called school: Prospects for the future*. New York: McGraw-Hill.

Harvard Educational Review.

Hill, J. P. (1980). *Understanding early adolescence: A framework*. Carrboro, NC: Center for Early Adolescence.

Lightfoot, S. L. (1983). *The good high school: Portraits of character and culture*. New York: Basic Books.

Lipsitz, J. (1984). *Successful schools for young adolescents*. New Brunswick, NJ: Transaction Books.

Mergendoller, J. R. (1982). To facilitate or impede? The impact of selected organizational features of secondary schools on adolescent development. In F. M. Newmann & C. E.

Sleeter (Eds.), *Proceedings from the Conference on Adolescent Development and Secondary Schooling* (pp. 77–105). Madison, WI: Wisconsin Center for Educational Research, University of Wisconsin-Madison.

Minuchin, P. P., & Shapiro, E. K. (1983). The school as a context for social development. In P. H. Mussen (Ed.), *Handbook of child psychology* (4th ed., Vol. 4, pp. 197–274). New York: Wiley.

National Commission on Excellence in Education. (1983). *A nation at risk: The imperative for educational reform.* Washington, DC: U.S. Government Printing Office.

Powell, A. G., Farrar, E., & Cohen, D. K. (1985). *The shopping mall high school.* Boston: Houghton Mifflin.

Rutter, M., Maughan, B., Mortimore, P., Ouston, J., with Smith, A. (1979). *Fifteen thousand hours: Secondary schools and their effects on children.* Cambridge: Harvard University Press.

Sizer, T. R. (1984). *Horace's compromise: The dilemma of the American high school.* Boston: Houghton Mifflin.

Youth and America's Future. (1988). *The forgotten half: Pathways to success for America's youth and young families.* Washington, DC: William T. Grant Foundation Commission on Work, Family, and Citizenship.

See Also

Academic Achievement; Achievement: Evidence from High School and Beyond; Dropouts, High School: Issues of Race and Sex; Dropouts, School; Educational Achievement and Tracking in High School; Educational Achievement, Tracking and; Family Life Education; Gifted Adolescents; Graduate School Attendance, Barriers to: Access and Equity along the Education Pipeline; Learning Disabilities in Adolescents: Description, Assessment, and Management; Minority and Female Participation in Math and Science, Increase in: The Importance of the Middle School Years; Parenthood and Marriage in Adolescence: Associations with Educational and Occupational Attainment; Preschool Programs, Impact of on Adolescent Development; Puberty Education; School-Linked Programs, Potential of; School Programs, Evaluation of; School Transitions, Secondary; Sex Education; Underachievers and Dropouts.

School-Linked Programs, Potential of

Laurie Schwab Zabin
Johns Hopkins University

A movement toward the establishment of school-linked health programs for teenagers has been predicated on a growing appreciation of the multiple problems facing adolescents in the United States, the importance of these formative years in establishing patterns of health behavior, and the failure of the medical system to reach many school-aged citizens with preventive care. Clusters of high-risk behaviors have been recognized, suggesting that problems of adolescent pregnancy, alcohol consumption, drug dependency, absenteeism, and premature school termination are not isolated phenomena (Jessor & Jessor 1977; Zabin, 1984; Zabin, Hardy, Smith, & Hirsch, 1986). They appear to form a complex of threats to which the nation's youth, and especially its economically disadvantaged young people, are exposed. The widespread nature of these problems and the comprehensive challenge they represent has made it seem necessary to reach adolescents where they can most readily be found, in the public schools. It should be recognized from the outset, however, that a large number of adolescent men and women are not to be found in that setting. Although in the nation at large the vast majority remain in school, in some locations disproportionate percentages terminate their educations before graduation. However successful school-linked health programs may be, they will not reach those who need them most: the 40% of high school-age young people who have dropped out of the inner-city schools.

For the many young people who can be reached through the schools, however, there are a wide range of interventions that have been implemented in individual schools in one or another part of the country. These include purely educational initiatives whose main purposes are to increase information and to expand understanding of the consequences of high-risk behavior. For example, these interventions may explicate the physiological effects upon which risks are predicated. They may include attempts to affect not merely knowledge but attitudes toward these behaviors, or attitudes toward the future upon which certain behaviors might impinge. Thus, the notion that education might improve the self-concept of individual students, and, by doing so, facilitate responsible decision making in areas of health, social conduct, and academic commitment, has gained some popularity. It seems clear that educational initiatives of these types are able to demonstrate increases in knowledge. It has not yet been demonstrated, however, that behavioral change will result, without the expansion of these programs beyond didactic or classroom intervention.

The varied quality of educational interventions is matched by equally great variety in the quantity of educational exposure. Thus, courses that are called "sex education" may consist of a brief visit by outside personnel, two or three unit curricula taught by a physical education teacher, or comprehensive, year-long discussion groups led by a highly trained health educator. Within that spectrum, courses may give specifics concerning contraceptive methods or may not mention them at all. This wide variation makes it difficult to assess their contribution without intensive study. It may be that the limited effects that have been reported, restricted as they are to increases in objective knowledge, underrate the effects of interventions more intensive in their offerings and in their potential impact.

A new area of activity within the schools is the provision of direct medical service. Although school health programs have long been a part of the scene, the introduction of full-scale, comprehensive clinics has been a recent development, predicated upon an understanding of the teenager's need for screening, diagnosis, treatment, and continuity of care. Some include a strong counseling or guidance component, while others are restricted to medical treatment and referral. In many cases the impetus for these programs has been the need to reduce problem behaviors such as drug use and adolescent pregnancy. The challenge is to create comprehensive programs, accepted by all members of the school community, that will address the specific needs of the student body.

Two experiments with reproductive health interventions have been able to report some reduction in pregnancy rates among students eligible for these services. The first was able to demonstrate the importance of the continued contact that was made possible in the school setting and its effect on the maintenance of contraceptive regimens (Edwards, Steinman, Arnold, & Hakanson, 1980). The second, which combined education, counseling, and medical service (Zabin et al., 1988), was able to demonstrate increased knowledge, increased utilization of clinic services, improved contraceptive effectiveness, and lower pregnancy rates; these changes among sexually active students were paralleled by a postponement of sexual onset among those who had not yet initiated intercourse (Zabin, Hirsch, Smith, Streett, & Hardy, 1986). Both these interventions made contraception and reproductive health explicit objectives of their services. Other programs have been funded with the hope that similar results would obtain, although they may not be as specifically directed. Their capacity for replication in the context of more comprehensive services is yet to be demonstrated.

Comprehensive health facilities are currently undergoing evaluation. Evidence exists that they are well received by parents and students alike. The components of individual projects vary widely, so that, even when they are well accepted and well utilized, it may be difficult to report on their impact in specific behavioral areas. This will not necessarily discredit them, because the need for continued access to care by large numbers of young people has been documented.

A third type of intervention that can take place in the schools, but which has been initiated more often in community-based projects, involves a wide range of interpersonal techniques. These programs seek to expand the young person's horizon of opportunity for the future, through job training, job placement, tutoring, augmented educational opportunities, mentorship and/or guidance. These initiatives are predicated on the belief that once young people perceive realistic future options, and internalize a belief in their potential for success, they will be better able to utilize the educational and social opportunities available to them. Literature on the association between schooling success and the perception of future options is well summarized by Hayes (1987). Once again, these initiatives are not well tested. However, because they seem to have merit in and of themselves, and are acceptable to the public, they appear to deserve trial. They may include objectives as diverse as upgrading the learning experience, improving recreational services, broadening job opportunities, discouraging premature termination of schooling, raising educational aspirations, involving communities in the social planning process, promoting parent-child communication, and helping young people adopt responsible preventive health behaviors. Whether or not mentoring and guidance programs can document effects upon premature school termination, unintended pregnancy, substance abuse, and other well-defined problems is not clear. However, the importance of these initiatives in expanding the horizons of disadvantaged youth has suggested that they may have a place within selected school districts while they attempt to demonstrate a specific, measurable impact. They are receiving increased attention. Partnerships between industry and schools, foundations and schools, and even individual benefactors and schools have led to the development of innovative experiments in motivation which have yet to be evaluated, but appear to hold promise.

There is, necessarily, some debate over the appropriate role of the school in areas that extend well beyond traditional academic disciplines. But, there is growing consensus that health education, education in the physiology of human sexuality, family life, and ethics are legitimate areas of academic concern. A role in the development of responsible citizens is a clear mandate to the schools. In the current climate it seems apparent that the promotion of preventive health behavior has a direct relationship with the ability of the school to retain students long enough to accomplish the fundamental tasks of education.

References

Edwards, L., Steinman, M., Arnold, K., & Hakanson, E. (1980). Adolescent pregnancy prevention services in high school clinics. *Family Planning Perspectives, 12*(1), 6–14.

Hayes, C. D. (Ed.). (1987). *Risking the future* (Vol. 1). Washington, DC: National Academy Press.

Jessor, R., & Jessor, S. L. (1977). *Problem behavior and psychosocial development: A longitudinal study of youth.* New York: Academic Press.

Zabin, L. S. (1984). The association between smoking and sexual behavior among teens in US contraceptive clinics. *American Journal of Public Health, 74,* 261–263.

Zabin, L. S., Hardy, J. B., Smith, E. A., & Hirsch, M. B. (1986). Substance use and its relation to sexual activity among inner-city adolescents. *Journal of Adolescent Health Care, 7,* 320–331.

Zabin, L. S., Hirsch, M. B., Smith, E. A., Streett, R., & Hardy, J. B. (1986). Evaluation of a pregnancy prevention program for urban teenagers. *Family Planning Perspectives, 18*(3), 119–126.

Zabin, L. S., Hirsch, M. B., Streett, R., Emerson, M. R., Smith, M., Hardy, J. B., & King, T. M. (1988). The Baltimore pregnancy prevention program for urban teenagers: How did it work? *Family Planning Perspectives, 20*(4), 182–187.

See Also

Academic Achievement; Achievement: Evidence from High School and Beyond; Dropouts, High School: Issues of Race and Sex; Dropouts, School; Educational Achievement and Tracking in High School; Educational Achievement, Tracking and; Family Life Education; Gifted Adolescents; Graduate School Attendance, Barriers to: Access and Equity along the Education Pipeline; Learning Disabilities in Adolescents: Description, Assessment, and Management; Minority and Female Participation in Math and Science, Increase in: The Importance of the Middle School Years; Parenthood and Marriage in Adolescence: Associations with Educational and Occupational Attainment; Preschool Programs, Impact of on Adolescent Development; Puberty Education; Schooling; School Programs, Evaluation of; School Transitions, Secondary; Sex Education; Underachievers and Dropouts.

Scientific Reasoning, Adolescent

Marcia C. Linn
University of California, Berkeley

Scientific reasoning is the ability to analyze and solve problems in such areas as energy conservation, disease transmission, nuclear power, or superconductivity. This entry addresses five issues in adolescent scientific reasoning: (1) what beliefs do adolescents typically hold about scientific phenomena?; (2) which complex reasoning skills are specific to scientific content, and which are general to all of reasoning?; (3) what aspects of scientific reasoning develop or change with age and instruction?; (4) what experiences and instructional activities contribute to effective scientific reasoning?; and (5) who acquires scientific reasoning skill, and what sorts of skill are required?

WHAT BELIEFS ABOUT SCIENCE DO ADOLESCENTS TYPICALLY HOLD?

■ Recent research shows that adolescents' ideas about science are less robust and cohesive than those of experts (di Sessa, 1988; Eylon & Linn, 1988; Larkin, McDermott, Simon, & Simon, 1980). Students' beliefs often reflect isolated observations and experiences rather than the underlying mechanisms. Thus, students believe that objects slow down rather than invoking the mechanism of friction used by experts. Students often hold conflicting ideas, believing, for example, that heat energy and temperature are the same thing, while at the same time saying that a tureen of soup has a higher temperature than a bowl of soup because there is more soup in the tureen. In contrast, physicists distinguish between temperature as an intensive property or the intensity at a given point, and heat energy as an extensive property. Students acquire an assortment of relatively disconnected ideas about scientific phenomena, whereas experts seek mechanisms or principles that make these ideas cohesive.

One reason for this lack of cohesion is that students memorize rather than organize and integrate scientific information. For example, in classical mechanics students memorize formulas, while expert physicists think qualitatively, draw free-body diagrams, and apply principles like conservation-of-energy. In thermodynamics, students learn that heat is measured in calories while temperature is measured in degrees centigrade, while experts often think about the distinction between heat energy and temperature in terms of heat flow. Thus, experts think in terms of qualitative models, while students focus on isolated bits of information.

ARE COMPLEX REASONING SKILLS GENERAL OR SPECIFIC TO SCIENCE? ■

Researchers have argued that knowledge is situated in the domain and that reasoning skills are not readily disentangled from the principles for which they are employed (Greeno & Simon, 1984). In contrast, Nickerson (1988) and Nisbett, Fong, Lehman, and Cheng (1987) point out that generalizable aspects of scientific reasoning are often overlooked in studies of situated learning. Nisbett et al. argue that students use principles about central tendency and random events learned in statistics classes when analyzing new probable situations. In contrast, work in thermodynamics demonstrates that students can gain a relatively sound understanding of the distinction between heat energy and temperature and not apply it to problems such as designing an energy-efficient home (Linn & Songer, in press). Adolescents will not generalize beyond the information given if they view scientific knowledge as isolated and unintegrated.

WHAT DEVELOPS OR CHANGES WITH AGE AND INSTRUCTION? ■

Piagetian investigations of reasoning describe similarities in performance of students at the same age. From this perspective, adolescents undergo a qualitative shift from concrete reasoning that is closely tied to the physical representation of the task to more formal or abstract and symbolic reasoning. The comprehensiveness of this hypothesized qualitative change has been seriously questioned (e.g., Driver & Erickson, 1983; Linn, 1982, 1983). Many of the tasks used to demonstrate a change from concrete to abstract thought are confounded with scientific content that only becomes available to students typically during the adolescent years.

Vygotsky offers a different developmental perspective, explaining that students have a zone of proximal development that determines the progress that they are likely to make in a given situation. This "construction zone" can be expanded by appropriate instruction and experience.

Both these views emphasize that learners construct an understanding of scientific phenomenon rather than absorb information about the world. Both argue that those wishing to foster adolescent reasoning consider developmental constraints.

WHAT CONTRIBUTES TO EFFECTIVE ADOLESCENT SCIENTIFIC REASONING? ■

Adolescents are constructing an understanding of the natural world and this process can be facilitated by appropriate informal and formal instruction. If students view science knowledge as cohesive and governed by a few mechanisms, they will attempt to construct an integrated view. To achieve this situation, science instruction must recognize the beliefs that students bring to science class and help students develop both a healthy skepticism about their own and others' ideas and a desire to identify mechanisms that govern a broad range of scientific events.

WHO ACQUIRES SCIENTIFIC REASONING SKILLS? ■

There is universal agreement that very few adolescents acquire effective scientific understanding, and furthermore, that in the past 20 years, adolescent reasoning about scientific phenomena has declined (Mullis & Jenkins, 1988). Even among 17-year-olds, the percent of students demonstrating competency at integrating scientific information was 7.5% in 1986, down from 8.5% in 1977. In addition, more than half were inadequately prepared to perform in jobs requiring technical skills or even to benefit from on-the-job training programs in technical areas.

Furthermore, there are substantial differences in science proficiency and science experience for groups defined by race, ethnicity, and gender. Black and Hispanic adolescents remain at least four years behind white adolescents in average scientific proficiency. In addition, females tend to drop behind males in the physical sciences at the onset of adolescence and continue to remain behind throughout adolescence (Mullis & Jenkins, 1988). There are disparities between both formal and informal science experiences of males and females and of at-risk populations. Those who lack competence in scientific reasoning also lack confidence in their ability to reason about scientific phenomenon. Many factors, no doubt, contribute to this confidence gap, including societal perceptions of the abilities of females and at-risk populations to perform scientific activities.

References

di Sessa, A. (1988). Knowledge in pieces. In G. Forman & P. Pufall (Eds.), *Constructivism in the computer age* (pp. 49–70). Hillsdale, NJ: Lawrence Erlbaum Associates.

Driver, R. H., & Erickson, G. L. (1983). Stability and change in student frameworks: Some empirical and theoretical issues. In A. L. Pines (Chair), *Stability and change in conceptual understanding*. Symposium conducted at the annual meeting of the American Educational Research Association.

Eylon, B., & Linn, M. C. (1988). Learning and instruction: An examination of four research perspectives in science education. *Review of Educational Research, 58*(3), 251–301.

Greeno, J. G., & Simon, H. A. (1984). Problem solving and reasoning. In R. C. Atkinson, R. Herrnstein, G. Lindzey, & R. D. Luce (Eds.), *Stevens' handbook of experimental psychology* (rev. ed., pp. 589–665). New York: John Wiley & Sons.

Larkin, J., McDermott, J., Simon, D. P., & Simon, H. A. (1980). Expert and novice performance in solving physics problems. *Science, 208,* 1335–1342.

Linn, M. C. (1982). Theoretical and practical significance of formal reasoning. *Journal of Research in Science Teaching, 19,* 727–742.

Linn, M. C. (1983). Content, context, and process in adolescent reasoning. *Journal of Early Adolescence, 3,* 63–82.

Linn, M. C., & Songer, N. B. (in press). Teaching thermodynamics to middle school students: What are appropriate cognitive demands? *Journal of Research in Science Teaching.*

Mullis, I. V. S., & Jenkins, L. B. (1988). *The science report card: Elements of risk and recovery* (Trends and achievement based on the 1986 National Assessment, Report No. 17-S-01). Princeton, NJ: Educational Testing Service.

Nickerson, R. S. (1988). *On improving thinking through instruction.* Cambridge, MA: Bolt Beranek and Newman Laboratories.

Nisbett, R. E., Fong, G. T., Lehman, D. R., & Cheng, P. W. (1987). Teaching reasoning. *Science, 238,* 625–631.

Songer, N. B., & Linn, M. C. (1988). *Everyday problem solving in thermodynamics.* Berkeley: University of California, Computer as Lab Partner Project.

See Also

Cognition, Adolescent; Cognition and Health; Cognitive Abilities and Physical Maturation; Cognitive and Psychosocial Gender Differences, Trends in; Cognitive Development; Egocentrism Theory and the "New Look" at the Imaginary Audience and Personal Fable in Adolescence; Formal Operational Thinking and Identity Resolution; Illness, Adolescents' Conceptualization of; Inhelder, Barbel; Introspectiveness, Adolescent; Memory; Piaget, Jean; Relativistic Thinking in Adolescence; Reasoning, Higher-Order, in Adolescence; Reasoning in the Adolescent; Social Intelligence in Adolescence; Spatial Ability and Maturation in Adolescence.

Scoliosis

J. W. Finkelstein
The Pennsylvania State University

Scoliosis is often called "curvature of the spine." This describes the situation accurately, for it is a condition in which the alignment of the vertebrae is abnormal, resulting in lateral curves of the spine that should not be present. A curve of the thoracic (chest level) spine whose apex is posterior, and a curve of the lumbar (lower back) spine whose apex is anterior, is normal in all individuals, but a lateral curve is normally not present at any level of the spine.

Scoliosis is not a disease, but is either secondary to some other disease or pathophysiologic process, or is idiopathic (the exact cause is unknown). Scoliosis that is not idiopathic accounts for less than 10% of all cases and may be due to either a malformation of the vertebrae themselves (5–7%) or to dysfunction of the neuromuscular units surrounding the spine (3–5%) (Kane & Moe, 1970; Renshaw, 1986). In the latter instance the nerve supply to the paraspinal muscles may be abnormal, causing the muscles to exert their forces asymmetrically, thus pulling the vertebrae out of alignment. Primary muscle disease affecting the paraspinal muscles may cause scoliosis via the same mechanism. A family history of scoliosis occurs in about 30% of cases.

Idiopathic scoliosis (which I will simply refer to as scoliosis in the remainder of this entry) is caused by unknown factors and results from both lateral displacement and abnormal rotation of the vertebrae. The condition occurs four to five times more frequently in girls than boys. It starts at about 8 to 10 years of age, a time when the early hormonal changes of puberty begin (Renshaw, 1986). It is tempting to ascribe a hormonal cause of scoliosis, but to date this has not been documented. Scoliosis rarely occurs and will rarely progress after growth has been completed. Completion of growth is usually estimated by determination of bone maturation. The method that has been used is to X-ray the iliac bone of the pelvis and to determine if the apophysis (growth plate) is fused to the ilium. If it is, growth is considered complete and there is little utility in following the progress of such an individual.

There are no symptoms that call the affected individual's attention to the presence of scoliosis and, therefore, the early cases of scoliosis most commonly go undetected until such time as the adolescent has a physical examination that includes an examination of the spine. Today, most middle and junior high schools perform routine screening for scoliosis in order to allow early detection and subsequent early treatment (Lonstein, Borklund, Wanninger, & Nelson, 1982; Tornell, 1981).

Detection of scoliosis during physical examination is simple. The adolescent needs to be clothed only in underclothes; the examiner sits facing the teen's back, with the teen standing. The examiner must make three basic observations. The first task is to observe the entire posterior surface of the body for asymmetries. Start at the neck and shoulders. Determine if the neck muscles, lower ends of the scapulae (shoulder blades), and shoulder heights are symmetrical. Then look for asymmetrical skin creases in the lateral aspects of the trunk, the lower folds of the buttocks, and the posterior aspects of the thighs. Any asymmetry is abnormal. Second, with the examiner's hands on the teen's hips, the teen is asked to stand on one foot at a time. Any tilting of the pelvis during this maneuver is abnormal. Third, the adolescent is asked to bend forward and the spine and rib cage are observed. Any lateral displacement of the spine or any asymmetry of the posterior rib cage (called a rib-hump) is abnormal. Bunnel (1984) has constructed a simple instrument to detect this abnormality. The most common abnormality is a thoracic curve with the apex to the left. Any other curve suggests a nonidiopathic cause.

If the examination is positive, spine X-rays are needed. These usually reveal the primary curve and usually one compensatory curve whose purpose is to keep the head aligned along the midline. The angles of the scoliotic curves are measured. Curves of less than 20 degrees are not treated and the patient is followed with X-rays every six months to determine if the curve is increasing or stable.

Curves between 20 and 40 degrees are treated with external bracing. This requires the teen to wear a brace extending from the chin to the pelvis all day and all night for several years, usually until growth is completed (Carr, Moe, Winter, & Lonstein, 1980). While this will prevent progression

in almost all cases, and thus prevent surgery, the teenager is likely to be highly resistant to this procedure. Bracing is highly visible and uncomfortable; teens do not like to be different from their peers and no one likes discomfort. Adolescents are not usually able to appreciate the preventive aspects of bracing (i.e., surgery, which involves a major procedure and long recovery, can be prevented) since they have difficulty in projecting themselves into the future. It is therefore important to provide support and counseling for those teens who require bracing. This should usually be provided by the adolescent's primary care physician, although some major medical centers provide counseling through their scoliosis program. However, it is rare for either primary care physicians or orthopedic surgeons to appreciate the need to take the psychosocial needs of teenagers with disabilities into consideration, and so counseling is commonly left out, to the detriment of the patient and his/her family.

If the curve is greater than 40 degrees, bracing is usually ineffective and surgery is required. This involves exposing the entire curve surgically. This usually calls for an incision of 30–60 cm along the spine. Spinal fusion is accomplished by removing superficial layers of bone along the affected vertebrae, obtaining bone from the iliac crest (pelvis) of the patient, and placing that bone along the exposed spines to graft the spine into a rigid, nonflexible, solid mass. In most instances, metal rods (Harrington or Luque rods or other similar devices) are placed along the spine to provide stability while the grafts take firmly and the bone heals. In many instances, the patient will stay in the hospital for about six months, usually in a spica plaster cast from neck to midthigh, lying on their stomach while solid fusion takes place (Renshaw, 1986). While surgery prevents further complications or progression of scoliosis, it results in a rigid spine and therefore limits movement in later life. Consequently, it is preferable to detect scoliosis early, and to use external bracing with all of its unpleasant social consequences, rather than to require surgery with its even more unpleasant consequences, surgical risks, and great expense.

Complications of untreated scoliosis can be significant. Thoracic curves of greater than 60 degrees usually cause pulmonary complications since the rib cage becomes severely deformed and one lung is usually significantly compressed. In addition, untreated scoliosis commonly causes arthritis of the spine and slippage of the vertebrae, both of which may become very painful (Weinstein, Zavala, & Ponsetti, 1981).

It seems obvious that early detection and treatment by bracing to prevent progression is preferable to surgery. In addition, the cost of a screening program is usually made up for by the prevention of cases requiring expensive surgical procedures. In one state the prevention of two surgeries paid for the entire screening program. Thus, early detection not only prevents morbidity and surgical mortality, but is cost effective (Lonstein, Borklund, Wanninger, & Nelson, 1982).

References

Bunnel, W. P. (1984). An objective criterion for scoliosis screening. *Journal of Bone and Joint Surgery, 66,* 1381–1386.

Carr, W. A., Moe, J. H., Winter, R. B., & Lonstein, J. E. (1980). Treatment of idiopathic scoliosis in the Milwaukee brace: Long-term results. *Journal of Bone and Joint Surgery, 62*(A), 559–563.

Kane, W. J., & Moe, J. W. (1970). A scoliosis prevalence survey. *Minnesota Clinical Orthopedics, 69,* 216–222.

Lonstein, J. E., Borklund, S., Wanninger, M. H., & Nelson, R. P. (1982). Voluntary school screening for scoliosis in Minnesota. *Journal of Bone and Joint Surgery, 64*(A), 481–487.

Renshaw, T. S. (1986). *Pediatric orthopedics in major problems in clinical pediatrics* (Vol. 28). Philadelphia: W. B. Saunders.

Tornell, G. (1981). The changing pattern of scoliosis due to effective screening. *Journal of Bone and Joint Surgery, 63*(A), 337–342.

Weinstein, S., Zavala, D. C., & Ponsetti, I. V. (1981). Idiopathic scoliosis: Long-term follow-up and prognosis in untreated patients. *Journal of Bone and Joint Surgery, 63*(A), 702–709.

See Also

AIDS and Adolescents; AIDS and HIV Infection in Adolescents: The Role of Education and Antibody Testing; Asthma in Puberty and Adolescence; Cystic Fibrosis in Puberty and Adolescence; Diabetes; Gynecomastia; Illness, Adolescents' Conceptualization of; Illness, Chronic; Injury during Adolescence, Risk Factors for; Injuries, Unintentional: Gender Differences in Accidents; Neurodevelopmental Variation and Dysfunction in Adolescence; Premenstrual Syndrome (PMS); Sexually Transmitted Diseases in Adolescence; Spina Bifida, the Adolescent with.

Self-Concept, Adolescent

William Damon
Brown University

Self-concept is a cognitive system with affective implications for how one evaluates oneself and behavioral implications for how one guides one's life. Like all cognitive systems, self-concept becomes transformed in the course of development. Children answer the question "What kind of person are you?" in very different ways as they grow older. Not only do they change the aspects of the self that they focus on (for example, the self's beliefs as opposed to the self's activities), but they also adopt more sophisticated means of organizing all the diversity of characteristics that they recognize as aspects of themselves.

During the adolescent period there are several dramatic changes in how the self is construed. These changes reflect, in part, a rapid growth in cognitive capacities that occurs at the end of childhood, a growth that enables the adolescent to pull together diverse sorts of information into formal categorical systems (Flavell, 1985; Piaget, 1983). In addition, these changes in self-concept also reflect the adolescent's awakening need to establish a coherent personal identity (Erikson, 1968). The resulting transformation in how the self is construed in turn plays an important role in reorganizing the nature of teenage social relationships.

Prior to the adolescent years young children view themselves in terms of their bodily characteristics, their actions, their family and group memberships, and their momentary moods (Damon & Hart, 1988; Flavell, 1985; Keller, Ford, & Meachum, 1978). For example, in response to a question like "What kind of person are you?," a young child might answer "I'm big for my age," or "Sometimes I wake up cranky from my naps." Generally such self-descriptors are not connected to one another; nor are they indicative of any overall notion of a stable self. Later in childhood children begin to use such statements a bit more strategically, as a way of comparing themselves with others, for example. A ten-year-old might say "I'm a better ball player than any of the other kids" (Damon & Hart, 1988; Ruble, 1983). Such statements, though, are still disconnected from one another and are mostly transient in character.

By the time of early adolescence the self begins to be understood in more enduring and general terms. Young adolescents often characterize themselves as having distinct personality traits (Bernstein, 1980; Damon & Hart, 1988; Harter, 1986; Montmeyer & Eisen, 1977). Such traits are seen to last across time and in various situations. The belief in such enduring personality traits enables young adolescents for the first time to remove the self from the immediate present and to establish links between their past, present, and future selves (Secord & Peevers, 1974). But although young adolescents' "trait theory" of self can help them pull together disparate aspects of personality into a few general notions, these notions often conflict with one another. For example, young adolescents might describe themselves by citing opposing traits such as "smart" and "dumb" or "shy" and "outgoing" at the same time (Harter, 1986). These adolescents may be quite disturbed about the contradiction and yet be wholly unable to explain or resolve it to their own satisfaction.

By late adolescence a marked trend toward systematizing the many disparate features of the self occurs. The older adolescent, armed with greater intellectual power, is able to find integrating principles that recognize the diversity but still maintain the coherence of the self-system (Bernstein, 1980; Harter, 1986). As one example, the older adolescent now might say: "I'm very adaptable. When I'm around my friends, who think that what I say is important, I'm very talkative; but around my family I'm quiet because they're never interested enough to really listen to me." Often the older adolescent invokes ideological beliefs, planned life-styles, or moral values as the key integrating principles of their self-systems (Bernstein, 1980; Damon & Hart, 1988). Their view of their own personality is then reformulated to reflect these enduring sets of beliefs and plans. This provides the adolescent with the kind of cognitive consistency and affective sense of unity that Erikson has written about in his personal identity theory (Erikson, 1968).

A model describing the development of self-concept through the late adolescent years is depicted in Figure 1. In this model development is portrayed as vertical move-ments along each of seven dimensions of self: the physical, active, social, and psychological self, and the continuity, distinctness, and agency of the self. The first four of these dimensions on the cube's front face represent the aspects of the self that may be seen as object by either self or other (the "self as known," or the "objective self"). The last three dimensions on the cube's side face represent the aspects of self that may be seen as subject by oneself (the "self as knower," or the "subjective self"—see Damon & Hart, 1988; James, 1898; Lewis & Brooks-Gunn, 1979). Development along each of the dimensions culminates in a "level 4," systematic, belief-driven construel of self that normally emerges at the end of adolescence. The model depicted in Figure 1 recently has been validated through a series of cross-sectional and longitudinal studies among several populations of children and adolescents (Damon & Hart, 1988).

The cognitive changes that transform adolescent self-concept set the stage not only for the construction of a unified personal identity but also for some uncomfortable emotional experiences that are typical of this age period. Research has found, for example, that self-criticism is strongest during adolescence and that throughout adulthood people tend to identify adolescence as the worst period of life (Lowenthal, Thurner, & Chiriboga, 1975). Moreover, other research has established that adolescence is the age at which affective conflicts and disturbances in self-concept are most likely to appear (Rosenberg, 1985).

Much of the adolescent's emotional turmoil springs from a new awareness of discrepancies between the ideal and the real self, an awareness created by the improved conceptual adequacy of the adolescent's self-understanding. Psychologists have found that the cognitive maturity of

The Self-As-Object

Developmental Level	General Organizing Principle	Physical Self	Active Self	Social Self	Psychological Self
Late Adolescence	*Systematic Beliefs and Plans*	Physical attributes reflecting volitional choices, or personal and moral standards.	Active attributes that reflect choices. Personal or moral standards.	Moral or personal choices concerning social relations or social-personality characteristics.	Belief systems, personal philosophy. Self's own thought processes.
Early Adolescence	*Inter-Personal Implications*	Physical attributes that influence social appeal and social interactions.	Active attributes that influence social appeal and social interactions.	Social-personality characteristics.	Social sensitivity, communicative competence, and other psychologically related social skills.
Middle and Late Adolescence	*Comparative Assessments*	Capability-related physical attributes.	Abilities relative to others. Self or normative standards.	Abilities or acts considered in light of others' reactions.	Knowledge, cognitive abilities, or ability-related emotions.
Early Childhood	*Catagorical Identifications*	Bodily patterns or material possessions.	Typical behavior.	Fact of membership in particular social relations or groups.	Momentary moods, feelings, preferences, and aversions.

The Self-As-Subject

Developmental Level	General Organizing Principle	Continuity	Distinctness	Agency
Late Adolescence	*Systematic Beliefs and Plans*	Relations between past, present, and future selves.	Unique subjective experience and interpretations of events.	Personal and moral evaluations influence self.
Early Adolescence	*Inter-Personal Implications*	Ongoing recognition of self by others.	Unique combination of psychological and physical attributes.	Communication and reciprocal interaction influence self.
Middle and Late Adolescence	*Comparative Assessments*	Permanent cognitive and active capabilities and immutable self-characteristics.	Comparisons between self and other along isolated dimensions.	Efforts, wishes, and talents influence self.
Early Childhood	*Catagorical Identifications*	Catagorical identifications.	Catagorical identifications.	External, uncontrollable factors determine self.

Source: Damon, W. and Hart, D. *Self-understanding in childhood and adolescence.* New York: Cambridge University Press, 1988.

FIGURE 1

the adolescent self-concept brings with it a sense of disparity between one's actual self and one's ideal self (Glick & Zigler, 1985). This sense of disparity is an intellectual achievement in the sense that it creates a more realistic view of self. But it can also yield some unique forms of emotional distress. Two such distinct forms, each linked to a particular type of ideal/real self-discrepancy, have been identified in developmental research. Perceived discrepancy between the actual self and the self that one *wants* to be can lead to disappointment, depression, and dejection (Higgins, 1987). Perceived discrepancy between the actual self and the self that one believes one *ought*

to be can lead to restlessness, fear, and generalized agitation (Higgins, 1987).

During adolescence the sense of disparity between real and ideal selves is particularly acute in the area of one's physical appearance (Harter, 1988). This poses a special emotional problem for the adolescent, since it is physical appearance that contributes most to self-esteem during this period (Lerner & Brackney, 1978; Lerner, Orlos, & Knapp, 1976; Simmons & Rosenberg, 1975). Moreover, this tendency is even more aggravated for adolescent girls than for boys. Not only do girls consider their physical attractiveness to be a more pressing issue than do boys, but girls often also feel less secure about their own appearances than do boys (Simmons & Blyth, 1987). It is not surprising, then, that teenage girls generally report lower self-esteem than teenage boys (Harter, 1988). In our culture girls who mature physically at an earlier age than other girls seem to be especially "at risk" for negative self-esteem, partly because they feel awkward and out-of-step with societal standards of attractiveness and partly because they are still unprepared to cope with the social and sexual expectations that their early maturity fosters (Peterson & Taylor, 1980; Simmons & Blyth, 1987).

For most adolescents, disturbances in self-concept usually result in nothing more serious than relatively transient emotional discomfort. But in some young people such disturbances can lead to severe psychological and behavioral disorders. Poor self-esteem has been implicated in depression (Harter, 1986; Rosenberg, 1985; Seligman, 1976); teenage suicide (Kazdin, French, Unis, & Esveldt-Dawson, 1983; Pfeffer, 1986); anorexia nervosa (Bruch, 1978; Damon & Hart, 1988); and delinquency (Bynner, O'Malley, & Bachman, 1981; Markus & Nurious, 1986; Melcher, 1986). The seriousness of the disorder depends not only on the nature of the self-concept disburbance but also on other co-occurring conditions in the adolescent's life. When negative self-esteem is compounded by difficult transitions in school or family life, or by other stressful events, behavioral breakdown can occur (Rutter & Garmezy, 1983; Simmons & Blyth, 1987).

But if the insecure adolescent receives strong social support from family and friends, the emotional discomfort is likely to pass without serious consequence. As the adolescent years unfold, peer support becomes increasingly important for the maintenance of positive self-esteem. Parental support assumes a secondary, though still vital, role in bolstering adolescents' feelings about themselves.

References

Bernstein, R. M. (1980). The development of the self-system during adolescence. *Journal of Genetic Psychology, 136*, 231–245.

Bruch, H. (1978). *The golden cage: The enigma of anorexia nervosa.* Cambridge: Harvard University Press.

Bynner, J. M., O'Malley, P. M., & Bachman, J. C. (1981). Self-esteem and delinquency revisited. *Journal of Youth and Adolescence, 10*, 407–441.

Damon, W., & Hart, D. (1988). *Self-understanding in childhood and adolescence.* New York: Cambridge University Press.

Erikson, E. (1968). *Identity: Youth and crisis.* New York: Norton.

Flavell, J. (1985). *Cognitive development* (2nd ed.). Englewood Cliffs, NJ: Prentice-Hall.

Glick, M., & Zigler, E. (1985). Self-image: A cognitive-developmental approach. In R. Leahy (Ed.), *The development of self* (pp. 1–47). Orlando, FL: Academic Press.

Harter, S. (1983). The development of the self and the self-system. In M. Hetherington (Ed.), *Handbook of child psychology* (4th ed., vol. 4, pp. 285–385). New York: Wiley.

Harter, S. (1986). Cognitive-developmental processes in the integration of concepts about emotions and the self. *Social Cognition, 4*, 119–151.

Harter, S. (1988). Developmental and dynamic changes in the nature of self-concept: Implications for child psychotherapy. In S. Shirk (Ed.), *Cognitive development and child psychotherapy* (pp. 28–54). New York: Plenum.

Higgins, E. T. (1987). Self-discrepancy: A theory relating self and affect. *Psychological Review, 94*, 319–340.

James, W. (1898). *Psychology.* New York: World Publishing.

Kazdin, A. E., French, N. H., Unis, A. S., & Esveldt-Dawson, K. (1983). Helplessness, depression, and suicidal intent among psychiatrically disturbed inpatient children. *Journal of Consulting and Clinical Psychology, 51*, 504–510.

Keller, A., Ford, L., & Meacham, J. (1978). Dimensions of self-concept in preschool children. *Developmental Psychology, 14*, 483–489.

Lerner, R. M., & Brackney, B. E. (1978). The importance of inner and outer body parts to attitudes in the self-concept of late adolescents. *Sex roles, 4*, 225–237.

Lerner, R. M., Orlos, J. B., & Knapp, J. (1976). Physical attractiveness, physical effectiveness, and self-concept of late adolescents. *Adolescence, 11*, 313–326.

Lewis, M., & Brooks-Gunn, J. (1979). *Social cognition and the acquisition of self.* New York: Plenum.

Lowenthal, M., Thurner, M., & Chiriboga, D. (1975). *Four stages of life.* San Francisco: Jossey-Bass.

Marcus, H., & Nurius, P. (1986). Possible selves. *American Psychologist, 41*, 954–969.

Melcher, B.. (1986). *Moral reasoning, self-identity, and moral action: A study of conduct disorder in adolescence.* Unpublished doctoral dissertation, University of Pittsburgh, Pittsburgh, PA.

Montemayor, R., & Eisen, M. (1977). The development of self-conceptions from childhood to adolescence. *Developmental Psychology, 13*, 314–319.

Peterson, A. C., & Taylor, B. (1980). Puberty: Biological change and psychological adaptation. In J. Adelson (Ed.), *Handbook of adolescent psychology.* New York: Wiley.

Pfeffer, C. (1986). *The suicidal child.* New York: Guilford Press.

Piaget, J. (1983). Piaget's theory. In P. H. Mussen (Ed.), *Handbook of child psychology* (Vol. 1, pp. 103–129). New York: Wiley.

Rosenberg, M. (1985). Self-concept and psychological well-being in adolescence. In R. Leahy (Ed.), *The development of the self.* (pp. 205–242). New York: Academic Press.

Ruble, D. (1983). The development of social-comparison processes and their role in achievement-related self-socialization. In E. T. Higgins, D. N. Ruble, & W. W. Hartup (Eds.), *Social cognition and social development* (pp. 82–110). New York: Cambridge University Press.

Rutter, M., & Garmezy, N. (1983). Developmental psychopathology. In M. Hetherington (Ed.), *Handbook of child psychology* (Vol. 4, pp. 775–911). New York: Wiley.

Secord, P., & Peevers, B. (1974). The development of person concepts. In T. Mischel (Ed.), *Understanding other persons* (pp. 65–97). Oxford: Blackwell.

Seligman, M. E. (1976). *Helplessness: On depression, development, and death.* San Francisco: W. Freeman.

Simmons, R. G., & Blyth, D. A. (1987). *Moving into adolescence: The impact of pubertal change and school context.* New York: Aldine de Gruyter.

Simmons, R. G., & Rosenberg, F. (1975). Sex, sex roles, and self-image. *Journal of Youth and Adolescence, 4*, 229–258.

See Also

Ego Development; Erikson, Erik Homburger; Motivations and Self-Perceptions, Changes in; Self-Regulation; Self-Efficacy, Impact of Perceptions on Adolescent Life Paths.

Self-Destructiveness, Chronic, Role of in Adolescence

Kathryn Kelley
Lori J. Dawson
University at Albany
State University of New York

Because adolescence is a time marked by sweeping changes physically, emotionally, and cognitively (Capes, 1975), the adolescent may turn to some self-destructive methods. These include both acute self-destructive measures, such as suicide, which has been decreasing in all age groups with the exception of those aged 15–24 (Berman, 1986), and more long-term, chronically self-destructive strategies.

Kelley (1985a) has proposed that individuals differ with respect to choice dilemmas in that some individuals respond to affective factors while others utilize a cognitive approach. Those individuals who respond to the immediate emotional factors are more likely to engage in chronically self-destructive strategies. Chronic self-destructiveness has been defined as the "generalized tendency to engage in acts that increase the probability of experiencing future negative consequences and/or reduce the probability of attaining future positive ones" (Kelley et al., 1985). Scores on the theoretically derived scale of chronic self-destructiveness are related to several factors commonly associated with the behavior of some adolescents, such as sensation seeking, risk taking, and impulsivity. Highly destructive adolescents did indeed report more incidents of rebelliousness, including scrapes with the legal system, commission of undetected crimes, and interpersonal dishonesty.

Adolescent males express more chronically self-destructive tendency than do females, as shown in a cross-cultural study conducted by Kelley, Singh, Rodriguez-Carrillo, and Cheung (1987). They studied adolescent and young adult males and females in Hong Kong, India, Venezuela, and the United States, and found that males in Hong Kong and the United States expressed higher chronic self-destructive tendencies than females. No gender differences were found in the sample in India and Venezuela.

Chronic self-destructiveness is related to a variety of negative behaviors among adolescents, including inadequate diet and health maintenance, abuse of drugs such as alcohol and marijuana, and poorer achievement in school. Kelley et al. (1985) surveyed 94 undergraduate college students with regard to their cheating behaviors. They found that chronic self-destructiveness was directly related to cheating. Additionally, when a median split was performed on the chronic self-destructiveness dimension, it was found that 100% of the males and 87% of the females low in chronic self-destructiveness indicated that they never or rarely cheated. None of the male respondents and only 22% of the female subjects high in chronic self-destructiveness reported cheating so infrequently.

Accidents, especially traffic accidents, are the leading cause of death among adolescents (Gordon, 1986). Kelley et al. (1985) suggest that since traffic safety depends on a number of mildly annoying acts such as wearing seat belts and obeying speed limits, as well as more crucial acts such as refraining from consuming alcohol and/or drugs before driving, high levels of chronic self-destructiveness would work against obeying these rules. Chronic self-destructiveness was directly related to the number of traffic and parking tickets received, and inversely related to seat belt usage. Additionally, those high in chronic self-destructiveness were less likely to endorse the mandatory use of seat belts and penalties for driving while intoxicated. The relationship between chronic self-destructiveness and number of violations was stronger for moving violations than for the less serious parking violations. A median split found that of those low in chronic self-destructiveness, over 90% report having received either none or only one ticket for a moving violation. Comparatively, 70% of the females and 83% of the males high in chronic self-destructiveness reported receiving three or more tickets for moving violations.

In the interpersonal sphere, female adolescents high in chronic self-destructiveness report a greater frequency of having experienced sexual coercion (Kelley, 1987; Dawson, 1988). A number of reasons may explain this finding. The chronically self-destructive young female may miss the signs of danger that her date displays, and ignore the threat that exists. Among females (but not males), chronic self-destructiveness and positive sexual attitudes are correlated, compounding the likelihood that these females would be motivated to approach sexual situations without appropriate defensiveness (Kelley, 1985b).

Chronic self-destructiveness and locus of control are also related. An individual with an internal locus of control believes that reinforcements are directly related to one's internal efforts, while those with an external locus of control believe that rewards are not contingent upon an individual's effort, but instead are controlled by external forces such as luck (Rotter & Hochreich, 1975). It was hypothesized that those high in chronic self-destructiveness would have an external locus of control, since they would be able to justify any negative consequences they might experience as a result of engaging in maladaptive behaviors to external causes and not to themselves. This hypothesis was confirmed using undergraduate students from two different universities in the U.S. (Kelley et al., 1985) and two other countries (Kelley et al., 1986).

The construct of chronic self-destructiveness appears to be a useful one for understanding the problems that may beset adolescents in a fast-paced, Western society. It provides a way of unifying these difficult, pervasive behaviors under one rubric: chronic self-destructiveness.

References

Berman, A. (1986). Helping suicidal adolescents: Needs and responses. In C. Corr and

J. McNeil (Eds.), *Adolescence and death* (pp. 151–166). New York: Springer.

Capes, M. (1975). Adolescence and change. In S. Meyerson (Ed.), *Adolescence: The crises of adjustment* (pp. 41–53). London: George Allen & Urwin Ltd.

Dawson, L. J. (1988). *Personality characteristics of sexually coerced females in a repeated-measures design.* Unpublished master's thesis, University at Albany, State University of New York.

Gordon, A. (1986). The tattered cloak of immortality. In C. Corr and J. McNeil (Eds.), *Adolescence and death* (pp. 16–31). New York: Springer.

Kelley, K. (1985a). *Conceptualizing chronic self-destructiveness.* Albany, NY: University at Albany, State University of New York. (ERIC Document Reproduction Service No. ED 261 286).

Kelley, K. (1985b, April). *Chronic self-destructiveness: Construct validity and empirical findings.* Paper presented at the William and Mary College, Norfolk, VA.

Kelley, K. (1987, September). *Chronic self-destructiveness: Research findings and theory.* Paper presented to the Department of Counseling Psychology, University at Albany, SUNY.

Kelley, K., Byrne, D., Przbyla, D., Eberly, C., Eberly, B., Greendlinger, V., Wan, C., and Gorsky, J. (1985). Chronic self-destruc-tiveness: Conceptualization, measurement, and initial validation of the construct. *Motivation and Emotion, 9,* 135–151.

Kelley, K., Cheung, F., Rodriguez-Carrillo, P., Singh, R., Wan, C., & Becker, M. (1986). Chronic self-destructiveness and locus of control in cross-cultural perspective. *Journal of Social Psychology, 126,* 573–577.

Kelley, K., Singh, R., Rodriguez-Carrillo, P., & Cheung, F. (1987, August). *Gender differences in chronic self-defeating tendencies.* Paper presented at the meeting of the American Psychological Association, New York, Washington, DC.

Rotter, J., & Hochreich, D. (1975). *Personality.* Plainview, Illinois: Scott, Foresman.

See Also

Aggressive Behavior in Adolescence; Attention Deficit Disorder and Hyperactivity; Bulimia Nervosa in Adolescence; Conflict, Adolescent-Parent: A Model and a Method; Delinquency; Handicapped Adolescents, Providing Services for; Learning Disabilities in Adolescents: Description, Assessment, and Management; Problem Behavior in Adolescence; Psychophysiological/Psychosomatic Problems; Runaways, Negative Consequences for; Stress and the Adolescent; Stress and Coping in the Adolescent; Suicide, Adolescent; Suicides, Cluster; Type A and Teenagers.

Self-Efficacy, Impact of Self-Beliefs on Adolescent Life Paths

Albert Bandura
Stanford University

Each period of human development brings with it new competency requirements and new challenges to coping capabilities. Adolescence is a crucial formative period in this developmental process because the roles of adulthood must begin to be addressed in almost every dimension of life. The task of choosing what course of lifework to pursue looms large during adolescence. Learning how to deal with emotionally invested partnerships and sexuality becomes a matter of considerable importance. As adolescents expand the nature and scope of their activities into the larger social community, they have to assume increasing responsibility for conduct that plays a more decisive role than do childhood involvements in fostering or foreclosing different life courses. The way in which adolescents develop and exercise their personal efficacy during this period can, therefore, play a key role in setting the course life paths take.

Operative competence is a generative capability that can be greatly enhanced or impaired by cognitive nonability factors rather than a fixed attribute. In any given domain successful psychosocial functioning requires not only sets of skills, but also self-beliefs of efficacy to ensure their successful development and use. Perceived self-efficacy is concerned with people's beliefs in their capabilities to mobilize the motivation, cognitive resources, and courses of action necessary to exercise control over environmental demands. People with the same skills may perform poorly, adequately, or extraordinarily depending on the strength of their self-judged efficacy that they can succeed in a given endeavor.

Sources of Self-Efficacy

People's beliefs in their efficacy can be enhanced in four principal ways (Bandura, 1986). The most effective way of developing a strong sense of efficacy is through *mastery experiences*. Performance successes build an efficacious outlook, while failures create self-doubts. If people experience only easy successes they come to expect quick results and are easily discouraged by failure. A resilient sense of efficacy requires experience in overcoming obstacles through perseverant effort. Some setbacks and difficulties in human pursuits, therefore, serve a useful purpose in teaching that success usually requires sustained effort. After people have become convinced they have what it takes to succeed, they persevere in the face of adversity and quickly rebound from setbacks.

The second way of strengthening self-beliefs of efficacy is by *modeling*. The models in people's lives serve as sources of interest, inspiration, and skills. Ready access to able models fosters competencies that strengthen beliefs in one's capabilities. Indeed, biographical study reveals that models who seek challenges and get deeply engrossed in what they do often leave lasting impressions on others that help to set the course of their life pursuits. People judge their capabilities partly in comparison with the achievements of others. Seeing people similar to oneself succeed by sustained effort raises observers' beliefs about their own efficacy. By the same token, negative modeling can be an undermining influence: the failures of similar others can instill self-doubts about one's own efficacy to master similar activities.

Social persuasion is a third way of strengthening people's beliefs that they possess the capabilities to achieve what they seek. Social support and realistic encouragements that lead people to exert greater effort increase their chances of success. Skilled efficacy builders do more than simply convey positive appraisals. In addition to cultivating people's beliefs in their own capabilities, they structure situations for them in ways that bring success and avoid placing them prematurely in situations where they are likely to experience repeated failure. To ensure progress in personal development, success is measured in terms of self-improvement rather than by triumphs over others.

People also rely partly on *judgments of their bodily states* in assessing their efficacy.

They read their stress and tension as signs of personal vulnerability to deficient performance. In activities involving strength and stamina, they use somatic information as indicators of physical capacity or limitations. The fourth way of modifying self-beliefs of efficacy is to enhance physical status, reduce stress levels, or alter how people interpret their bodily states. The accelerated rate of physical development during adolescence heightens attention to bodily states and structures. Physical changes that can affect physical prowess and social status among one's peers may produce significant cognitive changes in self-schemata of efficacy in physical and social domains of functioning.

Diverse Effects of Self-Efficacy

Beliefs of personal efficacy can affect psychosocial development and functioning in diverse ways (Bandura, 1986, 1989). First, they influence *choice of pursuits* and social milieus. People tend to avoid activities and situations that they believe exceed their capabilities, but they undertake and assuredly perform activities that they judge themselves capable of handling. Any factor that influences choice behavior can have profound effects on the course of personal development. A positive sense of personal efficacy promotes active engagement in activities that contribute to the growth of competencies. In contrast, beliefs of self-inefficacy that lead people to shun enriching environments and activities retard development of potentialities and shield self-handicapping beliefs from corrective change.

The impact of perceived self-efficacy on choice behavior is well documented in studies showing that student's beliefs in their efficacy influences their career decision making and occupational life paths (Betz & Hackett, 1986; Lent & Hackett, 1987). The stronger their self-belief in their capabilities, the more career options they consider possible, the greater the interest they show in them, and the better they prepare themselves educationally for different occupational pursuits. Biased cultural practices, stereotypic modeling of gender roles, and dissuading opportunity structures eventually leave their mark on women's beliefs about their occupational efficacy (Hackett & Betz, 1981). Female students are especially prone to limit their interests and range of career options by self-beliefs that they lack the necessary capabilities for occupations traditionally dominated by men, even though they do not differ from male students in actual ability. The self-limitation arises from perceived inefficacy, rather than from actual inability. However, changes in cultural attitudes and practices may be weakening the self-efficacy barriers. Students currently coming through the high school ranks reveal a much smaller disparity between males and females in their beliefs about their efficacy to pursue successfully varied careers (Post-Kammer & Smith, 1985).

A second important way in which self-efficacy beliefs govern psychosocial development is through their *effects on motivation* (Bandura, 1988a). The stronger the perceived self-efficacy, the more effort people invest in activities and the longer they persevere in the face of obstacles and failure experiences. Considerable research shows that a strong sense of efficacy fosters academic achievement, interpersonal competencies, and health-promoting habits (Bandura, 1986; 1988b; Leary & Atherton, 1986; O'Leary, 1985; Schunk, 1984; Strecher, DeVellis, Becker, & Rosenstock, 1986).

With growing independence during adolescence some experimentation with risky behavior is not all that uncommon (Jessor, 1984). Adolescents expand and strengthen their sense of efficacy by learning how to deal successfully not only with advantageous life events but also with potentially troublesome involvements in which they are unpracticed. Development of resilient self-efficacy requires some experience in mastering difficulties through perseverant effort. This is best achieved through guided mastery experiences (Bandura, 1986). Overcoming difficulties instills a strong belief in one's capabilities that provides the staying power in the face of difficulties. Insulation from problematic situations leaves one ill-prepared to cope with adversities. However, impoverished high-risk environments present harsh realities with minimal positive resources and social supports for culturally valued pursuits. But they provide extensive modeling, opportunity structures, incentives, and other social supports for the development of efficacy for transgressive life paths that may be self-impairing or socially detrimental. Such high-risk environments severely tax the coping efficacy of youth enmeshed in them to make it through adolescence in ways that do not irreversibly foreclose many beneficial life paths.

Self-beliefs of efficacy affect how much *stress and despondency* are experienced in coping with environmental demands, as well as choice of pursuits and level of motivation (Bandura, 1988b). People experience little stress either in anticipation or while managing potential threats they judge themselves to be capable of controlling. But when they cope with threats and taxing demands that exceed their perceived coping capabilities, they experience high subjective distress, autonomic arousal, and generate high levels of stress-related hormones.

The satisfactions people derive from what they do are determined, in large part, by the personal standards against which they measure their accomplishments. People who become easily depressed tend to set their personal standards of self-worth well above their perceived capabilities (Bandura, 1988a; Kanfer & Zeiss, 1983). High aspirations are self-motivating, rather than self-discouraging, provided that accomplishments are measured against attainable subgoals by which high aspirations are realized. Perceived self-inefficacy in cultivating desired interpersonal relationships can similarly breed despondency (Holahan & Holahan, 1987).

There is a growing body of evidence that human attainments and positive well-being require an optimistic sense of personal efficacy. This is because ordinary social realities are strewn with difficulties. They are full of impediments, adversities, failures, setbacks, frustrations, and inequities. People must have a robust sense of personal efficacy to sustain the perseverant effort needed to succeed without being unduly encumbered by stress and despondency. Indeed, anxious and depressed individuals differ little in their actual skills from those who are unburdened by such problems. But the nonanxious and nondepressed judge themselves more adept than they really are and take a more optimistic view of their efficacy to exercise influence over events.

Self-beliefs of efficacy additionally influence whether thought patterns while coping with difficult situations are self-debilitating or self-aiding. Those who have a strong sense of efficacy adopt a problem-solving approach in which they focus their attention on figuring out solutions to the problems they encounter (Wood & Bandura, 1989). In contrast, those who are beset by self-doubts tend to become self-preoccupied with evaluative concerns. They dwell on their personal deficiencies and envision failure scenarios that beget adverse consequences. Such intrusive thinking undermines effective use of capabilities by diverting attention from how best to overcome problems to concerns over personal deficiences and possible calamities (Sarason, 1975).

Adolescence has often been characterized as a period of psychosocial turmoil. While no period of life is ever free of problems, contrary to the stereotype of "storm and stress," most adolescents negotiate the important transitions of this period without undue disturbance or discord (Bandura, 1964; Petersen, 1988; Rutter, Graham, Chadwick, & Yule, 1976). Indeed, transitional school experiences generally sustain or even increase a sense of personal competence (Nottelmann, 1987). However, youngsters who enter adolescence beset by a disabling sense of inefficacy transport their vulnerability to distress and debility to the new environmental demands. For example, in managing the transition from the elementary to the junior high environment, efficacious students weather inefficacious teachers, whereas inefficacious students become even more self-doubting of their capabilities (Midgley, Feldlaufer, & Eccles, 1989). Adolescents who are insecure in their efficacy are less able to avoid or curtail involvement in problem behaviors that jeopardize beneficial life courses (Allen, Leadbeater, & Aber, in press). Thus, the ease with which the transition from childhood to the demands of adulthood is made depends, in no small measure, on the strength of personal efficacy built up through prior mastery experiences.

References

Allen, J. P., Leadbeater, B. J., & Aber, J. L. (1990, in press). The relationship of adolescent's expectations and values to delinquency, hard drug use and unprotected sexual intercourse. *Development and Psychopathology.*

Bandura, A. (1964). The stormy decade: Fact or fiction? *Psychology in the Schools, 1*, 224–231.

Bandura, A. (1986). *Social foundations of thought and action: A social cognitive theory.* Englewood Cliffs, NJ: Prentice-Hall.

Bandura, A. (1988a). Self-regulation of motivation and action through goal systems. In V. Hamilton, G. H. Bower, & N. H. Frijda (Eds.), *Cognitive perspectives on emotion and motivation* (pp. 37–61). Dordrecht, Netherlands: Martinus Nijhoff.

Bandura, A. (1988b). Perceived self-efficacy: Exercise of control through self-belief. In J. P. Dauwalder, M. Perrez, & V. Hobi (Eds.), *Annual series of European research in behavior therapy* (Vol. 2, pp. 27–59). Lisse, Netherlands: Swets & Zeitlinger.

Bandura, A. (1989). Perceived self-efficacy in the exercise of personal agency. *The Psychologist: Bulletin of the British Psychological Society, 2*, 411–424.

Bandura, A. (in press). Self-efficacy mechanism in physiological activation and health-promoting behavior. In J. Madden, IV, S. Matthysse, & J. Barchas (Eds.), *Adaptation, learning, and affect.* New York: Raven Press.

Betz, N. E., & Hackett, G. (1986). Applications of self-efficacy theory to understanding career choice behavior. *Journal of Social and Clinical Psychology, 4*, 279–289.

Hackett, G., & Betz, N. E. (1981). A self-efficacy approach to the career development of women. *Journal of Vocational Behavior, 18*, 326–339.

Holahan, C. K., & Holahan, C. J. (1987). Self-efficacy, social support, and depression in aging: A longitudinal analysis. *Journal of Gerontology, 42*, 65–68.

Jessor, R. (1984). Adolescent development and behavioral health. In J. D. Matarazzo, N. E. Miller, J. A. Herd, & S. M. Weiss (Eds.), *Behavioral health: A handbook of health enhancement and disease prevention* (pp. 69–90). Silver Spring, MD: Wesley.

Kanfer, R., & Zeiss, A. M. (1983). Depression,

interpersonal standard-setting, and judgments of self-efficacy. *Journal of Abnormal Psychology, 92*, 319–329.

Leary, M. R., & Atherton, S. C. (1986). Self-efficacy, social anxiety, and inhibition in interpersonal encounters. *Journal of Social and Clinical Psychology, 4*, 256–267.

Lent, R. W., & Hackett, G. (1987). Career self-efficacy: Empirical status and future directions. *Journal of Vocational Behavior, 30*, 347–382.

Midgley, C., Feldlaufer, H., & Eccles, J. S. (1989). Change in teacher efficacy and student self- and task-related beliefs in mathematics during the transition to junior high school. *Journal of Educational Psychology, 81*, 247–258.

Nottelmann, E. D. (1987). Competence and self-esteem during transition from childhood to adolescence. *Developmental Psychology, 23*, 441–450.

O'Leary, A. (1985). Self-efficacy and health. *Behaviour Research and Therapy, 23*, 437–451.

Petersen, A. C. (1988). Adolescent development. In M. R. Rosenzweig & L. W. Porter (Eds.), *Annual review of psychology* (Vol. 39, pp. 583–607). Palo Alto, CA: Annual Reviews.

Post-Kammer, P., & Smith, P. (1985). Sex differences in career self-efficacy, consideration, and interests of eighth and ninth graders. *Journal of Counseling Psychology, 32*, 551–559.

Rutter, M., Graham, P., Chadwick, O. F. D., & Yule, W. (1976). Adolescent turmoil: Fact or fiction? *Journal of Child Psychology and Psychiatry, 17*, 35–56.

Sarason, I. G. (1975). Anxiety and self-preoccupation. In I. G. Sarason & D. C. Spielberger (Eds.), *Stress and anxiety* (Vol. 2, pp. 27–44). Washington, DC: Hemisphere.

Schunk, D. H. (1984). Self-efficacy perspective on achievement behavior. *Educational Psychologist, 19*, 48–58.

Strecher, V. J., DeVellis, B. M., Becker, M. H.,

& Rosenstock, I. M. (1986). The role of self-efficacy in achieving health behavior change. *Health Education Quarterly, 13*, 73–91.

Wood, R. E., & Bandura, A. (1989). Impact of conceptions of ability on self-regulatory mechanisms and complex decision-making. *Journal of Personality and Social Psychology, 56*, 407–415.

See Also

Ego Development; Erikson, Erik Homburger; Motivations and Self-Perceptions, Changes in; Self-Regulation; Self Concept, Adolescent.

Self-Regulation

August Flammer
University of Bern, Switzerland

Self-regulation (or auto-regulation) is a defining characteristic of all living systems. Self-regulatory processes serve to maintain a given state (despite external disturbances), or to attain goal states, or even to set new goals. According to the actual conditions, self-regulatory processes have different concrete forms: hunger is followed by eating behavior, a desire for necessary information is followed by a trip to the library, or a threat to one's independence is followed by anger and attack behaviors.

Self-regulatory processes become diversified and strengthened during individual development. The adolescent period is considered to be one in which the most rapid development of self-regulation takes place.

There are mainly five areas in human development where the notion of self-regulation is applicable: increasing social independence, integrating social regulations in the individual's behavior, internalizing exterior actions into internal and abstract actions, developing a sense of personal control, and controlling one's own development.

Increasing emotional, intellectual, and economical autonomy is considered to be a primary developmental task of adolescents (Havighurst, 1948). Therefore, adolescents strive hard for increased *independence* from previous authorities. Despite the unpleasant fact that this may conflict with adults' plans to organize their own and other people's lives, the young generation's claim for independence is a necessity if it is true that the societal change and development is mainly to be carried out by each following "uncompromised" generation. In general terms, this task corresponds to a broadly shared conviction; therefore, if adolescents and young adults are held too far away from a share of real responsibilities, it is natural that they react violently and attack societal norms, institutions, and authorities.

Social independence is not meant to become social isolation, but should develop into a flexible equilibrium of social roles, either symmetrical or asymmetrical. The reorganization of social relations to parents is therefore a developmental task for the adolescent, his or her parents, and all other related persons (Stierlin, 1974).

The development of self-regulation can be conceived of as the *assimilation of the social regulation of the individual's behavior through the very individual* (S. Freud, 1917; Vygotsky, 1962; Wertsch, 1979). Language learning in infancy and beyond (Kohlberg, Yaeger, & Hjertholm, 1968; Luria, 1961; Luria & Yudowich, 1959), role playing by preschoolers (Flavell, 1968), and role experiencing by adolescents are important steps in this development. Group activities, especially problem solving in groups, favor later self-regulation and allow for emotional belonging, as well as offer public symbols to be used in social classification.

Adolescents invest a great amount of time and effort in peer-group activities, in endless telephone calls and in writing letters and sometimes diaries. One function of these activities is to experience social roles, to try out intellectual and emotional perspectives, to dialogue and to debate, activities which slowly can be mastered within one individual. Thus, work share may result in better organization of one's own working, role exchange may be reflected in thinking from different perspectives, debating may induce more distinct logical reasoning, socio-emotional participation may enhance clarifying and going about with one's emotions and needs.

Action regulation relies heavily on internal processes of action planning and controlling through cognitive information processing. The genesis of cognitive processing can be understood as an *interiorization of external activity*, social or not (Luria, 1961; Piaget, 1947; Vygotsky, 1962). In thinking and problem-solving, adolescents become more and more independent of overt actions and concrete imagination, they use abstract or formal mental operations and are eager to do so. They think and argue about the existing world and about possible and impossible worlds (Piaget & Inhelder, 1955). By this, thinking becomes critical, but very powerful and creative; it serves "mental" independence and prepares responsible self-regulated actions.

To accept new responsibilities is both attractive and threatening. Adolescents are especially concerned by their personal capacities, their social appearance and their personal characteristics. *Social as well as personal identity and self-appreciation* are at stake (Erikson, 1959). Both striving for more and for the better and narcisstic withdrawal may alternate. Drug use can serve as a means in coping with the threat of loss of control (Silbereisen & Kastner, 1987). Continued and generalized feelings of loss of control can lead to depression (Seligman, 1975; Peterson & Seligman, 1984).

The development in adolescence not only leads to increased self-regulation, but becomes itself more and more regulated by the individual self. Adolescents think about themselves and their development and set themselves development goals, that is, they set out and try hard to become an educated person, a loving and helpful partner, a strong and respectful personality, a healthy and equilibrated individual. There are many ways by which people "*produce their own development*" (Lerner & Busch-Rossnagel, 1981; Lerner, 1982), the most prominent ones being deliberate developmental actions. As far as people believe themselves to be in control of their own development they engage in long-term intentional actions (Brandtstädter, 1989). Development may then be the intended action goal. Much more frequent are developmental changes as results of unintended "side-effects" of actions which are undertaken for various intentional goals (Flammer, 1988). Adolescents start to be impressed by their control over their own development (Heckhausen, 1990) and probably overestimate the intended developmental effects of actions and underestimate the unintended "side-effects" of their actions.

References

Brandtstädter, J. (1989). Personal self-regulation of development: Cross-sequential analyses of development-related control beliefs and emotions. *Developmental Psychology, 25*, 96–108.

Erikson, E. H. (1959). *Identity and the life cycle.* New York: International Universities Press.

Flammer, A. (1988). *Entwicklungstheorien. Psychologische Theorien menschlicher Entwicklung.* Bern: Huber.

Flavell, J. H. (1968). *The development of role-taking and communication skills in children.* New York: Wiley.

Freud, S. (1917). *Vorlesungen zur Einführung in die Psychoanalyse. Gesammelte Werke XI.* London: Imago.

Havighurst, R. J. (1984). *Developmental task and education.* New York: McKay.

Heckhausen, J. (1990). Entwicklung im Erwachsenenalter aus der Sicht junger, mittelalter und alter Erwachsener. *Zeitschrift für Entwicklungspsychologie und Pädagogische Psychologie, 22*, 1–21.

Kohlberg, L., Yaeger, J., Hjertholm, E. (1968). Private speech: Four studies and a review of theories. *Child Development, 39*, 691–736.

Lerner, R. M. (1982). Children and adolescents as producers of their own development. *Developmental Review, 2*, 342–370.

Lerner, R. M. & Busch-Rossnagel, N. A., (Eds.) (1981). *Individuals as producers of their development: A life-span perspective.* New York: Academic.

Luria, A. R. (1961). *The role of speech in the regulation of normal and abnormal behavior.* New York: Basic Books.

Luria, A. R., Yudowich, F. J. (1959). *Speech and the development of mental processes in the child.* London: Staples Press (orig. 1956).

Peterson, C., Seligman, M. E. P. (1984). Causal explanations as a risk factor for depression: Theory and evidence. *Psychological Review, 91*, 347–374.

Piaget, J. (1947). *Psychologie de l'intelligence.* Paris: Colin.

Piaget, J., Inhelder, B. (1955). *De la logique de l'enfant à la logique de l'adolescent.* Paris: Presses universitaires de France.

Seligman, M. E. P. (1975). *Helplessness. On depression, development and death.* San Francisco: Freeman.

Silbereisen, R. K., Kastner, P. (1987). Jugend und Problemverhalten. Entwicklungspsychologische Perspektiven. In R. Oerter & L. Montada (Hg.), *Entwicklungspsychologie. 2. Auflage*, pp. 882–919. München: Psychologie Verlags Union.

Stierlin, H. (1974). *Separating parents and adolescents.* New York: Quadrangel.

Vygotsky, L. S. (1962). *Thought and language.* Cambridge: MIT Press (orig. 1934).

Wertsch, J. V. (1979). From social interaction to higher psychological processes. *Human Development, 22*, 1–22.

Sex Education

Patricia Barthalow Koch
The Pennsylvania State University

Sex, or sexuality, encompasses many expressions, ideas, feelings, and behaviors. It is certainly not limited to what a person does with his or her genitals. It also involves sex roles, gender identification, self-concept, body image, fantasies, reproduction, religious beliefs, societal mores, life-styles, and much more. Sexuality education begins at the moment of one's birth; for example, infants may first experience sensuousness through the touch of their parents. Even if a person does not receive any "formal" education about sexuality while growing up, she or he still receives a great deal of "informal" education through discussions with friends, the verbal and nonverbal reactions of parents, and media portrayals.

What are the major sources of sex education for adolescents? Researchers over the past fifty years have consistently found that adolescents identify their peers as their primary source of sex education, with parents and schools as significantly lesser sources (Bell, 1938; Lee, 1952; Thornburg, 1975). More recent research continues to support these earlier findings, indicating that no "sexual revolution" took place concerning sex education.

For example, Thornburg (1981) studied 1,152 students from a large midwestern high school to determine to whom adolescents initially turned in order to learn about sexuality. Peers emerged as the most often-cited source of sex information (37.1%). Literature, including all forms of the media, was the second most popular source (21.9%), followed by mother (17.4%), schools (15.2%), life experiences (5.4%), father (2.2%), minister (.5%), and physician (.3%). Gender differences were also examined. It was found that adolescent women and men were likely to seek out different sources of sex education; female adolescents were more dependent on their mothers for such information (22.3%) than male adolescents (6.9%), whereas the young men were more dependent on their peers (49.1%) than the young women were (33.4%).

This study also addressed the ages at which respondents first learned about twelve major sexual concepts. Results indicated that ages 12 and 13 were the peak times for first learning about sexual concepts, with 51.4% of the sexual information being acquired during this period. In fact, by age 13, 85.7% of the initial information on these topics had been learned.

Finally, the accuracy content of the information they had received was also rated by the adolescents. The overall accuracy rating for the twelve topics studied was 78.7%. The topics that the adolescents had defined most accurately were those reported to be provided by one's mother or literature, while topics with the lowest accuracy ratings were those provided by peers.

Other research focusing on the sex education occurring in the home generally finds it to be lacking (Fox 1981; Hass, 1979; Sorensen, 1973). However, some studies have indicated that when parents do talk to their children about sex, the adolescents tend to be less likely to engage in certain sexual behaviors (Goldfarb, Mumford, Schum, Smith, Flowers, & Schum, 1977; Lewis, 1973; Spanier, 1977). Further, if parent-educated teens did engage in sexual intercourse, they were more likely to use an effective, consistent means of birth control and to have fewer sexual partners (Fox, 1981; Furstenburg, 1971; Lewis, 1973; Shah & Zeknik, 1981; Spanier, 1977). In addition, high family sexual communication seems to be related to similarity in sexual attitudes between parents and their college-aged children (Fisher, 1987).

Because of the lack of sex education provided in the home and the abundance of misinformation provided by peers, the public schools have been called upon to fill this educational gap. Despite the heated controversy that the topic of sex education in the schools often evokes, a national survey of approximately 1,500 adults found that a majority of the total respondents (75%), including the majority of respondents who were parents with children attending public schools (81%), believed that public high schools should include sex education in their instructional program (Gallup, 1987).

The only national analysis of sex education programs in the United States was commissioned by the U. S. Department of Health, Education, and Welfare in 1979 (Kirby, Alter, & Scales, 1979). The researchers calculated that less than 10% of all students were receiving instruction about sexuality in their high schools. After completing an extensive evaluation of school-based programs throughout the country, the researchers documented the following outcomes from these programs: (1) an increase in students' knowledge about sexuality; (2) an increase in tolerance of the sexual practices of others, although there was no change in students' personal values that guide their own behavior; (3) little effect upon the amount of various types of sexual behavior; (4) increased use of effective contraception and decreased use of ineffective methods of contraception, plus a decline in intercourse without contraception for students in courses that emphasized contraception; and (5) probable reduced teenage pregnancy rates for students in courses that actually provide contraceptives. The report's overall conclusion stated: "Comprehensive programs must include far more than discussions of reproduction. They should cover other topics such as contraception, numerous sexual activities, the emotional and social aspects of sexual activity, values, and decision making and communication skills. In addition to being concerned with the imparting of knowledge, they should also focus on the clarifying of values, the raising of self-esteem, and the developing of personal and social skills. These tasks clearly require that sex education topics be covered in many courses in many grades" (Kirby, Alter, & Scales, 1979, p. 1).

In summary, it is evident that the sources of "informal" sex education, such as peers and the media, are abundant and that there is no way to isolate an adolescent from the barrage of sexual (mis)information in today's society. Everyone becomes sexually educated. The question is, is the sex education children receive inaccurate, negative, even destructive, or accurate, positive, and enhancing? To achieve the latter type of sex education, all sources (e.g., parents, peers, teachers, clergy, health and media professionals, etc.) need to be sexually educated themselves before they can effectively address the needs of the adolescents with whom they interact. All aspects of sex education, including the informational, the attitudinal, and the behavioral, need to be addressed honestly, openly, and naturally throughout one's life, from womb to tomb.

References

Bell, H. M. (1938). *Youth tell their story*. Washington, DC: American Council on Education.

Fisher, T. (1987). Family communication and the sexual behavior and attitudes of college students. *Journal of Youth and Adolescence, 16*, 481–495.

Fox, G. L. (1981). The family's role in adolescent sexual behavior. In Ooms, T. (Ed.), *Teenage pregnancy in a family context* (pp. 73–130). Philadelphia, PA: Temple University Press.

Furstenburg, F. F., Jr. (1971). Birth control experience among pregnant adolescents: The process of unplanned parenthood. *Social Problems, 19*, 192–203.

Gallup, G., Jr. (1987). *The Gallup poll: Public opinion 1986*. Wilmington, DE: Scholarly Resources.

Goldfarb, J. L., Mumford, D. M., Schum, D. A., Smith, P. B., Flowers, C., & Schum, C. (1977). An attempt to detect "pregnancy susceptibility" in indigent adolescent girls. *Journal of Youth and Adolescence, 6*, 127–144.

Hass, A. (1979). *Teenage sexuality*. New York: Macmillan.

Kirby, D., Alter, J., & Scales, P. (1979). *An analysis of U. S. sex education programs and evaluation methods: Executive summary*. Atlanta, GA: U. S. Department of Health, Education, and Welfare.

Lee, M. R. (1952). Background factors related to sex information and attitudes. *Journal of Educational Psychology, 43*, 467–485.

Lewis, R. A. (1973). Parents and peers: Socialization agents in the coital behavior of the young adult. *Journal of Sex Research, 9*, 156–170.

Shah, R., & Zelnik, M. (1981). Parent and peer influence on sexual behavior, contraceptive use, and pregnancy experience of young women. *Journal of Marriage and the Family, 43*, 339–348.

Sorensen, R. C. (1973). *Adolescent sexuality in contemporary America*. New York: World.

Spanier, G. B. (1977). Sources of sex information and premarital sexual behavior. *Journal of Sex Research, 13*, 73–88.

Thornburg, H. D. (1975). Sources in adolescents of initial sex information. In H. D. Thornburg, (Ed.), *Contemporary Adolescence: Readings* (2nd ed., pp. 384–390). Monterey, CA: Brooks/Cole.

Thornburg, H. D. (1981). Adolescent sources of information on sex. *Journal of School Health, 51*, 274–277.

See Also

Contraceptive Behavior as a Process; Dating during Adolescence; Family Planning Clinics: Efficacy for Adolescents; Gay and Lesbian Youth; Homosexuality, Adolescent; Safer Sex and Adolescence; Sexual Behavior in Black Adolescents, Initiation of; Sexual Onset, Early; Sexual Behavior, Sexual Attitudes and Contraceptive Use, Age Differences in Adolescent; Sexually Transmitted Diseases in Adolescence.

Sex Roles and Sex-Typing in Adolescence

Lisa J. Crockett
The Pennsylvania State University

Sex roles refer to differential expectations held for males and females in a given society. In the narrowest sense, sex roles are defined by the activities and tasks socially assigned to men and women (e.g., Spence & Helmreich, 1978), although many scholars employ a broader definition that includes not only sex-differentiated activities, but the different personal and social attributes believed to characterize males and females (e.g., Bem, 1974, 1981). *Sex-typed* characteristics and activities are those associated primarily with one gender. Similarly, a sex-typed individual is one who acts and appears in a manner congruent with cultural notions of what is appropriate for a person of his or her gender.

Sex roles and sex typing, then, must be understood on multiple levels, both social and individual. Sex roles are social expectations external to the individual. Sex typing, however, is partly dependent on a person's awareness and understanding of sex-role expectations. Both sex roles and sex typing may be expected to change developmentally. For example, sex roles may be age-graded, such that different behaviors define masculinity and femininity for different age-groups (Katz, 1979, 1986). Expectations may also depend on life stage, with certain events (e.g., becoming a parent or the onset of puberty) affecting the degree of sex-typed behavior expected. Moreover, a child's awareness and conceptualization of these expectations may change with developmental increases in cognitive sophistication (Huston, 1983). Finally, the perceived importance of conforming to these expectations may vary with age.

The multiple factors potentially affecting sex typing underscore the need to examine distinct dimensions of sex typing (e.g., behaviors, sex-role concepts, self-perceptions) and to examine them at multiple ages. Moreover, several scholars have noted that sex roles and sex typing are best conceptualized as a loosely related set of concepts, preferences, self-perceptions, and behaviors (e.g., Spence & Helmreich, 1978). Thus, developmental changes in attitudes and behavior may not coincide. Flexibility in attitudes may follow an initial period of extreme rigidity in attitudes and may coincide with fairly rigid sex typing of behavior or self-concept. Finally, the developmental patterns can not be assumed to be identical for boys and girls (e.g., Archer, 1984).

Sex Roles at Adolescence

Although the classic theories of development—the psychoanalytic (Freud, 1927), social learning (Mischel, 1966), and cognitive developmental (Kohlberg, 1966) formulations—focus on developments occurring earlier in childhood, more recent formulations based on a life-span perspective include changes in sex roles and sex typing that occur during adolescence and adulthood (e.g., Archer, 1984; Block, 1978; Brooks-Gunn & Matthews, 1979; Eccles, 1987; Katz, 1979; Rebecca, Hefner, & Oleshansky, 1976; Worell, 1981). The changes in sex roles and sex typing thought to occur during adolescence are closely tied to the developmental tasks and challenges of adolescence: pubertal development, the development of heterosexual relationships and sexuality, and the forging of a coherent sense of identity (e.g., Brooks-Gunn & Matthews, 1979; Katz, 1979, 1986).

Adolescence is a period of multiple individual and social changes potentially affecting sex-role expectations and sex typing. During adolescence the physiological changes of puberty lead to the development of a more adultlike physical appearance. Puberty accentuates the physical differences between boys and girls, increasing the salience of gender to them and to those around them. In addition, a more mature physique signals the impending assumption of sex-typed adult productive and reproductive roles. For these reasons, expectations for sex-typed "adult" behavior may be expected to increase during adolescence.

Adolescence is also a time of major cognitive advances (Keating, 1980; Piaget, 1972). These advances enable the adolescent to think in more sophisticated ways about possibilities, hypothetical situations, and abstract concepts; they also enable adolescents to think about themselves and others and to imagine how others perceive them. These increases in cognitive sophistication and accompanying changes in social cognition (Hill & Palmquist, 1978) are likely to influence both adolescents' understanding of sex roles and the importance they attach to these roles.

Finally, the cognitive advances of adolescence, in conjunction with increased social expectations for adultlike behavior, set the stage for a third major change potentially related to sex typing: the formation of a coherent sense of identity (e.g., Erikson, 1950, 1968). In attempting to develop a clear sense of themselves and their future goals, adolescents must come to terms with their maleness or femaleness and incorporate some version of sex roles into their developing identity (Brooks-Gunn & Matthews, 1979; Katz, 1986; Waterman, 1985).

There appears to be agreement among a number of scholars that sex roles (i.e., social expectations regarding boys' and girls' behavior) change at adolescence, especially for girls (e.g., Brooks-Gunn & Matthews, 1979; Hill & Lynch, 1983; Katz, 1979, 1986). One type of change involves changes in role content; specifically, sexuality becomes a core feature of sex roles during this time (Katz, 1979, 1986). Other hypothesized changes involve the intensity of social pressure to behave in accordance with sex-role stereotypes (i.e., for boys to behave in masculine ways and for girls to behave in feminine ways). The increase in role-related pressures is believed to be especially intense for girls. Throughout childhood adherence to gender roles is more strongly encouraged and role deviance more severely punished in boys than in girls (e.g., Huston, 1983; Maccoby & Jacklin, 1974). At adolescence, and particularly with the onset of puberty, the latitude previously accorded girls is thought to decrease and reinforcement of traditional feminine behaviors to increase (e.g., Brooks-Gunn & Matthews, 1979). This change in the intensity of sex-role related socialization, labeled "gender intensification" (Hill & Lynch, 1983), may result in part from changes in the expectations held within familiar social contexts (e.g., family and same-sex peer groups) but may also reflect adolescents' movement into new social settings, especially relationships with the other sex. Traditional role behavior may be especially encouraged in these new social settings.

Despite the plausibility of the gender-intensification hypothesis, few studies have attempted to assess changes in role-related expectations during adolescence. Consequently, evidence in support of the hypothesis is largely indirect. In a few cases parental expectations for sons and daughters have been measured and linked to the age or pubertal stage of the child. Block (1978) found that parents of adolescents had somewhat more differentiated expectations for sons and daughters than did parents of younger children in the areas of competition, participation in rough games, and fighting. Unfortunately, parents in Block's studies were not asked to focus their responses on specific periods of development, leaving open the possibility that the results for adolescents reflect general sex-related expectations rather than expectations linked to adolescence per se (Hill & Lynch, 1983). Nevertheless, Block's findings are consistent with an increase in gender-specific socialization pressures at adolescence, with parents encouraging competitiveness more and discouraging roughness and aggressiveness less in adolescent sons than in adolescent daughters.

A study of parents' expectations for their seventh-graders yielded similar results: parents of boys emphasized achievement-success, individualism and self-confidence more than parents of girls; and parents of girls were more likely to emphasize warmth, nurturance, courtesy, manners, and personality than parents of boys (Hill, 1964, cited in Hill & Lynch, 1983). Although consistent with the gender-intensification hypothesis, the results were based on a single age group; thus, developmental change in socialization pressures could not be examined.

Even fewer studies have looked at developmental change in peer pressure for sex-role conformity. The results of one study found that casual dating was related to compliant behavior among girls (Rosen & Aneshensel, 1976), suggesting that such relationships encourage stereotyped behavior. A study of sex-role identity indicated that androgynous early adolescent girls were most popular with their same-sex peers, while masculine boys were most popular (Massad, 1981). Thus, as in childhood, less stereotyped traits appear to be permitted and even encouraged among girls, while stereotypic masculinity is encouraged among boys. Taken together, the findings suggest that boys more than girls encourage sex-stereotyped behaviors in both their same-sex and other-sex peers.

Sex Typing in Adolescence

Apart from assessing gender role changes at adolescence, it is possible to examine the degree of sex typing (or stereotyping) adolescents exhibit in key domains, particularly, role-related behaviors, sex-role concepts and attitudes, and self-perceptions. Evidence of increased sex typing at adolescence would be consistent with the hypothesized increase in pressure to conform to gender roles. The evidence of sex typing in each domain is reviewed below.

SEX TYPING OF BEHAVIOR ■

Evidence that behavioral sex typing increases in adolescence comes primarily from studies of gender differences during this period. The emergence of new gender differences during adolescence and the enhancement of extant gender differences are taken as evidence of increased sex typing. In a recent review of this literature, Hill and Lynch (1983) concluded that some evidence exists for the emergence or enhancement of gender differences in 6 domains: susceptibility to anxiety; achievement-related behavior; self-concept; social relationships; risk taking; and aggression. Gender differences in the domains most closely related to sex-role stereotypes (achievement-related behavior and social relationships) are discussed in the following sections.

Achievement-related behaviors include standards for performance, actual performance, aspirations, and attributions about performance. Some evidence for enhanced sex typing at adolescence exists in each of these areas. In early adolescence standards for performance have been found to depend on whether a particular type of achievement is judged to be sex-appropriate: girls place more importance on achievement in feminine areas, and boys place more importance on achievement in masculine areas (Stein, 1971). This effect is more pronounced among ninth graders than sixth graders, suggesting an age-related increase in sex typing during early adolescence.

Actual performance among adolescents appears to parallel achievement standards. Sex differences in spatial skills favor boys, while sex differences in verbal skills favor girls. These differences, however, are already present in middle childhood (e.g., Linn & Petersen, 1985). Sex differences in mathematics performance emerge in adolescence, although they are not always found (e.g., Sherman & Fennema, 1977). It

is interesting, in this regard, that math and science are not consistently stereotyped as masculine until adolescence (Fennema & Sherman, 1977; Stein, 1971; Stein & Smithells, 1969).

Consistent gender differences in educational aspirations do not appear to exist among young adolescents (e.g., Bush, Simmons, Hutchinson & Blyth, 1977–1978). During the high school years, however, girls' educational aspirations tend to decrease whereas boys' tend to increase (Marini, 1978). Occupational aspirations may follow a similar pattern, although here the evidence is less clear. There is also some evidence that stereotyping in occupational aspirations increases during this period (Marini, 1978).

The stereotyping of achievement domains as masculine or feminine appears to affect attributions and expectancies regarding success and failure. In general, adolescent girls have lower expectancies of success, lower aspirations, greater anxiety about failure, and greater acceptance of responsibility for failure than do boys (Parsons, Ruble, Hodges, & Small, 1976; Stein & Bailey, 1973). Girls are also more likely than boys to attribute success to unstable causes, such as luck or effort, and to attribute failure to lack of ability. Many of these gender differences, however, appear in middle childhood (Huston, 1983).

Apart from these overall differences, boys' and girls' expectancies of success, their achievement standards, and their effort appear to be affected by the sex typing of achievement domains: expectancies and efforts are typically greater in "sex-appropriate" areas. For example, girls' attainment values are higher for artistic, verbal, and social skills, whereas boys' are higher for athletic and mechanical skills (Stein, 1971); boys' motivation and achievement in science also tends to be higher than girls' (Steinkamp & Maehr, 1984). Adolescent girls perceive math as being more difficult than do boys and have lower expectancies of success even if their performance is equal to boys' (e.g., Fennema, 1984; Meese, Parsons, Kaczala, Goff, & Futterman, 1982). Adolescent girls also view math as being less important for them (Fox, Brody, & Tobin, 1980). Similarly, adolescent girls have lower expectancies of success on spatial tasks than do boys, even when they are equal in ability (Gitelson, Petersen, & Tobin-Richards, 1982; Petersen, Crockett, & Tobin-Richards, 1982). In contrast, girls have higher expectancies of success in English than do boys (Huston, 1983).

Social relationships appear to become more gender-differentiated during adolescence. Girls appear to become more invested than boys in interpersonal relationships: they exhibit a higher social orientation in their self-descriptions (Berndt, 1982), and they place greater importance on popularity (Simmons & Rosenberg, 1975). The gender difference in concerns about popularity appears to increase during early adolescence (Rosenberg & Simmons, 1975).

During adolescence girls also demonstrate a greater capacity for intimacy than do boys, especially in terms of self-disclosure. As early as seventh grade, girls list more peers as being important and report more acceptance, understanding, and shared feelings in their peer relationships than do boys (Berndt, 1982; Blyth, Hill, & Thiel, 1982; Crockett, Losoff, & Petersen, 1984; Sharabany, Gershoni, & Hofman, 1981). Throughout high school, boys' relationships continue to be oriented around shared activities, the pattern also found with preadolescent girls (Douvan & Adelson, 1966). Notably, the level of intimacy with peers increases with age for both genders (Blyth et al., 1982; Sharabany et al., 1981), and the shared companionship among boys can lead to feelings of closeness similar to those associated with self-disclosure in girls (Camarena, Sarigiani, & Petersen, in press).

Researchers have also examined gender differences in one sex-role related behavior—responsiveness to babies—during adolescence. In one study gender differences in responses to baby pictures were found among 14–15 year olds, but not among 8–9 year olds, suggesting increasing gender divergence during adolescence (Feldman, Nash, & Cutrona, 1977); there was also a trend for girls to show greater responsiveness than boys to live infants. Frodi and Lamb (1978), however, found gender differences in amount of interaction with infants among both preadolescents and adolescents, with no age-related increase in the size of the gender difference. Thus, although the gender difference appears reliable, increasing gender divergence during adolescence has not been clearly established for this behavior.

SEX-ROLE CONCEPTS IN ADOLESCENCE ▪ The salience of sex roles and sex typing for adolescents may also be reflected in their sex-role concepts and stereotypes. Two aspects of sex-role concepts may be distinguished: (1) stereotypes concerning activities; and (2) stereotypes concerning personality characteristics. Developmental trends in stereotyping appear to differ somewhat for these two domains and will be discussed separately.

The domain of *activities* includes not only stereotypes concerning toy preferences and play activities, but occupational stereotypes, and stereotypes about other sex-typed behaviors. During adolescence there is evidence of several distinct but interrelated developmental trends in this domain. First, awareness of societal stereotypes regarding activities and occupations increases in adolescence, as it does throughout middle childhood (Huston, 1983).

Thus, when asked to indicate which gender typically performs an activity, adolescents' responses are more similar to adult stereotypes than are the responses of younger children (e.g., Stein, 1971; Stein & Smithells, 1969). At the same time, sex-role concepts become increasingly flexible. The understanding that sex roles are culturally relative and modifiable increases between childhood and adolescence (Carter & Patterson, 1982), and occupational stereotypes become less pronounced (e.g., Cummings & Taebel, 1980). Thus, adolescents are more likely than younger children to understand that both sexes can engage in many activities and to feel that some activities and occupations are appropriate for both genders.

Despite an increasing flexibility in sex-role concepts, however, there is evidence that young adolescents attach greater importance to sex-role conformity than do elementary school children. In one study, a clear U-shaped developmental pattern was observed in the perceived seriousness of sex-role transgressions: young children and early adolescents ranked sex-role transgressions (e.g., a boy wearing nailpolish) as being more wrong than did elementary school children (Stoddart & Turiel, 1985). The adolescents appeared to associate sex-role conformity with psychological normality and to view cross-gender behavior as deviant. Although they regarded sex-role uniformities as being flexible and culturally relative, they expressed a stronger personal commitment to these uniformities than did elementary school children (Stoddart & Turiel, 1985). A similar commitment to gender stereotypes among adolescents has been found in studies examining concepts of masculinity and femininity (e.g., Ullian, 1976), and studies of sexist attitudes (e.g., Benson & Vincent, 1980). Benson and Vincent (1980) found that sexist attitudes were more common among young adolescents than among older adolescents and adults, except for adults over age 50. The salience of gender-role stereotypes is also reflected in the finding that, although adolescents exhibit less occupational stereotyping than younger children, they do not exhibit less stereotyped views concerning current peer activities (Kleinke & Nicholson, 1979). Apparently, the importance attached to sex-role adherence is strong enough to override the abstract knowledge that many activities are appropriate for both genders.

Developmental patterns in the stereotyping of *personality attributes* are less well understood than stereotyping of activities, in large part because fewer studies have examined this issue (Huston, 1983). The available studies indicate increased awareness of social stereotypes during middle childhood and adolescence. By early adolescence, youngsters differ little from college students in their classification of traits by gender (Best et al., 1977). Some studies confirm this pattern of increased stereotyping with age during middle childhood and adolescence (e.g., Urberg, 1979), although others do not (Leahy & Eiter, 1980). Urberg (1979) studied early and late adolescents (seventh and twelfth graders, respectively) as well as adults and found that stereotyping with respect to ideal males and females was most pronounced among the late adolescents. These studies, however, are usually based on forced choice techniques, making impossible an assessment of developmental increase in sex-role flexibility. One interesting additional finding is that stereotyping occurs primarily in descriptions of the *other* gender rather than one's own gender (Rothbaum, 1977; Urberg & Labouvie-Vief, 1976). A similar pattern has been reported with respect to adolescents' concepts of same-sex versus other-sex labels (Crockett, Camarena, & Petersen, 1990).

SELF-PERCEPTIONS ▪ A final area of sex-typing concerns *self-perceptions*, including reports of personal preferences and descriptions of one's personal and social attributes. This domain may be referred to as sex-role identity—the degree to which one incorporates cultural definitions of masculinity and femininity into one's self-concept.

Far less is known about developmental changes in sex typing with respect to self-perceptions than about stereotyping of the activities and personality characteristics of others. Only a few studies are available on adolescents; in general, these studies suggest that sex typing is less evident with self-perceptions than with the activities and personalities of abstract males and females. Urberg (1979) found few gender differences in adolescents' self-reported personality attributes (far fewer than in their descriptions of ideal males and females). The only difference was found among 12th graders—in this group females perceived themselves as being more dependent than did males. Similarly, a recent study of sex-role identity during early adolescence found relatively small gender differences on scale scores tapping masculine and feminine characteristics, although large differences were found in self-ratings on the items "masculine" and "feminine" (Crockett et al., 1990).

When *gender differences in the degree of sex typing* are observed, boys typically exhibit a stronger adherence to traditional sex roles than do girls. For example, boys show a steady increase in preference for masculine activities during childhood, but girls do not show a parallel increase in preference for feminine activities (Huston, 1983). Rather, girls' preference for feminine activities often declines during the elementary school years while their interest in masculine activities increases (e.g., Huston-Stein & Higgins-Trenk, 1978; Kohlberg,

1966). At least two studies have found an age-related increase in masculine interests and preferences among adolescent girls as well (Kohlberg & Zigler, 1967; Leahy & Eiter, 1980).

Gender differences are also typically found in studies of sex-role concepts and attitudes, with adolescent boys having more traditional attitudes than adolescent girls (e.g., Benson & Vincent, 1980; Fennema & Sherman, 1977; Galambos, Petersen, Richards, & Gitelson, 1985). These findings are consistent with studies of younger children, in which boys consistently show more sex-typed choices than girls (Huston, 1983). It is not clear whether gender differences in sex typing also exist with adolescents' self-perceptions. Two studies found few gender differences in this domain (Crockett et al., 1990; Urberg, 1979).

Conclusions

There is a widely held belief that social pressure to conform to sex-role stereotypes increases in adolescence. Although there is little direct evidence supporting the validity of this assumption, much of the recent literature on sex typing in adolescence is at least partially consistent with it. Gender differences in achievement-related behaviors and in social relationships are in accordance with traditional gender roles, and, in several instances, there is evidence of an increase in gender divergence at or during adolescence. Sex-role concepts may also become more stereotyped in adolescence. Although adolescents often exhibit increased flexibility with respect to occupational roles, young adolescents view behavioral sex-role transgressions as serious and exhibit a personal commitment to sex-role adherence. Data on personal-social attributes also yield evidence of increased stereotyping, although, in this case, sex-role *flexibility* has not been routinely assessed. The least evidence for stereotyping is found with self-perceptions. In general, boys exhibit more sex-typed attitudes than do girls.

The increasing magnitude of gender differences in behavior at adolescence and the presumed increase in sex-role pressures at this time have led some scholars to suggest that sex typing increases at least during the early part of adolescence (e.g., Brooks-Gunn & Matthews, 1979; Katz, 1979). The increase in sex-role flexibility observed in occupational stereotypes and perhaps in self-perceptions, however, suggests that adolescents may become less tied to traditional stereotypes during the later subphases of adolescence. This possibility has led some scholars to view adolescence as the "gateway" to sex-role transcendence (e.g., Eccles, 1987; Rebecca, Hefner, & Oleshansky, 1976). Some evidence exists in support of each of these positions. A full understanding of sex typing in adolescence will require studies assessing multiple domains of sex typing (e.g., sex-role pressures, behavior, concepts, self-perceptions) across the multiple subphases of adolescence.

References

Archer, J. (1984). Gender roles as developmental pathways. *British Journal of Social Psychology, 23*, 245–256.

Bem, S. L. (1974). The measurement of psychological androgyny. *Journal of Consulting and Clinical Psychology, 42*, 155–162.

Bem, S. L. (1981). Gender schema theory: A cognitive account of sex typing. *Psychological Review, 88*, 354–364.

Benson, P. L., & Vincent, S. M. (1980). Development and validation of the Sexist Attitudes Toward Women Scale (SATWS). *Psychology of Women Quarterly, 5*, 276–291.

Berndt, T. J. (1982). Features and effects of friendship in early adolescence. *Child Development, 53*, 1447–1460.

Best, D. L., Williams, J. E., Cloud, J. M., Davis, S. W., Robertson, L. S., Edwards, J. R., Giles, H., & Fowles, J. (1977). Development of sex-trait stereotypes among young children in the United States, England, and Ireland. *Child Development, 48*, 1375–1384.

Block, J. H. (1978). Another look at sex differentiation in the socialization behaviors of mothers and fathers. In J. A. Sherman & F. L. Denmark (Eds.), *The psychology of women: Future directions of research* (pp. 29–87). New York: Psychological Dimensions.

Blyth, D. A., Hill, J. P., & Thiel, K. (1982). Early adolescents' significant others: Grade and gender differences in perceived relationships with familial and nonfamilial adults and young people. *Journal of Youth and Adolescence, 11*, 425–450.

Brooks-Gunn, J., & Matthews, W. S. (1979). *He and she: How children develop their sex-role identity.* Englewood Cliffs, NJ: Prentice-Hall.

Bush, D. E., Simmons, R., Hutchinson, B., & Blyth, D. (1977–1978). Adolescent perceptions of sex roles in 1968 and 1975. *Public Opinion Quarterly, 41*, 459–474.

Camarena, P. M., Sarigiani, P. A., & Petersen, A. C. (in press). Gender-specific pathways to intimacy in early adolescence. *Journal of Youth and Adolescence.*

Carter, D. B., & Patterson, C. J. (1982). Sex-roles as social conventions: The development of children's conceptions of sex-role stereotypes. *Developmental Psychology, 18*, 812–824.

Crockett, L. J., Camarena, P. M., & Petersen, A. C. (1990). Masculinity and femininity in early adolescence: Developmental change in self-perceptions. Unpublished manuscript.

Crockett, L. J., Losoff, M., & Petersen, A. C. (1984). Perceptions of the peer group and friendship in early adolescence. *Journal of Early Adolescence*, *4*, 155–181.

Cummings, S., & Taebel, D. (1980). Sexual inequality and the reproduction of consciousness: An analysis of sex-role stereotyping among children. *Sex Roles*, *6*, 631–644.

Douvan, E., & Adelson, J. (1966). *The adolescent experience*. New York: Wiley.

Eccles, J. (1987). Adolescence: Gateway to gender-role transcendence. In D. B. Carter (Ed.), *Current conceptions of sex roles and sex typing: Theory and research* (pp. 225–241). New York: Praeger.

Emmerich, W., & Shepard, K. (1982). Development of sex-differentiated preferences during late childhood and adolescence. *Developmental Psychology*, *18*, 406–417.

Erikson, E. E. (1950). *Childhood and society*. New York: Norton.

Erikson, E. E. (1968). *Identity: Youth and crisis*. New York: Norton.

Feldman, S. S., Nash, S., & Cutrona, C. (1977). The influence of age and sex on responsiveness to babies. *Developmental Psychology*, *13*, 675–676.

Fennema, E. (1984). Girls, women, and mathematics. In E. Fennema & M. J. Ayer (Eds.), *Women and education: Equity or equality?* (pp. 137–164). Berkeley, CA: McCutchan.

Fennema, E., & Sherman, J. A. (1977). Sex-related differences in mathematics achievement, spatial visualization, and affective factors. *American Educational Research Journal*, *14*, 51–71.

Fox, L. H., Brody, L., & Tobin, D. (1980). *Women and the mathematical mystique*. Baltimore: Johns Hopkins University Press.

Freud, S. (1927). Some psychological consequences of the anatomical distinction between the sexes. *International Journal of Psychoanalysis*, *8*, 133–142.

Frodi, A., & Lamb, M. (1978). Sex differences in responsiveness to infants: A developmental study of psychophysiological and behavioral responses. *Child Development*, *49*, 1182–1188.

Galambos, N. L., Petersen, A. C., Richards, M. H., & Gitelson, I. B. (1985). The Attitudes Toward Women Scale for Adolescents (AWSA): A study of reliability and validity. *Sex Roles*, *13*, 343–356.

Gitelson, I. B., Petersen, A. C., & Tobin-Richards, M. H. (1982). Adolescents' expectancies of success, self-evaluations, and attributions about performance on spatial and verbal tasks. *Sex Roles*, *8*, 411–419.

Hall, J. A., & Halberstadt, A. G. (1980). Masculinity and femininity in children: Development of the Children's Personal Attributes Questionnaire. *Developmental Psychology*, *16*, 270–280.

Hill, J. P. (1964). *Parental determinants of sex-typed behavior*. Unpublished doctoral dissertation, Harvard University. (Cited in Hill & Lynch, 1983.)

Hill, J. P., & Lynch, M. E. (1983). The intensification of gender-related role expectations during early adolescence. In J. Brooks-Gunn & A. C. Petersen (Eds.), *Girls at puberty: Biological and psychosocial dimensions* (pp. 201–228). New York: Plenum.

Hill, J. P., & Palmquist, W. (1978). Social cognition and social relations in early adolescence. *International Journal of Behavioral Development*, *1*, 1–36.

Huston, A. C. (1983). Sex-typing. In E. M. Hetherington (Ed.), *Handbook of child psychology: Vol. 4. Socialization, personality, and social development* (4th ed., pp. 387–467). New York: Wiley.

Huston-Stein, A. C., & Higgins-Trenk, A. (1978). Development of females from childhood through adulthood: Career and feminine role orientations. In P. B. Baltes (Ed.), *Life-span development and behavior* (Vol. 1, pp. 258–296). New York: Academic Press.

Katz, P. A. (1979). The development of female identity. *Sex Roles*, *5*, 155–178.

Katz, P. A. (1986). Gender identity: Development and consequences. In R. D. Ashmore & F. R. Del Boca (Eds.), *The social psychol-*

ogy of female-male relations (pp. 21–67). New York: Academic Press.

Keating, D. (1980). Thinking processes in adolescence. In J. Adelson (Ed.), *Handbook of adolescent psychology* (pp. 211–246). New York: Wiley.

Kleinke, C. L., & Nicholson, T. A. (1979). Black and white children's awareness of de facto race and sex differences. *Developmental Psychology, 15*, 84–86.

Kohlberg, L. (1966). A cognitive developmental analysis of children's sex-role concepts and attitudes. In E. E. Maccoby (Ed.), *The development of sex differences* (pp. 81–172). Stanford: Stanford University Press.

Kohlberg, L., & Zigler, E. (1967). The impact of cognitive maturity on the development of sex-role attitudes in the years 4 to 8. *Genetic Psychology Mongraphs, 75*, 89–165.

Leahy, R. L., & Eiter, M. (1980). Moral judgment and the development of real and ideal androgynous self-image during adolescence and young adulthood. *Developmental Psychology, 16*, 362–370.

Linn, M. C., & Petersen, A. C. (1985). Emergence and characterization of sex differences in spatial ability: A meta-analysis. *Child Development, 56*, 1479–1498.

Maccoby, E. E., & Jacklin, C. N. (1974). *The psychology of sex differences*. Stanford: Stanford University Press.

Marini, M. M. (1978). Sex differences in the determinants of adolescent aspirations: A review of the research. *Sex Roles, 4*, 723–753.

Massad, C. M. (1981). Sex-role identity and adjustment during adolescence. *Child Development, 52*, 1290–1298.

Meece, J. L., Parsons, J. E., Kaczala, C. M., Goff, S. B., & Futterman, R. (1982). Sex differences in math achievement: Toward a model of academic choice. *Psychological Bulletin, 91*, 324–348.

Meyer, B. (1980). The development of girls' sex-role attitudes. *Child Development, 51*, 508–514.

Mischel, W. (1966). A social-learning view of sex differences in behavior. In E. E. Maccoby (Ed.), *The development of sex differences* (pp. 56–81). Stanford: Stanford University Press.

Nemerowicz, G. M. (1979). *Children's perceptions of gender and work roles*. New York: Praeger.

Parsons, J. E., Ruble, D. N., Hodges, K. L., & Small, A. W. (1976). Cognitive-developmental factors in emerging sex differences in achievement-related expectancies. *Journal of Social Issues, 32*, 47–61.

Petersen, A. C., Crockett, L. J., & Tobin-Richards, M. H. (1982). Sex differences. In H. E. Mitzel (Ed.), *Encyclopedia of educational research* (Vol. 4, pp. 1696–1712). New York: Free Press.

Piaget, J. (1972). Intellectual evolution from adolescence to adulthood. *Human Development, 15*, 1–12.

Rebecca, M., Hefner, R., & Oleshansky, B. (1976). A model of sex-role transcendence. *Journal of Social Issues, 32*(3), 197–206.

Rosen, B. C., & Aneshensel, C. S. (1976). The chameleon syndrome: A social psychological dimension of the female sex role. *Journal of Marriage and the Family, 38*, 605–617.

Rosenberg, F. R., & Simmons, R. G. (1975). Sex differences in the self-concept during adolescence. *Sex Roles, 1*, 147–160.

Rothbaum, F. (1977). Developmental and gender differences in the sex stereotyping of nurturance and dominance. *Developmental Psychology, 13*, 531–532.

Simmons, R. G., & Rosenberg, F. R. (1975). Sex, sex roles, and self-image. *Journal of Youth and Adolescence, 4*, 229–258.

Sharabany, R., Gershoni, R., & Hofman, J. E. (1981). Girlfriend, boyfriend: Age and sex differences in intimate friendship. *Developmental Psychology, 17*, 800–808.

Sherman, J. A., & Fennema, E. (1977). The study of mathematics by high school girls and boys: Related variables. *American Educational Research Journal, 14*, 159–168.

Spence, J. T., & Helmreich, R. L. (1978). *Masculinity and femininity: Their psychological dimensions, correlates, and antecedents.* Austin, TX: University of Texas Press.

Stein, A. H. (1971). The effects of sex-role standards for achievement and sex-role preference on three determinants of achievement motivation. *Developmental Psychology, 4,* 219–231.

Stein, A. H., & Bailey, M. M. (1973). The socialization of achievement orientation in females. *Psychological Bulletin, 80,* 345–366.

Stein, A. H., & Smithells, J. (1969). Age and sex differences in children's sex-role standards about achievement. *Developmental Psychology, 1,* 252–259.

Steinkamp, M. W., & Maehr, M. L. (1984). Gender differences in motivational orientations toward achievement in school science: A quantitative analysis. *American Educational Research Journal, 21,* 39–59.

Stoddart, T., & Turiel, E. (1985). Children's concepts of cross-gender activities. *Child Development, 56,* 1241–1252.

Ullian, D. (1976). The development of conceptions of masculinity and femininity. In B. Lloyd & J. Archer (Eds.), *Exploring sex differences* (pp. 25–48). New York: Academic Press.

Urberg, K. A. (1979). Sex role conceptualizations in adolescents and adults. *Developmental Psychology, 15,* 90–92.

Urberg, K. A., & Labouvie-Vief, G. (1976). Conceptualizations of sex roles: A life-span developmental study. *Developmental Psychology, 12,* 15–23.

Waterman, A. S. (1985). Identity in the context of adolescent psychology. In A. S. Waterman (Ed.), *Identity in adolescence: Processes and contents* (pp. 5–24). San Francisco: Jossey-Bass.

Worell, J. (1981). Life-span sex roles: Development, continuity, and change. In R. M. Lerner & N. Busch-Rossnagel (Eds.), *Individuals as producers of their development: A life-span perspective* (pp. 313–347). New York: Academic Press.

See Also

Cognitive and Psychosocial Gender Differences, Trends in; Depression in Adolescence, Gender Differences in; Emotion, Gender Differences in; Family Interaction, Gender Differences in; Gender Intensification; Health and Substance Abuse in Adolescence: Ethnic and Gender Perspectives; Injuries, Unintentional: Gender Differences in Accidents; Maturational Timing, Antecedents of in Girls; Maturational Timing Variations in Adolescent Girls, Consequences of; Minority and Female Participation in Math and Science, Increase in: The Importance of the Middle School Years.

Sexual Behavior, Sexual Attitudes, and Contraceptive Use, Age Differences in Adolescent

Dominique A. Treboux
Nancy A. Busch-Rossnagel
Fordham University

The proportion of sexually experienced adolescents increases with age. For females ages 15 to 19, 19% of whites and 37% of blacks report having their first intercourse experience at the age of 15 or younger, while 62% of whites and 56% of blacks report that intercourse occurred for the first time between the ages of 15 and 17 years. For males ages 15 to 19, 32% of whites and 65% of blacks report first intercourse at 15 or under, and 54% of whites and 28% of blacks report a first intercourse between the ages of 15 and 17 (Zelnick & Shah, 1983). Hence by age 18 most adolescents are sexually experienced.

Similarly, age differences in contraceptive use are consistent findings in the research. Specifically, the longer adolescents postpone sexual intercourse the more likely they are to (1) use contraception at first intercourse (Cvetkovich & Grote, 1983; Faulkenberry, Vincent, James, & Johnson, 1987; Zelnick, Kanter, & Ford, 1981; Zel-nick & Shah, 1983); (2) use a medical method such as the pill at first intercourse (Cvetkovich & Grote, 1981; Zelnick & Shah, 1983); (3) currently be using contraception (Cvetkovich & Grote, 1983; Zelnick et al., 1981); and (4) use contraceptives consistently and effectively (Faulkenberry et al., 1987; Finkel & Finkel, 1978; Zelnick et al., 1981). In a national study, Zelnick and his colleagues (1981) found that there was a delay of 1.4 years between the onset of intercourse and of contraceptive use for females ages 15 and younger, whereas females aged 18 to 19 years delayed using contraception for 5 months.

Contraception knowledge and sexual attitudes also change as a function of age. One study (Reichelt & Werley, 1981) found that sexual and contraceptive information increased for both sexes up to age 17. Freeman, Rickels, Huggins, Mudd, Garcia, and Dickens (1980) found that contraceptive information increased significantly with school grade for females in grades 9 to 12. Fisher (1986) found that middle adolescents had more permissive sexual attitudes than early or late adolescents. In Reiss's study (1967) sexual attitudes differed as a function of dating age. White males who began dating at an early age, 12 years or less, held more permissive sexual attitudes than males who began dating later, at 16 or older. Those males who began dating between the ages of 13 and 15 were the least permissive in their sexual attitudes. DelCampo, Sporakowski, and DelCampo (1976) also found that college students who began dating the earliest held more permissive sexual attitudes.

The two primary socialization agents in adolescence are parents and peers; research has indicated that their behaviors related to sexuality also change as a function of the age of the adolescents. Parents were more likely to provide information about contraception to older adolescents than to younger adolescents (Rothenberg, 1980). In a study of 12- to 20-year-olds Fisher (1986) found high correlations between the sexual attitudes of children and parents in early adolescence, but low correlations in middle adolescence. In late adolescence, parents and children with high communication levels had high correlations between their attitudes, but the attitudes of parents and children with low communication levels were not related. In a longitudinal study, Jessor and Jessor (1975) found that perceived parental and peer approval of respondents engaging in sexual behavior increased as the adolescent became older. Adolescents who perceived their parents and friends as permissive in their sexual attitudes were more likely to engage in sexual intercourse (DeLamater & MacCorquordale, 1979; Jessor & Jessor, 1975) and to use contraception (Jorgensen & Sonestegard, 1984; Thomson, 1982). Adolescents who discussed sex and contraception with their parents were more likely to use contraception (Fox, 1981; Thomson, 1982). These studies suggest that the environment for the older adolescent is more supportive of sexual involvement and contraceptive use.

Who has more influence on adolescent sexual behavior—parents or peers?—is a question that has intrigued many researchers. Douvan and Adelson (1964) proposed a theoretical formulation of changes that occur in parent-child and peer relationships as a function of the age of the adolescent. Based on semistructured interviews, Douvan and Adelson argued that young adolescents (11–13 years) are still "tied" emotionally to their parents and "cling" to parental values. Middle adolescents (14–16 years) substitute their emotional dependency on parents for a dependency on peers and, consequently, choose their peers as guides of values, attitudes, and behaviors. By later adolescence (17–18 years) individuals are less dependent on both parents and peers as guides for their values, attitudes, and behavior, and thus are more self-directed.

Empirical research has supported the theoretical formuations postulated by Douvan and Adelson. Berndt (1979) found that conformity to peers reached its peak in ninth grade. The opposition between parents and peers was also the strongest in ninth grade and decreased by eleventh and twelfth grades. Another study found that eighth and ninth graders were less autonomous in relation to their peers than younger adolescents (Steinberg & Silverberg, 1986). Likewise, Hunter and Youniss (1982) found that in fourth, seventh, and tenth graders and college students, friends' control increased up to the tenth grade and then decreased. This research suggests that the relative importance of parents and peers on adolescent sexuality may change as the adolescent grows older, yet many researchers have tended to neglect the variable of age in their formulations of adolescent sexuality, which may have confounded their results.

References

Berndt, T. J. (1979). Developmental changes in conformity to peers and parents. *Developmental Psychology, 15*, 608-616.

Cvetkovich, B., & Grote, B. (1981). Psychological maturity and teenage contraceptive use: An investigation of decision-making and communication skills. *Population and Environment: Behavioral and Social Issues, 4*, 211-226.

Cvetkovich, G., & Grote, B. (1983). Adolescent development and teenage fertility. In D. Byrne & W. A. Fisher (Eds.), *Adolescents, sex, and contraception* (pp. 109-124). Hillsdale, NJ: Lawrence Erlbaum Associates.

DeLamater, J., & MacCorquordale, P. (1979). *Premarital sexuality.* Madison: University of Wisconsin Press.

DelCampo, R. L., Sporakowski, M. J., & DelCampo, P. S. (1976). Premarital sexual permissiveness and contracpetive knowledge: A biracial comparison of college students. *Journal of Sex Research, 12*, 180-192.

Douvan, E., & Adelson, J. (1966). *The adolescent experience.* New York: John Wiley.

Faulkenberry, R. J., Vincent, M., James, A., & Johnson, W. (1987). Coital behaviors, attitudes, and knowledge of students who experience early coitus. *Adolescence, 22*, 321-332.

Finkel, M. L., & Finkel, D. J. (1978). Male adolescent contraceptive utilization. *Adolescence, 13*, 443-451.

Fisher, T. D. (1986). An exploratory study of parent-child communication about sex and the sexual attitudes of early, middle, and late adolescents. *Journal of Genetic Psychology, 147*, 543-557.

Fox, G. L. (1981). The family's role in adolescent sexual behavior. In T. Ooms (Ed.), *Teenage pregnancy in a family context: Implications for policy* (pp. 73-103). Philadelphia: Temple University Press.

Freeman, E. W., Rickels, K., Huggins, G. R., Mudd, E. H., Garcia, C. R., & Dickens, H. O. (1980). Adolescent contraceptive use: Comparisons of male and female attitudes and information. *American Journal of Public Health, 70*, 790-797.

Hunter, F. T., & Youniss, J. (1982). Changes in functions of three relations during adolescence. *Developmental Psychology, 18*, 806-811.

Jorgensen, S. R., & Sonstegard, J. S. (1984). Predicting adolescent sexual and contraceptive behavior: An application of the Fishbein model. *Journal of Marriage and the Family, 46*, 43-55.

Jessor, S., & Jessor, R. (1975). Transition from virginity to nonvirginity among youth: A social psychological study over time. *Developmental Psychology, 11*, 473-484.

Reichelt, P. A., & Werley, H. B. (1981). Contraception, abortion, and venereal disease: Teenagers' knowledge and the effect of education. In F. F. Furstenberg, R. Lincoln, & J. Menken (Eds.), *Teenage sexuality, pregnancy, and childbearing* (pp. 305-316). Philadelphia: University of Pennsylvania Press.

Reiss, I. L. (1967). *The social context of premarital sexual permissiveness.* New York: Holt, Rinehart and Winston.

Rothenberg, B. P. (1980). Communication about sex and birth control between mothers and their adolescent children. *Population and Environment: Behavioral and Social Issues, 3*, 35-50.

Steinberg, L., & Silverberg, S. B. (1986). The vicissitudes of autonomy in early adolescence. *Child Development, 57*, 841-851.

Thomson, E. (1982). Socialization for sexual and contraceptive behavior: Moral absolutes versus relative consequences. *Youth and Society, 14*, 103-128.

Zelnick, M., Kanter, J. F., & Ford, K. (1981). *Sex and pregnancy in adolescence.* Beverly Hills, CA: Sage Publications.

Zelnick, M., & Shah, F. K. (1983). First intercourse among young Americans. *Family Planning Perspectives, 15,* 64–70.

See Also

Contraceptive Behavior as a Process; Dating during Adolescence; Family Planning Clinics: Efficacy for Adolescents; Gay and Lesbian Youth; Homosexuality, Adolescent; Safer Sex and Adolescence; Sex Education; Sexual Behavior in Black Adolescents, Initiation of; Sexual Onset, Early; Sexually Transmitted Diseases in Adolescence.

Sexual Behavior in Black Adolescents, Initiation of

Renee R. Jenkins
Ouida E. Westney
Howard University

Adolescent sexuality including its antecedents and sequela has been the focus of many popular and scholarly works over the past two decades. Significant progress has been made in the documentation of sexual behavior and its association with biological, psychological, social, and economic phenomena, but much work remains to be done. The initiation of sexual behavior in black adolescents is an especially compelling issue given the disproportionate representation of this population in statistics regarding adolescent sexual issues and their associated adverse outcomes.

There are at least two major theoretical perspectives one can use to conceptualize issues related to initiation of sexual behavior in adolescence. The most common theory is to consider adolescent sexual activity as deviant behavior. Udry and Billy's (1987) work in adolescent sexual behavior constructs a model using this perspective. The initiation of intercourse during adolescence is considered a failure of age-graded social controls. This model postulates three parameters that help to override these social controls: (1) motivation of the adolescent, (2) restriction or opportunities provided by these social controls, and (3) attractiveness of the adolescent to potential sexual partners, in which case the adolescent may be a less willing participant in the sexual behavior. The second theoretical perspective is developmental. According to this theory, sexuality is one of the major psychosocial issues in normal adolescence. Learning sex roles occurs prior to adolescence, with the remaining evolution of solidified gender identity and social roles, as related to sexual behavior, becoming a primary focus during adolescence. The most common outcome anticipated by late adolescence is the establishment of a relationship with a chosen mate, which may or may not involve sexual intercourse.

Regardless of the theoretical framework they choose, researchers tend to look at similar variables in relation to initiation of sexual intercourse. The most common variables analyzed are age at intercourse, race, socioeconomic status, family structure, pubertal development, school or academic performance, and peer relations. This entry will review major findings useful in understanding the initiation of sexual behavior in black adolescents and make suggestions for further areas of exploration.

Sex and the Young Black Adolescent

Most of the literature on sexual activity in teenagers concentrates on intercourse activity in females and its continuum relationships to contraceptive use and pregnancy. Less information is available on precoital activity and sexual activity in males. The earliest papers on the sexual behavior of white adolescents that included precoital behavior suggested that there were patterns of progression moving stepwise from less intimate behaviors (i.e., holding hands, hugging, kissing) to more intimate behaviors (i.e., light and heavy petting) (Ramsey, 1943; Vener & Stewart, 1974; Vener, Stewart, & Hager, 1972). More recent data (Smith & Udry, 1985) from a biracial population suggests that the patterns for blacks and whites leading up to intercourse are different. The sequential progressions for whites is consistent with earlier descriptions. Black teenagers were less predictable in their patterns, however, and intercourse occurred more frequently than some heavy petting behaviors. There is still the possibility that black teens may have a different set of precoital behaviors than whites, and that researchers have yet to identify these behaviors.

Data on a smaller sample of black preadolescents followed through their early adolescence suggests that timing is also an issue of importance in sexual progression. The earlier a preadolescent starts precoital behaviors, the more likely she/he is to begin early intercourse. In contrast, if an early adolescent begins precoital behaviors in a timing pattern that is consistent with his/her peer group, it is less likely to be followed by early intercourse. Findings from this longitudinal study that included interviews with youngsters during preadolescence (9–11 years old) and again at early adolescence (12–14 years old) revealed that the prevalence of at least one episode of sexual intercourse had increased from 2% to 50% in boys and from 0% to 25% in girls (Westney & Jenkins, 1988). This observation suggests that for a significant proportion of black boys and girls, the years from 11 to 14 may be an important transition period for sexual behavior.

On a national scale, according to a recent analysis of patterns of premarital sexual behavior in 13- to 19-year-old women over the past three decades, there appears to be a slowing of the rate of increase in sexual intercourse. However, teenagers continue to experience intercourse at younger and younger ages. For white teens, there was a significant increase in activity for those entering adolescence during the late 1960s and early 1970s. For black teens, there was a less significant increase due to the already high levels in the previous decade. By 1982 the rates of increase appeared to be leveling off; for blacks there was even a small but statistically nonsignificant decline between 1979 and 1982 (Hofferth, Kahn, & Baldwin, 1987). The trends that reflect increasing sexual activity are less alarming when one considers that these statistics are for girls reporting intercourse at least once. The patterns of intercourse for younger teens is generally more sporadic and less frequent than for older teens and adults. Over 40% of all unmarried U.S. female teens report never having any sexual activity at all (Hayes, 1987).

The data on initiation of intercourse in males is limited when compared to females. The National Longitudinal Survey of Youth (NLSY) has data on females and males from age 15, but by that time 42.4% of black teen males are already reporting intercourse (Hayes, 1987). In a smaller sample of inner-city black teen boys, 23.4% reported intercourse prior to age 9, with a mean age for the total group of 11.8 years (Clark, Zabin, & Hardy, 1984). In contrast, by age 15, only 9.7% of black girls in the NLSY report intercourse, but the gap narrows by age 20 (for boys, 93.9%; for girls, 84.6% [Hayes, 1987]).

Factors Influencing Sexual Behavior

There is consistency among adolescent sexual behavior theorists and researchers regarding biological, social, and psychological factors: everyone agrees that all these factors influence the sexual behavior of developing adolescents. However, not all variables studied have been explored consistently across race and gender, and studies including preadolescents are sparse.

Several investigators have looked at the influence of pubertal maturation on sexual behavior in blacks (Udry & Billy, 1987; Westney, Jenkins, Butts, & Williams, 1984; Leigh, Weddle, & Loewen, 1988). The results are inconclusive, most likely due to variation in age of population and the cross-sectional versus longitudinal design of the studies. Two studies of black female adolescents found no significant association between pubertal maturation and sexual behavior (Westney et al., 1984; Leigh et al., 1988). But Udry and Billy (1987) found that pubertal development predicted intercourse transition for black females. For black males, there was a consistent association between the development of secondary sex characteristics (genital and pubic hair development) and involvement in noncoital and coital behavior at the preadolescent and early adolescent levels of development (Westney et al., 1984). There is no available data for black developing adolescents linking the elaboration of sex hormones to sexual behavior although such documentation exists for white adolescent males and females (Udry, Billy, Morris, Groff, & Raj, 1985; Udry, Talbert, & Morris, 1985).

Social and psychological factors related to sexual behavior are very complex, and the nature of relationships often limits investigators' ability to separate individual factors versus factors that have synergistic effects. In examining data on black teens, race and socioeconomic status (SES) often comingle, given many of the early studies targeting the lower socioeconomic stratum adolescents. Although there is some improvement when comparing the consideration of socioeconomic status in the current literature with the majority of reports on black lower-income adolescents and their parents in the 1970s, there is still less detailed study of the effects of an upward shift in the SES status of black families in the last decade and its impact on teen sexuality.

The major messages that come through with some consistency for blacks relate to parental factors, school/academic achievement in relation to self-concept/self-esteem, and peer relations. Parental socioeconomic status defined in terms of income and education influence the initiation of sexual behavior in youngsters (Newcomer & Udry, 1983; Zelnik, Kantner, & Ford, 1981; Furstenberg, Moore, Morgan & Peterson, et al., 1985). Many black low-income pre- and early adolescents are at a distinct disadvantage because of the socioeconomic status of their families and the environments in which they live. In such environments, exposure to overcrowding, inappropriate modeling, inadequate opportunity for obtaining appropriate education regarding sexual development, and regarding the biological/socioemotional interplay and disequilibrium that is a normal part of growth during puberty and adolescence may contribute to early sexual involvement.

Psychological factors such as self-concept, career aspirations, and academic achievement have been found to be related to adolescent sexual behavior. Beginning at about age 11 years, there is a decline in self-esteem for both boys and girls (Simmons, Rosenberg, & Rosenberg, 1973). Black preadolescent girls who view themselves in a negative manner, both generally and physically, show more involvement in heterosexual activity than those who view themselves more positively. These associations are not apparent for preadolescent boys. Early adolescent boys in a longitudinal study who were sexually active tended to express lower professional aspirations and achieved lower scores on standardized spelling and reading tests while they were preadolescents (Jenkins, Westney, & Butts, 1983). Other research studies have shown that adolescents who scored high on intelligence tests, were highly motivated, and were doing well in school were less likely to have initiated sexual activity at an early age (Devaney & Hubley, 1981; Furstenberg, 1976; Moore, Petersen, & Furstenberg, 1985; Mott, 1983; Udry, Bauman, & Morris, 1975).

Both same- and opposite-sex peers are important in the sexual socialization of developing youngsters. At the preadolescent stage of development black boys and girls who report having girlfriends and boyfriends also report more involvement in heterosexual behavior (Jenkins, Westney, & Butts, 1983). Those who report more heterosexual interaction with peers as preadolescents are also more likely to be involved in sexual activity as early adolescents than those less involved in such interaction. There is evidence that early adolescents are influenced toward transition to sexual activity by their peers (Lewis & Lewis, 1984). In this respect, the initiation of sexual activity among white adolescent girls is related more to peer influence than

is the case for white boys and black girls and boys (Billy & Udry, 1984). In a recent study (Leigh, Weddle & Loewen, 1988), consistent with earlier findings, the timing of transition to dating was found to be the most significant factor in the timing of transition to intercourse for black female adolescents.

Summary

Major biological and psychosocial factors that are strongly related to the initiation of sexual behavior in black pre- and early adolescents have been discussed. The data presented here suggests that there are still large gaps in our understanding of initiation of sexual behavior in black adolescents. Adapting a theoretical context with a developmental structure such as the life-span perspective may be more useful in understanding issues related to timing of precoital and coital behaviors, other co-occurring adolescent behaviors both deviant and nondeviant, and environmental, cultural, and historical influences. It is unlikely that a single theory will be capable of an analysis of all of these influences; that larger picture may be pieced together by smaller snapshots that have a common background.

The cultural and historical context is a vital element in interpreting data related to behavior, especially sexual behavior. For blacks, there are a distinct set of historical and cultural dynamics that are very different than those for whites. These dynamics account for some of the difference in sexual behavior for the adolescents in their respective settings. The African ethos of positive procreation, where survival of the group was paramount, still exists at varying levels of consciousness. The slavery experience perpetuated this ethos, as did the economics of the rural South. As blacks migrated to the North in the early 1930s and 1940s, these values came with them, but the economic and material realities of a different economy began to modify these values (Washington, 1982). As blacks gain further educational and economic advances, their values and to some extent their sexual behaviors parallel the larger American culture—hence the gaps become narrower in statistics which compare measures of sexual behavior.

The dearth of information on sexual behavior in black males is especially alarming, given the stereotypes present in our society regarding black males. One would expect a larger effort to replace these stereotypes with objective, scientific observations and data. While this strategy is evident in more recent analyses of national data (Peterson, Moore, & Furstenberg, 1985) and smaller sociologic studies (Fox, 1986), the trend has yet to be accepted on a wider basis. The absence of this data to compare with that for black females leaves us with an incomplete picture of the complexity of sexual behavior and its related factors in this population.

References

Billy, J. O. G., & Udry, J. R. (1984). Adolescent sexual behavior and friendship choice. *Social Forces, 62*, 653–687.

Clark, S. D., Jr., Zabin, L. S., & Hardy, J. B. (1984). Sex, contraception, and parenthood: Experience and attitudes among urban black young men. *Family Planning Perspectives, 16*, 77–82.

Devaney, B. L., & Hubley, K. S. (1981). *Determinants of adolescent pregnancy and childbearing* (final report to the National Institute of Child Health and Human Development). Washington, DC: Mathematica Policy Research.

Fox, G. L. (1986). *Intrafamilial sexual socialization patterns and outcomes* (Final Report. Grant No. APR000925-01). Washington, DC: Office of Adolescent Pregnancy Projects, Department of Health and Human Services.

Furstenberg, F. F., Jr. (1976). *Unplanned parenthood: The social consequences of teenage childbearing.* New York: Free Press.

Furstenberg, F. F., Morgan, S. P., Moore, K. A., & Peterson, J. (1985). *Exploring race differences in the timing of intercourse.* Unpublished manuscript. University of Pennsylvania.

Hayes, C. D. (Ed.). (1987). *Risking the future: Adolescent sexuality, pregnancy, and childbearing* (Vol. 1). Washington, DC: National Academy Press.

Hofferth, S. L., Kahn, J. R., & Baldwin, W. (1987). Premarital sexual activity among U.S. teenage women over the past three decades. *Family Planning Perspectives, 19*, 6–53.

Jenkins, R. R., Westney, O. E., & Butts, J. D. (1983). *Sociosexual development of black preadolescents within a family context* (Final Report. Contract No. 1-HD-82840). Bethesda, MD: National Institute of Child Health and Human Development.

Leigh, G. K., Weddle, K. D., & Loewen, I. R. (1988). Analysis of the timing of transition to sexual intercourse for black adolescent females. *Journal of Adolescent Research, 3*, 333–344.

Lewis, C. E., & Lewis, M. A. (1984). Peer pressure and risk taking behaviors in children. *American Journal of Public Health, 74*, 580–584.

Moore, K. A., Peterson, J. L., & Furstenberg, F. F., Jr. (1985). *Starting early: The antecedents of early, premarital intercourse.* Revised draft of a paper presented at the annual meeting of the Population Association of America, Minneapolis.

Mott, F. L. (1983). *Early fertility behavior among American youth: Evidence from the 1982 National Longitudinal Surveys of Labor Force Behavior of Youth.* Paper presented at the annual meeting of the American Public Health Association.

Newcomer, S. F., & Udry, J. R. (1983). Adolescent sexual behavior and popularity. *Adolescence, 18*, 515–522.

Peterson, J. L., Moore, K. A., & Furstenberg, F. F. (1985). *Starting early: The antecedents of early premarital intercourse* (Final Summary Report. Contract No. APR000916-01-1). Washington, DC: Office of Adolescent Pregnancy Programs, Department of Health and Human Services.

Ramsey, G. V. (1943). Sexual development of boys. *American Journal of Psychology, 56*, 217–233.

Simmons, R. G., Rosenberg, F., & Rosenberg, M. (1973). Disturbance of the self-image at adolescence. *American Sociological Review, 38*, 553–568.

Smith, E. A., & Udry, J. R. (1985). Coital and noncoital sexual behaviors of white and black adolescents. *American Journal of Public Health, 75*, 1200–1203.

Udry, J. R., Bauman, K. E., & Morris, N. M. (1975). Changes in premarital coital experience of recent decade-of-birth cohorts of American women. *Journal of Marriage and the Family, 37*, 783–787.

Udry, J. R., Billy, J. O. G., Morris, N. M., Groff, T. R., & Raj, M. H. (1985). Serum androgenic hormones motivate sexual behavior in adolescent boys. *Fertility and Sterility, 43*, 90–94.

Udry, J. R., Talbert, L., & Morris N. M. (1985). *Biosocial foundations for adolescent female sexuality.* Paper presented at the annual meeting of the American Sociological Association, Washington, DC.

Udry, J. R., & Billy, J. O. G. (1987). Initiation of coitus in early adolescence. *American Sociological Review, 52*, 841–855.

Vener, A. M., Stewart, C. S., & Hager, D. L. (1972). The sexual behavior of adolescents in middle America: Generational and American-British comparisons. *Journal of Marriage and the Family, 34*, 696–705.

Vener, A. M., & Stewart, C. S. (1974). Adolescent sexual behavior in middle America revisited: 1970–1973. *Journal of Marriage and the Family, 36*, 728–735.

Washington, A. C. (1982). A cultural and historical perspective on pregnancy-related activity among U.S. teenagers. *Journal of Black Psychology, 9*, 1–28.

Westney, O. E., Jenkins, R. R., Butts, J. D., & Williams, I. (1984). Sexual development and behavior in black preadolescents. *Adolescence, 19*, 557–568.

Westney, O. E., & Jenkins, R. R. (1988). *Transitioning sociosexually from preadolescence to early adolescence: Findings from a longitudinal study.* Unpublished manuscript. Howard University, Washington, D.C.

Zelnik, M., Kantner, J., & Ford, K. (1981). *Sex and pregnancy in adolescence.* Beverly Hills, CA: Sage Publications.

See Also

Black Adolescents At-Risk: Approaches to Prevention; Black Adolescents, the Impact of Federal Income Assistance Policies on; Black Female Adolescents, Socialization of; Drug Use, Minority Youth and; Health and Substance Abuse in Adolescence: Ethnic and Gender Perspectives; Hispanic Adolescents; Identity, Minority Development of; Minority and Female Participation in Math and Science, Increase in: The Importance of the Middle School Years; Socialization of African-American Adolescents.

Sexually Transmitted Diseases in Adolescence

Cherrie B. Boyer

University of California, San Francisco

Karen Hein

Albert Einstein College of Medicine
Montefiore Medical Center

Scope of the Problem

Sexually transmitted diseases (STDs) are a major cause of morbidity among sexually active adolescents. Over 60% of the STD cases reported yearly are individuals under the age of 25, with one-fourth between ages 15 and 19 (Kroger & Wiesner, 1981; Centers for Disease Control, personal communication, 1988). STDs, including the sequelae of pelvic inflammatory disease (PID), are highest among sexually active female adolescents and decline significantly with increasing age (Bell & Hein, 1984; Bell & Holmes, 1984; Washington, Sweet, & Shafer, 1985; Metropolitan Insurance Company, 1986). The data suggest that STDs are the most pervasive, destructive, and costly communicable disease problem confronting adolescents in the United States (Kroger & Wiesner, 1981). Further, the rapid spread of Human Immunodeficiency Virus (HIV) in areas of high viral prevalence poses an even greater threat of disease morbidity and premature mortality to many adolescents.

Epidemiology of STDs

HISTORICAL TRENDS ▪ Rates of reported STDs were high during World War I and World War II, but declined dramatically during the early 1950s, probably as a result of two factors. First, the development of penicillin and other antibiotics proved to be effective in treating gonorrhea and early syphilis, two frequently reported STDs. Second, a national campaign to increase awareness about STDs, with associated programs for partner notification and more treatment centers, became available. However, as the 1950s progressed, these resources were withdrawn and once again the rates of STDs increased (Brandt, 1985). Changes in sexual practices in the 1960s are thought to have contributed further to the resurgence of reported cases of STDs. See Figure 1 for gonorrhea rates reported from 1960 to 1979.

During the 1970s rates continued at very high levels. During the past decade there was an encouraging decline in the early 1980s (Centers for Disease Control,

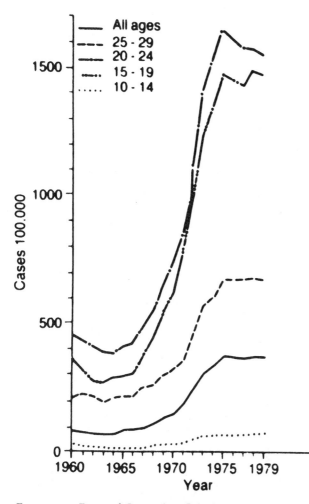

FIGURE 1 Rates of Gonorrhea Calculated by Total Population for Each Age Group

From *Sexually Transmitted Diseases* (73–84) by K. K. Holmes, P. Mardh, P. F. Sparling, & P. J. Wiesner (1984). New York: McGraw-Hill. Copyright 1984 by McGraw-Hill. Reprinted by permission.

1988; Handsfield, 1985; Krogh, Hellstron, & Bottiger, 1986; Poulsen & Ullman, 1985). However, despite the increasingly well-publicized pandemic of HIV infection and AIDS, rates of other STDs, including gonorrhea, syphilis, chlamydia, and PID, have shown an alarming increase in the most recent years (Brady, Baker, & Nein-

stein, 1988; Centers for Disease Control, 1988; Shafer, Beck, Blain, Dole, Irwin, Sweet, & Schachter, 1984; Washington, 1986).

SOCIODEMOGRAPHIC FACTORS ASSOCIATED WITH STDS ■ STDs are associated with younger age, gender, inner-city poverty, and minority group status. Rates of reported STDs among different age groups are misleading unless calculations are adjusted to account for the percent of sexually active individuals in each age group. For example, as shown in Figure 1, 10- to 14-year-old girls have the lowest rates of gonorrhea when rates are calculated on the basis of the total population in this age group.

However, when national data on rates of STDs are analyzed by age and adjusted to account for sexual activity relative to the total population, the previous underestimation of STDs in adolescents is underscored (see Figures 2, 3, and 4). It is clear that adolescents, not adults, have the highest rates of gonorrhea, syphilis, and concomitant hospitalizations for PID.

The artificially low rate of STDs among adolescents are due largely to two factors: (1) a higher proportion of individuals in the younger age group who are sexually inexperienced, and (2) a higher percentage of younger sexually active adolescents who sporadically engage in sexual intercourse (Aral, Schaffer, Mosher, & Cates, 1988).

Other data on the prevalence of STDs among adolescents indicate that inner-city minority adolescents have extremely high

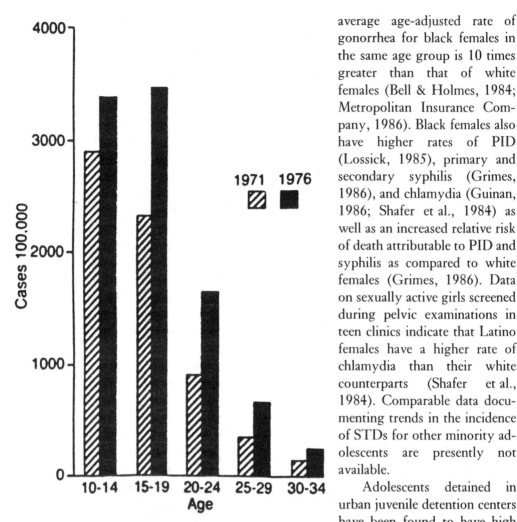

FIGURE 2   Rates of Gonorrhea for Sexually
Experienced Females

From *Sexually Transmitted Diseases* (73–84) by K. K.
    Holmes, P. Mardh, P. F. Sparling, & P. J.
    Wiesner (1984). Atlanta, GA: RE Johnson,
    Centers for Disease Control.

average age-adjusted rate of gonorrhea for black females in the same age group is 10 times greater than that of white females (Bell & Holmes, 1984; Metropolitan Insurance Company, 1986). Black females also have higher rates of PID (Lossick, 1985), primary and secondary syphilis (Grimes, 1986), and chlamydia (Guinan, 1986; Shafer et al., 1984) as well as an increased relative risk of death attributable to PID and syphilis as compared to white females (Grimes, 1986). Data on sexually active girls screened during pelvic examinations in teen clinics indicate that Latino females have a higher rate of chlamydia than their white counterparts (Shafer et al., 1984). Comparable data documenting trends in the incidence of STDs for other minority adolescents are presently not available.

Adolescents detained in urban juvenile detention centers have been found to have high rates of STDs. Many of these youth are poor and belong to inner-city minority groups. Rates of gonorrhea and syphilis among incarcerated youth in New York City was first documented to be high in the 1970s (Hein, Marks, & Cohen, 1977) and still remain equally high in the the 1980s (Alexander-Rodriquez & Vermund, 1987). In the recent report the prevalence of gonorrhea was 3% for boys and 18% for girls; the prevalence of syphilis was .63% for boys and 2.5% for girls ages 9 to 16 years who were screened during routine physical examinations. Similarly high rates were found in asymptomatic boys ages 12 to 18 who were detained in a

rates of STDs (Hardy, 1987; Holmes, Bell, & Berger, 1984; Oh, Feinstein, & Poss, 1988; Shafer et al., 1984). Epidemiological data also support these findings. The average age-adjusted gonorrhea rate in black males aged 15 to 19 is approximately 15 times greater than the rate for white males in the same age category. Similarly, the

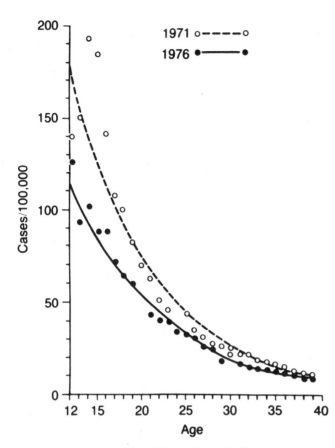

Figure 3 Rates of Syphilis for Sexually Experienced Females

From *Sexually Transmitted Diseases* (73–84) by K. K. Holmes, P. Mardh, P. F. Sparling, & P. J. Wiesner (1984). New York: McGraw-Hill. Copyright 1984 by McGraw-Hill. Reprinted by permission.

Los Angeles youth detention center. The prevalence of chlamydia was 14% for both black and Latino males and 10% for white males. The prevalence of gonorrhea for the same population was 1.5% (Brady, Baker, & Neinstein, 1988).

Risk Factors

Adolescence is characterized by rapid psychosocial and physical development. It is also a time when many teenagers perceive themselves to be invulnerable to disease and often engage in a variety of risk-taking behaviors that set the stage for many negative health outcomes, including the acquisition and transmission of STDs. The behaviors that place adolescents at increased risk for STDs include premature sexual activity, inadequate utilization of barrier-method contraceptives, and use of the intrauterine device (IUD) and oral contraceptives. In addition, the lack of complete physiologic development during adolescence may place adolescents at increased risk for acquiring STDs. Each of these risk factors is discussed below.

SEXUAL ACTIVITY ▪

More adolescents are initiating sexual intercourse at earlier ages than their counterparts did 10 years ago (Cates & Rauh, 1985; O' Reilly & Aral, 1985). The average age of first intercourse is 16 years (Zelnik & Shah, 1983), but as young as 12 years in some urban settings (Clark, Zabin, & Hardy, 1984). During adolescence 80% of males and 70% of females initiate sexual intercourse (Zelnik & Kantner, 1980), with 19% of them having more than four different sexual partners (Miller, 1987; Zelnik, 1983). Some adolescents have homosexual experiences that may increase their risk for acquiring STDs (cf. Darrow, 1986; Zenilman, 1988). As adolescents try to define their sexual identity, they experiment with a variety of sexual life-styles that may also put them at risk for STDs.

Sexual abuse among adolescents poses yet another risk for the acquisition of STDs. Although it is difficult to estimate

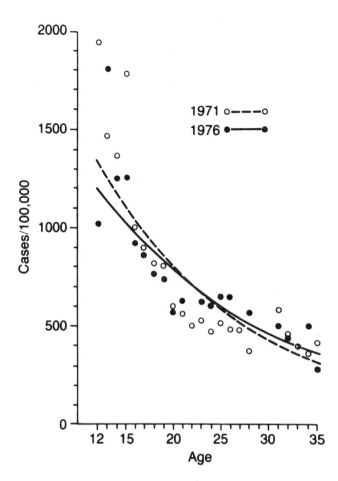

the exact number of adolescents who are being sexually abused, it is suggested that 3% of all teenagers are being sexually abused. Moreover, over half of all rape victims are adolescent females (Hamptom & Newberger, 1985).

CONTRACEPTIVE USE ■ The estimated one million teenage pregnancies occurring each year represent the apparent high rates of unprotected sexual intercourse among adolescents. Two-thirds of sexually active female adolescents aged 15 to 19 use nonbarrier-method contraceptives or none at all. Of the adolescents who use contraceptives, only 22% report using condoms (Zelnik & Kantner, 1980), the most effective method for preventing the transmission of STDs (Conant, Hardy, Sernatinger, & Spices, 1986).

The use of IUDs and oral contraceptives have also been identified as risk factors for infections associated with STDs (Johnson, 1987; Lee, Rubin, Ory, & Burkman, 1983; Newton & Keith, 1985; Oh et al., 1988; Washington, Sweet, & Shafer, 1985; Washington, Gove, Schachter, & Sweet, 1985). Women who use IUDs have a three- to fivefold increased risk for PID over women who use other forms of contraception or use no method at all. Although IUDs are not generally prescribed for adolescents, those under age 20 are reported to have an even greater risk for PID than those who use other forms of birth control (Washington, Sweet, et al., 1985). The findings on use of oral contraceptives appear to be contradictory; it appears that oral contraceptives provide some protection against gonococcal PID, but may increase susceptibility for chlamydia-related PID (Johnson, 1987; Washington, 1986; Washington, Sweet, et al., 1985). Given the extremely high rates of symptomatic and asymptomatic cervical chlamydia infection in women under age 20 and the use of oral contraceptives by over one million women in the same age group, oral contraceptives may be the most important risk factor for chlamydia-related PID (Washington, 1986).

PHYSIOLOGIC FACTORS ■ The early age of sexual debut of some female adolescents means that the physiologic maturational process will be incomplete when faced with exposure to organisms linked to STDs. Some investigators contend that the "inexperienced" immune system predisposes adolescents to STDs (McGregor, 1985). Levels of secretory IgA and other immune globulins differ in adolescents compared to adult women, and thus may render them more susceptible to infections. Other researchers suggest that sexually active female adolescents are particularly vulnerable to STDs, in part because of the histology of the cervical epithelium (Hernandez, 1987). During early puberty the columnar epithelium extends outward from the vaginal portion of the cervix, and is therefore exposed to pathogens (Bell & Hein, 1984). Once pubertal development is complete, a thick protective layer of squamous cells lines the vagina and the "transition zone" where vaginal and endometrial cells meet. As a result, gonorrhea, for example, causes vaginitis in prepubertal females, but cervicitis in postpubertal women. Also, the "transition zone" is the location where cervical intraepithitial neoplasia (CIN) arises. Exposure to STDs like human papillomavirus (HPV), a common STD in teenagers, is now thought to be a cofactor, if not a cause, of CIN (Howley, 1986).

Complications Related to STDs

The increasing numbers of STDs have been accompanied by a parallel increase in the complications occurring as a result of STDs. The physiological consequences are grave for adolescents, who are in the early stages of their reproductive life. Clinical complications range in severity from minor skin problems to systemic infections leading to increased morbidity, and, in some cases, mortality. The serious long-term consequences include chronic pelvic pain, repeated infections, infertility, ectopic pregnancies, neonatal transmission of infections causing fetal loss or illness during early infancy, as well as cervical carcinoma (cf. Hernandez, 1987; Johnson, 1987; Oriel, 1984; Pitegoff & Cathro, 1986).

The sequelae of PID is a leading cause of involuntary infertility among women. Estimates indicate that one episode of acute PID may cause 21% of its female victims to become involuntarily infertile (Washington, Gove, et al., 1985; Washington, Sweet, et al., 1985), and after three episodes 75% of women will become infertile because of obstruction to the Fallopian tubes (Oriel, 1984). Similarly, the risk of ectopic pregnancy is 6 to 10 times greater in women who have had at least one episode of PID than in those who have not had PID (Westrom, 1980). Statistical projections for the year 2000 suggest that if current trends of PID continue among female adolescents, as many as 10% of women will be sterile, and 3% will have had an ectopic pregnancy as a result of PID (Washington, Sweet, et al., 1985).

STD Treatment and Management

When discussing appropriate treatment of STDs in adolescence, it is important to go beyond medical aspects of care to include barriers to obtaining treatment. Access to services that are affordable, confidential, and attractive to youth are the first stages of effective therapy.

Effective medical treatment for STDs involves accurate and timely diagnosis, safe, acceptable treatment with adequate follow-up assessment for complications and compliance to prescribed regimens. For some STDs (gonorrhea, syphilis, and chlamydia), there are specific medicines that are curative. For others (herpes, HPV, HIV), however, eradication methods remain elusive. A summary of treatment modalities is provided in Table 1.

Prevention and Education

Prevention and education strategies are the primary hope for decreasing the high incidence of STDs among adolescents. Not all STDs are readily cured by antibiotics; therefore, it is imperative that adolescents consider delaying sexual intercourse and modifying behaviors that increase their risk of acquiring STDs. Prevention and risk-reduction programs are necessary and must be designed, implemented, and supported by parents, schools, health care providers, and the media. Such programs should target cognitive and behavioral skills aimed at enhancing adolescents' ability to communicate, problem-solve, and make appropriate decisions about engaging in sexual intercourse.

Adolescents should be accurately informed about the prevention of STDs; they need to learn about "safer sex" techniques, especially the use of condoms, the transmission and symptoms of STDs, the importance of compliance with treatment and behavioral recommendations, and the sequelae of untreated STDs. Prevention and risk-reduction programs should, in addition, clearly and unequivocally dispel myths and misconceptions about STDs. Information should be discussed in the context of comprehensive health education, including discussions about sex, sexuality, and birth control. To increase the likelihood that adolescents will accept the information being conveyed to them, these programs should be developed to account for individual and group differences among adolescents and be sensitive to cultural values, religious beliefs, and social customs.

In addition to educating adolescents, widespread education of health professionals who treat adolescents is also essential. These individuals must be aware of the risk factors associated with acquiring STDs, maintain a high level of suspicion for asymptomatic infection—as well as for the wide range of clinical signs and symptoms associated with STDs and its concomitant consequences—and provide timely effective treatment to patients and their sexual partners. During routine physical examinations health care providers should obtain thorough sexual histories and screen adolescents for STDs, paying particular attention to adolescents who initiated sexual intercourse at an early age, have multiple sexual partners, are pregnant, or have a history of previous STDs (Hernandez, 1987).

Conclusions

STDs among adolescents in the United States are of epidemic proportions. The highest rates of STDs are among younger adolescent females and inner-city minority youth. Many of these adolescents face severe psychosocial and physical consequences as a result of STDs. Broad-based educational programs to prevent or modify behaviors that put adolescents at risk for STDs are essential to stem the tide of this epidemic. In addition, cost-effective medical programs that are confidential, affordable, and accessible must be made readily available for adolescents who need such services.

TABLE 1
TREATMENT OF SEXUALLY TRANSMITTED DISEASES

TYPE OR STAGE	DRUG OF CHOICE	DOSAGE	ALTERNATIVES
GONORRHEA			
Urethritis or Cervicitis[1]	Ceftriaxone	125–250 mg IM once	Amoxicillin 3 grams oral once plus probenecid 1 gram oral once Spectinomycin 2 grams IM once
Rectal	Ceftriaxone	125–250 mg IM once	Penicillin G procaine 4.8 million U IM[2] once plus probenecid 1 gram oral once Spectinomycin 2 grams IM once
Pharyngeal	Ceftriaxone	125–250 mg IM once	Penicillin G procaine 4.8 million U IM[2] once plus probenecid 1 gram oral once Trimethoprim-sulfamethoxazole 9 tablets[3] daily in one dose × 5 days
Ophthalmia (adults)	Ceftriaxone plus saline irrigation	1 gram IM daily × 5 days	Penicillin G 10 million U IV daily × 5 days plus saline irrigation
Bacteramia and arthritis	Ceftriaxone	1 gram IV daily × 7 days	Penicillin G 10 million U IV daily × 3 days followed by amoxicillin 500 mg oral qid × 4 days Doxycycline[4] 100 mg oral bid × 7 days
Meningitis	Ceftriaxone	2 grams IV daily for at least 10 days	Penicillin G at least 10 million U IV daily for at least 10 days Chloramphenicol 4–6 grams/day for at least 10 days
Endocarditis	Ceftriaxone	2 grams IV daily for at least 3 to 4 weeks	Penicillin G at least 10 million U IV daily for at least 3 to 4 weeks
Neonatal —Ophthalmia	Cefotaxime plus saline irrigation	25 mg/kg q8–12h × 7 days	Penicillin G 100,000 U/kg/day IV in 4 doses × 7 days plus saline irrigation
	OR Ceftriaxone plus saline irrigation	125 mg IM once	

TABLE 1 (*continued*)

TYPE OR STAGE	DRUG OF CHOICE	DOSAGE	ALTERNATIVES
—Arthritis and septicemia	Cefotaxime	25–50 mg/kg q8–12h × 10–14 days	Penicillin G 75,000 to 100,000 U/kg/day IV in 4 doses × 7 days
—Meningitis	Cefotaxime	50 mg/kg q8–12h × 10–14 days	Penicillin G 100,000 U/kg/day IV in 3 or 4 doses for at least 10 days
Children (under 45 kg)			
—Urogenital, rectal and pharyngeal	Ceftriaxone	125 mg IM once	Amoxicillin 50 mg/kg oral once plus pro-benecid 25 mg/kg (max. 1 gram) oral once Penicillin G procaine 100,000 U/kg IM once plus probenecid 25 mg/kg (max. 1 gram) once Spectinomycin 40 mg/kg IM once
—Arthritis	Ceftriaxone	50 mg/kg/day (max. 2 grams) IV × 7 days	Penicillin G 150,000 U/kg/day IV × 7 days
	OR Cefotaxime	50 mg/kg/day IV in divided doses × 7 days	Tetracycline (over 8 years old) 10 mg/kg oral qid × 7 days
—Meningitis	Ceftriaxone	100 mg/kg/day (max. 2 grams) IV × 7 days	Penicillin G 250,000 U/kg/day IV in 6 divided doses for at least 10 days
	OR Cefotaxime	200 mg/kg/day IV for at least 10 days	Chloramphenicol 100 mg/kg/day IV for at least 10 days
CHLAMYDIA TRACHOMATIS			
Urethritis or cervicitis	Doxycycline[4]	100 mg bid × 7 days	Sulfisoxazole 500 mg oral qid × 10 days
	OR Erythromycin	500 mg oral qid × 7 days	
Oculogenital syndrome			
Proctitis	as for urethritis		
Neonatal	as for urethritis		
—Ophthalmia	Erythromycin	12.5 mg/kg oral or IV qid × 14 days	

TABLE 1 (*continued*)

TYPE OR STAGE	DRUG OF CHOICE	DOSAGE	ALTERNATIVES
—Pneumonia	Erythromycin	12.5 mg/kg oral or IV qid × 14 days	Sulfisoxazole 100 mg/kg/day oral or IV in divided doses (after 4 weeks of age)
Lymphogranuloma veneraum	Doxycycline[4] OR Erythromycin	100 mg bid × 21 days 500 mg oral qid × 21 days	
EPIDIDYMITIS	Ceftriaxone followed by doxycycline[4]	250 mg IM once 100 mg oral bid × 10 days	Amoxicillin 3 grams oral once plus probenecid 1 gram oral once followed by doxycycline[4] 100 mg oral bid × 10 days
PELVIC INFLAMMATORY DISEASE			
—outpatients	Cefoxitin plus probenecid OR Ceftriazone either one followed by doxycycline	2 grams IM once 1 gram oral once 250 mg Im once 100 mg oral bid × 10 days	
—hospitalized patients	Cefoxitin plus doxycycline followed by doxycycline	2 grams IV qid 100 mg IV bid until improvement 100 mg oral bid to complete 10 days	Clindamycin 600 mg IV qid plus gentamicin 2 mg/kg IV once followed by gentamicin 1.5 mg/kg IV tid until improvement followed by clindamycin 450 mg oral qid to complete 10–14 days
VAGINAL INFECTIONS			
Trichomoniasis	Metronidazole	2 grams oral once or 250 mg oral tid × 7 days	
—in pregnancy	Clotrimazole	100 mg intravaginally at bedtime × 7 days	
Bacterial vaginosis	Metronidazole	500 mg oral bid × 7 days	Amoxicillin 500 mg oral tid × 7 days
Vulvovaginal candidiasis	Clotrimazole	100 mg intravaginally at bedtime × 7 days, or 200 mg × 3 days	Nystatin 100,000 units intravaginally at bedtime × 14 days

1037 ∎

TABLE 1 (*continued*)

TYPE OR STAGE	DRUG OF CHOICE	DOSAGE	ALTERNATIVES
	OR Miconazole	100 mg intravaginally at bedtime × 7 days, or 200 mg × 3 days	
SYPHILIS			
Early (Primary, secondary, or latent less than one year)	Penicillin G benzathine	2.4 million U IM once	Tetracycline 500 mg oral qid × 15 days Erythromycin 500 mg oral qid × 15 days
Late (more than one year's duration, cardiovascular)	Penicillin G benzathine	2.4 million U IM weekly × 3 weeks	Tetracycline 500 mg oral qid × 30 days Erythromycin 500 mg oral qid × 30 days
Neurosyphilis	Penicillin G	2 to 4 million U IV q4h × 10 days	Tetracycline 500 mg oral qid × 30 days Erythromycin 500 mg oral qid × 30 days
	OR Penicillin G procaine plus probenecid	2.4 million U IM daily 500 mg qid orally both × 10 days	
	either one followed by penicillin G benzathine	2.4 million U IM weekly × 3 weeks	
Congenital	Penicillin G	25,000 U/kg IM or IV bid for at least 10 days	
	OR Penicillin G procaine	50,000 U/kg Im daily for at least 10 days	
CHANCROID	Ceftriaxone	250 mg IM once	Trimethoprim-sulfamethoxazole 2 tablets[3] bid × 7 days
	OR Erythromycin	500 mg oral qid × 7 days	

[1]Since a high percentage of women and heterosexual men with gonorrhea have coexisting *Chlamydia trachomatis* infection, these patients should also receive a seven-day course of doxycycline or tetracycline, as recommended for treatment of *Chlamydia.*

[2]Divided into two injections at one visit.

[3]Each tablet contains 80 mg trimethoprim and 400 mg sulfamethoxazole.

[4]Or tetracycline 500 mg qid.

Source: Treatment of Sexually Transmitted Diseases, 1982, *The Medical Letter on Drugs and Therapeutics, 30,* pp. 5–10. Copyright by the Medical Letter. Reprinted by permission.

References

Alexander-Rodriguez, T., & Vermund, S. H. (1987). Gonorrhea and syphilis in incarcerated urban adolescents: Prevalence and physical signs. *Pediatrics, 80*, 561–564.

Aral, S. O., Schaffer, J. E., Mosher, W. D., & Cates, W. (1988). Gonorrhea rates: What denominator is most appropriate? *American Journal of Pediatric Health, 78*, 702–703.

Bell, T. A., & Holmes, K. K. (1984). Age-specific risks of syphilis, gonorrhea, and hospitalized pelvic inflammatory disease in sexually experienced U.S. women. *Sexually Transmitted Dieseases, 11*, 291–295.

Bell, T., & Hein, K. (1984). Adolescents and sexually transmitted diseases. In K. K. Holmes, P. Mardh, P. F. Sparling, & P. J. Wieser (Eds.), *Sexually transmitted diseases* (pp. 73–84). New York: McGraw-Hill.

Brady, M., Baker, C., & Neinstein, L. S. (1988). Asymptomatic chlamydia trachomatic infections in teenage males. *Journal of Adolescent Health Care, 9*(1), 72–75.

Brandt, A. M. (1985). *No magic bullet: A social history of venereal disease in the United States since 1980.* New York: Oxford University Press.

Cates, W., & Rauh, J. L. (1985). Adolescents and sexually transmitted diseases: An expanding problem. *Journal of Adolescent Health Care, 6*(4), 257–261.

Centers for Disease Control. (1988). Syphilis and congenital syphilis—United States, 1985–1986. *Morbidity and Mortality Weekly Report,* August 19, *37*, 486–489.

Centers for Disease Control. (1988, July). Personal communication.

Clark, S. D., Zabin, L. S., & Hardy, J. B. (1984). Sex, contraception, and parenthood. *Family Planning Perspectives, 15*(2), 77–82.

Conant, M., Hardy, J., Sernatinger, D., & Spices, D. (1986). Condoms prevent transmission of AIDS-associated retrovirus. *Journal of the American Medical Association, 255*, 1706.

Darrow, W. W. (1986). Sexual behavior in America: Implications for the control of sexually transmitted disease. In Y. M. Felman (Ed.), *Sexually transmitted diseases* (pp. 261–280). New York: Churchill-Livingstone.

Grimes, D. A. (1986). Death due to sexually transmitted diseases. *Journal of the American Medical Association, 255*, 1727–1729.

Guinan, M. (1986). Sexually transmitted diseases may reverse the "revolution." *Journal of the American Medical Association, 255*, 1665–1667.

Hampton, R. L., & Newberger, E. H. (1985). Child abuse incidence and reporting by hospitals: Significance of severity, class, and race. *American Journal of Public Health, 75*, 55–60.

Handsfield, H. H. (1985). Decreasing incidence of gonorrhea in homosexually active men—minimal effect on risk of AIDS. *Western Journal of Medicine, 143*, 469–470.

Hardy, J. B. (1987). Sexually transmitted diseases among adolescents. *Maryland Medical Journal, 36*, 938–942.

Hein, K., Marks, A., & Cohen, M. I. (1977). Asymptomatic gonorrhea: Prevalence in a population of urban adolescents. *Journal of Pediatrics, 90*, 634–635.

Hernandez, T. J. (1987). Adolescents and sexually transmitted disease. *American Federal Physicians, 36*(2), 127–132.

Holmes, K. K., Bell, T. A., & Berger, R. E. (1984). Epidemiology of sexually transmitted diseases. *Urologic Clinics of America, 11*(1), 3–13.

Howley, P. (1986). On human papillomaviruses. *New England Journal of Medicine, 315*, 1089–1090.

Johnson, J. (1987). Sexually transmitted diseases in adolescents. *Adolescent Medicine, 14*(1), 101–120.

Krilov, L. R. (1988). Sexually transmitted diseases in adolescents. *Medical Aspects of Human Sexuality, 22*, 67–77.

Kroger, F., & Wiesner, P. J. (1981). STD education: Challenge for the 80's. *Journal of School Health, 51*, 242–246.

Krogh, G. V., Hellstron, L., & Bottiger, M. (1986). Declining incidence of syphilis among homosexual men in Stockholm. *Lancet, 2*, 920–921.

Lee, N. C., Rubin, G. L., Ory, A. W., & Burkman, W. J. (1983). Type of intrauterine device and the risk of pelvic inflammatory disease. *Obstetrics and Gynecology, 62*, 1–6.

Lossick, J. G. (1985). Epidemiology of sexually transmitted diseases. In B. A. Spagna & R. B. Prior (Eds.), *Sexually transmitted diseases: A clinical syndrome approach* (pp. 21–62). New York: Marcel Decker.

McGregor, J. A. (1985). Adolescent misadventures with urethritis and cervitis. *Journal of Adolescent Health Care, 6*, 286–297.

Metropolitan Insurance Company. (1986). Sexually transmitted diseases in the US. *Statistical Bulletin, 67*, 1–9.

Miller, G. (1987). Chair of the U.S. House of Representatives Select Committee on Children, Youth, and Families, introductory statement before the Committee hearing "AIDS and Teenagers: Emerging Issues." Congressional Record, June 17, 1987.

Newton, W., & Keith, L. G. (1985). Role of sexual behavior in the development of pelvic inflammatory disease. *Journal of Reproductive Medicine, 30*(2), 82–88.

Oh, M. K., Feinstein, R. A., & Pass, R. F. (1988). Sexually transmitted diseases and sexual behavior in urban adolescent females attending a family planning clinic. *Journal of Adolescent Health Care, 9*, 67–71.

O'Reilly, K. R., & Aral, S. O. (1985). Adolescence and sexual behavior: Trends and implications for STD. *Journal of Adolescent Health Care, 6*, 298–310.

Oriel, J. D. (1984). Public health aspects of sexually transmitted diseases. *Public Health Reviews, 12*, 131–157.

Pitegoff, J. G., & Cathro, D. M. (1986). Chlamydial infections and other sexually trans-

mitted diseases in adolescent pregnancy. *Seminars in Adolescent Medicine, 2*(3), 215–229.

Poulsen, A., & Ullman, S. (1985). AIDS-induced decline of the incidence of syphilis in Denmark. *Acta Dermato Venereologica, 65*, 567–568.

Shafer, M. A., Beck, A., Blain, B., Dole, P., Irwin, C. E., Sweet, R., & Schachter, S. (1984). Chlamydia trachomatis: Important relationships to race, contraception, lower genital tract, and Papanicolaou smears. *Journal of Pediatrics, 104*, 141–146.

Washington, A. E. (1986). Pelvic inflammatory disease in adolescents. *Research Highlights, 4*(1), 1–3.

Washington, A. E., Gove, S., Schachter, J., & Sweet, R. L. (1985). Oral contraceptives, chlamydia trachomatis infection, and pelvic inflammatory disease: A word of caution about protection. *Journal of the American Medical Association, 253*, 2246–2250.

Washington, A. E., Sweet, R. K., & Shafer, M. A. (1985). Pelvic inflammatory disease in the adolescent female and its sequelae. *Journal of Adolescent Health Care, 6*, 298–310.

Westrom, L. (1980). Incidence, prevalence, and trends of acute pelvic inflammatory disease and its consequences in industrialized countries. *American Journal of Obstetrics and Gynecology, 138*, 880.

Zelnik, M. (1983). Sexual activity among adolescents: Perspective of a decade. In E. R. McArnarney (Ed.), *Premature Adolescent Pregnancy and Parenthood*, pp. 21–33. New York: Grune and Stratton.

Zelnik, M., & Kantner, J. F. (1980). Sexual activity, contraceptive use, and pregnancy among metropolitan-area teenagers: 1971–1979. *Family Planning Perspectives, 12*(5), 230–237.

Zelnik, M., & Shah, F. (1983). First intercourse among young Americans. *Family Planning Perspectives, 15*(2), 64–70.

Zenilman, J. (1988). Sexually transmitted diseases in homosexual adolescents. *Journal of Adolescent Health Care*, *9*, 129–138.

See Also

Contraceptive Behavior as a Process; Dating during Adolescence; Family Planning Clinics: Efficacy for Adolescents; Gay and Lesbian Youth; Homosexuality, Adolescent; Safer Sex and Adolescence; Sex Education; Sexual Behavior in Black Adolescents, Initiation of; Sexual Onset, Early; Sexual Behavior, Sexual Attitudes and Contraceptive Use, Age Differences in Adolescent.

Sexual Onset, Early

Laurie Schwab Zabin

The Johns Hopkins University

The term "teen pregnancy" has suggested that conception during the teens is a single phenomenon, and has thereby tended to mask the fact that the years between puberty and age 20 are years of constant, even dramatic, change. Sexual activity among prepubertal and pubertal females and males, and conception in the early postpubertal years is not the same in its etiology or consequences as coital initiation at age 16 or 17, and differs radically from the sexual liaisons of young women who, initiating intercourse at age 18 or 19, may have graduated from high school and entered into marriage and/or the labor force. In order to understand adolescent fertility, one must focus on the early years after menarche, even though, in absolute numbers, more young women initiate intercourse at ages 16 and 17 than at ages 13, 14, and 15. What precipitates early coital exposure, and why is it more prevalent in some groups than in others?

Age of sexual onset is influenced by a personal biological time clock on the one hand and by social or normative patterns on the other. It has been demonstrated that androgen levels, the source of sexual motivation or libido, have an influence on the timing of sexual behavior (Udry, Billy, Morris, Graff and Madhwa 1985; Udry, Talbert, & Morris, 1986). However, if that were the only pressure, we would not see the wide variants in age of onset observed among those with similar pubertal ages, nor the long delays to sexual onset following puberty that are common among those whose social settings encourage restraint. Clearly, several influences interact in complex ways, not only affecting social groups as a whole but the individuals within social groups, each of whom works out a "sexual script" in a process that is both internal and social in nature (Simon & Gagnon 1986, 1987).

Menarche and other areas of sexual development are related, and the ordering of various physical manifestations of puberty appears to be constant. Menarche comes fairly late in puberty, following well after the onset of breast development, which may take four to five years to complete. Menarche always follows peak height velocity, whatever the chronological ages at which those two benchmarks occur. A recent decline in mean age of menarche in the developed world continued for almost a hundred years, leveling off about one generation ago. That process is still at work in parts of the developing world. The decline suggests that all physical changes are occurring at earlier ages, and that fertility, too, is achieved at younger ages than it was in the past.

A young age at puberty appears to exert downward pressure on the age of sexual initiation. Among students in an urban, black school population of males and females, the relationship between the two events was shown to be particularly strong in the early teen years; it attenuated over time, disappearing by 17 years of age among females and 15 among males (Zabin, Smith, Hirsch, & Hardy, 1986). It is possible that the fact that the relationship does attenuate has masked its effect when exploring the teen years as a whole, but the strength of the relationship at 13 and 14 years of age makes it important, nonetheless. Udry and Cliquet (1982) showed a relationship between menarche, marriage, first intercourse, and first birth that was evident cross-culturally; Buck and Stavraky (1967) showed parallel associations between age of menarche and age of marriage among childbearing women.

There are clear variations in age of coital onset in the United States between various geographic, social, ethnic and/or racial, and economic subgroups, suggesting that a social process as well as a biological process is at work. There have been some small differences reported between ages of maturation in one racial subgroup and another, but these differences do not approach the differences observed in age at first intercourse. Similarly, the increases in early sexual activity in the United States from the late 1960s to the present are much greater than would have been expected had they been due to changes in biological development—even had those changes been a response to decreases in age at menarche that had taken place a generation earlier.

Between 1971 and 1979 there was a 50% increase in the percentage of 15-year-old-girls who had experienced intercourse; whereas 14.4% of 15- to 19-year-olds in a national probability sample reported coitus by age 15 in 1971, the number had risen to 22.5% in 1979 (Zelnik & Kantner, 1980). There was a 30% increase, to approximately 50%, in the percentage of young women 15- to 19-years-old, living in metropolitan areas of the United States, who reported ever having engaged in coitus. By age 19, 69.0% of never married females and 77.5% of never married males had experienced coitus, according to the same report. While differences between males and females, and between racial groups, are extremely great in the early teen years, with blacks at each age more likely than whites or Hispanics to have experienced intercourse (Hayes, 1987), these discrepancies tend to become smaller over the teen years. It seems clear that there was a downward normative pressure on age of first intercourse throughout the United States during the 1970s, expressed among all social, economic, and racial subgroups, with the largest continuing decrease among young white females. The trend toward greater permissiveness throughout the country not only affected premarital and extramarital behavior at older ages, but influenced youthful premarital sexual behavior as well. However, there also appear to be cultural influences at work, with behavioral patterns in certain ethnic, religious, racial, and geographic subgroups precipitating young people into earlier sexual contact. These pressures can denote a range of social influences beyond those exerted through the media and the larger society.

The influence of family on sexual behavior is not well understood, but is apparent in the intergenerational aspect of early sexual contact and early fertility. Whether the influence of parents is biological (i.e., inherited through early pubertal development), communicated by example, or communicated verbally is not well demonstrated. Some effects of parental supervision, and/or of the family's expectations for the current behavior and future achievement of the adolescent, are documented (Hayes, 1987), but the nature of those influences is not clear. Similarly, the effects of peers are reported but not well understood. Billy and his colleagues have shown independent relationships between a best friend's sexual behavior and the conduct of young males and females (Billy & Udry, 1985a, 1985b; Billy, Rodgers, & Udry, 1984). Perhaps the most important peer effects are those exerted by sexual partners; when discussion with a sexual partner relative to contraception is seen as acceptable, he can have a strong effect on the decision to avoid a pregnancy (Zabin, 1985).

The effects of biology and social norms are not mutually exclusive, but interact in interesting ways. For example, physical maturation, because it determines the appearance of the growing individual, has a distinct effect on the perception of that individual by others, and on his or her self-perception. The sexually mature male or female may be able to acknowledge his/her sexual identity, and may be more attractive to potential partners, than the late maturer. Those perceptions, in turn, help create the environment in which the young person develops a "sexual script."

The process is extremely complex, and, although its role is not well described, self-perception appears to be a part of the calculus of choice. Individual decisions may be influenced by biology, and constrained or encouraged by social setting, but it is clear that the individual, nonetheless, plays an important role in the serial decision-making process that leads from virginity to childbearing. Whether or not to engage in coitus, whether or not to contracept, whether or not to bear a child when faced with an unintended conception—are all decisions. Unfortunately, they are often not true "choices"; for example, they may have been forced, accidental, a response to pressure, or influenced by substance use. Even when the adolescent has had a clear role in those decisions, they are often perceived as the choices they are.

It has been hypothesized that self-esteem, self-perception, aspirations and expectations for the future, and a sense of personal identity are factors in the sexual decision-making process (Hayes, 1987). However self-concept is defined, individuals from the same cultural settings, with the same ages of puberty, demonstrate a wide variety of sexual behaviors, with very different ages of sexual onset. The model proposed here would suggest that, over time, both the cultural/family setting and biological maturation have an effect on that self-concept, which is influenced by a past history of achievement or failure, by aspirations and expectations, and by personal efficacy. In turn, when the young person reaches puberty, the pressures of biology and environment are processed through that personal view of self, which affects the many decisions made when the opportunity to initiate sexual contact presents itself.

Understanding the importance of early sexual onset is critical to an understanding of adolescent pregnancy. Not only does early onset allow a longer period of exposure to unintended conception, but the developmental stages of youth increase the probability of conception in the early years of sexual exposure (Zabin, 1979). The cognitive, emotional, psychological, and pubertal development of adolescents each proceed on separate tracks, each operating with a timetable of its own. To the extent that early puberty is accelerated, the discrepancy between physical development, on the one hand, and cognitive and emotional development, on the other, becomes greater. The implications of this discrepancy for the provision of preventive services is clear. The difficulty in reaching young people in time to prevent conception is reflected in the heightened risk of unintended conception experienced by those who initiate intercourse at age 15 or earlier (Zabin, 1979).

References

Billy, J. O. G., Rodgers, J. L., & Udry, J. R. (1984). Adolescent sexual behavior and friendship choice. *Social Forces, 62,* 653–678.

Billy, J. O. G., & Udry, J. R. (1985a). The influence of male and female best friends on adolescent sexual behavior. *Adolescence, 20,* 21–31.

Billy, J. O. G., & Udry, J. R. (1985b). Patterns of adolescent friendships and effects on sexual behavior. *Social Psychology Quarterly, 48,* 27–31.

Buck, C., & Stavraky, K. (1967). The relationship between age at menarche and age at marriage among childbearing women. *Human Biology, 39,* 93–102.

Hayes, C. D., (Ed.). (1987). *Risking the future* (Vol. 1). Washington, DC: National Academy Press.

Simon, W., & Gagnon, J. H. (1986). Sexual scripts: Determinants and change. *Archives of Sexual Behavior, 15*(2), 97–120.

Simon, W., & Gagnon, J. H. (1987). A sexual scripts approach. In J. H. Geer & W. T. O'Donahue (Eds.), *Theories of human sexuality,* 363–383. New York: Plenum.

Udry, J. R., Billy, J. O. G., Morris, N. M., Graff, T. R., & Madhwa, R. H. (1985). Serum androgenic hormones motivate sexual behavior in adolescent boys. *Fertility and Sterility, 43,* 90–94.

Udry, J. R., & Cliquet, R. L. (1982). A cross-cultural examination of the relationship between ages at menarche, marriage, and first birth. *Demography, 19*(1), 53–63.

Udry, J. R., Talbert, L. M., & Morris, N. M. (1986). Biosocial foundations for adolescent female sexuality. *Demography, 23,* 217–230.

Zabin, L. S. (1985). Correlates of effective contraception among black inner-city high school students (Final Report to National Institute of Child Health and Human Development, RO1-HD-17183-02).

Zabin, L. S., Kantner, J. F., & Zelnik, M. (1979). The risk of adolescent pregnancy in the first months of intercourse. *Family Planning Perspectives, 11,* 215–222.

Zabin, L. S., Smith, E. A., Hirsch, M. B., & Hardy, J. B. (1986). Ages of physical maturation and first intercourse in black teenage males and females. *Demography, 23,* 595–605.

Zelnik, M., & Kantner, J. F. (1980). Sexual activity, contraceptive use, and pregnancy among metropolitan-area teenagers: 1971–1979. *Family Planning Perspectives, 12,* 230–237.

See Also

Contraceptive Behavior as a Process; Dating during Adolescence; Family Planning Clinics: Efficacy for Adolescents; Gay and Lesbian Youth; Homosexuality, Adolescent; Safer Sex and Adolescence; Sex Education; Sexual Behavior in Black Adolescents, Initiation of; Sexual Behavior, Sexual Attitudes, and Contraceptive Use, Age Differences in Adolescent; Sexually Transmitted Diseases in Adolescence.

Sibling Relationships in Adolescence

Clare Stocker
Judy Dunn
The Pennsylvania State University

Interest in the relationship between siblings centers on two general questions. First, is the relationship important as a developmental influence? Second, what qualities characterize the relationship, and what accounts for differences in sibling relationships?

To date research on siblings has focused chiefly on preschool and school-aged children, so answers to these questions for adolescent siblings remain tentative. However, in relation to the first question, a large survey of high school students found that 77% of adolescents reported that their sibling was an important influence in their lives (Blyth, Hill, & Thiel, 1982). But adolescents do not spend much time with their siblings. Raffaelli and Larson (1987) found that 10- to 14-year-olds spent 5.3% of their time alone with siblings, as compared with 19.5% alone with peers, and 5.9% alone with parents. Children's companionship with siblings appears to decrease steadily between third and twelfth grades (Buhrmester & Furman, 1989).

Some research indicates that firstborn children influence their younger siblings, especially in the areas of deviance and sex-uality (Patterson, 1986; Rowe, Rodgers, Meseck-Bushey, & St. John, 1989; Sutton-Smith & Rosenberg, 1970). Children who report high levels of hostility and rivalry with their siblings have also been found to be more anxious, more depressed, and to have lower self-esteem than those with more positive relationships (Stocker & McHale, 1988). However, the direction of causal influence here is unclear.

Sibling influence has also been inferred from studies of the striking differences between siblings in personality and psychopathology (Plomin & Daniels, 1987). To explain these differences, Schachter (1982) has proposed that siblings engage in a process of "deidentification" as a defense against sibling rivalry. It has also been suggested that siblings "niche-pick" to seek situations that foster their different talents (Scarr & Grajek, 1982). Systematic empirical evidence for such processes is not yet available. However, differences between adolescent siblings' relationships with parents and peers are marked and have been found to be associated with differences in siblings' psychological adjustment (Daniels, Dunn, Furstenberg, & Plomin, 1985).

In relation to the second question, the quality of the relationship between young adolescent siblings has been characterized by Furman and Buhrmester (1985), in terms of four independent dimensions: warmth/closeness, relative power/status, rivalry, and conflict. There is some evidence that sibling relationships become less conflictual and more egalitarian during the course of adolescence. But these changes may differ as a function of children's birth order (Buhrmester & Furman, 1989).

Characteristics of adolescents' sibling relationships, according to most reports, are not influenced by family structure variables such as gender, age gap between siblings, or family size (Hetherington, 1988; Raffaelli & Larson, 1987; Stocker & McHale, 1990). Young adolescents' relationships with their brothers and sisters do vary as a function of their parents' marital status. Hetherington (1988) found that biological siblings in stepfamilies had more problematic relationships than siblings in divorced or intact families. In all three types of families sibling relationships that included a boy were more troubled than those involving a girl. The quality of sibling relationships is also linked to characteristics of adolescents' relationships with their parents. Two studies report that adolescents whose parents were unaffectionate, hostile, and unresponsive were less affectionate and more hostile to their siblings than those who had warm relationship with their parents. More conflictual and rivalrous sibling relationships were also found in families in which parents treated their two children differently rather than similarly (Hetherington, 1988; Stocker & McHale, 1990).

It is important to note that these conclusions are based chiefly on cross-sectional, self-report data from a small number of studies. Clearly, more research is needed to clarify the nature of this relationship during a period when siblings are developing rapidly.

References

Blyth, D., Hill, J., & Thiel, K. (1982). Early adolescents' significant others: Grade and gender differences in perceived relationships with familial and nonfamilial adults and young people. *Journal of Youth and Adolescence, 11,* 425–450.

Buhrmester, D., & Furman, W. (1989). *The developmental course of sibling relationships.* Manuscript submitted for publication.

Daniels, D., Dunn, J., Furstenberg, F., & Plomin, R. (1985). Environmental differences within the family and adjustment differences within pairs of adolescent siblings. *Child Development, 56,* 764–774.

Furman, W., & Buhrmester, D. (1985). Children's perceptions of the qualities of sibling relationships. *Child Development, 56,* 448–461.

Hetherington, E. M. (1988). Parents, children, and siblings: Six years after divorce. In R. Hinde & J. Stevenson-Hinde (Eds.), *Relationships within families: Mutual influences* (pp. 311–331). Oxford University Press.

Patterson, G. R. (1986). The contribution of siblings to training for fighting: A microscopic analysis. In D. Olwens, J. Block, and M. Radke-Yarrow (Eds.), *Development of antisocial and prosocial behavior: Research, theories and issues* (pp. 235–261). New York: Academic Press.

Plomin, R., & Daniels, D. (1987). Why are children in the same family so different from one another? *Behavioral and Brain Sciences, 10,* 1–16.

Raffaelli, M., & Larson, R. (1987, April). *Sibling interaction in late childhood and early adolescence.* Paper presented at the Biennial Meeting of the Society for Research in Child Development, Baltimore, MD.

Rowe, D., Rodgers, J. L., Meseck-Bushey, S.,

& St. John, C. (1989). Sexual behavior and non-sexual deviance: A sibling study of their relationship. *Developmental Psychology, 25(1)*, 61–69.

Scarr, S., & Grajeck, S. (1982). Similarities and differences among siblings. In M. E. Lamb & B. Sutton-Smith (Eds.), *Sibling relationships: Their nature and significance across the life span* (pp. 357–381). Hillsdale, NJ: Lawrence Erlbaum Associates.

Schachter, F. F. (1982). Sibling deidentification and split-parent identification: A family tetrad. In M. E. Lamb & B. Sutton-Smith (Eds.), *Sibling relationships: Their nature and significance across the life span* (pp. 123–152). Hillsdale, NJ: Lawrence Erlbaum Associates.

Stocker, C., & McHale, S. (1988, March). *Sibling relationships in early adolescence.* Paper presented at the biennial meeting of the Society for Research in Adolescence, Alexandria, VA.

Stocker, C., & McHale, S. (1990). *The nature and family correlates of preadolescents' perceptions of their sibling relationships.* Manuscript submitted for publication.

Sutton-Smith, B., & Rosenberg, B. G. (1970). *The sibling.* New York: Holt, Rinehart & Winston.

See Also

Conflict, Adolescent-Parent: A Model and a Method; Divorce, Effects on Adolescents; Divorce, Parental during Late Adolescence; Family Interaction, Gender Differences in; Family Life Education; Family Structure; Generation Gap; Generational Continuity and Change; Grandparent-Grandchild Relations; Parent-Adolescent Relations; Parent-Adolescent Relations in Mid and Late Adolescence; Parental Influence; Parenting Styles and Adolescent Development.

Smoking and Drug Prevention with Early Adolescents, Programs for

Cheryl L. Perry
University of Minnesota

Early adolescence is the time for initiating tobacco, alcohol, and drug use (Johnston, O'Malley, & Bachman, 1985). Earlier onset generally means greater eventual involvement; therefore, primary prevention programs have as their goal to delay or discourage onset of use (Johnson, 1986). Until the mid-1970s smoking and drug abuse prevention programs provided factual information on the physiological effects of use or focused on affective issues such as self-esteem and values that were seen as correlates to use (Goodstadt, 1978). These programs were based on the premise that knowledge affected attitudes which, in turn, affected behavior. Intervention, at the level of knowledge or at the level of attitudes, ought to affect drug use behavior. The conclusion from over a decade of research evaluating these approaches is that they were not effective in influencing these behaviors (Schaps, DiBartolo, Moskowitz, Palley, & Churgin, 1981), even when knowledge and attitude change was achieved.

A dramatic shift in how adolescent smoking, alcohol, and drug use were viewed was accompanied by substantial progress in primary prevention. Instead of these behaviors being viewed as health behaviors or deviant behaviors, they began to be regarded as social behaviors with meaning or purpose within adolescents' lives. Social psychological theory guided etiological research in the 1970s that served to explain why adolescents begin to smoke or to use drugs (Kandel, 1978; Perry & Murray, 1985). This etiological work suggests that factors that influence the onset of smoking and drug use evolve as the child matures through adolescence, and that this developmental stage is a critical period for intervention prior to behavioral adoption and consolidation. Experimentation with drug use has become normative in American society and a community-wide or public health approach to prevention appears to be warranted (Perry, 1986). Drug use is associated with other problem behaviors, such as rebelliousness or precocious sexuality, and prevention efforts need to consider this constellation or syndrome of related behaviors and their underlying causes (Jessor & Jessor, 1977). Finally, attention to predictive factors for drug use at three levels of analysis—environment, personality, and behavior—appears to be critical in the design of effective intervention strategies (Perry & Jessor, 1985). In the social environment, predictive factors include significant role models, opportunities and barriers to use, societal norms, and social support for use or nonuse. Personality predictive factors include values, functional meanings of these behaviors, self-efficacy to avoid use, and level of knowledge. Behavioral factors include a repertoire of necessary skills or alternative behaviors, and incentives or reinforcements for use. These factors have been labeled psychosocial risk factors and are also the primary targets for change in current intervention programs (Jessor, 1985).

Recent reviews of the prevention literature indicate that most promising smoking and drug abuse prevention approaches available today focus on these more social influences to use or not use, and skills to deal with those influences (Flay, 1985; Botvin, 1986). The school-based strategies that have been developed for young adolescents have six major components. The programs generally involve 6 to 12 45-minute sessions of classroom time. First, the students identify the short-term social consequences of use, such as smelling badly, ruining their appearance, acting out-of-control. This is generally done through small group discussions so that the "consequences" are seen as relevant to this age group. Second, the reasons that adolescents use tobacco, alcohol, or drugs are explored. These reasons or functions include as a way to have fun, as a way of making friends, as a signal of maturity or adulthood, or as a method of coping with personal problems

(Perry & Murray, 1985). Third, the students learn how these meanings are established by advertising, peers, and adult role models. Methods used by advertisers to convince adolescents of tobacco or alcohol's functional value are presented through discussions of selected advertisements. Mock social situations are analyzed to identify the type of influences that exist. Fourth, the students learn and practice skills to resist these influences. They create antitobacco advertisements or skits (role playing) around possible social encounters. Fifth, they discover that smoking, alcohol, or drug use is *not* normative for young adolescents by comparing their expectations with actual data on use and discussing their overestimation of prevalence. Finally, these activities are made experiential—designed to require active participation—and are often led by trained same-age peer leaders (Klepp, Halper, & Perry, 1986).

The systematic use of peer leaders in smoking and drug abuse prevention programs is a notable component. Several researchers have found peer-led programs to be significantly more successful in reducing onset or use than the same program taught by the classroom teacher (Murray, Johnson, Luepker, & Mittelmark, 1984; Botvin, Baker, Renick, Filazzalo, & Botvin, 1984). Generally, five students who are "liked and respected" are elected in each of the intervention classrooms. These students are trained to conduct about half of the activities in the prevention program, particularly activities that involve the sharing of social information. They lead the small group discussions, read and give directions for activities, report students' views on issues to the class, organize role plays and skits, and lead brainstorming sessions. Early adolescents can easily be trained to perform these functions and the inclusion of peer leaders appears to be particularly efficacious.

Most of the research studies that have tested these social influence approaches have done so with 6th to 8th grade students and have demonstrated a significant impact on smoking onset rates (Flay, 1985; Botvin, 1986). The results reported range from reductions of 33% to 39% in the proportion of students who begin to smoke when compared with an equivalent or randomly assigned control group. In these studies the impact on regular (weekly) smoking ranged from reductions of 43% to 47%, with maintenance of these effects generally up to one year postintervention. These effects do appear to decay over time, and suggest that additional "booster" educational programs are needed in middle adolescence. Still, the repeated success of these programs, in over 20 research studies, in at least delaying onset of cigarette smoking is encouraging.

The reported impact of these approaches on adolescent alcohol and drug use is more limited. Botvin (1986) suggests that an expansion of the social influences approach to include other life skills might be necessary. These additional skills include general problem-solving or decision-making skills, skills to increase self-control and self-esteem, adaptive coping strategies for relieving stress, greater interpersonal communication skills, and assertiveness training. These are taught in a similar experiential method to the smoking prevention programs. Botvin and colleagues (1984) reported significant effects, reducing heavy drinking and marijuana use with young adolescents. Pentz (1983) reported her intervention program also had a positive effect on alcohol use and academic performance. Thus preliminary evidence suggests some optimism for a social competency, social skills approach, but further research to test these methods with alcohol and drug use are needed.

Several smoking and drug abuse pre-vention programs have gone beyond the classroom into the larger school and community environment. Mass media has been utilized to disseminate social influence messages, to attract audience attention, to increase interpersonal communication, and to augment school-based programs (Flay, 1986). Pentz, Cormack, Flay, Hansen, and Johnson (1986) describes an ongoing community-wide drug abuse prevention program in Kansas City, Missouri, that includes school-based education (using the social influences model), parental involvement, and mass media, and thereby aims at social support and maintenance of changes that have been made within the classroom program. Perry (1986) suggests that changes at multiple levels in the community are important to optimize impact. These include individualized or self-help instruction, such as direct messages given by pediatricians; family involvement, school environmental changes, such as explicit smoking policies for students and teachers; and community-wide campaigns in which adolescents have an active role. As seen in Figure 1, this multiple level approach already appears promising in preventing the decay in effects noted in classroom-only programs (Perry, Murray, & Klepp, 1987).

In summary, the past decade of smoking and drug abuse prevention research provides an optimistic picture. The prevention programs assume that these behaviors are social and functional in adolescents' lives and provide opportunities to learn and practice social skills. Young adolescents exposed to these programs appear to be less likely to smoke cigarettes. An extension of these approaches may also be promising for delaying and minimizing alcohol and drug use as well. Continued investigations and refinement of these approaches beyond the classroom are needed; this is an appropriate research agenda for the 1990s.

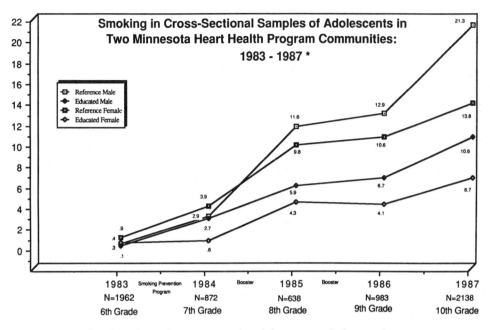

* Smoking refers to the average number of cigarettes smoked per week.

FIGURE 1
(From Perry, C. L., Klepp, K. I., and Sillers, C. *Cross-sectional sample community-wide strategies for cardiovascular health*: The Minnesota heart health program youth program. HER 4 (1), 1989. Reprinted with permission.)

References

Botvin, G. J. (1986). Substance abuse prevention research: Recent developments and future directions. *Journal of School Health, 56,* 369–374.

Botvin, G. J., Baker, E., Renick, N. L., Filazzalo, A. D., & Botvin, E. M. (1984). A cognitive behavioral approach to substance abuse prevention. *Addictive Behaviors, 9,* 137–147.

Flay, B. R. (1985). Psychosocial approaches to smoking prevention: A review of findings. *Health Psychology, 4,* 449–488.

Flay, B. R. (1986). Mass media linkages with school-based programs for drug abuse prevention. *Journal of School Health, 56,* 402–406.

Goodstadt, M. S. (1978). Alcohol and drug education. *Health Education Monographs, 6,* 263–279.

Jessor, R. (1985). Psycho-social risk, adolescent lifestyles, and implications for young adulthood. John B. Hawley lecture series, Division of Epidemiology, University of Minnesota.

Jessor, R., & Jessor, S. L. (1977). *Problem behavior and psychosocial development: A longitudinal study of youth.* New York: Academic Press.

Johnson, C. A. (1986). Objectives of community programs to prevent drug abuse. *Journal of School Health, 56,* 364–368.

Johnston, L., O'Malley, P., & Bachman, J. (1985). *Use of licit and illicit drugs by America's high school students, 1975–1984* (U.S. Department of Health and Human Services Publication No. [ADM] 85–1394). Washington, DC: U.S. Government Printing Office.

Kandel, D. B. (1978). Convergences in prospective longitudinal surveys of drug use in normal populations. In D. Kandel (Ed.). *Longitudinal research on drug use: Empirical findings and methodological issues* (pp. 3–38).

Washington, DC: Hemisphere (Halsted-Wiley).

Klepp, K. I., Halper, A., & Perry, C. L. (1986). The efficacy of peer leaders in drug abuse prevention. *Journal of School Health*, *56*, 407–411.

Murray, D. M., Johnson, C. A., Luepker, R. V., & Mittlemark, M. B. (1984). The prevention of cigarette smoking in children: A comparison of four strategies. *Journal of Applied Social Psychology*, *14*, 274–288.

Pentz, M. A. (1983). Prevention of adolescent substance abuse through social skill development. In T. J. Glynn, C. Luekefeld, & J. P. Ludford (Eds.): *Preventing adolescent drug abuse: Intervention strategies* (NIDA Research Monograph No. 47, pp. 195–232). Washington, DC: U.S. Government Printing Office.

Pentz, M. A., Cormack, C., Flay, B., Hansen, W. B., & Johnson, C. A. (1986). Balancing program and research integrity in community drug abuse prevention: Project STAR approach. *Journal of School Health*, *56*, 389–393.

Perry, C. L. (1986). Community-wide health promotion and drug abuse prevention. *Journal of School Health*, *56*, 359–363.

Perry, C. L., & Jessor, R. (1985). The concept of health promotion and the prevention of adolescent drug abuse. *Health Education Quarterly*, *12*(2), 169–184.

Perry, C. L., & Murray D. M. (1985). The prevention of adolescent drug abuse: Implications from etiological, developmental, behavioral, and environmental models. *Journal of Primary Prevention*, *6*(1), 31–52.

Perry, C. L., Murray D. M., & Klepp, K. I. (1987). Predictors of adolescent smoking and implications for prevention. *Morbidity and Mortality Weekly*, *36*(45), 41–45.

Schaps, E., DiBartolo, R. D., Moskowitz, J., Palley, C. S., & Churgin, S. (1981). A review of 127 drug abuse prevention program evaluations. *Journal of Drug Issues*, *11*, 17–43.

See Also

Anabolic–Androgenic Steroids, the Nonmedical Use by Adolescents; Cocaine Use among Adolescents and Young Adults, Antecedents/Predictors of; Drug Use, Adolescent; Drug Use, Epidemiology and Developmental Stages of Involvement; Drug Use, Minority Youth and; Drug Use, Predictors and Correlates of Adolescent; Hallucinogens; Health and Substance Abuse in Adolescence: Ethnic and Gender Perspectives; Pharmacology, Developmental; Smokeless Tobacco Use among Adolescents.

Smokeless Tobacco Use Among Adolescents

Phillip J. Marty
University of Arkansas

Robert J. McDermott
University of South Florida College of Public Health

Background

Public education to acquaint Americans with the health hazards of cigarette smoking has been carried out for over 20 years. But until recently little attention has been focused on snuff and chewing tobacco, their health consequences, and the factors that contribute to their use. The 1986 report of the Advisory Committee to the Surgeon General concluded, however, that users of smokeless tobacco products, particularly snuff, are at elevated risk for oral cancer and a host of noncancerous oral conditions (U.S. Department of Health and Human Services [USDHHS], 1986).

Moist snuff is finely ground tobacco, of which the user takes a "pinch" or "dip," and positions it between the cheek and gum, or between the lower lip and teeth of the lower jaw. Moist snuff may also be packaged in cachets, similar to tea bags; the entire cachet is designed to be placed in the mouth. Dry snuff, a powdered form of tobacco inhaled through the nostrils, also gets occasional use in parts of the U.S. Chewing tobacco consists of shredded tobacco leaves packed in a pouch, or compressed into a brick (plug) or twist. It is placed in the back of the mouth, and held against the cheek by the molars and tongue. With both snuff and chewing tobacco, the products combine with saliva to release nicotine, which is then absorbed through the oral mucosa.

Smokeless tobacco sales increased 52% between 1978 and 1985 (Connolly, 1985). Most of this increase was due to the increased popularity of moist snuff, the predominant form of smokeless tobacco consumed by youth (Connolly, Winn, Hecht, Henningfield, Walker, & Hoffman, 1986). Smokeless tobacco users in the U.S. number about 12 million (USDHHS, 1986). The current popularity of smokeless tobacco actually represents a reemergence. Until the early 20th century its use was more widespread than smoking tobacco. Smokeless tobacco fell out of vogue because the necessary expectoration associated with it was linked to transmission of tuberculosis (Connolly et al., 1986). By 1921 smokeless tobacco was surpassed in popularity by what was believed to be a "safe" alternative—the cigarette.

Among much of the general public

today "dipping" and "chewing" are not viewed as particularly dangerous activities, and are considered to be less of a "social evil" than smoking (Binnie, Rankin, & MacKenzie, 1983; Heth, 1982). Squier (1984) attributes the popularity of smokeless tobacco to effective advertising that links use with strong masculine images. The most impressionable recipients of these media messages have been children and youth, especially adolescent males. Among adolescent males, smokeless tobacco use is considered to be "macho," and thus a positive social adaptation (Christen, Swanson, Glover, & Henderson, 1982; Glover, Christen, & Henderson, 1981).

Although smokeless tobacco is used by children as young as kindergarten age (Young & Williamson, 1985) and by old women in some parts of the country (Winn, Blot, Shy, Pickle, Toledo, & Fraumeni, 1981), the group most "at risk" for initiation is the adolescent and young adult male (Glover, Johnson, Laflin, Edwards, & Christen, 1986; Marty, McDermott, & Williams, 1986; McDermott & Marty, 1986). In various studies of adolescent boys, prevalence of use on at least a weekly basis ranges from 1% to as high as 37% (Boyd & Associates, 1987; Greer & Poulson, 1983; Marty, McDermott, & Williams, 1986; Williams, Guyton, Marty McDermott, & Young, 1986). A Wisconsin study revealed that daily use of smokeless tobacco by boys increased from 3% in 7th grade to 15% in 12th grade (Centers for Disease Control, 1986). Weekly use of smokeless tobacco by adolescent girls is on the order of 2% or less (Boyd & Associates, 1987).

Persons in this age group, while well informed about the negative health effects of smoking, are often ignorant of the health consequences of smokeless tobacco use (Marty, McDermott, Young, & Guyton, 1986; McDermott & Marty, 1986). Peer pressure and role modeling by parents and siblings contribute to smokeless tobacco initiation (Ary, Lichtenstein, & Severson, 1987; Marty, McDermott, & Williams, 1986; Williams et al., 1986). Both the psychoactive and physiological effects of the products, along with psychosocial reinforcements, may play significant roles in the continued use of smokeless tobacco once experimentation begins (McDermott & Marty, 1986). Smokeless tobacco use also has been associated with having family problems, poor school performance, cigarette smoking, alcohol use, and deviant/delinquent behavior (Jones & Moberg, 1988). Despite enactment of P.L. 99-252, which banned smokeless tobacco advertisements from television in 1986, and required warning labels on smokeless tobacco products in 1987, there is concern that such deterrents are, by themselves, inadequate control measures (Koop, 1986).

Oral Pathology and Smokeless Tobacco

Undesirable effects linked to smokeless tobacco use include nicotine dependence (Gritz, Baer-Weiss, Benowitz, Van Vunakis, & Jarvik, 1981; Russell, Jarvis, Devitt, & Feyerabend, 1981), pregnancy complications (Verma, Chansoriya, & Kaul, 1983), suppressed immunologic response (Milstam, 1981), pancreatic cancer (Heuch, Kvale, Jacobson, & Bjelke, 1983), pharyngeal cancer (Christen & Glover, 1981; Winn, Blot, Shy, & Fraumeni, 1982; Winn, Ziegler, Pickle, Gridley, Blot, & Hoover, 1984) and acute episodes of elevated blood pressure (Hampson, 1985; Schroeder & Chen, 1985). However, most of the negative health effects from use of smokeless tobacco manifest themselves in the oral cavity.

Evidence of a relationship between smokeless tobacco use and oral changes is provided by Greer and Poulson (1983) who found that 48.7% of the users aged 14 to 19 that they examined had lesions. Poulson, Lindenmuth, and Greer (1984) detected oral lesions in 62.5% of the users they identified. One of the most frequent clinical observations made in smokeless tobacco users was the presence of oral leukoplakia, white plaquelike lesions that develop in response to local irritation from tobacco placement.

Statistical associations between use of smokeless tobacco products and oral cancer are established (Bartsch & Montesano, 1986; McGuirt, 1983). Oral cancer risk is higher for snuff dippers than for tobacco chewers (USDHHS, 1986). Compelling evidence for snuff dipping giving rise to oral cancer is revealed in a North Carolina study (Winn et al., 1981). This investigation found an oral and pharyngeal cancer mortality risk approaching fiftyfold among women who were chronic snuff users. Among persons studied by Stockwell and Lyman (1986), users of smokeless tobacco experienced 11 times the relative risk of cancers of the mouth and gum as nonusers of any tobacco product. Moreover, concerning cancers of the oral cavity, smokeless tobacco users were more at risk than smokers of up to 20 cigarettes per day.

The mechanism of cancer development in snuff dippers is not well understood. Cancer-causing chemicals in snuff, such as nitrosamines, probably are implicated (Hoffman, Lavoie, & Hecht, 1985). The total concentration of tobacco-specific nitrosamines with cancer-causing potential in snuff is 500 to 14,000 times higher than the level allowed by the U.S. Food and Drug Administration and the U.S. Department of Agriculture in consumer products such as beer and bacon (Connolly et al., 1986).

Another frequently occurring observation in snuff dippers is gum tissue recession at the site where snuff is habitually placed

(Greer & Poulson, 1983; Poulson et al., 1984). Gum recession may give rise to root caries, infection, and other undesirable oral conditions. Tooth loss or necessary extraction may result.

Although some reports have shown an association between smokeless tobacco use and gum inflammation (gingivitis), current data do not fully support this relationship (USDHHS, 1986). One study suggests that smokeless tobacco use may not produce inflammation in healthy mouths, but may aggravate an existing condition (Offenbacher & Weathers, 1985).

Some case reports suggest a relationship between smokeless tobacco use and dental caries. In their study of 565 adolescent boys, Offenbacher and Weathers (1985) saw a 2.4-fold relative risk of caries among youths with gingivitis who dipped snuff and chewed tobacco, compared to their nonuser, gingivitis-free peers. The average sucrose content in chewing tobacco products may be as high as 15% (Hsu, Pollack, Hsu, & Going, 1980). A separate study indicated that extract from chewing tobacco enhanced the growth of two strains of streptococcal bacteria implicated in caries formation (Lindemeyer, Baum, Hsu, & Going, 1981). Greer and Poulson (1983), however, found no tobacco-associated caries. Shannon and Trodahl (1978) have even suggested that the fluoride content of some smokeless tobacco and the salivary action produced during tobacco use may reduce caries susceptibility. The role of smokeless tobacco in either caries development or prevention remains controversial (USDHHS, 1986).

Education and Prevention

For youths who use smokeless tobacco, education of parents needs to be addressed. The perception of parental approval of smokeless tobacco is a regular feature of studies examining patterns of adolescent use (Marty, McDermott, & Williams, 1986; McDermott & Marty, 1986; Williams et al., 1986). This relationship is cause for concern if parents foster use in their children by being users themselves, or by giving a subtle endorsement to these products by viewing them as less of an evil than cigarettes, alcohol, or "hard" drugs.

Parental education extends to other adults who may be role models for youth, including sports figures, coaches, teachers, and other family members. Youngsters who aspire to be athletes may hold erroneous beliefs about a physiological "lift" or improved reaction time attributed to smokeless tobacco use. Research in this area indicates no neuromuscular performance enhancement from these products (Edwards & Glover, 1986). Misconceptions need to be identified and explained for coaches and athletes.

Some studies indicate an interest among adolescent and young adult snuff dippers and tobacco chewers to explore cessation programs (Marty, McDermott, & Williams, 1986; McDermott & Marty, 1986). While smoking cessation programs exist in many forms, and enjoy varying success rates, attempts at "smokeless cessation" programs have been made only recently (Glover, 1986). The use of chewing gum containing nicotine has shown promise in smoking cessation programs, since its main function is to alleviate symptoms of nicotine dependence (Christen, McDonald, Olson, Drook, & Stookey, 1984). However, Glover (1986) achieved only a 2.3% cessation rate after six months in two groups of smokeless tobacco users who tried nicotine gum. Withdrawal symptoms were of even greater intensity than those experienced by persons going through smoking withdrawal. In the future, pharmacological factors, psychosocial factors, and environmental factors may need to be addressed if smokeless tobacco cessation efforts are to be successful.

References

Ary, D. V., Lichtenstein, E., & Severson, H. H. (1987). Smokeless tobacco use among male adolescents: Patterns, correlates, predictors, and the use of other drugs. *Preventive Medicine, 16*, 385–401.

Bartsch, H., & Montesano, R. (1984). Relevance of nitrosamines to human cancer. *Carcinogenesis, 5*, 1381.

Binnie, W. H., Rankin, K. V., & MacKenzie, I. C. (1983). Etiology of oral squamous cell carcinoma. *Journal of Oral Pathology, 12*, 11–29.

Boyd, G., & Associates. (1987). Use of smokeless tobacco among children and adolescents in the United States. *Preventive Medicine, 16*, 402–421.

Centers for Disease Control. (1986). Use of smokeless tobacco—Wisconsin. *Morbidity and Mortality Weekly Report, 35*, 641–644.

Christen, A. G. (1980). The case against smokeless tobacco: Five facts for the health professional to consider. *Journal of the American Dental Association, 101*, 464–469.

Christen, A. G., & Glover, E. D. (1981). Smokeless tobacco: Seduction of youth. *World Smoking and Health, 6*, 20.

Christen, A. G., McDonald, J. L., Jr., Olson, B. L., Drook, C. A., & Stookey, G. K. (1984). Efficacy of nicotine chewing gum in facilitating smoking cessation. *Journal of the American Dental Association, 108*, 594.

Christen, A. G., Swanson, B. Z., Glover, E. D., & Henderson, A. H. (1982). Smokeless tobacco: The folklore and social history of snuffing, sneezing, dipping, and chewing. *Journal of the American Dental Association, 105*, 821–829.

Connolly, G. N. (1985). Tobacco and snuff: Growing health threats. *The Nation's Health, 15*(4), 6.

Connolly, G. N., Winn, D. M., Hecht, S. S., Henningfield, J. E., Walker, B., Jr., & Hoffman, D. (1986). The reemergence of smokeless tobacco. *New England Journal of Medicine, 314,* 1020–1027.

Edwards, S. W., & Glover, E. D. (1986). Snuff and neuromuscular performance. *American Journal of Public Health, 76,* 206.

Glover, E. D. (1986). Conducting smokeless tobacco cessation clinics. *American Journal of Public Health, 76,* 207.

Glover, E. D., Christen, A. G., & Henderson, A. H. (1981). Just a pinch between the cheek and gum. *Journal of School Health, 51,* 415–418.

Glover, E. D., Johnson, R., Laflin, M., Edwards, S. W., & Christen, A. G. (1986). Smokeless tobacco use trends among college students in the United States. *World Smoking and Health, 11,* 4–9.

Greer, R. O., & Poulson, T. C. (1983). Oral tissue alterations associated with the use of smokeless tobacco by teenagers, 1. Clinical findings. *Oral Surgery, 56,* 275–284.

Gritz, E. R., Baer-Weiss, V., Benowitz, N. L., Van Vunakis, H., & Jarvik, M. E. (1981). Plasma nicotine and cotinine concentration in habitual smokeless tobacco users. *Clinical Pharmacological Therapy, 30,* 201–209.

Hampson, N. B. (1985). Smokeless is not saltless. *New England Journal of Medicine, 312,* 919–920.

Heth, J. (1982, June 6). Kids think it's macho to chew. *Des Moines Register,* 6.

Hoffman, D., Lavoie, E. J., & Hecht, S. S. (1985). Nicotine: A precursor for carcinogens. *Cancer Letters, 26*(1), 67.

Hsu, S. C., Pollack, R. L., Hsu, A-F. C., & Going, R. E. (1980). Sugars present in tobacco extracts. *Journal of the American Dental Association, 101,* 915–918.

Huech, E., Kvale, G., Jacobsen, B. K., & Bjelke, E. (1983). Use of alcohol, tobacco, and coffee and risk of pancreatic cancer. *British Journal of Cancer, 48,* 637–643.

Jones, R. B., & Moberg, D. P. (1988). Correlates of smokeless tobacco use in a male adolescent population. *American Journal of Public Health, 78,* 61–63.

Koop, C. E. (1986). The campaign against smokeless tobacco. *New England Journal of Medicine, 314,* 1042–1044.

Lindemeyer, R. G., Baum, R. H., Hsu, S. C., & Going, R. E. (1981). In vitro effect of tobacco on the growth of oral carciogenic streptococci. *Journal of the American Dental Association, 103,* 719–722.

Marty, P. J., McDermott, R. J., & Williams, T. (1986). Patterns of smokeless tobacco use in a population of high school students. *American Journal of Public Health, 76,* 190–192.

Marty, P. J., McDermott, R. J., Young, M., & Guyton, R. (1986). Prevalence and psychosocial correlates of dipping and chewing behavior in a group of rural high school students. *Health Education, 17*(2), 28–31.

McDermott, R. J., & Marty, P. J. (1986). Dipping and chewing behavior among university students: Prevalence and patterns of use. *Journal of School Health, 56,* 175–177.

McGuirt, W. F. (1983). Snuff dipper's carcinoma. *Archives of Otolaryngology, 109,* 757–760.

Milstam, T. (1981). Uber die auswirkunger des zigarrenund tabakrauches auf die orale hygiene, plaqueentwicklung, gingiva und mundschleimhaut. *Quintessenz, 2,* 301–305.

Offenbacher, S., & Weathers, D. R. (1985). Effects of smokeless tobacco on the periodontal, mucosal and caries status of adolescent males. *Journal of Oral Pathology, 14,* 169–181.

Poulson, T. C., Lindenmuth, J. E., & Greer, R. O. (1984). A comparison of the use of smokeless tobacco in rural and urban teenagers. *CA-A Cancer Journal for Clinicians, 34,* 248–261.

Russell, M. A., Jarvis, M. J., Devitt, G., & Feyerabend, C. (1981). Nicotine intake by snuff users. *British Medical Journal, 282,* 814–817.

Schroeder, K. L., & Chen, M. S. Jr. (1985). Smokeless tobacco and blood pressure. *New England Journal of Medicine, 312*, 919.

Shannon, I. L., & Trodahl, J. N. (1978). Sugars and flouride in chewing tobacco and snuff. *Texas Dental Journal, 96*(1), 6–10.

Squier, C. A. (1984). Smokeless tobacco and oral cancer: A cause for concern. *CA-A Cancer Journal for Clinicians, 34*, 242–247.

Stockwell, H. G., & Lyman, G. H. (1986). Impact of smoking and smokeless tobacco on the risk of cancer of the head and neck. *Head and Neck Surgery, 9*, 104–110.

U.S. Department of Health and Human Services. (1986). *The health consequences of smokeless tobacco. A report of the Advisory Committee to the Surgeon General.* Bethesda, MD: Author. (NIH Publication No. 86-2874).

Verma, R. C., Chansoriya, M., & Kaul, K. K. (1983). Effect of tobacco chewing by mothers on fetal outcome. *Indian Pediatrics, 20*, 105–111.

Williams, T., Guyton, R., Marty, P. J., McDermott, R. J., & Young, M. E. (1986). Smokeless tobacco use among rural high school students in Arkansas. *Journal of School Health, 56*, 282–285.

Winn, D. M., Blot, W. J., Shy, C. M., & Fraumeni, J. F. Jr. (1982). Occupation and oral cancer among women in the South. *American Journal of Industrial Medicine, 3*, 161–167.

Winn, D. M., Blot, W. J., Shy, C. M., Pickle, L. W., Toledo, A., & Fraumeni, J. F. Jr. (1981). Snuff dipping and oral cancer among women in the southern United States. *New England Journal of Medicine, 304*, 745–749.

Winn, D. M., Ziegler, R. G., Pickle, L. W., Gridley, G., Blot, W. J., & Hoover, R. N. (1984). Diet in the etiology of oral and pharyngeal cancer among women from the southern United States. *Cancer Research, 44*, 1216–1222.

Young, M., & Williamson, D. (1985). Correlates of use and expected use of smokeless tobacco among kindergarten children. *Psychological Reports, 56*, 63–66.

See Also

Anabolic–Androgenic Steroids, the Nonmedical Use by Adolescents; Cocaine Use among Adolescents and Young Adults, Antecedents/Predictors of; Drug Use, Adolescent; Drug Use, Epidemiology and Developmental Stages of Involvement; Drug Use, Minority Youth and; Drug Use, Predictors and Correlates of Adolescent; Hallucinogens; Health and Substance Abuse in Adolescence: Ethnic and Gender Perspectives; Pharmacology, Developmental; Smoking and Drug Prevention with Early Adolescents, Programs for; Stimulants.

Social Development, Sex and Ethnic Differences in

Toni C. Antonucci
James S. Jackson
The University of Michigan

Adolescent social development theory and research has suffered in comparison to work on other periods of the life span. Historically, there was no period of adolescence. Teenagers, through early and prearranged marriages and apprenticeships, emerged from an invisible childhood to young adulthood. In more recent times only the stage theorists have devoted special attention to the period of adolescence. Even this attention has been limited, for most research has had a singular focus, emphasizing physical changes or role changes, for example. Speculation or theorizing has rarely been accompanied by empirical investigations and still more rarely has it been accompanied by empirical investigations of normal or representative samples.

Freud labeled adolescence the genital stage, that period in life when the individual is basically concerned with establishing a sexual identity. Erikson emphasized the importance of establishing self-identity. Both perspectives, of course, offer important insights into the major factors influencing the social development of the adolescent, but each is also limited in significant ways.

Although the need for a life-span perspective in human development has now been widely accepted, research on adolescents from this orientation has had few proponents. It is perhaps most useful to consider stage-oriented theoretical work within a life-span developmental context. Specifically, social development in the adolescent is best viewed within the broader framework of his/her individual, family, school, and community interaction and development. Unfortunately, most past research has been limited to only one of these levels, thereby providing a fragmented and incomplete picture of social development in the adolescent. In addition, in the past the small amount of systematic, empirical research on adolescent social development has tended to be problem-focused, concentrating on unplanned pregnancies, for example, or on drug addiction, juvenile delinquency, or other forms of social deviancy. More recently, however, a great deal of normative adolescent research is being conducted within the context of individual and family development and change.

Adolescence has traditionally been seen as a period of storm and strife, but life-span developmental theorists have shown that much of what is experienced in the adolescent years represents more life-span continuity than discontinuity. Sex and ethnic differences in social development can be seen in much the same way, although special attention should be given to those things that are unique to the subgroup (e.g., boys, girls, blacks, whites) of interest.

It should be recognized that this unique period of social development is part of an ongoing process of socialization and interpersonal interaction that occurs over the life course. Characteristics that best contribute to our understanding of social development can be understood as part of the individual as a developing organism. For most adolescents in Western industrial society, this period is marked by advanced capabilities and a greater behavioral or experiential repertoire. The adolescent has higher levels of intellectual and abstract reasoning capacity, and has also acquired a resource bank of interpersonal experiences. While the individual develops over time and reaches adolescence with unique characteristics, the family within which the adolescent develops has a unique interactive past. The adolescent does not emerge into this family tabula rasa, but instead evolves from a past of continuous interactive sequences that have been, for example, warm and nurturant or cold and nonsupportive. In fact, intergenerational research, responding to the popular view of adolescence as a period of rebellion or as the source of a widespread generation gap, has documented the similarity between the adolescent and his or her family in comparison with other adolescents or with other families. Similarities have been documented in politics, religion, sex-role attitudes, work, and achievement. It is likely that additional similarities could be documented were this area to receive widespread empirical attention.

Infant social development data suggests that the young child is exposed to systematic interactive styles that evolve through childhood and young adulthood. In attachment terminology the infant who had a secure relationship with his or her mother has a better chance of developing similar relationships with others, both in style and in security. Although there are no extensive long-term life-span data, the longitudinal studies available support the proposition that there is more consistency than change in interactive styles. Adolescents who exhibit insecure attachment and social development are likely to respond less positively fifteen to twenty years later on questions assessing their current satisfaction with social relationships. Caspi, Elder, and Bem (1987) found that ill-tempered children became ill-tempered adults with lower occupational status, an erratic work life, and increased likelihood of divorce. This is thought to be a part of a continuous life-span pattern, although no data yet exist to directly test this assumption.

Adolescents interact not only with their families but also with their peers in the broader community. Peer relationships have long been the subject of substantial empirical investigation (e.g., Coleman, 1961). Some have gone so far as to suggest that adolescent relationships with school and neighborhood age-mates form a special subculture of the society. Adolescents place a high value on friendship and tend to view their friends as more supportive than do younger children. Their peers, although often seen as an influence that is separate, discrete, and in relative conflict with the adolescents' families, may in actuality be more similar than different (Douvan & Adelson, 1966). Since the family in many ways structures the environment to which the adolescent is exposed, the influences of peers and community is often consistent with family values. For example, the tendency for some ethnic groups to live in geographically limited areas, and to hold traditionally stereotypic views of sex-roles or sex-specific social behaviors, may severely limit or shape their adolescents' social development. The extent to which the family of the adolescent influences the peers and community to which the adolescent is exposed may itself be influenced by the resources available to the parents. Thus, middle-class families are in a secure financial position and therefore likely to be able to choose resource-laden neighborhoods, school districts, and broader communities in which the adolescent will live. At the same time, to the extent that racial and ethnic groups are disproportionately represented in the lower end of the financial spectrum, these parents may be less likely to have this control, since they do not have the same range of choice about their neighborhoods, communities, or schools.

The role of adolescence as a vehicle for bringing social change and development into the family is also unique and deserves special recognition. Research in the 1960s and early 1970s, a period of rapid social change, showed that although radical teenagers were more like their parents than not, they were also an important influence on their parents' social awareness and attitude changes. Parents frequently reported being exposed to social issues in a compelling way for the first time through their adolescent children.

A life-span view of adolescent development may be especially important to understanding social development among minority adolescents. Americans of African descent face peculiar problems due to their unique social and economic histories in this country. While the nature and problems of minority adolescent development have been of long-standing scientific interest, normative empirical research on this topic has been sorely lacking. The research that

does exist has been of the problem-focused variety (i.e., studies of adolescent pregnancies or of juvenile delinquency). For the most part authors have pointed to the difficulties and strengths of African-American family life and how this might influence the social development and experiences of the adolescent. Problems in the educational and occupational attainment among African-American adolescents and their families suggest the unique characteristics of major influences on the normal social development of the adolescent, but little empirical evidence is available. Parental status among all adolescents, but especially the limits of parental status among minority adolescents, is likely to have a significant impact on social development.

Adolescence is a period of substantial and noticeable physical change. Physical changes in primary and secondary sex characteristics influence the social and family experiences of the adolescent. This holds particularly true in the examination of sex differences. Girls who mature physically at young ages may be more likely to engage in earlier dating behavior than their later-maturing peers, which in turn may influence important aspects of their social development. For example, early or unplanned pregnancy among adolescents has been shown to have substantial influence on the life course trajectory of girls. However, family reaction and support is one of the most important indicators of how successfully a girl will cope with this type of life crises and transition point. Although early maturity in boys may also be related to early dating behavior and early sexual activity, research indicates that it does not have the same limiting effects on their life-course trajectory.

Previous problem-focused social development research on adolescents has provided very little information concerning the normative experiences of the majority of male and female adolescents, a situation which is finally being rectified by ongoing studies. Research based on problematic adolescent behavior has been enormously sex-linked. Thus, for adolescent girls, early sexual activity or pregnancies historically have been the subject of most of the empirical literature; and for adolescent boys, gangs, juvenile delinquency, truancy, or drug addiction have received the greatest share of attention. There is some indication more recently that problem behaviors among adolescents are less sex-linked and show greater similarity among girls and boys than was previously the case. Particularly poignant examples are the problems resulting from the availability of crack cocaine and the presence of the AIDS epidemic.

One "modern" influence on the social development of the adolescent is a rapidly increasing change in their childhood and adolescent nuclear family experiences. A very high proportion of adolescents are experiencing major changes in their parents' behavior. Whereas a primary source and resource in the social development of adolescents in the past has been the primary nuclear family, it is clear that increasing numbers of adolescents are now experiencing the separation and divorce of their parents, and are being reared in single-parent families or as members of two nuclear families (i.e., mother, stepfather, siblings, and step- or half-siblings; father, stepmother, siblings, and step- or half-siblings). Of course, the implications of these changes extend beyond the social development of the adolescent, but the impact on the adolescent's experiences must be profound.

Several external characteristics both of the adolescent and the environment deserve special mention as probable important contributors to the social development and experiences of the young adolescent male and female. These include the early transition from grade or primary school to either a middle school or a junior high and the later transition to senior high school. The characteristics of the school itself will have important influences on the adolescent's experiences. The environment could permit a smooth transition from the primary to secondary school with very little actual change in terms of the peers with whom the adolescent interacts. Other possibilities also exist, however, including a transition with very little overlap in friends and little opportunity to make new friends. Adolescents in this type of environment tend to rely on their old friends, either from their neighborhood or from their former school. On the other hand, the new school might facilitate the development of new friendships, thereby forging an important avenue of social development that allows the adolescent to pursue the often-experienced need for a transformation in family and friend relationships in anticipation of an autonomous identity and adult status.

And finally, it would be impossible not to mention the role of clothes, haircuts, and especially music in the lives of adolescents. As seen in the various beatnik, hippie, punk, and now heavy metal labels, it is clear that adolescents affect distinctive clothes and hair-styles. The role of music is only rarely considered formally, but is believed by many to play an important self-identifying and distinguishing role for adolescents. Although often seen as a relatively new phenomena, perhaps emerging with the heavy metal or hard rock groups, this development reveals an element of consistency. Today's grandparents identified with blues music, swing, or Frank Sinatra, and today's parents had the Beatles, the Rolling Stones, the Temptations, and the Supremes. Although difficult to quantify, there is no doubt that music tends to exert a major influence on the life, especially the social life, and individual self-identity of adolescents.

The social development of the adolescent can thus be summed up as a confluence of experiences that are both highly similar to and evolve from previous experiences in childhood. Although adolescents are best known for their needs to be distinctive and autonomous from the principal influences of their childhood, most data suggest continuity, albeit with the trappings of autonomy. Theory and empirical evidence are not plentiful in this area, but there is reason to believe that the social development of the adolescent proceeds on a relatively normal or regular path from childhood through adulthood. But it must also be recognized that adolescence is a distinctive period in life-span development during which important characteristics of social relationships evolve into adult prototypes. Society variously views the adolescent as a child and adult, most probably an accurate reflection of the adolescent's own view of self. The influences upon the social development of the adolescent are either the same or evolve from the major influences on the social development of the child. It is a critical period in social development because choices that might be seen as temporary or unimportant—school, friends, hobbies, sports, dating—have profound implications for the social development and general life experiences throughout adulthood.

References

Bengtson, V. L., & Troll, L. (1978). Youth and their parents: Feedback and intergenerational influence in socialization. In R. M. Lerner & G. B. Spanier (Eds.), *Child influences on marital and family interaction: A life-span perspective* (pp. 215–240). New York: Academic Press.

Berndt, T. J. (1982). The features and effects of friendship in early adolescence. *Child Development, 53*, 1447–1470.

Burton, L. M. (1990). Teenage childbearing as an alternative life-course strategy in multi-generation black families. *Human Nature.*

Cairns, R. B., Neckerman, H. J., & Cairns, B. D. (1989). Social networks and shadows of synchrony. In G. R. Adams, R. Montemayor, & T. P. Gullotta (Eds.), *Biology of adolescent behavior and development* (pp. 275–305).

Caspi, A., Elder, G. H., Jr., & Bem, D. J. (1987). Moving against the world: Life-course patterns of explosive children. *Developmental Psychology, 23*, 308–313.

Coleman, J. S. (1961). *The adolescent society.* New York: Free Press.

Douvan, E., & Adelson, J. (1966). *The adolescent experience.* New York: Wiley.

Elder, G. H., Jr. (1980). Adolescence in historical perspective. In J. Adelson (Ed.), *Handbook of adolescent psychology.* New York: Wiley.

Furstenberg, F. F., Jr., Brooks-Gunn, J. & Chase-Lansdale, L. (1989). Teenage pregnancy and childbearing. *American Psychologist, 44*, 313–320.

Grotevant, H. D., & Cooper, C. R. (1986). Individuation in family relationships. *Human Development, 29*, 82–100.

Hill, J. P. (1987). Research on adolescents and their families: Past and prospect. In C. E. Irwin, Jr. (Ed.), *Adolescent social behavior and health* (pp. 13–32). San Francisco: Sage.

Marini, M. M., Shin, H.-C., & Raymond, J. (1989). Socioeconomic consequences of the process of transition to adulthood. *Social Science Research, 18*, 89–135.

Petersen, A. (1988). Adolescent development. *Annual Review of Psychology, 39*, 583–607.

Spence, J. T., Deaux, K., Helmreich, R. L. (1987). Sex roles in contemporary American society. In G. Lindzey & E. Aronson (Eds.), *The handbook of social psychology* (3rd ed., vol. 11, pp. 149–178). New York: Random House.

Steinberg, L. (1987). Impact of puberty on family relations: Effects of pubertal status and pubertal timing. *Developmental Psychology*, *23*, 451–460.

Wilson, M. N. (1989). Child development in the context of the Black extended family. *American Psychologist*, *44*, 380–385.

Youniss, J. & Smollar, J. (1985). *Adolescent relations with mothers, fathers, and friends*. Chicago: University of Chicago Press.

See Also

Black Adolescents At-Risk: Approaches to Prevention; Black Adolescents, the Impact of Federal Income Assistance Policies on; Black Female Adolescents, Socialization of; Drug Use, Minority Youth and; Health and Substance Abuse in Adolescence: Ethnic and Gender Perspectives; Hispanic Adolescents; Identity, Minority Development of; Minority and Female Participation in Math and Science, Increase in: The Importance of the Middle School Years; Sexual Behavior in Black Adolescents, Initiation of; Socialization of African-American Adolescents.

Social Intelligence in Adolescence

Martin E. Ford
Stanford University

Conceptions of Social Intelligence

Over the course of the past sixty years social intelligence has been defined in essentially two different ways (Ford & Tisak, 1983). Cognitive definitions of social intelligence have emphasized skills such as the ability to make insightful social inferences or to reason about social issues in a sophisticated way (e.g., O'Sullivan, Guilford, & DeMille, 1965). Such skills are typically assessed using paper-and-pencil tests or pictorial stimuli. Alternatively, behavioral definitions of social intelligence have focused on people's effectiveness in accomplishing social goals (e.g., Ford, 1986). Assessments of social-behavioral effectiveness are generally conducted using personality measures, observational techniques, or, more commonly, by asking knowledgeable people to make judgments about the target individual on relevant dimensions.

To date only the behavioral effectiveness conception of social intelligence has been validated as a separate, empirically coherent domain of human abilities (Ford & Tisak, 1983). This way of conceptualizing social intelligence is also the one most congruent with the implicit theories of laypersons and experts in the field of intelligence (Sternberg, Conway, Ketron, & Bernstein, 1981). It is therefore apparent that the most appropriate way to define and assess social intelligence is to focus on social goal attainment. Although sophisticated reasoning and inferencing skills *may* contribute to the attainment of social goals in novel or ambiguous circumstances, it appears that such skills are neither necessary nor sufficient for social success in most situations (Ford, 1984).

In applying this conception of social intelligence it is important to avoid a narrow definition of behavioral effectiveness, since otherwise one would have to regard unethical behavior that produces desired outcomes or behavior that is effective in the short run but that produces long-term negative consequences as intelligent behavior. Contextual and developmental boundary conditions should therefore be placed on evaluations of social-behavioral effectiveness, as Ford (1986) has suggested in defining social intelligence as "the attainment of relevant social goals in specified social environments, using appropriate means and resulting in positive developmental outcomes." This definition underlines the fact that *social intelligence is a socially judged phe-*

nomenon. Such judgments become useful when criteria for determining what constitutes socially intelligent behavior are clearly identified, well justified, and culturally shared.

Criteria for Defining and Assessing Social Intelligence in Adolescence

The Ford and Nichols (1987) Taxonomy of Human Goals provides a useful heuristic for making a general specification of the social goals most relevant to adolescent behavior and development. Ten of the 24 goals in the taxonomy are particularly germane to the domain of social intelligence; these are described in Table 1. The subset of social goals that have received the greatest attention in the adolescence literature appear in upper-case letters. The accomplishment of these five goals—individuality, self-determination, belongingness, social responsibility, and safety—may be regarded as providing the core meaning of social intelligence in adolescence. It is again important to point out, however, that because social intelligence represents a *valued set of accomplishments*, rather than something intrinsic to the person, one can expect significant variations on these five themes across different socioeconomic, ethnic, and cultural groups. Moreover, the specific content of each goal to be accomplished and the appropriate means for attaining these goals will be determined in large part by the particular social contexts in which the adolescent must function.

INDIVIDUALITY ■ has been a major focus of the adolescence literature in terms of relatively superficial qualities like dress and appearance as well as with regard to more fundamental personality processes

such as identity development. Indeed, some theorists (e.g., Erikson, 1968) view identity formation as the primary developmental task of adolescence. Adolescent identity development is largely organized around issues and values involving peer relations, sexuality and sex-role characteristics, and occupational status. Variations in the degree to which adolescents have accomplished the goal of developing coherent self-conceptions in these domains have been linked to a wide variety of attributes associated with personal agency, social maturity, and behavioral flexibility.

SELF-DETERMINATION ■ is a fundamental human motive (Deci & Ryan, 1985) that peaks developmentally first in early childhood and then again in adolescence. Self-determination emerges as an important aspect of social intelligence in this latter age group because of the need to make or contribute to major life decisions and to retain some autonomy in the face of powerful influences from peers and the media. The literature on moral development has also emphasized the importance of being able to resist social pressures to behave irresponsibly and to oppose adult rules or peer norms that support unjust or immoral behavior.

BELONGINGNESS ■ is frequently discussed in the adolescence literature in conjunction with the growing importance of peer group membership as a criterion for effective social functioning. Adolescents' strong concern with creating and maintaining social ties with peers is manifested in their valuing of friendships, their involvement in dating and intimate relationships, and their desire to belong to formal and informal groups at school. The maintenance of strong family bonds in the face of normative and nonnormative life changes may also be a priority for many adolescents

TABLE 1
CRITERIA FOR DEFINING AND ASSESSING SOCIAL INTELLIGENCE

Self-Assertive Accomplishments	These goals refer to the maintenance or promotion of the self in social situations.
INDIVIDUALITY	Defining one's identity as a separate person: developing patterns of functioning that do not depend on the defining features of other individuals or social groups.
SELF-DETERMINATION	Maintaining personal control over important aspects of one's life; resisting social efforts to inhibit or undermine such control.
Superiority	Gaining social status or importance; seeking to be better or higher than other people on relevant dimensions of comparison.
Resource Acquisition	Obtaining social-emotional support, material aid, information and advice, or validation from others.
Integrative Accomplishments	These goals refer to the maintenance or promotion of other people or the social groups of which one is a part.
BELONGINGNESS	Creating, maintaining, or enhancing the identity or integrity of the social units of which one is a part.
SOCIAL RESPONSIBILITY	Conforming to broad social and moral rules; fulfilling interpersonal commitments and obligations; accepting legitimate social control.
Equity	Promoting justice, fairness, or equality; ensuring that people are similar on relevant dimensions of comparison.
Resource Provision	Providing social-emotional support, material aid, information and advice, or validation to others.
Task Accomplishments	
Management	Organizing or influencing people to maintain or promote smooth social functioning and/or the attainment of particular task goals.
SAFETY	Avoiding social circumstances that produce personally damaging, threatening, or depriving consequences.

Note: Social intelligence criteria of particular relevance to adolescence appear in upper-case letters.

(e.g., those in divorced or reconstituted families, or those who have left home to begin college).

SOCIAL RESPONSIBILITY, ■

as recent research on developmental and educational priorities for adolescents (Krumboltz, Ford, Nichols, & Wentzel, 1987) suggests, may be the single most important criterion for adolescent social intelligence. Characteristics such as respect for others, dependability, and good citizenship are highly valued not only by adults who live and work with adolescents, but also by adolescents themselves. Moreover, unlike earlier phases of development, adolescence is a period in which a failure to make responsible decisions may result in very serious or even life-threatening consequences. A failure to develop habits of social responsibility may also jeopardize opportunities for the attainment of educational and occupational goals.

SAFETY ■ is another valued outcome
of adolescent behavior and development, one that is often closely associated with social responsibility (Krumboltz et al.,

1987). Safety-related issues are prominent in the literature because many public health problems such as sexually transmitted disease, unwanted pregnancy, alcohol and drug abuse, and automobile accidents are unusually prevalent in adolescence. This is also true of several less "public" negative health outcomes that nevertheless have social origins (e.g., eating disorders, suicide). Such outcomes clearly do not represent socially intelligent functioning, especially from a developmental perspective (i.e., unsafe behaviors may facilitate the attainment of short-term social objectives, but only at the expense of longer-term developmental outcomes).

Psychological Processes Associated With Social Intelligence in Adolescence

Before describing the person variables that appear to contribute most to the attainment of adolescent social goals, it is important to emphasize that *social intelligence is a joint product of a skillful, motivated person and a responsive environment.* Very capable people may often behave in unintelligent ways in contexts that are unfamiliar, unpredictable, or unusually stressful. Conversely, people with limited personal resources may be able to function quite adaptively in social contexts that are stable and supportive. Thus, in some cases the most successful interventions to enhance social intelligence may be those that try to improve the quality of the social environments in which adolescents must function.

Although the links between psychological processes and social outcomes depend in part on the particular outcomes being considered (Ford, 1987), it is possible to construct an overall profile of the socially intelligent adolescent by integrating the variety of literatures relevant to this topic. This profile includes seven components.

1. BEHAVIORAL REPERTOIRE ▪

A well-learned repertoire of social behavior patterns is a prerequisite for socially intelligent functioning (Goldstein, Sprafkin, Gershaw, & Klein, 1980). Such patterns allow one to guide behavior in complex social situations with efficiency and ease. The social skills training literature suggests that the most effective way to develop reliable and effective behavior patterns is to begin by observing and talking with experienced others, followed by direct behavioral practice in relevant contexts.

2. SOCIAL PLANNING AND PROBLEM-SOLVING CAPABILITIES ▪

In situations characterized by a significant degree of novelty or unpredictability, one must be able to create flexible plans of action that build upon or go beyond previously learned behavior patterns. Consequently, practical problem-solving skills such as means-ends thinking (constructing step-by-step solutions to interpersonal problems) and consequential thinking (anticipating the consequences of one's actions) are among the best predictors of effective social behavior in adolescence (Ford, 1982; Spivack, Platt, & Shure, 1976).

3. PERSONAL AGENCY BELIEFS ▪

These refer to two interrelated processes: control beliefs (i.e., the belief that the environment will be responsive to one's goal attainment efforts) and competence beliefs (i.e., the belief that one is capable of behaving effectively given the opportunity to do so). Adolescents who perceive themselves as competent, controlling agents are generally more successful on a wide range of social criteria. It appears that positive personal agency beliefs enable them to make the most of their existing capabilities and to maintain motivation in the face of obstacles to goal attainment or when new behavior patterns must be developed (Deci & Ryan, 1985; Lefcourt, 1976). Of particular significance is the possibility that personal agency beliefs may be crucial to long-term competence development as a result of their fundamental influence on self-system processes and interpersonal relationship patterns (Ford & Thompson, 1985).

4. GOAL IMPORTANCE ■

Although the links between social goals and intelligent behavior are complex, it appears that adolescents who express greater interest in or concern about such goals as self-determination and social responsibility are generally more likely to be successful in attaining these goals (Ford, 1987). This is presumably because social goals regarded as important are more likely to direct attention and effort and to activate the emotions, plans, and behavior patterns needed for effective action.

5. GOAL DIRECTEDNESS ■

Social goal directedness refers to a person's general tendency to set social goals, to be aware of these goals, and to persist effortfully in trying to attain these goals. Although a low level of goal directedness is associated with generalized social ineffectiveness, it appears that under some circumstances it may be adaptive to moderate one's goal-setting activity a bit in order to maintain some degree of flexibility and spontaneity (Ford, 1982, 1987).

6. EMOTIONAL WELL-BEING ■

Generalized emotional distress has been consistently linked to negative personal agency beliefs and disengagement from ef-

forts to attain social goals (Ford & Thompson, 1985; Klinger, 1975). In addition, anxiety and depression in adolescence are often associated with social irresponsibility and self-destructive behavior (Kaplan, 1980).

7. EMOTIONAL RESPONSIVENESS ■

The tendency for adolescents to respond emotionally to actual or anticipated social successes and failures appears to be an important factor in energizing efforts to be socially intelligent. For example, adolescents who are capable of feeling empathic concern when they encounter distress in others, guilt when they commit hurtful actions, and pride when they behave responsibly are much more likely to accomplish integrative goals than are those who do not experience or anticipate experiencing such emotions (Estrada, 1987; Ford, Wentzel, Wood, Stevens, & Siesfeld, 1989).

References

Deci, E. L., & Ryan, R. M. (1985). *Intrinsic motivation and self-determination in human behavior*. New York: Plenum.

Erickson, E. H. (1968). *Identity: Youth and crisis*. New York: Norton.

Estrada, P. (1987). Empathy and prosocial behavior in adolescence. Unpublished doctoral dissertation, Stanford University, Stanford, CA.

Ford, M. E. (1982). Social cognition and social competence in adolescence. *Developmental Psychology, 18*, 323–340.

Ford, M. E. (1984). Linking social-cognitive processes with effective social behavior: A living systems approach. In P. C. Kendall (Ed.), *Advances in cognitive-behavioral research and therapy* (Vol. 3, pp. 167–211). New York: Academic Press.

Ford, M. E. (1986). A living systems conceptualization of social intelligence: Processes, outcomes, and developmental change. In R. J. Sternberg (Ed.), *Advances in the psychology of human intelligence* (Vol. 3, pp. 119-171). Hillsdale, NJ: Lawrence Erlbaum Associates.

Ford, M. E. (1987). Processes contributing to adolescent social competence. In M. E. Ford & D. H. Ford (Eds.), *Humans as self-constructing living systems: Putting the framework to work* (pp. 199-234). Hillsdale, NJ: Lawrence Erlbaum Associates.

Ford, M. E., & Nichols, C. W. (1987). A taxonomy of human goals and some possible applications. In M. E. Ford & D. H. Ford (Eds.), *Humans as self-constructing living systems: Putting the framework to work* (pp. 289-311). Hillsdale, NJ: Lawrence Erlbaum Associates.

Ford, M. E., & Thompson, R. (1985). Perceptions of personal agency and infant attachment: Toward a life-span perspective on competence development. *International Journal of Behavioral Development, 8*, 377-406.

Ford, M. E., & Tisak, M. S. (1983). A further search for social intelligence. *Journal of Educational Psychology, 75*, 196-206.

Ford, M. E., Wentzel, K. R., Wood, D., Stevens, E., & Siesfeld, G. A. (1989). Processes associated with integrative social competence: Emotional and contextual influences on adolescent social responsibility. *Journal of Adolescent Research, 4*, 405-425.

Goldstein, A. P., Sprafkin, R. P., Gershaw, N. J., & Klein, P. (1980). *Skillstreaming the adolescent*. Champaign, IL: Research Press.

Kaplan, H. B. (1980). *Deviant behavior in defense of self*. New York: Academic Press.

Klinger, E. (1975). Consequences of commitment to and disengagement from incentives. *Psychological Review, 82*, 1-25.

Krumboltz, J., Ford, M. E., Nichols, C., & Wentzel, K. R. (1987). The goals of education. In R. C. Calfee (Ed.), *The study of Stanford and the schools: Views from the inside*. Stanford, CA: School of Education, Stanford University.

Lefcourt, H. M. (1976). *Locus of control: Current trends in theory and research*. Hillsdale, NJ: Lawrence Erlbaum Associates.

O'Sullivan, M., Guilford, J. P., & DeMille, R. (1965). *The measurement of social intelligence* (Report No. BR-5-0 198). Los Angeles: University of Southern California. (ERIC Document Reproduction Service No. ED 010 278).

Spivack, G., Platt, J. J., & Shure, M. B. (1976). *The problem-solving approach to adjustment*. San Francisco: Jossey-Bass.

Sternberg, R. J., Conway, B. E., Ketron, J. L., & Bernstein, M. (1981). People's conceptions of intelligence. *Journal of Personality and Social Psychology, 41*, 37-55.

See Also

Cognition, Adolescent; Cognition and Health; Cognitive Abilities and Physical Maturation; Cognitive and Psychosocial Gender Differences, Trends in; Cognitive Development; Egocentrism Theory and the "New Look" at the Imaginary Audience and Personal Fable in Adolescence; Formal Operational Thinking and Identity Resolution; Illness, Adolescents' Conceptualization of; Inhelder, Barbel; Introspectiveness, Adolescent; Memory; Piaget, Jean; Relativistic Thinking in Adolescence; Reasoning, Higher-Order, in Adolescence; Reasoning in the Adolescent; Scientific Reasoning, Adolescent; Spatial Ability and Maturation in Adolescence.

Socialization of African-American Adolescents

Geraldine Kearse Brookins
Jackson State University

African-American youth are socialized in the same manner as are their white counterparts with one major exception: African-American youth must be socialized to negotiate effectively two realities, that of mainstream America and the castelike status of black America. Accordingly, the ecological systems in which they are embedded play a deciding role in influencing the outcome of these youth. Because these systems interact in a variety of ways and are interpreted somewhat idiosyncratically by the adolescents, it is important that we begin by acknowledging that African-American youth are not a monolithic group, but a diversity of individuals, each with his or her unique repertoire of behaviors and attitudes. Keeping this proviso in mind, we shall proceed in an aggregate fashion to address some of the issues regarding socialization of African-American youth. Specifically, we shall focus on socialization and its outcomes regarding education, occupational goals, and sexuality. These three areas of development are inextricably connected, and the confluence of behaviors associated with them has significant influence on the subsequent life course development of these youth.

Education

The African-American family, like most families, is often portrayed as the single most important element in determining the educational and occupational aspirations of its youth. Lower educational and occupational outcomes are often viewed as a result of the disorganization of the African-American family (Moynihan, 1966) rather than as a result of a problem in American society and its institutions. African-American parents hold expectations and desires for success of their children similar to those of white parents. In a 1978 study Allen noted that the aspirations of African-American fathers equalled those of white fathers, while the aspirations of African-American mothers were slightly higher than those of white mothers.

Research indicates that a discrepancy exists between African-American adolescent aspirations, achievement orientations and actual attainment (Allen, 1980). African-American adolescents, like their white counterparts, have high achievement orientations, but when faced with the realities of discrimination, prejudice, and educational inequality, they often reduce their aspirations to a level that they feel is attainable (Ogbu, 1987).

With respect to education for their youth, most African-American parents express a desire to have their children complete high school and to continue on with more formal training, whether it be college or vocational education (Scanzoni, 1971; Ogbu, 1978). Nonetheless, in spite of the expressed desires of parents and youth themselves, African-American youth are more likely to fall behind in school, and to drop out of school, and are evidencing a general decline in numbers matriculating to college (Children's Defense Fund, 1985). These major demographic shifts may be attributed to several factors. Ogbu (1987) suggested that many African-American youth experience failure and reject the schooling process because of the lack of equality of results when compared to the equality of opportunity. In spite of federal antidiscrimination legislation, many African-Americans who have participated in the educational process have not fared well economically relative to their white counterparts. This has not gone unnoticed by African-American youth, and some have interpreted the employment outcomes for their peers and predecessors as an indication that investing the time or energy in education is fruitless (Ogbu, 1987).

On another level, schools contribute to and socialize for—perhaps unwittingly so—negative educational outcomes for African-American youth, especially males. According to self-reports, a substantial number of African-American males indicated that they had dropped out because they did not like school. The issue of males not liking school may be related to how they are perceived by the school systems, teachers, and peers. Research indicates that a disproportional number of African-American students are placed in classes for the educable mentally retarded (Children's Defense Fund, 1985). Unfortunately, factors other than educationally sound reasons

contribute to the decision making regarding student placement in these classrooms. It has been suggested that the lack of culturally responsive pedagogy contributes to a misinterpretation of classroom expectations on the part of both students and teachers (Erickson, 1987).

Low global self-esteem is also often advanced as an explanation for lower academic achievement among African-American adolescents (Giffore & Parsons, 1983). More recent studies indicate that African-American youngsters compartmentalize self-esteem relative to specific areas. For example, these youth view academic achievement and self as separate entities (Hare & Castenell, 1985; Mboya, 1986; Spencer, 1985). It is thus not unusual for African-American teenagers to maintain positive self-concepts while doing poorly in school.

In many instances peer pressure among African-American adolescents encourages a lack of academic motivation. It is a commonly held belief among some youth that exhibiting studious behavior is an expression of being "white oriented." As such, even those who possess the capabilities for academic achievement and mastery will eschew good study habits in order to be accepted and considered as "cool."

Occupational Goals

The adult roles that African-American youth eventually assume in society depend largely on the quality and amount of education received, the availability of access to occupational resources, and access to occupational models. Trying out the work world before one becomes an adult is a developmentally appropriate endeavor (Erikson, 1963). Young children will happily tell of what they want to be when they grow up. African-American children also express interest in obtaining jobs, with many of the positions to which they aspire falling into the higher prestige categories (Brookins, 1977, 1985).

Job experience obtained during adolescence can be viewed as critical to future occupational development. Having a job during adolescence facilitates career explorations and fosters personal responsibility. Working during adolescence increases the chances of finding employment and earning higher wages after graduation from high school and/or college (Meyer & Wise, 1982). Race, however, plays a major role in determining whether the adolescent will find employment. White youth have the highest employment rates, Hispanic youth the next highest, and African-American teens the lowest employment rate for the three major racial/ethnic groups in the United States. As suggested by the W. T. Grant Commission on Work, Family and Citizenship, in 1988 similar proportions of whites, African-Americans, and Hispanics sought employment, but white adolescents were more successful at finding jobs. Discriminatory practices, place of residence, discouragement, and lack of opportunity are but a few of the reasons cited for high unemployment among African-American youth.

Sexuality and Child Bearing

Family configuration and process is important in determining whether early sexual activity will occur. While father absence or presence has been suggested as an important determinant of sexual behavior of females among whites, it does not seem to be a major factor that influences the African-American female's sexual behavior (Eberhardt & Shill, 1984). The absence of the father during the preschool years is most likely to affect the behavior of sons. The mother appears to exert the strongest influence on the daugh-

ters' sexual attitudes and behavior patterns (Fox, 1980). Because the topic of sex causes discomfort and anxiety, many parents withdraw from taking an active role in the sexual socialization of their adolescents. Parents seldom serve as the primary source of information for their teenagers, particularly the male child. Studies indicate that parents fall behind peers, teachers, and reading material in providing advice on sex (Freeman et al., 1980).

Sexual activity among adolescents has increased over the last decade, and has occurred among younger and younger adolescents (Furstenberg, Lincoln & Menken, 1981). This is due in part to the availability of birth control and to relaxed mores regarding sexual behavior in society at large. In a 1979 survey of urban females, Zelnik and Kantner (1980) reported that, by the age of 19, 65% of white youth and 90% of African-American youth had engaged in sexual intercourse at least once. Socioeconomic variables accounted for more of the percentage variance than did race. Higher socioeconomic status, higher levels of education, and faithful church attendance were related to lower rates of coital activity, while poverty and residence in large metropolitan cities were correlated with higher rates of premarital intercourse (Zelnik & Kantner, 1980).

A large number of these sexual encounters result in pregnancy. Since the majority of African-American adolescent females elect to carry their pregnancies to term, the consequences are often quite disruptive to their lives and their adult life chances. Parental or welfare dependency, repeat pregnancies, marital instability, and slower cognitive development of their children are some of the adverse consequences of adolescent childbearing (Chilman, 1980). In spite of these consequences, lower-income status African-American females most frequently project themselves into the role of mother rather than into a career role (Starkshall,

1987). This projection partially explains why African-American teenage females choose not to abort. Motherhood for many of these youth may be seen as a means of accomplishment in the face of seeming insurmountable obstacles.

While most of the discussion on adolescent sexuality focuses on females (in large part because of the consequences to their life chances), African-American males serve as the nexus, wittingly and willingly, in the sexuality, pregnancy, and childbearing process. Thus, it is important to address those factors that have impact on their lives relative to this issue. While physiological maturation seems not to contribute to early sexual behavior among African-American females, hormonal and other physiological changes do seem to influence sexual behavior among African-American male adolescents (Westney, Jenkins, Butts, & Williams, 1984). Thus, maturational factors may, without the intervention of parental supervision and advice, propel these youth into early sexual behavior patterns that may foreclose options across the life course (Chilman, 1983; Furstenberg, Lincoln & Menken, 1981).

Parenthood also poses many problems for adolescent fathers. The majority of these young men express pride in fatherhood; however, they are not usually psychologically, emotionally, or financially prepared for the responsibilities associated with fatherhood. Teenage parenting also interferes with the educational process, which in turn has a serious impact on subsequent occupational opportunities and future income.

As noted previously, socialization for African-American youth requires their being responsive to mandates from mainstream society as well as "subcultural underpinnings," while also maintaining a healthy sense of self. This is not an easy task, and oftentimes places severe demands on the developing individual. Outcomes regarding sexuality, education, and occupational opportunity form a nexus for African-American life-course trajectories. Many of these youth, especially the young males, have poor outlooks for the future. Families and social structural entities within our society, such as schools, media, churches, and community agencies, play a major role in creating the developmental landscape along which these youth travel. For many African-American youth, the "road not taken" is the one that will have afforded the most productive life. Many have to share the burden of responsibility for that less than productive life.

References

Allen, W. R. (1980). Preludes to attainment: Race, sex and student achievement orientations. *The Sociological Quarterly, 21,* 65–79.

Brookins, G. K. (1977). *Maternal employment: Its impact on the sex roles and occupational roles of black children.* Doctoral dissertation, Harvard University. Cambridge, MA.

Brookins, G. K. (1985). Black children's sex-role ideologies and occupation choices in families of employed mothers. In M. B. Spencer, G. K. Brookins, & W. R. Allen (Eds.), *Beginnings: The social and effective development of black children.* Hillsdale, NJ: Lawrence Erlbaum Associates.

Brookover, W. B. (1985). Can we make schools effective for minority students. *Journal of Negro Education, 54,* 257–268.

Children's Defense Fund (1985). *Black and white children in America.* Washington, DC: Children's Defense Fund.

Chilman, C. S. (1980). Social and psychological research concerning adolescent childbearing: 1970–1980. *Journal of Marriage and the Family, 42,* 793–805.

Chilman, C. S. (1983). *Adolescent sexuality in a changing American society.* New York: John Wiley & Sons.

Eberhardt, C. A., & Shill, T. (1984). Differences in sexual attitudes and likeliness of sexual behavior in black lower-socioeconomic father-present vs. father-absent female adolescents. *Adolescence, 19*, 99–105.

Erickson, F. (1987). Transformation and school success: The politics and culture of education achievement. *Anthropology and Education Quarterly, 18*(4), 312–334.

Erikson, E. (1963). *Childhood and society.* New York: W. W. Norton.

Fox, G. L., & Inazu J. K. (1980). Mother-daughter communication about sex. *Family Relations, 29*, 347–352.

Freeman, E. W., Rickels, K., Huggins, M. R., Mudd, E. H., Garcia, C. R., & Dickens, H. O. (1980). Adolescent contraceptive use: Comparison of male and female attitudes and information. *American Journal of Public Health, 70*, 790–797.

Furstenberg, F. F., Lincoln, R., & Menken, J. (1981). *Teenage pregnancy and childbearing.* Philadelphia: University of Philadelphia Press.

Giffore, R. J., & Parsons, M. A. (1983). Student characteristics and achievement in desegregated schools. *Urban Education, 17*, 431–438.

Hare, B. R., & Castenell, L. A. (1985). No place to run, no place to hide: Comparative status and future prospects of black boys. In M. B. Spencer, G. K. Brookins, & W. R. Allen, (Eds.), *Beginnings: The social and effective development of black children.* Hillsdale, NJ: Lawrence Erlbaum Associates.

Hetherington, E. M. (1972). Effects of father absence on personality development in adolescent daughters. *Developmental Psychology, 7*, 313–326.

Mboya, M. M. (1986). Black adolescents: A descriptive study of their self-concept and academic achievement. *Adolescence, 21*, 689–696.

Meyer, R., & Wise D. (1982). High school preparation and early labor force experience. In R. Freeman, & D. Wise, (Eds.), *The youth labor market and problem: Its nature, causes, and consequences.* Chicago: University of Chicago Press.

Moynihan, D. P. (1966). *The Negro family: The case of national action.* Washington, DC: U.S. Government Printing Office.

Ogbu, J. U. (1978). *Minority education and caste: The American system in cross-cultural perspective.* New York: Academic Press.

Ogbu, J. (1987). Variability in minority school performance: A problem in search of an explanation. *Anthropology and Education Quarterly, 18*(4), 312–334.

Scanzoni, J. H. (1971). *The black family in modern society.* Boston, MA: Allyn and Bacon.

Starkshall, R. A. (1987). Motherhood as a dominant feature in the self-image of female adolescents of low-socioeconomic status. *Adolescence, 22*, 565–570.

Spencer, M. B. (1985). Cultural cognition and social cognition as identifying correlates of black children's personal social development. In M. B. Spencer, G. K. Brookins, & W. R. Allen, (Eds.), *Beginnings: The social and effective development of black children.* Hillsdale, NJ: Lawrence Erlbaum Associates.

Westney, O. E., Jenkins, R. R., Butts, J. D., & Williams, M. D. (1984). Sexual development and behavior in black preadolescents. *Adolescence, 19*, 557–568.

Zelnik, M., & Kantner, J. F. (1980). Sexual activity, contraceptive use, and pregnancy among metropolitan area teenagers: 1971–1979. *Family Planning Perspectives, 12*, 230–237.

See Also

Black Adolescents At-Risk: Approaches to Prevention; Black Adolescents, the Impact of Federal Income Assistance Policies on; Black Female adolescents, Socialization of; Drug Use, Minority Youth and; Health and Substance Abuse in Adolescence: Ethnic and Gender Perspectives; Hispanic Adolescents; Identity, Minority Development of; Minority and Female Participation in Math and Science, Increase in: The Importance of the Middle School Years; Sexual Behavior in Black Adolescents, Initiation of.

Social Networks in Adolescence

Deborah L. Coates
The Catholic University of America

Definition and Historical Perspectives

Social networks refer to an individual's links to persons to whom they feel significantly connected and to other less important social contacts. The social network has emerged as a psychological construct that refers to an individual's perceptions of, and the actual characteristics of, a broad array of social relationships. A personal social network includes family, peers, and nonfamilial adults who are socialized within home, school, community, and other settings. Social structure, social experiences, and social interaction are assumed to influence the development of a person's identity or self. Some empirical evidence supports the view that social environment acts as an influence on behavior by serving as a mirror that shows the person her- or himself and thus shapes expectations, perceptions, identity, and overt behavior (Cooley, 1902; Margolin, Blyth, & Carbone, 1988; Mead, 1934; Merton, 1957; Shrauger & Schoeneman, 1979).

At any period in a person's life a social context or network exists that can be viewed as a collection of social contacts and an index of that person's social world or life space (Feiring & Coates, 1987). Adolescence is a period of increased social contacts and the adolescent's social relationships are of paramount importance to him/her. The social network concept provides a useful conceptual tool for exploring the nature of emerging social relationships during adolescence. In both, research and service applications of the personal social network paradigm social relationships can be schematically or summarily represented. These representations indicate how the individual's social world is organized, how persons in it function to provide the individual with desired or necessary social interactions, and how they are interrelated (Coates, 1985). These social contacts can be based on blood or marital kinship, sentiment, the need to exchange material, emotional, or informational resources, or other less well-defined social functions.

The social network construct has been discussed extensively in the adult sociology and family socialization literature (see Bott, 1971; Boissevain, 1974; Boissevain & Mitchell, 1973; Leinhart, 1977; Whitten & Wolfe, 1973). According to Oliveri and Reiss (1987), early social network analysis provided descriptions of the overall organization of relationships within an intact community. Mathematical models have also been used to examine the structures of self-selected, psychologically close groups. More recently the "personal social network," or the set of persons having special significance for a specific target individual, have been explored (Brownell & Shumaker, 1984; Feiring & Coates, 1987; Thoits, 1986).

Other early social network analyses examined relationships between the social world in which a family existed and the characteristics of the social relationships between individuals in that family (Nadel, 1951; Oliveri & Reiss, 1981). The focus of much of this work was on how the larger social world influences family processes and how this, in turn, influences individuals. Social network influence on mental health in adulthood has also been explored extensively (Biegel, McCardle, & Mendelson, 1985; Gottlieb, 1981).

The personal social network has its roots in the sociological study of social structure. Studies of social structure have examined regularity in discernible social patterns (Blau, 1975). An interest in the choices an individual makes to maximize his/her social rewards formed the basis for the study of social structure (Merton, 1957).

Social Networks and Adolescent Development Theory

Most developmental theorists identify development of identity and social roles as a major task of adolescence (Greenberger & Sorensen, 1974; Grotevant, 1987). It is assumed that personality characteristics and social roles are influenced by the social environment in which the adolescent has functioned as a child and in which he/she functions as an adolescent (Bronfenbrenner, 1979; Sebald, 1977). The influence of family and of peers, in the immediate social environment, on adolescent development has received considerable attention (see Berndt, 1981; Cooper, 1987; Hunter, 1985; Kidwell, Dunham, Peppin, & Passarello, 1986; Nitz, Lerner, Lerner, & Talwar, 1988; Youniss, 1980; Youniss & Smollar, 1985).

Two predominant aspects of the social environment have been described: "reference group" and "significant other." The concept of reference group refers to processes associated with deriving values, perceptions, and norms from association with a myriad of membership groups that may include family, cultural or ethnic, religious affiliation, gender, or youth culture groups. These reference groups are assumed to directly and indirectly influence behavior. They may be self-selected, as in the case of gangs or clubs, or they may occur because of constraints that are not controlled by the adolescent, as, for example, ethnic and family groups. Reference groups may be shifting, multiple, and sometimes even may be in conflict with one another.

The "significant other" concept has been used to refer to the ways by which individual members of groups influence attitudes and behavior. Personality theorist H. S. Sullivan first suggested that the "significant other" was a useful way of describing the meaning derived from the most important relationships available to an adolescent (see Youniss, 1980). As with reference groups, the "significant other" concept does not necessarily imply choice and allows for great variety in socialization processes. It is assumed that significant others provide models for behavior, information that influences behavior, emotional support, and/or material support, and may be either a positive or a negative influence.

The concept of significant other has been described extensively and provides the explicit or implicit basis of most adolescent social network studies (e.g., Blyth, Hill, & Theil, 1982; Coates, 1985; Fischer, 1981; Galbo, 1983; Garbarino, Burston, Raber, Russell, & Crouter, 1978; Hinde, Perret-Clermont, & Stevenson-Hinde, 1985; Serafica & Blyth, 1985; Shade, 1983).

The social network construct is a convenient paradigm for organizing the related constructs of "reference group" and "significant other" and for integrating these with parent and peer influences on development. Social relationships have been explored as they relate to normative development (as described above), and to determine how social relationships mediate stress, and are related to social, cognitive, and personality development.

Behavioral scientists interested in social relationships, stress, and developmental outcomes have explored how social networks function to provide social support. Social support has also been explored as a moderator of normative functioning. Adult social networks and their relationship to mental health, coping, and adjustment have been discussed extensively (see Biegel et al., 1985; Brownell & Shumaker, 1984; Thoits, 1986). Social support, which is provided through the relationships present in one's social network, is thought to provide a psychological buffer for stress. Social support theories suggest that if adequate support is present, it provides a feedback mechanism through which meaningful information can be obtained and personal decisions influenced. If support is not present, stressful reactions, such as poor psychological adjustment and health, may result (see Coates, in press; Thoits, 1986). This theoretical approach has been extended to adolescents; some studies of social support, coping, and stress during adolescence have focused on the ways in which these processes are similar to those which occur for adults (Coates, in press; Compas, 1987). Recent studies of social support and adjustment in adolescence have described specific factors in the adolescent social environment, relationships between life events and health, self-concept and social environment-adolescent congruence (see Felner, Aber, Primavera, & Cauce, 1985; Hirsch & Rapin, 1987; Simmons, Burgeson, Carlton-Ford, & Blyth, 1988; Stevens, 1988, for examples).

The distinction between perceived and actual support and the significance of gender and race differences in social support and health and in social support patterns are important issues in the adolescent literature (see, for example, Feiring & Coates, 1987). A developmental basis for understanding and studying social support from infancy through adolescence and into maturity has also been proposed (Bruhn & Philips, 1987). This developmental perspective suggests that social support is a psychological need that is learned through life events and that significantly shapes adjustment and health. Developmental research has also considered the way in which social relationships provide different aspects of support at different developmental periods (e.g., Hunter, 1985; Hunter & Youniss, 1982).

Measurement of the Social Network and Its Functions

Most studies of social support networks in adolescence have used self-report measures. Some of these measures ask adolescents to identify persons they know, sometimes with reference to distinct categories (e.g., family or friends). The adolescent can be asked to list as many persons as they feel they know, or to list some limited number, or to identify some limited subset such as family, friends, or nonfamilial adults. Once the list is constructed, respondents are typically asked to describe the primary characteristics of these persons and how they interact with them. Adolescents are asked to describe who they see, how often they see them, where they see them, and the demographic features of these persons. These reports are then used to derive social network and/or social support scales that indicate the array or some limited subset of structural and functional characteristics of the network. Studies of network structure have described the size of the network, its durability, or how long it has existed for the adolescent (e.g., how long have persons in the network been known?), how frequently network members are seen, where they are seen, whether or not members in the network are known to each other and see each other in a variety of places, the geographic proximity of network members, and the number of persons available who can serve as emotional and/or material resources to the adolescent (e.g., Andrews, 1986; Blyth & Foster-Clarke, 1987; Blyth, Hill, & Thiel, 1982; Coates, 1985, 1986; Fischer, Sollie & Morrow, 1986; Rosen, 1982). Often these relationships are described graphically. In some limited instances a simple list of "significant others" in relationship to some important event, decision, or problem is generated (e.g., Peterson, Strivers, & Peters, 1986).

Studies of the friendship portion of social networks have asked a target adolescent and other adolescents within the same social reference group, such as a classroom, to list with whom they are friends. This sociometric technique allows one to identify whether perceptions of social affiliation are shared or perceived as significant by one person only (e.g., Berndt, 1985; Bukowski & Newcomb, 1983; Cairns, Perrin, & Cairns, 1985; Feltham, Doyles, Schwartzman, & Serbin, 1985; Shrum & Cheek, 1987). In this measurement approach nominations are examined to determine how many nominations are mutually linked, and these linkages are then used to describe mutually linked social groups.

Social support is considered the primary purpose of social networks. Studies of social network support focus on how those networks function to provide direct or indirect assistance. Vaux (1987) has discussed how social support has been conceptualized and describes three distinct support dimensions: love, respect, and involvement. These aspects of support have special developmental significance for adolescents. Vaux (1987) also reviews three social-support appraisal scales. Social support is often measured by presenting an adolescent with hypothetical problems and asking him/her to describe to whom they would go for help with the hypothetical serious problem or to whom they went for help with a similar problem they had recently experienced. Other approaches ask adolescents to identify to whom they feel close or how they interact with various members of their social network. These studies often ask adolescents to describe the stressors and problems they have recently experienced and to describe how their social relationships helped them to cope with these stressors. Still other approaches to measuring social support have used questions that describe how people can relate to each other. Many of these friendship descriptions focus on how friendship is perceived (e.g., Hirsch & Rapin, 1987; LaGaipa, 1979; LaGaipa & Wood, 1985). Others focus on the differences between the nature of peer and parental relationships (Felner, Aber, Primavera, & Cauce, 1985; Hunter, 1985; Hunter & Youniss, 1982). Some focus on the quality of relationships and interactions that characterize the network as supportive system (e.g., Coates, 1985; Compas, 1987; Rosen, 1982).

Adequate psychometric or replicated data is scarce in studies of adolescent social networks and social support. Some reliability data is available and one study demonstrates half-split sample replication (Blyth & Foster-Clark, 1987; Cairns et al., 1985; Coates, 1985; Fischer, Sollie, & Morrow, 1986; Shrum & Cheek, 1987). The validity of perceived network characteristics and their relationship to the actual social structure in which an adolescent is embedded is an important yet neglected assessment issue. Some notable studies have explored these issues. Cairns and his colleagues have identified some behavioral correlates of social network perceptions and have developed methods for describing social clusters that occur in natural settings (Cairns, Gariepy, & Kindermann, in press; Cairns, Perrin, & Cairns, 1985). Montemayer and Van Komen (1985) have also used observations of naturally occurring friendship groups and correlated these observations with adolescent perceptions of these friendship groups to describe the social structure of these groups during adolescence. Oliveri and Reiss (1981, 1987) have examined the congruence between adolescent and familial adult perceptions of social support networks.

Another measurement issue is psychometric scaling of social support items. In most instances social support items have not been linked item-by-item with any significant developmental outcomes such as sense of well-being or adjustment of social competence. Donald and Ware (1984) describe these issues in extensive detail and suggest ways of scaling measures of social support. This may contribute to a better understanding of the phenomenon being measured by paper and pencil measures of social relationships.

Social Networks, Social Support, and Adolescent Development

Research on adolescent social support and social networks is still in its infancy. Numerous studies are available that describe and validate descriptions of social networks or of the friendship subset of a social network. Fewer studies are available that relate social networks or social support to an aspect of development in adolescence, and many of these concern adjustment to adolescent pregnancy. Studies that have considered the developmental consequences of social network characteristics or social support in adolescence have explored self-concept and identity (Bukowski & Newcomb, 1983; Coates, 1985; Hirsch & Rapkin, 1987; Margolin et al., 1988) drug use (Newcomb & Bentler, 1988), clinical disorder (Feltham, Doyles, Schwartzman, & Serbin, 1985; Rosen, 1982), popularity (LaGaipa & Wood, 1985), and adjustment to pregnancy (e.g., Barth, 1988; Stevens, 1988; Unger & Wandersman, 1988).

Social Network Analysis as an Intervention with Adolescents

The social network paradigm has been suggested as a useful tool for preventing social problems in adolescence and for intervening with adolescents, who may be at risk for normative development (Coates, in press; Gottlieb & Hall, 1980; Speck & Speck, 1985). Adolescence is a time when major transitions occur in biological, cognitive, and social functioning (Lerner & Lerner, 1989). Interest in social roles and social relationships are at a peak during this developmental stage. This natural interest in social roles suggests that analysis of the personal social network may have intrinsic appeal to adolescents and thus facilitate intervention and prevention efforts on behalf of adolescents.

Social network analysis and therapeutic intervention have been described extensively with adult populations (see Biegel et al., 1985). Coates (in press) and Speck and Speck (1985) present a rationale for the relevance of this approach to adolescent prevention and intervention efforts and describe how to mobilize networks to treat adolescents. Speck and Speck describe the therapeutic role in network therapy and present case studies that illustrate how social network mapping provides the basis for intervention activities. Coates discusses the potential content of network interventions and suggests directions for future research that would enhance knowledge about effective social network analysis as an intervention mechanism during adolescence. Barth (1988), Crouse (1985), and Trimble (1981) have used network therapy with high school and college students at risk for adjustment, college success, and antisocial behavior respectively. They report moderate short-term effectiveness using this approach.

The Carnegie Council on Adolescent Development, located in Washington, D.C., has established a working group on social support networks as a part of their effort to examine effective and promising preventive interventions. The council chair, David Hamburg, has stated that the erosion of family social support has changed adolescent experience significantly. Hamburg has suggested that perhaps alternative social support networks such as churches, schools, and community organizations can be creatively mobilized to meet the developmental needs of adolescents. The council is exploring the potential of social support networks as an intervention that would prevent adolescent problems and promote healthy adolescent functioning. However, the council has identified a number of research and policy questions that need to be addressed prior to implementing social support programs for adolescents.

References

Andrews, H. F. (1986). The effects of neighbourhood mix on adolescents' social networks and recreational activities. *Urban Studies, 23,* 501–517.

Barth, R. (1988). Social skill and social support among young mothers. *Journal of Community Psychology, 16,* 132–143.

Berndt, T. (1981). Relations between social cognition, nonsocial cognition, and social behavior: The case of friendship. In J. Flavell & L. Ross (Eds.), *Social cognitive development: Frontiers and possible futures* (pp. 176–199). Cambridge: Cambridge University Press.

Berndt, T. (1985). Prosocial behavior between friends in middle childhood and early adolescence. *Journal of Early Adolescence, 5,* 307–317.

Biegel, D. E., McCardle, E., & Mendelson, S. (1985). *Social networks and mental health: An annotated bibliography.* Beverly Hills, CA: Sage.

Blau, P. (Ed.). (1975). *Approaches to the study of social structure: A collection of original essays.* New York: Free Press.

Blyth, D., & Foster-Clarke, F. (1987). Gender differences in perceived intimacy with different members of adolescents' social networks. *Sex Roles, 17,* 689–718.

Blyth, D., Hill, J., & Theil, K. (1982). Early adolescents' significant others: Grade and gender differences in perceived relationships with familial and nonfamilial adults and young people. *Journal of Youth and Adolescence, 11,* 425–450.

Boissevain, J. (1974). *Friends of friends: Networks, manipulators, and coalitions.* Oxford: Basil, Blackwell, & Mott.

Boissevain, J., & Mitchell, J. (1973). *Network analysis: Studies in human interaction.* The Hague, the Netherlands: Mouton.

Bott, E. (1971). *Family and social network: Roles, norms, and external relationships among ordinary urban families* (2nd ed.). New York: Free Press.

Bronfenbrenner, U. (1979). *The ecology of human development.* Cambridge: Harvard University Press.

Brownell, A., & Schumaker, S. (Eds.). (1984). Social support: New perspectives in theory, research, and intervention: Part 1. Theory and research (Special issue). *Journal of Social Issues, 40*(4).

Bruhn, J., & Philips, B. (1987). A developmental basis for social support. *Journal of Behavioral Medicine, 10,* 213–229.

Bukowski, W., & Newcomb, A. (1983). The association between peer experiences and identity formation in early adolescence. *Journal of Early Adolescence, 3,* 265–274.

Cairns, R., Gariepy, J., & Kindermann, T. (in press). Identifying social clusters in natural settings. *Psychological Bulletin.*

Cairns, R., Perrin, J., & Cairns, B. (1985). Social structure and social cognition in early adolescence: Affiliative patterns. *Journal of Early Adolescence, 5,* 339–355.

Coates, D. (1985). Relationships between self-concept measures and social network characteristics of black adolescents. *Journal of Early Adolescence, 5,* 319–338.

Coates, D. (1987). Gender differences in the structure and support characteristics of black adolescents' social networks. *Sex Roles, 17,* 667–687.

Coates, D. (1990). Social network analysis as mental health intervention with African-American adolescents. In F. C. Serafica, A. I. Schwebel, R. K. Russell, D. D. Isaac, & L. B. Meyers (Eds.), *Mental health of ethnic minorities.* New York: Praeger.

Compas, B. (1987). Coping with stress during childhood and adolescence. *Psychological Bulletin, 98,* 393–403.

Cooley, C. (1902). *Human nature and the social order.* New York: Scribners.

Cooper, C. (1987). Conceptualizing research on adolescent development in the family: Four root metaphors. *Journal of Adolescent Research, 2,* 321–330.

Crouse, R. (1985). Using peer network therapy with a residential program for Chicano students. *Journal of College Student Personnel, 26,* 549–550.

Donald, C., & Ware, J. (1984). The measurement of social support. *Research in Community and Mental Health, 4,* 325–370.

Feiring, C., & Coates, D. (Eds.). (1987). Social networks and gender differences in the life space of opportunity (Special issue). *Sex Roles, 17.*

Felner, R., Aber, M., Primavera, J., & Cauce, A. (1985). Adaptation and vulnerability in high-risk adolescents: An examination of environmental mediators. *American Journal of Community Psychology, 13,* 365–379.

Feltham, R., Doyles, A., Schwartzman, L., & Serbin, L. (1985). Friendship in normal and socially deviant children. *Jorunal of Early Adolescence, 5,* 371–382.

Fischer, J. (1981). Transitions in relationship style from adolescence to young adulthood. *Journal of Youth and Adolescence, 10,* 11–24.

Fischer, J., Sollie, D., & Morrow, K. (1986). Social networks in male and female adolescents. *Journal of Adolescent Research, 1,* 1–14.

Galbo, J. (1983). Adolescents' perceptions of significant adults. *Adolescence, 18,* 417–427.

Garbarino, J., Burston, N., Raber, S., Russell, R., & Crouter, A. (1978). The social maps of children approaching adolescence: Studying the ecology of youth and development. *Journal of Youth and Adolescence, 7,* 417–428.

Gottlieb, B. (Ed.). (1981). *Social networks and social support.* Beverly Hills, CA: Sage.

Gottlieb, B., & Hall, A. (1980). Social networks and the utilization of preventive mental health services. In R. Price, R. Ketterer, B. Bader, & J. Monahan (Eds.), *Prevention in mental health: Research, policy, and practice* (pp. 167–194). Beverly Hills, CA: Sage.

Greenberger, E., & Sorensen, A. (1974). Toward a concept of psychosocial maturity. *Journal of Youth and Adolescence, 3,* 329–358.

Grotevant, H. (1987). Toward a process model of identity formation. *Journal of Adolescent Research, 2,* 203–222.

Hinde, R., Perret-Clermont, A., & Stevenson-Hinde, J. (Eds.). (1985). *Social relationships and cognitive development.* Oxford: Clarendon Press.

Hirsch, B., & Rapin, B. (1987). The transition to junior high school: A longitudinal study of self-esteem, psychological symptomatology, school life, and social support. *Child Development, 58,* 1235–1243.

Hunter, F. (1985). Individual adolescents' perceptions of interactions with friends and parents. *Journal of Early Adolescence, 5,* 295–306.

Hunger, F., & Youniss, J. (1982). Changes in the functions of three relationships during adolescence. *Developmental Psychology, 18,* 806–811.

Kidwell, S., Dunham, R., Peppin, T., & Passarello, L. (1986). The adolescent-in-the-family: The effect of historical influence on the growth of a science. *Journal of Adolescent Research, 1,* 33–46.

LaGaipa, J. (1979). A developmental study of the meaning of friendship in adolescence. *Journal of Adolescence, 3,* 1–13.

LaGaipa, J., & Wood, D. (1985). An Eriksonian approach to conceptions of friendship of aggressive and withdrawn preadolescent girls. *Journal of Early Adolescence, 5,* 357–369.

Leinhart, S. (Ed.). (1977). *Social networks: A developing paradigm.* New York: Academic Press.

Lerner, J., & Lerner, R. (1989). Longitudinal analysis of biological, psychological, and social interactions across the transitions of

early adolescence. *Journal of Early Adolescence, 9,* 175–180.

Margolin, L., Blyth, D., & Carbone, D. (1988). The family as a looking glass: Interpreting family influences on adolescent self-esteem from a symbolic interactionist perspective. *Journal of Early Adolescence, 8,* 211–224.

Mead, G. (1934). *Mind, self, and society.* Chicago: University of Chicago Press.

Merton, R. (1957). *Social theory and social structure.* Glencoe, IL: Free Press.

Montemayer, R., & Van Komen, R. (1985). The development of sex differences in friendship patterns and peer group structure during adolescence. *Journal of Early Adolescence, 5,* 285–294.

Nadel, S. F. (1951). *The foundations of social anthropology.* London: Cohen & West.

Newcomb, M., & Bentler, P. (1988). Impact of adolescent drug use and social support on problems of young adults: A longitudinal study. *Journal of Abnormal Psychology, 79,* 64–75.

Nitz, K., Lerner, R., Lerner, J., & Talwar, R. (1988). Parental and peer ethnotheory demands, temperament, and early adolescent adjustment. *Journal of Early Adolescence, 8,* 243–264.

Oliveri, M., & Reiss, D. (1981). The structure of familes' ties to their kin: The shaping role of social constructions. *Journal of Marriage and the Family, 43,* 391–407.

Oliveri, M., & Reiss, D. (1987). Social networks of family members: Distinctive roles of mothers and fathers. *Sex Roles, 17,* 719–736.

Peterson, G., Stivers, M., & Peters, D. (1986). Family versus nonfamily significant others for the career decisions of low-income youth. *Family Relations, 35,* 417–424.

Rosen, R. (1982). Childhood support networks: A study of pediatric and psychiatric outpatients. *Clinical Proceedings, CHNMC, 38,* 314–329.

Sebald, H. (1977). *Adolescence: A social psychological analysis* (2nd ed.). Englewood Cliffs, NJ: Prentice-Hall.

Serafica, F., & Blyth, D. (Eds.). (1985). Contemporary approaches to friendship and peer relations in early adolescence (Special issue). *Journal of Early Adolescence, 5.*

Shade, B. (1983). The social success of black youth: The impact of significant others. *Journal of Black Studies, 14,* 137–150.

Shrauger, J., & Schoeneman, T. (1979). Symbolic interactionist view of the self-concept: Through the looking glass darkly. *Psychological Bulletin, 86,* 549–573.

Shrum, W., & Cheek, N. (1987). Social structure during the school years: Onset of the degrouping process. *American Sociological Review, 52,* 218–223.

Simmons, R., Burgeson, R., Carlton-Ford, S., & Blyth, D. (1988). The impact of cumulative change in early adolescence. *Child Development, 56,* 1220–1234.

Stevens, J., Jr. (1988). Social support, locus of control, and parenting in three low-income groups of mothers: Black teenagers, black adults, and white adults. *Child Development, 59,* 635–642.

Speck, J., & Speck, R. (1985). Social network intervention with adolescents. In M. Mirkin & S. Koman (Eds.), *Handbook of adolescence and family therapy* (pp. 149–160). New York: Garner.

Thoits, P. A. (1986). Social support as coping assistance. *Journal of Consulting and Clinical Psychology, 54,* 416–423.

Trimble, D. (1981). Social network intervention with antisocial adolescents. *International Journal of Family Therapy, 3,* 268–274.

Unger, D., & Wandersman, P. (1988). The relations of family and partner support for the adjustment of adolescent mothers. *Child Development, 59,* 1056–1060.

Vaux, A. (1987). Appraisals of social support: Love, respect, and involvement. *Journal of Community Psychology, 15,* 493–502.

Whitten, N., Jr., & Wolfe, A. (1973). Network analysis. In J. Honigman (Ed.), *Handbook of social and cultural anthropology* (pp. 717–746). Chicago: Rand-McNally.

Youniss, J. (1980). *Parents and peers in social development: A Sullivan-Piagetian perspective.* Chicago: University of Chicago Press.

Youniss, J., & Smollar, J. (1985). *Adolescent relations with mothers, fathers, and friends.* Chicago: University of Chicago Press.

See Also

Dating during Adolescence; Friendships; Peer Counseling: A Human Resource Program; Peer Group Status; Peer Relations and Influences.

Spatial Ability and Maturation in Adolescence

Deborah P. Waber
The Children's Hospital, Boston

The impact of the biological events of puberty on cognition has been a natural focus of interest for students of child development: the co-occurrence of dramatic changes in the physical and psychological domains in a population in whom measurement is relatively accessible and reliable (compared, for example, to infants) presents an ideal milieu for studying these fundamental relationships. Initially, attempts were made, some more successful than others, to relate global indices of maturation to global indices of cognitive development (Eichorn, 1963; Douglas, Ross, & Simpson, 1965; Bayley, 1950). Such relationships, however, were neither clear nor straightforward. And, as the theoretical climate in child development research shifted, with greater emphasis being placed on learning and experiential influences on behavioral development, interest in this issue waned and formal research became sparse. The concept of maturational factors as contributors to behavioral development fell out of favor.

In the 1970s, however, there began to be a shift away from the emphasis on environmental influences and toward behavioral development, now with more integrated approaches encompassing biological factors, such as genetics, hormonal influences, and neurological bases of behavior, in addition to experiential ones. In this context, the psychobiological aspects of adolescent development again attracted interest.

This approach to the question, unlike that of the earlier investigators, focused not on global indicators of maturation and cognition, but on more specific components. A hallmark of the adolescent transition—cognitive as well as physiological—is the emergence of clear patterns of sexual differentiation. Not only do males and females exhibit dramatic differences in terms of secondary sexual characteristics (Tanner, 1962), but they begin to exhibit sexually differentiated patterns of cognitive abilities, or skills, as well (Maccoby & Jacklin, 1974).

A pioneering series of studies was conducted by Donald Broverman and his colleagues (Broverman, Broverman, Vogel, Palmer, & Klaiber, 1964; Broverman, Klaiber, Kobayashi, & Vogel, 1968), who worked within the context of a cognitive style model, examining *intra*individual differences in the way children approach new and complex tasks. They administered an extensive test battery, whose scores were submitted to a statistical "ipsatization" procedure, the end result of which characterized the child as strong (relative to himself) at "automatization" (rapid, repetitive motor output) or "perceptual restructuring" (reorganization of visual perceptual material). They found that boys who exhibited greater androgenization, as measured by physical markers such as body hair, were likely to be stronger automatizers as well. Similarly, Petersen (1976) reanalyzed data from the Fels Growth Study and reported that a high degree of androgenization was associated with better spatial ability in females but weaker spatial ability in males.

A somewhat different perspective was introduced by Waber (1976, 1977), who noted that early-maturing males and late-maturing females were also likely to exhibit the physical markers of increased androgenization. She proposed that rate of maturation might be the relevant variable, with early maturation being associated with a pattern of better verbal (e.g., automatization, fluent production) than spatial skills (e.g., perceptual restructuring) and the reverse for late maturation. Since females as a group typically show an advantage for verbal skills and males for spatial skills, Waber hypothesized that these sex differences in cognitive skills might in fact reflect the sex difference in rate of physical maturation: females being the earlier maturing sex would be expected to show a predisposition for a verbal pattern superior to spatial pattern and males the reverse. Moreover, she proposed that the maturation-related differences were mediated by differences in cerebral organization of function, based on arguments that more complete laterali-

zation of language is associated with better spatial ability (Levy, 1969), and that males exhibit more complete lateralization (Bryden, 1979). In fact, late-maturing children of both sexes outperformed early maturers on spatial ability tasks and showed more pronounced lateralization on a dichotic listening task.

Since the initial report a number of investigators have replicated the basic finding that late maturation is associated with increased spatial ability by measuring the two domains concurrently in pubertal age children (Diamond, Carey, & Back, 1983; Newcombe & Bandura, 1983; Waber, Bauermeister, Cohen, Ferber, & Wolff, 1981; Waber, Mann, Merola, & Moylan, 1985) as well as retrospectively in young adults (Ray, Newcombe, Semon, & Cole, 1981; Sanders & Soares, 1986). Despite the fact that the basic finding has been replicated, however, it is by no means universal (i.e., occurring in every sample tested), nor is the effect typically a large one (Newcombe & Dubas, 1987).

Two questions, then, are pertinent. The first concerns factors that can influence the presence or absence of the effect; and the second the significance of this body of research and the maturation rate "phenomenon" itself.

There is a tendency to associate biological factors with determinism: it is often assumed that if biological factors are involved in behavioral development they are innate and will therefore determine the behavior in a fixed way. Thus, the expectation is that if a psychobiological relationship can be demonstrated it will inevitably appear. This is, of course, not the case, the evidence generally supporting a more systemic interpretation where biological, environmental, and behavioral factors comprise a unified *system* that has its own properties (see, for example, Bernstein & Waber, in press, and Waber, 1985, for extended discussion of systemic approaches). Within the context of such a perspective, changes in one component of the system can be expected to affect the others, such that the target relationship will appear in some circumstances but not others.

Thus, the central question to be asked in future research is not whether the phenomenon does or does not exist, but how and under what circumstances it can be expected to appear and, more important, what its appearance or failure to appear tells us about the broader properties of the system of which it is a component. Waber et al. (1981), for instance, found maturational status to be strongly related to performance on a map-walking task, but among middle-class children only; low SES children failed to show the effect. A companion finding of SES-related differences in indicators of the functional activity of the CNS (Waber, Carlson, Mann, Merola, & Moylan, 1984) suggests how experiential factors may serve to influence cognitive processing in important ways that may serve to alter the parameters of the system itself. Rather than focusing exclusively on direct correlations of one set of variables with another as if they were fixed entities, it is necessary to view these relationships in a more dynamic context.

Another related question is the choice of outcome measures. As Sanders and Soares (1986) pointed out, there is no reason to assume that any task that has face validity as a measure of visuospatial skill will necessarily be related to maturation rate. Waber et al. (1985), for example, reported that the maturation phenomenon could not be documented when the outcome measures were summary scores from complex, standardized tasks, but that there were nevertheless systematic differences between early- and late-maturing youngsters when more basic components of cog-

nitive processing were elicited. Thus, the biologically relevant behavior is probably not isomorphic with psychometrically derived measures of spatial skills but more likely reflects fundamental components of cognitive processing that contribute to performance on the more complex, standardized tasks.

Finally, the broader significance of the data on the relation between maturation rate and performance on spatial ability tasks needs to be addressed. Given the available data, the evidence is mounting that while there is a relationship between maturation rate and spatial ability, it does not explain the persistent sex differences in these abilities, as Waber had originally hypothesized (Sanders & Soares, 1986). Even so, there remains an intriguing phenomenon that has yet to be adequately explained. Physical maturation rate itself must, of course, be viewed as an epiphenomenon, that is, it is an end-result or manifestation of a constellation of endocrinological and ultimately genetic events, not a discrete biological phenomenon in itself. What the salient endocrinological events are, and, more specifically, the nature of the individual differences and how they affect CNS development at puberty, remain as elusive now as they were when the existence of such a relationship was first reported by Broverman. Whether there is some critical biological event early in development that later manifests itself as maturation rate and processing of visuospatial information, as might be suggested by work derived from animal models (Hines, 1982; Resnick, Berenbaum, Gottesman, & Bouchard, 1986), or whether the biological events themselves influence CNS function only at adolescence (not mutually exclusive possibilities) remain to be discovered. Given the research to date, therefore, the major significance of the maturation rate-spatial ability phenomenon lies not in its ability to explain sex differences, but in its potential as a vehicle for investigating the development of the CNS at puberty.

References

Bernstein, J. H., & Waber, D. P. (in press). Developmental neuropsychological assessment: The systemic approach. In A. A. Boulton, G. B. Baker, & M. Hiscock (Eds.), *Neuromethods: Vol. 15, Neuropsychology.* Clifton, NJ: Humana Press.

Broverman, D. M., Broverman, I. K., Vogel, W., Palmer, R. D., & Klaiber, E. L. (1964). The automatization cognitive style and physical development. *Child Development, 35,* 1343–1359.

Broverman, D. M., Klaiber, E. L., Kobayashi, Y., & Vogel, W. (1968). Roles of activation and inhibition in sex differences in cognitive abilities. *Psychological Review, 75,* 23–50.

Bryden, M. P. (1979). Evidence for sex-related differences in cerebral organization. In M. Wittig & A. C. Petersen (Eds.), *Sex-related differences in cognitive functioning: Developmental issues* (pp. 121–144). New York: Academic Press.

Diamond, R., Carey, S., & Back, K. (1983). Genetic influences on the development of spatial skills during early adolescence. *Cognition, 13,* 167–185.

Douglas, Ross, & Simpson, (1965). The relation between height and measured educational ability in school children of the same social class, family size, and stage of sexual development. *Human Biology, 37,* 178–186.

Eichorn, D. H. (1963). Biological correlates of behavior. In H. W. Stevenson (Ed.), *Yearbook of the National Society for the Study of Education, 62* (Part 1),

Hines, M. (1982). Prenatal gonadal hormones and sex differences in human behavior. *Psychological Bulletin, 92,* 56–80.

Jones, M. C., & Bayley, N. (1950). Physical maturing among boys as related to behavior. *Journal of Educational Psychology, 41,* 129–148.

Levy, J. (1969). Possible basis for the evolution of lateral specialization of the human brain. *Nature, 224,* 614–615.

Maccoby, E. E., & Jacklin, C. N. (1974). *The psychology of sex differences.* Stanford: Stanford University Press.

Newcombe, N., & Bandura, M. M. (1983). Effect of age at puberty on spatial ability in girls: A question of mechanism. *Developmental Psychology, 19,* 215–224.

Newcombe, N., & Dubas, J. S. (1987). Individual differences in cognitive ability: Are they related to timing of puberty? In R. M. Lerner & T. T. Foch (Eds.), *Biological-psychosocial interaction in early adolescence* (pp. 249–302). Hillsdale, NJ: Lawrence Erlbaum Associates.

Petersen, A. C. (1976). Physical androgyny and cognitive functioning in adolescence. *Developmental Psychology, 12,* 524–533.

Ray, W. J., Newcombe, N., Semon, J., & Cole, P. M. (1981). Spatial abilities, sex differences, and EEG functioning. *Neuropsychologia, 19,* 719–722.

Resnick, S. M., Berenbaum, S. A., Gottesman, I. I., Bouchard, T. J. (1986). Early hormonal influences on cognitive functioning in congenital adrenal hyperplasia. *Developmental Psychology, 22,* 191–198.

Sanders, B., & Soares, M. P. (1986). Sexual maturation and spatial ability in college students. *Developmental Psychology, 22,* 199–203.

Tanner, J. M. (1962). *Growth at adolescence.* London: Blackwell.

Waber, D. P. (1976). Sex differences in cognition: A function of maturation rate? *Science, 192,* 572–574.

Waber, D. P. (1977). Sex differences in mental abilities, hemispheric lateralization, and rate of physical growth at adolescence. *Developmental Psychology, 13,* 29–38.

Waber, D. P. (1985). The search for biological correlates of behavioural sex differences in humans. In J. Ghesquiere, R. D. Martin, & F. Newcombe (Eds.), *Human sexual dimorphism.* (pp. 251–282). London: Taylor & Francis.

Waber, D. P., Bauermeister, M., Cohen, C., Ferber, R., & Wolff, P. H. (1981). Behavioral correlates of physical and neuromotor maturity in adolescents from different environments. *Developmental Psychology, 14,* 513–522.

Waber, D. P., Carlson, D., Mann, M., Merola, J., & Moylan, P. (1984). SES-related aspects of neuropsychological performance. *Child Development, 55,* 1878–1886.

Waber, D. P., Mann, M. B., Merola, J., & Moylan, P. M. (1985). Physical maturation rate and cognitive performance in early adolescence: A longitudinal examination. *Developmental Psychology, 21,* 666–681.

See Also

Cognition, Adolescent; Cognition and Health; Cognitive Abilities and Physical Maturation; Cognitive and Psychosocial Gender Differences, Trends in; Cognitive Development; Egocentrism Theory and the "New Look" at the Imaginary Audience and Personal Fable in Adolescence; Formal Operational Thinking and Identity Resolution; Illness, Adolescents' Conceptualization of; Inhelder, Barbel; Introspectiveness, Adolescent; Memory; Piaget, Jean; Relativistic Thinking in Adolescence; Reasoning, Higher-Order, in Adolescence; Reasoning in the Adolescent; Scientific Reasoning, Adolescent; Social Intelligence in Adolescence.

Spermarche

Howard E. Kulin

*The Pennsylvania State University
College of Medicine*

The term *spermarche*, indicative of the age of onset of reproductive potential in the male, has been coined as an analogy to *menarche*. Remarkably few studies exist for the delineation of this important event in the male. Histologic data are sparse, but they generally indicate a time period between 12 to 16 years of age; no precise association with pubertal stage or hormone values has been published in histologic investigations.

Since ethical and social considerations have made it impossible to examine semen collections via masturbation, an indirect approach has been chosen. Over the past 10 years five published studies from three laboratories have attempted to observe sperm in overnight urine collections and thereby compute the age of spermarche. The fertilizing capacity of these gametes remains unknown, but—more than likely—urinary sperm are meaningful indicators of this potential. How sperm get into the urinary tract is also unclear, but spermaturia probably reflects urethral washings after an ejaculation—either from a nocturnal emission or by masturbation.

Despite the relatively few investigations available, techniques for observing sperm have varied considerably. There has been little standardization with respect to the amount of urine concentrated, microscopic observation techniques, or sensitivity of the procedure. Generally, the identification of a single sperm has been considered significant. Furthermore, the intermittent nature of spermaturia has long been recognized. For these reasons multiple collections spanning a week or more must be performed to ascertain the existence of sperm in urine during adolescence.

Notwithstanding these limitations, there is general agreement that spermarche is a relatively early maturational event. A longitudinal study that took into account the frequent false negative urine specimens as well as the sampling interval employed proposed a median age of spermarche of 13.4 years, with a range from 11.7 to 15.3 years. All studies agree that the median age of onset of spermaturia is usually by the 14th birthday. Of interest is the fact that this age is very similar to the time obtained in an investigation of the age of first conscious ejaculation (not nocturnal emission).

There are also data that relate spermarche to secondary sex characteristics. The event is midpubertal if pubic hair, genital stage, testes size, and the growth spurt are all taken together. Pubic hair is very variable in its appearance during adolescence, and many boys with spermaturia have only small amounts. However, testes size is usually well advanced and peak height velocity occurs in boys at approximately age 14.

The hormone constituents of spermarche are particularly understudied. Nonetheless, it would appear that mid-pubertal amounts of urinary testosterone and urinary luteinizing hormone (LH) are associated with the phenomenon. Our own results using overnight urine samples indicate follicle-stimulating hormone (FSH) has reached well into the adult range by the age of spermarche.

References

Hirsch, M., Lunenfeld, B., Modan, M., Ovadia, J., & Shemesh, J. (1985). Spermarche—The age of onset of sperm emission. *Journal of Adolescent Health Care 6*, 35–39.

Kulin, H. E., Frontera, M. A., Demers, L. M., Bartholomew, M. J. & Lloyd, T. A. (1989). The onset of sperm production in pubertal boys. *American Journal of Diseases of Children 143*, 190–193.

Laron, Z., Gurewitz, R., Grunebaum, M., & Dickerman, Z. (1980). Age of first conscious ejaculation: A milestone in male puberty. *Helvetica Paediatrica Acta 35*, 13–20.

Nielsen, C. T., Skakkebaek, N. E., Darling, J. A. B., Hunter, W. M., Richardson, D. W., Jorgensen, J., & Keiding, N. (1986). Longitudinal study of testosterone and luteinizing hormone (LH) in relation to spermarche, pubic hair, height, and sitting height in normal boys. *Acta Endocrinology 113*, 98–106.

Nielsen, C. T., Skakkebaek, N. E., Richardson, D. W., Darling, J. A. B., Hunter, W. M., Jorgensen, M., Nielsen, A., Ingerslev, O., Keiding, N., & Muller, J. (1986). Onset of the release of spermatozoa (spermarche) in boys in relation to age, testicular growth, pubic hair, and height. *Journal of Clinical Endocrinology and Metabolism, 62*, 532–535.

See Also

Cognitive Abilities and Physical Maturation; Growth Spurt, Adolescent; Maturational Timing, Antecedents of in Girls; Maturational Timing Variations in Adolescent Girls, Consequences of; Menarche and Body Image; Menarche, Secular Trend in Age of; Menstrual Cycle; Physical Status and Timing in Early Adolescence, Measurement of; Pubertal Development, Assessment of; Puberty, Body Fat and; Puberty Education; Puberty, Endocrine Changes at; Puberty, Hypothalamic-Pituitary Changes of; Puberty, Precocious, Treatment of; Puberty, Sport and; Spatial Ability and Maturation in Adolescence.

Spina Bifida, the Adolescent with

Robert W. Blum

University of Minnesota

Spina bifida is a defect in the development of the neural tube that occurs during fetal growth with the result that there is incomplete formation of the spinal cord and, frequently, an associated hydrocephalus. Depending on where along the spinal cord the defect occurs will determine, to a great extent, the degree of disability the child experiences: the higher up the spinal canal is the lesion, the greater tends to be the impairment of bladder, bowel, genital sensation, and ambulation.

Less than 30 years ago, the prevailing notion was that most children with this condition were doomed to severe mental retardation and profound disability. Advances in antibiotic and neurosurgical management of infants, coupled with more vigorous treatment, has resulted in an increasing number of individuals surviving childhood into adolescence and adulthood. In fact, over the past 25 years, the improved survival through the second decade of life is between 200 and 400%. As a consequence, there is an ever-increasing number of adolescents and young adults with a condition heretofore relatively unknown beyond childhood.

Developing with Spina Bifida

From a developmental perspective, the tempo of physical maturation for youths with spina bifida is out of pace with non-disabled peers. Specifically, as is the case with most neural tube defects, the majority of teens with this condition will start puberty significantly earlier than peers. For example, the average age for menarche among girls with spina bifida is 11.4 years compared with approximately 12.5 years for most American females. In addition, youths with spina bifida tend to be both shorter and heavier than peers.

The alterations in the timing of puberty have significant consequences for youths with spina bifida. At an age when appearing different runs a significant risk of social isolation, youths with spina bifida have both the stigmata of precocious puberty and their condition. Yet the relationship between social isolation and physical limitations is not linear. Rather, social relations are heavily influenced by the extent of *perceived* disability. It appears that it is one's self-image rather than the severity of disability that will determine social competence. And among teenagers with spina bifida, it appears that those with the *least* physical involvement have the most disturbed sense of self.

Peer and Friendship Patterns

When one looks closely at the nature of friendship patterns for youths with spina bifida, the image of social isolation becomes sharper: "best" friends are often significantly younger or older, out-of-school contacts with friends are rare, and very few date during adolescence. Most youths with spina bifida have "best" friends who are nondisabled; and few would choose to make friends with a peer with spina bifida over one who is nondisabled. The rejection of those with similar physical attributes to oneself has a marked impact on social isolation and on self-image.

Lack of contact with peers during the teenage years, low self-esteem, and overdependence on parents for meeting personal needs (e.g., bowel programs and mobility needs) have negative consequences for many teenagers with spina bifida. Suicidal ideation has been reported among 25 to 50% of this population.

Parent Relationships

Limited contact with peers tends to be compensated by prolonged dependence on, and affiliation with, parents. A dynamic that tends to characterize the parent-teen relationship in families where the adolescent has spina bifida is perceived harmony. Such was the perception of youth in a recent study in Minnesota where, almost without exception, all respondents reported close relationships with parents.

Additionally, most youths in the Minnesota study indicated that their parents treat them in an age-appropriate manner. Noticeable in its absence is a sense of adolescent rebellion. While a quarter of youths in the Minnesota study indicated that their parents tend to infantilize them, and an equal proportion believed that they were overprotected, parental dependence remains high, with over one-third of youths indicating continued dependence on parents for their bowel program.

While there is a perception of closeness with parents, few teens with spina bifida recall talking with their parents about personal issues such as sexuality. In the Minnesota study noted above, only one-third of the group ($n = 34$) ever recall discussing pubertal maturation with either parent. Interestingly, of those who had not spoken with a parent, only eight had ever spoken with anyone else—primarily friends and siblings. Among females, just over half reported discussing menstruation and, for most of those, the discussion was seen as brief and uninformative.

Another function that the family serves is to provide the adolescent with a sense of value and utility within a social system. Parental expectations are expressed both verbally and nonverbally. Almost all able-bodied adolescents have specific chores and delegations at home, but few teens with spina bifida have responsibilities beyond personal care (e.g., hygiene, making own bed).

What we are left with is a parent-adolescent relationship frequently intertwined with substantial needs for assistance with activities of daily life coupled with a perception of closeness in excess of actual behavior. While the perception of closeness and dependence is at times comforting, it may further serve to isolate the adolescent with spina bifida from his/her peers.

School

School represents the major setting of peer interactions for the adolescent with spina bifida. In comparing regular and special school settings, it has been found that teenagers with spina bifida who had attended both types of institutions unanimously preferred regular schools. They feel that normal school settings helped them develop some of the needed social skills to live in an able-bodied society. However, regular schools often are not without their problems. Peer relationships are frequently described as strained. Many spina bifida youth reported having been teased, stared at, and questioned excessively by able-bodied peers. The major deficit of regular schools noted by youth with spina bifida is in the area of vocational counseling.

Beyond the social function of the educational setting are the academic and intellectual requirements. The data are overwhelming that academically, as well as socially, regular schools are far superior to special educational settings. O'Moore and Carr found that youth with spina bifida in regular schools were academically far more advanced in both reading and mathematics than comparable youths in special schools.

It has been shown dramatically that academic performance of children and youth is closely correlated with teacher expectations. Having few, if any, prior encounters with youth with spina bifida, most teachers are poorly informed and ill-prepared to establish developmentally and intellectually appropriate expectations for these students. As a result, they can be manipulated by such students to establish lower performance requirements than should be appropriate. In the short run, spina bifida students might be relieved of specific school assignments, but the long-run consequence is that manipulation as a coping mechanism is reinforced at the cost of education and self-esteem.

Beyond its academic and social functions, the school setting represents an important locus of advice for both parents and youth for coping with day-to-day problems. School departure or graduation often represents a major source of support and continuity not only for the teenager but his/her parents as well.

Employment

Work and future employment represent a considerable source of anxiety for youth with spina bifida and their families. Vocational counseling is a major deficit in their education, and future employment also is a major concern of parents. These concerns appear well justified. In one study, less than 50% of adolescents with spina bifida who had left school had any prospect for desired employment. In another study, while 66% of young adults with spina bifida were employed, only 20% had a job with any security. The lack of mobility seemed to be the major liability to employment. Employers give many reasons for not hiring disabled individuals, including presumed increase of insurance rates; a need to make major adjustments in the work place to accommodate those with disabilities; resentment by able-bodied employees because of special advantages those with disabilities would receive; and lack of acceptance by other employees.

The data do not substantiate these concerns. The Du Pont Corporation, with an extensive program for hiring handicapped employees, found no increase in workmen's compensation costs as a result of their employment policies. The U.S. Chamber of Commerce, in a study conducted with the National Association of Manufacturers, found that of 279 companies, 90% experienced no increase in their insurance costs as a result of hiring handicapped individuals. This study also indicated that physical changes necessary in the work place were, in most situations, minimal, usually consisting of a special desk or installation of entrance ramps.

The DuPont study found that, of their 1400 handicapped employees, 96% had better safety records than their able-bodied counterparts. Fellow employees did not consider handicapped parking spaces or minor work place adjustments as representing special privileges.

In summary, the barriers that inhibit those with spina bifida from entering the work place seem to reside less in objective reality than in the minds of themselves and their potential employers.

Conclusion

What we are left with is a picture of the teenager with spina bifida who is precocious in physical development, arrested in social development, mobile yet often in need of assistance for ambulation. Almost without exception these youths live at home and view their relationships with parents as strong while dependence on parents for activities of daily living is significant. Despite the perceived closeness, few have discussed with their parents either issues of sexuality or menstruation. In fact, few have ever had the opportunity to discuss these issues with anyone.

As with all youths, for these teens peers are very important; however, the social contact with peers is relatively limited and social isolation is often a consequence. Social isolation, low self-esteem, delayed social development, and depression are often interrelated, and these factors tend to correlate more with perceived rather than actual disability.

While we have reason to celebrate the medical advances that have resulted in improved life expectancy for those with spina bifida, there is much yet to be done to bring these youths into the mainstream so as to maximize their potential as well as to improve the quality of their lives.

References

Blum, R. (1983). The adolescent with spina bifida. *Clinical Pediatrics, 22*(5), 331–335.

Blum, R., St. Germaine, A., Resnick, M., & Nelson, R. (in press). Family and peer issues among adolescents with spina bifida. *Pediatrics.*

Carr, J., et al. (1981). Educational attainments of spina bifida children attending ordinary or special schools. *Zeitschrift fur Kinderchirurgie 34*, 364–370.

Castree, B., & Walker, J. (1981). The young adult with spina bifida. *British Medical Journal, 283*, 1040–1042.

Dorner, S. (1977a). Problems of teenagers. *Physiotherapy, 63*, 190–192.

Dorner, S. (1977b). Sexual interest and activity in adolescents with spina bifida. *Journal of Child Psychology and Psychiatry, 18*, 229–237.

Hayden, P., Davenport, S., & Campbell, M. (1979). Adolescents with myelodysplasia: Impact of physical disability on emotional maturation. *Pediatrics, 64*, 53–59.

McAndres, I. (1979). Adolescents and young people with spina bifida. *Developmental Medicine and Child Neurology, 21*, 619–629.

National Association for Manufacturing. (1955). *Guide for employers in hiring the physically handicapped.* New York: Author.

Sears, J. (1958). *DuPont survey of handicapped employees.* Wilmington, DE: DuPont.

Shurtleff, D., & Sousa, J. (1977). Adolescent with myelodysplasia: Development achievement, sex, and deterioration. In R. McLaurin (Ed.), *Myelomeningocele.* Chicago: Grune and Stratton.

See Also

Stimulants

John D. Swisher
The Pennsylvania State University

Stimulants are central nervous system enhancers that increase heart rate, blood pressure, and pulmonary activity, dilate pupils, elevate mood, and decrease appetite. Stimulants range in potency from mild (e.g., caffeine) to strong (e.g., cocaine). The actual effects of various stimulants are interactive with dosage, administration, body characteristics, prior experience, and psychosocial expectations (Swisher, 1979).

Medical use of stimulants includes treatment for obesity, narcolepsy, and, paradoxically, hyperactivity. Stimulants are used illegally to enhance academic, social, and athletic performance, but their excessive use can interfere with psychological and physiological functioning. Cocaine snorting typically disrupts the mucosal membrane and irritates the nasal passageway. Regular inhalation can cause ulceration of the septum. Dependency on cocaine may be very rapid and sudden death from heart failure may occur. Injection of any stimulant is associated with AIDS and hepatitis. Dependency on stimulants is both physiological and psychological in nature and withdrawal is associated with depression and fatigue. Interference with adolescent development has not been clarified in current research.

Adolescent use of various stimulants has been given considerable attention by the mass media but usually without providing perspective on other concerns. The major issue centers on use of cocaine (including crack). An annual survey of stimulant use by high school seniors (Johnston, O'Malley, & Bachman, 1989) indicates that regular use (use in the last 30 days) of cocaine increased from 2% in 1975 to 7% in 1986. Unfortunately, use of caffeine (e.g., sodas) is not assessed, but would reflect greater regular use. Similarly, alcohol use (see Table 1) reflects much greater regular use than stimulants and is associated with highway deaths, suicide, and teenage pregnancy.

Table 1 compares stimulants and cocaine with alcohol and marijuana regarding regular use (i.e., use in the last 30 days), perceived degree of harmfulness, and use by best friends. The data indicate that alcohol and marijuana use are substantially greater and the perceived harmfulness is proportionally lower. Best friend use is approximately equal to levels of respondent's use.

TABLE 1
ADOLESCENT USE, FRIENDS USE AND PERCEIVED HARMFULNESS OF AMPHETAMINES, COCAINE, MARIJUANA AND ALCOHOL AMONG HIGH SCHOOL SENIORS IN 1986

	AMPHETAMINES	COCAINE	MARIJUANA	ALCOHOL
Self-reported use in last 30 days				
Males	5.1	7.2	26.8	69.0
Females	5.8	5.1	20.0	61.9
Friends Use				
none	58.2	54.4	20.8	4.4
most or all	3.4	6.2	18.2	68.0
Harmfulness if used				
1 or 2 times	25.1	33.5	15.1	4.6
regularly	67.3	82.2	71.3	39.1

References

Johnston, L. D., O'Malley, P. M., & Bachman, J. G. (1989). *Drug use, drinking, and smoking: National survey results from high school, college, and young adults populations, 1975–1988.* Rockville, MD: National Institute on Drug Abuse.

Swisher, J. (1979). Diagnosis and treatment of drug and alcohol dependency. In K. Hylbert & W. Hylbert (Eds.), *Medical information for human service workers* (pp. 469–502). State College, PA: Counselor Education Press.

See Also
Anabolic-Androgenic Steroids, the Nonmedical Use by Adolescents; Cocaine Use among Adolescents and Young Adults, Antecedents/Predictors of; Drug Use, Adolescent; Drug Use, Epidemiology and Developmental Stages of Involvement; Drug Use, Minority Youth and; Drug Use, Predictors and Correlates of Adolescent; Hallucinogens; Health and Substance Abuse in Adolescence: Ethnic and Gender Perspectives; Pharmacology, Developmental; Smokeless Tobacco Use among Adolescents; Smoking and Drug Prevention with Early Adolescents, Programs for.

Stress and Coping in Adolescence

Aaron T. Ebata
University of Illinois at Urbana-Champaign

As children grow into adolescents they experience marked changes and transitions, both within themselves and in their environments (Hamburg, 1974; Petersen & Spiga, 1982). While many of these changes are normal, expected, and experienced by most youths (e.g., puberty, changing from elementary school to middle or junior high school), others may be non-normative, sudden, or unexpected (e.g., death of a parent, divorce, accident, or injury). For some individuals in certain circumstances a major change or a combination of changes can be overwhelming, making adolescence a particularly stressful period. Most youth manage to meet the challenges of the teen years successfully and grow into healthy, competent adults. Others experience difficulties that may occasionally reoccur, but are resolved in time. Some, unfortunately, continue to have difficulties that become more serious as they face the challenges of adulthood (Petersen, 1988).

This entry provides a brief overview and introduction to the research in stress and coping during adolescence. Readers interested in a more detailed treatment or a list of primary sources are directed to several recent reviews by Compas (1987a, 1987b), Johnson (1986), and Johnson and Bradlyn (1988). Additional sources are listed at the end of this entry. These reviews present findings from a variety of studies, summarize the conceptual and methodological issues that have limited previous research, and provide agendas for future study. Additional perspectives on the study of stress, transitions, vulnerability, and resilience to stress can be found in Felner (1984), Garmezy (1983), Hauser, Vieyra, Jacobsen, and Wertlieb (1985), McCubbin and Patterson (1986), and Rutter (1983, 1987).

Stress

Operational definitions of stress vary, but studies that use the concept in one form of another generally consider an event "stressful" if it (1) is linked to a negative outcome, (2) requires social readjustment or adaptive effort, or (3) is appraised by the subject as being stressful or undesirable. Many studies have focused on the effects of specific events or changes, such as divorce or making school transitions, that may be disruptive and put individuals at risk for adjustment problems. Other studies have focused on the cumulative effects of major events and changes that require social readjustment and adaptive effort. Having to cope with multiple, simultaneous (or sequential) changes in a given period of time (whether they be normative or nonnormative) may put greater demands on individuals and put them at greater risk for experiencing distress.

A number of measures and checklists have been developed to assess the cumulative life events and changes experienced by older children and adolescents (Coddington, 1972; Compas, Davis, Forsythe, & Wagner, 1987; Johnson & McCutcheon, 1980; Newcomb, Huba, & Bentler, 1981; Patterson & McCubbin, 1987; Swearingen & Cohen, 1985; Yeaworth, York, Hussey, Ingle, & Goodwin 1980). Generally, respondents are presented with a checklist of events, changes, or situations and asked to indicate whether or not they have experienced each event in the recent past. Although there are methodological differences between studies, some consistent results have emerged.

Cross-sectional studies of normative populations have consistently found that a greater frequency of negative events is related to higher levels of psychological, behavioral, and physical dysfunction, including depression, anxiety, and conduct problems. The predictive power of life events, however, is quite low, with correlations most often falling in the range between .20 and .30. Negative life events are also found more frequently among youth with clinically identified psychiatric problems than among physically and psychologically healthy youth.

There have been relatively few prospective studies where life events are assessed prior to measuring adjustment outcomes. These studies are important for identifying the causal relationship between life events and later adjustment. Most of these studies do not find a relationship between prior life events and psychological symptoms once prior adjustment is controlled. In fact, several studies show that prior symptoms are better predictors of later events than events are of symptoms. The apparent discrepancy from results of cross-sectional studies may be due to a number of theoretical and methodological issues. However, two sets of findings appear to be especially relevant.

First, recent studies have shown that measures of "smaller" everyday events ("daily hassles") or chronic, ongoing stressors (e.g., arguments with parents, having too much homework, etc.) are more predictive of psychological adjustment than acute major events. Second, the effects of major events may not be direct, but mediated by daily events. Major negative events may thus exert their influence by setting off a chain of events that change long-term ongoing daily experiences. It is daily experiences that have more of a direct and lasting impact on development.

Prediction may also improve if factors that may moderate the stress-outcome relationship are taken into account. Although experiencing certain events or a greater number of events may place adolescents at a greater statistical risk for adjustment problems, certain personal characteristics, behaviors, and environmental circumstances may increase or reduce the likelihood that stressful events and circumstances lead to maladjustment.

Personal characteristics are hypothesized to be important because they affect how individuals may appraise and cope with events, situations, and conditions. Individuals differ in how they perceive events (whether an event is desirable or undesirable, how much of an impact it may have, whether it is seen as a threat versus a challenge, whether it is controllable or not) as well as how they respond to and attempt to manage the event and its consequences. Several studies have found that girls rate events as being more stressful and report more negative events and daily hassles than boys. Higher correlations between events and symptoms have also been found for girls as compared to boys.

The effects of acute or chronic events may also depend on the interaction between the characteristics of the stressors and the characteristics of the individual. Certain types of events or changes in certain domains may be more salient (have greater potential impact) than others, and there may be individual differences in vulnerability to events in certain domains. Only a few attempts have been made to categorize stressors and to relate these different categories to outcomes. These attempts show differential relationships between different stressor domains and indices of adjustment. For example, family/parent stressors are consistently related to measures of depression, while correlations with other categories of events are much lower or nonsignificant. Daniels and Moos (1990) examined negative life events and chronic stressors and resources in eight adolescent life domains (e.g., physical health, school, relationships with parents, peer relationships, etc.) and found only moderate correlations among stressors in different domains. Ongoing stressors and resources from certain domains (physical health, home/money, parent, extended family, and school) and not others (sibling, friend, boy/girlfriend) were found to distinguish clinically depressed adolescents from healthy controls. When used to examine individual differences in adjustment, only certain stressor domains contributed to the prediction. For example, ongoing physical health and parent stressors predicted depression, while extended family and school stressors did not.

Adolescents also differ in their particu-lar living situations and the financial, physical, and social resources that are available to them. In general, a greater availability of social resources has positive effects on adjustment, although the conditions under which social support can "buffer" the effects of stress are still uncertain.

Differences in characteristics of the stressor, person, situation, and their interaction, however, are useful in that they suggest differences in the process of coping with stress. Studies of adaptation and personal characteristics related to adjustment are common in the developmental literature, but only recently have efforts focused on what adolescents actually do to manage specific problems, events, or situations.

Coping

Several frameworks have been used to describe and classify coping efforts in adults and to examine the relationship between coping and adjustment (Lazarus & Folkman, 1984; Menaghan, 1983; Moos & Billings, 1982; Roth & Cohen, 1986). Researchers have begun to use these models to assess and classify coping in children and adolescents (e.g., Band & Weisz, 1988; Compas, Malcarne, & Fondacaro, 1988; Dise-Lewis, 1988; McCubbin & Patterson, 1986; Patterson & McCubbin, 1987; Wertlieb, Weigel, & Feldstein, 1987; Wills, 1985, 1986).

Coping efforts can be conceptualized as approach-versus avoidance-oriented strategies. Approach strategies include cognitive attempts to change ways of thinking about the problem and behavioral attempts to change ways of thinking about the problem and behavioral attempts to resolve events by dealing directly with the problem or its consequences. Avoidant strategies include cognitive attempts to deny or minimize the threat, and behavioral attempts to get away from or avoid confronting the situation, or to relieve tension by expressing one's emotions. Similarly, coping efforts can be seen as focusing on modifying the stressor (problem-focused) or on regulating emotional states that may accompany the stressor (emotion-focused).

While there are a number of methodological differences between studies of adolescents, similar dimensions of coping have been found. These studies have identified approach-oriented or problem-focused dimensions such as information gathering and problem solving, redefining situations to see the positive side of things, and seeking instrumental and emotional support from a variety of sources. These studies have also found avoidant- or emotion-focused dimensions such as distraction and denial, ventilating feelings or acting out as a means to manage tension, and seeking alternative sources of pleasure or diversion.

When faced with a problem, adolescents use a variety of coping strategies to manage the situation. However, certain coping strategies are more often linked to psychological well-being, while others are more often linked to indicators of distress. Greater reliance on approach-oriented or problem-focused responses and less reliance on avoidance- or emotion-focused responses is related to better adjustment on a variety of indices, including depression, anxiety, conduct problems, and substance use. Although there are some variations in coping by age, gender, and presence of identified clinical symptoms, the small number of studies and the methodological differences between them make generalizations difficult.

Although studies generally show that greater reliance on avoidance- or emotion-focused coping is related to poorer adjustment, these strategies may be effective in particular situations, with certain (particularly uncontrollable) stressors, or at specific stages of the coping process. For example, avoidant coping may reduce anxiety and allow for a gradual recognition of threat so that the problem does not become overwhelming or crippling. While the use of avoidance strategies may be adaptive in certain situations (especially in the short term), persistent reliance on these types of responses, particularly with recurrent or chronic stressors (e.g., problems with peers, parents arguing, etc.) may prove costly to long-term adjustment if it prevents the development of a range of coping skills that include more approach- or problem-focused strategies and the ability to flexibly try alternative strategies.

Conclusion

While the study of stress and coping during adolescence is not without controversy and criticism, it is an area of research that is rapidly growing. A certain amount of challenge may be necessary for healthy development, and the answer to whether certain events or circumstances impede or enhance functioning during adolescence may require not only more complex person-context process models, but a life-span perspective that takes prior as well as subsequent development into account. The study of these processes, the transaction between individuals and their environments, especially during periods of transitions, may help us predict whether subsequent challenges will become opportunities rather than obstacles to growth.

References

Band, E. B., & Weisz, J. R. (1988). How to feel better when it feels bad: Children's perspectives on coping with everyday stress. *Developmental Psychology, 24,* 247–253.

Billings, A. G., & Moos, R. H. (1981). The role of coping responses and social resources in attenuating the stress of life events. *Journal of Behavioral Medicine, 4,* 139–157.

Coddington, R. D. (1972). The significance of life events as etiological factors in the diseases of children: 2. A study of a normal population. *Journal of Psychosomatic Research, 16,* 205–213.

Coleman, J. C. (1978). Current contradictions in adolescent theory. *Journal of Youth and Adolescence, 7,* 1–11.

Compas, B. E. (1987a). Stress and life events during childhood and adolescence. *Clinical Psychology Review, 7,* 275–302.

Compas, B. E. (1987b). Coping with stress during childhood and adolescence. *Psychological Bulletin, 101,* 393–403.

Compas, B. E., Davis, G. E., Forsythe, C. J., & Wagner, B. M. (1987). Assessment of major and daily stressful events during adolescence: The Adolescent Perceived Events Scale. *Journal of Consulting and Clinical Psychology, 55,* 534–541.

Compas, B. E., Malcarne, V. L., & Fondacaro, K. M. (1988). Coping with stressful events in older children and young adolescents. *Journal of Consulting and Clinical Psychology, 56,* 405–411.

Compas, B. E., Wagner, B. M., Slavin, L. A., & Vannatta, C. (1986). A prospective study of life events, social support, and psychological symptomatology during the transition from high school to college. *American Journal of Community Psychology, 14,* 241–257.

Daniels, D., & Moos, R. H. (1990). Assessing life stressors and social resources among adolescents: Applications to depressed youth. *Journal of Adolescent Research, 5,* 208–289.

Dise-Lewis, J. (1988). The life events and coping inventory: An assessment of stress in children. *Psychosomatic Medicine, 50,* 484–499.

Ebata, A. T., & Moos, R. H. (in press). Coping and adjustment in distressed and healthy adolescents. *Journal of Applied Developmental Psychology.*

Ebata, A. T., & Petersen, A. C. (in press). The development of psychopathology in adolescence. In J. E. Rolf, A. Masten, D. Cicchetti, K. H. Neuchterlin, & S. Weintraub (Eds.), *Risk and protective factors in the development of psychopathology* (pp. 308–333). New York: Cambridge University Press.

Felner, R. D. (1984). Vulnerability in childhood. In M. C. Roberts & L. Peterson (Eds.), *Prevention of problems in childhood: Psychological research and applications* (pp. 133–169). New York: Wiley-Interscience.

Felner, R. D., Farber, S. S., & Primavera, J. (1983). Transitions and stressful events: A model for primary prevention. In R. D. Felner, L. A. Jason, J. N. Moritsugu, & S. S. Farber (Eds.), *Preventive psychology: Theory, research, and practice* (pp. 199–215). New York: Pergamon.

Friedrich, W., Reams, R., & Jacobs, J. (1982). Depression and suicidal ideation in early adolescence. *Journal of Youth and Adolescence, 11,* 403–407.

Garmezy, N. (1983). Stressors of childhood. In N. Garmezy & M. Rutter (Eds.), *Stress, coping, and development in children* (pp. 43–84). New York: McGraw-Hill.

Hamburg, B. A. (1974). Early adolescence: A specific and stressful stage of the life cycle. In G. V. Coelho, D. A. Hamburg, & J. E. Adams (Eds.), *Coping and adaptation* (pp. 101–124). New York: Basic Books.

Hauser, S. T., Vieyra, M. A. B., Jacobsen, A. M., & Wertlieb, D. (1985). Vulnerability and resilience in adolescence: Views from the family. *Journal of Early Adolescence, 5,* 81–100.

Johnson, J. H. (1986). *Life events as stressors in childhood and adolescence.* Newbury Park, CA: Sage.

Johnson, J. H., & Bradlyn, A. S. (1988). Life events and adjustment in childhood and adolescence. In L. H. Cohen (Ed.), *Life* events and psychological functioning: Theoretical and methodological issues (pp. 64–95). Newbury Park, CA: Sage.

Johnson, J. H., & McCutcheon, S. M. (1980). Assessing life stress in older children and adolescents: Preliminary findings with the Life Events Checklist. In I. G. Sarason & C. D. Spielberger (Eds.), Stress and anxiety (pp. 111–125). Washington, DC: Hemisphere.

Kanner, A. D., Feldman, S. S., Weinberger, D. A., & Ford, M. E. (1987). Uplifts, hassles, and adaptational outcomes in early adolescents. Journal of Early Adolescence, 7, 371–394.

Lazarus, R. S., & Folkman, S. (1984). Stress, appraisal, and coping. New York: Springer.

McCrae, R. R. (1984). Situational determinants of coping responses: Loss, threat, and challenge. Journal of Personality and Social Psychology, 46, 919–928.

McCubbin, H. I., & Patterson, J. M. (1986). Adolescent stress, coping, and adaptation: A normative family perspective. In G. K. Leigh & G. W. Petersen (Eds.), Adolescence in a family context (pp. 256–276). Cincinnati, OH: South-Western Publishers.

Menaghan, E. G. (1983). Individual coping efforts: Moderators of the relationship between life stress and mental health outcomes. In H. Kaplan (Ed.), Psychosocial stress: Trends in theory and research (pp. 157–191). New York: Academic Press.

Moos, R. H., & Billings, A. G. (1982). Conceptualizing and measuring coping resources and processes. In L. Goldberger & S. Breznitz (Eds.), Handbook of stress: Theoretical and clinical aspects (pp. 212–230). New York: Free Press.

Newcomb, M. D., Huba, G. J., & Bentler, P. M. (1981). A multidimensional assessment of stressful life events among adolescents: Derivation and correlates. Journal of Health and Social Behavior, 2, 400–415.

Newcomb, M. D., Huba, G. J., & Bentler, P. M. (1986). Life change events among adolescents: An empirical consideration of some methodological issues. Journal of Nervous and Mental Disease, 174, 280–289.

Patterson, J. M., & McCubbin, H. I. (1987). Adolescent coping style and behaviors: Conceptualization and measurement. Journal of Adolescence, 10, 163–186.

Pearlin, L. I., & Schooler, C. (1978). The structure of coping. Journal of Health and Social Behavior, 19, 2–21.

Petersen, A. C. (1988). Adolescent development. Annual Review of Psychology, 39, 583–607.

Petersen, A. C., & Spiga, R. (1982). Adolescence and stress. In L. Goldberg & S. Breznitz (Eds.), Handbook of stress: Theoretical and clinical aspects (pp. 515–528). New York: Free Press.

Roth, S., & Cohen, L. J. (1986). Approach, avoidance, and coping with stress. American Psychologist, 41, 813–819.

Rutter, M. (1983). Stress, coping, and development: Some issues and questions. In N. Garmezy & M. Rutter (Eds.), Stress, coping, and development in children (pp. 1–41). New York: McGraw-Hill.

Rutter, M. (1987). Psychosocial resilience and protective mechanisms. American Journal of Orthopsychiatry, 57, 316–331.

Rutter, M., Graham, P., Chadwick, O. F. D., & Yule, W. (1976). Adolescent turmoil: Fact or fiction? Journal of Child Psychology and Psychiatry, 17, 35–56.

Simmons, R. G., & Blyth, D. A. (1987). Moving into adolescence: The impact of pubertal change and school context. Hawthorne, NY: Aldine.

Simmons, R. G., Burgeson, R., Carlton-Ford, S., & Blyth, D. A. (1987). The impact of cumulative change in early adolescence. Child Development, 58, 1220–1234.

Steinhausen, H. C., & Radtke, B. (1986). Life events and child psychiatric disorders. Journal of the American Academy of Child Psychiatry, 25, 125–129.

Suls, J., & Fletcher, B. (1985). The relative efficacy of avoidant and nonavoidant coping strategies: A meta-analysis. *Health Psychology, 4,* 249–288.

Swearingen, E. M., & Cohen, L. H. (1985). Life events and psychological distress: A prospective study of young adolescents. *Developmental Psychology, 21,* 1045–1054.

Swindle, R. W., Heller, K., & Lakey, B. (1988). A conceptual reorientation to the study of personality and stressful life events. In L. H. Cohen (Ed.), *Life events and psychological functioning: Theoretical and methodological issues* (pp. 237–268). Newbury Park, CA: Sage.

Tyerman, A., & Humphrey, M. (1983). Life stress, family support, and adolescent disturbance. *Journal of Adolescence, 6,* 1–12.

Wagner, B. M., Compas, B. E., & Howell, D. C. (1988). Daily and major life events: A test of an integrative model of psychosocial stress. *American Journal of Community Psychology, 16,* 189–205.

Werner, E. E., & Smith, R. S. (1982). *Vulnerable but invincible: A longitudinal study of resilient children and youth.* New York: McGraw-Hill.

Wertlieb, D., Weigel, C., & Feldstein, M. (1987). Measuring children's coping. *American Journal of Orthopsychiatry, 57,* 548–560.

Wills, T. A. (1985). Stress, coping, and tobacco and alcohol use in early adolescence. In S. Shiffman & T. Wills (Eds.), *Coping and substance use* (pp. 67–94). New York: Academic Press.

Wills, T. A. (1986). Stress and coping in early adolescence: Relationships to substance use in urban school samples. *Health Psychology, 5,* 503–529.

Yeaworth, R. C., York, J., Hussey, M. A., Ingle, M. E., & Goodwin, T. (1980). The development of an adolescent life change event scale. *Adolescence, 57,* 91–97.

See Also

Aggressive Behavior in Adolescence; Attention Deficit Disorder and Hyperactivity; Bulimia Nervosa in Adolescence; Conflict, Adolescent-Parent: A Model and a Method; Delinquency; Handicapped Adolescents, Providing Services for; Learning Disabilities in Adolescents: Description, Assessment, and Management; Problem Behavior in Adolescence; Psychophysiological/Psychosomatic Problems; Runaways, Negative Consequences for; Self-Destructiveness, Chronic, Role of in Adolescence; Stress and the Adolescent; Suicide, Adolescent; Suicides, Cluster; Type A and Teenagers.

This work was supported by the William T. Grant Foundation, NIMH Grant MH16744, and Veterans Administration Medical Research Funds.

Stress and the Adolescent

Elizabeth J. Susman
The Pennsylvania State University

Beginning around the turn of the century, adolescence came to be characterized as a period of "storm and stress." This viewpoint predominated the field until the last decade, when diverse perspectives on adolescence began to emerge. More recent viewpoints include the notion that adolescence is not necessarily a turbulent and stressful period of development. The assumed stressfulness of adolescence may have arisen, in part, because of ambiguities in the concept of stress itself. Four issues related to stress and adolescence will be discussed in this entry: concepts of stress, the rationale for considering adolescence a stressful period of development, gender differences in stress, and recent perspectives on stress in adolescence.

Concepts of Stress

Stress has been conceptualized in multiple ways in this century. Cannon (1932) was one of the first to be concerned with stress, examining it in relation to lack of oxygen, temperature extremes, and other environmental factors. He viewed stress as involving processes that eventually led to a disturbance in homeostasis or breakdown of biological systems. Influenced by Cannon, Hans Selye devoted his career to examining the physiology of stress. Selye (1950) viewed stress as the precipitant for a cascade of physiological, bodily defenses that resulted from aversive environmental stimuli. Three phases of the stress response were identified: the alerting response, the resistance response, and the exhaustion response. Both Cannon and Selye emphasized the physiological aspects of stress.

Later theories of stress emphasized psychological processes, for instance, emotional arousal, as well as physically aversive stimuli, in initiating and moderating the physiological aspects of stress. Stress-related physiological changes are most likely to occur if the stimuli are novel and challenging (Mason, 1968). Re-exposure to the same stimulus may not result in comparable physiological changes as those occurring when the stimulus is novel. The decrease in physiological responses to identical stimuli indicates that individuals adapt to emotionally noxious stimuli.

Most earlier formulations of stress assumed that stress-related physiological changes are a result of emotional arousal. But others have argued that it is not specific emotions that lead to stress-related changes in physiology (Levine, 1984). Rather, uncertainty is the psychological provocation leading to the physiological response to a noxious stimulus.

Other theories of stress have been proposed that emphasize, alone or in combination, the psychological and physiological aspects of stress. Regardless of the diversity of its definition, the general consensus is that, as Perlin (1987) suggests, "[stress] helps to focus on a special kind of encounter that people have with their social environments—encounters that are difficult and emotionally bruising" (p. 53). Adolescents will, of course, encounter many difficult and emotionally bruising challenges as they progress from a secure and dependent status within a family to an unpredictable and independent status within diverse peer and social contexts.

Adolescence as a Stressful Period of Development

Until recently the prevailing theories of adolescent development suggested that children progressing from childhood to adolescence are thrown into a period of disarray (Blos, 1970), with their development interrupted, changing from peaceful growth to emotional turmoil (Freud, 1958). These theoretical perspectives led naturally to studies that focused on psychological upheaval and disturbances. Psychiatric disorders, as well as less serious adjustment problems, that occur during this period were considered different from those that occur at other periods of development (Rutter, Graham, Chadwick, & Yule, 1976). A unique feature of adolescent psychological problems was their presumed transient nature, a result of normal adolescent fluctuating emotions.

The rationales for the belief that adolescence is a stressful period of development are diverse, and include both biological and psychological explanations. The biological explanation focuses on the rapid change in biological processes as a precipitant for stress during adolescence. Starting in early adolescence, major changes in height, weight, and body proportions occur. Levels of hormones of gonadal and adrenal origin increase dramatically within a four- to five-year period. Testosterone, for instance, an androgen of gonadal origin, may increase eighteenfold in boys across the stages of pubertal development (Nottelmann et al., 1987). These physical and hormonal changes are thought to be related to perturbations in emotions.

The psychological explanation for adolescent stress focuses on adolescence as a period of rapid change in the nature of social behavior, emotions, and cognition. With regard to social and emotional development, a developmental task of adolescence is to achieve an identity formation (Erikson, 1950), a sense of one's own self and personality. An aspect of identity formation germane to stress is the task of becoming independent from parental identification. This process entails developing self-identity and one's own goals, a process which may be stressful and increase an adolescent's sense of alienation and self-worth. At the same time, adolescents are confronted with increasing demands for achieving excellence in academic performance and popularity with peers. With regard to cognitive changes, as elaborated by Piaget (e.g., Piaget & Inhelder, 1969), adolescents become competent in the ability to think abstractly, including the ability to perceive the future, to think of themselves in new roles, and to take the perspective of others. Finally, the ability to think abstractly has implications for the development of fears and anxieties. Thinking abstractly enables adolescents to project themselves into unknown situations and to hypothesize more possibilities for fearful outcomes. These newly developed cognitive abilities contribute to an increase in stress during adolescence to an unknown extent.

Some research findings do support arguments in favor of the inherent stressfulness of adolescence, but the findings are far from consistent. Feelings of distress and misery and affective disorders were reported to increase from childhood to adolescence (Rutter et al., 1976). But Rutter and colleagues qualify these findings by citing other studies that do not report increases in problems or report that problems during adolescence are less frequent than those seen during adulthood (Rutter et al., 1976). The proportion of adolescents in any age group exhibiting problems tends to be relatively small, suggesting that adolescence is not problematic for all. Offer and Offer (1975) reported that there are three pathways through adolescence: continuous growth (relatively no problems), surgent growth (problems sometimes), and tumultuous growth (social or emotional upheavals). The latter group consisted of 21% of the sample, suggesting that maladjustment may be problematic for only a few adolescents. Furthermore, the earlier cited increase in problems during adolescence may reflect an overall increase in problems that is continuous from childhood to adulthood, rather than an increase that is spurned by processes unique to adolescence. The studies needed to test this hypothesis have not yet been carried out.

Gender Differences in Stress

Adolescence is the time when girls and boys begin to experience the rigid requirements of sex-role standards (Barnett, Biener, & Baruch, 1987). Girls, in particular, may begin to feel the constraints of their gender role, less freedom than their opposite-sex peers, and the desirability of being liked, by boys as well as by girls. Boys, on the other hand, may begin to experience the increasing demands to achieve and take on career responsibilities. In general, girls are viewed as experiencing more stresses and have fewer resources for coping (Bush & Simmons, 1987). This view is derived from the belief that biological differences (as found in girls and boys) have different social meanings. Girls may experience more stress in the present decade than in the past because of new cultural demands to achieve in the public sphere and simultaneously to be successful at home (Bush & Simmons, 1987). Therefore, society, in combination with biology, leads to gender differences in how stressors are perceived and the consequences of stress.

Recent Perspectives on Stress in Adolescence

Contemporary theories of stress, although not formulated specifically for adolescence, appear promising for improving our understanding of stress in adolescents. Specifically, the view of stress as associated with novel, unpredictable, and challenging situations (Levine, 1984) may be especially appropriate for understanding stress in adolescence. Central to this perspective is the notion that novel or strange aversive psychological stimuli lead to a physiological response. The perception of situations as novel or aversive requires the ability to think abstractly and to imagine the potential harmfulness of the situation. The cognitive abilities required to appraise the potential harmfulness of a situation were not present in childhood. Adolescents are newly empowered with the ability to identify the unpredictability of situations. Novel situations previously viewed as benign now may be viewed as potentially harmful and become stressful to adolescents.

Although it is assumed that there are many novel, challenging, and uncertain experiences in the lives of adolescents that are stressful, the nature and frequency of these experiences are far from being verified by research. Greater specificity is needed in defining what is stressful for adolescents, how adolescents differ in their physiological and behavioral responses to stressful situations, and the long-term implications of differences in reactivity to stress. Advances in the behavioral (e.g., Greene, 1988) and physiological components of stress now make it possible to measure the physiological, as well as the behavioral, reactivity of adolescents to potentially stressful situations.

Specifically, the physiological cascade that occurs in humans in response to stressors has been studied in considerable detail by physiologists. In response to stressors, individuals alter both their behavior and their physiological systems to adapt to the new situation (see Susman, Nottelmann, Dorn, Gold, & Chrousos, 1989, for a discussion of these systems). Behavioral changes include heightened activity, increased vigilance, and decreased feeding and reproductive behavior. Physiological changes include the improvement of nutrition and oxygenation, and detoxification of the central nervous system (CNS) and other organ systems involved in the "fight or flight" response. The central nervous system both senses stressors and orchestrates the stress response. For instance, changes in stress-related hormones are initiated in the hypothalamus, which secretes a releasing hormone (corticotropin releasing hormone) in response to a stressful situation. In turn, this releasing hormone stimulates the pituitary to secrete adreno-

corticotropin hormone (ACTH), and consequently the adrenal gland to secrete cortisol. Other stress-related substances are secreted as well. These hormonal changes, as well as other complex physiological changes, are adaptive in terms of the survival of the species (Gray, 1987) because they prepare the organism for fleeing the stressful stimuli (or danger).

The physiological responses just described do not occur with the same intensity in all individuals when confronted with the same stressful situation. An important advance in the psychology of stress has been the growing recognition that cognition and emotions play a central role in moderating reactivity to stressful stimuli. Specifically, the stimuli must be appraised as stressful prior to the initiation of either psychological (Lazarus & Folkman, 1984) or physiological stress responses. Future efforts to study differences among adolescents when confronted with diverse types of novel and challenging situations may advance understanding of stress in adolescents.

Summary and Conclusions

Stress has been conceptualized in multiple ways in this century. Earlier theories concentrated almost exclusively on the physiological response to noxious stimuli. Later theories incorporated both the physiological and psychological aspects of stress. The view of stress associated with novel, unpredictable, and challenging situations may be especially appropriate for understanding stress in adolescents because of the multiple changes that occur in the lives of adolescents.

In spite of the many questions that remain regarding stress and adolescence, there appears to be wide variability among adolescents in their tendencies to react to the stressors of adolescence. The differences in reactions may reflect genetic differences and accumulated experience in learning to cope with novel and challenging situations. Because of these wide differences in reactivity, vigilance in monitoring the adverse reactions of adolescents to novel, unpredictable, and challenging situations may help to identify adolescents at risk for developing stress-related physical or emotional problems. Identifying adolescents who are at risk for these consequences will enable parents, teachers, and others to intervene early to help adolescents cope with the everyday challenges of adolescent life.

References

Barnett, R. C., Biener, L., & Baruch, G. K. (Eds.). (1987). *Gender and stress*. New York: Free Press.

Blos, P. (1970). *The young adolescent: Clinical studies*. London: Collier-Macmillan.

Bush, D. M., & Simmons, R. G. (1987). Gender and coping with entry into early adolescence. In R. C. Barnett, L. Biener, & G. K. Baruch (Eds.), *Gender and stress* (pp. 185–217). New York: Free Press.

Cannon, W. B. (1932). *The wisdom of the body*. New York: Norton.

Erikson, E. H. (1950). *Childhood and society*. New York: Norton.

Freud, A. (1958). Adolescence. In R. S. Eissler (Ed.), *Psychoanalytic studies of the child* (Vol. 13, pp. 255–278). New York: Plenum.

Gray, A. G. (1987). *The psychology of fear and stress*. Cambridge: Cambridge University Press.

Greene, A. L. (1988). Early adolescents' perceptions of stress. *Journal of Adolescent Health Care, 8*, 391–403.

Lazarus, R. W., & Folkman, S. (1984). *Stress, appraisal, and coping*. New York: Springer.

Levine, S. (1984). A psychobiological approach to the ontogeny of coping. In N. Garmezy & M. Rutter (Eds.), *Stress, coping, and development in children* (pp. 107–131). New York: McGraw-Hill.

Mason, J. W. (1968). A review of psychoendocrine research on the pituitary-adrenal cortical system. *Psychosomatic Medicine, 30*, 576–608.

Nottelmann, E. D., Susman, E. J., Inoff-Germain, G., Dorn, L. D., Loriaux, D. L., Cutler, G. B., Jr., & Chrousos, G. P. (1987). Developmental processes in early adolescence: Relations among chronologic age, pubertal stage, height, weight, and serum levels of gonadotropins, sex steroids, and adrenal androgens. *Journal of Adolescent Health Care, 8*, 246–260.

Offer, D., & Offer, J. (1975). *From teenage to young manhood: A study of normal adolescent boys*. New York: Basic Books.

Perlin, L. (1987). The stress process and strategies of intervention. In K. Hurrelmann & U. Engel (Eds.), *The social world of adolescents: International perspectives* (pp. 53–72). Betlin, NY: Walter de Gruyter.

Piaget, J., & Inhelder, B. (1969). *The psychology of the child*. New York: Basic Books.

Rutter, M., Graham, P., Chadwick, O. F. D., & Yule, W. (1976). Adolescent turmoil: Fact or fiction? *Journal of Child Psychology and Psychiatry, 17*, 35–56.

Selye, H. (1950). *Stress: The physiology and pathology of exposure to stress*. Montreal: Acta Medical Publishers.

Susman, E. J., Nottelmann, E. D., Dorn, L. D., Gold, P. W., & Chrousos, G. P. (1989). The physiology of stress and behavioral development. In D. S. Palermo (Ed.), *Coping with uncertainty: Behavioral and developmental perspectives* (pp. 17–37). Hillsdale, NJ: Lawrence Erlbaum Associates.

See Also

Aggressive Behavior in Adolescence; Attention Deficit Disorder and Hyperactivity; Bulimia Nervosa in Adolescence; Conflict, Adolescent-Parent: A Model and a Method; Delinquency; Handicapped Adolescents, Providing Services for; Learning Disabilities in Adolescents: Description, Assessment, and Management; Problem Behavior in Adolescence; Psychophysiological/Psychosomatic Problems; Runaways, Negative Consequences for; Self-Destructiveness, Chronic, Role of in Adolescence; Stress and Coping in the Adolescent; Suicide, Adolescent; Suicides, Cluster; Type A and Teenagers.

Suicide, Adolescent

David A. Cole

University of Notre Dame

Incidence

According to the National Center for Health Statistics (1987), 5,121 young people committed suicide in the United States in 1985. This translates into a rate of 12.9 suicides per 100,000, or an average of 14 adolescent suicides per day. In 1985, the 15- to 24-year-old age group constituted 16.6% of the U.S. population and committed 17.4% of the suicides. Clearly, adolescents are at least as likely to commit suicide as other U.S. age groups. However, this has not always been true. The nationwide rate of suicide for all age groups has been very stable over the past 30 years, ranging from 10 to 13 per 100,000. By comparison, the adolescent suicide rate has tripled over the same time span, moving from 4.1 per 100,000 in 1955, to 6.2 in 1965, to 11.8 in 1975, and to 12.9 in 1985 (Osgood & McIntosh, 1986). Consequently, in 1984 suicide surpassed homicide as the second leading cause of death among adolescents (accidents remain the primary cause). However, because many actual adolescent suicides may be reported as accidents, these rates are best regarded as lower-bound estimates.

In general, suicide rates in the United States have been comparable to those in Australia, Belgium, and Great Britain. Rates are lower in Canada, Italy, Norway, The Netherlands, and Ireland. However, the rates are substantially higher in Austria, Denmark, Hungary, Japan, and Switzerland. In the U.S., whites are more likely to commit suicide than are nonwhites, although the suicide rates among nonwhite groups are increasing. Black and Hispanic adolescents have a slightly lower suicide rate than whites in general; however, suicide rates peak for blacks during adolescence. The suicide rate for native Americans is higher than for blacks, Hispanics, and whites but also peaks during young adulthood. However, Asian-Americans have a generally lower rate of suicide in the U.S., and an especially low rate during adolescence (McIntosh & Santos, 1985–86).

In the U.S. population at large, there are an estimated 8 to 20 suicide attempts for every completed suicide. However, among U.S. adolescents, the ratio is much higher. Estimates are as high as 200 suicide attempts for every adolescent death by suicide. Adolescent females (like adult females) are three times more likely to attempt suicide than are males. Nevertheless, adolescent males are four times as likely to succeed. In part, this is due to the choice of method. Approximately 50% of adolescent male suicide completers use firearms. The second most common means is hanging. Only one-third of adolescent female suicides involve firearms. Another third involve some form of solid or liquid poisoning. Because poisoning is typically slower and potentially reversible, attempts by females are more apt to be interrupted than are those by males.

Correlates and Theories of Suicide

A wide variety of factors have been linked directly or indirectly to suicide. Some of these factors have been imbedded in theories attempting to explain or predict suicide in adolescence. Four of the primary factors will be discussed here: depression, hopelessness, problem-solving, and family environment.

DEPRESSION ■ Depression has long been recognized as a risk factor for suicide in adults. A similar association has also been noted in adolescents. Carlson and Cantwell (1980) reported that about 89% of children and adolescents with affective disorders admitted having suicidal ideations, whereas only 37% from other diagnostic categories did. Conversely, Clarkin, Friedman, Hurt, Corn, and Aronoff (1984) reported that 71% of adolescents who are hospitalized for attempting suicide are diagnosable as depressed. Similar results were reported by Robbins and Alessi (1985), in which 5 out of 6 adolescent inpatients who made serious suicidal attempts were diagnosed with major depressive disorder. The sixth was diagnosed with dysthymic disorder. Some depressive symptoms appear to be more highly correlated with suicide than others. These include depressed mood, low self-esteem, anhedonia, poor concentration, lack of decisiveness, psychomotor agitation or retardation, and substance abuse (Pfeffer, 1986).

HOPELESSNESS ■ Many people are depressed but not suicidal. Some people are suicidal but not depressed. Cognitive theorists have noted that hopelessness seems to be a critical variable, accounting for the apparent relation between depression and suicide among inpatient adults (e.g., Minkoff, Bergman, Beck, & Beck, 1973). Using a hopelessness inventory for children, Kazdin, French, Unis, Esveldt-Dawson, & Sherrick (1983) replicated these findings with inpatient children. However, other findings suggest that the preeminent role of hopelessness may be limited to individuals in treatment (Cole, 1988), and may not be as critical as other cognitive factors among normal adolescents (Cole, 1989).

PROBLEM-SOLVING ■ Clinicians have often remarked that their suicidal clients seem to have very limited and rigid approaches to problem-solving (Neuringer, 1974). A diathesis-stress model of suicide has been proposed wherein problem-solving deficits are the diathesis and negative life events are the stressors (Schotte & Clum, 1982). Although this model has been supported by research with children (Asarnow, Carlson, & Guthrie, 1987) and adults (Schotte & Clum, 1987), relatively little work has been conducted with adolescents (Levenson & Neuringer, 1971).

FAMILY ENVIRONMENTS ■ Most theories of adolescent suicide are little more than adult theories, modified slightly for application to a younger age group. Nevertheless, other factors such as the family environment may play a more central role in the lives of children and adolescents than they do in adults. Several studies have noted that children and early adolescents who manifest serious suicidal behavior are more likely to have family histories of suicide and/or depression (Garfinkel, Froese, & Hood, 1982; Schaffer, 1974). Recent research suggests that families of suicidal children are less cohesive, have more conflict, and are more chaotic than families of nonsuicidal children (Asarnow et al., 1987). Others have noted marked disorganization in families of suicidal adolescents (Shafii, Carrigan, Whittinghill, & Derrick, 1985). The implicit theory underlying these data is that the healthy family protects the adolescent from suicidal contemplation by providing emotional support and reducing isolation (Pfeffer, 1986; Schaffer, 1974).

References

Asarnow, J. R. Carlson, G. A., & Guthrie, D. (1987). Coping strategies, self-perceptions, hopelessness, and perceived family environments in depressed and suicidal children. *Journal of Consulting and Clinical Psychology*, *55*, 361–366.

Carlson, G. A., & Cantwell, D. P. (1980). A survey of depressive symptoms, syndromes, and disorder in a child psychiatric population. *Journal of Child Psychology and Psychiatry*, *21*, 19–25.

Clarkin, J. F., Friedman, R. C., Hurt, S. W., Corn, R., & Aronoff, M. (1984). Affective and character pathology of suicidal adolescent and young adult inpatients. *Journal of Clinical Psychiatry*, *45*, 19–22.

Cole, D. A. (1988). Hopelessness, social desirability, depression, and parasuicide in two college student samples. *Journal of Consulting and Clinical Psychology*, *56*, 131–136.

Cole, D. A. (1989). Psychopathology of adolescent suicide: Hopelessness, coping beliefs, and depression. *Journal of Abnormal Psychology*, *98*, 248–255.

Garfinkel, B. D., Froese, A., & Hood, J. (1982). Suicide attempts in children and adoles-

cents. *American Journal of Psychiatry*, *139*, 1257–1261.

Kazdin, A. E., French, N. H., Unis, A. S., Esveldt-Dawson, K., & Sherrick, R. B. (1983). Hopelessness, depression, and suicidal intent among psychiatrically disturbed inpatient children. *Journal of Consulting and Clinical Psychology*, *81*, 504–510.

Levenson, M., & Neuringer, C. (1971). Problem-solving behavior in suicidal adolescents. *Journal of Consulting and Clinical Psychology*, *37*, 433–436.

McIntosh, J. L., & Santos, J. F. (1985–86). Methods of suicide by age: Sex and race differences among the young and old. *International Journal of Aging and Human Development*, *22*, 123–139.

Minkoff, K., Bergman, E., Beck, A. T., & Beck, R. (1973). Hopelessness, depression, and attempted suicide. *American Journal of Psychiatry*, *130*, 455–459.

National Center for Health Statistics. (1987). Advance report of final mortality statistics, 1985. *NCHS Monthly Vital Statistics Report*, *36* (5, Suppl.).

Neuringer, C. (1974). *Psychological assessment of suicidal risk*. Springfield, IL: Charles C. Thomas.

Osgood, N. J., & McIntosh, J. L. (1986). *Suicide and the elderly: An annotated bibliography and review*. New York: Greenwood Press.

Pfeffer, C. R. (1986). *The suicidal child*. New York: Guilford Press.

Robbins, D. R., & Alessi, N. E. (1985). Depressive symptoms and suicidal behavior in adolescents. *American Journal of Psychiatry*, *142*, 588–592.

Shaffer, D. (1974). Suicide in childhood and early adolescence. *Journal of Child Psychology and Psychiatry*, *15*, 275–291.

Schotte, D. E., & Clum, G. A. (1982). Suicide ideation in a college student population: A test of a model. *Journal of Consulting and Clinical Psychology*, *50*, 690–696.

Schotte, D. E., & Clum, G. A. (1987). Problem-solving skills in suicidal psychiatric patients. *Journal of Consulting and Clinical Psychology*, *55*, 49–54.

Shafii, M., Carrigan, S., Whittinghill, J. R., & Derrick, A. (1985). Psychological autopsy of completed suicide in children and adolescence. *American Journal of Psychiatry*, *142*, 1061–1064.

See Also

Aggressive Behavior in Adolescence; Attention Deficit Disorder and Hyperactivity; Bulimia Nervosa in Adolescence; Conflict, Adolescent-Parent: A Model and a Method; Delinquency; Handicapped Adolescents, Providing Services for; Learning Disabilities in Adolescents: Description, Assessment, and Management; Problem Behavior in Adolescence; Psychophysiological/Psychosomatic Problems; Runaways, Negative Consequences for; Self-Destructiveness, Chronic, Role of in Adolescence; Stress and the Adolescent; Stress and Coping in the Adolescent; Suicides, Cluster; Type A and Teenagers.

Suicides, Cluster

Madelyn S. Gould

Columbia University
New York State Psychiatric Institute

The terms "clusters," "contagion," and "imitation" are often used interchangeably in the literature, leading to difficulties in communication and understanding of the contribution of these factors to suicide (Biblarz, 1988). A suicide *cluster* refers to an excessive number of suicides occurring in close temporal and/or geographic proximity. Suicide *contagion* is the process by which one suicide facilitates the occurrence of a subsequent suicide. Contagion assumes either direct or indirect awareness of the prior suicide. Various suicide contagion pathways may exist: direct contact or friendship with a victim, word-of-mouth knowledge, and indirect transmission through the media. *Imitation*, the process by which one suicide becomes a compelling model for successive suicides, is one underlying theory to explain the occurrence of contagion.

The importance of suicide "contagion" has been suggested by two diverse literatures: the reports of suicide "epidemics" or "cluster outbreaks," and research on the effects of suicide stories in the mass media. A review of these two bodies of literature is the focus of this entry.

Evidence of Suicide Cluster Outbreaks

Evidence of epidemic suicides has been reported in accounts from ancient times through the twentieth century (Bakwin, 1957; Popow, 1911; see Coleman, 1987, Davidson & Gould, 1989, and Gould & Davidson, 1988, for detailed accounts). The anecdotal reports of cluster suicides have addressed diverse populations, including psychiatric inpatients (Anonymous, 1977; Crawford & Willis, 1966; Kahne, 1968; Kobler & Stotland, 1964; Sacks & Eth, 1981), high school and college students (Robbins & Conroy, 1983; Seiden, 1967), community samples (Ashton & Donnan, 1981; Nalin, 1973; Rubinstein, 1983; Walton, 1978), native Americans (Ward & Fox, 1977), marine troops (Hankoff, 1961), prison inmates (Niemi, 1978), and religious sects (Rovinsky, 1898).

A number of studies highlight the choice of identical methods among suicides in a cluster (Ashton & Donnan, 1981; Crawford & Willis, 1966; Hankoff, 1961; Nalin, 1973; Rovinsky, 1898; Seiden, 1967; Walton, 1978). A clear imitation of method was seen in Seiden's (1967) report of five cases of suicide by jumping that occurred within a month on a college campus. Identical methods, however, may not always reflect direct imitation of another decedent in the cluster. Cultural factors may also predominate in the choice of method.

Recent clusters indicate that it is not necessary for the decedents to have had direct contact with each other (Davidson & Gould, 1988). Indirect knowledge of the suicides appears to have been obtained through the news media in some cluster situations. Other clusters have a mixture of members from one social network plus individuals unknown to each other directly. Among those who knew another decedent, the degree of acquaintanceship varied from closest friends to those in the same school or church who knew of each other but had little direct personal contact. A recent study (Davidson, et al., 1989) found that suicide victims had no more exposure to other suicides, either through friends or news reports, then did matched controls who did not commit suicide. However, the nature of the control limited the examination of the association of suicide with exposure to suicide as a risk factor (see Gould, 1990). The investigation (Davidson, et al., 1989) concluded that exposure to suicide may profoundly influence those individuals already at risk of killing themselves.

Behavioral and psychiatric problems are considered to increase susceptibility to suicide in a cluster (Ashton & Donnan, 1981; Davidson, et al., 1989; Niemi, 1978; Robbins & Conroy, 1983; Walton, 1978; Ward & Fox, 1977). However, the proportion of noncluster suicides with psychiatric problems (Robins, 1981) may not differ from proportions reported in case series of cluster suicides.

The anecdotal reports of "outbreaks" are difficult to interpret. There is no sys-

tematic surveillance or reporting system of suicide clusters. Therefore, these case series have selection biases that affect their representativeness. As descriptive studies, no comparison groups or statistical analyses have been included. Without reference to a comparison group descriptions of the demographic and psychological characteristics of suicides that occur within the context of a cluster are speculative. What may appear to be a ubiquitous characteristic of cluster suicides may not differentiate them from sporadic, noncluster suicides, and, therefore, may be of limited value in preventing this particular type of death. Moreover, even if suicides occurred essentially at random, some clustering would be bound to arise by chance alone, and if enough people are looking for it, some are sure to find it. What is necessary to determine is whether "outbreaks" are occurring to an extent greater than would be expected by chance variation. Until recently there has been no systematic research on the extent to which cluster outbreaks occur.

A recent project by the author (Gould, Wallenstein, & Kleinman, 1990a, 1990b) developed and adapted epidemiologic techniques to detect the occurrence and assess the significance of time-space clusters. These methods establish clustering by demonstrating an excess frequency of suicide in certain times and places or a significant relationship between the time and space distances between pairs of suicides. The epidemiologic techniques to detect clusters were applied to U.S. mortality data on suicides obtained from the National Center for Health Statistic Mortality Detail Files for 1978 through 1984. The analyses indicated that suicide clusters occur predominantly among teenagers and young adults; a cluster situation does not appear to accelerate suicidal behavior in individuals who would have killed themselves anyway as indicated by the lack of "vacuities" in the number of suicides following the clusters. Rather, the cluster represents a significant excess of suicides; and cluster suicides account for approximately 1–5% of all teenage suicides. The estimates do not reflect all clusters that occur because different clusters may have different geographic and time patterns than employed in the analysis. The variability in temporal and geographic patterns is indicated from anecdotal reports; however, the cluster analytic methods require a predefined set of time and space units to characterize a cluster (e.g., suicides occurring within a county). Moreover, these estimates do not include clusters of attempted suicides. It is not possible to enumerate suicide attempts adequately because no registry of attempts exists. Therefore, the estimates of clustering represent a lower bound due to the set definitions and the sole employment of mortality data.

In summary, anecdotal accounts and epidemiologic research of epidemic suicides indicate that significant clustering of suicides does occur. Cluster suicides appear to be multidetermined, as are noncluster suicides, but imitation and identification are factors hypothesized to increase the likelihood of cluster suicides.

Media Influences

NONFICTIONAL SUICIDE STORIES

■ Most of the research on imitative suicide has focused on the reporting of nonfictional suicides in the mass media (Baron & Reiss, 1985; Barraclough, Shepherd, & Jennings, 1977; Blumenthal & Bergner, 1973; Bollen & Phillips, 1981, 1982; Littman, 1985; Motto, 1967, 1970; Phillips, 1974, 1979, 1980; Phillips & Carstensen, 1986; Stack, 1984; Wasserman, 1984). Consistent findings in support of an imitation hypothesis have been reported by the majority of studies despite their variation in method, location, and type of variables. A number of studies examined an excess of deaths following the appearance of suicide stories (Barraclough, Shepherd, & Jennings, 1977; Bollen & Phillips, 1981, 1982; Gould & Shaffer, 1986; Phillips, 1974, 1979; Wasserman, 1984), while other studies examined the decrease in deaths during a newspaper strike when there was a cessation of newspaper stories (Blumenthal & Bergner, 1973; Motto, 1970). Different types of "control" periods have been employed, varying from control periods immediately prior to the suicide story (Bollen & Phillips, 1981), to control periods in different years (Motto, 1970; Phillips, 1979), to indirect control periods used in time series analyses (Wasserman, 1984). Both quasi-experimental designs (e.g., Phillips, 1974) and regressions analytic strategies (e.g., Bollen & Phillips, 1981) have been employed.

Prominent newspaper coverage of a suicide appears to have the effect of increasing suicide behavior within the readership area of the newspaper. The magnitude of the increase is related to the "attractiveness" of the individual whose death is being reported and the amount of publicity given to the story (Bollen & Phillips, 1981, 1982; Phillips, 1974, 1979, 1980; Phillips & Carstensen, 1986). This finding has been replicated with American (Bollen & Phillips, 1982) and Dutch data (Ganzeboom & de Haan, 1982).

FICTIONAL SUICIDE STORIES

■ Little research has been carried out on the impact of fictional stories. The few recent studies prove to be controversial, with findings of significant imitative effects (Holding, 1974, 1975; Schmidtke & Hafner, 1986), no imitative effects (Berman, 1986, 1988; Phillips & Paight, 1987), and sex- and age-specific imitative effects (Platt, 1987).

Previous research by the author suggested that an increase in teenage suicides in the greater New York area followed fictional films featuring suicidal behavior that were broadcast on television in the fall and winter of 1984–1985 (Gould & Shaffer, 1986). The examination of the variation in youth suicide was extended to the metropolitan regions of Cleveland, Dallas, and Los Angeles. The results indicated a significant interaction by location (Gould, Shaffer, & Kleinman, 1988).

Recently, Phillips and Paight (1987) published results that indicated that there was no significant effect of the same movies in the states of California and Pennsylvania. These results are not inconsistent with the present findings in that both sets of results might be explained by an interaction between the locations where the films were shown and the effect of the films. Berman (1988) has also reported variability in the impact of fictional television dramitizations by geographic locale. This is not an unreasonable supposition because the way the suicide broadcasts were presented varied according to location. The affiliates were encouraged to develop local education programs to go along with the film and these varied in intensity. Phillips and Paight (1987) have hypothesized that there is a dose-response effect between suicide and the media: more exposure produces more effect. If this is true, it might explain regional variation. However, the extent of affiliate coverage in the areas studied has not been documented.

Growing evidence forcefully supports the existence of imitative suicides following media coverage of nonfictional suicides. While there is evidence that fictional suicide stories can have a negative impact (Gould & Shaffer, 1986; Holding, 1974, 1975; Schmidtke & Hafner, 1986), there is clearly a need to engage in further careful research in this area to resolve the issue.

References

Anonymous. (1977). A suicide epidemic in a psychiatric hospital. *Journal of Diseases of the Nervous System, 38*, 327–331.

Ashton, V. R., & Donnan, S. (1981). Suicide by burning as an epidemic phenomenon: An analysis of 82 deaths and inquests in England and Wales in 1978–79. *Psychological Medicine, 11*, 735–739.

Bakwin, H. (1957). Suicide in children and adolescents. *Journal of Pediatrics, 50*, 749–769.

Baron, J. N., & Reiss, P. C. (1985). Reply to Phillips and Bollen. *American Sociological Review, 50*, 372–376.

Barraclough, B., Shepherd, D., & Jennings, C. (1977). Do newspaper reports of coroners' inquests incite people to commit suicide? *British Journal of Psychiatry, 131*, 259–532.

Berman, A. L. (1986, June). *Mass media and youth suicide prevention.* Paper prepared for the National Conference on Prevention and Interventions in Youth Suicide, Department of Health and Human Services' Task Force on Youth Suicide, Oakland, CA.

Berman, A. L. (1988). Fictional depiction of suicide in television films and imitation effects. *American Journal of Psychiatry, 145*, 982–986.

Biblarz, A. (1988, April). *Minimizing the contagion phenomenon.* Panel at the 21st Annual Conference of the American Association of Suicidology, Washington, DC.

Blumenthal, S., & Bergner, L. (1973). Suicide and newspaper: A replicated study. *American Journal of Psychiatry, 130*, 468–471.

Bollen, K. A., & Phillips, D. P. (1981). Suicidal motor vehicle fatalities in Detroit: A replication. *American Journal of Sociology, 87*, 404–412.

Bollen, K. A., & Phillips, D. P. (1982). Imitative suicides: A national study of the effects of television news stories. *American Sociological Review, 47*, 802–809.

Coleman, L. (1987). *Suicide Clusters.* Boston: Farber & Farber.

Crawford, J. P., & Willis, J. H. (1966). Double suicide in psychiatric hospital patients. *British Journal of Psychiatry*, *112*, 1231–1235.

Davidson, L., & Gould, M. S. (1989). Contagion as a risk factor for youth suicide. DHHS Pub. No. (ADM) 89-1622. *Report of the Secretary's Task Force on Youth Suicide* Washington, DC: U.S. Government Printing Office.

Davidson, L. E., Rosenberg, N. L., Mercy, J. A., Franklin, J., & Simmons, J. T. (1989). An epidemiologic study of risk factors in two teenage suicide clusters. *Journal of the American Medical Association*, *262*, 2687–2692.

Ganzeboom, H. B. G., & de Haan, D. (1982). Gepubliceerde zelfmoorden en verhoging van sterfte door zelfmoord en ongelukken in Nederland 1972–1980. *Mens en Maatschappij*, *57*, 55–69.

Gould, M. S. (1990). Teenage Suicide Clusters. Letter to the editor. *Journal of the American Medical Association*, *263*, p. 2051.

Gould, M. S., & Davidson, L. (1988). Suicide contagion among adolescents. In A. R. Stiffman & R. A. Felman (Eds.), *Advances in adolescent mental health: Vol. 2. Depression and suicide* 29–59. Greenwich, CT: Jai Press.

Gould, M. S., & Shaffer, D. (1986). The impact of suicide in television movies: Evidence of imitation. *New England Journal of Medicine*, *315*, 690–694.

Gould, M. S., Shaffer, D., & Kleinman, M. (1988). The impact of suicide in television movies: Replication and commentary. *Suicide and Life Threatening Behavior*, *18*(1), 90–99.

Gould, M. S., Wallenstein, S., & Kleinman, M. (1990a). Time-space clustering of teenage suicide. *American Journal of Epidemiology*, *131*, 71–78.

Gould, M. S., Wallenstein, S., & Kleinman, M. (1990b). Suicide clusters: An examination of age specific effects. *American Journal of Public Health*, *80*, 211–212.

Hankoff, L. D. (1961). An epidemic of attempted suicide. *Comprehensive Psychiatry*, *2*, 294–298.

Holding, T. A. (1974). The B.B.C. "Befrienders" series and its effects. *British Journal of Psychiatry*, *124*, 470–472.

Holding, T. A. (1975). Suicide and "The Befrienders." *British Medical Journal*, *3*, 751–753.

Kahne, M. J. (1986). Suicide among patients in mental hospitals. *Psychiatry*, *1*, 32–43.

Kobler, A. L. L., & Stotland, E. (1964). *The end of hope: A social-clinical study of suicide*. London: Free Press of Glencoe.

Littmann, S. K. (1985). Suicide epidemics and newspaper reporting. *Suicide and Life-Threatening Behavior*, *15*, 43–50.

Motto, J. A. (1967). Suicide and suggestibility—the role of the press. *American Journal of Psychiatry*, *124*, 252–256.

Motto, J. A. (1970). Newspaper influence on suicide. *Archives of General Psychiatry*, *23*, 143–148.

Nalin, D. R. (1973). Epidemic of suicide by malathion poisoning in Guyana. *Tropical and Geographical Medicine*, *25*, 8–14.

Niemi, T. (1978). The time-space distances of suicides committed in the lock-up in Finland in 1963–1967. *Israel Annals of Psychiatry and Related Disciplines*, *16*, 39–45.

Phillips, D. (1974). The influence of suggestion on suicide: Substantive and theoretical implications of the Werther effect. *American Sociological Review*, *39*, 340–354.

Phillips, D. P. (1979). Suicide, motor vehicle fatalities, and the mass media: Evidence toward a theory of suggestion. *American Journal of Sociology*, *84*, 1150–1174.

Phillips, D. P. (1980). Airplane accidents, murder, and the mass media: Toward a theory of imitation and suggestion. *Social Forces*, *58*, 1001–1004.

Phillips, D. P., & Carstensen, L. L. (1986). Clustering of teenage suicides after television news stories about suicide. *New England Jornal of Medicine*, *315*, 685–689.

Phillips, D. P., & Paight, D. J. 1987). The impact of televised movies about suicide: A replicative study. *New England Journal of Medicine, 317,* 809–811.

Platt, S. (1987). The aftermath of Angie's overdose: Is soap (opera) damaging to your health? *British Medical Journal, 294,* 954–957.

Popow, N. M. (1911). The present epidemic of school suicides in Russia. *Nevrol Nestnik (Kazan), 18,* 312–35, 592–646.

Robbins, D., & Conroy, R. C. (1983). A cluster of adolescent suicide attempts: Is suicide contagious? *Journal of Adolescent Health Care, 3,* 253–255.

Robins, E. (1981). *The final months.* New York: Oxford University Press.

Rovinsky, A. (1898). Epidemic suicides. *Boston Medical and Surgical Journal, 1898,* 238–239.

Rubinstein, D. H. (1983). Epidemic suicide among Micronesian adolescents. *Social Science Medicine, 17,* 657–665.

Sacks, M., & Eth, S. (1981). Pathological identification as a cause of suicide on an inpatient unit. *Hospital and Community Psychiatry, 32,* 36–40.

Schmidtke, A., & Hafner, H. (1986). Die vermittlung von selbstmordmotivation und selbstmordhandlung durch fiktive modelle. *Nervenarzt, 57,* 502–510.

Seiden, R. H. (1967). Suicidal behavior contagion on a college campus. In N. L. Farberow (Ed.), *Proceedings of Fourth International Conference for Suicide Prevention* (pp. 360–365), Los Angeles.

Stack, S. (1984). *The effect of suggestion on suicide: A reassessment.* Paper read at the Annual Meetings of the American Sociological Association, San Antonio, TX.

Walton, E. W. (1978). An epidemic of antifreeze poisoning. *Medicine, Science, and the Law, 18,* 231–237.

Ward, J. A., & Fox, J. (1977). A suicide epidemic on an Indian reserve. *Canadian Journal of the Psychiatric Association, 22,* 423–426.

Wasserman, I. M. (1984). Imitation and suicide: A reexamination of the Werther effect. *American Sociological Review, 49,* 427–436.

See Also

Aggressive Behavior in Adolescence; Attention Deficit Disorder and Hyperactivity; Bulimia Nervosa in Adolescence; Conflict, Adolescent-Parent: A Model and a Method; Delinquency; Handicapped Adolescents, Providing Services for; Learning Disabilities in Adolescents: Description, Assessment, and Management; Problem Behavior in Adolescence; Psychophysiological/Psychosomatic Problems; Runaways, Negative Consequences for; Self-Destructiveness, Chronic, Role of in Adolescence; Stress and the Adolescent; Stress and Coping in the Adolescent; Suicide, Adolescent; Type A and Teenagers.

This work was supported in part by CDC Contract #200-85-0834 (P) and Faculty Scholars Award #84-0954-84 from the William T. Grant Foundation.

Portions of this paper were adapted from Gould, M. S., and Davidson, L. Suicide contagion among adolescents. In A. R. Stiffman & R. A. Feldman (Eds.), Advances in Adolescent Mental Health, Volume III: Depression and Suicide. Greenwich, CT: JAI Press, 1988.

Television, Adolescents and

Patricia J. Bence
Tompkins Cortland Community College

Amount of time spent viewing television has traditionally been lower in adolescence than in any other period of life. In 1985, adolescents 12- to 17-years-old watched an average of 23½ hours of television per week compared to children 2- to 11-years-old, who averaged 28 hours per week, and adults, who viewed around 32 hours a week (Nielsen, 1986). Since 1965, however, the amount adolescents watch has shown an upward trend (see Figure 1) with adolescent males viewing slightly more than females. Thirty-four percent of adolescents' viewing time is during prime-time hours and 18% of viewing time is during weekday afternoons (Nielsen, 1986). Youth spend a great deal of time watching television with other members of their families. In general, adolescents prefer situation comedies and feature films. Individual variations in motivations to use television also exist: adolescents who seek arousal prefer more dramatic programs, while the more habitual viewers favor sitcoms and avoid the news. Older adolescents select programs more carefully than younger adolescents; in general, adolescents are more selective in their program choices than are children. Adolescents with better educated, higher income parents watch less television and are more critical of programming.

Television viewing is a prevalent leisure time activity among adolescents. They report using television to pass the time, to relax, and to seek relief from loneliness. Many adolescents study and do homework in front of the television. Of 11 major activities engaged in by adolescents (e.g., talking with friends, playing games/sports, etc.) television viewing placed second in terms of time spent in the activity. However, adolescents report feeling less excitement (and more boredom) when viewing television relative to listening to music. Compared to other activities (e.g., engaging in sports and games, or studying) television watching is associated with the least positive overall mood. Adolescents *do*, however, attend to television, and their reported concentration is as high while watching television programming as while listening to music (Larson & Kubey, 1983).

Many areas of adolescent life and television usage have been explored by scholars. Adolescents who are heavy viewers have fewer friends. Moreover, heavy television watching is associated with less overall time spent with peers. Heavy television use

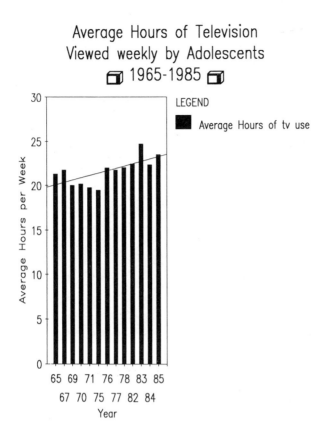

Average Hours of Television
Viewed weekly by Adolescents
1965-1985

LEGEND

■ Average Hours of tv use

FIGURE 1

roles). An historical analysis of prime-time television characters has shown that teenagers are depicted in a way that devalues this age group.

Television may also be an informal source of sexual socialization for adolescents with the potential to dilute other sex education programs. There has been a steady increase of sexual messages on television in general and soap operas in particular (Bence, 1989). Television programming frequently associates sex with violence. Since aspects of sexuality are of extreme concern and relevance to adolescents, their definition of a personal sexual role may be influenced by the sexual behaviors of their favorite television characters. Perceptions of televised sex and initial coital satisfaction among adolescent girls has been found to have a positive association, and 14- and 16-year-olds have been shown to understand sexual innuendos on prime-time programs. In a poll conducted by Planned Parenthood (1987), teens ranked television and movies as important sources of information regarding sex. It has also been suggested that television is a less threatening source of sexual information than either parents or peers, although it may not be any more accurate.

Many studies have indicated that heavy viewers of television tend to be more sex-typed and that it works to increase consistency between attitudes and sex-typed behavior, especially for adolescent males.

The voluminous works addressing the relationship between viewing televised violence and aggressive behavior in youth have been summarized in the National Institute of Mental Health [NIMH] report (1982, pp. 103–174). The report states

among high school students has also been associated with significantly more alcohol use as well as with poor physical fitness. The New England Medical Center and the Harvard School of Public Health have found that children who watch more television are more likely to become obese as they enter adolescence; several other studies have found a correlation between obesity and frequent television viewing (but at least one recent study did not find this relationship [Tucker, 1986]).

Several studies have examined the influence of television as a socializer to adult roles. Television may provide role models for adolescents, who rehearse these models and try to incorporate them into their own social worlds (e.g., dating and occupational that a large body of evidence supports the relationship. But a panel study conducted by researchers for the National Broadcasting Corporation (NBC) found no evidence that television violence was causally implicated in the development of aggressive behavior patterns among adolescents (NIMH, 1982). Some researchers believe that television's role in producing violence and violent crime is meager when compared to other social variables.

Most bivariate studies of amount of television viewing and academic achievement have shown a negative relationship, and that the relationship is strongest when adolescents view over 30 hours a week. When third variables such as IQ, gender, and age are controlled, the relationship between viewing and achievement weakens. Certain types of programming can actually increase academic achievement. For example, 8th through 12th graders' achievement scores have a positive correlation with viewing of news programs. Many adolescents, however, watch low-information, entertainment programs. There is a negative relationship between viewing these types of programs (e.g., music videos and sports) and academic achievement. Lower levels of overall knowledge are also associated with more time spent viewing soap operas by adolescents.

Recent changes in the television environment may be radically altering how adolescents use and are affected by the medium. Viewing options have proliferated through expanded cable access and videocassette ownership. Especially significant for adolescents are music video channels, other channels that offer films with R or X ratings, and the VCR. MTV and other music video channels and programs reach 43% of all teens nationwide (Sun & Lull, 1986); adolescents engage in this type of viewing with peers rather than with family. There is some evidence, however, that

music video viewing among 12- to 17-year-olds is declining and that music videos are enjoyed less than the songs alone. The music video may no longer be a novelty for contemporary adolescents.

VCRs have changed the weekend lifestyles of teenager viewers by providing a reason to get together, rent films, and party on Friday and Saturday nights. The results of a recent study of adolescent leisure found that 7th graders used the VCR for an average of 4.12 hours per week—representing 14.2% of television viewing time—the largest single category of program type. Ninth graders viewed the VCR an average of 4.27 hours per week, representing 15.9% of total viewing time. Eleventh graders used the VCR 3.14 hours per week, or 11.3% of television use time (Bence, 1987). This phenomenon and its developmental implications have yet to be studied.

Television, an ever-changing medium, is an important part of contemporary adolescent life and development, both in time spent viewing, and as a socializer of values.

References

A. C. Nielsen. (1986). *Nielsen yearly report.* Northbrook, IL: A. C. Nielsen.

Bence, P. (1989, April). *Adolescent dating behavior and TV soaps: Guided by "The Guiding Light"?.* Paper presented at the biennial meeting of the Society for Research in Child Development, Kansas City, MO.

Bence, P. (1987). *Adolescence and TV.* Unpublished data, Cornell University, Ithaca, NY.

Larson, R., & Kubey, R. (1983). Television and music: Contrasting media in adolescent life. *Youth and Society, 15,* 13–31.

National Institute of Mental Health. (1982). *Television and behavior: Ten years of scientific progress and implications for the eighties* (Vol. 2, DHHS Publication No. ADM 82-

1195). Washington, DC: U.S. Government Printing Office.

Planned Parenthood Federation of America. (1987). *American teens speak: Sex, myths, tv, and birth control* (poll). Washington, DC: Author.

Sun, S., & Lull, J. (1986). The adolescent audience for music videos and why they watch. *Journal of Communication, 36,* 115–125.

Tucker, L. (1986). The relationship of television viewing to physical fitness and obesity. *Adolescence, 21,* 797–806.

See Also

Twentieth-Century America, Adolescence in.

Temperament During Adolescence

Katherine Nitz
George Washington University

Jacqueline V. Lerner
The Pennsylvania State University

The study of temperament has been approached from several theoretical perspectives (i.e., Buss & Plomin, 1975, 1984; Goldsmith & Campos, 1982; Lerner & Lerner, 1983; Rothbart & Derryberry, 1981; Strelau, 1983; Thomas & Chess, 1977). Some of these views stress that temperament is an inherited, stable aspect of personality (Buss & Plomin, 1975, 1984) and others define temperament as behavioral style, or the "how" of behavior (Thomas & Chess, 1977). Despite these different approaches, it is generally agreed that temperament constitutes relatively stable individual differences in behavior and that it has import for a person's adaptive functioning.

While there has been considerable research on the functional significance of temperament during infancy and childhood, relatively little research has focused on adolescence. However, research that has addressed this period of development has most often used a *developmental-contextual* approach to assess temperament's functional implications. In developmental contextualism variables from biological, psychological, and social levels of analysis are believed to influence each other and, through so doing, provide the bases of behavior and development (Lerner, 1986; Lerner & Lerner, 1983). Such an approach to the functional significance of temperament during adolescence is important given the multiple hormonal, cognitive, and social changes that occur during this period. That is, these changes lead to the expectation that adjustment during adolescence entails some sort of congruence between changing organismic characteristics and changing contextual characteristics.

Based on the above perspective, one approach used to study temperament during adolescence is through testing the goodness of fit model (Lerner & Lerner, 1983; Thomas & Chess, 1977). This model emphasizes the need to consider both the temperament of the person and the demands of the social environment as indexed, for instance, by the expectations or attitudes of key significant others with whom the adolescent interacts (e.g., parents, peers, and teachers).

Adolescents, as do most people, show individual differences in their characteristics of temperament; for example, some adolescents show positive moods coupled with high activity levels and low thresholds of reactivity, while others may show characteristically negative moods, yet similar activity and threshold levels (Chess & Thomas, 1984). Such individual differences are central to understanding the goodness of fit model. As a consequence of characteristics of temperamental individuality, adolescents promote differential reactions in their key significant others. In turn, these reactions may feed back to the adolescent and provide a basis for further development. The goodness of fit model accounts for the type of feedback in these "circular functions" (Schneirla, 1957). That is, if a person's temperament matches or fits the demands of a particular social context then positive interactions and adjustment are expected. In contrast, negative adjustment and interactions are expected to occur when there is a poor fit between the demands of a particular social context and the person's temperament.

To illustrate, if a particular characteristic of temperament (e.g., regular sleeping habits) is expected within a given social context (e.g., the family) by a significant other (e.g., the mother), then an adolescent who possesses or develops that behavior will have a good fit with his or her environment. In such cases these adolescents are expected to show positive behavioral interactions in regard to this characteristic. If an adolescent does not possess or develop behavior that matches or fits the demands of the context, then negative outcomes are predicted.

As we have noted, just as an adolescent brings his or her temperamental characteristics to a particular social setting, there are demands placed on the adolescent by virtue of the physical and/or by the social components of the setting. These demands may take the form of, first, attitudes, values, or expectations held by parents, peers, or teachers regarding the adolescent's behavioral characteristics. Second, demands exist as a consequence of the behavioral attributes of these significant others. Parents, peers, and teachers are significant others with whom the adolescent must coordinate, or fit, his or her behavioral attributes for adaptive interactions to exist. Finally, the physical characteristics of a setting (e.g., such as the noise level of the home) constitute contextual demands. Such demands require the adolescent to possess certain behavioral attributes (e.g., high thresholds of reactivity to sound) for efficient interactions within the setting to occur (e.g., in regard to studying in a crowded, noisy home).

It is these demands that provide the functional significance for a given temperamental characteristic. Since parents, peers, and teachers may hold different demands for a given temperament characteristic, an adolescent's temperaments may fit these demands in some contexts and not in others. For example, teachers may want students who show little distractibility, since they would not want attention diverted from a lesson by the activity of adolescents in the classroom. Parents, however, might desire their adolescents to be moderately distractible—for example, when they want the adolescents to move from television watching to the dinner table. Adolescents whose behavioral individuality was either generally distractible or generally not distractible would thus differentially meet the demands of these two contexts. Problems of adjustment to school demands or to home demands might develop as a consequence of an adolescent's lack of match, or "goodness of fit," in either or both settings.

Tests of the goodness of fit model of the functional significance of temperament during adolescence have been conducted in the New York Longitudinal Study (NYLS), an ongoing study of behavioral development from infancy to adulthood (Chess & Thomas, 1984). In the NYLS it has been found that adolescents who have a poor fit with the demands of their parents in childhood continue to have a poor fit during adolescence. In addition, the behavior problems of childhood that result from this poorness of fit continue to be present in adolescence and may even be intensified as a consequence of the new demands that may emerge during this period of development (Carey, 1988).

The Pennsylvania Early Adolescent Transitions Study (PEATS) is another investigation that has contributed to the study of temperament during adolescence through testing of the goodness of fit model. The PEATS is a short-term longitudinal study involving a group of approximately 150 early adolescents who are undergoing physical, psychological, social, and school transitions. Results from the PEATS have shown that adolescents whose temperaments match the demands of their parents and peers tend to have higher academic and social competence, as viewed by teachers, more positive relationships with their peers, and fewer behavior problems in the home (e.g., East, Lerner, & Lerner, 1988; Nitz, Lerner, Lerner, & Talwar, in press). These results seem to emerge most often for the temperament dimension of mood. That is, adolescents whose mood is more congruent with the perferences for mood maintained by their parents and their peers (that is, the adolescents have generally more positive than negative moods) have better adjustment in school, in their peer group, and in their family.

As is evident from the NYLS and the PEATS investigations, the study of temperament during adolescence has involved a consideration of the person's organismic characteristics and the expectations for his or her temperament found in the social context. The results of these studies indicate that the functional significance of temperament involves a relationship between person and context. While the goodness of fit model is only one approach to the study of temperament, during adolescence temperament generally has not been studied through the application of other frameworks (e.g., a psychobiological or a behavioral-genetic framework). Despite the obvious importance of continuing to use the developmental-contextual, goodness of fit model in future adolescent temperament research, other approaches certainly may provide additional insight into the importance of temperament during this period of development. Thus, given the relative paucity of information about adolescent temperament, considerably more research is needed in order to more fully understand the functional significance of temperament during this transitional period of development.

References

Buss, A. H., & Plomin, R. (1975). *A temperament theory of personality development.* New York: Wiley.

Buss, A. H., & Plomin, R. (1984). *Temperament: Early developing personality traits.* Hillsdale, NJ: Lawrence Erlbaum Associates.

Carey, W. B. (1988). A suggested solution to the confusion in attention deficit diagnoses. *Clinical Pediatrics, 7,* 348–349.

Chess, S., & Thomas, A. (1984). *The origins and evolution of behavior disorders: Infancy to early adult life.* New York: Brunner/Mazel.

East, P. L., Lerner, R. M., & Lerner, J. V. (1988). *Early adolescent peer group fit, peer relations, and adjustment.* Unpublished manuscript.

Goldsmith, H. H., & Campos, J. J. (1982). Toward a theory of infant temperament. In R. N. Emde & R. Harmon (Eds.),

Attachment and affiliative systems: Neurobiological and psychobiological aspects (pp. 161–193). New York: Plenum.

Lerner, J. V., & Lerner, R. M. (1983). Temperament and adaptation across life: Theoretical and empirical issues. In P. B. Baltes & O. G. Brim, Jr. (Eds.), *Life-span development and behavior* (Vol. 5, pp. 197–230). New York: Academic Press.

Lerner, R. M. (1986). *Concepts and theories of human development* (2nd ed.). New York: Random House.

Nitz, K., Lerner, R. M., Lerner, J. V., & Talwar, R. (in press). Parental and peer demands, temperament, and early adolescent adjustment. *Journal of Early Adolescence.*

Rothbart, M. K., & Derryberry, D. (1981). Development of individual differences in temperament. In M. E. Lamb & A. L. Brown (Eds.), *Advances in developmental psychology* (Vol. 1, pp. 37–86). Hillsdale, NJ: Lawrence Erlbaum Associates.

Schneirla, T. C. (1957). The concept of development in comparative psychology. In D. B. Harris (Ed.), *The concept of development* (pp. 78–108). Minneapolis: University of Minnesota Press.

Strelau, J. (1983). A regulative theory of temperament. *Australian Journal of Psychology, 35,* 305–317.

Thomas, A., & Chess, S. (1977). *Temperament and development.* New York: Brunner/Mazel.

See Also

Conformity in Adolescence; Intimacy; Introspectiveness; Adolescent; Political Development; Rites of Passage; Self-Regulation; Temperament in Adolescence and Its Functional Significance.

Jacqueline V. Lerner's work on this paper was supported in part by a grant to Richard M. Lerner and Jacqueline V. Lerner from the William T. Grant Foundation and by NIMH Grant MH39957.

Temperament in Adolescence and Its Functional Significance

Alexander Thomas
Stella Chess
New York University Medical Center

Any normal adolescent's behavioral patterns are influenced by many factors: genetic inheritance, past and current life experiences, special talents, interests and ambitions, moral values, nature of the peer group, role models, etc. Among these many factors, the adolescent's temperament, or behavioral style, often plays a significant part in shaping the course of psychological development. Though this entry is specifically concerned with temperament in the adolescent, a clearer picture of this factor is possible if we start by briefly describing temperament in children. The studies of temperament, including our own, have emphasized its significance in the childhood period, where it can be more easily identified in the less complex behavioral patterns of that period as compared to adolescence and adult life.

The concept of temperament stands in contrast to abilities and motivations, two other broad categories of psychological attributes that are reflected in the adolescent's behavior. For example, two adolescents may show similar cognitive levels, learning ability, and intellectual interests, and their motivations and achievement goals may coincide. Yet, these two adolescents may differ significantly with regard to the quickness with which they move; the ease with which they approach a new environment, social situation, or task; and the effort required by others to distract them when they are absorbed in an activity. In other words, their abilities and motivations may be similar, but their temperaments (behavioral style) may be different. Or the opposite may be true. Temperaments may be similar and abilities or motivations may differ.

Individual differences in behavior due to differences in temperament can be identified even in very young infants, a finding noted by a number of investigators, going back many decades (Thomas, Chess, & Birch, 1968, p. 5). But none of these observations had been developed into a systematic, comprehensive study of temperament and its functional significance for normal and deviant psychological functioning until we initiated the New York Longitudinal

Study in 1956. We started with 133 very young infants and have now followed them with a number of data-gathering procedures and analyses into their middle and late twenties (Chess & Thomas, 1984). (Our attrition rate has been only 3%.) We did not start with newborns, even though individual differences are often evident even at birth, because behavior in the neonates is subject to a number of transient variables: the effect of the pregnancy procedures, the residual effect of maternal hormones and other chemicals on the neonate's behavior, and the unpredictability of the newborn's state of alertness from day to day and even from hour to hour. We obtained data from detailed objective reports from the parents on the children in the routines of daily life: sleeping, feeding, bathing, play, responses to familiar and unfamiliar places and people, reactions to unusual external stimuli, the nature and tempo of the response to any change in routine, and the child's response to any change in his or her routine.

Categories of Temperament

We established nine categories of temperament that appeared to us to have functional significance by an inductive content of the parent interviews. A quantitative scoring method was developed to rate each temperamental category quantitatively (Thomas, Chess, Birch, Hertzig, & Korn, 1963; Thomas, Chess, & Birch, 1968). The nine categories of temperament and their definitions are as follows:

1. *Activity level*: the level of motor component in a child's activities
2. *Rhythmicity* (regularity): the regularity or irregularity of biological functions, such as sleep, hunger cycles, bowel movements

3. *Approach or withdrawal*: the nature of the initial response to a new stimulus, be it a new food, place, toy or person—approach reactions are positive and withdrawal reactions are negative, whether displayed by mood expression or motor activity
4. *Adaptability*: the ease or difficulty with which the child adapts to change
5. *Sensory threshold*: the intensity of stimulation that is necessary to evoke a discernable response to an external stimulus such as sound, light, temperature and texture, and the intensity of such elicited response
6. *Intensity of reaction*: the energy level of response regardless of its quality or direction
7. *Quality of mood*: the amount of pleasant and friendly behavior, as contrasted with unpleasant and unfriendly behavior
8. *Distractibility*: the effectiveness of an extraneous external stimulus in interfering with or altering the direction of ongoing behavior
9. *Attention span and persistence*: these two categories are related—attention span identifies the length of time a child pursues a particular activity; persistence refers to the continuation of an activity direction in the face of obstacles.

We have also defined three temperamental patterns of functional significance by qualitative analysis and factor analysis of the data. One group is characterized by rhythmicity, positive approach responses to the new, quick adaptability to change, and mild or moderate mood intensity that is preponderantly positive. This pattern we have called "easy temperament," because such a child establishes regular sleep and feeding schedules, takes to most new foods quickly, is usually easily toilet-trained, adapts quickly to strangers, a move to a new home, and the entry to school. This group made up about 40% of our sample.

At the opposite end of the temperamental spectrum are the children with irregularity in biological functions, negative withdrawal responses to most new stimuli, slow adaptability to change, and intense mood expressions that are frequently negative in character. This pattern we have called "difficult temperament" because of the irregular sleep and feeding schedules, negative withdrawal reactions to the new, prolonged adjustment periods to change, and relatively frequent periods of loud crying that may lead to temper tantrums when the youngster is frustrated. This group makes up about 10% of our sample. This is indeed a difficult child for the caregivers, who frequently develop guilt feelings if they feel they are responsible in some way for the child's behavior, or express angry or even punitive behavior at the stress such a child is producing for them.

A third noteworthy temperamental pattern comprises a combination of negative responses of mild intensity to new situations or people, with slow adaptability after repeated contact. Such a child is often called "shy," but we have used the label "slow-to-warm-up" as a more descriptive term. About 15% of our sample fell into this category.

As can be seen from these percentages (40%, 10%, 15%), not all children fit into one of these temperamental groups. Individual children manifest varying and different combinations of temperament, and many cannot be classified as typically easy, difficult, or slow-to-warm-up. In addition, children who can be so categorized show a wide range in the degree of manifestation of one of those three patterns. Some are extremely temperamentally easy, difficult, or slow-to-warm-up in almost all situations; others show only some of these char-

acteristics, or their manifestations may be relatively mild or may differ from situation to situation.

It should be emphasized that even an extreme rating on a temperamental category or pattern is still within normal limits. The great variability in temperamental characteristics indicates the marked differences in behavioral styles of any group of individuals, no matter what age.

The nine temperamental categories and the three constellations have been by now identified in a large number of studies from many centers in this country, as well as in various European and other countries (Thomas & Chess, 1977; Porter & Collins, 1982; deVries & Sameroff, 1984; Maziade, Cote, Boudreault, Thivierge, & Coperaa, 1984).

Other concepts of temperament have been suggested by various workers (Goldsmith, Buss, Plomin, Rothbart, Thomas, Chess, Hinde, & McCall 1987), but their replicability and functional significance have yet to be demonstrated. There is general agreement that temperament is a biologically determined variable, but can be and is modified by its expression and even altered by environmental life experiences.

Our interview technique and item-scoring method, while invaluable for our basic study, is too time consuming for general use. A number of questionnaires to rate temperament in the various age periods of childhood, adolescence, and early adult life have now been devised by various workers (Chess & Thomas, 1986, pp. 238–239; Lerner, Palermo, Spiro, & Nesselroade, 1982; Thomas, Mittleman, Chess, Korn, & Cohen, 1982). The DOTS questionnaire of Lerner and coworkers, while it has been useful over a wide range of age-periods, is especially valuable and unique for the period of adolescence.

The influence of temperament on school functioning has been investigated by several research groups. They have modified our categories to develop teacher questionnaires that are more pertinent and useful to define the child's significant temperamental characteristics in the school setting (Keogh, 1982; Pullis & Caldwell, 1982; Martin, Nagle, & Paget, 1983).

Origins and Consistency Over Time

Temperament is a categorical term without any implications as to etiology. This formulation is accepted by most students of temperament, with the outstanding exceptions of Buss and Plomin (1975), who assume a genetic basis for temperament, and the Eastern European Pavlovian and neo-Pavlovian schools (Strelau, 1983), who derive the concept of temperament from the reactive properties of the central nervous system. It is our view that a most important direction for future research in temperament will be the effort to identify specific biological markers for individual categories of temperament. A promising start has been made by the work of Kagan and his coworkers (1987), who have found correlations between "behavior inhibition" (which corresponds closely to our approach/withdrawal category) and a number of physiological indexes: heart rate and its variability, pupillary dilation, and muscular tension. Several studies have suggested an appreciable but not exclusive genetic role (Torgersen & Kringlen, 1978). Sex differences are not striking, and the available data indicates that parental attitudes and practices are not decisive in shaping temperamental characteristics as they crystallize in the first few months of life (Thomas & Chess, 1980).

Continuity over time of one or another temperamental characteristic from infancy to early adult life has been strikingly evident in a number of our longitudinal study subjects. In others, significant change has taken place over time (Thomas & Chess, 1977). In this regard, temperament is similar to all other psychological factors, such as intellectual competence, motivations and goals, coping mechanisms, adaptive patterns, and value systems. Continuity over time is not the result of a fixed immutable intrapsychic attribute, but of stability in the dynamics of interplay between individual and environment. With such stability, temperamental attributes may be consistent at different age-periods. Without this stability, all types of change and discontinuity may be evident.

Temperament and Motivation

We have emphasized the concept of temperament as a biologically determined but environmentally influenced behavioral category that is *nonmotivational* in character. However, all human behavior is goal-directed and motivated, whether it be the sucking reflex of a neonate or the abstract highly symbolic equations formulated by a mathematician. With this in mind, it becomes evident that the influence of temperament does have motivational *consequences*, though not motivational origins. For example, the child with the temperamental trait of a negative reaction to a new situation will experience discomfort at the first entry to school, with its strange environment and unfamiliar children and adults. He may then cling to his mother to relieve his sense of discomfort. The discomfort has a nonmotivational origin, in his temperamental reaction, but the consequent behavior in clinging to his mother has a motivational basis. This distinction of origin and consequence is important both for our understanding the dynamics of behavioral functioning and for a proper strategy of treatment. If the child's behavior is correctly interpreted as having a temperamental origin, then counseling will consist of a plan whereby the child can be gradually introduced to this new situation, with his mother more and more receding into the background. When he has made a positive adjustment and can join the group with minor or no discomfort, his mother can then absent herself. If, on the other hand, the child's discomfort and clinging is interpreted as primarily motivational due to some subjective intrapsychic state such as chronic anxiety or an insecure attachment to his mother, then treatment will focus on identifying and treating a pathological state in the child—for which the mother is all too often assumed to be the cause. The differentiation of a temperamental versus a motivational basis for any behavioral pattern is usually not difficult, as long as the assumption is not made, as so many clinicians still do, that the behavior must be primarily motivational in origin. Data such as whether the child clings to the mother or not or is upset if she leaves him with other people he knows well is an example of the types of information that will clarify the basis of his behavior in the new school setting.

Although temperament, motivation, and abilities are conceptualized as separate factors, they inevitably interact with each other. A girl with persistence temperamentally but with strong interests and talents in music may pursue her musical works with even greater persistence than her other activities. A highly distractible child will be less distractible if he has a special motivation to perform well, and, by contrast, become especially distracted if he is bored or inept with some other specific activity.

The Functional Significance of Temperament

Tempermant by itself does not determine the level or quality of an individual's psychological functioning. Rather it is the "goodness or poorness of fit" that is crucial. Specifically, if the demands and expectations of the environment are consonant with the child's temperament, so that she/he can cope with such demands successfully, then there is a goodness of fit between child and environment, and healthy psychological development is likely. If, on the other hand, the demand and expectations of the environment are incompatible with the child's temperament, then excessive stress and failure in achievement are all too possible, causing unfavorable effects on the child's development. For example, if a demand is made on the youngster for quick adaptation to change, such as for immediate positive participation with a new peer group, this expectation can be met by the child with the temperamental attribute of quick adaptability and there will be a goodness of fit. But, for the child who adapts slowly to change, pressure to adapt quickly to a new and strange peer group will not be possible, resulting in a poorness of fit. Goodness or poorness of fit is not confined to the temperament-environment interaction. It can be an issue with academic demands or parental expectations for athletic or other accomplishments by their child.

The influence of temperament has to be viewed developmentally. A particular temperamental attribute may be important in early life and less so in later years, and vice versa. For example, rhythmicity of biological functions is an important factor in caregiving in early life. The infant who established regular sleep, nap, and feeding schedules quickly and is also easily toilet trained because his bowel movements are regular and predictable makes life much easier for her/his mother, and facilitates the development of a positive bond between them. The arythmic child, by contrast, whose sleep pattern is irregular, with frequent night-awakening, and whose naps are irregular as well, can leave many mothers groggy and irritable. Some parents even believe that somehow or other the infant's sleep behavior must have been caused by something wrong they are doing. Bowel training may also be a prolonged and even stressful procedure because of the child's irregularity. All in all, mothers or other caregivers of such a child may find it difficult to develop a warm, affectionate relationship to the infant, which may be a significant factor in the development of a less than optimistic mother-child relationship.

However, by adolescence, rhythmicity is rarely a significant temperamental attribute. Consistent sleep patterns have been achieved, as has toilet training, and variations are of minor or even no concern to the parents. In a few cases, an adolescent or adult with a very regular sleep pattern may find it difficult to stay up late to complete a school or work assignment, but this very rarely becomes a significant problem.

High distractibility is another example. The infant who fusses and squirms when dressed can be easily interested in a toy if she is highly distractible. If she is not distractible, however, dressing and undressing may be a prolonged chore for the caregiver. Similarly, the crawling infant who starts to pull at electric wires or other dangerous objects may be easily diverted if highly distractible. If she is nondistractible, and persistent as well, forceful removal of a shrieking, kicking child may be required. In school-age children, however, the issue may be reversed. The distractible child may find it difficult to fix his attention on his school work for prolonged periods,

though he can learn adequately if allowed to concentrate in short spurts. He may also "forget" after-school appointments with friends because something caught his attention on the way home and he arrived too late for his appointment. Nondistractibility, by contrast, is an asset in school or at work, or in remembering to keep appointments that have been made.

It should be emphasized, also, that the behavior of the child changes as he/she grows older, and, with this, so do the manifestations of temperament. Approach/withdrawal, for example, may be shown in infancy by the first reactions to the bath, a new food, or the first visit to the doctor. At an older age it will be evident in the reaction to a new school, a new peer group, or a move to a new neighborhood. The behavior changes with maturation, and so do the criteria for the temperamental criteria.

Temperament also plays an important role in the development of behavior disorders (we are not including the severe psychiatric syndromes such as autism, cyclical affective disorders, schizophrenia, etc.). As the eminent British psychiatrist, Michael Rutter, has put it, "The last decade has seen a burgeoning of interest in temperament. There has been an accompanying substantial growth in our knowledge and understanding of the importance of temperamental differences. Temperament constitutes a variable of considerable predictive power in developmental psychopathology, a power with both practical and theoretical implications" (1982, p. 1). Children with difficult temperament patterns are most vulnerable. Their intense negative withdrawal reactions to the new and their slow adaptability, together with biological irregularity, make the demands of early socialization highly stressful for these children. "Poorness of fit" is frequent for these children, since many if not most parents do not understand the nature of the child's behavior, and use pressure, intimidation, appeasement, or inconsistency in their approach, instead of calm, friendly, but firm and patient insistence. The risk of behavior disorder development is further increased if a child is mentally retarded, physically handicapped, or has a mentally ill parent.

However, behavior disorders can develop with any temperamental pattern, even with that of the easy child, if demands for change and adaptation are excessively dissonant with the particular child's temperament, and therefore highly stressful. No temperamental pattern confers an immunity to behavior disorder development, nor is it inevitably fated to create psychopathology.

An accurate knowledge of an individual's temperament can be very useful not only to parents, other caregivers, and mental health professionals, but also to other professionals who have specific responsibilities for the care and healthy development of children and adolescents: pediatricians, family physicians, hospital nurses, and educators (see Chess & Thomas, 1986, for detailed discussion of these issues).

Temperament in the Adolescent

The preceding sections of this entry, while emphasizing the issue of temperament in the child, apply equally as well to the adolescent. There are, however, some significant differences.

In early childhood the identification and rating of temperament is relatively easy. Motives and abilities are rudimentary and as yet underdeveloped, and easy to distinguish from temperament. As the child grows older this task of identifying and categorizing temperament becomes more and more complex. Increasingly elaborate repertoires of ability and talents mature and

become evident. Motivational patterns also become more complex as brain functioning develops, as life experiences become cumulative in their effect on goal directions, and as coping and defensive mechanisms become crystallized and elaborated. Furthermore, temperament, motivations, and abilities enter into increasingly complex processes so that individual items and patterns of behavior come more and more to reflect this interplay of influences. Thus, it may be relatively simple in a two-year-old to determine whether slow achievement in task performance, such as self-feeding and dressing, is due primarily to temperamental issues such as slow activity, distractibility or low persistence; or to motivational issues such as a fear that these accomplishments will attenuate his close contact with the mother if she needs less and less to do such caregiving activities; or to slow maturation of perceptual and neuromuscular dexterity.

As the child grows older, however, the nature of the parent-child interaction, other intra- and extrafamilial environmental influences, and the impact of special life experiences all play significant roles in shaping behavior and modifying temperament, motivations, and abilities and the dynamic interplay over time among these latter factors. As a result, an adolescent's (or an adult's) difficulties in school or with a job may, for example, be the result of the constantly evolving interaction between parental expectations and pressures, sibling and peer competition, characteristics of the school, socioeconomic problems of the family, cognitive and perceptual ability, self-image and self-judgments, or various temperamental characteristics such as very low or very high activity level, withdrawal responses to the new, slow adaptability, high distractibility, low persistence and/or short attention span.

The task of teasing out the temperamental factor in the complex behavior patterns of the adolescent thus becomes formidable. But it is a necessary task. In some instances temperament may not play a significant role in an adolescent's problems. But in other instances it may be a significant and even crucial factor in his difficulties in coping successfully with the tasks society and he himself expects to accomplish. This indentification of the adolescent's temperament may be evident to parents, teachers, or friends, who may point out that he gets too angry at minor annoyances, that he is too shy with a new group even when they are eager to accept him, that he is a "slow poke" and should make himself move faster to get things accomplished, etc. If the identification of temperament is difficult, it becomes the mental health professional's responsibility. Questionnaires such as the DOTS developed by Lerner and associates are helpful. Also, the answer may very often be found by exploring two questions in detail: first, does the adolescent show this troublesome behavior even when engaged in an activity of his own choice?, and second, is there any substantial evidence that the behavior is due to some identifiable motive or inadequacy in level of functioning?

Temperament, Self-Insight, and Mastery

To identify for an adolescent the temperamental factors in his/her behavior is no mere academic exercise. (The same is true of identification of motives and abilities.) Such self-insight, which the adolescent but not the child is capable of achieving, can have enormous benefits in a number of ways. The slow-to-warm-up adolescent who understands that she may be shy and uncomfortable in a new situation, but that these reactions will disappear gradually as she becomes familiar with this new setting, will be motivated to live through the initial phase of discomfort and to resist her impulse to withdraw by using some excuse. As a result, she will finally achieve a positive adaptation, reap the rewards that the new environment can bring her, and develop a sense of mastery and control of her life. She is also likely to find that as she succeeds in coping successfully with one new situation after another, that the initial periods of discomfort become shorter and less intense.

Another adolescent, with a similar slow-to-warm-up temperament, may, however, take a different course. She may lack self-insight into her temperament, either because she has not developed spontaneous insight into the meaning of her initial reactions to the new, or this insight has not been provided by parents, teachers, friends, or professional counselors. She may also have been sheltered by her parents and by limited life experiences with the new, with insufficient opportunities to discover that she could gradually adapt successfully to the new. She may even have been pressured by parents, teachers, or friends to involve herself quickly with the new, a pressure that could only result in increased discomfort and a dread of facing any new social aspects of the task demand. Such an adolescent will lack the positive self-insight of the girl described just above. Rather, she is all too likely to interpret her reactions to the new as a reflection of some mysterious defect within herself over which she has no control. With such distortion of self-insight, the adolescent will predictably try to avoid any new demands or expectations, or, if she cannot avoid such a situation, to function defensively, such as by standing at the periphery of a group or attaching herself to the person or element of the task that is not new for her. Such a pattern of behavior can have significant subjective consequences for the adolescent's self-image and self-esteem, and serious objective consequences for her social life, academic functioning, and career opportunities.

This example of the importance of self-insight into his temperament for an adolescent can be repeated for other temperamental attributes. To give a few other brief examples, the adolescent who knows he can explode with intense anger even with minor disagreements or frustrations can learn to "keep the lid on" until he is himself and also train himself to use other, more acceptable behavioral strategies when he finds himself about to face a confrontation or frustration; the highly distractible adolescent can call on his friends and family to remind him to get back to the task from which he has been diverted; the highly persistent adolescent can learn not to start an absorbing activity if he knows he will have to drop it quickly for some other unavoidable activity; the low-activity adolescent can learn that he should give himself extra time to finish a task or to be ready for a social or other appointment.

It is also important for the family and professional counselor to emphasize the positive aspects of the adolescent's temperamental attributes, even as the unfavorable consequences are identified. To be slow-to-warm-up in a new situation is not always undesirable. It can lead to cautiousness in evaluating whether and how to get involved, in contrast to the impulsive adolescent, who plunges immediately into something new that attracts him, without weighing the consequences of this quick commitment. To explode with anger is sometimes appropriate and effective. The highly distractible adolescent may "forget" appointments and assignments unless reminded, but his awareness of the behavior of others around him when he is presumably absorbed in some task, can be an asset in many situations. The slowly adaptive

adolescent is not likely to be a "pushover." The point is that any temperamental trait is not always unfavorable under all circumstances.

The key point to be emphasized is that by adolescence, normal individuals are capable of gaining this insight into their temperament and other behavioral attributes. If they use this insight constructively, it can lead to a sense of genuine self-esteem and confidence in coping successfully with the social and task demands that lie ahead of them. If, on the other hand, they fail to gain this insight, and most especially if they have one or another temperamental attribute or pattern that is toward the extreme end of the normal distribution, rather than average for their peer group and community, then they are not likely to gain the ability to control the extreme expression of their temperament when this is undesirable in specific social, academic, or work situations. Such lack of control and its consequences can only hinder or prevent the development of the positive self-esteem that is such a basic psychological asset for the adolescent as he begins to develop his own independent and mature life.

References

Buss, A. H., & Plomin, R. (1975). *A temperament theory of personality development.* New York: Wiley.

Chess, S., & Thomas, A. (1984). *Origins and evolution of behavior disorders: From infancy to early adult life.* New York: Brunner/Mazel.

Chess, S., & Thomas, A. (1986). *Temperament in clinical practice.* (1986). New York: Guilford Press.

deVries, M. W., & Sameroff, A. J. (1984). Culture and temperament: Influences on infant temperament in three East African societies. *American Journal of Orthopsychiatry, 54,* 83–96.

Goldsmith, H. H., Buss, A. H., Plomin, R., Rothbart, M., Thomas, A., Chess, S., Hinde, R., & McCall, R. (1987). Round-table: What is temperament? Four approaches. *Child Development, 58,* 515–529.

Kagan, J., Resnick, J. S., & Sniderman, N. (1987). The physiology and psychology of behavioral inhibition in children. *Child Development, 58,* 1459–1473.

Keogh, B. K. (1982). Children's temperament and teacher decisions. In R. Porter & G. Collins (Eds.), *Ciba Foundation Symposium 89: Temperamental differences in infants and young children* (pp. 267–278). London: Pitman.

Lerner, R. M., Palermo, M., Spiro, A., & Nesselroade, J. R. (1982). Assessing the dimensions of temperamental individuality across the life span: The Dimensions of Temperament Survey (DOTS). *Child Development, 53,* 149–159.

Martin, R. P., Nagle, R., & Paget, K. (1983). Relationships between temperament and classroom behavior, teacher attitudes, and academic achievement. *Journal of Psychoeducational Assessment, 1,* 377–386.

Maziade, M., Cote, R., Boudreault, M., Thivierge, J., & Caperaa, P. (1984). The New York Longitudinal studies model of temperament. Gender differences and demographic correlates in a French-speaking population. *Journal of the Academy of Child Psychiatry, 23,* 582–587.

Porter, R., & Collins, G. (Eds.). (1982). *Ciba Foundation Symposium 89: Temperamental differences in infants and young children.* London: Pitman.

Pullis, M., & Caldwell, J. (1982). The influence of children's temperament characteristics on teacher's decision strategies. *American Educational Research Journal, 19,* 165–181.

Rutter, M. (1982). Introduction. In R. Porter & G. Collins (Eds.), *Ciba Foundation Symposium 89: Temperamental differences in infants and young children.* London: Pitman.

Strelau, J. (1983). *Temperament personality activity.* New York: Academic Press.

Thomas, A., & Chess, S. (1977). *Temperament and development.* New York: Brunner/Mazel.

Thomas, A., & Chess, S. (1980). *The dynamics of psychological development.* New York: Brunner/Mazel.

Thomas, A., Chess, S., & Birch, H. G. (1968). *Temperament and behavior disorders in children.* New York: New York University Press.

Thomas, A., Chess, S., Birch, H. G., Hertzig, M. E., & Korn, S. (1963). *Behavioral individuality in early childhood.* New York: New York University Press.

Thomas, A., Mittleman, M., Chess, S., Korn, S., & Cohen, J. (1982). A temperamental questionnaire for early adult life. *Educational and Psychological Measurement, 42,* 593–600.

Torgersen, A. M., & Kringlen, E. (1978). Genetic aspects of temperamental differences in infants. *Journal of the American Academy of Child Psychiatry, 17,* 433–444.

See Also

Conformity in Adolescence; Intimacy; Introspectiveness, Adolescent; Political Development; Rites of Passage; Self-Regulation; Temperament during Adolescence.

Theories of Adolescent Development

Rachna Talwar
Jacqueline V. Lerner
The Pennsylvania State University

Numerous theories of development have been advanced to account for development during adolescence. These theories can be placed into three major explanatory categories: nature theories, nurture theories, and interaction theories (Lerner & Spanier, 1980). The nature theories of adolescent development were the first historically, and stress that biology, or the person's *nature*, is the source of adolescent development, and that experience and environment have little impact on the quality of behavior or on the sequence of change in behaviors occurring across adolescence. Nurture theories, on the other hand, stress that experience, learning, and environment are the major sources of variables influencing behavior and behavior change. Some of the nurture theorists emphasize the functional link between stimulus and response and eschew cognitive and mental factors in behavior change. Other theorists stress that attention, observation, and modeling of behaviors leads to the acquisition of new responses.

The third group, "interaction" theories of adolescent development, stress the interplay of both nature (biology) and nurture (environment) in shaping development. According to Lerner and Spanier (1980), interaction theories of adolescent development can be categorized as "weak," "moderate," and "strong." Weak interaction theories emphasize that either nature or nurture is more important. The moderate interaction theory gives equal conceptual weight to both nature and nurture, but views them as being independent of each other. The strong interaction theory sees nature and nurture as always embedded with each other, as dynamically interacting (Lerner, 1978). Examples of the above types of theories are presented below.

Nature Theories of Adolescent Development

Nature theories place primary stress on purportedly evolutionarily shaped, hereditary mechanisms in explaining individual behavior and development. As a consequence, such theories explain ontogenetic change on the basis of the presumed relevance of phylogenetic history and biogenetic mechanisms for the individual's life span. Although several instances of such theories exist (e.g., see Lerner, 1986, for reviews), one has been central across the history of the study of adolescence.

G. Stanley Hall's recapitulation theory (Hall, 1904), was the first scientific theory to define adolescence as a specific period in ontogeny after childhood. Hall asserted that human beings relive or pass through stages in their course of ontogenetic development that correspond to the major evolutionary stages involved in the history of mankind. That is, individuals repeat the development of the human race from its early primitive existence to its more recent, civilized state. Since, in this view, evolutionary-shaped biological (e.g., maturational) factors control and direct development, growth, and behavior, this theory paid little attention to the influence of environmental factors on the quality or sequential emergence of behavior.

Adolescence was a period of transition between childhood and adulthood. This ontogenetic period corresponded to a time when—in evolution—the human race was in a turbulent and transitional stage between its beastlike past and its current, civilized state. Thus, adolescence, in recapitulating this stage, involved stormy and stressful transition too, here a change involving being dominated by instinctual drives associated with physical growth while adapting to socializing demands made by significant others (Hall, 1904).

Nurture Theories of Adolescent Development

Generally, nurture theories suggest that there is a functional relationship that exists between stimulus and response (e.g., see Bijou & Baer, 1961). However, there is a great diversity in nurture theories, and no consensus exists about what is the nurture view of behavior (Lerner, 1986; Lerner & Spanier, 1980). This situation is complicated further because no general nurture theory has been specifically developed to deal with the phenomena of human development (White, 1970). However, some nurture theories are useful in understanding adolescent development.

DAVIS'S THEORY OF SOCIALIZED ANXIETY ▪ Davis (1944) has proposed a theory of socialized anxiety. He argues that individuals learn to anticipate punishment for behaviors that are disapproved. This anticipation of punishment, termed socialized anxiety, is experienced as an unpleasant state by the individual. Because of this unpleasant state, a person's behavior will be aimed at reducing or avoiding it, that is, behavior will be aimed at diminishing or eliminating this anxiety. Adolescence, according to Davis, is a period where there is less certainty about what behaviors are punished and what behaviors are rewarded. As such, there is no certain way of diminishing socialized anxiety. Accordingly, storm and stress may be involved during adolescence.

However, according to Davis, socialized anxiety during adolescence is important because it serves as a motivating and, through its reduction, as a reinforcing agent in the process of socialization. Nevertheless, too much or too little socialized anxiety during adolescence hinders the attainment of mature behavior.

McCANDLESS'S DRIVE THEORY ▪ A "drive theory" of adolescent behavior and development was proposed by McCandless (1970). This

theory was predicated on the view that all human behavior is based on drives (e.g., hunger or sex) and that the direction behavior takes is a consequence of a particular drive. Over time, the individual learns that certain behaviors reduce drive-states; while some of these behaviors are rewarded, others are punished by society (McCandless, 1970). Social learning involves, then, acquiring those drive-reducing behaviors that will likely attain rewards and eliminating or avoiding those drive-reducing behaviors likely to result in punishment.

The relevance of this theory to adolescence is that, during adolescence, a new drive, the sex drive, emerges. Because of this emergence, adolescents have to learn socially acceptable ways of reducing this drive. As males and females are differentially rewarded for male or female sex-appropriate behavior, adolescents will adopt specific roles appropriate for their sex (McCandless, 1970).

COGNITIVE SOCIAL LEARNING THEORIES OF ADOLESCENT DEVELOPMENT ■

As there is no one nurture view of human development, there is no one cognitive social learning theory of adolescent development. One cognitive social learning theory proposed by Albert Bandura (1977) used nurture-based learning principles to explain the role of the social environment in controlling human behavior. According to Bandura, human development is a lifelong process of socialization in which modeling and reinforcement of behavior shape biological drives. Through modeling, adolescents observe and imitate the behavior of others, and through reinforcement, adolescents learn that behaviors that are rewarded are approved while behaviors that are punished are disapproved.

Interaction Theories of Adolescent Development

Interaction theories stress the contributions of both nature and nurture in shaping development. Theories of this type differ, however, in whether this interaction is conceived of as weak, moderate, or strong. Weak interaction theories stress that one source, typically nature, is the prime mover of development and that the second source only acts to hamper or facilitate the action of the first. Moderate interaction theories see both nature and nurture as equal sources of change. However, each source is unaffected by the other over the course of their interaction. Strong interaction theories emphasize the dynamic, systemic, transactional, or dialectic relation between nature and nurture. Examples of each type exist in relation to the study of adolescent development.

SIGMUND FREUD'S PSYCHOSEXUAL STATE THEORY ■

According to the psychoanalytic theory of Sigmund Freud (1949), adolescent and adult development are determined in the first five years of life. Therefore, little emphasis is placed on pubescence and adolescence. Thus, in order to understand adolescent development one has to understand the libidinal fixations and conflicts that occurred in the first three psychosexual stages, namely the oral stage, the anal stage, and the phallic stage.

According to Freudian theory, during the time of pubertal development the libido, or psychic energy, resurfaces after being dormant, and it is localized in the genital area. This stage is termed the genital stage and is marked by the emergence of sexuality that may take an adult form (depending on prior fixations in earlier psychosexual stages). Thus, if the adolescent has been successful in his/her previous psychosexual development, there emerges the potential for adult reproductive sexuality, a sexuality directed towards heterosexual relationships and development.

Since the stages of psychosexual development occur in a predetermined and universal sequence, nature, or biological, factors predominate in the sequence of development. However, Freud contends that nature or experiential factors serve as inhibitors or facilitators of this nature-based sequence (that is, nurture is the source of fixations of nature-based changes). Thus, Freud's theory is a "weak" interaction theory.

ANNA FREUD'S THEORY OF ADOLESCENT DEFENSE MECHANISMS ■ Sigmund Freud's
theory placed relatively little emphasis on adolescence. Despite his neglect concerning this period of life, it has been a major concern of Freud's daughter, Anna. Anna Freud (1969) believed that adolescence is a period marked by turbulence because of new, internal demands on the adolescent arising from his/her sexual maturation and the intensified sexual drive associated with it. An increased sexual drive brings with it an increase in most impulse activity, a change leading to the enhancement of aggressiveness, inquisitiveness, and egocentricity in adolescence. Along with this set of changes comes a reactivation of the psychosexual conflicts of childhood, an occurrence leading to ambivalent behavior in adolescents; that is, adolescents tend to alternate between emotional extremes, such as excessive independence and clinging dependence.

In her discussion of adolescence Anna Freud (1969) emphasizes that the relationship between the id, the ego, and the superego undergoes qualitative change. The process of physiological growth and sexual maturation leads to a disequilibrium between the id and the ego, resulting in increased conflict during this period. In turn, the superego, which is developed through the assimilation of the moral values of the people with whom the adolescent identifies, comes into conflict with the ego that is yielding to the id impulses.

Since the conflicts of this period arouse much anxiety in the adolescent, the adolescent tries to cope through the development of new defense mechanisms as well as through the continuation of the use of prior defense mechanisms. As with the defense mechanisms used in earlier periods, new defense mechanisms are unconscious, but they are also influenced by learning. Since the adolescent learns that certain ways of acting out sexual impulses are not condoned by society (e.g., incest is forbidden), some defense against these manifestations of sexual impulses is established. One defensive strategy typically drawn from use in prior periods of life is sublimation, where sexual impulses are transformed into more socially acceptable endeavors such as intellectual and artistic activity. Displacement is another major defense, one wherein the adolescent displaces his/her impulses to other things or persons. Identification with others besides parents, including teachers and peers, may also occur.

Anna Freud held that not only does the adolescent try the above defenses, but he or she also forms new types of defense mechanisms, such as intellectualism and asceticism. In intellectualism the adolescent uses his/her newly developed abstract thinking and intellectual reasoning to justify his or her behavior. This helps in creating an emotional distance between ideas and impulses. In asceticism the adolescent unconsciously denies that he or she has any sexual desires. This is an effort to impose control on their sexual needs.

In sum, Anna Freud sees adolescence as a necessarily and universally developmentally turbulent period, a period having these features because of the emergence of the sexual drive during puberty. Her view is consistent with that of Sigmund Freud, who sees nurture as only an inhibitor or facilitator of nature. Both of their theories are therefore weak-interaction ones.

ERIK ERIKSON'S THEORY OF IDENTITY DEVELOPMENT ■

Erikson's (1959, 1968) theory is an expansion and modification of the Freudian theory of psychosexual development and can be characterized also as a "weak" interaction theory. This theory shifts the emphasis of development from an exclusively psychosexual, as in classical Freudian theory, to a psychosocial emphasis.

In his theory, Erikson describes eight stages of psychosocial development. In each stage the person has to develop a capacity (an ego function) to meet societal demands. Thus, each stage involves an "ego crisis," the resolution of which depends on whether the person meets the demands of the society and develops appropriate ego capabilities.

The core concept in Erikson's theory in regard to adolescence is the acquisition of ego-identity, and the identity crisis is the most prominent and essential characteristic of adolescence (Erikson, 1950). During adolescence the person has to adopt behaviors (that is, a *role*) that involves the perpetuation of society and, as such, the establishment of a sense of identity. Thus, the adolescent experiences a crisis between identity formation at one end and identity diffusion (or role confusion) at the other.

PIAGET'S THEORY OF MODERATE NATURE-NURTURE INTERACTION ■

A moderate interaction between nature and nurture involves the view that heredity and environment, acting independently of each other, are both equally important in development. Jean Piaget's theory of cognitive development falls into this moderate interaction category.

Piaget forwarded a stage theory of development, wherein the posited stages are universal and invariant. These stages are brought about by the organism acting on the environment and the environment acting on the organism. Although Piaget accepts the role of organism and environment in development, a close examination of this theory has led to the belief that experience or environment is not as fully considered as are maturational factors (Brainerd, 1978). Perhaps, for this reason, some consider Piaget's theory as a weak interaction theory.

Piaget (1950, 1970) believed that cognitive development, that is, the processes involved in the acquisition of knowledge, involve a progressive development through four stages. The fourth stage involves the attainment of formal operations, or abstract thought, during adolescence. Formal operations are most representative of adolescents in Western society. With the attainment of such abstract thinking abilities, the person can now deal with hypothetical situations, and can make deductions in order to find solutions to problems, both real and counterfactual. The emergence of this capacity constitutes a turning point in the development of the structure of adolescent thought. Indeed, because the individual centers so much on this newly acquired thinking ability, egocentricism in adolescents is believed, by some scientists, to emerge. That is, the adolescent believes that others are as preoccupied with the object of his or her thought (for example, his or her own physical appearance) as he or she is. The failure to distinguish between his or her thoughts and those of others leads to the construction of an imaginary audience (Elkind, 1967). Along with this emergence of an imaginary audience, the adolescent also constructs a personal fable, that is, a belief that he or she is a unique or special person.

In sum, with the attainment of formal operations, Piaget (1950, 1970, 1972) believes that the last stage of cognitive development is achieved. However, research indicates that not all people achieve formal operational ability. Moreover, some researchers believe that cognitive changes proceed beyond adolescence and involve a fifth stage of cognitive development (Arlin, 1975; Labouvie-Vief, 1980).

STRONG INTERACTION THEORIES ▪ Strong interaction theories see nature and nurture as dynamically or reciprocally interactive with each other, with each acting as a product and producer of the other (Lerner & Spanier, 1980). Adolescent development involves a combined influence of the inner-biological, individual-psychological, outer-physical, and sociocultural-historical levels of analyses (Riegel, 1975). The basis of adolescent development involves the interdependence among all levels, and is not the product of a single level (Lerner & Spanier, 1980; Petersen & Taylor, 1980).

Lerner and Spanier (1980) have elaborated this idea within the framework of a "dynamic interactional" model of adolescent development. From the point of view of this model, the potential for change is continual. The phenomena associated with puberty, for example, are not merely biological events. Rather, such changes are linked to changes in the social context of the adolescent. At a molar level these changes involve nutritional and medical care that can affect the timing and quality of pubertal change. In turn, the resulting changes in pubertal development can fur-ther impact on society and culture as it evolves across history. For instance, some possible implications for society of females experiencing puberty earlier in life—when they are less cognitively and emotionally developed—are increased incidences of illegitimate births and more teenagers dropping out of school. The implications for adolescents are also problematic because reaching puberty and reproductive maturity at an early age can result in an increase in stress for the adolescent. At a more molecular level pubertal changes can influence how others in the social context react to the adolescent and these different reactions may feed back to the youth and alter his or her ensuing psychosocial development (Lerner & Lerner, 1989).

Conclusions

Nature, nurture, and interaction theories of adolescent development represent quite contrasting orientations to understanding the phenomena involved in this period of development. Yet all theories put forward concepts that bear on the core conceptual issues of adolescent development, that is, of the role of biology and context in the lives of young people. Accordingly, the empirical ideas and concomitant research done by researchers associated with each respective approach are inevitably valuable in shedding light on these issues. Thus, these different theoretical approaches to conceptualizing adolescent development are vital for providing ideas and data needed to understand the complexities of this period of life.

References

Arlin, P. K. (1975). Cognitive development in adulthood: A fifth stage? *Developmental Psychology, 11*, 602–606.

Bandura, A. (1965). A stormy decade: Fact or fiction? *Psychology in the School, 1*, 224–231.

Bandura, A. (1977). *Social learning theory.* Englewood Cliffs, NJ: Prentice-Hall.

Bandura, A., & Walters, R. H. (1959). *Adolescent aggression.* New York: Ronald Press.

Bijou, S. W., & Baer, D. M. (1961). *Child development: A systematic and empirical theory* (Vol. 1). New York: Appleton-Century-Crofts.

Brainerd, C. J. (1978). The stage question in cognitive-developmental theory. *Behavioral and Brain Sciences, 2,* 173–182.

Davis, A. (1944). Socialization and the adolescent personality. *Forty-third year book of the National Society for the Study of Education* (Vol. 43). Chicago: University of Chicago Press.

Elkind, D. (1967). Egocentricism in adolescence. *Child Development, 38,* 1025–1034.

Erikson, E. H. (1950). *Childhood and society.* New York: W. W. Norton.

Erikson, E. H. (1959). Identity and the life-cycle. *Psychological Issues, 1,* 18–164.

Erikson, E. H. (1968). *Identity, youth, and crisis.* New York: Norton.

Freud, A. (1969). Adolescence as a developmental disturbance. In G. Caplan & S. Lebovice (Eds.), *Adolescence* (pp. 5–10). New York: Basic Books.

Freud, S. (1949). *Outline of psychoanalysis.* New York: Norton.

Hall, G. S. (1904). *Adolescence.* New York: Appleton.

Labouvie-Vief, G. (1980). Beyond formal operations: Uses and limits of pure logic in life-span development. *Human Development, 23,* 141–161.

Lerner, R. M. (1978). Nature, nurture, and dynamic interactionism. *Human Development, 21,* 1–20.

Lerner, R. M. (1986). *Concepts and theories of human development* (2nd ed.). New York: Random House.

Lerner, R. M., & Lerner, J. V. (1989). Organismic and social-contextual bases of development: The sample case of early adolescence.

In W. Damon (Ed.), *Child development today and tomorrow* (pp. 69–85). San Francisco: Jossey-Bass.

Lerner, R. M., & Spanier, G. B. (1980). *Adolescent development: A life-span perspective.* New York: McGraw-Hill.

McCandless, B. R. (1970). *Adolescents.* Hinsdale, IL: Dryden Press.

Petersen, A. C., & Taylor, T. (1980). The biological approach to adolescence: Biological change and psychological adaptation. In Adelson (Ed.), *Handbook of adolescent psychology* (pp. 117–155). New York: Wiley.

Piaget, J. (1950). *The psychology of intelligence.* London: Routledge & Kegan Paul.

Piaget, J. (1970). Piaget's theory. In P. H. Mussen (Ed.), *Carmichael's manual of child psychology* (Vol. 1, pp. 703–732). New York: Wiley.

Piaget, J. (1972). Intellectual evolution from adolescence to adulthood. *Human Development, 15,* 1–12.

Riegel, K. F. (1975). Toward a dialectical theory of development. *Human Development, 18,* 50–64.

Sampson, E. E. (1977). Psychology and the American ideal. *Journal of Personality and Social Psychology, 35,* 767–782.

White, S. H. (1970). The learning theory tradition and child psychology. In P. H. Mussen (Ed.), *Carmichael's manual of child psychology* (pp. 657–702). New York: Wiley.

See Also

Critical Periods; Developmental Contextualism and Adolescent Development; Developmental Tasks; Life-Span View of Human Development and Adolescent Development; Multivariate, Replicated, Single-Subject, Repeated Measures Design: Studying Change in the Adolescent; Psychoanalytic Theory.

Jacqueline V. Lerner's work on this paper was supported in part by a grant to Richard M. Lerner and Jacqueline V. Lerner from the William T. Grant Foundation, and by NIMH grant MH39957.

Turmoil, Adolescent

Daniel Offer
Northwestern University Medical School

R. B. Church
Michael Reese Hospital

Adolescent turmoil is defined as an emotional condition marked by two primary features: (1) a significant disruption in psychological equilibrium as indexed by fluctuation in moods, confusion in thought, and changeable, unpredictable behavior, and (2) serious conflicts and rebellion against one's parents. It is believed that if adolescents do not experience turmoil, they will stay overdependent on their parents, have trouble developing a sense of identity, and have difficulties relating well to peers. In addition, it has been commonly thought by mental health professionals and the population at large that typical or normal adolescents need to experience adolescent turmoil as a part of their normal development (see Offer, Ostrov, & Howard, 1981). In other words, it is more normal for children to go through adolescence experiencing a period of emotional disequilibrium than to experience emotional equilibrium.

Although these beliefs are intriguing and certainly have some intuitive appeal for those of us who have gone through adolescence ourselves or who have witnessed adolescent transition, one must ask whether systematic data exists that support the belief that the majority of youth actually do suffer "turmoil" as they pass through the stage of adolescence.

New Directions in Adolescent Research

There has been a recent upsurge in adolescent research suggesting that (1) adolescent turmoil does not, in fact, characterize the majority of adolescents, and that (2) adolescence is not characterized by the two features (psychological disequilibrium and deep-rooted parent-child conflicts) described above.

First, focusing on the distribution of emotional disturbance in adolescents, many studies examining the prevalence of emotional disturbance in adolescence have found that emotionally disturbed adolescents comprise only about 20% of the adolescent populations examined—clearly a minority (Krupinski, Baikie, Stoller, Graves, O'Day, & Polke, 1967; Langner, Gersten, & Eisenberg, 1974; Offer, Ostrov, & Howard, 1987; Rutter, Graham, Chadwick & Yule, 1976). Moreover, this 20% estimate of emotional disturbance is similar to that found in the adult population. Thus, adolescents are not any likelier than adults to experience emotional turmoil. It is important to note, however, that although this percentage has been found both here in the United States and in other countries, the estimate pertains to a limited sample of middle-class adolescents. It is not clear, therefore, what the distribution of emotional disturbance would be for other populations of adolescents. This issue clearly merits further examination.

Second, focusing on the nature of adolescent turmoil, Offer (1985), for example, comprehensively examined the psychological dispositions of a population of 30,000 adolescents. In his study he used: (1) The Offer Self-Image Questionnaire (OSIQ), which has adolescents rate themselves on items indexing psychological adjustment and family and social relationships; (2) interviews with both adolescents and parents; and (3) behavioral ratings of adolescents by their teachers. With respect to psychological disequilibrium, Offer found that the majority of adolescents observed exhibited no mood swings or behavioral unpredictability. Although they did exhibit some anxiety over situational variables such as an upcoming exam, there was no evidence of profound emotional conflict. In addition, they appeared to exhibit confidence about their own capacities and skills, as well as optimism about their futures.

With respect to parent-child conflict, many studies have found that most adolescent-parent conflict does not tend to be over serious and deep-rooted issues but instead tends to be over mundane matters such as household chores, dating, curfews, and personal appearance (e.g., Powers, Hauser, & Kilner, 1989). Moreover, Offer (1985) found that adolescents did not feel that they had any major problems with their parents. In fact, most adolescents had positive feelings about their parents and tended to share their parents values and attitudes.

It is important to point out that in many of the studies suggesting that emotional turmoil and parent-child conflict do not characterize the stage of adolescence, the method of assessment is typically a rating scale that requires an individual to report how he or she feels in general, out of the context of everyday life. That is, an individual is required to provide a "policy statement" about his or her psychological state rather than to provide a statement about what he or she is feeling at that very moment, in the context of a specific daily activity. Thus, these studies may not reflect actual psychological experiences of adolescents as they occur in the context of everyday events. Retrospectively, adolescents may report that they do not feel themselves to be in turmoil or in conflict with their parents. However, if observed "at the moment" in the context of everyday life, adolescents might report very different psychological experiences.

A unique method was devised to capture adolescents' psychological experiences and activities "at-the-moment" in the context of their everyday lives (Csikszentmihalyi & Larsen, 1984). Adolescents were asked to carry electronic beepers around with them as they went about their regular daily routines. The electronic pagers would send signals to these adolescents on a random basis; when paged, these adolescents would fill out questionnaires asking about their psychological experiences at the precise moment that they were paged. Even with this method, the same psychological profile of normal adolescence was revealed. Adolescents were neither exhibiting extreme psychological maladjustment nor were they involved in an inordinate number of serious conflicts with their parents (Csikszentmihalyi & Larsen, 1984).

Although most adolescents do not experience "turmoil" in the classical sense, there appears to be a small group of adolescents who do. Offer (1985) found in his study that a subsample of his adolescents (approximately 20%) exhibited dramatic mood swings and behavioral acting out of frustrations, low self-esteem, and inabilities to cope. In addition, this subsample tended to have difficulties communicating with their parents and saw the adult world from an adversarial point of view.

Moreover, it should be noted that because there has been such a common belief that emotional turmoil in adolescence is normal, we perhaps have neglected to properly attend to the 20% of adolescents who are experiencing emotional difficulty (Offer, 1987). After all, although emotional turmoil may characterize only 20% of the adolescent population, that percentage includes a large number of individuals (3.4 million teenagers if the data from the various studies examining frequency of emotional disturbance in adolescents is extrapolated to the larger population). Thus, a focus on adolescent disturbance should become a priority for those interested in mental health intervention.

Sources for the Myth of Adolescent Turmoil

How, one may ask, did this overwhelming impression that adolescence is a time characterized by emotional turmoil come about? There are a number of sources for this widespread belief, three of which we will discuss here.

HISTORICAL ROOTS ▪ The notion that the period of adolescence is characterized by turmoil has its historical roots in the work of Stanley Hall, one of the first American psychologists. Hall, influenced by nineteenth-century German romantic writings on youthful rebellion against the established ways of the adult generation,

first coined the phrase "adolescent turmoil" to characterize universally the stage of adolescence (Hall, 1904). Hall described the adolescent psyche as being characterized by extreme fluctuations in emotional states such that the adolescent will feel happy and optimistic one day and depressed and pessimistic the next.

Hall focused on a functional explanation for adolescent turmoil. He reasoned that adolescence was full of turbulence primarily because the child has to separate forcefully from the grasp of his parents in order to proceed from childhood to adulthood. Therefore, in order to grow up mentally healthy, the adolescent child must rebel against the established values of his or her parents.

Anna Freud further substantiated the theory of adolescent turmoil in her influential work with disturbed children and adolescents (Freud, 1958). She provided a mechanistic explanation for adolescent turmoil. She argued that the biological changes occurring during puberty lead to a conflict between the instinctual drives of the individual and the cultural forces surrounding the individual. This conflict, in turn, makes for an unbalanced psychic structure and disharmonious behavior.

Even more recently, Peter Blos, a major contributor to psychoanalytic theory on adolescent development, supported the belief that it is necessary for adolescents to experience "turmoil" in their development (Blos, 1961). Blos wrote that adolescence is characterized by turmoil that can only be alleviated with the acquisition of controlling, inhibiting, and evaluative principles that do not occur until after adolescence.

THE DATA ON WHICH THE "ADOLESCENT TURMOIL" THEORY IS BASED ▪ Contributing to this belief in adolescent turmoil was the fact that these theories of adolescence were based either on unsystematic observations of youth or on youth in a clinical setting. For example, Stanley Hall based his theories largely on philosophical beliefs rooted in evolutionary theory and his own unsystematic observations of youth. Anna Freud and Peter Blos generalized to the normal population of adolescents, from their extensive work with disturbed children and adolescents. In other words, no one had systematically determined whether the "turmoil" discovered in these select populations of adolescents was generalizable to the larger population of adolescents, nor were systematic examinations carried out to determine the frequency of adolescent turmoil in the larger population.

BIOLOGICAL, COGNITIVE, AND SOCIAL CHANGES IN ADOLESCENCE
■ Finally, there is substantial evidence suggesting that dramatic biological, psychological, and social changes are occurring as the adolescent progresses from childhood to adulthood. Biologically, it has been well-documented that the endocrine system is maturing into the adult system. This change results in, among other events, dramatic increases in hormone levels (Sussman & Loriaux, 1987). Moreover, recent research has found that these increases in hormone levels do have a relationship with changes in certain psychological states such as aggression, impulse inhibition, and tolerance for frustration, above and beyond what might be accounted for by the emotional significance of an adolescent's changing physical appearance (Sussman, Nottelmann, Inoff-Germain, Dorn, Cutler, Loriaux, & Chrousos, 1985). Psychologically, cognitive changes are marked by an increase in formal operational thinking (Piaget, 1967), allowing for the ability to question and analyze other's (most notably parents') assertions and logically argue for one's own point of view (cf. Montemayer, 1983). Socially, an adolescent's role in the family dynamic appears to change from a submissive and dependent role to a more egalitarian (and in some cases more dominant) and autonomous role (cf. Montemayer, 1983). Therefore, it is not surprising that we would find some amount of emotional turmoil given the occurrence of all of these dramatic changes. What is impressive is that the majority of adolescents appear to negotiate these multiple system changes with such emotional ease.

In sum, "adolescent turmoil" has been described as an emotional disturbance common to most adolescents, characterized by severe and dramatic mood swings and serious parent-child disagreements over basic values and attitudes. It has been thought that the mechanism of emotional turmoil had to do with the adolescent's psychic disintegration while negotiating multiple biological, psychological, and social changes. It has also been believed that the function of adolescent turmoil was to increase an adolescent's autonomy from the family so that the adult role can be adopted (Freud, 1958; Hall, 1904; Powers, Hauser, & Kilner, 1989). We suggest here that three primary sources contributed to this widespread belief that normal adolescence is characterized by emotional turmoil. These three sources include first, the fact that adolescent turmoil has its historical roots in Stanley Hall's work and the German romantic philosophy espousing rebellion against the adult generation; second, the tendency to base this belief primarily on unsystematic observations of a skewed population of adolescents—adolescents who were being treated for psychiatric disturbance; and third, the evidence suggesting that adolescence is characterized by dramatic changes in an adolescent's biological, cognitive, and social systems.

However, recent research suggests that emotional disturbance characterizing adolescent turmoil *does not* in fact apply to the majority of adolescents. Rather it characterizes only 20% of the adolescent population (cf. Offer, 1985). The majority of adolescents appear to be coping well, have positive self-esteem, and get along well with their parents (Offer, 1985). What is impressive is that the majority of adolescents appear to negotiate this time of transition with emotional ease rather than with emotional turmoil. Contrary to what has been the popular belief, the adolescent appears to be equipped with psychological devices that help maintain emotional equilibrium in the face of internal and external changes.

References

Blos, P. (1961). *On adolescence.* New York: Free Press of Glencoe.

Csikszentmihalyi, M., & Larsen, R. (1984). *Being adolescent.* New York: Basic Books.

Freud, A. (1958). Adolescence. *Psychoanalytic study of the child* (Vol. 13, p. 275). New York: International Universities Press.

Hall, G. S. (1904). *Adolescence: Its psychology and its relation to physiology, anthropology, sociology, sex, crime, religion, and education.* New York: D. Appleton.

Krupinski, J., Baikie, A. G., Stoller, A., Graves, J., O'Day, D. M., & Polke, P. (1967). A community health survey of Heyfield, Victoria. *Medical Journal of Australia, 54,* 1204–1211.

Langner, T. S., Gersten, J. C., & Eisenberg, J. G. (1974). Approaches to measurement and definition in epidemiology of behavior disorders: Ethnic background and child behavior. *International Journal of Health Services, 4,* 483–501.

Montemayer, R. (1983). Parents and adolescents in conflict: All families some of the time and some families all of the time. *Journal of Early Adolescence, 3*(1–2), 83–103.

Offer, D. (1985). A portrait of normal adolescents. *American Educator, 9*(2), 34–37.

Offer, D. (1987). In defense of adolescents. *Journal of the American Medical Association, 257,* 3407–3408.

Offer, D., Ostrov, E., & Howard, K. I. (1987). Epidemiology of mental health and mental illness among adolescents. In J. D. Noshpitz (Ed.). *Basic handbook of child psychiatry: Vol. 5: Advance and New Directions* (pp. 82–88). New York: Basic Books, Inc.

Offer, D., Ostrov, E., & Howard, K. (1981). The mental health professional's concept of the normal adolescent. *Archives of General Psychiatry, 38,* 149–152.

Piaget, J. (1967). *Six psychological studies.* New York: Vintage Books.

Powers, S. I., Hauser, S. T., & Kilner, L. A. (1989). Adolescent mental health. *American Psycyhologist,* Vol. 2, 200–208.

Rutter, M., Graham, P., Chadwick, D. F. D., & Yule, W. (1976). Adolescent turmoil: Fact or fiction. *Journal of Child Psychology and Psychiatry, 17,* 35–36.

Sussman, E. J., & Loriaux, D. L. (1987). Hormones, emotional dispositions, and aggressive attributes in young adolescents. *Child Development, 58,* 1114–1134.

Sussman, E. J., Nottelmann, E. D., Inoff-Germain, G. E., Dorn, L. D., Cutler, G. B., Loriaux, D. L., & Chrousos, G. P. (1985). The relation of relative hormonal levels and physical development and social-emotional behavior in young adolescents. *Journal of Youth and Adolescence, 14*(3), 245–263.

See Also

Affective Disorders; Depression in Adolescence, Gender Differences in; Developmental Psychopathology and the Adolescent; Fears and Phobias in Adolescence; Moodiness, Adolescent; Psychophysiological/Psychosomatic Problems; Schizophrenia in Adolescence and Young Adulthood, Antecedents/Predictors of.

Twentieth-Century America, Adolescence in

Jeffrey E. Mirel
Northern Illinois University

The twentieth century has witnessed a rapid and profound change in the institutions and relationships used to define the experience of adolescence in America. As late as 1920 the demands of family and work dominated the lives of most young people in the United States. Schooling played an important role in the development of young children, but it was only a marginal experience for the vast majority of teenagers, most of whom entered the full-time labor market by age 16 or 17. Social reformers and child advocates, believing that young people entered the working world too early, sought methods to slow that process. By the 1950s, due to enormous changes in the American economy and the largely successful efforts of reformers and educators, the majority of American adolescents spent most of their teenage years in school. Teachers, rather than employers or co-workers, became the nonfamilial adults with whom teenagers most frequently interacted. As school became more central to the adolescent experience, family and work receded in importance. In addition, the peer group emerged as a major force in adolescent development. As a consequence of these changes, teenagers became increasingly segregated from adult society. This segegation encouraged the creation of a distinctive youth culture that simultaneously sought the trappings of adulthood and rebelled against adult authority. By the 1980s the norms, values, and behavior patterns of the youth culture had become an undeniable, dynamic element in American society. Unfortunately, at the same time there was growing evidence of pathology in aspects of the youth culture. By the late 1980s there were numerous calls for change aimed at solving the problems of American youth.

Adolescence from 1900 to 1930

From the turn of the century until the Great Depression most American adolescents followed the deeply carved grooves of the 19th-century life course. Family, work, and community were the dominant institutions in young peoples' lives. Public institutions such as schools played an important, but, in terms of time, relatively small role for most adolescents. Throughout most of this period the great majority of children received only about eight years of formal education, with most leaving school in their early teens, In 1900, for example, only 11.4% of young people aged 14–17 were in secondary school. Ten years later, that figure was just 15.4%. On the eve of the depression, after two decades of enormous increases in school enrollment, still barely half of the age group was in high school (Mirel & Angus, 1986).

Adolescents left school to enter the adult, working world. Generally, young women assumed household responsibilities, either by aiding their mothers in caring for younger siblings or by becoming domestic workers in the homes of other families. In urban areas, however, labor force participation by young women was increasing rapidly, particularly in office and factory work. Young men helped their fathers in the fields, apprenticed in crafts and trades, or worked in the expanding manufacturing and service industries (Lapsley, Enright, & Serlin, 1985; Rury, 1990; Zelizer, 1985). There was, however, considerable variation in these patterns. Children from wealthier homes, whose families could forego the income from adolescent workers, tended to stay in school longer than their poorer counterparts. Similarly, adolescents in the South entered the work force earlier than those in the North (Angus & Mirel, 1985). Race also played a major role in determining the options available to young people. The experience of black adolescents has often differed markedly from that of whites. For much of this century, widespread, at times violent, racial discrimination restricted the opportunities available to black adolescents in education, employment, and social relations (Davis & Dollard, 1940; Homel, 1984; Perlmann, 1985; Wright, 1945).[1]

Throughout the first quarter of the century large numbers of Americans still subscribed to the 19th-century perspective that early entry of young people into the working world was both economically and educationally vital. Young workers could substantially increase their family's income since they generally earned about one-third to one-half of what adult workers earned. Many families relied on this income, some for actual survival, others for improved living standards (Angus & Mirel, 1985; Hogan, 1985; Lapsley, Enright, & Serlin, 1985; Perlmann, 1983). Beyond these obvious economic benefits, the conventional wisdom of the era held that early work experiences were essential for shaping character and values. Work provided a genuine sense of accomplishment, taught real skills, and encouraged habits that would lead to future success. Adult-adolescent interactions in the workplace provided young people with mature role models and eased the socialization of the young into the demands and responsibilities of adulthood (Sparkes, 1936; Zelizer, 1985).

In 1920 over 51% of 14- to 19-year-old males were employed (Spring, 1982). That year, however, proved to be the high-water mark of youth employment. Over the next few decades several economic, political, and social changes that had been developing since the turn of the century combined to gradually push adolescents out of the full-time labor market. The most important changes were economically based. The technological innovations that companies introduced to increase productivity and profits eliminated large numbers of youth jobs. The telephone, for example, quickly made the Western Union delivery boy obsolete. Similarly, the cash register and pneumatic tube put an end to the

---

[1]Even after the Civil Rights movement ended the most blatant forms of racial discrimination, the problems of American adolescents seem to afflict black youths more severely and for longer periods of time than whites (Wilson, 1987).

armies of adolescent "cash runners" in department stores (Troen, 1985; Zelizer, 1985).

These economic changes were direct and immediately apparent, at times eliminating huge numbers of adolescent jobs almost overnight. The political movement to end child labor was more evolutionary, gradually working to change American values and attitudes about youth employment. Though slower in effect than economic changes, the consequences of this movement were equally profound. Between 1890 and 1920 an increasing number of social reformers and educators denounced child labor as a barbarous practice unfit for a civilized society. They labeled child labor the "slaughter of the innocents" and "child slavery" (Bremner, 1971; McKelway, 1911). In 1904, a group of prominent reformers created the National Child Labor Committee (NCLC) to press for state and national legislation to restrict the employment of young workers (Trattner, 1970). In addition to the NCLC, the U.S. Children's Bureau, created in 1912, began publishing an ongoing series of reports on the status of child labor and child labor legislation throughout the country (e.g., U.S. Children's Bureau, 1932).

The NCLC frequently relied on muckraking journalism to expose the most heinous forms of child and adolescent exploitation. Refuting the idea that early entry into the work force built character and instilled positive values, these articles described youth labor as mind-numbing, physically exhausting, and often exceedingly dangerous. One famous expose, for example, described the permanent physical harm sustained by children as young as 12 as they carried red-hot bottles eight hours at a stretch in a glass-blowing factory (Sprago, 1971). Reformers pointed to similar outrages in the canning, meat packing,

coal, and textile industries (Davidson, 1939; Illinois Inspectors of Factories, 1971; Hine, 1971). All combined, the studies, articles, lobbying efforts of the NCLC, photographs of Lewis Hine, and nationwide attention to such disasters as the 1911 Triangle Shirtwaist Company fire (most of whose 148 victims were teenage girls and young women) spurred the gradual transformation of American attitudes about youth labor (Bremner, 1971).

Beyond publicizing the abuses of child workers, the NCLC and its allies in public education and organized labor vigorously campaigned for legal restrictions on child labor. Despite setbacks on the national level, such as the U.S. Supreme Court ruling that declared the 1916 Keating-Owen Act unconstitutional and the failure to get the Child Labor Amendment ratified, anti-child labor advocates did win numerous battles on the state and local levels. By 1929, for example, almost every industrial state had legislation that limited the hours children could work (Bremner, 1971). In addition, child labor was further restricted by the passage of compulsory education laws that were in force in every state of the union by 1918 (Deffenbaugh & Keesecker, 1935).

These political efforts were bolstered by the pathbreaking intellectual pursuits of several scholars, who articulated a new school of thought that viewed "adolescence" as a special developmental stage of life, in need of nurture and protection. G. Stanley Hall, the most important of these thinkers, argued that urban, industrial society distorted the natural pattern of adolescent development by forcing young people to "leap rather than grow into maturity" (Hall, 1904, xviii). While many educators and child advocates were suspicious of Hall's curious blend of science, romanticism, repression, and permissiveness, his basic idea of the "sanctity" of adolescence was tremendously influential (Kett, 1977; Kliebard, 1985). Jane Addams, for example, echoed Hall's ideas when she condemned urban life because it turned innate adolescent idealism away from its natural search for social justice (Addams, 1972; Kett, 1977; Troen, 1985).

These economic, political, and intellectual trends ultimately combined in the first few decades of the twentieth century to inspire a broad-based movement to improve society through the formal ordering of the experiences of young people. Throughout the last part of the 19th century Americans had increasingly viewed the child as the central figure in social and political progress (Wishy, 1968; Wiebe, 1967). By 1910 reformers had forged that inchoate sensibility into a series of practical measures focusing on improving education, juvenile justice, and the leisure activities of young people. At the heart of these efforts were "intermediary" adult guidance figures such as teachers or juvenile court officers who would replace parents and/or adult co-workers as the most important role models for adolescents (Grubb & Lazerson, 1982; Katz, 1986; Kett, 1977; Schlossman, 1977). Virtually all of these measures relied on large bureaucratic organizations, such as juvenile courts or the Boy Scouts, to carry out their programs. Each invariably expanded the role of professionals trained specifically for work with children and adolescents.

By far the most important of these reform efforts focused on public education. Progressive-era reformers expansively claimed that education could solve almost every problem afflicting American youth. As mechanization forced young workers out of unskilled jobs, they argued, schools would step in and train them for new, more rewarding careers. Schools also would provide the haven for adolescents that both anti-child labor advocates and the disciples of Hall desired (Chadsey, 1919; Kett, 1977; Troen, 1985). Throughout the first quarter of the twentieth century educational reformers sounded these themes in their campaign to restructure public education. By 1930 these often elite, business-oriented activists had gained control of most urban public school systems and had introduced changes destined to profoundly alter the lives of adolescents (Bowles & Gintis, 1976; Ravitch, 1974; Tyack & Hansot, 1982). Large public school systems became exemplars of bureaucratic order and administrative efficiency, and, above all, arenas where professionals could shape the life experiences of young people (Tyack, 1974; Tyack & Hansot, 1982). For adolescents, the most important changes centered on the high school, which was gradually assuming a crucial role in the adolescent life course.

Progressive-era educational reformers focused on expanding the high school curriculum. In this effort, they were guided by a series of overlapping theories. They first claimed that young people left school for work because of educational rather than economic reasons. Thus, reformers introduced courses that would have greater relevance to adolescence. Second, educators sought to scientifically match young people with the most appropriate curriculum through the use of standardized tests. Third, school leaders introduced vocational tracks, believing that as youth labor declined the school would replace the work place as the primary institution for vocational socialization (Bowles & Gintis, 1976; Cremin, 1961; Krug, 1969; Moehlman, 1925; Spring, 1982; Violas, 1978).

Reformers implemented these changes rapidly. By 1925 most urban school districts had replaced the traditional high school curriculum that stressed such established academic disciplines as English, history, mathematics, science, and foreign language with a bewildering array of new tracks, programs, and courses of study (Tyack, 1974). In Grand Rapids, Michigan, for example, the number of available high school courses almost tripled in two decades, from 22 in 1900 to 65 in 1920. Almost all this expansion was in the commercial, industrial arts, home economics, physical education, and music curricula (Angus, 1982). These curricular changes were part of the larger process of economic and educational change in which preparation for work eventually supplanted actual engagement in work as the primary vocational experience of adolescents.

Between 1910 and 1920 the percentage of all 14- to 17-year-olds enrolled in secondary school almost doubled to include nearly a third of the age-group (Mirel & Angus, 1986). While the family and work place still remained the dominant institutions for adolescents in this period, high school enrollment was rising proportionately higher and faster than ever before. It is impossible to precisely identify the social origins of this flood of high school students but it appears that they were disproportionately drawn from the growing American middle class. While the actual numbers of working-class adolescents in high school clearly increased between 1900 and 1930, the ratio of young people from white-collar and blue-collar homes who attended high school appears to have held constant at roughly two to one throughout the era (Angus, 1981).

At the same time that the high school was becoming the central educational institution for a growing proportion of American adolescents, it was also gradually emerging as the pivotal social center for youth. The Lynds point out in their classic study of Middletown that "The high school, with its athletics, clubs, sororities and fraternities, dances and parties, and other 'extracurricular activities', is a fairly complete social cosmos in itself, and about this city within a city the social life of the intermediate generation centers" (Lynd & Lynd, 1929; p. 211). Thus, by 1930, essentially every "modern" aspect of what would soon become the most important adolescent-serving institution of the twentieth century was in place.

Adolescence from 1930 to 1950

The Great Depression was the turning point in the history of adolescence in the twentieth century. The economic collapse profoundly influenced the course of adolescent development as the virtual disappearance of the youth labor market drastically reduced young people's choices regarding work, school, and starting a family—indeed changing the entire process of social maturity. Because teenagers were usually the last hired and the first fired, they felt the most immediate impact of the depression. In fact, by 1931, adolescent workers were virtually eliminated from the work force. In Detroit, for example, applications for work permits in 1929 averaged 86 per month for 15-year-olds and 334 per month for 16-year-olds; in 1931, the applications were 19 and 105, respectively; and, in 1933, 4 and 30 (Mirel & Angus, 1985). Black youth suffered most from the economic collapse, burdened with discrimination based on both age and race (Bell, 1938). While there were occasional instances where employers sought to drastically cut labor costs by hiring adolescents (Trattner, 1970), for the most part teenagers rarely found full-time work in the 1930s. Under the circumstances, the passage of the Fair Labor Standards Bill in 1938, which outlawed child labor in interstate commerce, appeared to simply codify existing practice (Bremner, 1971).

By the mid-1930s, educators and policy makers began to categorize the effects of these depression-era conditions under the heading of the "youth problem" (Bell, 1938). A number of dramatic developments revealed the depth of the problem to the American people. By 1932, for example, as many as 300,000 teenage tramps, 10% of them young women, left home to wander aimlessly around the country (Baker, 1932; Minehan, 1934). Other young people stayed closer to home, wandering the streets in despair, unable to find work (Davis, 1936). Some adolescents, mostly in large cities, vented their rage against the system by embracing political radicalism. During the 1930s the Communist and Socialist parties attracted a segment of young American intellectuals who eventually exercised considerable influence on the national scene (Cowley, 1981; Rawick, 1957).

The depression also played havoc with basic family relationships. Most severely affected were adolescents whose fathers experienced long periods of unemployment. In these households, the loss of income and status combined to undercut the traditional role of fathers as authority figures, an experience that left an indelible mark on the character of many adolescents. Many of these "children of the Great Depression" came to especially prize such things as job security and family dependability in their later lives (Elder, 1974, 1980).

At the heart of the youth problem was the question of how to bridge the widening gap between adolescence and adulthood in a society where youth unemployment rather than child labor was the common experience of huge numbers of young people. For many Americans schools seemed the obvious institution to bridge that gap. Young people clearly recognized that schools were the one constant shelter in the economic storm. Between 1930 and 1934 high school enrollments jumped almost 30%, with most of the increase coming in the eleventh and twelfth grades (Angus, 1965). In a decade-to-decade comparison of the ratio of high school enrollment increase to growth in the 14- to 17-year-old population, the 1930-40 decade shows twice the growth rate of 1910-20, the next fastest growing decade, 611% to 269%, respectively (Mirel & Angus, 1986). This flood of students, rather than the dramatic surge in enrollments during the Progressive era, appears to have included large numbers of working-class youth (Karpinos, 1941). Indeed, in the 1939-40 school year, over 73% of 14- to 17-year-olds were in secondary school (O'Neil & Sepielli, 1985).

This leap in high school enrollment by students who would normally have entered the work force at age 16 or 17 presented educators with serious discipline and curricular problems. In trend-setting urban school districts educators responded to this influx of new students by substantially altering the high school curriculum, by diluting the content and rigor of traditional academic courses, and by adding a variety of new, "relevant" courses. These new courses, largely offered through social studies or vocational programs, catered to students' immediate interests and stressed the acquisition of social rather than academic or vocational skills (Franklin, 1982; Mirel & Angus, 1986; Ravitch, 1983). The class bias inherent in many of these curricular changes was apparent by the early 1940s as the placement of students in the various courses of study tended to follow social class lines (Hollingshead, 1949).

Beyond curricular reform, these course changes reflected a profound shift in both the lives of American adolescents and in the nature and the function of the high school. By destroying the youth labor market, the depression had closed off virtually every legitimate avenue except the high school through which adolescents could grow to adulthood. Many educators saw this trend as the ultimate realization of their ambition to serve "all American youth." They even spoke of the high school as the "cure" for youth unemployment. Recognizing a sea-change in the history of American adolescence, educators vastly expanded the custodial role of the school and ensured that the school would take responsibility for addressing all the problems and needs of youth (Educational Policy Commission, 1944; Krug, 1972).

The major challenge to that solution to the youth problem came from the American Youth Commission (AYC), a privately funded policy research group that commissioned several important studies of youth in the late 1930s (Angus, 1965; Flack, 1969). These studies convinced the AYC that the proper response to the problem of youth unemployment was not more schooling but rather an institution designed to bridge the gap between leaving school and securing a full-time job (American Youth Commission, 1942). The closest approximations of such an institution were the Civilian Conservation Corps and the National Youth Administration. These federally funded programs provided jobs as well as educational and vocational training to 16- to 24-year-olds whose families were on relief. In 1943, however, due in part to intense lobbying by educational organizations, Congress abolished both these programs (Rawick, 1957; Salmond, 1967; Zeitlan, 1958). With that act, the high school became the centerpiece of American youth policy.

Youth employment did have a "last hurrah" during World War II when the severe shortage of adult workers lured millions of young people into the defense industry. Winning the war quickly took precedence over enforcement of child labor laws. Between 1940 and 1944, the number of teenage workers jumped from about 1 million to 2.9 million. Many of these young workers dropped out of high school to enter the labor force (Polenberg, 1972). Following the war, however, the depression-era pattern of teenage unemployment and growing high school attendance returned. By 1950 over 82% of 14- to 17-year-olds were in high school (U.S. Bureau of the Census, 1955).

Throughout the 1940s national attention was drawn to a new issue, the rising incidence of juvenile delinquency. The first indications of this probem came in communities experiencing the war-time economic boom, but increasing juvenile crime soon became a national phenomenon. While boys were generally arrested for theft and girls for what was called "sex delinquency," there was a disturbing increase in violent crimes such as assault as well. Many of the young people arrested for juvenile crimes were from working-class backgrounds. Socioligists explained delinquent behavior by pointing to the moral uncertainties created by the war, the breakdown of community support structures that accompanied the massive wartime migrations, and the loss of an important authority figure as fathers went off to war (Blum, 1976; Kandel, 1948; Polenberg, 1972). Nevertheless, when juvenile delinquency persisted after the war and, perhaps more importantly, when it spread to middle-class adolescents, educators and policy makers began to see the phenomenon as evidence of the changing nature of the youth problem.

Adolescence from 1950 to 1988

In the 1950s the economic and political changes in American life that began in the Great Depression finally succeeded in making the high school an "inescapable institution" for American adolescents. As the high school became the main institution for the education and socialization of adolescents, curriculum reform became a prominent and recurrent political issue. Underlying much of the controversy were contending definitions of adolescence. People who saw adolescents as "adults-in-holding" paid most attention to developing skills that young people would need to succeed in adult social relationships and the working world. An opposing faction argued that adolescents were "children-in-transition" who needed to master the basic subject areas that defined American culture before they could enter adult society. Since the high school had become the sole institution for dealing with the problems of American youth, advocates of these two schools of thought often framed their debates in millennial terms, arguing that the very survival of the nation was at stake in every curricular change (e.g., Hirsch, 1987; Silberman, 1970). Each side believed that if only educators could get the curriculum right, solutions to the problems of youth would be within reach (e.g., Adler, 1982, p. 36).

Since World War II one form or the other of these schools of thought have dominated American secondary education. The social skills–oriented Life Adjustment Movement influenced high schools well into the 1950s (Ravitch, 1983). In the panic that followed the launching of Sputnik, Life Adjustment was replaced by curricula that stressed subject mastery, particularly in mathematics, the sciences, and foreign languages (Bestor, 1953; Hofstader, 1963). During the turbulent 1960s that rigorous content-oriented curricula gave way to more "relevant" courses and increased student choices within high school programs (Silberman, 1970). Much as Sputnik led to the demise of the Life Adjustment movement, however, so the

economic crises of the late 1970s encouraged a "back-to-basics" reaction against the reforms of the late 1960s. Providing fuel for the "back-to-basics" movement was startling evidence that the quality of academic achievement had declined markedly since the 1960s. Between 1967 to 1981, for example, the mean Scholastic Aptitude Test scores for high school seniors dropped from 466 to 424 in the Verbal section of the test and from 492 to 466 in the Mathematics Section (O'Neil & Sepielli, 1985). The latest reform movement has refocused the curriculum on learning specific content areas and on reducing students' choices about high school programs (Adler, 1982; Boyer, 1983; Hampel, 1986; Powell, Farrar, & Cohen, 1985).

The fact that practically all adolescent Americans were enrolled in high school—94% of 14- to 17-year-olds by 1980 (O'Neil & Sepielli, 1985)—also helped transform the high school into the main social service agency for youth. Beyond providing such traditional services as academic and vocational counseling, for example, in the postwar years high schools began offering psychological counseling as well as programs dealing with adolescent suicide, drug and alcohol addiction, teenage pregnancy, and the problems of unwed adolescent mothers (Sedlak & Church, 1982). In some places schools even provided students with birth control clinics (Vinovskis, 1988).

Coinciding with the massive "warehousing" of adolescents in high schools was the development of a distinctive adolescent subculture. The most important element of that subculture was the peer group. As contacts with adults were reduced to interactions with parents and teachers, the peer group became increasingly important as the source of values, attitudes and identity (Coleman, 1961; Kett, 1977; Panel on Youth 1973). The peer group established its own code of conduct, stressing loyalty to the group and status based on resistance to the norms and values of adult society (Cross & Kleinhesselink, 1985). Indeed, the most notable elements of the youth subculture have been its simultaneous quest for the appearances of adulthood and its rebellion against adult authority (Friedenberg, 1959; Goodman, 1956).

Initially, the subculture drew its inspiration from a variety of sources, particularly working-class teenage gangs, blacks, and beatniks—all socially marginal groups that opposed either overtly or covertly important elements of the dominant white, middle-class culture (Gilbert, 1985; Roszak, 1968; Spring, 1982). Adolescents identified with these groups, in part because they also saw themselves as marginal, fulfilling no social role other than as consumers and condemned to a "passive dependency imposed on [them] by schools" (Kett, 1977, p. 268). The most visible features of the subculture quickly became apparent in the 1950s—distinctive hair styles, special clothing such as jeans and t-shirts, the use of profanity and slang, smoking, drinking, and blatant sexuality. Getting a driver's license became a significant rite of passage, an act that provided the possibility of physical independence (Gilbert, 1985; Kett, 1977). As elements of this culture became increasingly prevalent among middle-class adolescents, and as juvenile delinquency spread to more affluent neighborhoods, numerous educators and social commentators raised alarms about the direction in which the younger generation was heading (Gilbert, 1985). Films such as *Rebel without a Cause* and *The Wild One* reflected adult concerns while ironically providing new "antiestablishment" heroes for young people (Cohen, 1982). The most important artistic reflection of adolescent rebellion, however, was not film but music. By the late 1950s, rock n'roll, with

its themes of love, sex, alienation, and opposition to adult authority, became the dominant form of youthful expression and identification (Bloom, 1987; Roszak, 1968; Ward, Stokes, & Tucker, 1986).

For all its rebellion against adult society, perhaps the most important aspect of the postwar youth culture was its dynamic relationship with the American economy. New products, marketing strategies, even industries were created in response to the enormous baby-boom market. In this trend, American adolescents had moved full circle from the turn of the century—no longer producers in the economic world, the adolescent became economically important only as a consumer. Throughout the 1960s retailers increasingly used the symbols and heroes of the youth culture to sell products and services (Cohen, 1982; Cross & Kleinhesselink, 1985). By the 1970s it was impossible to distinguish where the youth culture ended and creative marketing began.

The 1960s marked the political awakening of the adolescent subculture. Adolescents easily shifted their general rebellion against adult authority to specific causes such as opposition to racial segregation and the Vietnam War. The phrase "Don't trust anyone over thirty" became symbolic of the political and generational conflict of the era (Rubin, 1970). During the 1960s and 1970s, drug use and promiscuous sex became badges of youthful rebellion. Between 1972 and 1979, for example, drug use among white 12- to 17-year-olds jumped almost 139% (Uhlenberg & Eggebeen, 1986). One survey found that the proportion of sexually active teenage girls in metropolitan areas jumped from 30 to 50% between 1971 and 1979 (Wilson, 1987).

Most of the young rebels of the 1960s and 1970s were children from white, middle-class homes. They engaged in protest and antiestablishment behaviors within the security of suburban high schools and colleges. Many of their poor and minority counterparts faced a much harsher world. Even during the period of substantial economic growth in the 1960s, unemployment for black teenagers was twice the rate as that of whites (Spring, 1982). Also, during the late 1960s and early 1970s, the lives of many black and working-class adolescents were transformed by efforts to desegregate urban public school systems. Hundreds of thousands of these high school students bore the brunt of the fierce political conflict over neighborhood autonomy and racial equality that gripped the nation during this era (Lukas, 1985). The most serious event confronting these young people, however, was the Vietnam War, which was fought by a disproportionately high percentage of young, poor, and minority soldiers. The average age of Americans who served in Vietnam was only 19, compared to 26 in World War II (Baritz, 1985; Terry, 1984).

In the 1970s, as the leading edge of the baby-boom generation crossed into adulthood and the American economy slowed, the adolescent subculture turned inward. Some critics labeled these young people the "Me generation" and accused them of selfishness, narcissism, and excessive materialism (Lasch, 1979; Wolfe, 1976). Whatever values guided adolescents of the 1970s and early 1980s, mounting evidence indicated that aspects of the youth culture were becoming pathological. The delinquency rate for 10- to 17-year-olds, for example, jumped almost 131% between 1960 and 1980. Drug use soared during the same period. In 1987, for example, one study found that 42% of all high school seniors had used illicit drugs in the previous year (Goldberg, 1988). The most chilling statistics reveal increases in teenage homicide and suicide. Between 1960 and 1980 homi-

cide deaths of white 15- to 19-year-olds climbed more than 232%, while suicide jumped 140% (Greenberg, Carey, & Popper, 1987; Uhlenberg & Eggebeen, 1986).

Two particular adolescent problems dominated national attention in the late 1970s and the 1980s: teenage pregnancy and high school dropouts. The rise in teenage pregnancy was especially troubling because it occurred among the youngest adolescents. Between 1966 and 1977, while the birth rate among 15- to 19-year-olds was declining, the birth rate for girls ages 10 to 14 increased by a third (Vinovskis, 1988). This problem was most acute among black teenage girls, whose rate of out-of-wedlock births has increased from 42% in 1960 to 89% in 1983 (Wilson, 1987). High school dropouts were also disproportionately drawn from minority groups. In Chicago, for example, only 47% of ninth graders who enrolled in school in 1980 graduated in 1984, with blacks and Hispanics making up the vast majority of those leaving school (Wilson, 1987).

The dramatic increase in these problems has led to a series of calls for action in the 1980s. While much of the attention still focuses on the high school, a number of policy analysts have begun to consider other approaches for dealing with youth problems. Some social scientists, for example, have called attention to divorce and changes in parenting as causes of "the declining well-being of American adolescents" (Uhlenberg & Eggebeen, 1986). Others have urged the reform of welfare policies in order to encourage options such as teenage marriages (Vinovskis & Chase-Lansdale, 1987). Still others have pointed to the desperate need for jobs, primarily for inner-city, minority teenagers (Wilson, 1987). Now, in the last years of the 1980s, there appears to be little consensus on youth policy, but there are some signs that policy analysts are recognizing that more education or different types of education will not be enough to deal with the changing problems of adolescents.

Conclusions

The most dramatic development in the lives of American adolescents in the twentieth century has been the shift from the home-and-work-centered experience of the early part of the century to the school-and-peer-group-centered experience of the more recent decades. During these years adolescents went economically from being producers to becoming consumers; psychologically, from bearing the burdens of premature adulthood to confronting the problems of prolonged childhood; socially, from easy integration into adult society to an ever-lengthening period of age segregation; and politically, from being the object of campaigns to end child labor to being the focus of efforts to reduce teenage unemployment. At the center of these changes is the American high school, which itself has evolved from a largely academic and vocational institution into one increasingly concerned with the custodial care of adolescents. Today the strain upon the high school to both educate young people and solve their problems threatens to overwhelm the institution. In the coming years educators and youth policy makers will have to look beyond the high school in order to provide adolescents with more fulfilling avenues to adulthood.

References

Addams, J. (1972). *The spirit of youth and the city streets*. Urbana, IL: University of Illinois Press. (Originally published 1909.)

Adler, M. J. (1982). *The paideia proposal: An educational manifesto*. New York: Macmillan.

American Youth Commission. (1942). *Youth and the future*. Washington, DC: American Council on Education.

Angus, D. L. (1965). *The dropout problem: An interpretive history*. Unpublished doctoral dissertation, Ohio State University, Columbus, OH.

Angus, D. L. (1981). A note on the occupational backgrounds of high school students prior to 1940. *Journal of the Midwest History of Education Society, 9*, 158–183.

Angus, D. L. (1982, October). *Vocationalism and the blueing of the high school: Grand Rapids, Michigan, 1900–1920*. Unpublished conference paper, History of Education Society, Pittsburgh.

Angus, D. L., & Mirel, J. E. (1985). From spellers to spindles: Work-force entry by children of textile workers, 1888–1890. *Social Science History, 9*, 123–143.

Baker, N. D. (1932, December 1). Homeless wanderers create a new problem for America. *New York Times*.

Baritz, L. (1985). *Backfire: A history of how American culture led us into Vietnam and made us fight the way we did*. New York: Ballantine.

Bell, H. (1938). *Youth tell their story*. Washington, DC: American Council on Education.

Bestor, A. (1953). *Educational wastelands: The retreat from learning in our public schools*. Urbana, IL: University of Illinois Press.

Bloom, A. (1987). *The closing of the American mind*. New York: Simon and Schuster.

Blum, J. M. (1976). *V was for victory: Politics and American culture during World War II*. New York: Harcourt Brace Jovanovich.

Bowles, S., & Gintis, H. (1976). *Schooling in capitalist America: Educational reform and the contradictions of economic life*. New York: Basic Books.

Boyer, E. L. (1983). *High school: A report on secondary education in America*. New York: Harper and Row.

Bremner, R. H. (Ed.). (1971). *Children and youth in America: A documentary history: Vol.*

2. *1866–1932*. Cambridge: Harvard University Press.

Chadsey, C. E. (1919). Child labor and our public schools. *Detroit Educational Bulletin, 2*, 1.

Cohen, R. D. (1982). Schooling and age grading in American society since 1800: The fragmenting of experience. In J. Salzman, (Ed.), *Prospects*, pp. 347–364. New York: Burt Franklin and Co.

Coleman, J. S. (1961). *The adolescent society: The social life of teenagers and its impact on education*. New York: Free Press.

Cowley, M. (1981). *The dream of the golden mountains*. New York: Penguin.

Cremin, L. A. (1961). *The transformation of the school: Progressivism in American education, 1876–1957*. New York: Alfred A. Knopf.

Cross, H. J., & Kleinhesselink, R. R. (1985). The impact of the 1960s on adolescence. *Journal of Early Adolescence, 5*, 517–531.

Csikszentmihalyi, M., & Larson, R. (1984). *Being adolescent: Conflict and growth in the teenage years*. New York: Basic Books.

Davidson, E. H. (1939). *Child labor legislation in the southern textile states*. Chapel Hill: University of North Carolina Press.

Davis, A., & Dollard, J. (1940). *Children of bondage*. Washington, DC: American Council on Education.

Davis, M. (1936). *The lost generation*. New York: Macmillan.

Deffenbaugh, W. S., & Keesecker, W. W. (1935). *Compulsory school attendance laws and their administration*. Washington, DC: U.S. Office of Education.

Educational Policy Commission. (1944). *Education for "all" American youth*. Washington, DC: National Education Association.

Elder, G. H., Jr. (1974). *Children of the Great Depression*. Chicago: University of Chicago Press.

Elder, G. H., Jr. (1980). Adolescence in historical perspective. In J. Adelson (Ed.), *The handbook of adolescent psychology*, pp. 3–46. New York: John Wiley and Sons.

Finn, C. E., Jr. (1987). The high school dropout puzzle. *Public Interest, 87*, 3–22.

Flack, B. C. (1969). *The work of the American Youth Commission, 1935–42*. Unpublished doctoral dissertation, Ohio State University, Columbus, OH.

Franklin, B. M. (1982). The social efficiency movement reconsidered: Curriculum change in Minneapolis, 1917–1950. *Curriculum Inquiry, 12*, 9–33.

Friedenberg, E. Z. (1959). *The vanishing adolescent*. New York: Dell.

Gilbert, J. (1985). Mass culture and the fear of delinquency in the 1950s. *Journal of Early Adolescence, 5*, 505–516.

Goldberg, K. (1988, January 20). Sharp drop seen in cocaine abuse. *Education Week*, p. 6.

Goodman, P. (1956). *Growing up absurd*. New York: Vintage.

Greenberg, M. R., Carey, G. W., & Popper, F. J. (1987). The violent deaths of American youths. *Public Interest, 87*, 38–48.

Grubb, W. N., & Lazerson, M. (1982). *Broken promises: How Americans fail their children*. New York: Basic Books.

Hall, G. S. (1904). *Adolescence and psychology and its relations to physiology, anthropology, sociology, sex, crime, religion, and education*. New York: D. Appleton.

Hampel, R. (1986). *The last citadel: American high schools since the 1940s*. Boston: Houghton Mifflin.

Hine, L. W. (1971). Baltimore to Biloxi and back. In Robert Bremner (Ed.), *Children and youth in America: A documentary history* (Vol. 2, pp. 621–23). Cambridge: Harvard University Press. (Originally published 1913.)

Hirsch, E. D., Jr. (1987). *Cultural literacy: What every American needs to know*. Boston: Houghton Mifflin Company.

Hofstader, R. (1963). *Anti-intellectualism in American life*. New York: Alfred A. Knopf.

Hogan, D. J. (1985). *Class and reform: School and society in Chicago, 1880–1930*. Philadelphia: University of Pennsylvania Press.

Hollingshead, A. B. (1949). *Elmstown's youth: The impact of social class on adolescents.* New York: John Wiley and Sons.

Homel, M. W. (1984). *Down from equality: Black Chicagoans and the public schools, 1920–41.* Urbana, IL: University of Illinois Press.

Illinois Inspectors of Factories. (1971). Third Annual Report, 1895. In R. Bremner (Ed.), *Children and youth in America: A documentary history* (Vol. 2, p. 619). Cambridge: Harvard University Press. (Originally published 1896.)

Kandel, I. (1948). *The impact of the war upon American education.* Chapel Hill: University of North Carolina Press.

Karpinos, B. (1941). *The socio-economic and employment status of urban youth in the United States, 1935–36.* Washington, DC: U.S. Government Printing Office.

Katz, M. B. (1986). *In the shadow of the poorhouse: A social history of welfare in America.* New York: Basic Books.

Kett, J. F. (1977). *Rites of passage: Adolescence in America 1790 to the present.* New York: Basic Books.

Kleibard, H. M. (1985). Psychology . . . the teacher's blackstone: G. Stanley Hall and the effort to build a developmental curriculum for youth. *Journal of Early Adolescence, 5,* 467–478.

Krug, E. (1969). *The shaping of the American high school, 1880–1920.* Madison, WI: University of Wisconsin Press.

Krug, E. (1972). *The shaping of the American high school, 1920–41.* Madison, WI: University of Wisconsin Press.

Lapsley, D. K., Enright, R. D., & Serlin, R. C. (1985). Toward a theoretical perspective on the legislation of adolescence. *Journal of Early Adolescence, 5,* 441–466.

Lasch, C. (1979). *The culture of narcissism.* New York: Norton.

Lukas, J. A. (1985). *Common ground: A turbulent decade in the lives of three American families.* New York: Random House.

Lynd, R. S., & Lynd, H. M. (1929). *Middletown: A study in modern American culture.* New York: Harcourt Brace Jovanovich.

Minehan, T. (1934). *Boy and girl tramps of America.* New York: Farrar and Rinehart.

Mirel, J. E., & Angus, D. L. (1985). Youth, work, and schooling in the Great Depression. *Journal of Early Adolescence, 9,* 489–504.

Mirel, J. E., & Angus, D. L. (1986). The rising tide of custodialism: Enrollment increases and curriculum reform in Detroit, 1928–40. *Issues in Education, 4,* 101–120.

Moehlman, A. (1925). *Public education in Detroit.* Bloomington, IL: Public School Publishing.

O'Neil, D. M., & Sepielli, P. (1985). *Education in the United States, 1940–1983.* Washington, DC: U. S. Government Printing Office.

Panel on Youth of the President's Science Advisory Committee. (1973). *Youth: Transition to adulthood.* Washington, DC: U.S. Government Printing Office.

Perlmann, J. (1983). Working-class homeownership and schooling in Providence, Rhode Island, 1880–1925. *History of Education Quarterly, 23,* 175–191.

Perlmann, J. (1985, November). Aspects of the social origins and school achievement in a northern city; Providence, Rhode Island, 1880–1925. Unpublished paper presented at the Social Science History Association, Chicago.

Polenberg, R. (Ed.). (1968). *America at war: The home front, 1941–45.* Englewood Cliffs, NJ: Prentice-Hall.

Polenberg, R. (1972). *War and society: The United States, 1941–45.* Philadelphia: J. B. Lippencott.

Powell, A. G., Farrar, E., & Cohen, D. K. (1985). *The shopping mall high school: Winners and losers in the educational marketplace.* Boston: Houghton Mifflin.

Ravitch, D. (1974). *The great school wars.* New York: Basic Books.

Ravitch, D. (1983). *The troubled crusade: American education, 1945–1980*. New York: Basic Books.

Rawick, G. P. (1957). *The New Deal and youth: The Civilian Conservation Corps, the National Youth Administration, and the American Youth Congress*. Unpublished doctoral dissertation, University of Wisconsin, Madison, WI.

Roszak T. (1968). *The making of a counter-culture: Reflections on the technocratic society and its youthful opposition*. New York: Anchor Books.

Rubin, J. (1970). *Do it!* New York: Simon and Schuster.

Rury, J. L. (1990). *Education and womens work: Female schooling and the division of labor in urban America, 1870–1930*. Albany, NY: SUNY Press.

Salmond, J. A. (1967). *The Civilian Conservation Corps, 1933–42*. Durham, NC: Duke University Press.

Schlossman, S. L. (1977). *Love and the American delinquent: The theory and practice of "progressive" juvenile justice, 1825–1920*. Chicago: University of Chicago Press.

Sedlak, M. W., & Church, R. L. (1982). *A history of social services delivered to youth, 1880–1977* (NIE Contract No. 400–79–0017). Washington, DC: National Institute of Education.

Silberman, C. E. (1970). *Crisis in the classroom: The remaking of American education*. New York: Random House.

Spargo, J. (1971). The bitter cry of the children. In R. Bremner (Ed.), *Children and youth in America: A documentary history* (Vol. 2, pp. 620–23). Cambridge: Harvard University Press. (Originally published 1906.)

Sparkes, B. (1936, May 2). Horatio Alger at the bridge. *Saturday Evening Post* (pp. 20–21, 70, 72, 74).

Spring, J. (1982). *American education: An introduction to social and political aspects*. New York: Longman.

Terry, W. (1984). *Bloods: An oral history of the Vietnam War by black veterans*. New York: Random House.

Trattner, W. I. (1970) *Crusade for the children: A history of the National Child Labor Committee and child labor reform in America*. Chicago: Quadrangle Books.

Troen, S. K. (1985). Technological development and adolescence: The early twentieth century. *Journal of Early Adolescence, 5*, 429–439.

Tyack, D. (1974). *The one best system: A history of American urban education*. Cambridge: Harvard University Press.

Tyack, D., & Hansot, E. (1982). *Managers of virtue: Public school leadership in America, 1820–1980*. New York: Basic Books.

U. S. Bureau of the Census. (1955). *Statisitical abstract of the United States: 1955*. Washington, DC: U. S. Government Printing Office.

U. S. Children's Bureau. (1932). Trend of child labor in the United States, 1920–1931. *Monthly Labor Review, 35*, 1322–1336.

Uhlenberg, P., & Eggebeen, D. (1986). The declining well-being of American adolescents. *Public Interest, 25–38*.

Vinovskis, M. A. (1988). *An "epidemic" of adolescent pregnancy? Some historical and policy considerations*. New York: Oxford University Press.

Vinovskis, M. A., & Chase-Lansdale, P. L. (1987). Should we discourage teenage marriage? *Public Interest, 87*, 23–37.

Violas, P. (1978). *The training of the urban working class*. Chicago: Rand McNally.

Ward, E., Stokes, G., & Tucker, K. (1986). *Rock of ages: The Rolling Stone history of rock and roll*. New York: Rolling Stone Press/Summit Books.

Wiebe, R. H. (1967). *The search for order, 1877–1920*. New York: Hill and Wang.

Wilson, W. J. (1987). *The truly disadvantaged: The inner city, the underclass, and public policy*. Chicago: University of Chicago Press.

Wishy, B. (1968). *The child and the republic: The dawn of American child nurture*. Philadelphia: University of Pennsylvania Press.

Wolfe, T. (1976). *Mauve gloves and madmen, clutter and vine*. New York: Farrar, Straus and Giroux.

Wright, R. (1945). *Black boy*. New York: Harper and Row.

Zeitlin, H. (1958). *Federal relations in American education, 1933–1943: A study of New Deal efforts and innovations*. Unpublished doctoral dissertation, Columbia University, New York.

Zelizer, V. A. (1985). *Pricing the priceless child: The changing social value of children*. New York: Basic Books.

See Also

Colonial America, Adolescence in; History of Research on Adolescence; Menarche, Secular Trend in Age of; Nineteenth-Century America, Adolescence in; Preindustrial World, Adolescence in.

Type A and Teenagers

Carl E. Thoresen

Stanford University

Concern with the origins of the Type A behavior pattern (TA) and adults has encouraged the study of younger people, especially adolescents.[1] As a complex syndrome composed of excessive levels of competitiveness, time urgency/impatience, and hostility, coupled with a strong need for perceived control, the TA has been the subject of considerable scientific as well as public interest (Cooper, Detre & Weiss, 1981; Friedman & Rosenman, 1974; and Houston & Snyder, 1988). Despite controversy, especially the status of TA as a predictor or cause of coronary heart disease (CHD), results of recent critical reviews show that the TA is a significant risk factor for premature CHD in white adult males (Booth-Kewley & Friedman, 1987; Friedman & Booth-Kewley, 1988; Matthews, 1988; Matthews & Haynes, 1986). For women, however, the evidence is much less clear (Thoresen & Graff-Low, 1990). By and large, adult women assessed as Type A display some of the physiological and psychosocial characteristics associated with CHD risk, but well-controlled studies using validated measures of TA have been lacking. In addition, little is known about TA among minority-group male and female adults, such as blacks, Hispanics and Asian-Americans (Matthews & Haynes, 1986).

Two things seem clear. First, the TA appears to be a culturally influenced and socially acquired style of coping, probably emerging from life experiences in the first two decades of life (Margolis, McElroy, Runyan, & Kaplan, 1983). Individual differences in terms of physiological and social cognitive factors also seem involved (Thoresen & Pattillo, 1988). Second, when TA has been reduced in adults such changes have been directly associated with reduced morbidity and mortality along with lessened psychosocial problems (e.g., Friedman et al., 1986; see Nunes, Frank, & Kornfeld, 1987, for review).

Why Study Type A in Youth?

At present the most compelling answer concerns the possible relationship of TA and coronary heart disease. Matthews and Woodall (1988), for example, describe how the

---

1. I am indebted to the work of several colleagues whose ideas have been very helpful in preparing this article, especially Meyer Friedman, who originated the Type A construct along with Ray Rosenman, and Karen Matthews and her seminal work in studying TA in children; Jean Eagleston and Kathy Kirmil-Gray, formerly at Stanford, for their leadership in conducting studies of TA at Stanford; and to Jerry Pattillo, whose sensitive insights about TA in younger persons have proved invaluable.

processes of coronary atherosclerosis (hardening of the coronary arteries) in youth commonly set the stage for coronary heart disease (CHD) in adulthood. They argue that, unless demonstrated otherwise, TA in younger people should be taken seriously as a possible risk for CHD in adulthood.

Several researchers have suggested that various psychosocial and behavior patterns of children and adolescents deserve careful consideration since the origins of "risk factors" for chronic disease in adults are commonly found in the childhood and adolescent years (e.g., Glueck, 1986; Henry & Stephens, 1977; Weiner, 1977). Examples of risk factors for chronic disease include high fat dietary patterns, excessive body mass, elevated blood pressure, cigarette smoking, and higher serum cholesterol levels. A number of tracking or longitudinal studies have demonstrated a surprising degree of stability in some behaviors and characteristics assessed in older childhood and early adolescence into the adult years (e.g., Webber, Cresanta, Voors, & Berenson, 1983). To the extent that the TA is a fairly stable behavior pattern over time, it deserves careful consideration among young people (Hunter et al., 1989). Implication of TA for other physical as well as several mental and social health indicators also merit investigation given the "clinical picture" of the TA in adults (Houston & Snyder, 1988; Price, 1982).

Overview of Findings

What is currently known about the relationship of TA with older children and adolescents? If we recognize that important conceptual and assessment limitations exist, then some tentative assertions based on research reported to date can be offered. I will briefly sketch a partial portrait of TA in older children and adolescents, noting that more detailed reviews are available elsewhere (e.g., Matthews & Woodall, 1988; Ney & Wagner, 1987; Thoresen & Pattillo, 1988). Some major features of the portrait will be discussed—physiological reactivity, heritability, ethnicity, family demographics, parental influences, academic performance, and anger and hostility—recognizing that parts of the picture remain blurred or uninvestigated. Following this, some conceptual and assessment issues will be cited, followed by reflections and recommendations for future research.

PHYSIOLOGICAL REACTIVITY ■

In general, older TA children and adolescents have been found to show greater physical reactions, that is, physiologic reactivity, to various challenging or demanding tasks (e.g., mental arithmetic, video games) compared to non–TA youth (Krantz, Lundberg, & Frankenhaeuser, 1988).[2] This research has commonly used systolic and/or diastolic blood pressure and heart rate changes as measures and, to a lesser extent, certain neuroendocrines, such as urinary cortisol and catecholamines. Some gender differences occur, such that girls may show more increases in heart rate than diastolic blood pressure changes to a mental arithmetic task, compared to boys whose reactivity to video games might be greater (Matthews, Rakaczky, Stoney, & Manuck, 1987). Note that under resting or nondemanding situations no differences are typically found (e.g., Eagleston et al., 1986). Generally, in laboratory studies, when the demands of the task have been increased by making it more difficult or more competitive, TA adolescents have shown greater physiologic reactivity.

2. For purposes of space economy, the phrase TA children or teens will be often used. This does not denote, however, support for a fixed traitlike concept of TA nor a dichotomous view that all children or adolescents are either Type A or not Type A.

Importantly, a few studies have shown that reactivity in the laboratory setting corresponds with measures of reactivity in the natural environment. In one study (Southard, Coates & Kolodner 1986), changes were found in systolic blood pressure in the laboratory that corresponded with systolic blood pressure changes in the natural setting. Further, such changes were positively associated with the adolescent's self-related feelings of hostility, depression, tension, and worry. Adolescents who perceived the environment as more hostile and demanding also showed greater blood pressure changes. Another study (Matthews, Manuck, & Saab, 1986) found that changes in blood pressure and heart rate during laboratory tests in some cases correlated with changes during a public speaking task in a high school English classroom. The results showed that the changes varied by type of stressor and by the particular physiological measure used (e.g., changes in heart rate vs. changes in systolic blood pressure).

In physiological reactivity studies, the perceived salience of the task to the adolescent deserves much more careful study (e.g., not all 14-year-olds consider mental arithmetic a personally challenging task) as does the connection of reactivity in a laboratory setting to everyday life situations. Further, gender differences are important as reactivity often varies by the type of task or stressor involved for males and females. Females, for example, typically do not show as much change in various neurotransmitters or hormones, such as norepinephirine in laboratory tasks, as do males (Krantz & Manuck, 1984).

HERITABILITY ▪ Little is currently known about how genetics influences the origins and the expression of TA in children and adolescents. While a few adult studies suggest modest levels of inherited traits, such as certain speech characteristics

among Type A adults (Rahe, Hervig, & Rosenman, 1978), the complexity of the TA syndrome coupled with the need to use twin studies methodology (MG vs. DG twins) prevents firm conclusions about genetic factors. Matthews and Woodall (1988) suggest, however, that heritability might be a factor for cardiovascular reactivity to certain behavioral stressors, such as blood pressure change.

Confounding the heritability issue is how to disentangle what an infant, or fetus, may learn from experience compared to inherited characteristics. Further, the emerging complexity in the field of genetics, with the growing recognition of the subtle and complex influences of how genes interract with and are influenced by experience, makes the classic heredity versus environment dichotomy somewhat meaningless (Changeux, cited in Lewin, 1986). At present, much of the TA appears acquired through experiences in family, school, community, and mass media settings.

ETHNICITY ▪ Findings on ethnic differences concerning TA have been inconsistent. White children, for example, have commonly rated themselves higher on TA measures than black children (e.g., Hunter et al., 1989). Teachers, however, have also consistently rated black children as more TA than white or Hispanic children (e.g., Hunter, Parker, Williamson, Downey, Webber, & Berenson, 1985). Some inconsistencies across ethnic groups may be explained by different perceptions of teachers and other observers as well as by students themselves about what constitutes socially acceptable behavior. For example, are TA qualities and characteristics viewed as more or less desirable by different ethnic groups? Evidence to date with children and adolescents generally supports the existence of TA in adolescents across ethnic groups, although the prevalence probably varies by

educational level, socioeconomic status (SES), and parental education, as it does with adults (Moss et al., 1986). An interesting question concerns ethnicity and SES: does the prevalance of TA vary more by SES level than by ethnicity in older children and adolescents?

FAMILY DEMOGRAPHICS ▪ At present a clear picture of family demographics to TA in adolescents remains unavailable, in large part because the TA in older children and adolescents has been assessed using different measures (self-report vs. teacher rating vs. structured interview). Modest correlations exist between these types of assessments, suggesting each may be measuring a different facet of the TA syndrome.

To date, family income, father's occupation, parental history of cardiovascular disease, and educational level have not been strongly associated with TA status of adolescents. For example, Matthews, Stoney, Rakaczky, and Jamison (1986) found no differences in families of TA and non–TA children in terms of SES level and history of CHD. Similarly, Bracke and Thoresen (1989) found no differences among young adolescents in 40 families in terms of family SES, parental occupation, and educational level. However, Manning, Balson, Hunter, Berenson and Welles (1987) found more TA students (male and female) in an upper SES urban setting than a lower SES rural setting. I suspect that future studies will confirm the strong relationship between SES level and TA, paralleling adult findings when more heterogeneous samples of adolescents are studied.

PARENTAL ATTITUDES AND BEHAVIORS ▪ Enviromental factors early on undoubtedly contribute to a variety of adolescent behaviors and attitudes. Studies to date suggest that TA behaviors

and characteristics of parents contribute to the prevalence of TA in their children. An early study (Bortner, Rosenman & Friedman, 1970) found a strong positive relationship between TA fathers and TA in their sons. Treiber et al. (1990), however, found mother's verbal hostility level predicted children's Type A status, especially in families with a history of cardiovascular disease.

Almost all studies to date, looking at specific parental and child behaviors and attitudes, have involved elementary school children (Thoresen & Pattillo, 1988). Developmentally, however, these studies create a portrait that seems valid for parent and adolescent experience. Evidence with children, for example, suggests that mothers have been observed to "push" TA children harder and more often than non–TA children on tasks, yet these adults did not otherwise act differently toward TA or non–TA children. Further, mothers of TA children have also been found to give fewer positive evaluations to their child, to encourage the child to try harder, despite the child's successful performance, and to offer more critical evaluations of their child (Matthews, 1977; Matthews, Glass, & Richins, 1977). Thus, parents of TA children appear to encourage their children to try harder as well as to avoid mistakes more often than parents of non–TA children. In addition, parents of TA children also seem to be less discriminating about their child's performance in that they offer more encouragement as well as more criticism regardless of how well the child is performing (Bracke & Thoresen, 1989).

TRYING HARDER AND HARDER ▪ These findings suggest an explanation for the tendency of many adult TAs to continue making efforts to succeed, even if their efforts are ineffective in solving problems (Price, 1982). Understandably, some TA children may be learning that

success comes from making greater and greater efforts to succeed, in contrast to clarifying what a task requires them to do in a particular situation. This tendency for parents of TA children to play a more active if not controlling role by encouraging and by criticizing the child's performance may contribute to the child's inability to make valid discriminations about how well tasks are being done. This inability may thus set the internal stage about how to self-evaluate, especially in terms of what standards or criteria for self-evaluation should be used.

Matthews (1977) noted that mothers of TA children frequently provided very ambiguous or confusing standards for children to evaluate their own performance. In a developmental sense what may emerge from childhood into adolescence is growing confusion about what constitutes success in their work, contributing to a belief that under this kind of uncertainty more effort coupled with more control is the answer to performing better and being successful (Matthews & Volkin, 1981; Strube, Lott, Heilizer, & Gregg, 1986). Such beliefs acquired earlier in life would seem to explain, in part, the frequently observed "joyless striving" of many adult TAs and their frequent confusion about what constitutes a good performance (Friedman & Rosenman, 1974; Price, 1982; Thoresen, 1989).

SOCIAL COMPARISONS AND ATTRIBUTIONS ▪ Coupled with issues of ambiguity about self-evaluations and parental demands to try harder is evidence suggesting that TA children and their parents seek information more often to compare the child's performance against a child identified as an excellent performer (e.g., Bracke & Thoresen, 1989; Matthews & Siegel, 1983). By contrast, less TA children and their parents are more likely to use the child's previous performance as the comparison (Heft et al., 1988). Common use of social comparisons would explain in part the socially competitive and time-urgent actions of many Type As. That is, given unclear inner standards of what constitutes a successful performance, coupled with pressure from parents and others always to try harder (this often translates to work faster than others), acting in a Type A manner seems both logical and adaptive. Indeed, the younger person may learn that the TA helps alleviate the anxious and perhaps fearful thoughts and feelings experienced when one's sense of success and security are so ambiguous and so uncertain.

TA children have also been found to make different attributions about their performance under clear versus ambiguous conditions. They often attribute their success under clear performance conditions to their personal effort but give the credit to luck or external factors when working under more ambiguous conditions (Murray, Matthews, Blake, Prineas, & Gillum, 1986). TA children have also been noted to make more negative self-statements when working under ambiguous conditions compared to non–TA children, yet more positive self-statements when performing under clearly defined conditions of success.[3]

---

3. The work of M. E. F. Seligman and his colleagues on explanatory styles for negative events and how these social cognitive processes are predictive of negative health status, including mortality, is intriguing. For example, the attribution of the explanatory style may link to the Type A belief of always trying harder to succeed and the "global" attribution (i.e., bad events are due to major forces beyond my control) may fit with the Type A's unrealistic struggle to be in control of situations. Currently a study of negative explanatory style in adult Type As at Stanford is finding that a negative "stable" explanatory style predicts mortality in males. If confirmed, the need to examine this kind of social cognition in younger persons as related to TA will be supported.

Finally, parents of high TA young adolescents have also been found to differ in some of their specific attitudes about achievement training and discipline, as well as in the social modeling of TA behavior (Bracke & Thoresen, 1989). For example, parents of young TA adolescents were found to expect much more overt achievement and independent behavior by their children than parents of non–TA children. When observed working with their child on a task, parents of the TA children demonstrated more TA-related actions (e.g., speech stylistics, frequency of giving directions). While parents of both high and low TA adolescents provided reward and encouragement for successful performance and shared high aspirations for their children, parents of high TA youth also used more punishment, primarily in the form of criticism, for less successful performance.

What emerges is a tentative picture of how parents may promote the TA. The social modeling and reinforcing of TA behaviors and characteristics by parents seems evident: indiscriminately "pushing" their children to perform well, encouraging greater effort to try harder and work faster instead of taking more time to reflect on what needs to be done if current efforts are not working. Further, given the common ambiguity of what constitutes success in many life situations, children appear forced to use social comparisons of those who are perceived as top-notch performers. In this way parents may indeed be instilling an excessive sense of social competitiveness and comparison with others, coupled with an aggravated sense of time urgency, given that one is expected to do more and more in a finite amount of time. Thus, what has been called the "pressured drive" facet of TA may indeed be, in part, a product of parental attitudes and actions (Thoresen & Ohman, 1987).

PERFORMANCE: DO TYPE As DO BETTER?

Many adults believe that high performance, if not success, is due to TA characteristics (Friedman & Ulmer, 1984; Price, 1982). In general, studies of TA in children and adolescents have not demonstrated a superiority in terms of performance on a variety of academic, intellectual, and athletic tasks and performance measures (Thoresen & Pattillo, 1988). Some data have suggested that the competitive component of TA is associated with a superior performance on some tasks, such as doing math problems under unlimited time conditions (e.g., Matthews & Volkin, 1981). However, the vast majority of studies to date have failed to demonstrate a strong relationship between TA status and performance outcomes (e.g., Bracke & Thoresen, 1989; Corrigan & Moscowitz, 1982; Fontana & Davidio, 1984). Rodeo and Thoresen (1988) found, for example, no performance differences between TA and non–TA male and female college athletes. Further, the athletic potential and athletic talent independently rated by their coaches showed no differences by level of TA. Differences between TA male athletes and nonathletes showed that the athletes were more Type A only on competition-related issues, not on time-related or hostility-related issues. Further, this higher competitiveness in male athletes was limited to the athletic context; no differences were found for academic or social competitiveness. These results suggest that performance differences associated with the TA may indeed exist but are probably limited to doing certain tasks and in particular contexts.

In sum, TA does not at this point appear to be strongly associated with significantly higher classroom grades, achievement test scores, and other kinds of performance variables. Interestingly, some evidence from adult studies (e.g., Jamal,

1985) suggests that *quality* of performance (compared to quantity) as rated by supervisors may be lower for Type A adults. Needed are studies that include quality of performance measures not just readily quantified performance markers concerning the TA-performance issue.

ANGER AND HOSTILITY ■

Anger and hostility has clearly emerged as perhaps the most powerful or pathogenic component of the TA, particularly as it relates to cardiovascular disease (e.g., Williams, Barefoot & Shekelle, 1985). However, the study of anger and hostility related to the TA in children and adolescents has received very little attention. Siegel (1984), in one of the few studies, found that TA adolescents did not express their anger outwardly more often than non–TA adolescents, but did report experiencing more anger in a greater variety of situations (i.e., they felt more angry in more different settings). In addition, TA adolescents were also found to smoke more, to be more overweight, and to be less physically active, particularly boys. They also reported lower self-esteem and less life satisfaction. Thoresen, Eagleston, Kirmil-Gray, Wiedenfeld, and Bracke (1989) also found substantial differences in self-reported anger and hostility among young high vs. low Type A adolescents using a variety of self-report measures. High TA children and adolescents reported considerably more anger arousal in terms of frequency, intensity, and duration, as well as experiencing more anger in a greater variety of situations. Further, the high TA students reported much more "anger-in" (getting angry but not openly expressing it) similar to the findings of Siegel (1984).

How anger is actually expressed and experienced by adolescents in everyday situations remains unexamined. We lack information on anger gathered by observational and naturalistic studies. Further, at this point, we do not know how the experience of anger covaries with other major TA components, such as degree of competitiveness and level of time urgency. Conceivably, it may be the more angry TA adolescent, compared to a more time-urgent adolescent, who is at greatest risk for a variety of physical and psychosocial disorders.

Also unexamined is the construct of hostility in adolescents. Although some researchers and clinicians equate hostility with physical aggressiveness, most view it as a cognitive schema, a complex set of social cognitive processes ("deep seated attitudes") that perceive and anticipate events from a more suspicious, distrustful, if not cynical perspective (Williams & Barefoot, 1988). As such, the more transient emotional state of anger differs from the more enduring attitude of hostility. The study of anger and hostility in children and adolescents, especially in terms of its relationship to the TA, deserves the highest priority. Indeed, the early establishment of hostile schema by the child, carried into adolescence, may profoundly determine much of what is experienced in adulthood.

Assessment Issues

TA in children and adolescents has been assessed in a variety of ways, including self-report measures, structured interviews, and classroom teacher ratings (see Ney & Wagner, 1987; Thoresen & Pattillo, 1988). Unfortunately, with rare exception, studies of children and adolescents have used only one type of assessment, such as the MYTH, which is an elementary teacher's rating of the child in an elementary classroom on such questions as "This child does things in a hurry" and "This child is competitive" (Matthews & Angullo, 1980). Fewer studies have used self-report ratings, such as the Hunter-Wolfe Type Scale (Wolfe, Sklove, Wenzel, Hunter & Berenson, 1981) or the Student Type Behavior Scale (STABS) (Kirmil-Gray, Eagleston, Thoresen, Heft, Arnow, & Bracke, 1987). Rarely have studies combined either teacher ratings or self-report measures with audiotaped structured interviews to assess TA (Kirmil-Gray et al., 1987; Siegel, 1984).

Unfortunately, the relationship between classroom teacher ratings and self-report measures is modest (ranging from .05 to .25) as is the association of teacher ratings with the structured interview. Thus, different measures of TA in youth appear to be tapping different facets of the Type A syndrome. As already noted, none of the current TA measures for children and adolescents adequately assess anger and hostility, particularly anger that is not openly expressed ("anger-in"). Most of the variance in current TA assessments is accounted for by either self-reported or teacher-rated competitiveness and time-urgent impatience.

Despite these limitations, current measures have offered data that is reasonably reliable and fairly valid to the extent that expected relationships paralleling the characteristics of TA in adults have been found among younger people. Optimally, future studies will use more than one mode of assessment (e.g., more than a single self-report questionnaire) and will also include longitudinal or prospective designs so that assessment will be repeated over occasions. Currently, for example, such a project is underway by Karen Matthews and her colleagues at the University of Pittsburgh.

Perhaps the basic assessment issue is a conceptual one: how do investigators think of the TA in adolescents? If it is viewed as primarily a fixed personality trait, then global, single-occasion assessments would seem appropriate. If, however, TA is construed to be more of a "person-by-environment" interaction phenomena, that is, where personal and contextual factors interact to yield a certain pattern of behavior, then a more contextually sensitive assessment strategy is required. It is intriguing, for example, to consider an assessment strategy that would include ways of tapping the adolescent's social cognitions about self and others in particular situations, much in the way that Dodge and his colleagues have done in examining cognitive and perceptual differences in physically aggressive and nonaggressive boys (e.g., Dodge & Frame, 1982). Optimally, assessment strategies are directed by conceptual models of the phenomena in question. Hopefully, the need for clearer conceptualizations of the TA will be recognized in studies with adolescents.

Reflections and Recommendations

Type A–like behaviors and characteristics are clearly observable in adolescents as well as in children, even during the preschool years. Differences seem to exist in the prevalence of TA by gender and possibly ethnicity as well as region (urban vs. rural), level of education, and SES. Does TA in adolescence represent a significant or noteworthy problem? The answer is probably yes if viewed in terms of cardiovascular risk in adulthood. No direct evidence has yet demonstrated TA in adolescence to be predictive of increased CHD in adulthood. Still, the pattern of evidence indicates a strong possibility of risk and should be taken seriously unless demonstrated otherwise in controlled empirical studies. TA in adolescence, however, is also a possible risk for a variety of other disorders—social, emotional, personal, and vocational (Thoresen, 1989).

Despite obvious limitations and shortcomings of studies in terms of assessment, conceptualization, and research design—for example, almost all studies are cross-sectional in design—little if any compelling evidence exists to show that higher levels of TA in adolescence promotes *positive* outcomes. Further, no evidence supports the conjecture that TA status predicts or enhances quality of life indicators among adolescents. Indeed, what evidence does exist suggests TA status is related to problems of lower self-esteem, higher anger, disrupted social relationships, negative major life events, and a variety of physical symptoms of stress and discomfort (e.g., Eagleston et al., 1986; Eagleston et al., 1989; Heft et al., 1988; Johnson et al. 1989).

I suspect that many adolescents manifesting higher levels of TA are, in effect, gradually creating self-schema, a working conceptual model of self and of others that guides perceptions and evaluations, that could prove very debilitating over time in terms of physical, personal, social, and career-related issues (Markus, 1977). If conjectures trying to explain the etiology of TA are supported (e.g., the need for excessively high levels of perceived control, coupled with often inappropriate sustained effort in ambiguous situations with confused criteria for making self-evaluations) then a variety of questions emerge about TA in adolescence. For example, is the excessively individualistic and self-focused orientation of many adult Americans recently documented by Bellah and his colleagues (1985) a product of parental, academic, and mass media–based influences on children and adolescents, influences that foster TA–like characteristics? One has

only to inspect the popular role models, frequently presented in prime-time commercial television and popular films as well as the newspaper advertisements, to appreciate how the dominant contemporary culture in many ways is socially marketing a Type A–like life-style, one that is highly individualistic, sharply competitive, and obsessed with time (Rifkind, 1987). Friedman and Booth-Kewley (1988) recently argued that promising evidence is now available to consider seriously the conjecture that a "disease-prone personality" exists, one combining three components: anger/hostility, depression, and anxiety. Conceivably, the TA may emerge in the next decade as a fitting part of this disease-prone style of living, a dynamic blend of individualistically focused competitiveness, hostility, and impatience. It is also conceivable that depressive and anxious patterns in people characterized as high on the TA have gone unrecognized, especially in women (Thoresen & Graff-Low, 1990).

Some Recommendations

Continue studies of the TA in adolescence with much more concern for assessment and evaluation, especially relative to gender, context, ethnicity, SES level, region, and family. Initially, investigators should use more than one mode of assessment on more than one occasion with selected adolescent groups.

Increase the number of direct observation studies, both in terms of controlled laboratory settings and naturalistic contexts. Studies are needed in which adolescents self-monitor selected actions, thoughts, and emotional states along with systematic observations by teachers and parents. The advent of reasonably inexpensive ambulatory monitoring devices has greatly increased the viability of doing observation studies outside of the laboratory. Both settings, however, are essential.

Conduct well-conceptualized, controlled clinical case studies of adolescents who clearly manifest excessive levels of TA compared to adolescents who clearly do not. No such studies are available. Several subtleties and nuances of the TA in adults have emerged from the clinical insights and case materials. Richly documented, qualitatively focused case material on adolescents would be very useful.

Initiate prospectively designed studies of TA children and adolescents and their parents across several years. In this way, the development of TA and its various correlates—physiologically, behaviorally, emotionally, academically—can be tracked over time. The expense of such designs may be diminished if networks of collaborating researchers will cooperate in carefully selecting cohorts, and cooperating in their assessment efforts.

Abandon theory and assessment that views the TA as a fixed personality trait that is assessed globally. Instead, think of TA as a complex social, cognitive, and behavioral pattern that is very sensitive to particular contexts. Study the components of the pattern, such as hostility or time urgency, and examine how these components relate to important psychosocial and physiological markers and endpoints.

Finally, recognize that powerful social and cultural factors, manifested in school, worksite, and community settings, including the mass media, are at work in the development, maintenance, and generalization of the TA and related behaviors. In the same way that such factors markedly can influence prevailing life-style patterns, such as food preferences, leisure time, and use of drugs, including alcohol and cigarettes, they also seem to be encouraging more individualistic competitiveness, time urgency, and a diminishing sense of trust, respect and caring for others as well as for oneself.

References

Bellah, R. N., Madson, R., Sullivan, W. M., Savidler, A., & Tipton, S. M. (1985). *Habits of the heart: Individualism and commitment in American life.* Berkeley and Los Angeles: University of California Press.

Booth-Kewley, S., & Friedman, H. S. (1987). Psychological predictors of heart disease: A quantitative review. *Psychological Bulletin, 101,* 343–362.

Bortner, R. W., Rosenman, R. H., & Friedman, M. (1970). Familiar similarity in pattern A behavior. *Journal of Chronic Disease, 23,* 39–43.

Bracke, P., & Thoresen, C. E. (1989). Parental attitudes and behaviors of Type A and non–Type A children and adolescents. Unpublished manuscript.

Cooper, T., Detre, T., & Weiss, S. M. (1981). Coronary-prone behavior and coronary heart disease. *Circulation, 63,* 1199–1215.

Corrigan, S. A., & Moskowitz, D. S. (1982). Type A behavior in preschool children: Construct validation evidence for the MYTH. *Child Development, 54,* 1513–1521.

Dodge, K. A., & Frame, C. L. (1982). Social cognitive biases and deficits in aggressive boys. *Child Development, 53,* 620–635.

Eagleston, J. R., Kirmil-Gray, K., Thoresen, C. E., Wiedenfeld, S. A., Bracke, P., Heft, L., & Arnow, B. (1986). Physical health correlates of Type A behavior in children and adolescents. *Journal of Behavioral Medicine, 9,* 341–362.

Eagleston, J. R., Thoresen, C. E., Kirmil-Gray, K., Bracke, P., Heft, L., Wiedenfeld, S., & Arnow, B. (1989). Major life events and daily hassles: Stressful experiences of Type A children and adolescents. Unpublished manuscript, Stanford University.

Eagleston, J. R., Thoresen, C. E., Kirmil Gray, K., Wiedenfeld, S. A. & Bracke, P. (1989). Major life events and daily hassles: Stressful experiences of Type A children and adolescents. Unpublished manuscript.

Fontana, A., & Davidio, J. (1984). The relationship between stressful life events and school-related performances of Type A and Type B adolescents. *Journal of Human Stress, 10*, 50–55.

Friedman, H., & Booth-Kewley, S. (1988). Validity of the Type A construct: A reprise. *Psychological Bulletin, 104*, 381–384.

Friedman, M., & Rosenman, R. H. (1974). *Type A behavior and your heart.* New York: Alfred A. Knopf.

Friedman, M., Thoresen, C. E., Gill, J. J., Ulmer, D., Powell, L. H., Price, V. A., Brown, B., Thompson, L., Rubin, D. D., Breall, W. S., Bourg, E., Levy, R., & Dixon, T. (1986). Alteration of Type A behavior and its effect on cardiac recurrences in postmyocardial infarction patients: Summary results of the Recurrent Coronary Prevention Project. *American Heart Journal, 112*, 653–665.

Friedman, M., & Ulmer, D. (1984). *Treating Type A behavior—and your heart.* New York: Alfred A. Knopf.

Glueck, C. J. (1986). Pediatric primary prevention of atherosclerosis. *New England Journal of Medicine, 314*, 175–177.

Heft, L., Thoresen, C. E., Kirmil-Gray, K., Wiedenfeld, S. A., Eagleston, J. R., Bracke, P., & Arnow, B. (1988). Emotional and temperamental correlates of Type A in children and adolescents. *Journal of Youth and Adolescence, 17*, 461–475.

Henry, J., & Stephens, P. (1977). *Stress, health, and the social environment.* New York: Springer-Verlag.

Houston, B. K., & Snyder, C. R. (Eds.). (1988). *Type A behavior pattern: Theory, research, and intervention.* New York: John Wiley.

Hunter, S. M., Johnson, C. C., Vigelberg, B. A., Webber, L. S., Berenson, G. S. (1989). Establishment of norms and tracking of Type A behavior in children and young adults: The Bogalusa Heart Study. Unpublished manuscript, Department of Medicine, Louisiana State University, New Orleans.

Hunter, S. M., Parker, F. C., Williamson, G. D., Downey, A. M., Webber, L. S., & Berenson, G. S. (1985). Measurement assessment of the Type A coronary prone behavior pattern and hyperactivity/problem behaviors in children: Are they related? The Bogalusa Heart Study. *Journal of Human Stress, Vol. 11*, 177–183.

Jamal, M. (1984). Type A behavior and job performance: Some suggestive findings. *Journal of Human Stress, 11*, 60–68.

Johnson, C. C., Hunter, S. M., Amos, C. I., Elden, S. T., Berenson, G. S. (1989). Cigarette smoking, alcohol, and oral contraceptive use by Type A adolescent—The Bogalusa Heart Study. *Journal of Behavioral Medicine, 12*, 13–24.

Kirmil-Gray, K., Eagleston, J. R., Thoresen, C. E., Heft, L., Arnow, B., & Bracke, P. (1987). Developing measures of Type A behavior in children and adolescents. *Journal of Human Stress, 13*, 5–15.

Krantz, D. S., Lundberg, U., & Frankenhaeuser, M. (1988). Stress and Type A behavior: Interactions between environmental and biologic factors. In A. Baum & J. E. Singer (Eds.), *Handbook of psychology and health: Vol. 5. Stress and coping* (pp. 74–115). Hillsdale, NJ: Lawrence Erlbaum Associates.

Krantz, D. S., & Manuck, S. B. (1984). Acute psychophysiologic reactivity and risk of cardiovascular disease: A review and methodologic critique. *Psychological Bulletin, 96*, 435–464.

Lewin, R. (1986). Brain architecture: Beyond genes. *Science, 233*, 155–156.

Manning, D. T., Balson, P. M., Hunter, S. M., Berenson, G. S., Willis, A. S. (1987).

Comparison of the prevalence of Type A behavior in boys and girls from two contrasting socioeconomic groups. *Journal of Human Stress*, *13*, 116–120.

Margolis, L. H., McElroy, K. R., Runyan, C. W., & Kaplan, B. H. (1983). Type A behavior: An ecological approach. *Journal of Behavioral Medicine*, *6*, 245–258.

Matthews, K. (1988). Coronary heart disease and Type A behaviors: Update on and alternative to the Booth-Kewley and Friedman (1987) review. *Psychological Bulletin*, *104*, 373–380.

Matthews, K. A. (1977). Caregiver-child interactions and the Type A coronary-prone behavior pattern. *Child Development*, *48*, 1752–1756.

Matthews, K. A., & Angullo, J. (1980). Measurement of the Type A behavior pattern in children: Assessment of children's competitiveness, impatience-anger, and aggression. *Child Development*, *51*, 466–475.

Matthews, K. A., Glass, D. C., & Richins, M. (1977). The other-son observation study. In D. C. Glass (Ed.). *Behavior patterns, stress, and coronary disease*. Hillsdale, NJ: Lawrence Erlbaum Associates.

Matthews, K., & Haynes, S. G. (1986). Type A behavior pattern and coronary disease risk. *American Journal of Epidemiology*, *123*, 923–959.

Matthews, K. A., Manuck, S. B., & Saab, P. G. (1986). Cardiovascular responses of adolescents during a naturally occurring stressor and their behavioral and psychophysiological predictors. *Psychophysiology*, *23*, 198–209.

Matthews, K. A., Rakaczky, C. J., Stoney, C. M., & Manuck, S. B. (1987). Are cardiovascular responses to behavioral stressors a stable individual difference variable in childhood? *Psychophysiology*, *24*, 464–473.

Matthews, K. A., & Siegel, M. J. (1983). Type A behaviors for children, social comparison, and standards for self-evaluation. *Developmental Psychology*, *19*, 135–140.

Matthews, K. A., Stoney, C. M., Rakaczky, C. J., & Jamison, W. (1986). Family characteristics and school achievements of Type A children. *Health Psychology*, *5*, 453–467.

Matthews, K. A., & Volkin, J. I. (1981). Efforts to excel and the Type A behavior pattern in children. *Child Development*, *52*, 1283–1289.

Matthews, K. A., & Woodall, K. L. (1988). Childhood origins of overt Type A behaviors and cardiovascular reactivity to behavioral stressors. *Annals of Behavioral Medicine*, *10*, 71–77.

Moss, G. E., Dielman, T. E., Campanelli, P. C., Leech, S. L., Harlan, W. R., Van Harrison, R., & Horvath, W. J. (1986). Demographic correlates of SI assessments of Type A behavior. *Psychosomatic Medicine*, *48*.

Murray, D. M., Matthews, K. A., Blake, S. M., Prineas, R. J., & Gillum, R. F. (1986). Type A behavior in children: Demographic, behavioral, and physiological correlates. *Health Psychology*, *5*, 159–169.

Ney, R. E., & Wagner, M. K. (1987). The assessment of Type A behavior in children and adolescents: An overview. *Journal of Psychopathology and Behavioral Assessment*, *9*, 1–12.

Nunes, E. V., Frank, K. A., & Kornfeld, D. S. (1987). Psychological treatment for the Type A behavior pattern and for coronary heart disease: A meta-analysis of the literature. *Psychosomatic Medicine*, *48*, 159–173.

Price, V. A. (1982). *Type A behavior pattern: A model for research and practice*. New York: Academic Press.

Rahe, R. H., Hervig, L., & Rosenman, R. H. (1978). The heritability of Type A behavior. *Psychosomatic Medicine*, *40*, 478–486.

Rodeo, S., & Thoresen, C. E. (1988). Type A behavior and collegiate athletes: Relationship to non-athletes, gender, over-use injuries, and performance. Unpublished manuscript, Stanford University.

Siegel, J. M. (1984). Anger and cardiovascular

risk in adolescents. *Health Psychology, 3,* 293–313.

Southard, D. R., Coates, T. J., Kolodnes, K. (1986). Relationship between mood and blood pressure in the natural environment: An adolescent population. *Health Psychology, 5,* 469–480.

Spielberger, C. D., Johnson, E. H., Russell, S. F., Crane, R., & Worden, T. (1985). The experience and expression of anger. In M. Chesney & R. H. Rosenman (Eds.), *Anger and hostility in cardiovascular and behavioral disorder* (pp. 5–30). New York: Hemisphere/McGraw-Hill.

Strube, M. J., Lott, C. L., Heilizer, R., & Gregg, B. (1986). Type A behavior and the judgement of control. *Journal of Personality and Social Psychology, 50,* 403–412.

Thoresen, C. E. (1989). Counseling and Type A: Reflections on theory, assessment, and treatment. Symposium presented at the American Psychological Association Annual Meeting, New Orleans.

Thoresen, C. E., Eagleston, J. R., Kirmil-Gray, K., & Wiedenfeld, S. A. (1989). Examining anger in low and high Type A children and adolescents. Poster session, Society of Behavioral Medicine 10th annual meeting. San Francisco, CA.

Thoresen, C. E., & Graff-Low, K. (1990). Women and the Type A behavior pattern: Review and commentary. *Journal of Social Behavior and Personality, 5,* 117–133.

Thoresen, C. E., & Ohman, A. (1987). The Type A behavior pattern: A person-environment interaction perspective. In D. Magnusson & A. Ohman (Eds.), *Psychopathology: An interaction perspective* (pp. 140–156). New York: Academic Press.

Thoresen, C. E., & Pattillo, J. (1988). Exploring the Type A behavior pattern in children and adolescents. In B. K. Houston & C. R. Snyder (Eds.), *Type A behavior: Research and intervention* (pp. 98–145). New York: John Wiley.

Treiber, F. A., Mabe, P. A., Riley, W. T., McDuffie, M., Strong, W. B., Levy, M. (1990). Children's Type A behavior: The role of parental hostility and family history of cardiovascular disease. *Journal of Social Behavior and Personality, 5,* 182–199.

Webber, L. S., Cresanta, J. L., Voors, A. W., Berenson, G. S. (1983). Tracking of cardiovascular disease risk factor variables in school-age children. *Journal of Chronic Diseases, 36,* 647–660.

Weiner, H. (1977). *Psychobiology and human disease.* New York: Elsevier.

Williams, R. B., & Barefoot, J. C. (1988). Coronary-prone behavior: The emerging role of the hostility complex. In B. K. Houston & C. R. Snyder (Eds.), *Type A behavior pattern: Research, theory and intervention* (pp. 189–211). New York: Wiley.

Williams, R. B., Barefoot, J. C., & Shekelle, R. B. (1985). The health consequences of hostility. In M. Chesney and R. Rosenman (Eds.), *Anger and hostility in cardiovascular and behavioral disorders* (pp. 175–183). New York: Hemisphere.

Wolf, T. M., Sklov, M. C., Wenzel, P. A., Hunter, S. M., & Berenson, G. S. (1982). Validation of a measure of Type A behavior pattern in children: Bogalusa Heart Study. *Child Development, 53,* 126–135.

See Also

Aggressive Behavior in Adolescence; Attention Deficit Disorder and Hyperactivity; Bulimia Nervosa in Adolescence; Conflict, Adolescent-Parent: A Model and a Method; Delinquency; Handicapped Adolescents, Providing Services for; Learning Disabilities in Adolescents: Description, Assessment, and Management; Problem Behavior in Adolescence; Psychophysiological/Psychosomatic Problems; Runaways, Negative Consequences for; Self-Destructiveness, Chronic, Role of in Adolescence; Stress and the Adolescent; Stress and Coping in the Adolescent; Suicide, Adolescent; Suicides, Cluster.

Underachievers and Dropouts

Robert B. McCall
University of Pittsburgh

Parents of children and adolescents report that school achievement is one of their primary concerns along with drug, alcohol, and sexual problems. One out of four adolescents does not graduate from high school. Poor academic achievement may occur for many reasons, including limited mental ability and retardation, specific learning disorders, social or emotional problems, and poor motivation associated with personality, family, school, and societal factors.

Poorly achieving students, especially those who have only motivational problems, are called *underachievers* if they perform worse in school than one would expect on the basis of their mental abilities. Several kinds of underachievers, plus some students with other problems, may not finish high school. They are often called *dropouts*, although some may be "pushed out," fail to fulfill graduation requirements, or fade out of school for many other reasons.

Underachievement

The most rigorous definition of underachievers includes those students who fall one standard deviation below the regression of school performance (i.e., typically measured by grades) on mental ability (i.e., typically measured by intelligence, aptitude, or even achievement tests). In large samples of high school students, this criterion embraces the bottom 16% of youth who perform most poorly (approximately one grade point or more) relative to the level expected on the basis of ability.

Defining underachievers in this way means that the number of underachievers in the country is arbitrary, because the one-standard-deviation cutoff itself is arbitrary. Also, underachievers will come from all ability groups, not just from the ranks of the "gifted," who have been the primary focus of study.

CHARACTERISTICS ■ Using the above definition, underachievement has the following characteristics (see review by McCall, Evahn, & Kratzer, 1988).

Sex distribution. Approximately two boys are designated as underachievers for every girl, but this may be partly because boys generally get poorer grades than girls.

Age of onset. Technically, the above definition will identify approximately 16% of the students as underachievers at any age at which grades and ability measures are available. But parents and school teachers tend to complain about underachievement during late elementary and junior high school, which coincides with the beginning of adolescence and the beginning of homework assignments. Failure to do homework is often the first clear sign to teachers and parents of a student's flagging motivation.

Stability. Adequate studies are not available, but boys who are underachievers in junior high school have often shown a pattern of underachievement since at least third grade, whereas underachieving junior high girls have not. After junior high, the persistence of underachievement in individuals is believed to increase, with long-term consequences for adult educational and occupational success (see below).

Socioeconomic status (SES). While high SES parents who value education are more likely to be concerned, complain to school personnel, and seek professional assistance when their children underachieve, broad-based samples tend to show underachievers are more likely to have families with lower socioeconomic status and parents who provide less encouragement for achievement.

Family configuration. Underachievers come from slightly larger families, which may be associated with lower SES. While counselors and clinicians report that under-achievers often have siblings (especially older ones) who are very accomplished in school, this is not found in broad-based samples. Also, underachievers are not more likely to be children of divorced parents or working mothers.

School behavior. Underachievers have poor study habits, are often deficient in basic skills and problem-solving techniques, display inconsistent effort and quality of performance, show a lack of concentration and much daydreaming and restlessness, are disorganized and distractible, are often sloppy and impulsive in their work or do just enough to get by, do not try, fail to do homework, and avoid challenges. They may appear immature and maladjusted, disruptive, and/or talkative; they may be tardy and absent frequently; and some are a discipline problem.

Personal characteristics. Clinicians describe underachievers as having low self-esteem and extremely poor self-concepts, especially low perceptions of their abilities. As a result they lack persistence, giving an impulsive reaction and/or dropping the task at the first sign of challenge or difficulty.

They often set unrealistic goals and standards for themselves, which are displayed in self-critical behavior, dissatisfaction with every performance, and unrealistic perfectionism. They have a fear of failure and a fear of success, and they often become anxious or nervous before they are asked to perform.

They are either shy, withdrawn, immature, and ineffectual in social skills, or they are aggressive and disruptive. Emotionally, they can be flat, apathetic, unhappy, and depressed, or they can be emotionally explosive and poorly controlled. While a few are socially popular, most lack friends and many are lonely or alienated.

The aggressive underachiever is often hostile and rejecting of authority figures, obsessed with being independent, lacking in self-control, manipulative, irresponsible and unreliable, and sometimes delinquent. Other underachievers are passive-aggressive, getting back at parents and authority figures by not achieving or "playing their game."

Finally, many are externally controlled, blaming and criticizing others for their own problems and failures.

Parental characteristics. Parents of underchievers seem to be of two general kinds. One type is indifferent, disinterested, and distant, with neutral to negative attitudes toward education. They also may be authoritarian, restrictive, and rejecting, or they may be extremely permissive or lax, granting the child extraordinary freedom as if he or she were an adult.

The second kind of parent, one more likely to be seen by private therapists, is preoccupied with achievement, directly or indirectly setting high standards and pressuring their children to achieve. They may be overindulgent, oversolicitous, overprotective, and too helpful. While they are well-meaning and may have other children who achieve very well, such parents can give children the impression that they are loved only if they achieve and that they are not capable of going it alone without the parent to guide them and prevent them from failing.

School characteristics. The school environment may contribute in at least two ways. First, Whitmore (1980) argued that gifted children have special needs for intellectual independence and creativity that may clash with a restrictive classroom atmosphere that emphasizes rote and repetitive learning. Second, schools may be apathetic to the needs of unmotivated students in general. Most school systems have no special programs for students who are "simply" unmotivated or underachieving, unless they also have mental retardation, specific learning disabilities, or social-emotional and disruptive behavioral problems.

CAUSES ■

While many theories and explanations of underachievement have been offered, no single approach is widely accepted and none has been empirically tested. On the surface, many underachievers are simply disinterested in school, because they come from home environments that do not value education and/or attend a school system that permits them to fall by the wayside. Some are predominantly shy and lack the self-confidence, persistence, and resiliency to failure that are necessary to conquer challenges. Others are rebellious, aggressively or passively getting back at their parents who want them to achieve at levels the youth perceives as personally unattainable. Some are just interested in other things (e.g., athletics, social life).

LONG-TERM PROGNOSIS ■

In the absence of any special program, high school underachievers as a group attain the same number of years of education and the same occupational status 13 years later as their nonunderachieving peers who had the same grade averages but lower mental abilities (McCall, Evahn, & Kratzer, 1988). In terms of adult accomplishment, high school grades are everything while mental ability is nothing.

This general result is in stark contrast to the predictions often made by high school administrators to parents of underachieving students that they will grow out of it once they are away from home. This is true for approximately 10–15%, especially those who have highly educated parents, are not underachieving by more than 1.5 grade points, and are personally self-confident and expect to do well in college and in life. But, generally, a diamond in the rough stays a diamond in the rough.

INTERVENTION AND TREATMENT ■

Treatment for underachievement has consisted of many different approaches.

Specifically, almost no evaluation data exist on the success of *individual psychotherapy*. *Group therapeutic sessions*, typically conducted in schools, occasionally have shown some benefit, especially if parents are involved and the sessions focus on parent-child relations.

Social skills training tends to improve social and classroom behavior but not academic achievement. Similarly, programs providing *tutoring* plus activities designed to *improve self-esteem* consistently have produced improvements in these areas, but not necessarily in general academic performance.

The *periodic progress report system*, which provides students and parents with a detailed report card each day or week, with rewards at home contingent upon adequate performance, consistently has been shown to improve classroom behavior and academic performance across the age span (Atkeson & Forehand, 1979). No data exist, however, on its influence on other aspects of underachievement or on the long-term outcomes of its use as the primary remedial approach to underachievement.

Finally, *comprehensive special classrooms* with parent involvement for gifted underachievers have a checkered history, but carefully designed programs implemented in the primary grades can be effective (Whitmore, 1980).

Dropouts

According to one national study, approximately one out of four adolescents entering high school as a freshman does not graduate. But rates vary greatly as a function of the school (as high as 40% for some inner-city districts), how "dropout" is defined, and how the data are collected (see review by Bickel, Bond, & LeMahieu, 1986).

CHARACTERISTICS OF THE POPULATION ■ The High School and Beyond Study (HSBS) followed 30,000 high school sophomores through graduation (Ekstrom, Goertz, Pollack, & Rock, 1986). They found higher rates of early school exit for students from low socioeconomic classes, students in vocational programs, males (only slightly), minority

students except Asian-Americans, students in the West and South, and students in urban as opposed to rural or suburban schools.

In addition, such students typically had lower school grades and tests scores (especially in reading), more disciplinary problems, lower rates of homework completion, lower self-concepts, lower educational expectations, and more externalized sense of control. They were slightly more likely to be employed during their sophomore year and to work more hours per week at a job they found more enjoyable than school.

These characteristics are national averages and some trends are not large, so the situation may be very different from one locale to another. For example, not all students who leave school have poor ability or poor school performance. Specifically, in Project Talent, a national longitudinal study of school-aged children started in 1960, 20% of students who left school before graduation were in the top half of the population on the "General Academic Ability Composite" used in the study (Combs & Cooley, 1968).

REASONS FOR LEAVING SCHOOL ■ Students who leave school early cite a variety of reasons pertaining to themselves, their families, the schools, and society.

Student reasons. The most frequently reported reasons pertain to poor academic performance (e.g., poor grades, failing too many courses, lack of interest in school subjects, and poor reading ability). Estimates are that between 50 and 75% of all early school departures are associated partly with these academic factors.

Such students also list nonacademic reasons, including discipline problems (e.g., constant fighting, drug use, stealing, vandalism), inability to get along with school personnel (especially males), poor or irregular attendance, desire to get married (especially females), desire to follow close peers who have left school, and pregnancy (more than one-fourth of the girls who leave school).

Family reasons. A disproportionate number of dropouts have experienced the actual or psychological divorce of their parents. Also, many have parents who do not support or emphasize school achievement. One-fourth of the students who chose to leave school were encouraged to do so by their parents and another one-fourth had indifferent parents. Many parents of nongraduates did not finish secondary school themselves. Finally, failure to finish school is associated with low family income, including unemployment, welfare participation, and unskilled work.

School reasons. Higher rates of school departures occur for schools that lack an "early warning" mechanism, are perceived as "too dangerous," do not have in-school alternatives to disciplinary suspension, and have teachers who students feel do not care and lack fairness and effectiveness in their disciplinary policies and practices.

Societal reasons. While they are difficult to evaluate empirically, many observers believe that racial, ethnic, gender, and class biases in society contribute to the problem by diluting the quality of education and rendering the potential socioeconomic rewards of education unattainable for some groups of people.

INTERVENTIONS ▪

Prevention. Few direct attempts have been made to prevent school departures before the youth is clearly at risk. However, early childhood compensatory education programs have been shown to reduce school failure. Less directly, recent school improvements and reforms of classroom instructional methods might reduce the problem to the extent that they improve actual student success in school. Also, efforts to track students systematically with a computer data-base management system might improve early warning systems.

Remediation. Most intervention efforts are not imposed until students are at crisis levels. Such programs emphasize trying to change the students, the school, teacher attitudes, school operating procedures, and/or the home and community environments.

Bickel, Bond, and LeMahieu (1986) and Hamilton (1986) have reviewed these programs and find a great diversity of approaches but some common themes related to success: (1) placement of the target students in separate programs that differ markedly from the ordinary school experience; (2) strong emphasis on vocational training and community-vocational experiences; (3) intensive programs with low student/teacher ratios, individualized instruction and counseling, and small class sizes; and (4) multiple motivational approaches and the use of alternative environments that increase the perceived relevance of the school experience to the community or to employment.

Successful programs also seem to create a special atmosphere among the administrators, teachers, and students. For example, the program has separate space and identity; administrators and teachers are given relatively more power and autonomy; staff are optimistic about student success and expect students to behave and perform; teachers accept being accountable for student improvement; the teachers believe in educating the "whole" student and advocating for him or her; the program is viewed as a cooperative team effort between administrators, teachers, students, and parents; and the students support the program and its goals.

Generally, however, such last-ditch intervention efforts are very intensive and costly. Given the high rates of early school departure and its enormous social and financial consequences, it would be worthwhile to invest in prevention programs that systematically identify students at early ages and provide them with the motivation, skills, and successes they need.

References

Atkeson, B. M., & Forehand, R. (1979). Home-based reinforcement programs designed to modify classroom behavior: A review and methodological evaluation. *Psychological Bulletin, 86,* 1298–1308.

Bickel, W. E., Bond, L., & LeMahieu, P. (1986). *Students at risk of not completing high school.* Authors, University of Pittsburgh, Pittsburgh, PA.

Combs, J., & Cooley, W. W. (1968). Dropouts: In high school and after school. *American Educational Research Journal, 5,* 343–363.

Ekstrom, R. B., Goertz, M. E., Pollack, J. M., & Rock, D. A. (1986). Who drops out of high school and why? Findings from a national study. *Teachers College Record, 87,* 356–373.

Hamilton, S. F. (1986). Raising standards and reducing dropout rates. *Teachers College Record, 87,* 410–429.

McCall, R. B., Evahn, C., & Kratzer, L. (1988). The adult educational and occupational status of chronic high school underachievers. Unpublished manuscript, authors.

Whitmore, J. R. (1980). *Giftedness, conflict, and underachievement.* Boston: Allyn and Bacon.

See Also

Unemployment

Thomas Kieselbach

University of Bremen

The Social Background to Unemployment

Until about a decade ago, unemployment was not a scientifically recognized object of psychological research, or a field that attracted much continuous research. This may be related, on the one hand, to the widespread disinclination that psychological research has shown towards addressing socially significant problems, or, on the other hand, to the cyclical resurgence of mass unemployment in the Western industrialized nations. The rates of unemployment in most of these countries have risen considerably since the mid-70s. They have, in some areas, exceeded the levels reached during the Great Depression of the 1930s (as in Great Britain, for example), whereby long-term unemployment (defined as unemployment of more than one year) has increased dramatically. In the OECD countries the number of unemployed persons in the year 1988 was estimated to be 31 million, and in the European OECD countries alone the figure was 20 million (OECD, 1988).

Unemployment, with its cyclical fluctuations, is a permanent feature that accompanies the capitalist economic system, based on private ownership of the means of production. Comparable forms of underemployment and hidden unemployment were not seriously recognized as problems in the socialist countries until recently (Gniazdowski, 1987). Different forms of unemployment can be distinguished, depending on their origins and the accompanying circumstances (Labica, 1983, p. 101). Cyclical unemployment arises in conjunction with the cyclical crises of the capitalist economy. Structural unemployment results from the discrepancy between the qualifications required for jobs and the actual structure of qualifications existent among the workforce. Seasonal variations in the demand for labor result in seasonal unemployment. Hidden unemployment refers to the reduced degree of productivity of the worker, who continues, however, to be employed. Technologically determined unemployment means the substitution of human labor by machines.

The Effects of Unemployment as Consequences of the Function of Work

The most negative aspects of unemployment for the individual concerned are the reduction of financial means and uncertainty about the future. Release from work stress, and the fact that there is more time available for hobbies, family, and friends, are the most important positive aspects. Many unemployed people initially experience a feeling of freedom from burdens (evidenced, especially in terms of physical health, in some unemployed people as a so-called "gain in health"; Brinkmann & Potthoff, 1983), but this progressively wears off the longer the unemployment situation lasts. As negative aspects accumulate, the perception of a "vacation effect" quickly disappears.

The effects of unemployment can only be understood by taking into account the social and individual meaning of work. Jahoda (1979, 1982), assuming that work represents the most important connection to reality, has tried to define the latent functions of work—as distinct from the manifest function of earning one's living—in terms of five categories. The activity of work incorporates the following psychological dimensions: it imposes a time structure; it compels contacts and shared experiences with others outside the nuclear family; it represents goals and purposes beyond the scope of an individual; it enforces activity; and it imposes status and social identity that combines occupational prestige with the central social system of value—namely money (Jahoda & Rush 1980).

The central question is, what can one substitute to fulfill these functions, once one becomes unemployed? The "psychologically privileged" (Jahoda) or "proactive" unemployed workers (Fryer & Payne 1984), can cope with unemployment in very positive and creative ways. In spite of serious financial difficulties, he/she is not demoralized at all and demonstrates, on the contrary, a positive basic attitude and state of psychosocial well-being. But few unemployed workers can be character-ized as proactive. Any complete substitution of the psychological functions of paid work cannot be visualized under current social conditions, except in the rarest of cases. At this point in time, no activity can be imagined that could attain the psychological functions of work described above in the same way or to the same extent.

Social Features and Mental Health

The characteristics of the social environment have special significance for the maintenance or the development of mental health. Warr (1987) names the following factors in this respect: the opportunity for control, the opportunity for skill use, externally generated goals, variety, environmental clarity, availability of money, physical security (accommodation, food, etc.), opportunity for interpersonal contact and valued social position.

For the unemployed the opportunity for control is reduced by failures while looking for employment, the impossibility of influencing employers, and dependence on the social bureaucracy. A deterioration in the opportunities for skill use, and a decrease in externally generated goals takes place; this is due to the low use and decline of vocational qualifications, the fact that only a minority of the unemployed use their leisure time actively, the low level of external demands made on them, the reduction of goals and the decrease in significance of previously important goals.

Lowered need to leave the family environment and the home, loss of the stimulating contrast between work and leisure, and reduction in financial possibilities—all lead to a reduction in variety. Uncertainty about which behavior leads to success in finding a job, and the necessity of presenting oneself in a different light with each application that one makes, result in loss of environmental clarity. The clarity of the social environment is further reduced by leading a "life characterised by short-term thinking" (Biermann, Schmerl & Ziebell, 1985), caused by uncertainty regarding any future plans. The reduction of financial means can lead to deterioration of nutrition, and, to an extent, the necessity of moving into a different neighbourhood (physical security), which in turn can reduce the level of support from the unemployed person's usual social network.

Interpersonal contacts can increase in number due to more available time, particularly in the case of the young unemployed. For other groups of the unemployed, however, self-isolating tendencies, resulting from financial restrictions or shameful withdrawal have been proven empirically. The work ethic in our society tends to devalue the unemployed socially. This situation is often reinforced through individualistic ideologies such as the "just world belief" (Lerner, 1974), according to which everybody gets what he deserves. In this way the valued social position of the unemployed is considerably reduced, their claims on society are deprived of legitimacy, and they themselves are rendered incapable of asserting themselves in conflict situations (Kieselbach, 1987b). This weakened social position is supplemented by dependence on state institutions and the bureaucracy of welfare organizations, which put those dependent on them into the role of humble petitioners and cause feelings of worthlessness and helplessness.

Unemployment and Health

Macrosociological surveys conducted in the 1970s have demonstrated, on the basis of longitudinal analyses in the Anglo-American world, a relationship between economic indicators (rate of unemployment, rate of inflation, average earnings levels) and health indicators (rate of psychiatric hospitalization, rate of deaths due to heart diseases, cirrhosis of the liver, and suicide) (Brenner, 1973; 1976). More recent analyses, over different periods of time and for other countries, have not always supported this result (Schwefel, 1983), although a summary report for the World Health Organization on vulnerability among the long-term unemployed, recently came to the following conclusion: "The current and predicted levels of unemployment must be perceived as a major epidemiological catastrophe for many societies" (WHO 1985, p. 13; see also John, Schwefel & Zöllner, 1983; Kieselbach & Wacker, 1985; Kieselbach & Svennsson, 1988).

Studies carried out in the United Kingdom evidenced that the long-term unemployed have more para-suicides than employed people or the short-term unemployed (Platt, 1985). It has been shown in the Federal Republic of Germany that unemployment facilitates the incidence of alcoholism, reinforces already existent forms of alcoholism, and significantly increases the relapse rate of alcoholics during the process of rehabilitation (Henkel, 1985, 1987). Observations have also been made in other institutions, dealing with vocational and psychiatric rehabilitation, indicating that rehabilitation efforts that were previously successful generally fail when the chances of reintegration into the labor market are low (Morgan & Cheadle, 1975; Thomann, Freese & Walter, 1985).

A further indicator of the effects of loss of work can be seen in the often dramatic improvements in psychosocial health manifested by previously unemployed persons when they obtain re-employment (Lahelma & Kangas 1989; Verkleij 1989).

Moderators in Coping with Unemployment

Corresponding to the lack of uniformity among the unemployed themselves with regard to demographic and psychological features, there exist different forms of coping with unemployment. In the following summary I present some research results relating to the influence of those moderating variables which determine how individuals cope with unemployment (see also Warr, 1984a):

FINANCIAL RESTRICTIONS ■

This factor was best able to explain, in a number of studies, the negative psychosocial implications of unemployment. However, this result does not in any way automatically lead to the conclusion that the financial restrictions imposed by unemployment are solely responsible for the negative effects of unemployment. Research results from those countries where exemplary social welfare systems in terms of financial security for the unemployed exist disprove this. In Sweden, for example, where unemployed persons receive 90% of their previous net income as an unemployment benefit during the first year, empirical evidence of serious negative effects on health has been found (e.g., reduced immunological resistance after 9 months of unemployment; Arnetz et al., 1987).

EMPLOYMENT COMMITMENT ■

Those unemployed who show a strong commitment toward employment are especially exposed to strain during periods of unemployment (Jackson, Stafford, Banks, & Warr, 1983). Psychological stress (Brinkmann, 1984), low levels of personal self-esteem (Feather & Bond, 1984), and depressive tendencies could be found to a higher degree among this group (Feather & Barber, 1983). In a longitudinal study, employment commitment proved to be the best predictor for the change in levels of self-esteem and depression (Schultz-Gambard, Balz, Drewski, & Mowka, 1986).

AGE ■

The unemployed who experience the severest distress are the middle-aged, who generally have stronger family commitments, and who have no alternative, socially acceptable roles available (Hepworth, 1980; Brinkmann, 1984). The association between age and psychosocial distress appears to be a curvilinear relationship with the highest values found among the middle-aged, medium values for the young, and the lowest values among those reaching retirement age (Jackson & Warr, 1984). In other studies, however, prevalence rates of psychiatric morbidity were also found to be very high among young unemployed people (Banks & Jackson, 1982; Cullen, Ryan, Cullen, Ronayne, & Wynne, 1989; for an overview, see Kieselbach, 1988a).

GENDER ■

In general, women report less stress due to unemployment than men (Brinkmann 1976, 1984; Warr, Jackson, & Banks, 1982; Lahelma & Kangas, 1989). Perhaps the social allocation of roles ("socially accepted alternative roles") facilitates and supports a woman's withdrawal better than a man's withdrawal from the labor market (to join the "still reserve"), and that feelings of self-esteem are created by adopting domestic and childcaring roles. On the other hand, in more detailed comparative studies, it has been found that for single women and for women whose non-occupational environment is relatively deprived, occupational work has a markedly positive influence on psychological well-being (Warr & Parry, 1982).

DURATION OF UNEMPLOYMENT ■

Differing results from various countries with respect

to coping with long-term unemployment can probably partly be accounted for by a lack of methodological precision. The respective differences also depend heavily on the effect of nationally specific variables such as financial security and the future perspectives of the labor market. The thesis generally accepted is that the longer the duration of unemployment lasts, the worse the psychosocial situation becomes. This process of deterioration does slow down with increasing duration (Harrison, 1976) especially in the male 20–59 age group (Jackson & Warr, 1984). An increase of this kind could be found in the stress levels among the long-term unemployed in the Federal Republic of Germany (Brinkmann, 1984). However, Swedish and British studies found, in contrast to the above, a slight average improvement reducing average levels of distress (Warr, Jackson & Banks, 1982; Brenner & Levi, 1987; Warr, 1989). In a Dutch investigation an adaptation was found after a period of three years, although even after four years a renewed increase in stress (physical complaints, negative feelings, or depression) could be observed (Verkleij, 1989). While average distress values may provide evidence of positive adaptation, they also may conceal groups who are particularly vulnerable (e.g., unemployed youths with serious financial problems, for whom a further worsening of their situation can be expected in the long term) (Ronayne, Ryan, & Cullen, 1989).

LEVEL OF QUALIFICATION ■

Unemployment research literature in the United States is dominated by the view that those who fall the furthest are also those who show the severest strain under unemployment (Goodchilds & Smith, 1963; Kaufman, 1982). This idea can no longer be substantiated by the current state of research: the highest levels of stress are experienced by those who have low qualifications (i.e., blue-collar workers with little or no occupational training; Brinkmann, 1984; Warr, 1984a; Wuggenig, 1985).

CAUSAL ATTRIBUTION AND OPPORTUNITY FOR CONTROL ■

The kind of explanation the individual has for his or her own unemployment has an important influence on the level of distress he or she perceives. In this context, internal and external explanations (blaming oneself vs. making society responsible) do not necessarily exclude each other, but can coexist and mix (Frese, 1985; Ulich, Hausser, Mayring, Strehmel, Kandler, & Degenhardt, 1985). Those who blame themselves are more vulnerable (Feather & Barber, 1983; Gurney, 1981). A further important modifying variable is one's degree of expectation regarding ability to control one's own position on the labor market (i.e. to find a job through one's own efforts). People who have high expectation levels regarding hope for control are less prone to depression or are less vulnerable (Pelzmann, Winkler, & Zewell, 1985); when they remain unemployed, however, the reverse is the case: compared with those unemployed with lower expectations, they show higher levels of psychosocial distress (Frese, 1979).

LEVEL OF PERSONAL ACTIVITY ■

Unemployed persons who had problems with structuring their time before they became unemployed demonstrate higher stress levels during unemployment (Hepworth, 1980). In contrast, there are forms of actively coping with unemployment to be found in the so-called "proactive" unemployed, who can be distinguished by their virtual lack of psychosocial stress (Fryer & Payne, 1984). An important protective function can be performed in this respect by activity in the "grey economy" (Pelzmann, Winkler, & Zewell, 1985); it should not be overlooked, however, that this can be associated with new long-term health risks due to the lack or absence of social control, and forms of gross exploitation (Lemkow, 1987; Lemkow & Torns, 1989).

SOCIAL SUPPORT ■ It is easier to cope with stressful life events if there is a supportive social environment (Cobb, 1976). Coping with unemployment also seems to be easier for those who are not single and unattached, and who do feel supported by family or friends (Gore, 1978; Kasl & Cobb, 1979). Unemployed young people are more positive and optimistic in their orientation to the future if they feel they are supported by family, friends or the community (Clark & Clissold, 1982). At the same time, they experience less support from their families than employed young people receive (Schober, 1978). It should also be realized that social networks have both supportive as well as controlling functions, that members of the family are also indirectly involved as "victims-by-proxy," and that their resources of support can therefore become exhausted (Kieselbach, 1988b).

HELP-SEEKING AND THE AVAILABILITY OF HELP ■ The specific stress that unemployment engenders can, in spite of a real need for help, hinder the unemployed person from seeking help from the institutions that provide it. Unemployed people often try to avoid seeking any professional help, until a point is reached where such behavior can be characterized as extremely self-damaging, in order not to lower their remaining self-respect any further by seeking and accepting help (Kieselbach, 1986, 1990; Liem, 1988); they fear that professional helpers in particular may palliatively "normalize"

their situation (Spruit, 1983) More than other people with psychological difficulties, they tend to conceal these problems from others on account of their particular experience of feelings such as shock, stigmatization, or shame associated with unemployment (Buss & Redburn, 1983). The effectivity of help on offer to the unemployed has not as yet been systematically studied, but there are indications, that many such offers are neither accessible, acceptable nor effective (Arnetz et al., 1987; Buss & Redburn, 1983; Kieselbach 1988c).

LEVEL OF UNEMPLOYMENT ■ A high level of unemployment can normalize unemployment and lead to a reduction of personally experienced stress, but it can at the same time produce an atmosphere of hopelessness. In one British study significant differences in levels of psychiatric morbidity were found between regions of high compared with regions of low unemployment. In areas with chronically high unemployment the levels of psychosocial distress were found to be significantly lower, presumably because of cultural changes and community adaptation to mass unemployment (Jackson & Warr, 1987). The lower distress scores obtained in a comparison of unemployed school leavers in the U.K. between 1978 and 1983 in the second study provide a further indication of collective adjustment to poor employment prospects (Banks & Ullah, 1988, p. 69).

PREVIOUS EXPERIENCE OF UNEMPLOYMENT ■ It is possible that previous experience of unemployment can alleviate a renewed experience of unemployment, but if that former experience was a traumatic one, this can also lead to increased anticipatory distress. In the same way, it can be supposed that coping with unemployment is facilitated if earlier crises were successfully overcome.

Typologies and Stages of Coping

The description of the moderators involved in coping makes it clear that, just as unemployment itself is no uniform event, no uniform reactions can be predicated of the persons directly affected by unemployment (Wacker, 1983). Two directions have been taken by unemployment research in the attempt to develop typologies of the forms of reaction. As early as the historically most important study of the effects of unemployment on an entire community, namely the "Marienthal Study" by Jahoda et al. (1933, 1975), which became famous on account of its methodological differentiation, the attempt was made to develop a typology of different forms of reaction. Jahoda et al. distinguished between resignation, brokenness (sub-divided into apathy and despair), and unbrokenness.

Bakke (1940) formulated the following "cycle of adaptation" in unemployed families: momentum stability–unstable equilibrium–disorganization–experimental readjustment–permanent readjustment. The sequence shock–optimism–pessimism–fatalism, as described by Harrison (1976), has become perhaps the best known formula. The presumption of any such ideal/typical sequence has been criticized more recently on various grounds. First, there is no sufficient empirical basis for such a presumption, and second, because in this manner a stereotyped picture of the behavior of unemployed people is created (Kelvin & Jarrett, 1985).

Warr (1989), criticizing any concept of adaptation that merely implies a reduction in psychological morbidity without referring to the extent to which individual development is excluded by unemployment, distinguishes between "resigned" and "constructive" adaptation. In the case of constructive adaptation the person affected develops interests and activities outside the conventional labor market, spends more time on hobbies, extends his social activities and gets involved in voluntary or community organizations, whereas the more widespread form, resigned adaptation, consists of self-isolation and a more far-reaching reduction in expectations in many areas of life.

Young and Unemployed— A Special Problem?

In many Western countries youth unemployment is presently characterized by a transition from unemployment of a predominantly temporary kind to consolidation and structuralization. In the member states of the European Community, there were five million unemployed young people between 15 and 25 years of age (in 1987). Of these, about one third must be counted among the long-term unemployed (i.e., those unemployed for longer than one year). The average rate of youth unemployment is three times as high as the overall rate.

Significant research on youth unemployment comes mainly from Great Britain and Australia and, to a lesser degree, from the FRG. Besides Italy and Spain, Australia and Great Britain are among those Western countries with an exceptionally high rate of youth unemployment. Astonishingly little research on the impact of youth unemployment has been done in the USA. This may possibly be explained by a different type of transition, as compared with other countries like the FRG, between the educational system and employment, which leads to temporary unemployment (interrupted by several short-term, low-paid jobs) being regarded as quite ordinary for a young person's biography. That particular stage, which lasts up to the age of about 22, has been named "floundering period" (Hamilton, 1985, 1987).

A number of contributions have raised the question of a specific vulnerability of young people to the experience of unemployment (Roberts, 1984; Schwefel, 1984; Spruit & Svensson, 1984; Warr, 1984b). This means asking, on the one hand, which age group suffers more from psychosocial stress associated with unemployment and, on the other, whether there are age-dependent qualitative differences. A few arguments will, in the following, be put forward in order to elucidate the particular features of psychosocial stress with juveniles, emphasizing possible long-term effects (cf. Roberts, 1984).

Whether young people or adults suffer more badly from the condition of unemployment cannot, considering the existing body of research, be stated unequivocally. Although there are indications that affliction with psychiatric symptoms is correlated with age in a nearly curvilinear way, i.e., that affliction is strongest for the unemployed of medium age, weaker for the young and weakest for the older unemployed (Jackson & Warr, 1984), merely to ask for the most vulnerable group does not make sense. The purpose behind a question like this is to identify one group among the unemployed which is particularly vulnerable to psychosocial damage. By trying to grasp and to compare effects one-dimensionally only, however, the question is too short-sighted.

A lower vulnerability of young people with regard to psychiatric morbidity contrasts with higher ratings in other dimensions of stress. In a content analysis of qualitative data Viney (1983) found significantly higher rates for young unemployed below 20 years of age with regard to anxiousness, anger, helplessness, guilt and shame than for older ones. Schober (1978), concludes from a comparison of stress profiles that unemployed juveniles suffer considerably more from domestic tensions and attributions of blame, whereas adults more intensively perceive social isolation and stigmatization induced by unemployment. So we are obviously more precise in talking of age-dependent differential stress profiles.

Young people experience unemployment as a frustration of expectations which, in their previous educational career, they had been made to regard as crucial goals and orientations and which had been a major motivational basis for previous achievements. Being unemployed, to them, does not mean losing the positive concomitants of having a job. Furthermore, school leavers may indeed, initially, welcome unemployment as a relief from the exactions of the final stage of their school career.

One of the important results is that we find a widening developmental gap opening between unemployed and employed young people. This gap is determined, on the part of the unemployed, by stagnation and regression as a consequence of not being allowed to work as well as by the experience of unemployment as a cumulation of "daily hassles" and, on the other hand, by the effects of working (like greater independence, acquisition and utilization of skills, etc.) on employed juveniles.

When comparing the health hazards of unemployment for adults and young people we must take into account the good state of health of juveniles which may mitigate immediate negative health consequences of a critical life event such as unemployment. However, a riskier health behavior on the part of unemployed juveniles (with regard to eating and sleeping habits, alcohol and tobacco consumption, personal hygiene, and sporting activities) may well lead to delayed damage to their health, the extent of which cannot, at present, easily be estimated (Olafsson & Svensson, 1986). Two Finnish researchers did find differences in the health behavior of unemployed and employed 19-year-old males; they expressed the belief that the unemployed young people of today are likely to be the sick middle-aged men of tomorrow because they differ in precisely those health behavioral aspects that we already know to have a major impact on future health (Kannas & Hietarharju, 1979; quoted in Janlert, 1985, p. 18).

Furthermore, we are justified in assuming that empirical data on unemployed young people are somewhat marred by a conservative (under-)estimation of psychosocial stress because of a stronger selection of samples within that group (due to disappearance or refusal in cases of very bad affliction).

"Victims-by-Proxy": Partners and Children

Not only are unemployed people themselves affected by unemployment and its consequences, their family or partners are also exposed, albeit indirectly, to the stress of unemployment (Kieselbach, 1988b; Kieselbach, Lödige-Röhrs & Lünser, 1989; McLoyd, 1989). They may often represent an important source of social support for the directly affected unemployed person, but they may also produce increased stress for the unemployed insofar as responsibility for others is involved and the uncertainty about the future extends to dependants as well.

The consequences, often loaded with potential conflict for the families of the unemployed, result from deterioration of financial conditions, greater proximity, which can be associated with increased control, as well as changes in everyday routines and the distribution of power and roles within the family. Critical for familial coping with unemployment is, however, the previous quality of the conjugal relationship. A relationship is affected adversely by economic loss particularly when tensions were already present before such changes took place, or if the husband possesses low resources for coping (Liker & Elder, 1983).

It was noted as early as the studies carried out in the 1930s that the effects on children of paternal unemployment include emotional instability, development of nervous symptoms and functional disturbances, involvement in antisocial activities, and deterioration of performance in school; these effects are frequently more pronounced among girls than boys. In addition to this, the behavior of the unemployed father was more authoritarian (Komarovsky, 1940). Various studies have shown the relationship between economic stress and child maltreatment and abuse (Garbarino & Crouter, 1978; Steinberg, Catalano & Dooley, 1981). It can be concluded from this that the high level of mass unemployment in the highly industrialized countries implies a threat to the conditions under which many children live and grow up, whereby the number of registered cases of cruelty to children—itself only the tip of the iceberg—is an indicator of the pressure that is exerted by economic conditions.

In one investigation into the development over time of the health of children of unemployed parents, it was shown that they were generally more often affected by illness, especially infections and chronic diseases (Margolis & Farran, 1981). Unemployment may have more far-reaching effects on children, because it not only damages the present state of health or performance (such as school performance) (Baarda, Frowijn, de Goede, & Postma, 1983), but also, more extensively, young people's feeling of self-esteem in general

(Coopersmith, 1967). It has also been shown to significantly influence the career expectations of girls (Galambos & Silbereisen, 1987). These effects which extend the consequences of unemployment to a distant future, even for the indirectly affected, demonstrate the "long arm of unemployment."

References

Arnetz, B. B., Wasserman, J., Petrini, B., Brenner, S.-O., Levi, L., Eneroth, P., Salovaara, H., Hjelm, R., Salovaara, L., Theorell, T., & Petterson, I.-L. (1987). Immune function in unemployed women. *Psychosomatic Medicine, 49,* 3–12.

Baarda, P. B., Frowijn, A. P. M., de Goede, M. P. M., & Postma, M. E. (1983). Schoolprestaties van Kinderen van werkloze Vaders. *Pedagogische Studies, 60,* 473–484.

Bakke, E. W. (1940). *Citizens without work. A study of the effects of unemployment upon the workers' social relations and practices.* New Haven.

Banks, M. H., & Jackson, P. R. (1982). Unemployment and risk of minor psychiatric disorder in young people. *Psychological Medicine, 12,* 789–798.

Banks, M. H., & Ullah, P. (1988). *Youth unemployment in the 1980's. Its psychological effects.* London: Croom Helm.

Biermann, I., Schmerl, C., & Ziebell, L. (1985). *Leben mit kurzfristigem Denken. Eine Untersuchung zur Situation arbeits loser Akademikerinnen.* Weinheim: Beltz.

Brenner, M. H. (1973). *Mental illness and the economy.* Cambridge: Harvard University Press.

Brenner, M. H. (1976). *Estimating the social costs of national economic policy: Implications for mental and physical health, and criminal aggression* (Vol. 1: Employment, Paper No. 5). Washington, DC: U.S. Government Printing Office.

Brenner, S.-O., & Levi, L. (1987). Vulnerability among long-term unemployed. A longitudinal study of mental and physical health among Swedish women at different phases of unemployment—some preliminary results. In D. Schwefel, P.-G. Svensson, & H. F. K. Zöllner (Eds.), *Unemployment, social vulnerability, and health in Europe* (pp. 239–256). New York: Springer.

Brinkmann, C. (1976). Finanzielle und psychosoziale Belastungen während der Arbeitslosigkeit. *Mitteilungen aus der Arbeitsmarkt- und Berufsforschung, 9,* 397–413.

Brinkmann, C. (1984). Die individuellen Folgen längerfristiger Arbeitslosigkeit. *Mitteilungen aus der Arbeitsmarkt- und Berufforschung, 17,* 454–473.

Brinkmann, C., & Potthoff, P. (1983). Gesundheitliche Probleme in der Eingangsphase der Arbeitslosigkeit. *Mitteilungen aus der Arbeitsmarkt- und Berufsforschung, 17,* 378–394.

Buss, T. F., & Redburn, F. S. (with Waldron, J.). (1983). *Mass unemployment. Plant closings and community mental health.* Beverly Hills: Sage.

Clark, A. W., & Clissold, M. P. (1982). Correlates of adaptation among unemployed and employed young men. *Psychological Reports, 50,* 887–893.

Cobb, S. (1976). Social support as a moderator of life stress. *Psychosomatic Medicine, 38,* 300–314.

Coopersmith, S. (1967). *The antecedents of self-esteem.* San Francisco: Freeman.

Cullen, J. H., Ryan, G. M., Cullen, K. M., Ronayne, T., & Wynne, R. F. (1987). Unemployed youth and health: Findings from the pilot phase of a longitudinal study. In L. Levi (Ed.), Unemployment and health (Special Issue). *Social Science and Medicine, 25,* 133–146.

Feather, N. T., & Barber, J. G. (1983). Depressive reactions and unemployment. *Journal of Abnormal Psychology, 92,* 185–195.

Feather, N. T., & Bond, M. J. (1983). Time structure and purposeful activity among employed and unemployed university graduates. *Journal of Occupational Psychology*, *56*, 241–254.

Frese, M. (1979). Arbeitslosigkeit, Depressivität und Kontrolle: eine Studie mit Wiederholungsmessung. In T. Kieselbach & H. Offe (Eds.). *Arbeitslosigkeit - Individuelle Verarbeitung und gesellschaftlicher Hintergrund* (pp. 222–241). Darmstadt: Steinkopff.

Frese, M. (1985). Zur Verlaufsstruktur der psychischen Auswirkungen von Arbeitslosigkeit. In T. Kieselbach & A. Wacker (Eds.), *Individuelle und gesellschaftliche Kosten der Massenarbeitslosigkeit - Psychologische Theorie und Praxis* (pp. 224–255). Weinheim: Beltz.

Fryer, D., & Payne, R. L. (1984). Proactive behaviour in unemployment: Findings and implications. *Leisure Studies*, *3*, 273–295.

Galambos, N. L., & Silbereisen, R. K. (1987). Income change, parental outlook, and adolescent expectations for job success. *Journal of Marriage and the Family*, *49*, 141–149.

Garbarino, J., & Crouter, A. (1978). Defining the community context of parental-child relations: The correlates of child maltreatment. *Child Development*, *49*, 604–616.

Gniazdowski, A. (1988). Full-employment policy in Poland and some of its effects related to workers' health. Paper presented to the WHO workshop "Unemployment, Poverty, and Quality of Working Life—Innovative Interventions to Counteract Damaging Health Effects", Vienna 12-13 May 1987. Unpublished manuscript.

Goodchilds, J. D., & Smith, E. E. (1963). The effects of unemployment by social status. *Sociometry*, *26*, 287–293.

Gore, S. (1978). The effect of social support in moderating the health consequences of unemployment. *Journal of Health and Social Behavior*, *19*, 157–165.

Gurney, R. M. (1981). Leaving school, facing unemployment and making attributions about the causes of unemployment. *Journal of Vocational Behaviour*, *18*, 79–91.

Hamilton, S. F. (1985). Arbeit und Erwachsenwerden in den USA und der BRD. *Bremer Beiträege zur Psychologie*, No. 49.

Hamilton, S. F. (1987). Adolescent problem behavior in the United States and the Federal Republic of Germany: Implications for prevention. In K. Hurrelmann, F. X. Kaufmann & F. Lösel (Eds.), *Social intervention: Potential and constraints* (pp. 185–204). Berlin: Walter de Gruyter.

Harrison, R. (1976). The demoralizing experience of prolonged unemployment. *Department of Employment Gazette* (April), 339–348.

Henkel, D. (1985). Arbeitslosigkeit als Risikofaktor für Alkoholgefährdung und Hindernis für Rehabilitationsprozesse. In T. Kieselbach & A. Wacker (Eds.), *Individuelle und gesellschaftliche Kosten der Massenarbeitslosigkeit—Psychologische Theorie und Praxis* (pp. 66–83). Weinheim: Beltz.

Henkel, D. (1987). Arbeitslosigkeit und Alkoholismus. *Drogalkohol* (*ISPA-Press*), *11*(2), 79–106.

Hepworth, S. J. (1980). Moderating factors of the psychological impact of unemployment. *Journal of Occupational Psychology*, *53*, 139–146.

Jackson, P. R., Stafford, E. M., Banks, M. H., & Warr, P. B. (1983). Unemployment and psychological distress in young people: The moderating role of employment commitment. *Journal of Applied Psychology*, *68*, 525–535.

Jackson, P. R., & Warr, P. B. (1984). Unemployment and psychological illhealth: The moderating role of duration and age. *Psychological Medicine*, *14*, 605–614.

Jackson, P. R., & Warr, P. B. (1987). Mental health of unemployed men in different parts of England and Wales. *British Medical Journal*, *295*, 422.

Jahoda, M. (1979). The impact of unemployment in the 1930's and the 1970's. *Bulletin* of the British Psychological Society, 32, 309–314.

Jahoda, M. (1982). *Employment and unemployment.* Cambridge: Cambridge University Press.

Jahoda, M., Lazarsfeld, P., & Zeisel, H. (1975). *Die Arbeitslosen von Marienthal. Ein soziographischer Versuch.* Frankfurt: Suhrkamp. (Originally published 1933.)

Jahoda, M., & Rush, H. (1980). *Work, employment, and unemployment* (Occasional Paper Series, No. 12). New York: SPRU, University of Sussex.

Janlert, U. (1985). Unemployment and health. In G. Westcott, P.-G. Svensson, & H. F. K. Zöllner, (Eds.), *Health policy implications of unemployment* (pp. 7–26). Copenhagen: World Health Organization.

John, J., Schwefel, D., & Zöllner, H. F. K. (Eds.). (1983). *Influence of economic instability on health.* New York: Springer.

Kasl, S. V., & Cobb, S. (1970). Blood pressure in men undergoing job loss: A preliminary result. *Psychosomatic Medicine, 32,* 19–38.

Kaufman, H. G. (1982). *Professionals in search of work. Coping with the stress of job loss and underemployment.* New York: Wiley.

Kelvin, P., & Jarrett, J. E. (1985). *Unemployment. Its social psychological effects.* Cambridge: Cambridge University Press.

Kieselbach, T. (1985). Die gesellschaftliche Verarbeitung von Massenarbeitslosigkeit: Gesundheits- und sozialpolitische Konsequenzen aus der Arbeitslosenforschung. *Theorie und Praxis der sozialen Arbeit, 36*(4), 122–134.

Kieselbach, T. (1986). Zwischen "blaming the victim" und "social victim": Forschung und Intervention im Bereich Arbeitslosigkeit. In A. Schorr (Ed.), *Psychologie Mitte der 80er Jahre: Geschichte, Berufsrecht, Weiterbildung, Neue Tätigkeitsfelder, Integration in der Psychotherapie* (pp. 211–228). Proceedings of the 13th Congress for Applied Psychology of the Association of German Psychologists (BDP), Bonn, Sept. 1985, vol. 3. Bonn: Deutscher Psychologen-Verlag.

Kieselbach, T. (1987a). Self-disclosure and help-seeking as determinants of vulnerability. Case studies of unemployed from social-psychiatric services and demands for health and social policy. In D. Schwefel, P.-G. Svensson & H. F. K. Zöllner (Eds.), *Unemployment, social vulnerability, and health in Europe* (pp. 281–303). New York: Springer.

Kieselbach, T. (1987b). Gesellschaftliche und individuelle Bewältigung von Arbeitslosigkeit. In H. Moser (Ed.), *Bedrohung und Beschwichtigung. Die politische und die seelische Gestalt technischer, wirtschaftlicher und gesundheitlicher Gefährdungen (Fortschritte der Politischen Psychologie, Sonderband 1)* (pp. 28–55). Weinheim: Deutscher Studien Verlag.

Kieselbach, T. (1988a). Youth unemployment and health effects. *International Journal of Social Psychiatry, 34*(2), 83–96.

Kieselbach, T. (1988b). Familie unter dem Druck der Arbeitslosigkeit: "Opfer-durch-Nähe" und Quelle sozialer Unterstützung. In K. Menne & K. Alter (Eds.), *Gesellschaft im Umbruch - Antworten der Erziehungsberater* (pp. 47–76). München: Juventa.

Kieselbach, T. (1988c). A multisectoral approach for the improvement of the psychosocial situation of the unemployed. In B. Starrin, P.-G. Svensson, & H. Wintersberger (Eds.), *Unemployment, poverty, and quality of working life—Some European experiences* (pp. 295–334). Berlin: Edition Sigma.

Kieselbach, T. (1990). Help-seeking and coping with unemployment. In R. A. Young & W. A. Borgen (Eds.), *Methodological approaches to the study of career* (pp. 163–184). New York: Praeger Publishers.

Kieselbach, T., Lödige-Röhrs, L., & A. Lünser (1989). Die Kinder von Arbeitslosen - "Opfer-durch-Nähe". Ergebnisse der psychologischen Arbeitslosenforschung zu den

Auswirkungen von Arbeitslosigkeit auf die Familie. Theoretisches Hintergrundpapier zum Forum der Sozialdemokratischen Partei Deutschlands (SPD) "Gestohlene Kindheit - Verborgene Folgelasten der Langzeitarbeitslosigkeit", Bonn, 16. November 1989. Bonn: Author.

Kieselbach, T., & Svensson, P.-G. (1988). Health and social policy responses to unemployment in Europe. In D. Dooley & R. Catalano (Eds.), Psychological reactions to unemployment (Special Issue). *Journal of Social Issues, 44*(4), 173–191.

Kieselbach, T., & Wacker, A. (Eds.). (1985). *Individuelle und gesellschaftliche Kosten der Massenarbeitslosigkeit - Psychologische Theorie und Praxis.* Weinheim, Basel: Beltz (2nd ed. Weinheim: Deutscher Studien Verlag 1987).

Komarowsky, M. (1940). The unemployed man and his family: The effects of unemployment upon the status of the man in fifty-nine families. New York: Dryden Press.

Labica, G. (1983). *Kritisches Wörterbuch des Marxismus* (Vol. 1). Berlin: Argument.

Lahelma, E., & Kangas, R. (1989). Unemployment, reemployment and psychic well-being in Finland. In B. Starrin, P.-G. Svensson, & H. Wintersberger (Eds.), *Unemployment, poverty, and quality of working life. Some European experiences* (pp. 135–164). Berlin: Edition Sigma.

Lemkow, L. (1987). The subterranean economy as a survival strategy: The Spanish case. In D. Schwefel, P. G. Svensson & H. F. K. Zöllner (Eds.), *Unemployment, social vulnerability and health in Europe* (pp. 143–150). New York: Springer.

Lemkow, L., Torns, T. (1989). Continuity and change in the submerged economy. In B. Starrin, P. -G. Svensson & H. Wintersberger (Eds.), *Unemployment, poverty, and quality of working life. Some European experiences* (pp. 277–284). Berlin: Edition Sigma.

Lerner, M. J. (1974). Social psychology of justice and interpersonal attraction. In T. L. Huston (Ed.), *Foundations of interpersonal attraction* (pp. 331–351). New York: Academic Press.

Liem, R. (1988). Unemployed workers and their families: Social victims or social critics? In P. Voydanoff & L. J. Majka (Eds.), *Families and economic distress. Coping strategies and social policy* (pp. 135–151). Beverly Hills: Sage.

Liker, J. K., & Elder, G. H. Jr. (1983). Economic hardship and marital relations in the 1930's. *American Sociological Review, 48,* 343–359.

Margolis, L. H., & Farran, D. (1981). Unemployment: The health consequences in children. *North Carolina Medical Journal, 42,* 849–850.

McLoyd, V. (1989). Socialization and development in a changing economy. The effects of paternal job and income loss on children. *American Psychologist, 44,* 293–302.

Morgan, R., & Cheadle, A. J. (1975). Unemployment impedes resettlement. *Social Psychiatry, 10*(2), 63–67.

OECD, Organization of Economic Development (1988). *Economic outlook.* Paris: OECD.

Olafsson O., & Svensson P.-G. (1986). Unemployment-related lifestyle changes and health disturbances in adolescents and children in the Western countries. *Social Science and Medicine, 22,* 1105–1113.

Pelzmann, L., & Winkler, N. & Zewell, E. (1985). Antizipation von Arbeitslosigkeit. In T. Kieselbach & A. Wacker (Eds.), *Individuelle und gesellschaftliche Kosten der Massenarbeitslosigkeit - Psychologische Theorie und Praxis* (pp. 256–268). Weinheim: Beltz.

Platt, S. (1985). Suicidal behaviour and unemployment: A literature review. In G. Westcott, P.-G. Svensson, & H. F. K. Zöllner, (Eds.), *Health policy implications of unemployment* (pp. 87–132). Copenhagen: World Health Organization.

Roberts, K. (1984). Problems and initiatives in youth unemployment. *Journal of Community Health Care, 62*, 320–326.

Ronayne, T., Ryan, G. M., & Cullen, J. H. (1989). Health effects of work and exclusion from work. Approaches to understanding, monitoring and intervening. In B. Starrin, P.-G. Svensson, & H. Wintersberger (Eds.), *Unemployment, poverty, and quality of working life. Some European experiences* (pp. 197–234). Berlin: Edition Sigma.

Schober, K. (1978). Arbeitslose Jugendliche: Belastungen und Reaktionen der Betroffenen. *Mitteilungen aus der Arbeitsmarkt- und Berufsforschung, 11*(2), 198–215.

Schultz-Gambard, J., Balz, H. J., Drewski, R., & Mowka, K. (1986). *Weitere Ergebnisse der Bielefelder Längsschnittstudie zu Auswirkungen von Arbeitslosigkeit.* Unpublished manuscript, University of Bielefeld.

Schwefel, D. (1983). Arbeitslosigkeit und Gesundheit. Ein europäisches (Forschungs-) Problem. *Sozialer Fortschritt, 32*(8), 169–173.

Schwefel, D. (1984). Unemployment, health and health services in German-speaking countries. *Social Science and Medicine, 22*, 409–430.

Schwefel, D., Svensson, P.-G., & Zöllner, H. F. K. (Eds.). (1987). *Unemployment, social vulnerability, and health in Europe.* New York: Springer.

Spruit, I. (1983). To be employed, to be unemployed, and health in families in Leiden. In I. Spruit (Ed.), *Unemployment, employment, and health* (pp. 137–177). Leiden: Instituut voor Sociale Geneeskunde.

Spruit, I. P., & Svensson, P. G. (1987). Young and unemployed: Special problems? In D. Schwefel, P.-G. Svensson (Eds.), *Unemployment, social vulnerability, and health in Europe.* New York: Springer.

Starrin, B., Svensson, P.-G., & Wintersberger, H. (Eds.). (1989). *Unemployment, poverty, and quality of working life—Some European*

experiences. Berlin: Edition Sigma.

Steinberg, L., Catalano, R., & Dooley, D. (1981). Economic antecedents of child abuse and neglect. *Child Development, 52*, 975–985.

Thomann, K.-D., Freese, M., & Walter, J. (1985). Hohe Sockel arbeitslosigkeit—Perspektiven der medizinischen und beruflichen Rehabilitation. In T. Kieselbach & A. Wacker (Eds.), *Individuelle und gesellschaftliche Kosten der Massenarbeitslosigkeit—Psychologische Theorie und Praxis* (pp. 390–402). Weinheim: Beltz.

Ulich, D., Hausser, K., Mayring, P., Strehmel, P., Kandler, M., & Degenhardt, B. (1985). *Psychologie der Krisenbewältigung. Eine Längsschnittuntersuchung mit arbeitslosen Lehrern.* Weinheim: Beltz.

Viney, L. (1983). Psychological reactions of young people to unemployment. *Youth and Society, 14*, 457–474.

Verkleij, H. (1989). Vulnerabilities of very long-term unemployed in the Netherlands: Results of a longitudinal study. In B. Starrin, P.-G. Svensson, & H. Wintersberger, (Eds.), *Unemployment, poverty, and quality of working life—Some European experiences* (pp. 79–100). Berlin: Edition Sigma.

Wacker, A. (1983). Differentielle Verarbeitungsformen von Arbeitslosigkeit - Anmerkungen zur aktuellen Diskussion in der Arbeitslosenforschung. *Prokla, 53*, 77–88.

Warr, P. B. (1984a). Job loss, unemployment, and psychological well-being. In K. L. Allen & J. van de Vliert (Eds.), *Role transitions: Explorations and explanations.* New York: Plenum.

Warr, P. B. (1984b). Economic recession and mental health: A review of research. *Journal of Community Health Care, 62*, 298–308.

Warr, P. B. (1987). *Work, unemployment, and mental health.* London: Oxford University Press.

Warr, P. B. (1989). Individual and community adaptation to unemployment. In Starrin, B., Svensson, P.-G., & Wintersberger, H.

(Eds.), *Unemployment, poverty and quality of working life—Some European experiences* (pp. 27–44). Berlin: Edition Sigma.

Warr, P. B., Jackson, P., & Banks, M. (1982). Duration of unemployment and psychological well-being in young men and women. *Current Psychological Research, 2,* 207–214.

Warr, P. B., & Parry, G. (1982). Paid employment and women's psychological well-being. *Psychological Bulletin, 91,* 498–516.

Westcott, G., Svensson, P.-G., & Zöllner, H. F. K. (Eds.). (1985). *Health policy implications of unemployment.* Copenhagen: World Health Organization.

World Health Organization (1985). *Report on a WHO meeting "Vulnerability among long-term unemployed.* Ljubljana, October 1985 (ICP/HSR 801/mo2 244OV).

Wuggenig, U. (1985). Sozialer Rang und Arbeitslosigkeit—Gemeinsamkeiten und Unterschiede der Arbeitslosigkeitserfahrung bei Arbeitern und Akademikern. In T. Kieselbach & A. Wacker (Eds.), *Individuelle und gesellschaftliche Kosten der Massenarbeitslosigkeit—Psychologische Theorie und Praxis* Weinheim: Beltz.

See Also

Employment; Maternal Employment Influences on Adolescent Development; Parenthood and Marriage in Adolescence: Associations with Educational and Occupational Attainment: Vocational Development and Choice in Adolescence; Vocational Training.

Vocational Development And Choice In Adolescence

Fred W. Vondracek

The Pennsylvania State University

Among the developmental tasks described so eloquently by Erikson (1963) and by Havighurst (1951), none is more far reaching in its implications for adult life than the transition to work, or, using Erikson's term, the development of industry. In spite of the importance of vocational development it has not received as much attention from adolescence researchers and theoreticians as one might expect. This is due, in large part, to a somewhat artificial division among those researchers most concerned with the phenomena of vocational development, namely developmental and vocational psychologists. Fortunately, there are indications that joint efforts by developmental and vocational psychologists will lead to an improved understanding of this important area (Jepsen, 1984; Vondracek, Lerner, & Schulenberg, 1986).

Before taking a closer look at vocational development during adolescence a number of observations must be made. First, it should be clear that vocational development in the United States and in Western industrialized countries is very dif- ferent from vocational development in other parts of the world. For example, vocational choice has long been a rare luxury in the People's Republic of China, where individuals are assigned to work not on the basis of their preferences but on the basis of their abilities and where they are needed in the economic structure. Another course of vocational development could be observed in the hunter-gatherer societies of Africa, where the transition to work for males and females coincides with age-old rituals of induction into the ranks of manhood and womanhood. Thus, it is clear that vocational development is a process that is limited and defined not only by the biological properties of the developing person and his/her immediate socioeconomic and familial circumstances but also by the larger sociocultural context within which it is occurring.

The cultural relativity of adolescent vocational development described above suggests a second major observation, namely, that vocational development does not take place in a vacuum, but that it is a consequence of the dynamic interaction between individual and environment (Lerner, 1984). What this means is that the determinants of vocational development include the genetic/biological endowment of the person, as well as the environmental contexts within which it unfolds. It also means that individuals make choices (or have choices made for them) throughout their development that can result in enhancing vocational development on the one hand or in retarding it on the other. Viewed from this perspective, making vocational choices is seen as an integral component of the overall process of development, leading to the conclusion that vocational development is best understood if viewed as part and parcel of development in general.

Just as vocational development should not be conceptually separated from other important features of development, vocational development in adolescence should not be isolated from the life-span processes involved in career development. Although it may be argued that the most important decisions about careers are made during adolescence, this stereotyped view of career development is no longer tenable at a time when such catchy phrases as "serial careers," "midlife career change," and "retirement careers" are commonplace in the headlines of the national media. Thus, it should be understood that vocational development in adolescence is firmly based on the foundation of cognitive and social development that occurs prior to adolescence, and that while adolescence represents an important period of vocational development in its own right, this period of life is also the precursor of important, meaningful, and consequential career decisions that are made later in life.

A number of theories have been proposed to account for the various features that are important in adolescent vocational development (see Osipow, 1983, for a review). The most influential of these theories are those of Holland (1973) and Super (1953, 1980). Both theories postulate that it is essential for optimal vocational development to achieve a good match between an individual's attributes and the characteristics of his or her chosen career. The principal difference between the two theories lies in the fact that Holland views the accomplishment of such a match as the first step toward an enduring, often life-long career commitment, while Super views such a match as simply one event in a life-long series of events that ultimately constitute the person's career.

Researchers interested in adolescent vocational development and choice have, over the years, examined a number of variables thought to be salient in this area. Prominent among them have been vocational interests (Walsh & Osipow, 1986), vocational maturity (Westbrook, 1983), and work values (Super, 1973). Other areas that have received increasing attention by researchers are the vocationl development of women (Fitzgerald & Betz, 1983) and of minorities (Smith, 1983). Future research on adolescent vocational development will include increasing utilization of sophisticated, multivariate longitudinal research designs to examine the complex interplay between the family and sociocultural context on the one hand, and the developing adolescent in search of a vocation on the other.

References

Erikson, E. H. (1963). *Childhood and society* (2nd ed.). New York: W. W. Norton.

Fitzgerald, L. F., & Betz, N. E. (1983). Issues in the vocational psychology of women. In W. B. W. Walsh & S. H. Osipow (Eds.), *Handbook of vocational psychology: Vol. 1. Foundations* (pp. 83–159). Hillsdale, NJ: Lawrence Erlbaum Associates.

Havighurst, R. J. (1951). *Developmental tasks and education.* New York: Longman.

Holland, J. L. (1973). *Making vocational choices: A theory of careers*. Englewood Cliffs, NJ: Prentice-Hall.

Jepsen, D. A. (1984). The developmental perspective on vocational behavior: A review of theory and research. In S. D. Brown & R. W. Lent (Eds.), *Handbook of counseling psychology* (pp. 178–215). New York: John Wiley & Sons.

Lerner, R. M. (1984). *On the nature of human plasticity*. New York: Cambridge University Press.

Osipow, S. H. (1983). *Theories of career development* (3rd ed.). Englewood Cliffs, NJ: Prentice-Hall

Smith, E. J. (1983). Issues in racial minorities' career behavior. In W. B. Walsh & S. H. Osipow (Eds.), *Handbook of vocational psychology: Vol. 1. Foundations* (pp. 161–122). Hillsdale, NJ: Lawrence Erlbaum Associates.

Super, D. E., (1953). A theory of vocational development. *American Psychologist, 8*, 185–190.

Super, D. E. (1973). The Work Values Inventory. In D. G. Zytowsky (Ed.), *Contemporary approaches to interest measurement* (pp. 189–205). Minneapolis: University of Minnesota Press.

Super, D. E. (1980). A life-span, life-space approach to career development. *Journal of Vocational Behavior, 16*, 282–298.

Vondracek, F. W., Lerner, R. M., & Schulenberg, J. E. (1986). *Career development; A life-span developmental approach*. Hillsdale, NJ: Lawrence Erlbaum Associates.

Walsh, W. B., & Osipow, S. H. (Eds.). (1986). *Advances in vocational psychology: Volume 1. The assessment of interests*. Hillsdale, NJ: Lawrence Erlbaum Associates.

Westbrook, B. W. (1983). Career maturity: The concept, the instrument, and the research. In W. B. Walsh & S. H. Osipow (Eds.), *Handbook of vocational psychology: Vol. 1. Foundations* (pp. 263–303). Hillsdale, NJ: Lawrence Erlbaum Associates.

See Also

Employment; Maternal Employment Influences on Adolescent Development; Parenthood and Marriage in Adolescence: Associations with Education and Occupational Attainment; Unemployment; Vocational Training.

Vocational Training

Stephen F. Hamilton
Cornell University

Before graduating from high school, adolescents in the United States have opportunities to learn specific job skills in three contexts: vocational high school programs; workplaces; and subsidized employment training programs. Available evidence suggests that vocational training is most effective when it is combined with schooling and leads to related employment, a combination that is far more prevalent in German-speaking than in English-speaking countries (Hamilton, 1987; Reubens, 1980).

SECONDARY VOCATIONAL SCHOOLING ■
Vocational courses are taught in comprehensive high schools, in specialized vocational high schools, and in vocational centers serving students from several high schools. Transcripts of 1982 graduates in the High School and Beyond sample showed that 97% had taken some vocational courses. Vocational courses accounted for 20% of the cohort's coursework. Nearly half of vocational enrollees were college bound, demonstrating that vocational courses serve a general education function (National Assessment of Vocational Education, 1988).

Vocational schooling's original proponents in the United States viewed it as an alternative form of general education, but it gained support primarily as a means of staffing the nation's factories and offices, a purpose codified by the Smith-Hughes Act of 1917 (Lazerson & Grubb, 1974; Wirth, 1972). Research comparing the employment and earnings of vocational and general track graduates fails to confirm its value in the labor market. Finer-grained studies have demonstrated that young women who learn office skills and young men in some industrial courses earn more and suffer less unemployment (Berryman, 1982; Grasso & Shea, 1979). But the largest and most consistent benefits are found among graduates who take a coherent vocational program and then succeed in finding employment related to their training; these graduates constitute about one-third of vocational concentrators (Bishop, 1986). These gains, however, appear to carry some costs in the form of reduced academic learning (Ekstrom, Goertz, Pollack, & Rock, 1986).

Vocational schooling's limited benefits are partly attributable to instructional weaknesses, including lack of access to up-to-date equipment. More important, however, is its failure to mesh with the labor market for recent high school graduates. Employers in the United States are reluctant to offer career-entry positions to applicants under the age of 20. As a result, non–

college youth experience a period of "floundering" in the labor market, working in a series of low-skill jobs, often the same kinds of jobs they held before graduation (Osterman, 1980). By the time they are considered mature enough for adult jobs, their high school vocational training may be forgotten or irrelevant.

ON-THE-JOB TRAINING ▪

Although employment during high school has become nearly universal (Lewin-Epstein, 1981), adolescent workers receive little formal training because their jobs require only minimal skills (Borus, 1984; Greenberger & Steinberg, 1986; Lillard & Tan, 1986). The most useful form of workplace training is Cooperative Education, which combines vocational schooling with work experience (Bottoms & Copa, 1983).

SUBSIDIZED EMPLOYMENT TRAINING PROGRAMS ▪

Most federal job training programs for youth have demonstrated only limited effectiveness (Betsey, Hollister, & Papageorgiou, 1985). The most effective program is the Job Corps, which has proved cost-effective with disadvantaged dropouts by combining job training with a wide range of supportive services and education (Mallar, Karachsky, & Thornton, 1982). The current Job Training Partnership Act (JTPA) serves few youth. A promising innovation for in-school youth is the Summer Training and Education Program (STEP), which combines two summers of subsidized employment with required summer school (Sipe, Grossman, & Milliner, 1988).

References

Berryman, S. E. (1982). The effectiveness of secondary vocational education. In H. F. Silberman & K. J. Rehage (Ed.). *Education and work* (81st yearbook of the National Society for the Study of Education, pp. 169–203). Chicago: University of Chicago Press.

Betsey, C. L., Hollister, R. B., Jr., & Papageorgiou, M. R. (Eds.). (1985). *Youth employment and training programs: The YEDPA years*. Washington, DC: National Academy Press.

Bishop, J. (1986). *High school vocational education: A review of research on its impacts with recommendations for improvement*. Unpublished paper prepared for Research for Better Schools, Inc., Cornell University.

Borus, M. E. (1984). A description of employed and unemployed youth in 1981. In M. E. Borus (Ed.), *Youth and the labor market: Analyses of the National Longitudinal Survey* (pp. 13–55). Kalamazoo, MI: W. E. Upjohn Institute for Employment Research.

Bottoms, G., & Copa, P. (1983). A perspective on vocational education today. *Phi Delta Kappan, 64*, 348–354.

Ekstrom, R. B., Goertz, M. E., Pollack, J. M., & Rock, D. A. (1986). Who drops out of high school and why? Findings from a national study. *Teachers College Record, 87*, 356–373.

Grasso, J., & Shea, J. R. (1979). *Vocational education and training: Impact on youth*. Berkeley, CA: Carnegie Council on Policy Studies in Higher Education.

Greenberger, E., & Steinberg, L. (1986). *When teenagers work: The psychological and social costs of adolescent employment*. New York: Basic Books.

Hamilton, S. F. (1987). Apprenticeship as a transition to adulthood in West Germany. *American Journal of Education, 95*, 314–345.

Lazerson, M., & Grubb, W. N. (Eds.) (1974). *American education and vocationalism: A documentary history, 1870–1970*. New York: Teachers College Press.

Lewin-Epstein, N. (1981). *Youth employment during high school*. Washington, DC: National Center for Education Statistics.

Lillard, L. A., & Tan, H. W. (1986). *Private sector training: Who gets it and what are its effects?* Santa Monica, CA: The Rand Corporation.

Mallar, C., Karachsky, S., & Thornton, C. V. D. (1982). *Evaluation of the economic impact of the Job Corps Program* (Third Follow-up Report). Princeton, NJ: Mathematica Policy Research. (National Technical Information Service: PB83-145441)

National Assessment of Vocational Education. *First Interim Report from the National Assessment of Vocational Education*, (January, 1988). Washington, DC: U. S. Department of Education.

Osterman, P. (1980). *Getting started: The youth labor market.* Cambridge: MIT Press.

Reubens, B. G. (1980). *Apprenticeship in foreign countries* (R&D Monograph 77, U. S. Department of Labor, Employment and Training Administration). Washington, DC: U. S. Government Printing Office.

Sipe, C. L., Grossman, J. B., & Milliner, J. A. (1988). *Summer Training and Education Program: Report on the 1987 experience.* Philadelphia: Public/Private Ventures.

Wirth, A. G. (1972). *Education in a technological society: The vocational-liberal studies controversy in the early twentieth century.* Scranton, PA: Intext Educational Publishers.

See Also

Employment; Maternal Employment Influences on Adolescent Development; Parenthood and Marriage in Adolescence: Associations with Educational and Occupational Attainment; Unemployment; Vocational Development and Choice in Adolescence.

Subject Index